Mike Meyers'

CompTIA Network+®
Guide to Managing and Troubleshooting Networks

Second Edition

▪ CompTIA Authorized Quality Curriculum

The logo of the CompTIA Authorized Quality Curriculum (CAQC) program and the status of this or other training material as "Authorized" under the CompTIA Authorized Quality Curriculum program signifies that, in CompTIA's opinion, such training material covers the content of CompTIA's related certification exam.

The contents of this training material were created for the CompTIA Network+ exams covering CompTIA certification objectives that were current as of April 2009. CompTIA has not reviewed or approved the accuracy of the contents of this training material and specifically disclaims any warranties of merchantability or fitness for a particular purpose. CompTIA makes no guarantee concerning the success of persons using any such "Authorized" or other training material in order to prepare for any CompTIA certification exam.

How to Become CompTIA Certified

This training material can help you prepare for and pass a related CompTIA certification exam or exams. In order to achieve CompTIA certification, you must register for and pass a CompTIA certification exam or exams. To become CompTIA certified, you must:

1. Select a certification exam provider. For more information, please visit http://certification.comptia.org/resources/registration.aspx.

2. Register for and schedule a time to take the CompTIA certification exam(s) at a convenient location.

3. Read and sign the Candidate Agreement, which will be presented at the time of the exam(s). The text of the Candidate Agreement can be found at http://www.comptia.org/certification/general_information/candidate_agreement.aspx.

4. Take and pass the CompTIA certification exam(s).

For more information about CompTIA's certifications, such as its industry acceptance, benefits, or program news, please visit http://certification.comptia.org.

CompTIA is a not-for-profit information technology (IT) trade association. CompTIA's certifications are designed by subject matter experts from across the IT industry. Each CompTIA certification is vendor-neutral, covers multiple technologies, and requires demonstration of skills and knowledge widely sought after by the IT industry.

To contact CompTIA with any questions or comments, please call (1) (630) 678-8300 or e-mail questions@comptia.org.

Mike Meyers'

CompTIA Network+®
Guide to Managing and
Troubleshooting Networks

Second Edition

Mike Meyers

New York   Chicago   San Francisco
Lisbon   London   Madrid   Mexico City   Milan
New Delhi   San Juan   Seoul   Singapore   Sydney   Toronto

The McGraw·Hill Companies

Cataloging-in-Publication Data is on file with the Library of Congress

Sponsoring Editor
TIMOTHY GREEN

Editorial Supervisor
JODY MCKENZIE

Project Editor
LAURA STONE

Acquisitions Coordinator
MEGHAN RILEY

Technical Editor
CHRISTOPHER CRAYTON

Developmental Editor
LAURA STONE

Copy Editor
BILL MCMANUS

Proofreader
PAUL TYLER

Indexer
JACK LEWIS

Production Supervisor
JIM KUSSOW

Composition
INTERNATIONAL TYPESETTING AND COMPOSITION

Illustration
INTERNATIONAL TYPESETTING AND COMPOSITION

Art Director, Cover
JEFF WEEKS

McGraw-Hill books are available at special quantity discounts to use as premiums and sales promotions, or for use in corporate training programs. To contact a special sales representative, please visit the Contact Us page at www.mhprofessional.com.

Mike Meyers' CompTIA Network+® Guide to Managing and Troubleshooting Networks, Second Edition

4567890 QDB QDB 10

ISBN: Book p/n 978-0-07-161485-6
  and CD p/n 978-0-07-161486-3
  of set 978-0-07-161483-2

MHID: Book p/n 0-07-161485-0
  and CD p/n 0-07-161486-9
  of set 0-07-161483-4

■ About the Author

Michael Meyers is the industry's leading authority on CompTIA Network+ certification. He is the president and founder of Total Seminars, LLC, a major provider of PC and network repair seminars for thousands of organizations throughout the world, and a member of CompTIA.

Mike has written numerous popular textbooks, including the best-selling *Mike Meyers' CompTIA A+® Guide to Managing & Troubleshooting PCs*, *Mike Meyers' CompTIA A+® Guide to Essentials*, and *Mike Meyers' CompTIA A+® Guide to PC Technician*.

About the Contributors

Scott Jernigan wields a mighty red pen as Editor in Chief for Total Seminars. With a Master of Arts degree in Medieval History, Scott feels as much at home in the musty archives of London as he does in the warm CRT glow of Total Seminars' Houston headquarters. After fleeing a purely academic life, he dove headfirst into IT, working as an instructor, editor, and writer. Scott has edited and contributed to more than a dozen books on computer literacy, hardware, operating systems, networking, and certification. His latest book is *Computer Literacy – Your Ticket to IC³ Certification*. Scott co-authored the best-selling *A+ Certification All-in-One Exam Guide, Fifth Edition*, and the *Mike Meyers' A+ Guide to Managing and Troubleshooting PCs* (both with Mike Meyers). He has taught computer classes all over the United States, including stints at the United Nations in New York and the FBI Academy in Quantico.

Alec Fehl (BM, Music Production and Engineering, and MCSE, A+, NT-CIP, ACE, ACI certified) has been a technical trainer, computer consultant, and Web application developer since 1999. After graduating from the prestigious Berklee College of Music in Boston, he set off for Los Angeles with the promise of becoming a rock star. After ten years gigging in Los Angeles, teaching middle-school math, and auditioning for the Red Hot Chili Peppers (he didn't get the gig), he moved to Asheville, North Carolina with his wife Jacqui, where he teaches computer classes at Asheville-Buncombe Technical Community College and WCI/SofTrain Technology Training Center. Alec is author or co-author of several titles covering Microsoft Office 2007, Microsoft Vista, Web design and HTML, and Internet systems and applications.

About the Technical Editor

Christopher A. Crayton (MCSE, MCP+I, CompTIA A+, CompTIA Network+) is an author, technical editor, technical consultant, security consultant, and trainer. Formerly a computer and networking instructor at Keiser College (2001 Teacher of the Year), Chris has also worked as network administrator for Protocol and at Eastman Kodak Headquarters as a computer and network specialist. Chris has authored several print and online books on topics ranging from CompTIA A+ and CompTIA Security+ to Microsoft Windows Vista. Chris has provided technical edits and reviews for many publishers, including McGraw-Hill, Pearson Education, Charles River Media, Cengage Learning, Wiley, O'Reilly, Syngress, and Apress.

■ Acknowledgments

I'd like to acknowledge the many people who contributed their talents to make this book possible:

To Tim Green, my acquisitions editor at McGraw-Hill: Please tell me, as I have to know: is there or is there not a Mike voodoo doll in your home, and if so, have you used it? Every time I tried to stop typing, my back started to hurt—and I know you've been to Jamaica. No other explanation makes sense.

To my in-house Editor-in-Chief, Scott Jernigan: Sorry to take you away from the mighty Tsarion so much. Level 80 is just around the corner. Oh, and we're done now, so just go buy the MINI.

To Chris Crayton, technical editor: As far as I'm concerned, I've found my permanent tech editor. Now to the bigger question: "Do you want the job?"

To Alec Fehl, contributing author: Alec, I truly appreciate you taking the time to go "outside the job," catching errors and challenging me on concept. Never again will I confuse "The Two Auth's."

To Bill McManus, copy editor: You, sir, are the fastest, most accurate copyeditor I've ever seen. Like scary fast. One of these days you have got to tell me your secret.

To Michael Smyer, Total Seminars' resident tech guru and photographer: You've learned the secret: good technology research means clear concepts, delivered in nice, tidy thought boxes. I am content.

To Ford Pierson, graphics maven and editor: See! I told you it was fun. You did such a great job that I'm going to add a full eight feet to your chain. Plus I'm personally going to warm your gruel. You've earned it!

To Dudley Lehmer, my partner at Total Seminars: Thanks for keeping things running smoothly so we had time to put together another great book.

To Meghan Riley, acquisitions coordinator at McGraw-Hill: What do you mean, "We need that manuscript today!" HAHAHAHA! You crack us up!

To Laura Stone and Jody McKenzie, project editors: You truly fulfill the axiom: "Speak quietly, but carry a big stick." You almost can't see any bruises on me anymore. Thank you both so much for your skill, patience, and perseverance! It was a joy to work with you again.

To the ITC production team: Thank you for producing a marvelous book that I'm proud to call my own.

■ *This book is dedicated to Ms. K and Rat Dog.*

About This Book

■ Important Technology Skills

Information technology (IT) offers many career paths, leading to occupations in such fields as PC repair, network administration, telecommunications, Web development, graphic design, and desktop support. To become competent in any IT field, however, you need certain basic computer skills. Mike Meyers' Network+ Guide to Managing and Troubleshooting Networks *builds a foundation for success in the IT field by introducing you to fundamental technology concepts and giving you essential computer skills.*

Cross-Check *questions develop reasoning skills: ask, compare, contrast, and explain.*

Key Terms, *identified in red, point out important vocabulary and definitions that you need to know.*

Tech Tip *sidebars provide inside information from experienced IT professionals.*

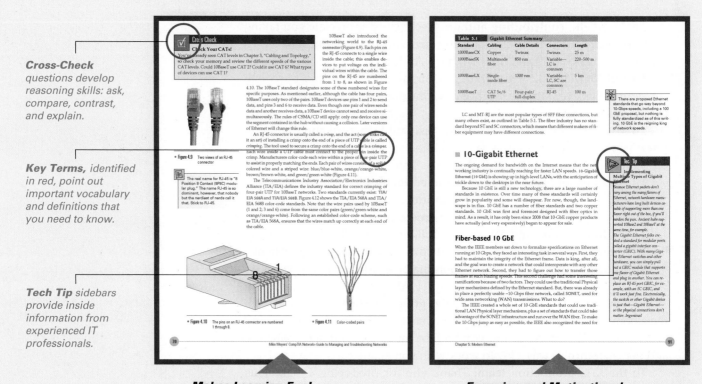

Makes Learning Fun! — *Rich, colorful text and enhanced illustrations bring technical subjects to life.*

Engaging and Motivational — *Using a conversational style and proven instructional approach, the authors explain technical concepts in a clear, interesting way using real-world examples.*

Proven Learning Method Keeps You on Track

Mike Meyers' Network+ Guide to Managing and Troubleshooting Networks *is structured to give you comprehensive knowledge of computer skills and technologies. The textbook's active learning methodology guides you beyond mere recall and—through thought-provoking activities, labs, and sidebars—helps you develop critical-thinking, diagnostic, and communication skills.*

Effective Learning Tools

This pedagogically rich book is designed to make learning easy and enjoyable and to help you develop the skills and critical thinking abilities that will enable you to adapt to different job situations and troubleshoot problems.

Mike Meyers' proven ability to explain concepts in a clear, direct, even humorous way makes this book interesting, motivational, and fun.

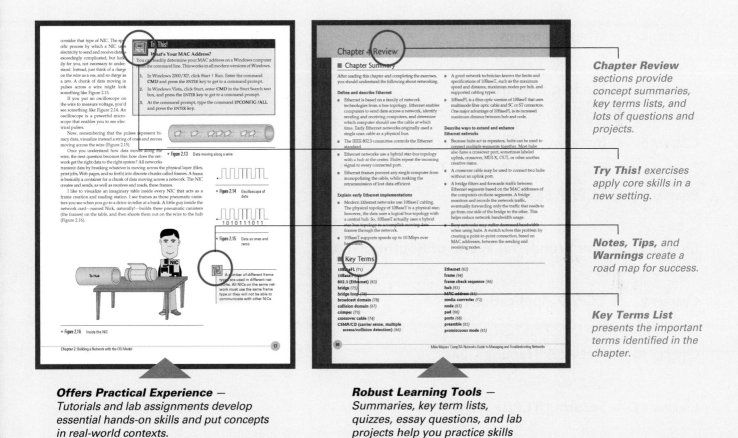

Chapter Review sections provide concept summaries, key terms lists, and lots of questions and projects.

Try This! exercises apply core skills in a new setting.

Notes, Tips, and **Warnings** create a road map for success.

Key Terms List presents the important terms identified in the chapter.

Offers Practical Experience —
Tutorials and lab assignments develop essential hands-on skills and put concepts in real-world contexts.

Robust Learning Tools —
Summaries, key term lists, quizzes, essay questions, and lab projects help you practice skills and measure progress.

Each chapter includes:

- **Learning Objectives** that set measurable goals for chapter-by-chapter progress

- **Illustrations** that give you a clear picture of the technologies

- **Tutorials** that teach you to perform essential tasks and procedures hands-on

- **Try This!, Cross-Check,** and **Tech Tip** sidebars that encourage you to practice and apply concepts in real-world settings

- **Notes, Tips,** and **Warnings** that guide you through difficult areas

- **Chapter Summaries** and **Key Terms Lists** that provide you with an easy way to review important concepts and vocabulary

- **Challenging End-of-Chapter Tests** that include vocabulary-building exercises, multiple-choice questions, essay questions, and on-the-job lab projects

CONTENTS AT A GLANCE

CONTENTS

Chapter 18
■ Network Management 484

Appendix A
■ Objectives Map: CompTIA Network+ 510

Appendix B
■ About the CD-ROM 520

■ Glossary 522

■ Index 554

I was a teacher long before I was ever an author. I started writing computer books for the simple reason that no one wrote the kind of books I wanted to read. The books were either too simple (Chapter 1, "Using Your Mouse") or too complex (Chapter 1, "TTL Logic and Transistors") and none of them provided a motivation for me to learn the information. I guessed that there were geeky readers just like me who wanted to know *why* they needed to know the information in a computer book.

Good books motivate the reader to learn what he or she is reading. If a book discusses binary arithmetic but doesn't explain why I need to learn it, for example, that's not a good book. Tell me that understanding binary makes it easier to understand how an IP address works or why we're about to run out of IP addresses and how IPv6 can help, then I get excited, no matter how geeky the topic. If I don't have a good reason, a good motivation to do something, then I'm simply not going to do it (which explains why I haven't jumped out of an airplane!).

In this book, I teach you why you need to understand the wide world of networking. You'll learn everything you need to start building, configuring, and supporting networks. In the process, you'll gain the knowledge you need to pass the CompTIA Network+ certification exam.

Enjoy, my fellow geek.

—Mike Meyers

For instructor and student resources, check out http://novella.mhhe.com/sites/0071628835. Students will find chapter quizzes that will help them learn more about troubleshooting and fixing networks, and teachers can access support materials.

■ Additional Resources for Teachers

Resources for teachers are provided via an Online Learning Center that maps to the organization of the textbook. This site includes the following:

- Answer keys to the end-of-chapter activities in the textbook
- Answer keys to the lab manual activities
- Access to testbank files and software that allows you to generate a wide array of paper- or network-based tests, and that features automatic grading
- Hundreds of practice questions and a wide variety of question types and difficulty levels, enabling you to customize each test to maximize student progress
- Blackboard cartridges and other formats may also be available upon request; contact your sales representative
- Engaging PowerPoint slides on the lecture topics (include full-color artwork from the book)

CompTIA Network+ in a Nutshell

"Networking is an essential part of building wealth."
—ARMSTRONG WILLIAMS

In this chapter, you will learn how to

- Describe the importance of CompTIA Network+ certification
- Illustrate the structure and contents of the CompTIA Network+ certification exam
- Plan a strategy to prepare for the exam

By picking up this book, you've shown an interest in learning about networking. But be forewarned. The term *networking* describes a vast field of study, far too large for any single certification, book, or training course to cover. Do you want to configure routers for a living? Do you want to administer a large Windows network at a company? Do you want to install wide area network connections? Do you want to set up Web servers? Do you want to secure networks against attacks?

If you're considering a CompTIA Network+ certification, you probably don't yet know exactly what aspect of networking you want to pursue, and that's okay! You're going to *love* preparing for the CompTIA Network+ certification.

Attaining CompTIA Network+ certification provides you three fantastic benefits. First, you get a superb overview of networking that helps you decide what part of the industry you'd like to pursue. Second, it acts as a prerequisite toward other, more advanced certifications. Third, the amount of eye-opening information you'll gain just makes getting CompTIA Network+ certified plain old *fun*.

Nothing comes close to providing a better overview of networking than CompTIA Network+. The certification covers local area networks (LANs), wide area networks (WANs), the Internet, security, cabling, and applications in a wide-but-not-too-deep fashion that showcases the many different parts of a network and hopefully tempts you to investigate the aspects that intrigue you by looking into follow-up certifications.

Both Cisco and Microsoft—the two main choices for follow-up training—treat CompTIA Network+ as a prerequisite toward at least some of their own certifications, and in some cases provide certification credit for attaining CompTIA Network+ certification. These benefits sometimes change, so check out the Cisco (www.cisco.com) and Microsoft (www.microsoft.com) Web sites for details. Just do a search for **training**.

The process of attaining CompTIA Network+ certification will give you a solid foundation in the whole field of networking. Mastering the competencies will help fill in gaps in your knowledge and provide an ongoing series of "ah ha!" moments of grasping the big picture that make being a tech so much fun.

Ready to learn a lot, grab a great certification, and have fun doing it? Then welcome to CompTIA Network+ certification!

■ Who Needs CompTIA Network+? I Just Want to Learn about Networks!

Whoa up there, amigo! Are you one of those folks who either has never heard of the CompTIA Network+ exam or just doesn't have any real interest in certification? Is your goal only to get a solid handle on the idea of networking and get a jump start on the basics? Are you looking for that "magic bullet" book that you can read from beginning to end and then start installing and troubleshooting a network? Do you want to know what's involved with running network cabling in your walls or getting your new wireless network working? Are you tired of not knowing enough about what TCP/IP is and how it works? If these types of questions are running through your mind, then rest easy—you have the right book. Like every book with the Mike Meyers name, you'll get solid concepts without pedantic details or broad, meaningless overviews. You'll look at real-world networking as performed by real techs. This is a book that understands your needs, well beyond the scope of a single certification.

If the CompTIA Network+ exam isn't for you, you can skip the rest of this chapter, shift your brain into learn mode, and dive into Chapter 2. But then, if you're going to have the knowledge, why *not* get the certification?

■ What Is CompTIA Network+ Certification?

CompTIA Network+ certification is an industry-wide, vendor-neutral certification program developed and sponsored by the Computing Technology Industry Association (CompTIA). The CompTIA Network+ certification shows that you have a basic competency in the physical support of networking systems and knowledge of the conceptual aspects of networking. The test covers the knowledge that a network technician with at least nine months of networking experience should have. CompTIA recommends CompTIA A+ knowledge or background but does not require a CompTIA A+ certification to take the CompTIA Network+ exam. You achieve a CompTIA Network+ certification by taking one computer-based, multiple-choice examination. To date, many hundreds of thousands of technicians have become CompTIA Network+ certified.

CompTIA Network+ certification enjoys wide recognition throughout the IT industry. At first, it rode in on the coattails of the successful CompTIA A+ certification program, but it now stands on its own in the networking industry and is considered the obvious next step after CompTIA A+ certification.

What Is CompTIA?

CompTIA is a nonprofit, industry trade association based in Oakbrook Terrace, Illinois, on the outskirts of Chicago. Tens of thousands of computer resellers, value-added resellers, distributors, manufacturers, and training companies from all over the world are members of CompTIA.

CompTIA was founded in 1982. The following year, CompTIA began offering the CompTIA A+ certification exam. CompTIA A+ certification is now widely recognized as a *de facto* requirement for entrance into the PC industry. Because the A+ exam covers networking only lightly, CompTIA decided to establish a vendor-neutral test covering basic networking skills. So, in April 1999, CompTIA unveiled the CompTIA Network+ certification exam.

CompTIA provides certifications for a variety of areas in the computer industry, offers opportunities for its members to interact, and represents its members' interests to government bodies. CompTIA certifications include A+, Network+, Security+, and RFID+, to name a few. Check out the CompTIA Web site at www.comptia.org for details on other certifications.

CompTIA is *huge*. Virtually every company of consequence in the IT industry is a member of CompTIA: Microsoft, Dell, Cisco…name an IT company and it's probably a member of CompTIA.

The Current CompTIA Network+ Certification Exam Release

CompTIA constantly works to provide tests that cover the latest technologies and, as part of that effort, periodically updates its test objectives, domains, and test questions. This book covers all you need to know to pass the 2009 revision of the CompTIA Network+ exam.

How Do I Become CompTIA Network+ Certified?

To become CompTIA Network+ certified, you simply pass one computer-based, multiple-choice exam. There are no prerequisites for taking the CompTIA Network+ exam, and no networking experience is needed. You're not required to take a training course or buy any training materials. The only requirements are that you pay a testing fee to an authorized testing facility and then sit for the exam. Upon completion of the exam, you will immediately know whether you passed or failed. Once you've passed, you become CompTIA Network+ certified for life, just like with CompTIA A+ certification. That's it—there are no annual dues and no continuing education requirements.

Now for the details: CompTIA recommends that you have at least nine months of networking experience and CompTIA A+ knowledge, but this is not a requirement. Note the word "recommend." You may not need experience or CompTIA A+ knowledge but they help! The CompTIA A+ certification competencies have a small degree of overlap with the CompTIA Network+ competencies, such as types of connectors. As for experience, keep in mind that CompTIA Network+ is mostly a practical exam. Those who have been out there supporting real networks will find many of the questions reminiscent of the types of problems they have seen on LANs. The bottom line is that you'll probably have a much easier time on the CompTIA Network+ exam if you have some CompTIA A+ experience under your belt.

■ What Is the Test Like?

The CompTIA Network+ test contains 100 questions, which you have 90 minutes to complete. To pass, you must score at least 720 on a scale of 100–900. The exam questions are divided into six areas that CompTIA calls domains. This table lists the CompTIA Network+ domains and the percentage of the test that each represents.

CompTIA Network+ Domain	Percentage
1.0 Network Technologies	20%
2.0 Network Media and Topologies	20%
3.0 Network Devices	17%
4.0 Network Management	20%
5.0 Network Tools	12%
6.0 Network Security	11%

The CompTIA Network+ exam is extremely practical. Questions often present real-life scenarios and ask you to determine the best solution. CompTIA Network+ loves troubleshooting. Let me repeat: many of the test objectives deal with direct, *real-world troubleshooting*. Be prepared to troubleshoot both hardware and software failures, and to answer both "What do you do next?" and "What is most likely the problem?" types of questions.

A qualified CompTIA Network+ test candidate can install and configure a PC to connect to a network. This includes installing and testing a network card, configuring drivers, and loading all network software. The exam will test you on the different topologies, standards, and cabling.

Expect conceptual questions about the Open Systems Interconnection (OSI) seven-layer model. If you've never heard of the OSI seven-layer model, don't worry! This book will teach you all you need to know. While this model rarely comes into play during the daily grind of supporting a network, you need to know the functions and protocols for each layer to pass the CompTIA Network+ exam. You can also expect questions on most of the protocol suites, with heavy emphasis on the TCP/IP suite.

CompTIA occasionally makes changes to the content of the exam, as well as the score necessary to pass it. Always check the Web site of my company, Total Seminars (www.totalsem .com), before scheduling your exam.

How Do I Take the Test?

To take the test, you must go to an authorized testing center. You cannot take the test over the Internet. Prometric and Pearson VUE administer the actual CompTIA Network+ tests. You'll find thousands of Prometric and Pearson VUE testing centers scattered across the United States and Canada, as well as in over 75 other countries around the world. You may take the exam at any testing center. In the United States and Canada, call Prometric at 888-895-6116 or Pearson VUE at 877-551-7587 to locate the nearest testing center and schedule the exam. International customers should go to CompTIA's Web site at www.comptia.org, navigate to the CompTIA Network+ area of the site, and look under the **Ready to take the Exam** area for a link called **Find your test center**.

While you can't take the exam over the Internet, both Prometric and Pearson VUE provide easy online registration. Go to www.prometric.com or www.vue.com to register online.

How Much Does the Test Cost?

CompTIA fixes the price, no matter what testing center you use. The cost of the exam depends on whether you work for a CompTIA member. At press time, the cost for non-CompTIA members is $239 (U.S.).

If your employer has a CompTIA membership, you can save money by obtaining an exam voucher. In fact, even if you don't work for a CompTIA member, you can purchase a voucher from member companies and take advantage of significant member savings. You simply buy the voucher and then use the voucher to pay for the exam. Most vouchers are delivered to you on paper, but the most important element is the unique voucher number that you'll generally receive via e-mail from the company that sells the voucher to you. That number is your exam payment, so protect it from prying eyes until you're ready to schedule your exam.

CompTIA requires any company that resells vouchers to bundle them with some other product or service. Because this requirement is somewhat vague, voucher resellers have been known to throw in some pretty lame stuff, just to meet the requirement and keep their overhead low. My company, Total Seminars, is an authorized CompTIA member and voucher reseller, and we bundle our CompTIA Network+ vouchers with something you can actually use: our excellent test simulation software. It's just like the CD-ROM in the back of this book, but with hundreds more questions to help you prepare for the CompTIA Network+ exam.

If you're in the United States or Canada, you can visit www.totalsem.com or call 800-446-6004 to purchase vouchers. As I always say, "You don't have to buy your voucher from us, but for goodness' sake, get one from somebody!" Why pay full price when you have a discount alternative?

You must pay for the exam when you schedule, either online or by phone. If you're scheduling by phone, be prepared to hold for a while. Have ready your Social Security number (or the international equivalent) and either a credit card or a voucher number when you call or begin the online scheduling process. If you require any special accommodations, both Prometric and Pearson VUE will be able to assist you, although your selection of testing locations may be a bit more limited.

International prices vary; see the CompTIA Web site for international pricing. Of course, prices are subject to change without notice, so always check the CompTIA Web site for current pricing!

■ How to Pass the CompTIA Network+ Exam

The single most important thing to remember about the CompTIA Network+ certification is that CompTIA designed it to test the knowledge of a technician with as little as nine months of experience—so keep it simple! Think in terms of practical knowledge. Read the book, practice the questions at the end of each chapter, take the practice tests on the CD-ROM in the back of the book, review any topics you missed, and you'll pass with flying colors.

Is it safe to assume that it's probably been a while since you've taken an exam? Consequently, has it been a while since you've had to study for an exam? If you're nodding your head yes, you'll probably want to read the next sections. They lay out a proven strategy to help you study for the CompTIA Network+ exam and pass it. Try it. It works.

Obligate Yourself

The first step you should take is to schedule the exam. Ever heard the old adage that heat and pressure make diamonds? Well, if you don't give yourself a little "heat," you might procrastinate and unnecessarily delay taking the exam. Even worse, you may end up not taking the exam at all. Do yourself a favor. Determine how much time you need to study (see the next section), then call Prometric or Pearson VUE and schedule the exam, giving yourself the time you need to study, adding a few extra days for safety. Afterward, sit back and let your anxieties wash over you. Suddenly, it will become a lot easier to turn off the television and crack open the book! Keep in mind that Prometric and Pearson VUE let you schedule an exam only a few weeks in advance, at most. If you schedule an exam and can't make it, you must reschedule at least a day in advance or lose your money.

Set Aside the Right Amount of Study Time

After helping thousands of techs get their CompTIA Network+ certification, we at Total Seminars have developed a pretty good feel for the amount of study time needed to pass the CompTIA Network+ exam. Table 1.1 will help you plan how much study time you must devote to the CompTIA Network+ exam. Keep in mind that these are averages. If you're not a great student or if you're a little on the nervous side, add another 10 percent. Equally, if you're the type who can learn an entire semester of geometry in one night, reduce the numbers by 10 percent. To use this table, just circle the values that are most accurate for you and add them up to get the number of study hours.

A complete neophyte will need at least 120 hours of study time. An experienced network technician already CompTIA A+ certified should only need about 24 hours.

Keep in mind that these are estimates. Study habits also come into play here. A person with solid study habits (you know who you are) can reduce the number by 15 percent. People with poor study habits should increase that number by 20 percent.

The total hours of study you need is _____.

Table 1.1 Determining How Much Study Time You Need

	Amount of Experience			
Type of Experience	**None**	**Once or Twice**	**On Occasion**	**Quite a Bit**
Installing a SOHO wireless network	4	2	1	1
Installing an advanced wireless network (802.1X, RADIUS, etc.)	2	2	1	1
Installing structured cabling	3	2	1	1
Configuring a home router	5	3	2	1
Configuring a Cisco router	4	2	1	1
Configuring a software firewall	3	2	1	1
Configuring a hardware firewall	2	2	1	1
Configuring an IPv4 client	8	4	2	1
Configuring an IPv6 client	3	3	2	1
Working with SOHO WAN connection (DSL, cable)	2	2	1	0
Working with advanced WAN connection (Tx, OCx, ATM)	3	3	2	2
Configuring a DNS server	2	2	2	1
Configuring a DHCP server	2	1	1	0
Configuring a Web application server (HTTP, FTP, SSH, etc.)	4	4	2	1
Configuring a VLAN	3	3	2	1
Configuring a VPN	3	3	2	1
Configuring a dynamic routing protocol	2	2	1	1

Study for the Test

Now that you have a feel for how long it's going to take, you need a strategy for studying. The following has proven to be an excellent game plan for cramming the knowledge from the study materials into your head.

This strategy has two alternate paths. The first path is designed for highly experienced technicians who have a strong knowledge of PCs and networking and want to concentrate on just what's on the exam. Let's call this group the Fast Track group. The second path, and the one I'd strongly recommend, is geared toward people like me: the ones who want to know why things work, those who want to wrap their arms completely around a concept, as opposed to regurgitating answers just to pass the CompTIA Network+ exam. Let's call this group the Brainiacs.

To provide for both types of learners, I have broken down most of the chapters into two parts:

- **Historical/Conceptual** It's not on the CompTIA Network+ exam, but it's knowledge that will help you understand more clearly what is on the CompTIA Network+ exam.
- **Test Specific** Topics that clearly fit under the CompTIA Network+ certification domains.

The beginning of each of these areas is clearly marked with a large banner that looks like the following.

Historical/Conceptual

If you consider yourself a Fast Tracker, skip everything but the Test Specific section in each chapter. After reading the Test Specific sections, jump immediately to the End of Chapter questions, which concentrate on information in the Test Specific sections. If you run into problems, review the Historical/Conceptual sections in that chapter. After going through every chapter as described, do the free practice exams on the CD-ROM that accompanies the book. First, do them in practice mode, and then switch to final mode. Once you start hitting in the 80–85 percent range, go take the test!

Brainiacs should first read the book—the whole book. Read it as though you're reading a novel, starting on Page 1 and going all the way through. Don't skip around on the first read-through, even if you are a highly experienced tech. Because there are terms and concepts that build on each other, skipping around will make you confused, and you'll just end up closing the book and firing up your favorite PC game. Your goal on this first read is to understand concepts—to understand the whys, not just the hows.

It's helpful to have a network available while you're doing each read-through. This gives you a chance to see various concepts, hardware, and configuration screens in action when you read about them in the book. Nothing beats doing it yourself to reinforce a concept or piece of knowledge!

You will notice a lot of historical information—the Historical/Conceptual sections—that you may be tempted to skip. Don't! Understanding how some of the older stuff worked or how something works conceptually will help you appreciate the reason behind networking features and equipment, as well as how they function.

After you have completed the first read-through, cozy up for a second. This time, try to knock out one chapter at a sitting. Concentrate on the Test Specific sections. Get a highlighter and mark the phrases and sentences that bring out major points. Take a hard look at the pictures and tables, noting how they illustrate the concepts. Then, do the end of chapter questions. Repeat this process until you not only get all the questions right, but also understand *why* they are correct!

Once you have read and studied the material in the book, check your knowledge by taking the practice exams included on the CD-ROM at the back of the book. The exams can be taken in practice mode or final mode. In practice mode, you are allowed to check references in the book (if you want) before you answer each question, and each question is graded immediately. In final mode, you must answer all the questions before you are given a test score. In each case, you can review a results summary that tells you which questions you missed, what the right answer is, and where to study further.

Use the results of the exams to see where you need to bone up, and then study some more and try them again. Continue retaking the exams and reviewing the topics you missed until you are consistently scoring in the 80–85 percent range. When you've reached that point, you are ready to pass the CompTIA Network+ exam!

If you have any problems or questions, or if you just want to argue about something, feel free to send an e-mail to me at michaelm@totalsem.com.

For additional information about the CompTIA Network+ exam, contact CompTIA directly at its Web site: www.comptia.org.

Good luck!

—Mike Meyers

> Be aware that you may need to skip back to previous chapters to get the Historical/Conceptual information you need for a later chapter.

> We have active and helpful discussion groups at www.totalsem.com/forums. You need to register to participate (though not to read posts), but that's only to keep the spammers at bay. The forums provide an excellent resource for answers, suggestions, and just socializing with other folks studying for the exam.

Building a Network with the OSI Model

chapter

2

"First we thought the PC was a calculator. Then we found out how to turn numbers into letters with ASCII—and we thought it was a typewriter. Then we discovered graphics, and we thought it was a television. With the World Wide Web, we've realized it's a brochure."

—DOUGLAS ADAMS

In this chapter, you will learn how to

- Describe models such as the OSI seven-layer model
- Explain the major functions of network hardware with OSI Layers 1–2
- Describe the functions of network software with OSI Layers 3–7

The CompTIA Network+ certification challenges you to understand virtually every aspect of networking—not a small task. Luckily for you, there's a long-used method to conceptualize the many parts of a network called the Open Systems Interconnection (OSI) seven-layer model.

The **OSI seven-layer model** is a guideline, a template that breaks down how a network functions into seven parts called layers. If you want to get into networking—and if you want to pass the CompTIA Network+ certification exam—you must understand the OSI seven-layer model in great detail.

The OSI seven-layer model provides a practical model for networks. The model provides two things. For network techs, the OSI seven-layer model provides a powerful tool for diagnosing problems. Understanding the model enables a tech to determine quickly at what layer a problem can occur and thus zero in on a solution without wasting a lot of time on false leads. The model also provides a common language to describe networks—a way for us to communicate with each other about the functions of a network. Figure 2.1 shows a sample Cisco Systems Web page about configuring routing—a topic this book covers in detail later on. A router operates at Layer 3 of the OSI seven-layer model, for example, so you'll hear techs (and Web sites) refer to it as a "Layer 3 switch." That's a use of the OSI seven-layer model as language.

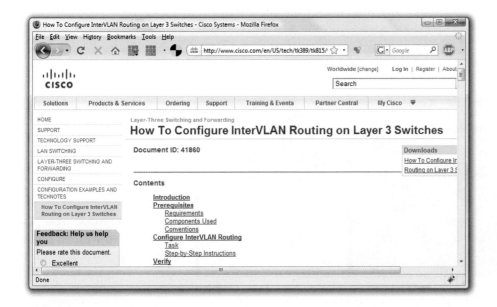

● **Figure 2.1**   Using the OSI terminology—Layer 3—in a typical setup screen

This chapter looks first at models, and specifically at the OSI seven-layer model to see how it helps make network architecture clear for techs. The second and third portions of the chapter apply that model to the practical pieces of networks, the hardware and software common to all networks.

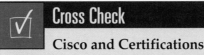

Cross Check

Cisco and Certifications

You learned a little about Cisco, the major player in Internet hardware, in Chapter 1, "CompTIA Network+ in a Nutshell," so check your knowledge. What does Cisco say about CompTIA Network+ certification? Where would you go to get more details?

Historical/Conceptual

■ Working with Models

The best way to learn the OSI seven-layer model is to see it in action. For this reason, I'll introduce you to a small network that needs to copy a file from one computer to another. This example goes through each of the OSI layers needed to copy that file, taking time to explain each step and why it is necessary. By the end of the chapter you should have a definite handle on using the OSI seven-layer model as a way to conceptualize networks. You'll continue to build on this knowledge throughout the book and turn it into a powerful troubleshooting tool.

Biography of a Model

What does the word "model" mean to you? Does the word make you think of a beautiful woman walking down a catwalk at a fashion show or some hunky guy showing off the latest style of blue jeans on a huge billboard? Maybe it makes you think of a plastic model airplane? What about those computer models that try to predict weather? We use the term "model" in a number of ways, but each use shares certain common themes.

All models are a simplified representation of the real thing. The human model ignores the many different types of body shapes, using only a single "optimal" figure. The model airplane lacks functional engines or the internal framework, and the computerized weather model might disregard subtle differences in wind temperatures or geology (Figure 2.2).

• **Figure 2.2**   Types of models (images from left to right courtesy of NOAA, Mike Schinkel, and Albert Poawui)

Additionally, a model must have at least all the major functions of the real item, but what constitutes a major rather than a minor function is open to opinion. Figure 2.3 shows a different level of detail for a model. Does it contain all the major components of an airplane? There's room for argument that perhaps it should have landing gear to go along with the propeller, wings, and tail.

In modeling networks, the OSI seven-layer model faces similar challenges. What functions define all networks? What details can be omitted and yet not render the model inaccurate? Does the model retain its usefulness when describing a network that does not employ all the layers?

In the early days of networking, different manufacturers made unique types of networks that functioned fairly well. But each network had its own cabling, hardware, drivers, naming conventions, and many other unique features. In fact, most commonly, a single manufacturer would provide everything for a customer: cabling, NICs, hubs, and drivers, even all the software, in one complete and expensive package!

• **Figure 2.3**   Simple model airplane

Although these networks worked fine as stand-alone networks, the proprietary nature of the hardware and software made it difficult—to put it mildly—to connect networks of multiple manufacturers. To interconnect networks and improve networking as a whole, someone needed to create a guide, a model that described the functions of a network, so that people who made hardware and software could work together to make networks that worked together well.

The International Organization for Standardization, known as ISO, proposed the OSI seven-layer model. The OSI seven-layer model provides precise terminology for discussing networks—so let's see it!

ISO may look like a misspelled acronym, but it's actually a word, derived from the Greek word *isos*, which means equal.

The Seven Layers in Action

Each layer in the OSI seven-layer model defines a challenge in computer networking, and the protocols that operate at that layer offer solutions to those challenges. **Protocols** define rules, regulations, standards, and procedures so that hardware and software developers can make devices and applications that function properly. The OSI model encourages modular design in networking, meaning that each protocol is designed to deal with a specific layer and to have as little to do with the operation of other layers as possible. Each protocol needs to understand the protocols handling the layers directly above and below it, but it can, and should, be oblivious to the protocols handling the other layers.

The seven layers are

- **Layer 7** Application
- **Layer 6** Presentation
- **Layer 5** Session
- **Layer 4** Transport
- **Layer 3** Network
- **Layer 2** Data Link
- **Layer 1** Physical

The best way to understand OSI is to see it in action—let's see it work at the fictional company of MHTechEd, Inc.

Welcome to MHTechEd!

Mike's High-Tech Educational Supply Store and Post Office, or MHTechEd for short, has a small network of PCs running Windows, a situation typical of many small businesses today. Windows runs just fine on a PC unconnected to a network, but it also comes with all the network software it needs to connect to a network. All the computers in the MHTechEd network are connected by special network cabling.

As in most offices, virtually everyone at MHTechEd has his or her own PC. Figure 2.4 shows two workers, Janelle and Tiffany, who handle all the administrative functions at MHTechEd. Because of the kinds of work they do, these two often need to exchange data between their two PCs. At the moment, Janelle has just completed a new employee handbook in Microsoft Word, and she wants Tiffany to check it for accuracy. Janelle could transfer a copy of the file to Tiffany's computer by the tried-and-true sneakernet method, saving the file on a thumb drive and walking it over to her, but thanks to the wonders of computer networking, she doesn't even have to turn around in her chair. Let's watch in detail each piece of the process that gives Tiffany direct access to Janelle's computer, so she can copy the Word document from Janelle's system to her own.

> Be sure to memorize both the name and the number of each OSI layer. Network techs use terms such as "Layer 4" and "Transport layer" synonymously. Students have long used mnemonics for memorizing such lists. One of my favorites for the OSI seven-layer model is Please Do Not Throw Sausage Pizza Away. Yum!

> Keep in mind that these layers are not laws of physics—anybody who wants to design a network can do it any way he or she wants. While many protocols fit neatly into one of the seven layers, others do not.

> This section is a conceptual overview of the hardware and software functions of a network. Your network may have different hardware or software, but it will share the same functions!

● **Figure 2.4** Janelle and Tiffany, hard at work

Long before Janelle ever saved the Word document on her system—when the systems were first installed—someone who knew what they were doing set up and configured all the systems at MHTechEd to be part of a common network. All this setup activity resulted in multiple layers of hardware and software that can work together behind the scenes to get that Word document from Janelle's system to Tiffany's. Let's examine the different pieces of the network, and then return to the process of Tiffany grabbing that Word document.

Test Specific

■ Let's Get Physical—Network Hardware and Layers 1–2

Clearly the network needs a physical channel through which it can move bits of data between systems. Most networks use a cable like the one shown in Figure 2.5. This cable, known in the networking industry as **unshielded twisted pair (UTP)**, usually contains four pairs of wires that transmit data.

Another key piece of hardware the network uses is a special box-like device called a **hub** (Figure 2.6), often tucked away in a closet or an equipment room. Each system on the network has its own cable that runs to the hub. Think of the hub as being like one of those old-time telephone switchboards, where operators created connections between persons who called in wanting to reach other telephone users.

Layer 1 of the OSI model defines the method of moving data between computers. So the cabling and hubs are part of the **Physical layer** (Layer 1). Anything that moves data from one system to another, such as copper cabling, fiber optics, even radio waves, is part of the Physical layer. Layer 1 doesn't care what data goes through; it just moves the data from one system to another system. Figure 2.7 shows the MHTechEd network in the OSI seven-layer model thus far. Note that each system has the full range of layers, so data from Janelle's computer can flow to Tiffany's computer.

● **Figure 2.5**   UTP cabling

● **Figure 2.6**   Typical hub

The real magic of a network starts with the **network interface card**, or **NIC** (pronounced "nick"), which serves as the interface between the PC and the network. While NICs come in a wide array of shapes and sizes, the ones at MHTechEd look like Figure 2.8.

On older systems, a NIC truly was a separate card that snapped into a handy expansion port, which is why they were called network interface *cards*. Even though they're now built into the motherboard, we still call them NICs.

When installed in a PC, the NIC looks like Figure 2.9. Note the cable running from the back of the NIC into the wall; inside that wall is another cable running all the way back to the hub.

Cabling and hubs define the Physical layer of the network, and NICs provide the interface to the PC. Figure 2.10 shows a diagram of the network cabling system. I'll build on this diagram as I delve deeper into the network process.

You might be tempted to categorize the NIC as part of the Physical layer at this point, and you'd have a valid argument. The NIC clearly is necessary for the physical connection to take place! The CompTIA Network+ exam and most authors put the NIC into Layer 2, the Data Link layer, though, so clearly something else is happening inside the NIC. Let's take a closer look.

Tiffany		Janelle
Layer 7–Application		Layer 7–Application
Layer 6–Presentation		Layer 6–Presentation
Layer 5–Session		Layer 5–Session
Layer 4–Transport		Layer 4–Transport
Layer 3–Network		Layer 3–Network
Layer 2–Data Link		Layer 2–Data Link
Layer 1–Physical	Cabling Hubs	Layer 1–Physical

• **Figure 2.7**   The network so far, with the Physical layer hardware installed

The NIC

To understand networks, you must understand how NICs work. The network must provide a mechanism that gives each system a unique identifier—like a telephone number—so that data is delivered to the right system. That's one of the most important jobs of a NIC. Inside every NIC, burned onto some type of ROM chip, is special firmware containing a

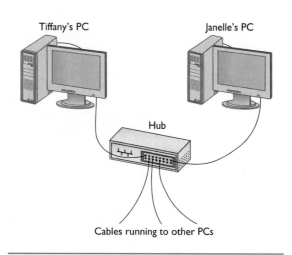

• **Figure 2.8**   Typical NIC

• **Figure 2.9**   NIC with cable connecting the PC to the wall jack

Tiffany's PC

Janelle's PC

Hub

Cables running to other PCs

• **Figure 2.10**   The MHTechEd network

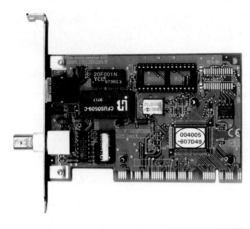

• Figure 2.11   MAC address

unique identifier with a 48-bit value called the *media access control address*, or **MAC address**.

No two NICs ever share the same MAC address—ever. Any company that makes NICs must contact the Institute of Electrical and Electronics Engineers (IEEE) and request a block of MAC addresses, which the company then burns into the ROMs on its NICs. Many NIC makers also print the MAC address on the surface of each NIC, as shown in Figure 2.11. Note that the NIC shown here displays the MAC address in hexadecimal notation. Count the number of hex characters—because each hex character represents 4 bits, it takes 12 hex characters to represent 48 bits.

The MAC address in Figure 2.11 is 004005-607D49, although in print, we represent the MAC as 00–40–05–60–7D–49. The first six digits, in this example 00–40–05, represent the number of the manufacturer of the NIC. Once the IEEE issues to a manufacturer those six hex digits—often referred to as the **organizationally unique identifier (OUI)**—no other manufacturer may use them. The last six digits, in this example 60–7D–49, are the manufacturer's unique serial number for that NIC; this portion of the MAC is often referred to as the **device ID**.

Would you like to see the MAC address for your NIC? If you have a Windows system, type **IPCONFIG /ALL** from a command prompt to display the MAC address (Figure 2.12). Note that IPCONFIG calls the MAC address the **physical address**, which is an important distinction, as you'll see a bit later in the chapter.

Okay, so every NIC in the world has a unique MAC address, but how is it used? Ah, that's where the fun begins! Recall that computer data is binary, which means it's made up of streams of ones and zeroes. NICs send and receive this binary data as pulses of electricity, light, or radio waves. The NICs that use electricity to send and receive data are the most common, so let's

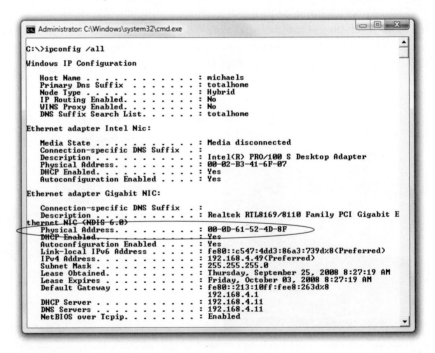

• Figure 2.12   Output from IPCONFIG /ALL

consider that type of NIC. The specific process by which a NIC uses electricity to send and receive data is exceedingly complicated, but luckily for you, not necessary to understand. Instead, just think of a *charge* on the wire as a *one*, and *no charge* as a *zero*. A chunk of data moving in pulses across a wire might look something like Figure 2.13.

If you put an oscilloscope on the wire to measure voltage, you'd see something like Figure 2.14. An oscilloscope is a powerful microscope that enables you to see electrical pulses.

Now, remembering that the pulses represent binary data, visualize instead a string of ones and zeroes moving across the wire (Figure 2.15).

Once you understand how data moves along the wire, the next question becomes this: how does the network get the right data to the right system? All networks transmit data by breaking whatever is moving across the physical layer (files, print jobs, Web pages, and so forth) into discrete chunks called frames. A **frame** is basically a container for a chunk of data moving across a network. The NIC creates and sends, as well as receives and reads, these frames.

I like to visualize an imaginary table inside every NIC that acts as a frame creation and reading station. I see frames as those pneumatic canisters you see when you go to a drive-in teller at a bank. A little guy inside the network card—named Nick, naturally!—builds these pneumatic canisters (the frames) on the table, and then shoots them out on the wire to the hub (Figure 2.16).

Try This!

What's Your MAC Address?

You can readily determine your MAC address on a Windows computer from the command line. This works in all modern versions of Windows.

1. In Windows 2000/XP, click Start | Run. Enter the command **CMD** and press the ENTER key to get to a command prompt.
2. In Windows Vista, click Start, enter **CMD** in the Start Search text box, and press the ENTER key to get to a command prompt.
3. At the command prompt, type the command **IPCONFIG /ALL** and press the ENTER key.

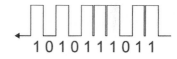

• **Figure 2.13** Data moving along a wire

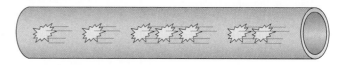

• **Figure 2.14** Oscilloscope of data

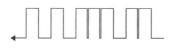

1 0 1 0 1 1 1 0 1 1

• **Figure 2.15** Data as ones and zeroes

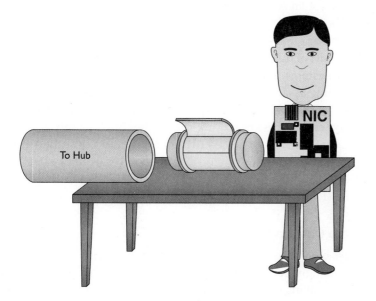

NIC
To Hub

• **Figure 2.16** Inside the NIC

A number of different frame types are used in different networks. All NICs on the same network must use the same frame type or they will not be able to communicate with other NICs.

Recipient's MAC address	Sender's MAC address	Data	CRC

● **Figure 2.17** Generic frame

● **Figure 2.18** Frame as a canister

Here's where the MAC address becomes important. Figure 2.17 shows a representation of a generic frame. Even though a frame is a string of ones and zeroes, we often draw frames as a series of rectangles, each rectangle representing a part of the string of ones and zeroes. You will see this type of frame representation used quite often, so you should become comfortable with it (even though I still prefer to see frames as pneumatic canisters!). Note that the frame begins with the MAC address of the NIC to which the data is to be sent, followed by the MAC address of the sending NIC. Then comes the data, followed by a special bit of checking information called the **cyclic redundancy check (CRC)** that the receiving NIC uses to verify that the data arrived intact.

So, what's inside the data part of the frame? We neither know nor care. The data may be a part of a file, a piece of a print job, or part of a Web page. NICs aren't concerned with content! The NIC simply takes whatever data is passed to it via its device driver and addresses it for the correct system. Special software will take care of *what* data gets sent and what happens to that data when it arrives. This is the beauty of imagining frames as little pneumatic canisters (Figure 2.18). A canister can carry anything from dirt to diamonds—the NIC doesn't care one bit (pardon the pun).

Like a canister, a frame can hold only a certain amount of data. Different networks use different sizes of frames, but generally, a single frame holds about 1500 bytes of data. This raises a new question: what happens when the data to be sent is larger than the frame size? Well, the sending system's software must chop the data up into nice, frame-sized chunks, which it then hands to the NIC for sending. As the receiving system begins to accept the incoming frames, it's up to the receiving system's software to recombine the data chunks as they come in from the network. I'll show how this disassembling and reassembling is done in a moment—first, let's see how the frames get to the right system!

When a system sends a frame out on the network, the frame goes into the hub. The hub, in turn, makes an exact copy of that frame, sending a copy of the original frame to every other system on the network. The interesting part of this process is when the copy of the frame comes into all the other systems. I like to visualize a frame sliding onto the receiving NIC's "frame assembly table," where the electronics of the NIC inspect it. Here's where the magic takes place: only the NIC to which the frame is addressed will process that frame—the other NICs simply erase it when they see that it is not addressed to their MAC address. This is important to appreciate: *every* frame sent on a network is received by *every* NIC, but only the NIC with the matching MAC address will process that particular frame (Figure 2.19).

Getting the Data on the Line

The process of getting data onto the wire and then picking that data off the wire is amazingly complicated. For instance, what happens to keep two NICs from speaking at the same time? Because all the data sent by one NIC is read by every other NIC on the network, only one system may speak at a time. Networks use frames to restrict the amount of data a NIC can send at

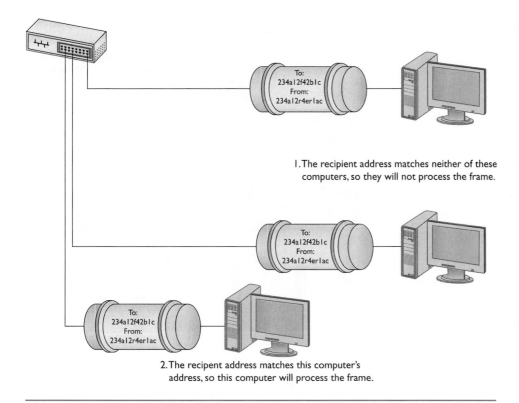

1. The recipient address matches neither of these computers, so they will not process the frame.

2. The recipient address matches this computer's address, so this computer will process the frame.

● Figure 2.19   Incoming frame!

once, giving all NICs a chance to send data over the network in a reasonable span of time. Dealing with this and many other issues requires sophisticated electronics, but the NICs handle these issues completely on their own without our help. So, thankfully, while the folks who design NICs worry about all these details, we don't have to!

Getting to Know You

Using the MAC address is a great way to move data around, but this process raises an important question. How does a sending NIC know the MAC address of the NIC to which it's sending the data? In most cases, the sending system already knows the destination MAC address, because the NICs had probably communicated earlier, and each system stores that data. If it doesn't already know the MAC address, a NIC may send a *broadcast* onto the network to ask for it. The MAC address of FF-FF-FF-FF-FF-FF is the **broadcast address**—if a NIC sends a frame using the broadcast address, every single NIC on the network will process that frame. That broadcast frame's data will contain a request for a system's MAC address. The system with the MAC address your system is seeking will read the request in the broadcast packet and respond with its MAC address.

The Complete Frame Movement

Now that you've seen all the pieces used to send and receive frames, let's put these pieces together and see how a frame gets from one system to another. The basic send/receive process is as follows.

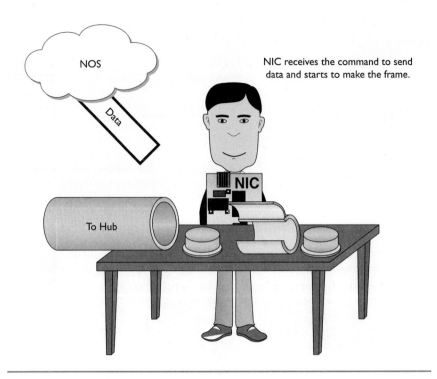

• **Figure 2.20**   Building the frame

First, the sending system network operating system (NOS) software—such as Windows Vista—hands some data to its NIC. The NIC begins building a frame to transport that data to the receiving NIC (Figure 2.20).

After the NIC creates the frame, it adds the CRC, and then dumps it and the data into the frame (Figure 2.21).

• **Figure 2.21**   Adding the data and CRC to the frame

Next, the NIC puts both the destination MAC address and its own MAC address onto the frame. It waits until no other NIC is using the cable, and then sends the frame through the cable to the network (Figure 2.22).

The frame propagates down the wire into the hub, which creates copies of the frame and sends it to every other system on the network. Every NIC receives the frame and checks the MAC address. If a NIC finds that a frame is addressed to it, it processes the frame (Figure 2.23); if the frame is not addressed to it, the NIC erases it.

So, what happens to the data when it gets to the *correct* NIC? First, the receiving NIC uses the CRC to verify that the data is valid. If it is, the receiving NIC strips off all the framing information and sends the data to the software—the network operating system—for processing. The receiving NIC doesn't care what the software does with the data; its job stops the moment it passes on the data to the software.

Any device that deals with a MAC address is part of the OSI **Data Link layer**. Let's update the OSI model to include details about the Data Link layer (Figure 2.24).

Note that the cabling and the hub are located in the Physical layer. The NIC is in the Data Link layer, but spans two sublayers.

● **Figure 2.22**   Sending the frame

The Two Aspects of NICs

Consider how data moves in and out of a NIC. On one end, frames move into and out of the NIC's network cable connection. On the other end, data moves back and forth between the NIC and the network operating system software. The many steps a NIC performs to keep this data moving—sending and

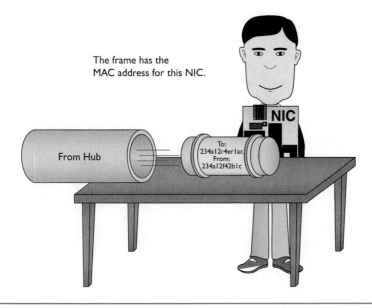

● **Figure 2.23**   Reading an incoming frame

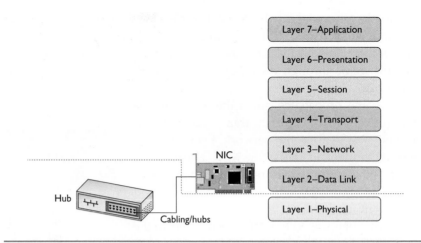

• Figure 2.24   Layer 1 and Layer 2 are now properly applied to the network.

receiving frames over the wire, creating outgoing frames, reading incoming frames, and attaching MAC addresses—are classically broken down into two distinct jobs.

The first job is called the Logical Link Control (LLC). The LLC is the aspect of the NIC that talks to the operating system, places data coming from the software into frames, and creates the CRC on each frame. The LLC is also responsible for dealing with incoming frames: processing those that are addressed to this NIC and erasing frames addressed to other machines on the network.

The second job is called the Media Access Control (MAC), and I bet you can guess what it does! That's right—it remembers the NIC's own MAC address and handles the attachment of MAC addresses to frames. Remember that each frame the LLC creates must include both the sender's and recipient's MAC addresses. The MAC also ensures that the frames, now complete with their MAC addresses, are then sent along the network cabling. Figure 2.25 shows the Data Link layer in detail.

> The CompTIA Network+ exam tests you on the details of the OSI seven-layer model, so know that the Data Link layer is the only layer that has any sublayers.

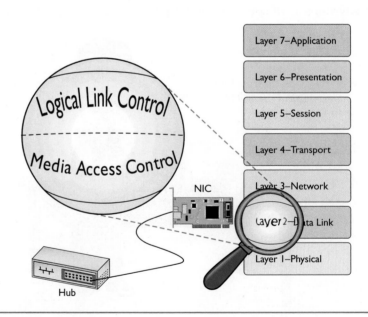

• Figure 2.25   LLC and MAC, the two parts of the Data Link layer

Tech Tip

NIC and Layers

Most networking materials that describe the OSI seven-layer model put NICs squarely into the Data Link layer of the model. It's at the MAC sublayer, after all, that data gets encapsulated into a frame, destination and source MAC addresses get added to that frame, and error checking occurs. What bothers most students with placing NICs solely in the Data Link layer is the obvious other duty of the NIC—putting the ones and zeroes on the network cable. How much more physical can you get?

Many teachers will finesse this issue by defining the Physical layer in its logical sense—that it defines the rules for the ones and zeroes—and then ignore the fact that the data sent on the cable has to come from something. *The first question when you hear a statement like that—at least to me—is, "What component does the sending?" It's the NIC of course, the only device capable of sending and receiving the physical signal.*

Network cards, therefore, operate at both Layer 2 and Layer 1 of the OSI seven-layer model. If cornered to answer one or the other, however, go with the more common answer, Layer 2.

■ Beyond the Single Wire—Network Software and Layers 3–7

Getting data from one system to another in a simple network (defined as one in which all the computers connect to one hub) takes relatively little effort on the part of the NICs. But one problem with simple networks is that computers need to broadcast to get MAC addresses. It works for small networks, but what happens when the network gets big, like the size of the entire Internet? Can you imagine millions of computers all broadcasting? No data could get through. When networks get large, you can't use the MAC addresses any-more. Large networks need a logical addressing method that no longer cares

MAC addresses are also known as physical addresses.

about the hardware and enables us to break up the entire large network into smaller networks called **subnets**. Figure 2.26 shows two ways to set up a network. On the left, all the computers connect to a single hub. On the right, however, the LAN is separated into two five-computer subnets.

To move past the physical MAC addresses and start using logical addressing requires some special software, usually called a **network protocol**. Network protocols exist in every operating system. A network protocol not only has to create unique identifiers for each system, but must also create a set of communication rules for issues like how to handle data chopped up

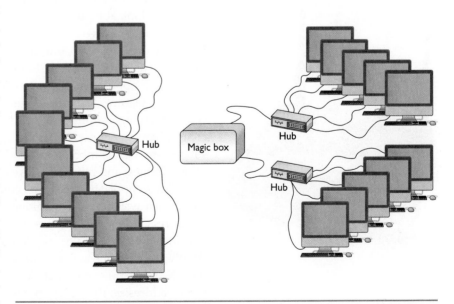

● **Figure 2.26** Large LAN complete (left) and broken up into two subnets (right)

TCP/IP is the most famous network protocol, but there are others.

into multiple packets, and how to make sure that those packets get from one subnet to another. Let's take a moment to learn a bit about the most famous network protocol—TCP/IP—and its unique universal addressing system.

To be accurate, TCP/IP is really several network protocols designed to work together—but two protocols, TCP and IP, do so much work the folks who invented all these protocols named the whole thing TCP/IP. TCP stands for **Transmission Control Protocol**, and IP stands for **Internet Protocol**. IP is the network protocol I need to discuss first; rest assured, however, I'll cover TCP in plenty of detail later.

IP—Playing on Layer 3, the Network Layer

The IP protocol is the primary protocol that TCP/IP uses at Layer 3 (Network) of the OSI model. The IP protocol makes sure that a piece of data gets to where it needs to go on the network. It does this by giving each device on the network a unique numeric identifier called an **IP address**. An IP address is known as a **logical address** to distinguish it from the physical address, the MAC address of the NIC.

Every network protocol uses some type of naming convention, but no two protocols use the same convention. IP uses a rather unique dotted decimal notation (sometimes referred to as a dotted-octet numbering system) based on four 8-bit numbers. Each 8-bit number ranges from 0 to 255, and the four numbers are separated by periods. (If you don't see how 8-bit numbers can range from 0 to 255, don't worry. By the end of this book, you'll understand these naming conventions in more detail than you ever believed possible!) A typical IP address might look like this:

192.168.4.232

No two systems on the same network share the same IP address; if two machines accidentally receive the same address, they won't be able to send or receive data. These IP addresses don't just magically appear—they must be configured by the end user (or the network administrator).

Take a look at Figure 2.26. What makes logical addressing powerful are the magic boxes—called **routers**—that separate each of the subnets. Routers work like a hub, but instead of forwarding packets by MAC address they use the IP address. Routers enable you to take one big network and chop it up into smaller networks. Routers also have a second, very important feature. They enable you to connect networks with different types of cabling or frames. Figure 2.27 shows a typical router. This router enables you to connect a network that uses MAC addresses—a small subnet—to a cable modem network. You can't do that with a hub—the cables, frames, and physical addressing are totally different!

What's important here is for you to appreciate that in a TCP/IP network, each system has two unique identifiers: the MAC address and the IP address. The MAC address (the physical address) is literally burned into the chips on the NIC, while the IP address (the logical address) is simply stored in the software of the system. MAC addresses come with the NIC, so we don't configure MAC addresses, whereas we must configure IP addresses through software. Figure 2.28 shows the MHTechEd network diagram again, this time with the MAC and IP addresses displayed for each system.

● **Figure 2.27**   Typical small router

This two-address system enables IP networks to do something really cool and powerful: using IP addresses, systems can send each other data without regard to the physical connection!

This capability requires more than the simple assignment of an IP address for each computer. The network protocol must also know where to send the frame, no matter what type of hardware the various computers are running. To do this, a network protocol also uses frames—actually, frames within frames!

Anything that has to do with logical addressing works at the OSI **Network layer**. At this point there are only two items we know of that operate at the Network layer— routers and the part of the network protocol on every computer that understands the logical addressing (Figure 2.29).

MAC address 00-A0-C9-98-12-F4
IP address   192.168.6.5

Computer A

MAC address 00-A9-D8-98-12-F5
IP address   192.168.6.6

Computer B

Hub

MAC address 00-A0-C9-77-10-C3
IP address   192.168.6.7

MAC address 00-C3-B9-47-08-C3
IP address   192.168.6.8

● **Figure 2.28**   MHTechEd addressing

Head to Chapter 7, "TCP/IP Basics," and Chapter 8, "The Wonderful World of Routing," to get much deeper into routers.

There's Frames in Them Thar Frames!

Whoa! Frames within frames? What are you talking about, Mike? Never fear—I'll show you. Visualize the network protocol software as a layer between the system's software and the NIC. When the IP network protocol gets hold of data coming from your system's software, it places its own frame around that data. We call this inner frame an IP **packet**, so it won't be confused with the *frame* that the NIC will add later. Instead of adding MAC addresses to its packet, the network protocol adds sending and receiving IP addresses. Figure 2.30 shows a typical IP packet; notice the similarity to the frames you saw earlier.

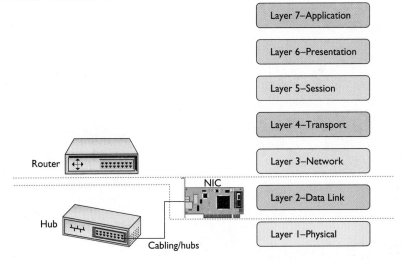

Router

NIC

Hub

Cabling/hubs

Layer 7–Application

Layer 6–Presentation

Layer 5–Session

Layer 4–Transport

Layer 3–Network

Layer 2–Data Link

Layer 1–Physical

● **Figure 2.29**   Router now added to the OSI model for the network

This is a highly simplified IP packet. I am not including lots of little parts of the IP packet in this diagram because they are not important to what you need to understand right now—but don't worry, you'll see them later in the book!

Data type	Packet Count	Recipient's IP address	Sender's IP address	Data

● **Figure 2.30**   IP packet

• **Figure 2.31**   IP packet in a frame (as a canister)

But IP packets don't leave their PC home naked. Each IP packet is handed to the NIC, which then encloses the IP packet in a regular frame, creating, in essence, a *packet within a frame*. I like to visualize the packet as an envelope, with the envelope in the pneumatic canister frame (Figure 2.31). A more conventional drawing would look like Figure 2.32.

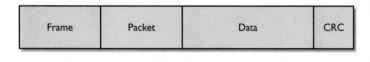

| Frame | Packet | Data | CRC |

• **Figure 2.32**   IP packet in a frame

All very nice, you say, but why hassle with this *packet in a frame* business when you could just use MAC addresses? For that matter, why even bother with this IP thing in the first place? Good question! Let's get back to talking about routers!

Let's say that Janelle wants to access the Internet from her PC using her cable line. A tech could add a cable modem directly to her computer, but the boss wants everyone on the network to get on the Internet using a single cable modem connection. To make this possible, the MHTechEd network will connect to the Internet through a router (Figure 2.33).

The router that MHTechEd uses has two connections. One is just a built-in NIC that runs from the router to the hub. The other connection links the router to a cable modem. Therein lies the answer: cable networks *don't use MAC addresses*. They use their own type of frame that has nothing to do with MAC addresses. If you tried to send a regular network frame on a cable modem network—well, I don't know exactly what would happen, but I assure you, it wouldn't work! For this reason, when a router receives an IP packet inside a frame added by a NIC, it peels off that frame

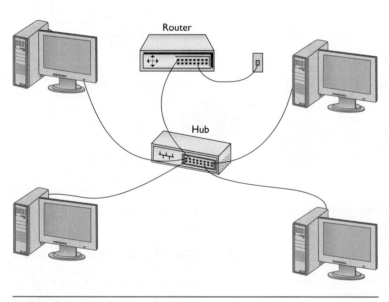

• **Figure 2.33**   Adding a router to the network

and replaces it with the type of frame the cable network needs (Figure 2.34).

Once the network frame is gone, so are the MAC addresses! Thus, you need some *other* naming system the router can use to get the data to the right computer—and that's why you use IP addresses on a network. After the router strips off the MAC addresses and puts on whatever type of addressing used by the cable modem network, the frame flies through the cable modem network, using the IP address to guide the frame to the router connected to the receiving system. At this point, the process reverses. The router rips off the cable modem frame, adds the MAC address for the receiving system, and sends it on the network, where the receiving system picks it up (Figure 2.35).

The receiving NIC strips away the MAC address header information and passes the remaining packet off to the software. The networking software built into your operating system handles all the rest of the work. The NIC's driver software is the interconnection between the hardware and the software. The NIC driver knows how to communicate with the NIC to send and receive frames, but it can't do anything with the packet. Instead, the NIC driver hands the packet off to other programs that know how to deal with all the separate packets and turn them into Web pages, e-mail messages, files, and so forth.

The Network layer is the last layer that deals directly with hardware. All the other layers of the OSI seven-layer model work strictly within software.

Assembly and Disassembly—Layer 4, the Transport Layer

Because most chunks of data are much larger than a single frame, they must be chopped up before they can be sent across a network. When a serving computer receives a request for some data, it must be able to chop the requested data into chunks that will fit into a packet (and eventually into the NIC's frame), organize the packets for the benefit of the receiving system, and hand them to the NIC for sending. The receiving system must be able to recognize a series of incoming packets as one data transmission, reassemble the packets correctly based on information included in the packets by the sending system, and verify that all the packets for that piece of data arrived in good shape.

This part is relatively simple—the network protocol breaks up the data into packets and gives each packet some type of sequence number. I like to compare this process to the one that my favorite international shipping company uses. I receive boxes from UPS almost every day; in fact, some days I receive many, many boxes from UPS! To make sure I get all the boxes for one shipment, UPS puts a numbering system, like the one shown in Figure 2.36, on the label of each box. A computer sending data on a network does the same thing. Embedded into the

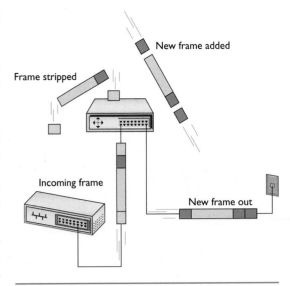

• **Figure 2.34** Router removing network frame and adding one for the cable line

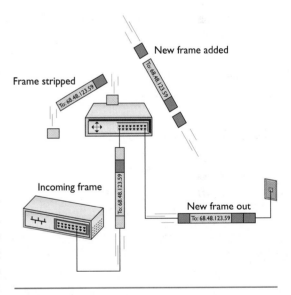

• **Figure 2.35** Router in action

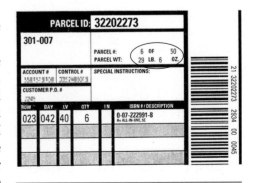

• **Figure 2.36** Labeling the boxes

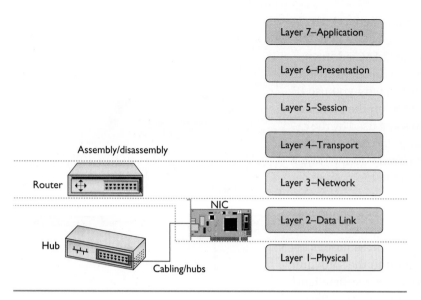

Layer 7–Application

Layer 6–Presentation

Layer 5–Session

Layer 4–Transport

Layer 3–Network

Layer 2–Data Link

Layer 1–Physical

Assembly/disassembly

Router

Hub

NIC

Cabling/hubs

● **Figure 2.37** OSI updated

data of each packet is a sequencing number. By reading the sequencing numbers, the receiving system knows both the total number of packets and how to put them back together.

The MHTechEd network just keeps getting more and more complex, doesn't it? And you still haven't seen the Word document get copied, have you? Don't worry; you're almost there—just a few more pieces to go!

Layer 4, the **Transport layer** of the OSI seven-layer model, has only one big job: it's the assembler/disassembler software. As part of its job, the Transport layer also initializes requests for packets that weren't received in good order (Figure 2.37).

Talking on a Network—Layer 5, the Session Layer

Now that you understand that the system uses software to assemble and disassemble data packets, what's next? In a network, any one system may be talking to many other systems at any given moment. For example, Janelle's PC has a printer used by all the MHTechEd systems, so there's a better than average chance that as Tiffany tries to access the Word document, another system will be sending a print job to Janelle's PC (Figure 2.38). Janelle's system must direct these incoming files, print jobs, Web pages, and so on to the

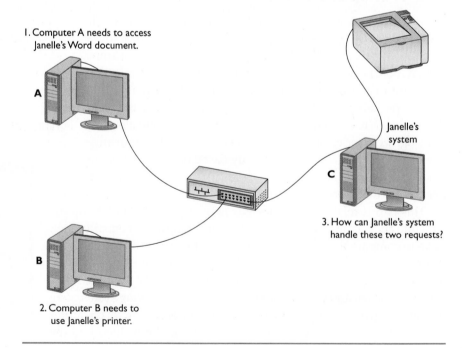

1. Computer A needs to access Janelle's Word document.

A

B

C

Janelle's system

2. Computer B needs to use Janelle's printer.

3. How can Janelle's system handle these two requests?

● **Figure 2.38** Handling multiple inputs

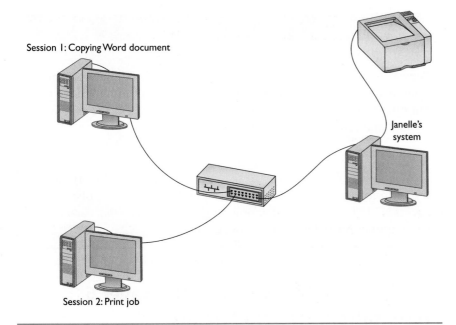

Session 1: Copying Word document

Janelle's system

Session 2: Print job

● **Figure 2.39**   Each request becomes a session.

right programs (Figure 2.39). Additionally, the operating system must enable one system to make a connection to another system to verify that the other system can handle whatever operation the initiating system wants to perform. If Bill's system wants to send a print job to Janelle's printer, it first contacts Janelle's system to ensure that it is ready to handle the print job. The **session software** handles this part of networking.

Layer 5, the **Session layer** of the OSI seven-layer model, handles all the sessions for a system. The Session layer initiates sessions, accepts incoming sessions, and opens and closes existing sessions. The Session layer also keeps track of computer naming conventions, such as calling your computer SYSTEM01 or some other type of name that makes more sense than an IP or MAC address (Figure 2.40).

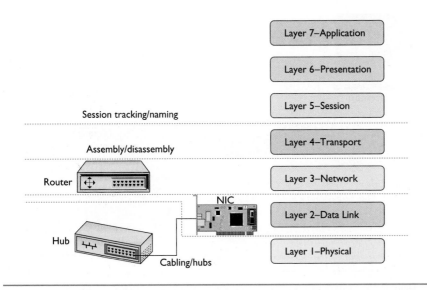

● **Figure 2.40**   OSI updated

Standardized Formats, or Why Layer 6, Presentation, Has No Friends

One of the most powerful aspects of a network lies in the fact that it works with (almost) any operating system. Today's networks easily connect, for example, a Macintosh system to a Windows PC, despite the fact that these different operating systems use different formats for many types of data. Different data formats used to drive us crazy back in the days before word processors (like Microsoft Word) could import or export a thousand other word processor formats (Figure 2.41).

This created the motivation for standardized formats that anyone—at least with the right program—could read from any type of computer. Specialized file formats, such as Adobe's popular Portable Document Format (PDF) for documents and PostScript for printing, provide standard formats that any system, regardless of the operating system, can read, write, and edit (Figure 2.42).

Tech Tip

Acrobat as Open Standard
Adobe released the PDF standard to ISO in 2007 and PDF became the ISO 32000 open standard. Adobe Acrobat remains the premier application for reading and editing PDF documents, so most folks call PDF documents Acrobat files.

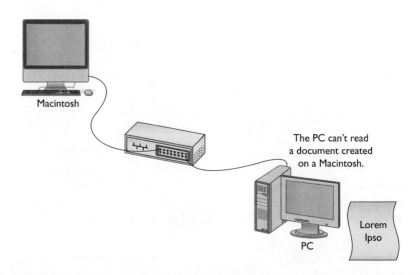

• **Figure 2.41**   Different data formats were often unreadable between systems.

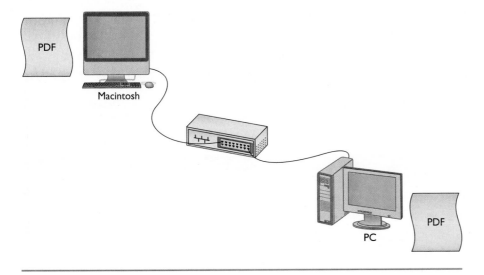

Layer 6, the **Presentation layer** of the OSI seven-layer model, handles converting data into formats that are readable by the system. Of all the OSI layers, the high level of standardization of file formats has made the Presentation layer the least important and least used (Figure 2.43).

Network Applications—Layer 7, the Application Layer

The last, and most visible, part of any network is the software applications that use it. If you want to copy a file residing on another system in your network, you need an application like Network in Windows Vista (or My Network Places in earlier versions of Windows) that enables you to access files on remote systems. If you want to view Web pages, you need a Web browser like Internet Explorer or Mozilla Firefox. The people who use a network experience it through an application. A user who knows nothing about all the other parts of a network may still know how to open an e-mail application to retrieve mail (Figure 2.44).

Applications may include a number of additional functions, such as encryption, user authentication, and tools to control the look of the data. But these functions are specific to the given applications. In other words, if you want to put a password on your Word document, you must use the password functions of Word to do so.

Layer 7, the **Application layer** of the OSI seven-layer model, refers to the code built into all operating systems that enables network-aware applications. All operating systems have Application Programming Interfaces (APIs) that

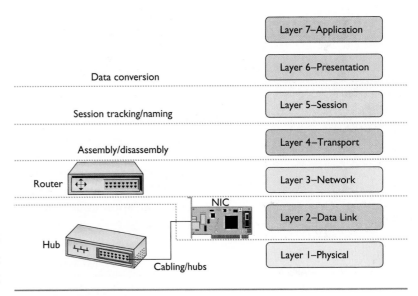

● **Figure 2.43** OSI updated

• **Figure 2.44**   Network applications at work

programmers can use to make their programs network aware (Figure 2.45). An API in general provides a standard way for programmers to enhance or extend an application's capabilities.

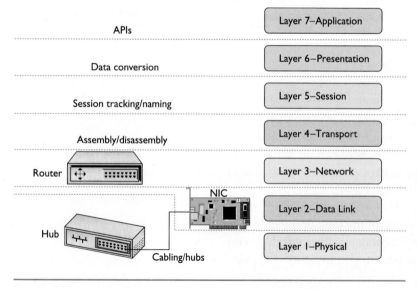

| APIs |
| Data conversion |
| Session tracking/naming |
| Assembly/disassembly |
| Router |
| NIC |
| Hub |
| Cabling/hubs |

Layer 7–Application

Layer 6–Presentation

Layer 5–Session

Layer 4–Transport

Layer 3–Network

Layer 2–Data Link

Layer 1–Physical

• **Figure 2.45**   OSI updated

How Tiffany Gets Her Document

Okay, you've now seen all the different parts of the network; keep in mind that not all networks contain all these pieces. Certain functions, such as encryption (which is used to make readable text unreadable), may or may not be present, depending on the needs of the particular network. With that understanding, let's watch the network do its magic as Tiffany gets Janelle's Word document.

The Application layer gives Tiffany choices for accessing Janelle's Word document. She can access the document by opening Word on her system, selecting File | Open, and taking the file off Janelle's desktop; or she can use Network,

Computer, or Windows Explorer to copy the Word file from Janelle's desktop to her computer, and then open her own copy of the file in Word. Tiffany wants to make changes to the document, so she chooses to copy it over to her system. This will leave an original copy on Janelle's system, so Janelle can still use it if she doesn't like Tiffany's changes.

Tiffany's goal is to copy the file from Janelle's shared Desktop folder to her system. Let's watch it happen. The process begins when Tiffany opens her Network application. The Network application shows her all the computers on the MHTechEd network (Figure 2.46).

Both systems are PCs running Word, so Tiffany doesn't need to worry about incompatible data formats, which means the Presentation layer (Layer 6) doesn't come into play here. As soon as Tiffany clicks the icon for Janelle's system in Network, the two systems begin to use the OSI Session layer (Layer 5) and establish a session. Janelle's system checks a database of user names and privileges to see what Tiffany can and cannot do on Janelle's system. This checking process takes place a number of times during the process as Tiffany accesses various shared folders on Janelle's system. By this time, a session has been established between the two machines. Tiffany now opens the shared folder and locates the Word document. To copy the file, she drags and drops the Word document icon from her Network application onto her desktop (Figure 2.47).

This simple act starts a series of actions. First, Janelle's OSI Transport layer (Layer 4) software begins to chop the Word document into packets

● **Figure 2.46**   Network application showing computers on the MHTechEd network

● **Figure 2.47**   Copying the Word document

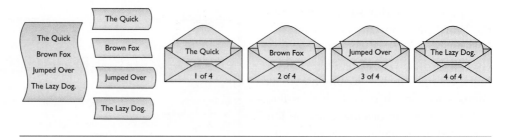

• **Figure 2.48**   Chopping the Word document

and assign each a sequence number, so that Tiffany's system will know how to reassemble the packets when they arrive on her system (Figure 2.48).

After Janelle's system chops the data into numbered packets, the OSI Network layer (Layer 3) software adds to each packet the address of Tiffany's system, as well as Janelle's address (Figure 2.49).

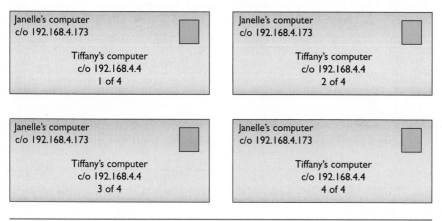

• **Figure 2.49**   Creating and addressing packets

The packets now get sent to the NIC for transfer. The NIC's OSI Data Link layer (Layer 2) adds around each packet a frame that contains the MAC addresses for Tiffany's and Janelle's systems (Figure 2.50).

As the NIC assembles each frame, it checks the network cabling to see if the cable is busy. If not, it sends the frame down the wire, finally using the Physical layer (Layer 1). Now it's time to reverse the process as the frames arrive at Tiffany's system. The frame goes through the hub and off to every other NIC in the network. Each NIC looks at the MAC address. All the other systems discard the frame, but Tiffany's system sees its MAC address and grabs it (Figure 2.51).

As Tiffany's NIC begins to take in frames, it checks each one using the CRC to ensure the validity of the data in the frame. After verifying the data, the NIC strips off both the frame and the CRC and passes the packet up to the next layer. Tiffany's system then begins to reassemble the individual packets back into the complete Word document. If Tiffany's system fails to receive one of the packets, it simply requests that Janelle's computer resend it.

Once Tiffany's system reassembles the completed Word document, it sends the document to the proper application—in this case, Windows Explorer. Once the system copies the file to the desktop, the network applications erase the session connection information

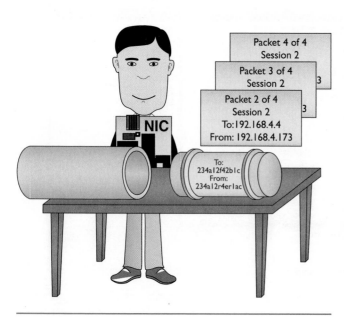

• **Figure 2.50**   Creating frames

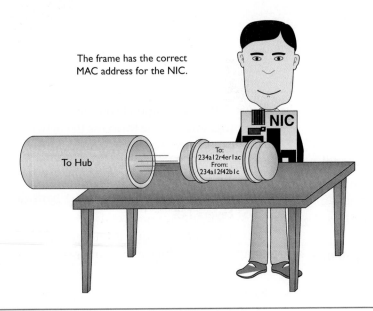

The frame has the correct MAC address for the NIC.

To Hub

NIC

To:
234a12r4er1ac
From:
234a12f42b1c

● **Figure 2.51**   Tiffany's system grabbing a frame

from each system and prepare for what Tiffany and Janelle may want to do next.

The most amazing part of this process is that the users see virtually none of it. Tiffany simply opened her Network application, located Janelle's system, located the shared folder containing the Word document, and then dragged and dropped the Word document onto her desktop. This is the beauty and mystery of networks. The complexities of the different parts of software and hardware working together aren't noticed by users—nor should they be!

The Tech's Troubleshooting Tool

The OSI seven-layer model provides you with a way to conceptualize a network to determine what could cause a specific problem when the inevitable problems occur. Users don't need to know anything about this, but techs can use the OSI model for troubleshooting.

If Jane can't print to the networked printer, for example, the OSI model can help solve the problem. If her NIC shows activity, then you can set aside both the Physical layer (Layer 1) and Data Link layer (Layer 2) and go straight to the Network layer (Layer 3). If her computer has a proper IP address, then Layer 3 is done and you can move on up to check other layers to solve the problem.

By understanding how network traffic works throughout the model, you can troubleshoot with efficiency. You can use the OSI model during your career as a network tech as the basis for troubleshooting.

Chapter 2 Review

■ Chapter Summary

After reading this chapter and completing the exercises, you should understand the following about networking.

Describe models such as the OSI seven-layer model

■ The OSI seven-layer model defines the role played by each protocol. The OSI model also provides a common jargon that network techs can use to describe the function of any network protocol.

■ Layer 1, the Physical layer, includes anything that moves data from one system to another, such as cabling or radio waves.

■ Layer 2, the Data Link layer, defines the rules for accessing and using the Physical layer. The Data Link layer is divided into two sublayers: Media Access Control (MAC) and Logical Link Control (LLC). The MAC sublayer controls access to the Physical layer, or shared media. It encapsulates (creates the frames for) data sent from the system, adding source and destination MAC addresses and error-checking information; it also decapsulates (removes the MAC addresses and CRC from) data received by the system. The LLC sublayer provides an interface with the Network layer protocols. It is responsible for the ordered delivery of frames, including retransmission of missing or corrupt packets, and for flow control (moderating data flow so one system doesn't overwhelm the other). Any device that deals with a MAC address is part of the Data Link layer.

■ Layer 3, the Network layer, is the last layer to work directly with hardware. It adds to the packets unique identifiers (such as IP addresses) that enable routers to make sure the packets get to the correct system without worrying about the type of hardware used for transmission. Anything having to do with logical addressing works at the Network layer.

■ Layer 4, the Transport layer, breaks up data received from the upper layers into smaller pieces for transport, called packets.

■ Layer 5, the Session layer, manages the connections between machines on the network.

■ Layer 6, the Presentation layer, presents data from the sending system in a form that the applications on the receiving system can understand.

■ Layer 7, the Application layer, defines a set of tools that programs can use to access the network. Application layer programs provide services to the programs that the users see.

Explain the major functions of network hardware with OSI Layers 1–2

■ Network hardware consists most often of three components: cabling, a hub, and network interface cards (NICs).

■ Every NIC has a hard-coded, unique identifying 48-bit number, called a media access control address (MAC address). The MAC address can be broken down into an organizationally unique identifier (OUI) and a device ID.

■ All networks transmit data by breaking whatever is moving across the network (files, print jobs, Web pages, and so forth) into discrete chunks called *frames*. A frame is basically a container for a chunk of data moving across a network. The NIC creates and sends, as well as receives and reads, these frames.

■ A frame begins with the MAC address of the NIC to which the data is to be sent, followed by the MAC address of the sending NIC. Then comes the data, followed by a special bit of checking information called the cyclic redundancy check (CRC) that the receiving NIC uses to verify that the data got to it correctly.

■ Hubs make copies of frames they receive and forward them to every system on the network. Only the system for which the frame was destined disassembles the frame. All other systems ignore the frame.

■ If the sending system does not know the MAC address of the receiving system, it broadcasts the frame using the broadcast address. In this case, every system inspects the frame and no system ignores it.

Describe the functions of network software with OSI Layers 3–7

■ Network protocols create software-addressing schemes that enable network traffic to cross routers, which can connect networks of differing cabling or frame types. TCP/IP is a well-known suite of network protocols, of which TCP and IP are the individual protocols that do most of the work in the suite.

■ The Internet Protocol (IP) makes sure that a piece of data gets to where it needs to go on the network. It does this by giving each device on the network a unique numeric identifier, called, appropriately, an IP address. The IP address is a logical address stored in the software of the system, whereas a MAC address is a physical address burned into the NIC. Both the IP address and MAC address can be viewed by running the command-line IPCONFIG program.

■ When packaging data, IP creates a packet containing the receiving and sending computers' IP addresses, and then places that packet into a network frame.

■ The network protocol breaks up data into packets and gives each packet some type of sequence number so that the receiving PC can reassemble the data properly.

■ Session software handles the process of differentiating between various types of connections on a PC. The NETSTAT program can be used to view existing sessions.

■ Standardized data formats, such as PDF, enable computers running on different platforms to share data across a network, the result of which is that the Presentation layer is the least important and least used of the seven layers.

■ Network applications, such as Network (or My Network Places), enable you to access files or features on remote systems.

■ Key Terms

Application layer *(29)*
broadcast address *(17)*
cyclic redundancy check (CRC) *(16)*
Data Link layer *(19)*
device ID *(14)*
frame *(15)*
hub *(12)*
Internet Protocol (IP) *(22)*
IP address *(22)*
logical address *(22)*
MAC address *(14)*
network interface card (NIC) *(13)*
Network layer *(23)*
network protocol *(21)*

OSI seven-layer model *(8)*
organizationally unique identifier (OUI) *(14)*
packet *(23)*
physical address *(14)*
Physical layer *(12)*
Presentation layer *(29)*
protocol *(11)*
router *(22)*
Session layer *(27)*
session software *(27)*
subnet *(21)*
Transmission Control Protocol (TCP) *(22)*
Transport layer *(26)*
unshielded twisted pair (UTP) *(12)*

■ Key Term Quiz

Use the Key Terms list to complete the sentences that follow. Not all terms will be used.

1. The _____ is an example of software that creates packets for moving data across networks.

2. Most often, the _____ provides the physical connection between the PC and the network.

3. Using the _____ enables a computer to send a packet that every other PC on the network will process.

4. You can connect two very different networks by using a(n) _____.

5. Every NIC has a hard-coded identifier called a(n) _____.

6. The _____ provides an excellent tool for conceptualizing how a network works.

7. On a sending machine, data gets broken up at the _____ of the OSI seven-layer model.

8. NICs encapsulate data into a(n) _____ for sending that data over a network.

9. A(n) _____ enables multiple machines to connect over a network.

10. The _____ provides the key interface between the Physical and Network layers.

■ Multiple-Choice Quiz

1. Which of the following OSI layers converts the ones and zeroes to electrical signals and places these signals on the cable?

    A. Physical layer

    B. Transport layer

    C. Network layer

    D. Data Link layer

2. The term "unshielded twisted pair" describes which of the following network components?

    A. Cable

    B. Hub

    C. Router

    D. NIC

3. From the options that follow, select the one that best describes the contents of a typical network frame.

    A. Sender's MAC address, recipient's MAC address, data, CRC

    B. Recipient's MAC address, sender's MAC address, data, CRC

    C. Recipient's IP address, sender's IP address, data, CRC

    D. Recipient's e-mail address, sender's e-mail address, data, CRC

4. Which of the following is most likely to be a MAC address assigned to a NIC?

    A. 192.168.1.121

    B. 24.17.232.7B

    C. 23.4F.17.8A.4C.10

    D. 713.555.1212

5. Which layer of the OSI model involves routing?

    A. Physical layer

    B. Transport layer

    C. Network layer

    D. Data Link layer

6. How much data can a typical frame contain?

    A. 500 bytes

    B. 1500 bytes

    C. 1500 kilobytes

    D. 1 megabyte

7. Which of the following best describes an IP address?

    A. A unique dotted decimal notation burned into every NIC

    B. A unique 48-bit identifying number burned into every NIC

    C. A dotted decimal notation assigned to a NIC by software

    D. A 48-bit identifying number assigned to a NIC by software

8. Which layer of the OSI model makes sure the data is in a readable format for the Application layer?

    A. Application layer

    B. Presentation layer

    C. Session layer

    D. Transport layer

9. Which of the following enables you to connect a PC via modem to an IP network?

    A. NIC

    B. Hub

    C. Router

    D. TCP

10. What handles the initial connection between two computers to verify that the receiving system can handle the network request of the sending system?

    A. NIC

    B. IP

    C. TCP

    D. Session software

11. What is Layer 3 of the OSI seven-layer model?

    A. Presentation layer

    B. Session layer

    C. Transport layer

    D. Network layer

12. What component of Layer 2 of the OSI seven-layer model is responsible for the ordered delivery of frames, including retransmission of missing or corrupt packets?

    A. MAC sublayer

    B. LLC sublayer

    C. CRC sublayer

    D. Data Link sublayer

13. Which components work at Layer 1 of the OSI seven-layer model? (Select two.)

    A. Cables

    B. Hub

    C. Network protocol

    D. Session software

14. Andalyn says complete 48-bit MAC addresses are allocated to NIC manufacturers from the IEEE. Buster says the IEEE only assigns the first 24 bits to manufacturers. Carlos says the IEEE assigns only the last 24 bits to manufacturers. Who is correct?

    A. Only Andalyn is correct.

    B. Only Buster is correct.

    C. Only Carlos is correct.

    D. No one is correct.

15. If a sending system does not know the MAC address of the intended recipient system, it sends a broadcast frame with what MAC address?

    A. 192.168.0.0

    B. FF-FF-FF-FF-FF-FF

    C. 11-11-11-11-11-11

    D. 00-00-00-00-00-00

■ Essay Quiz

1. Some new techs at your office are confused by the differences between a NIC's frame and an IP packet. Write a short essay describing the two encapsulations, including the components that do the encapsulating.

2. Your boss has received a set of files with the file extension .WP and is worried because he's never seen that extension before. He wants people to have access to the information in those files from anywhere in the network. Write a short memo describing how Microsoft Word can handle these files, including discussion of how that fits with the OSI seven-layer model.

3. After reading this chapter over your shoulder, your co-worker is not clear about how the Tiffany and Janelle story connects with the OSI seven-layer model. Write an essay that describes each layer and include an example from the Tiffany and Janelle story that fits at each layer.

Lab Projects

• Lab Project 2.1

Examine your classroom network. What components does it have? How would you classify those components according to the OSI seven-layer model?

• Lab Project 2.2

Create a mnemonic phrase to help you remember the OSI seven-layer model. With two layers beginning with the letter *P*, how will you differentiate in your mnemonic between Presentation and Physical? How will you incorporate the two sublayers of the Data Link layer?

Cabling and Topology

"It's from someone who says she's a fan of my work on low-dimensional topology. And she's a fan of my . . . hair."

—CHARLIE EPPES, *NUMB3RS*

In this chapter, you will learn how to

■ **Explain the different types of network topologies**

■ **Describe the different types of network cabling**

■ **Describe the IEEE networking standards**

Every network must provide some method to get data from one system to another. In most cases, this method consists of some type of cabling (usually copper or fiber-optic) running between systems, although many networks skip wires and use wireless methods to move data. Stringing those cables brings up a number of critical issues you need to understand to work on a network. How do all these cables connect the computers together? Does every computer on the network run a cable to a central point? Does a single cable snake through the ceiling, with all the computers on the network connected to it? These questions need answering! Furthermore, we need some standards so that manufacturers can make networking equipment that works well together. While we're talking about standards, what about the cabling itself? What type of cable? What quality of copper? How thick should it be? Who defines the standards for cables so that they all work in the network?

This chapter answers these questions in three parts. First, you will learn about **network topology**—the way that cables and other pieces of hardware connect to one another. Second, you will tour the most common standardized cable types used in networking. Third, you will discover the IEEE committees that create network technology standards.

Test Specific

◼ Topology

Computer networks employ many different *topologies*, or ways of connecting computers together. This section looks at both the historical topologies—bus, ring, and star—and the modern topologies—hybrid, mesh, point-to-multipoint, and point-to-point.

Bus and Ring

The first generation of wired networks used one of two topologies, both shown in Figure 3.1. A **bus topology** uses a single bus cable that connects all of the computers in line. A **ring topology** connects all computers on the network with a central ring of cable.

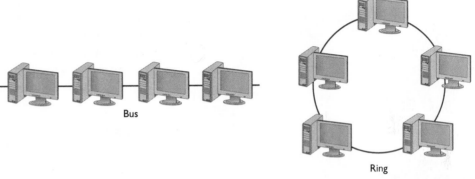

Note that topologies are diagrams, much like an electrical circuit diagram. Real network cabling doesn't go in perfect circles or perfect straight lines. Figure 3.2 shows a bus topology network that illustrates how the cable might appear in the real world.

Data flows differently between bus and ring networks, creating different problems and solutions. In bus topology networks, data from each computer simply goes out on the whole bus. A network using a bus topology needs termination at each end of the cable to prevent a signal sent from one computer from reflecting at the ends of the cable, creating unnecessary traffic (Figure 3.3). In a ring topology network, in contrast, data traffic moves in a circle from one computer to

• **Figure 3.1**   Bus and ring topologies

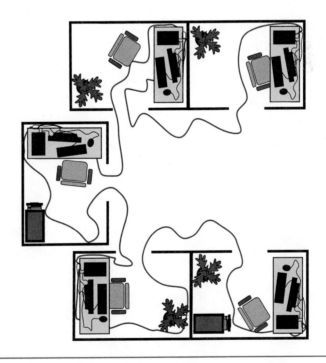

• **Figure 3.2**   Real-world bus topology

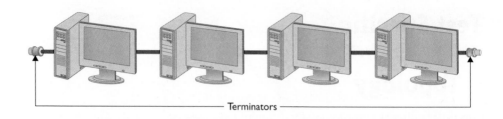

• **Figure 3.3** Terminated bus topology

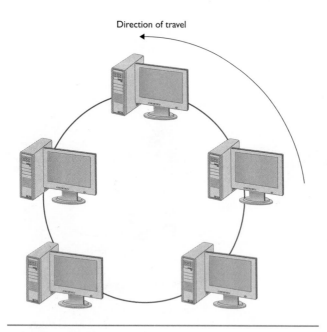

Direction of travel

• **Figure 3.4** Ring topology moving in a certain direction

the next in the same direction (Figure 3.4). With no end of the cable, ring networks require no termination.

Bus and ring topology networks worked well, but suffered from the same problem: the entire network stopped working if the cable broke at any point. The broken ends on a bus topology aren't terminated, causing reflection between computers still connected. A break in a ring topology network simply breaks the circuit and stops the data flow (Figure 3.5).

Star

The **star topology** uses a central connection for all the computers on the network (Figure 3.6). Star topology had a huge benefit over ring and bus by offering **fault tolerance**—if one of the cables broke, all of the other computers could still communicate. Bus and ring were popular and inexpensive to implement, so the old-style star topology wasn't very successful. Network hardware designers couldn't easily redesign their existing networks to use star topology.

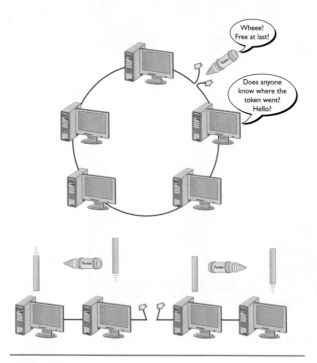

• **Figure 3.5** Nobody is talking!

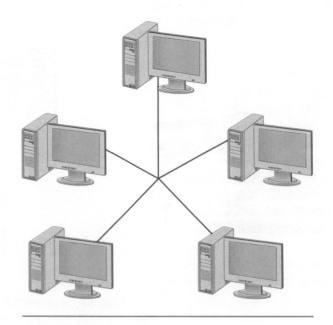

• **Figure 3.6** Star topology

Hybrids

Even though network designers couldn't use a star topology, the benefits of star were overwhelming, motivating smart people to come up with a way to use star without a major redesign—and the way they did so was ingenious. The ring topology networks struck first by taking the entire ring and shrinking it into a small box, as shown in Figure 3.7.

This was quickly followed by the bus topology folks, who in turn shrunk their bus (better known as the **segment**) into their own box (Figure 3.8).

Physically, they looked like a star, but if you looked at it as an electronic schematic, the signals acted like a ring or a bus. Clearly the old definition of topology needed a little clarification. When we talk about topology today, we separate how the cables physically look (the **physical topology**) from how the signals travel electronically (the **signaling topology**).

We call any form of networking technology that combines a physical topology with a signaling topology a **hybrid topology**. Hybrid topologies have come and gone since the earliest days of networking. Only two hybrid topologies, **star-ring topology** and **star-bus topology**, ever saw any amount of popularity. Eventually star-ring lost market and star-bus reigns as the undisputed king of topologies.

Mesh and Point-to-Multipoint

Topologies aren't just for wired networks. Wireless networks also need a topology to get data from one machine to another, but using radio waves instead of cables makes for somewhat different topologies. Almost all wireless networks use one of two different topologies: mesh topology or point-to-multipoint topology (Figure 3.9).

Mesh

In a **mesh topology** network, every computer connects to every other computer via two or more routes. Some of the routes between two computers may require traversing through another member of the mesh network.

There are two types of meshed topologies: partially meshed and fully meshed (Figure 3.10). In a **partially meshed topology** network, at least two machines have redundant connections. Every machine doesn't have to connect to every other machine. In a **fully meshed topology** network, every computer connects directly to every other computer.

If you're looking at Figure 3.10 and thinking that a mesh topology looks amazingly resilient and robust, it is—at least on paper. Because every computer connects to every other computer on the fully meshed network, even if half the PCs crash, the network still functions as well as ever (for the survivors). In a practical sense, however, implementing a fully meshed topology in a wired network would be an expensive mess. For example, even for a tiny fully meshed network with only 10 PCs, you would need *45* separate and distinct pieces of cable to connect every PC to every other PC. What a

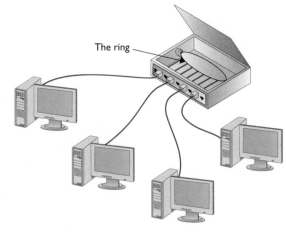

● Figure 3.7　Shrinking the ring

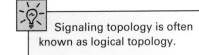

Signaling topology is often known as logical topology.

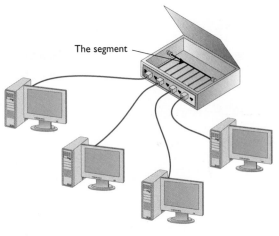

● Figure 3.8　Shrinking the segment

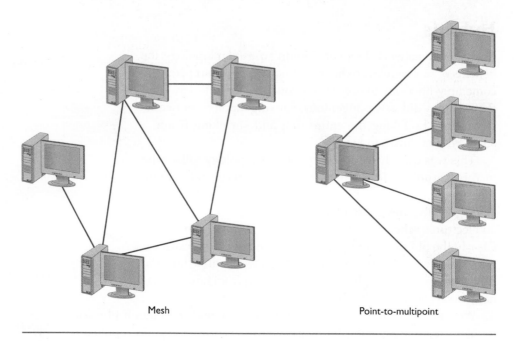

Mesh   Point-to-multipoint

● **Figure 3.9**   Mesh and point-to-multipoint

mesh mess! Because of this, mesh topologies have never been practical in a cabled network.

Make sure you know the formula to calculate the number of connections needed to make a fully meshed network, given a certain number of computers. Here's the formula:

y = number of computers

Number of connections = $y(y - 1)/2$

So, if you have six computers, you need $6(6 - 1)/2 = 30/2 = 15$ connections to create a fully meshed network.

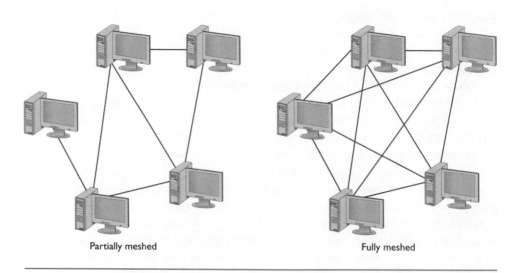

Partially meshed   Fully meshed

● **Figure 3.10**   Partially and fully meshed topologies

Point-to-Multipoint

In a **point-to-multipoint topology**, a single system acts as a common source through which all members of the point-to-multipoint network converse. If you compare a star topology to a slightly rearranged point-to-multipoint topology, you might be tempted to say they're the same thing. Granted, they're similar, but look at Figure 3.11. See what's in the middle? The subtle but important difference is that a point-to-multipoint topology requires an intelligent device in the center, while the device or connection point in the center of a star topology has little more to do than send or provide a path for a signal down all the connections.

You'll sometimes find mesh or point-to-multipoint topology wired networks, but they're rare. The two topologies are far more commonly seen in wireless networks.

> Point-to-multipoint topology is sometimes also called star topology, even though technically they differ.

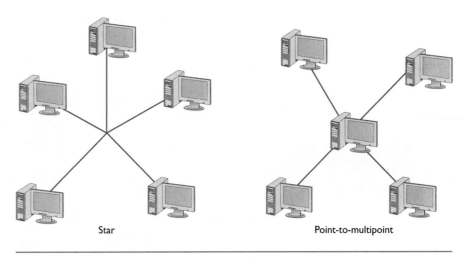

Star   Point-to-multipoint

• **Figure 3.11** Comparing star and point-to-multipoint

Point-to-Point

In a **point-to-point topology** network, two computers connect directly together with no need for a central hub or box of any kind. You'll find point-to-point topologies implemented in both wired and wireless networks (Figure 3.12).

• **Figure 3.12** Point-to-point

Parameters of a Topology

While a topology describes the method by which systems in a network connect, the topology alone doesn't describe all of the features necessary to enable those networks. The term *bus topology*, for example, describes a network that consists of some number of machines connected to the network via a single linear piece of cable. Notice that this definition leaves a lot of questions unanswered. What is the cable made of? How long can it be? How do the machines decide which machine should send data at a specific moment? A network based on a bus topology can answer these questions in a number of different ways—but it's not the job of the topology to define issues like these. A functioning network needs a more detailed standard.

Over the years, particular manufacturers and standards bodies have created several specific network technologies based on different topologies. A *network technology* is a practical application of a topology and other critical technologies to provide a method to get data from one computer to another on a network. These network technologies have names like 10BaseT, 1000BaseF, and 10GBaseLX. You will learn all about these in the next two chapters.

> Make sure you know all your topologies: bus, ring, star, hybrid, mesh, point-to-multipoint, and point-to-point!

Cabling

The majority of networked systems link together using some type of cabling. Different types of networks over the years have used a number of different types of cables—and you need to learn about all these cables to succeed on the CompTIA Network+ exam! This section explores both the cabling types used in older networks and those found in today's networks.

All cables used in the networking industry can be categorized in three distinct groups: coaxial (coax), twisted pair, and fiber-optic. Let's look at all three.

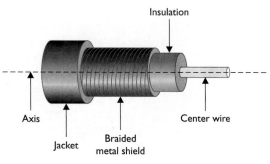

• **Figure 3.13**   Cutaway view of coaxial cable

Coaxial Cable

Coaxial cable contains a central conductor wire surrounded by an insulating material, which in turn is surrounded by a braided metal shield. The cable is referred to as coaxial (coax for short) because the center wire and the braided metal shield share a common axis or centerline (Figure 3.13).

Coaxial cable shields data transmissions from **electromagnetic interference (EMI)**. Many devices in the typical office environment generate magnetic fields, including lights, fans, copy machines, and refrigerators. When a metal wire encounters these magnetic fields, electrical current is generated along the wire. This extra current—EMI—can shut down a network because it is easily misinterpreted as a signal by devices like NICs. To prevent EMI from affecting the network, the outer mesh layer of a coaxial cable shields the center wire (on which the data is transmitted) from interference (Figure 3.14).

Early bus topology networks used coaxial cable to connect computers together. The most popular back in the day used special bayonet-style connectors called **BNC connectors** (Figure 3.15). Even earlier bus networks used thick cable that required vampire connections—sometimes called *vampire taps*—that literally pierced the cable.

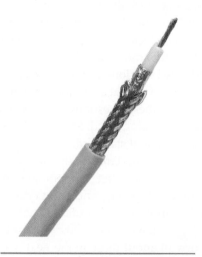

• **Figure 3.14**   Coaxial cable showing braided metal shielding

• **Figure 3.15**   BNC connector on coaxial cable

You'll find coaxial cable used today primarily to enable a cable modem to connect to an Internet service provider (ISP). Connecting a computer to the cable modem enables that computer to access the Internet. This is the same type of cable used to connect televisions to cable boxes or to satellite receivers. These cables use an F-type connector that screws on, making for a secure connection (Figure 3.16).

Cable modems connect using either RG-6 or, rarely, RG-59. RG-59 was used primarily for cable television rather than networking. Its thinness and the introduction of digital cable motivated the move to the more robust RG-6, the predominant cabling used today (Figure 3.17).

All coax cables have an **RG rating**; the U.S. military developed these ratings to provide a quick reference for the different types of coax. The only important measure of coax cabling is its **Ohm rating**, a relative measure of the resistance (or more precisely, characteristic impedance) on the cable. You may run across other coax cables that don't have acceptable Ohm ratings, although they look just like network-rated coax. Fortunately, most coax cable types display their Ohm ratings on the cables themselves (see Figure 3.18). Both RG-6 and RG-59 cables are rated at 75 Ohms.

Given the popularity of cable for television and Internet in homes today, you'll run into situations where people need to take a single coaxial cable and split it. Coaxial handles this quite nicely with coaxial splitters like the one shown in Figure 3.19. It's also easy to connect two coaxial cables together using a barrel connector when you need to add some distance to a connection (Figure 3.20).

Twisted Pair

The most overwhelmingly common type of cabling used in networks consists of twisted pairs of cables, bundled together into a common jacket. Networks use two types of twisted-pair cabling: shielded twisted pair and

● **Figure 3.16**   F-type connector on coaxial cable

Coaxial cabling is also very popular with satellite, over-the-air antennas and even some home video devices. The book covers cable and other Internet connectivity options in great detail in Chapter 14, "Remote Connectivity."

The Ohm rating of a particular piece of cable describes the characteristic impedance of that cable. *Impedance* describes a set of characteristics that define how much a cable resists the flow of electricity. This isn't simple resistance, though. Impedance also factors in things like how long it takes the wire to get a full charge—the wire's *capacitance*—and other things.

● **Figure 3.17**   RG-6 cable

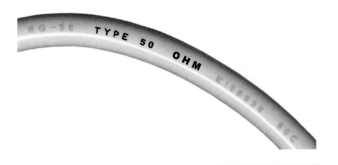

● **Figure 3.18**   Ohm rating (on an older, RG-58 cable used for networking)

• **Figure 3.19** Coaxial splitter

• **Figure 3.20** Barrel connector

Have you ever picked up a telephone and heard a distinct crackling noise? That's an example of crosstalk.

unshielded twisted pair. Twisted-pair cabling for networks is composed of multiple pairs of wires, twisted around each other at specific intervals. The twists serve to reduce interference, called **crosstalk**: the more twists, the less crosstalk.

• **Figure 3.21** Shielded twisted pair

Shielded Twisted Pair

Shielded twisted pair (STP), as its name implies, consists of twisted pairs of wires surrounded by shielding to protect them from EMI. STP is pretty rare, primarily because there's so little need for STP's shielding; it only really matters in locations with excessive electronic noise, such as a shop floor with lots of lights, electric motors, or other machinery that could cause problems for other cables. Figure 3.21 shows the most common STP type: the venerable IBM Type 1 cable used in Token Ring network technology.

Unshielded Twisted Pair

Unshielded twisted pair (UTP) is by far the most common type of network cabling used today. UTP consists of twisted pairs of wires surrounded by a plastic jacket (see Figure 3.22). This jacket does not provide any protection from EMI, so when installing UTP cabling, you must be careful to avoid interference from light, motors, and so forth. UTP is much cheaper than, and in most cases does just as good a job as, STP.

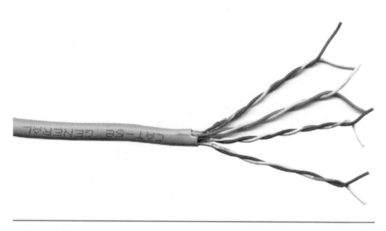

• **Figure 3.22** Unshielded twisted pair

Although more sensitive to interference than coaxial or STP cable, UTP cabling provides an inexpensive and flexible means to cable networks. UTP cable isn't exclusive to networks; many other technologies (such as telephone systems) employ the same cabling. This makes working with UTP a bit of a challenge. Imagine going up into a ceiling and seeing two sets of UTP cables: how would you determine which is for the telephones and which is for the network? Not to worry—a number of installation standards and tools exist to help those who work with UTP get the answer to these types of questions.

Not all UTP cables are the same! UTP cabling has a number of variations, such as the number of twists per foot, which determine how quickly data can propagate on the cable. To help network installers get the right cable for the right network technology, the cabling industry has developed a variety of grades called **category (CAT) ratings**. CAT ratings are officially rated in *megahertz (MHz)*, indicating the highest frequency the cable can handle. Table 3.1 shows the most common categories.

UTP cables are rated to handle a certain frequency, such as 100 MHz or 1000 MHz, which originally translated as the maximum throughput for a cable. Each cycle, each hertz basically accounts for one bit of data. For example, a 10 million cycle per second (10 MHz) cable could accommodate 10 million bits per second (10 Mbps)—1 bit per cycle. The maximum amount of data that goes through the cable per second is called the **bandwidth**. Through the use of *bandwidth-efficient encoding schemes*, however, manufacturers squeeze more bits into the same signal, as long as the cable can handle it. Thus the CAT 5e cable can handle throughput of up to 1000 Mbps, even though it's rated to handle a bandwidth of only up to 100 MHz.

Because most networks can run at speeds of up to 1000 MHz, most new cabling installations use Category 5e (CAT 5e) cabling, although a large number of installations use CAT 6 to future-proof

Table 3.1		CAT Ratings for UTP	
CAT Rating	**Max Frequency**	**Max Bandwidth**	**Status with TIA/EIA**
CAT 1	< 1 MHz	Analog phone lines only	No longer recognized
CAT 2	4 MHz	4 Mbps	No longer recognized
CAT 3	16 MHz	16 Mbps	Recognized
CAT 4	20 MHz	20 Mbps	No longer recognized
CAT 5	100 MHz	100 Mbps	No longer recognized
CAT 5e	100 MHz	1000 Mbps	Recognized
CAT 6	250 MHz	10000 Mbps	Recognized

> ### Tech Tip
>
>
>
> #### CAT 6a
>
> *If you have a need for speed, the latest update to the venerable UTP cable is Category 6a. This update doubles the bandwidth of CAT 6 to 550 MHz to accommodate 10-Gbps speeds up to 100 meters. Take that, fiber! (The 100-meter limitation, by the way, refers to the Ethernet standard, the major implementation of UTP in the networking world. Chapter 4 covers Ethernet in great detail.)*

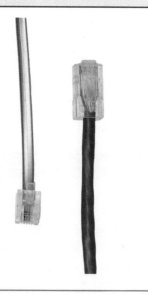

• Figure 3.25   RJ-11 (left) and RJ-45 (right) connectors

• Figure 3.24   CAT level on UTP

the network. CAT 5e cabling currently costs much less than CAT 6, although as CAT 6 gains in popularity, it's slowly dropping in price.

Make sure you can look at UTP and know its CAT rating. There are two places to look. First, UTP is typically sold in boxed reels, and the manufacturer will clearly mark the CAT level on the box (Figure 3.23). Second, look on the cable itself. The category level of a piece of cable is usually printed on the cable (Figure 3.24).

Anyone who's plugged in a telephone has probably already dealt with the registered jack (RJ) connectors used with UTP cable. Telephones use **RJ-11** connectors, designed to support up to two pairs of wires. Networks use the four-pair **RJ-45** connectors (Figure 3.25).

Fiber-Optic

Fiber-optic cable transmits light rather than electricity, making it attractive for both high-EMI areas and long-distance transmissions. While a single copper cable cannot carry data more than a few hundred meters at best, a single piece of fiber-optic cabling will operate, depending on the implementation, for distances of up to tens of kilometers. A fiber-optic cable has four components: the glass fiber itself (the **core**); the **cladding**, which is the part that makes the light reflect down the fiber; *buffer* material to give strength, and the **insulating jacket** (Figure 3.26).

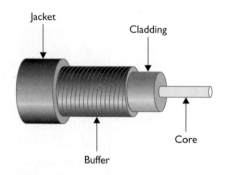

Jacket

Cladding

Core

Buffer

• Figure 3.26   Cross section of fiber-optic cabling

Fiber-optic cabling is manufactured with many different diameters of core and cladding. In a convenient bit of standardization, cable manufacturers use a two-number designator to define fiber-optic cables according to their core and cladding measurements. The most common fiber-optic cable size is 62.5/125 µm. Almost all network technologies that use fiber-optic cable require pairs of fibers. One fiber is used for sending, the other for receiving. In response to the demand for two-pair cabling, manufacturers often connect two fibers together like a lamp cord to create the popular duplex fiber-optic cabling (Figure 3.27).

Fiber cables are pretty tiny! Light can be sent down a fiber-optic cable as regular light or as laser light. The two types of light require totally different fiber-optic cables. Most network technologies that use fiber-optics use LEDs (light emitting diodes) to send light signals. Fiber-optic cables that use LEDs are known as **multimode**.

Fiber-optic cables that use lasers are known as **single-mode**. Using laser light and single-mode fiber-optic cables prevents a problem unique to multimode fiber-optics called **modal distortion** and enables a network to achieve phenomenally high transfer rates over incredibly long distances.

Fiber-optics also define the wavelength of light used, measured in nanometers (nm). Almost all multimode cables transmit 850-nm wavelength, while single-mode transmit either 1310 or 1550 nm, depending on the laser.

Fiber-optic cables come in a broad choice of connector types. There are over one hundred different connectors, but the three you need to know for the CompTIA Network+ exam are ST, SC, and LC (Figure 3.28). LC is unique because it is a duplex connector, designed to accept two fiber cables.

Other Cables

Fiber-optic and UTP make up almost all network cabling, but there are a few other types of cabling that may come up from time to time as alternatives to these two: the ancient serial and parallel cables from the earliest days of PCs and the modern high-speed serial connection, better known as FireWire.

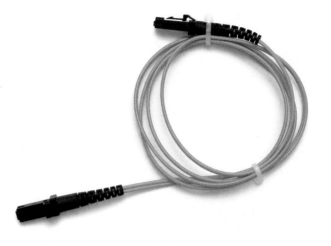

● **Figure 3.27**   Duplex fiber-optic cable

 For those of you unfamiliar with it, the odd little u-shaped symbol describing fiber cable size (µ) stands for *micro*, or 1/1,000,000th.

Tech Tip

What's in a Name?

Most technicians call common fiber-optic connectors by their initials—such as ST, SC, or LC—perhaps because there's no consensus about what words go with those initials. ST probably stands for straight tip, but SC and LC? How about subscriber connector, standard connector, or Siemon connector for the former; local connector or Lucent connector for the latter?

If you want to remember the connectors for the exam, try these: stick and twist *for the bayonet-style ST connectors;* stick and click *for the straight push-in SC connectors; and* little connector *for the . . . little . . . LC connector.*

● **Figure 3.28**   From left to right: ST, SC, and LC fiber-optic connectors

These cables are only used with quick-and-dirty temporary connections, but they do work, so they bear at least a quick mention.

Classic Serial

Serial cabling not only predates networking, it also predates the personal computer. **RS-232**, the recommended standard (RS) upon which all serial communication takes places on your PC, dates from 1969 and hasn't substantially changed in around 40 years. When IBM invented the PC way back in 1980, serial connections were just about the only standard input/output technology available, and IBM added two serial ports to every PC. The most common serial port is a 9-pin, male D-subminiature connector, as shown in Figure 3.29.

Serial ports offer at best a poor option for networking, with very slow data rates—only about 56,000 bps—and only point-to-point connections. In all probability it's faster to copy something on a flash drive and just walk over to the other system, but serial networking does work if needed. Serial ports are quickly fading away and you rarely see them on newer PCs.

• Figure 3.29   Serial port

Parallel

Parallel connections are almost as old as serial. Parallel can run up to around 2 Mbps, although when used for networking it tends to be much slower. Parallel is also limited to point-to-point topology, but uses a 25-pin female—rather than male—DB type connector (Figure 3.30). The **IEEE 1284** committee sets the standards for parallel communication. (See the section "Networking Industry Standards—IEEE," later in this chapter.)

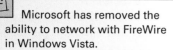

• Figure 3.30   Parallel connector

FireWire

FireWire (based on the **IEEE 1394** standard) is the only viable alternative cabling option to fiber-optic or UTP. FireWire is also restricted to point-to-point connections, but it's very fast (currently the standard is up to 800 Mbps). FireWire has its own unique connector (Figure 3.31).

Microsoft has removed the ability to network with FireWire in Windows Vista.

Concentrate on UTP—that's where the hardest CompTIA Network+ exam questions lie. Don't forget to give coax, STP, and fiber a quick pass, and make sure you understand the reasons for picking one type of cabling over another. Even though the CompTIA Network+ exam does not test too hard on cabling, this is important information that you will use in the real networking world.

• Figure 3.31   FireWire connector

Mike Meyers' CompTIA Network+ Guide to Managing and Troubleshooting Networks

Fire Ratings

Did you ever see the movie *The Towering Inferno*? Don't worry if you missed it—*The Towering Inferno* was one of the better infamous disaster movies of the 1970s, but it was no *Airplane!* Anyway, Steve McQueen stars as the fireman who saves the day when a skyscraper goes up in flames because of poor-quality electrical cabling. The burning insulation on the wires ultimately spreads the fire to every part of the building. Although no cables made today contain truly flammable insulation, the insulation is made from plastic, and if you get any plastic hot enough, it will create smoke and noxious fumes. The risk of burning insulation isn't fire—it's smoke and fumes.

To reduce the risk of your network cables burning and creating noxious fumes and smoke, Underwriters Laboratories and the National Electrical Code (NEC) joined forces to develop cabling *fire ratings*. The two most common fire ratings are PVC and plenum. Cable with a **polyvinyl chloride (PVC)** rating has no significant fire protection. If you burn a PVC cable, it creates lots of smoke and noxious fumes. Burning **plenum**-rated cable creates much less smoke and fumes, but plenum-rated cable—often referred to simply as "plenum"—costs about three to five times as much as PVC-rated cable. Most city ordinances require the use of plenum cable for network installations. The bottom line? Get plenum!

The space between the acoustical tile ceiling in an office building and the actual concrete ceiling above is called the plenum—hence the name for the proper fire rating of cabling to use in that space. A third type of fire rating, known as **riser**, designates the proper cabling to use for vertical runs between floors of a building. Riser-rated cable provides less protection than plenum cable, though, so most installations today use plenum for runs between floors.

■ Networking Industry Standards—IEEE

The **Institute of Electrical and Electronics Engineers (IEEE)** defines industry-wide standards that promote the use and implementation of technology. In February of 1980, a new committee called the 802 Working Group took over from the private sector the job of defining network standards. The IEEE 802 committee defines frames, speed, distances, and types of cabling to use in a network environment. Concentrating on cables, the IEEE recognizes that no single cabling solution can work in all situations, and thus provides a variety of cabling standards.

IEEE committees define standards for a wide variety of electronics. The names of these committees are often used to refer to the standards they publish. The IEEE 1284 committee, for example, sets standards for parallel communication. Have you ever seen a printer cable marked "IEEE 1284–compliant," as in Figure 3.32? This means the manufacturer followed the rules set by the IEEE 1284 committee. Another committee you

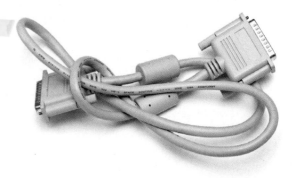

● **Figure 3.32** Parallel cable marked IEEE 1284–compliant

may have heard of is the IEEE 1394 committee, which controls the FireWire standard.

The IEEE 802 committee sets the standards for networking. Although the original plan was to define a single, universal standard for networking, it quickly became apparent that no single solution would work for all needs. The 802 committee split into smaller subcommittees, with names such as IEEE 802.3 and IEEE 802.5. Table 3.2 shows the currently recognized IEEE 802 subcommittees and their areas of jurisdiction. I've included the inactive subcommittees for reference. The missing numbers, such as 802.4 and 802.12, were used for committees long ago disbanded. Each subcommittee is officially called a Working Group, except the few listed as a Technical Advisory Group (TAG) in the table.

Some of these committees deal with technologies that didn't quite make it, and the committees associated with those standards, such as IEEE 802.4, Token Bus, have become dormant. When preparing for the CompTIA Network+ exam, concentrate on the IEEE 802.3 and 802.11 standards. You will see these again in later chapters.

Memorize the 802.3 and 802.11 standards. Ignore the rest.

Table 3.2	IEEE 802 Subcommittees
IEEE 802	LAN/MAN Overview & Architecture
IEEE 802.1	Higher Layer LAN Protocols
802.1s	Multiple Spanning Trees
802.1w	Rapid Reconfiguration of Spanning Tree
802.1x	Port Based Network Access Control
IEEE 802.2	Logical Link Control (LLC); now inactive
IEEE 802.3	Ethernet
802.3ae	10 Gigabit Ethernet
IEEE 802.5	Token Ring; now inactive
IEEE 802.11	Wireless LAN (WLAN); specifications, such as Wi-Fi
IEEE 802.15	Wireless Personal Area Network (WPAN)
IEEE 802.16	Broadband Wireless Access (BWA); specifications for implementing Wireless Metropolitan Area Network (Wireless MAN); referred to also as WiMax
IEEE 802.17	Resilient Packet Ring (RPR)
IEEE 802.18	Radio Regulatory Technical Advisory Group
IEEE 802.19	Coexistence Technical Advisory Group
IEEE 802.20	Mobile Broadband Wireless Access (MBWA)
IEEE 802.21	Media Independent Handover
IEEE 802.22	Wireless Regional Area Networks

Chapter 3 Review

■ Chapter Summary

After reading this chapter and completing the exercises, you should understand the following about cabling and topology.

Explain the different types of network topologies

■ A network's *topology* describes how computers connect to each other in that network. The most common network topologies are called *bus*, *ring*, *star*, and *mesh*.

■ In a bus topology, all computers connect to the network via a main line. The cable must be terminated at both ends to prevent signal reflections.

■ In a ring topology, all computers on the network attach to a central ring of cable. A single break in the cable stops the flow of data through the entire network.

■ In a star topology, the computers on the network connect to a central wiring point, which provides fault tolerance.

■ Modern networks use one of two hybrid topologies: *star bus* or *star ring*. Star bus is overwhelmingly the most common topology used today.

■ In a mesh topology, each computer has a dedicated line to every other computer. Mesh networks can be further categorized as partially meshed or fully meshed, both of which require a significant amount of physical cable. Networks techs are able to determine the amount of cable segments needed with a mathematical formula.

■ In a point-to-multipoint topology, a single system acts as a common source through which all members of the network converse.

■ Mesh and point-to-multipoint topologies are common among wireless networks.

■ In a point-to-point topology, two computers connect directly together.

Describe the different types of network cabling

■ Coaxial cable, or coax, shields data transmissions from EMI. Coax was widely used in early bus networks and used BNC connectors. Today, coax is used mainly to connect a cable modem to an ISP.

■ Coax cables have an RG rating, with RG-6 being the predominant coax today.

■ Twisted pair, which comes shielded or unshielded, is the most common type of networking cable today. UTP is less expensive and more popular than STP, though it doesn't offer any protection from EMI.

■ UTP is categorized by its CAT rating, with CAT 5, CAT 5e, and CAT 6 being the most commonly used today.

■ Telephones use RJ-11 connectors, while UTP uses RJ-45 connectors.

■ Fiber-optic cabling transmits light instead of the electricity used in CAT cable or coax. It is thin and more expensive, yet less flexible and more delicate, than other types of network cabling.

■ There are two types of fiber-optic cable based on what type of light is used. LEDs require multimode cable, while lasers generally require single-mode cable.

■ All fiber-optic cable has three parts: the fiber itself; the cladding, which covers the fiber and helps it reflect down the fiber; and the outer insulating jacket. Additionally, there are over one hundred types of connectors for fiber-optic cable, but ST, SC, and LC are the most common for computer networking.

■ Plenum-rated UTP is required by most cities for network installations.

■ Serial cables adhering to the RS-232 standard and parallel cables adhering to the IEEE-1284 standard may be used to network two computers directly together. You can also use IEEE 1394 (FireWire) connections for direct connection, although not with Windows Vista.

Describe the IEEE networking standards

■ Networking standards are established and promoted by the Institute of Electrical and Electronics Engineers (IEEE).

- The IEEE 802 committee defines frames, speeds, distances, and types of cabling to use in networks. IEEE 802 is split into several subcommittees, including IEEE 802.3 and IEEE 802.11.

- The IEEE 1284 committee defines the standards for parallel communications, while the IEEE 1394 committee defines the standards for FireWire High-Performance Serial Bus.

■ Key Terms

bandwidth *(47)*
bus topology *(39)*
BNC connector *(44)*
category (CAT) rating *(47)*
cladding *(48)*
coaxial cable *(44)*
core *(48)*
crosstalk *(46)*
electro-magnetic interference (EMI) *(44)*
fault tolerance *(40)*
fiber-optic cable *(48)*
fully meshed topology *(41)*
hybrid topology *(41)*
Institute of Electrical and Electronics Engineers (IEEE) *(51)*
IEEE 1284 *(50)*
IEEE 1394 *(50)*
insulating jacket *(48)*
mesh topology *(41)*
modal distortion *(49)*
multimode *(49)*
network topology *(38)*

Ohm rating *(45)*
partially meshed topology *(41)*
physical topology *(41)*
plenum *(51)*
point-to-multipoint topology *(43)*
point-to-point topology *(43)*
polyvinyl chloride (PVC) *(51)*
RG rating *(45)*
ring topology *(39)*
riser *(51)*
RJ-11 *(48)*
RJ-45 *(48)*
RS-232 *(50)*
segment *(41)*
shielded twisted pair (STP) *(46)*
signaling topology *(41)*
single-mode *(49)*
star topology *(40)*
star-bus topology *(41)*
star-ring topology *(41)*
unshielded twisted pair (UTP) *(46)*

■ Key Term Quiz

Use the Key Terms list to complete the sentences that follow. Not all terms will be used.

1. The _____ is a network topology that relies on a main line of network cabling, normally coaxial cable.

2. The _____ of a cable will determine its speed.

3. A(n) _____ provides more fault tolerance than any other basic network topology.

4. When your network has all computers connected to a centrally located wiring closet, you have a physical _____ network.

5. _____ networks use more than one type of basic network topology.

6. CAT 5e cable is a type of _____ wiring.

7. Coaxial cable uses a braided metal shield to protect data from _____.

8. Network cabling can use either light or electricity to transmit data. The faster of these types uses light along _____.

9. _____-grade UTP must be installed in ceilings, while _____-grade UTP is often used to connect one floor to another vertically in a building.

10. The twisting of the cables in UTP and STP reduces _____.

■ Multiple-Choice Quiz

1. Which of the following are standard network topologies? (Select three.)

    A. Bus

    B. Star

    C. Ring

    D. Dual-ring

2. John was carrying on at the water cooler the other day, trying to show off his knowledge of networking. He claimed that the company had installed special cabling to handle the problems of crosstalk on the network. What kind of cabling did the company install?

    A. Coaxial

    B. Shielded coaxial

    C. Unshielded twisted pair

    D. Fiber-optic

3. Jill needs to run some UTP cable from one office to another. She found a box of cable in the closet and wants to make sure it's CAT 5 or better. How can she tell the CAT level of the cable? (Select two.)

    A. Check the box.

    B. Scan for markings on the cable.

    C. Check the color of the cable—gray means CAT 5, yellow means CAT 6e, and so on.

    D. Check the ends of the cable.

4. What topology provides the most fault tolerance?

    A. Bus

    B. Ring

    C. Star-bus

    D. Mesh

5. What organization is responsible for establishing and promoting networking standards?

    A. Institute of Electrical and Electronics Engineers (IEEE)

    B. International Standards Organization (ISO)

    C. Federal Communications Commission (FCC)

    D. International Telecommunications Association (ITA)

6. What aspects of network cabling do the IEEE committees establish? (Select three.)

    A. Frame size

    B. Speed

    C. Color of sheathing

    D. Cable types

7. What are types of coax cabling that have been used in computer networking? (Select three.)

    A. RG-8

    B. RG-45

    C. RG-58

    D. RG-62

8. What applications are best suited for fiber-optic cabling? (Select two.)

    A. Short distances

    B. Wireless networks

    C. High-EMI areas

    D. Long distances

9. What are the main components of fiber-optic cabling? (Select three.)

    A. Cladding

    B. Insulating jacket

    C. Copper core

    D. Fiber

10. What is the most popular size fiber-optic cabling?

    A. 62.5/125 µm

    B. 125/62.5 µm

    C. 50/125 µm

    D. 125/50 µm

11. Most fiber-optic installations use LEDs to send light signals and are known as what?

    A. Single-mode

    B. Multimode

    C. Complex mode

    D. Duplex mode

12. Why must the main cable in a bus topology be terminated at both ends?

    A. To allow the signal to be amplified so it can reach both ends of the network

    B. To prevent the signal from dropping off the network before reaching all computers

    C. To prevent the signal from bouncing back and forth

    D. To convert the signal to the proper format for a bus network

13. Where are you most likely to encounter a mesh network?

    A. On any network using fiber-optic cable

    B. On any network using plenum cable

    C. On wireless networks

    D. On wired networks

14. You are asked by your boss to research upgrading all the network cable in your office building. The building manager requires the safest possible cabling type in case of fire, and your boss wants to future-proof the network so cabling doesn't need to be replaced when network technologies faster than 1 Gbps are available. You decide to use CAT 5e plenum cabling throughout the building. Which objective have you satisfied?

    A. Neither the building manager's nor your boss's requirements have been met.

    B. Only the building manager's requirement has been met.

    C. Only your boss's requirement has been met.

    D. Both the building manager's and your boss's requirements have been met.

15. Which committee is responsible for wireless networking standards?

    A. IEEE 802.2

    B. IEEE 802.3

    C. IEEE 802.5

    D. IEEE 802.11

■ Essay Quiz

1. You work in the computer training department at your company. A newly developed mobile training program is being planned. The plan requires setting up five training computers in a particular department you use to train on weekly. Write a short essay that describes which network topology would be quickest to set up and tear down for this type of onsite training.

2. Your boss has decided to have cable run to every computer in the office, but doesn't know which type to use. In an effort to help bring the company into the 21st century, write a short essay comparing the merits of UTP and fiber-optic cabling.

3. The NICs on your company's computers all have dual 10-Mbps and 100-Mbps capability, yet users complain that the network is slow. Write a brief essay that explains what could be the cause of the problem.

4. Write a short essay describing how you would acquire 1500 feet of RG-58 coaxial cabling for use in your nonprofit organization's office space.

5. Your company has hired a group of new network techs and you've been tasked to do their training session on networking standards organizations. Write a brief essay detailing the IEEE and its various committees.

Lab Projects

• Lab Project 3.1

This lab project requires you to demonstrate knowledge of the four basic network topologies. Obtain four blank pieces of paper. Proceed to draw six boxes on each page to represent six computers—neatness counts! At the top of each sheet, write one of the following: bus topology, mesh topology, ring topology, or star topology. Then draw lines to represent the physical network cabling required by each network topology.

• Lab Project 3.2

In your studies of network cabling for the CompTIA Network+ certification exam, you realize you could use a simplified chart to study from and memorize. Build a reference study chart that describes the features of network cabling. Create your completed chart using a spreadsheet program, or simply a sheet of paper, with the column headings and names shown below. If you wish, you can start by writing your notes here.

Cable Type	Description	Benefits	Drawbacks
CAT 5			
CAT 5e			
CAT 6			
Thinnet			
Thicknet			
Fiber-optic			

• Lab Project 3.3

In this lab project, you will demonstrate knowledge of the different IEEE committees that are most prevalent today. Use the Internet to research each of these subcommittees: IEEE 802.3, IEEE 802.5, and IEEE 802.11. Give an example of where each type of technology might best be used.

Ethernet Basics

"In theory there is no difference between theory and practice. In practice there is."
—YOGI BERRA

In this chapter, you will learn how to

- **Define and describe Ethernet**
- **Explain early Ethernet implementations**
- **Describe ways to extend and enhance Ethernet networks**

In the beginning, there were no networks. Computers were isolated, solitary islands of information in a teeming sea of proto-geeks, who used clubs and wore fur pocket protectors. Okay, maybe it wasn't that bad, but if you wanted to move a file from one machine to another—and proto-geeks were as much into that as modern geeks—you had to use *Sneakernet*, which meant you saved the file on a disk, laced up your tennis shoes, and hiked over to the other system. All that walking no doubt produced lots of health benefits, but frankly, proto-geeks weren't all that into health benefits—they were into speed, power, and technological coolness in general. (Sound familiar?) It's no wonder, then, that geeks everywhere agreed on the need to replace Sneakernet with a faster and more efficient method of sharing data. The method they came up with is the subject of this chapter.

Historical/Conceptual

■ Ethernet

In 1973, Xerox answered the challenge of moving data without sneakers by developing **Ethernet**, a networking technology standard based on a bus topology. The Ethernet standard dominates today's networks and defines all of the issues involved in transferring data between computer systems. The original Ethernet used a single piece of coaxial cable in a bus topology to connect several computers, enabling them to transfer data at a rate of up to 3 Mbps. Although slow by today's standards, this early version of Ethernet was a huge improvement over Sneakernet methods, and served as the foundation for all later versions of Ethernet.

Ethernet remained a largely in-house technology within Xerox until 1979, when Xerox decided to look for partners to help promote Ethernet as an industry standard. Xerox worked with Digital Equipment Corporation (DEC) and Intel to publish what became known as the Digital-Intel-Xerox (DIX) standard. Running on coaxial cable, the DIX standard enabled multiple computers to communicate with each other at a screaming 10 Mbps. Although 10 Mbps represents the low end of standard network speeds today, at the time it was revolutionary. These companies then transferred control of the Ethernet standard to the IEEE, which in turn created the **802.3 (Ethernet)** committee that continues to control the Ethernet standard to this day.

Given that Ethernet's been around for so long, we need to start at a common point. I've chosen to use 10BaseT, the earliest version of Ethernet designed to use UTP cabling. At this point, don't worry what 10BaseT means—this chapter will cover the definition. For right now, just get into the idea of how Ethernet works.

Ethernet's designers faced the same challenges as the designers of any network: how to send data across the wire, how to identify the sending and receiving computers, and how to determine which computer should use the shared cable at what time. The engineers resolved these issues by using data frames that contain MAC addresses to identify computers on the network, and by using a process called CSMA/CD (discussed shortly) to determine which machine should access the wire at any given time. You saw some of this in action in Chapter 2, "Building a Network with the OSI Model," but now I need to introduce you to a bunch of new terms, so let's look at each of these solutions.

Topology

Every version of Ethernet invented since the early 1990s uses a hybrid star-bus topology. At the center of the network is a **hub**. This hub is nothing more than an electronic **repeater**—it interprets the ones and zeros coming in from one port and repeats the same signal out to the other connected ports. Hubs do not send the same signal back down the port that originally sent it (Figure 4.1). Repeaters are not amplifiers! They read the incoming signal and send new copies of that signal out to every connected port on the hub.

There have been many versions of Ethernet over the years. The earliest versions, named 10Base5 and 10Base2, are long obsolete. As of 2009, CompTIA finally dropped these ancient technologies from the CompTIA Network+ exam. Rest in peace, 10Base5 and 10Base2!

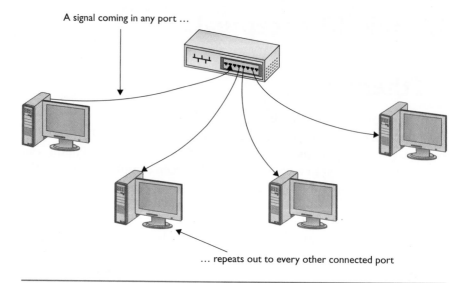

A signal coming in any port ...

... repeats out to every other connected port

• **Figure 4.1**   Ethernet hub

Test Specific

Organizing the Data: Ethernet Frames

All network technologies break data transmitted between computers into smaller pieces called **frames**, as you'll recall from Chapter 2. Using frames addresses two networking issues. First, it prevents any single machine from monopolizing the shared bus cable. Second, frames make the process of retransmitting lost data more efficient.

The process you saw in Chapter 2 of transferring a word processing document between two computers illustrates these two issues. First, if the sending computer sends the document as a single huge frame, it will monopolize the cable and prevent other machines from using the cable until the entire file gets to the receiving system. Using relatively small frames enables computers to share the cable easily—each computer listens on the **segment**, sending a few frames of data whenever it detects that no other computer is transmitting. Second, in the real world, bad things can happen to good data. When errors occur during transmission, the sending system must retransmit the frames that failed to get to the receiving system in good shape. If a word processing document were transmitted as a single massive frame, the sending system would have to retransmit the entire frame—in this case, the entire document. Breaking the file up into smaller frames enables the sending computer to retransmit only the damaged frames. Because of their benefits—shared access and more efficient retransmission—all networking technologies use frames, and Ethernet is no exception to that rule.

In Chapter 2, you saw a generic frame. Let's take what you know of frames and expand on that knowledge by inspecting the details of an Ethernet frame. A basic Ethernet frame contains seven pieces of information: the preamble, the MAC address of the frame's recipient, the MAC address of the sending system, the length of the data, the data itself, a pad, and a frame check

The terms *frame* and *packet* are often used interchangeably, especially on exams! This book uses the terms more strictly. You'll recall from Chapter 2, "Building a Network with OSI," that frames are based on MAC addresses; packets are generally associated with data assembled by the IP protocol at Layer 3 of the OSI seven-layer model.

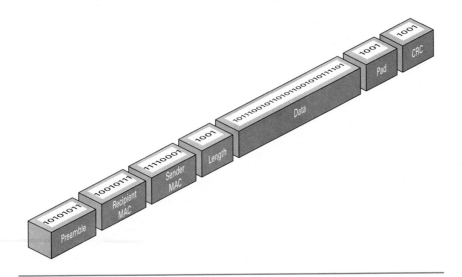

● **Figure 4.2**   Ethernet frame

sequence, generically called a cyclic redundancy check (CRC). Figure 4.2 shows these components.

Preamble

All Ethernet frames begin with a **preamble**, a 64-bit series of alternating ones and zeroes that ends with 11. The preamble gives a receiving NIC time to realize a frame is coming and to know exactly where the frame starts. The preamble is added by the sending NIC.

MAC Addresses

Each NIC, more commonly called a **node**, on an Ethernet network must have a unique identifying address. Ethernet identifies the NICs on a network using special 48-bit (6-byte) binary addresses known as **MAC addresses**.

MAC addresses give each NIC a unique address. When a computer sends out a data frame, it goes into the hub that repeats an exact copy of that frame to every connected port, as shown in Figure 4.3. All the other computers on the network listen to the wire and examine the frame to see if it contains their MAC address. If it does not, they ignore the frame. If a machine sees a frame with its MAC address, it opens the frame and begins processing the data.

>
> The CompTIA Network+ exam might describe MAC addresses as 48-bit binary addresses or 6-byte binary addresses.

Cross Check

NICs and OSI

You learned about NICs and MAC addresses in Chapter 2, "Building a Network with the OSI Model," so check your memory with these questions. Where does the NIC get its MAC address? How does the MAC address manifest on the card? At what layer or layers of the OSI seven-layer model does the NIC operate?

This system of allowing each machine to decide which frames it will process may be efficient, but because any device connected to the network cable can potentially capture any data frame transmitted across the wire, Ethernet networks carry a significant security vulnerability. Network diagnostic programs, commonly called **sniffers**, can order a NIC to run in **promiscuous mode**. When running in promiscuous mode, the NIC processes all the

>
> There are many situations in which one computer might have two or more NICs, so one physical system might represent more than one node.

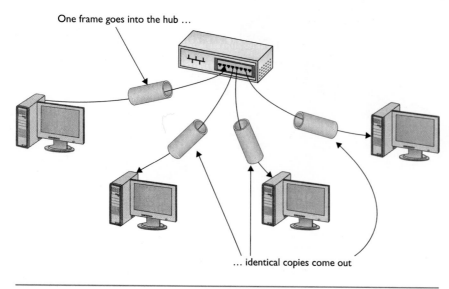

One frame goes into the hub ...

... identical copies come out

● **Figure 4.3**   Frames propagating on a network

frames it sees on the cable, regardless of their MAC addresses. Sniffers are valuable troubleshooting tools in the right hands, but Ethernet provides no protections against their unscrupulous use.

Length

An Ethernet frame may carry up to 1500 bytes of data in a single frame, but this is only a maximum. Frames can definitely carry fewer bytes of data. The length field tells the receiving system how many bytes of data this frame is carrying.

Data

The data part of the frame contains whatever data the frame carries. (If this is an IP network, it will also include extra information, such as the IP addresses of both systems, sequencing numbers, and other information.)

Pad

The minimum Ethernet frame is 64 bytes in size, but not all of that has to be actual data. If an Ethernet frame has fewer than 64 bytes of data to haul, the sending NIC will automatically add extra data—a **pad**—to bring the data up to the minimum 64 bytes.

Frame Check Sequence

The **frame check sequence**—Ethernet's term for the cyclic redundancy check—enables Ethernet nodes to recognize when bad things happen to good data. Machines on a network must be able to detect when data has been damaged in transit. To detect errors, the computers on an Ethernet network attach a special code to each frame. When creating an Ethernet frame, the sending machine runs the data through a special mathematical formula and attaches the result, the frame check sequence, to the frame. The receiving machine opens the frame, performs the same calculation, and compares its answer with the one included with the frame. If the answers do not match, the receiving machine asks the sending machine to retransmit that frame.

At this point, those crafty network engineers have solved two of the problems facing them: they've created frames to organize the data to be sent, and put in place MAC addresses to identify machines on the network. But the challenge of determining which machine should send data at which time required another solution: CSMA/CD.

CSMA/CD

Ethernet networks use a system called **carrier sense multiple access/collision detection (CSMA/CD)** to determine which computer should use a shared cable at a given moment. *Carrier sense* means that each node using the network examines the cable before sending a data frame (Figure 4.4). If another machine is using the network, the node detects traffic on the segment, waits a few milliseconds, and then rechecks. If it detects no traffic—the more common term is to say the cable is "free"—the node sends out its frame.

Multiple access means that all machines have equal access to the wire. If the line is free, any Ethernet node may begin sending a frame. From the point of view of Ethernet, it doesn't matter what function the node is performing: it could be a desktop system running Windows XP, or a high-end file server running Windows Server 2008 or even Linux. As far as Ethernet is concerned, a node is a node is a node, and access to the cable is assigned strictly on a first-come, first-served basis.

So what happens if two machines, both listening to the cable, simultaneously decide that it is free and try to send a frame? A collision occurs, and both of the transmissions are lost (Figure 4.5). A collision resembles the effect of two people talking at the same time: the listener hears a mixture of two voices, and can't understand either one.

It's easy for NICs to notice a collision. Collisions create nonstandard voltages that tell each NIC another node has transmitted at the same time. If they detect a collision, both nodes immediately stop transmitting. They then each generate a random number to determine how long to wait before trying again. If you imagine that each machine rolls its magic electronic dice and waits for that number of seconds, you wouldn't be too far from the truth, except that the amount of time an Ethernet node waits to retransmit is much shorter than one second (Figure 4.6). Whichever node generates the lowest random number begins its retransmission first, winning the competition to use the wire. The losing node then sees traffic on the wire, and waits for the wire to be free again before attempting to retransmit its data.

Collisions are a normal part of the operation of an Ethernet network. Every Ethernet network wastes some amount of its available bandwidth dealing with these collisions. A properly running average Ethernet network has a maximum of 10 percent collisions. For every 20 frames sent, approximately

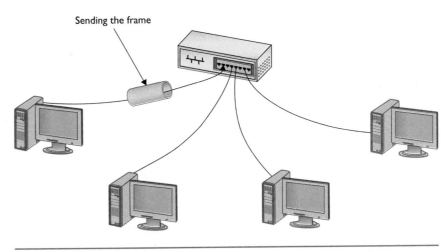

• **Figure 4.4**   No one else is talking—send the frame!

CSMA/CD is a network access method that maps to the IEEE 802.3 standard for Ethernet networks.

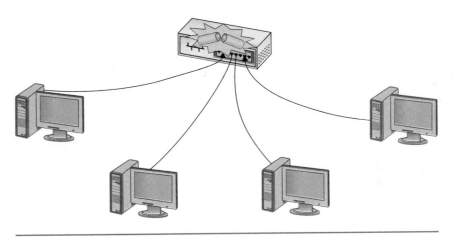

• **Figure 4.5**   Collision!

In an Ethernet network, a **collision domain** is a group of nodes that hear each other's traffic. A segment is certainly a collision domain, but there are ways to connect segments together to create larger collision domains. If the collision domain gets too large, you'll start running into traffic problems that manifest as general network sluggishness. That's one of the reasons to break up networks into smaller groupings.

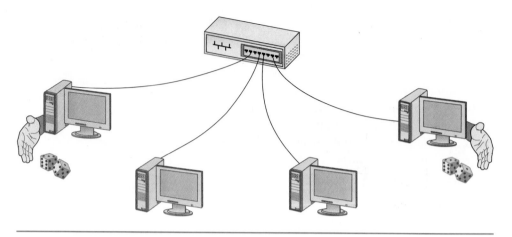

● **Figure 4.6** Rolling for timing

2 frames will collide and require a resend. Collision rates greater than 10 percent often point to damaged NICs or out-of-control software.

■ Early Ethernet Networks

Now we have the answers to many of the questions that faced those early Ethernet designers. MAC addresses identify each machine on the network. CSMA/CD determines which machine should have access to the cable when. But all this remains in the realm of theory—we still need to build the thing! Contemplating the physical network brings up numerous questions. What kind of cables should be used? What should they be made of? How long can they be? For these answers, turn to the IEEE 802.3 standard and two early implementations of Ethernet, 10BaseT and 10BaseFL.

10BaseT

In 1990, the IEEE 802.3 committee created a new version of Ethernet called **10BaseT** to modernize the first generations of Ethernet. Very quickly 10BaseT became the most popular network technology in the world, replacing competing and now long-gone competitors with names like Token Ring and AppleTalk. Over 99 percent of all networks use 10BaseT or one of its faster, newer, but very similar versions. The classic 10BaseT network consists of two or more computers connected to a central hub. The NICs connect with wires as specified by the 802.3 committee.

10BaseT hubs come in a variety of shapes and sizes to support different sizes of networks. The biggest differentiator between hubs is the number of **ports** (connections) that a single hub provides. A small hub might have only 4 ports, while a hub for a large network might have 48 ports. As you may imagine, the more ports on a hub, the more expensive the hub. Figure 4.7 shows two hubs. On the top is a small, 8-port

● **Figure 4.7** Two 10BaseT hubs

Cross Check

Physical vs. Logical

You might be tempted at this moment to define 10BaseT in terms of physical topology versus logical topology—after all, it uses a physical star, but a logical bus. But refer to Chapter 3, "Cabling and Topology," and cross-check your memory. What's a physical topology? And a logical topology? What would you say if you walked into an office building that implemented a 10BaseT network? Yes, if you actually *walked into* it, you'd probably say "Ouch!" But beyond that, think about how you would describe the wires and connectors you would see in terms of physical or logical topology.

hub for small offices or the home. It rests on a 12-port rack-mount hub for larger networks.

Regardless of size, all 10BaseT hubs need electrical power. Larger hubs will take power directly from a power outlet, while smaller hubs often come with an AC adapter. In either case, if the hub loses power, the entire segment will stop working.

The name 10BaseT follows roughly the naming convention used for earlier Ethernet cabling systems. The number *10* refers to the speed: 10 Mbps. The word *Base* refers to the signaling type: baseband. The letter *T* refers to the type of cable used: twisted-pair. 10BaseT uses unshielded twisted-pair (UTP) cabling.

> If you ever run into a situation on a 10BaseT or later network in which none of the computers can get on the network, always first check the hub!

UTP

Officially, 10BaseT requires the use of CAT 3 (or higher), two-pair, unshielded twisted-pair (UTP) cable. One pair of wires sends data to the hub while the other pair receives data from the hub. Even though 10BaseT only requires two-pair cabling, everyone installs four-pair cabling to connect devices to the hub as insurance against the possible requirements of newer types of networking (Figure 4.8). Most UTP cables come with stranded Kevlar fibers to give the cable added strength, which in turn enables installers to pull on the cable without excessive risk of literally ripping it apart.

> The names of two earlier true bus versions of Ethernet, 10Base5 and 10Base2, gave the maximum length of the bus. 10Base5 networks could be up to 500 meters long, for example, whereas 10Base2 could be almost 200 meters (though in practice topped out at 185 meters).

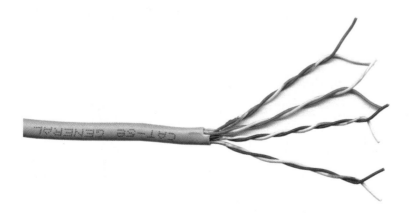

● **Figure 4.8**   A typical four-pair CAT 5e unshielded twisted-pair cable

10BaseT also introduced the networking world to the **RJ-45 connector** (Figure 4.9). Each pin on the RJ-45 connects to a single wire inside the cable; this enables devices to put voltage on the individual wires within the cable. The pins on the RJ-45 are numbered from 1 to 8, as shown in Figure 4.10.

The 10BaseT standard designates some of these numbered wires for specific purposes. As mentioned earlier, although the cable has four pairs, 10BaseT uses only two of the pairs. 10BaseT devices use pins 1 and 2 to send data, and pins 3 and 6 to receive data. Even though one pair of wires sends data and another receives data, a 10BaseT device cannot send and receive simultaneously. The rules of CSMA/CD still apply: only one device can use the segment contained in the hub without causing a collision. Later versions of Ethernet will change this rule.

An RJ-45 connector is usually called a *crimp*, and the act (some folks call it an art) of installing a crimp onto the end of a piece of UTP cable is called *crimping*. The tool used to secure a crimp onto the end of a cable is a **crimper**. Each wire inside a UTP cable must connect to the proper pin inside the crimp. Manufacturers color-code each wire within a piece of four-pair UTP to assist in properly matching the ends. Each pair of wires consists of a solid-colored wire and a striped wire: blue/blue-white, orange/orange-white, brown/brown-white, and green/green-white (Figure 4.11).

The Telecommunications Industry Association/Electronics Industries Alliance (TIA/EIA) defines the industry standard for correct crimping of four-pair UTP for 10BaseT networks. Two standards currently exist: **TIA/EIA 568A** and **TIA/EIA 568B**. Figure 4.12 shows the TIA/EIA 568A and TIA/EIA 568B color-code standards. Note that the wire pairs used by 10BaseT (1 and 2; 3 and 6) come from the same color pairs (green/green-white and orange/orange-white). Following an established color-code scheme, such as TIA/EIA 568A, ensures that the wires match up correctly at each end of the cable.

• **Figure 4.9**   Two views of an RJ-45 connector

The real name for RJ-45 is "8 Position 8 Contact (8P8C) modular plug." The name RJ-45 is so dominant, however, that nobody but the nerdiest of nerds calls it by its real name. Stick to RJ-45.

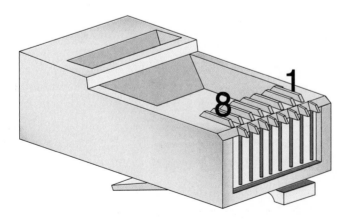

• **Figure 4.10**   The pins on an RJ-45 connector are numbered 1 through 8.

• **Figure 4.11**   Color-coded pairs

The ability to make your own Ethernet cables is a real plus for a busy network tech. With a reel of CAT 5e, a bag of RJ-45 connectors, a moderate investment in a crimping tool, and a little practice, you can kiss those mass-produced cables goodbye! You can make cables to your own length specifications, replace broken RJ-45 connectors that would otherwise mean tossing an entire cable—and in the process, save your company or clients time and money.

Why do the 568 standards say to split one of the pairs to the 3 and 6 positions? Wouldn't it make more sense to wire them sequentially (1 and 2; 3 and 4; 5 and 6; 7 and 8)? The reason for this strange wiring scheme stems from the telephone world. A single telephone line uses two wires, and a typical RJ-11 connector has four connections. A single line is wired in the 2 and 3 positions; if the RJ-11 is designed to support a second phone line, the other pair is wired at 1 and 4. TIA/EIA kept the old telephone standard for backward compatibility. This standardization doesn't stop at the wiring scheme: you can plug an RJ-11 connector into an RJ-45 outlet.

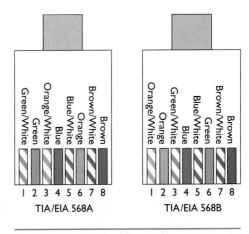

• Figure 4.12 The TIA/EIA 568A and 568B standards

10BaseT Limits and Specifications

Like any other Ethernet cabling system, 10BaseT has limitations, both on cable distance and on the number of computers. The key distance limitation for 10BaseT is the distance between the hub and the computer. The twisted-pair cable connecting a computer to the hub may not exceed 100 meters in length. A 10BaseT hub can connect no more than 1024 computers, although that limitation rarely comes into play. It makes no sense for vendors to build hubs that large—or more to the point, that *expensive*—because excessive collisions can easily bog down Ethernet performance with far fewer than 1024 computers.

10BaseT Summary

- **Speed** 10 Mbps
- **Signal type** Baseband
- **Distance** 100 meters between the hub and the node
- **Node Limit** No more than 1024 nodes per hub
- **Topology** Star-bus topology: physical star, logical bus
- **Cable type** Uses CAT 3 or better UTP cabling with RJ-45 connectors

Tech Tip

568A and 568B

An easy trick to remembering the difference between 568A and 568B is the word "GO." The green and orange pairs are swapped between 568A and 568B, whereas the blue and brown pairs stay in the same place!

For the CompTIA Network+ exam, you won't be tested on the TIA/EIA 568A or B color codes. Just know that they are industry-standard color codes for UTP cabling.

10BaseFL

Just a few years after the introduction of 10BaseT, a fiber-optic version appeared, called **10BaseFL**. As you know from the previous chapter, fiber-optic cabling transmits data packets using pulses of light instead of using electrical current. Using light instead of electricity addresses the three key weaknesses of copper cabling. First, optical signals can travel much farther. The maximum length for a 10BaseFL cable is up to 2 kilometers, depending on how it is configured. Second, fiber-optic cable is immune to electrical interference, making it an ideal choice for high-interference environments. Third, the cable is much more difficult to tap into, making it a good choice for environments with security concerns. 10BaseFL uses *multimode* fiber-optic and employs either an SC or an ST connector.

10BaseFL is often just called 10BaseF.

Figure 4.13 shows a typical 10BaseFL card. Note that it uses two fiber connectors—one to send, and one to receive. All fiber-optic networks use at least two fiber-optic cables. While 10BaseFL enjoyed some popularity for a number of years, most networks today are using the same fiber-optic cabling to run far faster network technologies.

10BaseFL Summary

- **Speed**   10 Mbps
- **Signal type**   Baseband
- **Distance**   2000 meters between the hub and the node
- **Node limit**   No more than 1024 nodes per hub
- **Topology**   Star-bus topology: physical star, logical bus
- **Cable type**   Uses multimode fiber-optic cabling with ST or SC connectors

• **Figure 4.13**   Typical 10BaseFL card

So far you've seen two different flavors of Ethernet, 10BaseT and 10BaseFL. Even though these use different cabling and hubs, the actual packets are still Ethernet packets. As a result, it's common to interconnect different flavors of Ethernet. Since 10BaseT and 10BaseFL use different types of cable, you can use a **media converter** (Figure 4.14) to interconnect different Ethernet types.

• **Figure 4.14**   Typical copper-to-fiber Ethernet media converter (photo courtesy of TRENDnet)

Extending and Enhancing Ethernet Networks

Once you have an Ethernet network in place, you can extend or enhance that network in several ways. You can install additional hubs to connect multiple local area networks, for example. A network bridge can connect two Ethernet segments, effectively doubling the size of a collision domain. You can also replace the hubs with better devices to reduce collisions.

Connecting Ethernet Segments

Sometimes, one hub is just not enough. Once an organization uses every port on its existing hub, adding additional nodes requires additional hubs or a device called a bridge. Even fault tolerance can motivate an organization to add more hubs. If every node on the network connects to the same hub, that hub becomes a single point of failure—if it fails, everybody drops off the network. There are two ways to connect hubs: an uplink port or a crossover cable. You can also connect Ethernet segments using a bridge.

Uplink Ports

Uplink ports enable you to connect two hubs together using a straight-through cable. They're always clearly marked on the hub, as shown in Figure 4.15. To connect two hubs, insert one end of a cable to the uplink and the other cable to any one of the regular ports. To connect more than two hubs, you must daisy-chain your hubs by using one uplink port and one regular port. Figure 4.16 shows properly daisy-chained hubs. As a rule, you cannot daisy-chain more than four hubs together.

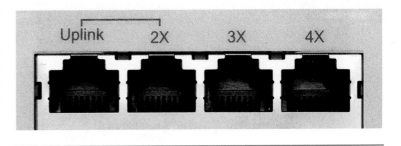

• **Figure 4.15**   Typical uplink port

You also cannot use a single central hub and connect multiple hubs to that single hub, as shown in Figure 4.17. It simply won't work.

Working with uplink ports is sometimes tricky, so you need to take your time. It's easy to mess up and use a central hub. Hub makers give their uplink ports many different names, such as crossover, MDI-X, and OUT. There are also tricks to using uplink ports. Refer to Figure 4.15 again. See the line connecting the uplink port and the port labeled 2X? You may use only one of those two ports, not both at the same time. Additionally, some hubs

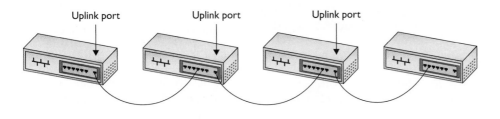

• **Figure 4.16**   Daisy-chained hubs

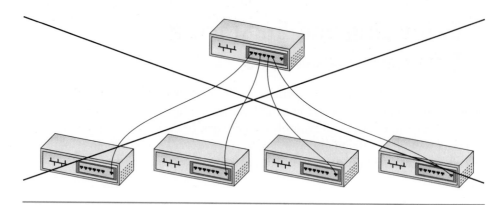

● **Figure 4.17**   Hierarchical hub configuration. This will not work!

● **Figure 4.18**   Press-button port

place on one of the ports a switch that you can press to make it either a regular port or an uplink port (Figure 4.18). Pressing the button electronically reverses the wires inside the hub. Be sure to press the button so it works the way you want it to work.

When connecting hubs, remember the following:

■ Only daisy-chain hubs.

■ Take time to figure out the uplink ports.

■ If you plug hubs in incorrectly, no damage will occur—they just won't work.

Crossover Cables

Hubs can also connect to each other via special twisted-pair cables called crossover cables. A standard cable cannot be used to connect two hubs without using an uplink port, because both hubs will attempt to send data on the second pair of wires (3 and 6) and will listen for data on the first pair (1 and 2). A **crossover cable** reverses the sending and receiving pairs on one end of the cable. One end of the cable is wired according to the TIA/EIA 568A standard, while the other end is wired according to the TIA/EIA 568B standard (Figure 4.19). With the sending and receiving pairs reversed, the hubs can hear each other; hence the need for two standards for connecting RJ-45 jacks to UTP cables.

● **Figure 4.19**   A crossover cable reverses the sending and receiving pairs.

A crossover cable connects to a regular port on each hub. Keep in mind that you can still daisy-chain even when you use crossover cables. Interestingly, many hubs, especially higher-end hubs, do not come with any uplink ports at all. In these cases your only option is to use a crossover cable.

Try This!

Examine Your Uplink Ports

While most hubs come with uplink ports, they all seem to have different ways to use them. Some hubs have dedicated uplink ports, and some have uplink ports that convert to regular ports at the press of a button. Take a look at some hubs and try to figure out how you would use an uplink port to connect it to another hub.

In a pinch, you can use a crossover cable to connect two computers together using 10BaseT NICs with no hub between them at all. This is handy for the quickie connection needed for a nice little home network or when you absolutely, positively must chase down a friend in a computer game!

Be careful about confusing crossover cables with uplink ports. First, never connect two hubs by their uplink ports. Take a regular cable; connect one end to the uplink port on one hub and the other end to any regular port on the other hub. Second, if you use a crossover cable, just plug each end into any handy regular port on each hub.

Bridges

The popularity and rapid implementation of Ethernet networks demanded solutions or workarounds for the limitations inherent in the technology. An Ethernet segment could only be so long and connect a certain number of computers. What if your network went beyond those limitations?

A **bridge** acts like a repeater or hub to connect two Ethernet segments, but it goes one step beyond—filtering and forwarding traffic between those segments based on the MAC addresses of the computers on those segments. This preserves precious bandwidth and makes a larger Ethernet network possible. To *filter* traffic means to stop it from crossing from one network to the next; to *forward* traffic means to pass traffic originating on one side of the bridge to the other.

A newly installed Ethernet bridge initially behaves exactly like a repeater, passing frames from one segment to another. Unlike a repeater, however, a bridge monitors and records the network traffic, eventually reaching a point where it can begin to filter and forward. This makes the bridge more "intelligent" than a repeater. A new bridge usually requires only a few seconds to gather enough information to start filtering and forwarding.

Although bridges offer a good solution for connecting two segments and reducing bandwidth usage, these days you'll mainly find bridges used in wireless, rather than wired, networks. (I cover more on those kinds of bridges in Chapter 16, "Wireless Networking.") Most networks instead have turned to a different magic box, a switch, to extend and enhance an Ethernet network.

Switched Ethernet

As any fighter pilot will tell you, sometimes you just feel the need—the need for speed. While plain-vanilla 10BaseT Ethernet performed well enough for first-generation networks (which did little more than basic file and print sharing), by the early 1990s networks used more-demanding applications, such as Lotus Notes, SAP business management software, and Microsoft Exchange, which quickly saturated a 10BaseT network. Fortunately, those crazy kids over at the IEEE kept expanding the standard, giving the network tech in the trenches a new tool that provided additional bandwidth—the switch.

Tech Tip

Crossing Crossovers

If you mess up your crossover connections, you won't cause any damage, but the connection will not work. Think about it. If you take a straight cable (that is, not a crossover cable) and try to connect two PCs directly, it won't work. Both PCs will try to use the same send and receive wires. When you plug the two PCs into a hub, the hub electronically crosses the data wires, so one NIC sends and the other can receive. If you plug a second hub to the first hub using regular ports, you essentially cross the cross and create a straight connection again between the two PCs! That won't work. Luckily, nothing gets hurt (except your reputation if one of your colleagues notes your mistake!).

  Because bridges work with MAC addresses, they operate at Layer 2, the Data Link layer of the OSI networking model.

  SAP originally stood for Systems Applications and Products when the company formed in the early 1970s. Like IBM, SAP is now just referred to by the letters.

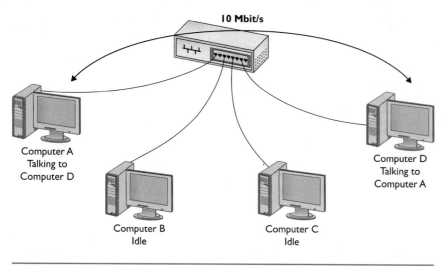

Figure 4.20 One conversation gets all the bandwidth.

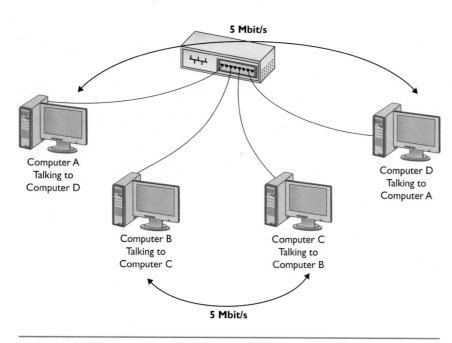

Figure 4.21 Two conversations must share the bandwidth.

The classic difference between a hub and a switch is in the repeating of packets during *normal use*. Although it's true that switches *initially* forward all frames, in regular use they filter by MAC address. Hubs never learn and always forward all frames.

The Trouble with Hubs

In a classic 10BaseT network, the hub, being nothing more than a multiport repeater, sends all packets out on all ports. While this works well, when you get a busy network with multiple conversations taking place at the same time, you lose speed. The problem with hubs is that the total speed of the network—the bandwidth—is 10 Mbps. To appreciate the problem with hubs, take a look at the two computers sending data in Figure 4.20.

Since only one conversation is taking place, the connection speed between Computer A and Computer D runs at 10 Mbps. But what happens if Computer B and Computer C wish to talk at the same time? Well, CSMA/CD kicks in and each conversation runs at only ~5 Mbps (Figure 4.21).

Imagine a network with 100 computers, all talking at the same time! The speed of each conversation would deteriorate to a few hundred thousand bits per second, way too slow to get work done.

Switches to the Rescue

An Ethernet **switch** looks and acts like a hub, but comes with extra smarts that enable it to take advantage of MAC addresses, creating point-to-point connections between two conversing computers. This effectively gives every conversation between two computers the full bandwidth of the network.

To see a switch in action, check out Figure 4.22. When you first turn on a switch, it acts exactly as though it were a hub, passing all incoming frames right back out to all the other ports. As it forwards all frames, however, the switch copies the source MAC addresses and quickly (usually in less than one second) creates an electronic table of the MAC addresses of each connected computer.

As soon as this table is created, the switch begins to do something amazing. The moment it detects two computers talking to each other, the switch starts to act like a telephone operator, creating an on-the-fly, hard-wired

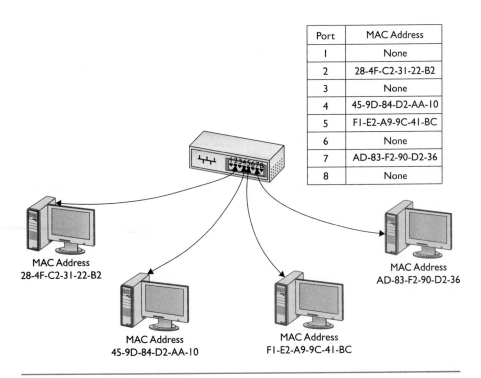

Port	MAC Address
1	None
2	28-4F-C2-31-22-B2
3	None
4	45-9D-84-D2-AA-10
5	F1-E2-A9-9C-41-BC
6	None
7	AD-83-F2-90-D2-36
8	None

MAC Address
28-4F-C2-31-22-B2

MAC Address
AD-83-F2-90-D2-36

MAC Address
45-9D-84-D2-AA-10

MAC Address
F1-E2-A9-9C-41-BC

• **Figure 4.22**   A switch tracking MAC addresses

connection between the two devices. While these two devices communicate, it's as though they are the only two computers on the network. Figure 4.23 shows this in action. Since each conversation is on its own connection, each runs at 10 Mbps.

Speed isn't the only benefit switches bring to a 10BaseT network. When you use switches instead of hubs, the entire CSMA/CD game goes out the window. Forget about daisy-chain only! Feel free to connect your switches pretty much any way you wish (Figure 4.24).

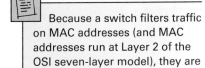

Because a switch filters traffic on MAC addresses (and MAC addresses run at Layer 2 of the OSI seven-layer model), they are often called *Layer 2 switches*.

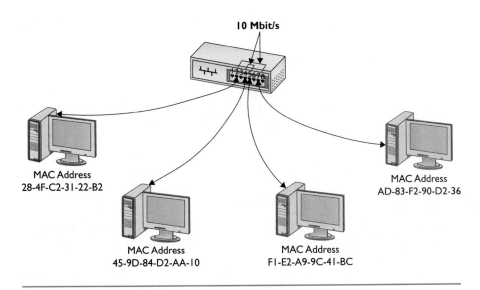

10 Mbit/s

MAC Address
28-4F-C2-31-22-B2

MAC Address
AD-83-F2-90-D2-36

MAC Address
45-9D-84-D2-AA-10

MAC Address
F1-E2-A9-9C-41-BC

• **Figure 4.23**   A switch making two separate connections

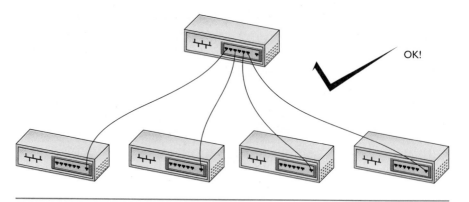

OK!

• **Figure 4.24**   Switches are very commonly connected in a tree organization.

• **Figure 4.25**   Hub (top) and switch (bottom) comparison

Physically, an Ethernet switch looks much like an Ethernet hub (Figure 4.25). Logically, because the switch creates a point-to-point connection between any two computers, eliminating CSMA/CD, the entire concept of collision domain disappears because there are no longer any collisions. Instead, the common term used today is **broadcast domain**, because all devices connected to a switch will hear a broadcast sent from any one system.

Spanning Tree Protocol

The ease of interconnecting switches makes them prone to a nefarious little problem called **bridge loops**. As its name implies, a bridge loop is nothing more than an interconnection of switches in such a fashion that they create a loop. In the network shown in Figure 4.26, for example, packets going between switches A, B, and C have multiple paths. This creates a problem.

A bridge loop using the first generations of Ethernet switches was a very bad thing, creating a path sending packets in an endless loop and preventing the network from working. To stop this, the Ethernet standards body

> Collisions (and CSMA/CD) can still take place on a switched Ethernet network, for example, if two devices tried to broadcast at the same time and collided. In these rare situations, switches still fall back to CSMA/CD.

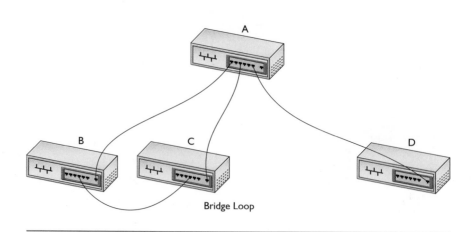

A

B   C   D

Bridge Loop

• **Figure 4.26**   Bridge loops are bad!

adopted the **Spanning Tree Protocol (STP)**. STP adds a little more intelligence to switches that enables them to detect bridge loops. If detected, the switches communicate with each other and, without any outside interaction, turn off one port on the loop (Figure 4.27).

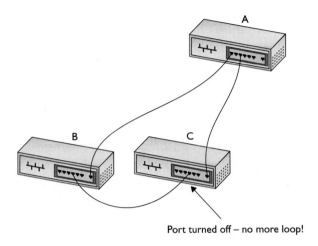

Port turned off – no more loop!

• **Figure 4.27**   Port turned off, disaster averted

Chapter 4 Review

■ Chapter Summary

After reading this chapter and completing the exercises, you should understand the following about Ethernet.

Define and describe Ethernet

- Ethernet is based on a family of network technologies from a bus topology. Ethernet enables computers to send data across a network, identify sending and receiving computers, and determine which computer should use the cable at which time. Early Ethernet networks originally used a single coax cable as a physical bus.

- The IEEE 802.3 committee controls the Ethernet standard.

- Ethernet networks use a hybrid star-bus topology with a hub at the center. Hubs repeat the incoming signal to every connected port.

- Ethernet frames prevent any single computer from monopolizing the cable, while making the retransmission of lost data efficient.

- Ethernet frames contain seven basic parts: the preamble, the MAC address of the destination computer, the MAC address of the sender, the length of data, the data itself, a pad, and a frame check sequence.

- CSMA/CD stands for carrier sense multiple access/collision detection. Carrier sense means that the node checks the network cable before sending to see if anyone else is transmitting. Multiple access means all computers have equal access to the network cable. Collision detection is when nodes detect that a transmission did not complete.

Explain early Ethernet implementations

- Modern Ethernet networks use 10BaseT cabling. The physical topology of 10BaseT is a physical star; however, the data uses a logical bus topology with a central hub. So, 10BaseT actually uses a hybrid star-bus topology to accomplish moving data frames through the network.

- 10BaseT supports speeds up to 10 Mbps over baseband.

- 10BaseT requires the use of CAT 3 or higher, two-pair, unshielded twisted-pair cable. These cables utilize RJ-45 connectors, which are crimped to the cable.

- Correct crimping follows either the TIA/EIA 568A or the TIA/EIA 568B color-code standard.

- A good network technician knows the limits and specifications of 10BaseT, such as the maximum speed and distance, maximum nodes per hub, and supported cabling types.

- 10BaseFL is a fiber-optic version of 10BaseT that uses multimode fiber-optic cable and SC or ST connectors. One major advantage of 10BaseFL is its increased maximum distance between hub and node.

Describe ways to extend and enhance Ethernet networks

- Because hubs act as repeaters, hubs can be used to connect multiple segments together. Most hubs also have a crossover port, sometimes labeled uplink, crossover, MDI-X, OUT, or other another creative name.

- A crossover cable may be used to connect two hubs without an uplink port.

- A bridge filters and forwards traffic between Ethernet segments based on the MAC addresses of the computers on those segments. A bridge monitors and records the network traffic, eventually forwarding only the traffic that needs to go from one side of the bridge to the other. This helps reduce network bandwidth usage.

- Busy networks may suffer decreased bandwidth when using hubs. A switch solves this problem by creating a point-to-point connection, based on MAC addresses, between the sending and receiving nodes.

- Switches eliminate collision domains and instead create broadcast domains where all devices connected to a switch hear a broadcast sent from any other node.

- Connecting switches the wrong way can lead to bridge loops, which in turn can break the network. Switches that support the Spanning Tree Protocol are immune to bridge loops, even if wired in a physical loop.

Key Terms

10BaseFL *(67)*

10BaseT *(64)*

802.3 (Ethernet) *(59)*

bridge *(71)*

bridge loop *(74)*

broadcast domain *(74)*

carrier sense multiple access/collision detection (CSMA/CD) *(62)*

collision domain *(63)*

crimper *(66)*

crossover cable *(70)*

Ethernet *(59)*

frame *(60)*

frame check sequence *(62)*

hub *(59)*

MAC address *(61)*

media converter *(68)*

node *(61)*

pad *(62)*

ports *(64)*

preamble *(61)*

promiscuous mode *(61)*

repeater *(59)*

RJ-45 connector *(66)*

segment *(60)*

sniffer *(61)*

Spanning Tree Protocol (STP) *(75)*

switch *(72)*

TIA/EIA 568A *(66)*

TIA/EIA 568B *(66)*

uplink port *(69)*

Key Term Quiz

Use the Key Terms list to complete the sentences that follow. Not all terms will be used.

1. The _____ is unique to each individual NIC.

2. When extra "filler" data is needed in a packet, a(n) _____ is added.

3. Another name for a packet is a(n) _____.

4. A NIC that is listening for all packets sent along the wire is said to be in _____.

5. The first item in a data packet is the _____.

6. A hub acts as a(n) _____ in that it copies all incoming signals to every connected port.

7. Connecting switches incorrectly can create a(n) _____, which can make the whole network stop working.

8. Hubs can be daisy-chained through their _____, or the use of a(n) _____.

9. _____ has a maximum distance between node and hub of 100 meters while _____ has a maximum distance of 2000 meters.

10. A(n) _____ can be used to interconnect different Ethernet types.

Multiple-Choice Quiz

1. What is another term commonly used for frame?

   A. Network

   B. Packet

   C. Pad

   D. Segment

2. How are the connectors wired on a crossover cable?

   A. One end is TIA/EIA 568A; the other end is TIA/EIA 568B.

   B. Both ends are TIA/EIA 568A.

   C. Both ends are TIA/EIA 568B.

   D. One end is an RJ-45; the other end is an RG-6.

3. What items below make up the CSMA/CD system used in Ethernet networks? (Select three.)

   A. Collision avoidance

   B. Carrier sense

   C. Multiple access

   D. Collision detection

4. What happens when two computers transmit through a hub simultaneously?

   A. Nothing happens.

   B. The terminators prevent any transmission problems.

   C. Their signals are reflected back down the cable to their points of origin.

   D. A collision occurs.

5. What is a group of nodes that hear each other's traffic?

   A. Collision domain

   B. Ethernet

   C. Fast Ethernet

   D. Sneakernet

6. Which committee is responsible for Ethernet standards?

   A. IEEE 803.2

   B. IEEE 803.3

   C. IEEE 802.2

   D. IEEE 802.3

7. What type of cabling do modern Ethernet networks use?

   A. 10Base2

   B. 10Base5

   C. 10BaseT

   D. 10Base-Cat5

8. What is the purpose of a preamble in an Ethernet frame?

   A. It gives the receiving NIC time to realize a frame is coming and to know when the frame starts.

   B. It provides the receiving NIC with the sending NIC's MAC address so communication can continue.

   C. It provides error-checking to ensure data integrity.

   D. It contains a description of the data that is to follow so the receiving NIC knows how to reassemble it.

9. What is a valuable network tool that can be used to examine all frames on the network, regardless of their intended recipient?

   A. Repeater

   B. Media converter

   C. STP

   D. Sniffer

10. For what purpose is a crimping tool used?

    A. To splice a 10BaseT cable with a 10BaseFL cable.

    B. To attach an RJ-45 connector to a UTP cable.

    C. To attach a 10BaseT cable to a media converter.

    D. To connect two hubs together.

11. Which of the following is not a limitation on 10BaseT cable?

    A. Maximum speed of 10 Mbps

    B. Maximum distance between hub and node of 100 feet

    C. Maximum of 1024 nodes per hub

    D. Minimum CAT 3 or better UTP with RJ-45 connectors

12. Which of the following is not a limitation on 10BaseFL cable?

    A. Maximum speed of 10 Mbps

    B. Maximum distance between hub and node of 2000 meters

    C. Maximum of 1024 nodes per hub

    D. Minimum CAT 3 or better UTP with RJ-45 connectors

13. Upon looking at the front of a hub, you notice something labeled as MDI-X. What is this for?

    A. It is a special receptacle for the power cable.

    B. It is a regular port used to connect computers.

C. It is an uplink port used to connect the hub to another hub.

D. It is the brand name of the hub.

14. Which statement best describes the main difference between hubs and switches?

A. A hub repeats signals whereas a switch amplifies them.

B. A hub repeats incoming signals to all connected ports whereas a switch only repeats an incoming signal to the destination port.

C. Hubs use 10BaseT but switches use 10BaseFL.

D. Hubs can be daisy-chained but switches cannot.

15. What feature of switches prevents the problem of bridge loops?

A. STP

B. TCP/IP

C. IEEE 802.3

D. UTP

■ Essay Quiz

1. Describe two ways that using frames helps move data along a network.

2. Define the term *CSMA/CD*, using simple descriptions to explain each of the three parts: CS, MA, and CD.

3. Describe what a hub does and some of its limitations. Then explain how a switch works to overcome the problems of a hub.

Lab Projects

• Lab Project 4.1

On a blank sheet of paper, use one side to list the basic facts you must know about 10BaseT for the CompTIA Network+ certification exam. Use the other side to list the essential facts you must know about 10BaseFL. Double-check your work, either by yourself or with a classmate, to ensure its accuracy. Save this sheet to use as a quick-reference study aid when you're preparing to sit for your exam—it will help!

• Lab Project 4.2

In this chapter you learned about the basic functionality of switches. Use the Internet to delve deeper and research the difference between a managed switch, an unmanaged switch, and a smart switch. Create a chart to compare the similarities and differences between them. In addition to the differences in features and functionality, research and report on the pricing differences for similarly sized switches. For example, what is more expensive, a 24-port managed, unmanaged, or smart switch? What do you get for the extra money? Is it worth it?

• Lab Project 4.3

Use the Internet to research freeware or shareware programs that will "sniff" the data on your network. With your instructor's permission, download a program that you find, and then install it on your classroom lab network. Try to sniff data going to and from your machine, as well as other traffic. Have fun, and document your findings.

Modern Ethernet

*"To expect the unexpected shows
a thoroughly modern intellect."*

—OSCAR WILDE

**In this chapter, you will learn
how to**

- **Describe the varieties of 100-
megabit Ethernet**

- **Discuss copper- and fiber-based
Gigabit Ethernet**

- **Compare the competing varieties
of 10-Gigabit Ethernet**

Within a few years of introduction, 10BaseT proved inadequate to meet the growing networking demand for speed. As with all things in the computing world, bandwidth is the key. Even with switching, the 10-Mbps speed of 10BaseT, seemingly so fast when first developed, quickly found a market clamoring for even faster speeds. This chapter looks at the improvements in Ethernet since 10BaseT. You'll read about 100-megabit standards and the several standards in Gigabit Ethernet. The chapter wraps up with the newest speed standards, 10-Gigabit Ethernet.

Test Specific

Before diving into the newer standards, let's get a few facts about Ethernet out of the way:

- There are only four Ethernet speeds: 10 megabit, 100 megabit, 1 gigabit, and 10 gigabit.

- Every version of Ethernet uses either unshielded twisted pair (UTP) or fiber. (There were a few exceptions to this rule, but they were rare and weird.)

- Every version of Ethernet uses a hub or a switch, although hubs are incredibly rare today.

- Only 10- and 100-megabit Ethernet may use a hub. Gigabit and 10-Gigabit Ethernet networks must use a switch.

- Every version of Ethernet has a limit of 1024 nodes.

- Every UTP version of Ethernet has a maximum distance from the switch or hub to the node of 100 meters.

▣ 100-Megabit Ethernet

The quest to break 10-Mbps network speeds in the Ethernet world started in the early 1990s. By then 10BaseT Ethernet had established itself as the most popular networking technology (although other standards, such as IBM's Token Ring, still had some market share). The goal was to create a new speed standard that made no changes to the actual Ethernet frames themselves. By doing this, the 802.3 committee ensured that different speeds of Ethernet could interconnect, assuming you had something that could handle the speed differences and a media converter if the connections were different.

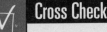

> **Cross Check**
>
> ### Interconnecting Ethernet Networks
>
> You learned about the devices used to connect different types of Ethernet networks—hubs and switches—in Chapter 3, "Cabling and Topology." Check your memory now. What's the difference between the two devices? Which would you prefer for connections and why?

100BaseT

If you want to make a lot of money in the technology world, create a standard and then get everyone else to buy into it. For that matter, you can even give the standard away and still make tons of cash if you have the inside line on making the hardware that supports the standard.

When it came time to come up with a new standard to replace 10BaseT, network hardware makers forwarded a large number of potential standards, all focused on the prize of leading the new Ethernet standard. As a result, two UTP Ethernet standards appeared, **100BaseT4** and **100BaseTX**. 100BaseT4 used CAT 3 cable while 100BaseTX used CAT 5. By the late 1990s, 100BaseTX became the dominant 100-megabit Ethernet standard. 100BaseT4 disappeared from the market and today it's forgotten. As a result, we almost never say 100BaseTX today, simply choosing to use the term **100BaseT**.

 100BaseT was at one time called Fast Ethernet. The term still sticks to the 100-Mbps standards—including 100BaseFX, which you'll read about in an upcoming section—even though there are now much faster versions of Ethernet.

100BaseTX (100BaseT) Summary

- **Speed** 100 Mbps
- **Signal type** Baseband
- **Distance** 100 meters between the hub and the node
- **Node limit** No more than 1024 nodes per hub
- **Topology** Star-bus topology: physical star, logical bus
- **Cable type** Uses CAT 5(e) or better UTP cabling with RJ-45 connectors

Upgrading a 10BaseT network to 100BaseT is not a small process. First you need to make sure you have CAT 5 cable or better. This isn't a big deal, because almost all network cables installed in the past decade are at least CAT 5. Second, you must replace all the old 10BaseT NICs with 100BaseT NICs. Third, you need to replace the 10BaseT hub or switch with a 100BaseT hub/switch. Making this upgrade cost a lot in the early days of 100BaseT, so people clamored for a way to make the upgrade a little easier. This was done via multispeed, auto-sensing NICs and hubs/switches.

Figure 5.1 shows a typical multispeed, auto-sensing 100BaseT NIC from the late 1990s. When this NIC first connects to a network it starts to negotiate automatically with the hub or switch to determine the other device's highest speed. If they both do 100BaseT, then you get 100BaseT. If the hub/switch only does 10BaseT, then the NIC does 10BaseT. All of this happens automatically (Figure 5.2).

It is impossible to tell a 10BaseT NIC from a 100BaseT NIC without close inspection. Look for something on the card to tell you the card's speed. Some NICs may have extra link lights to show the speed (see Chapter 6, "Installing a Physical Network," for the scoop on link lights). Of course, you can always

• **Figure 5.1** Typical 100BaseT NIC

Tech Tip

Lingo

If you want to sound like a proper tech, you need to use the right words. Techs don't actually say, "multispeed, auto-sensing," but rather "10/100." As in, "Hey, is that a 10/100 NIC you got there?" Now you're talking the talk!

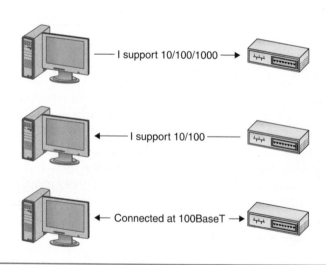

I support 10/100/1000 →

← I support 10/100

← Connected at 100BaseT →

• **Figure 5.2** Auto-negotiation in action

just install the card as shown in Figure 5.3 and see what the operating system says it sees!

It's very difficult to find a true 10BaseT NIC any longer because 100BaseT NICs have been around long enough to have pretty much replaced 10BaseT. All modern NICs are multispeed and auto-sensing. That applies to 100BaseT NICs and faster NICs as well.

100BaseFX

Most Ethernet networks use UTP cabling, but quite a few use fiber-based networks instead. In some networks, using fiber simply makes more sense.

UTP cabling cannot meet the needs of every organization for three key reasons. First, the 100-meter distance limitation of UTP-based networks is inadequate for networks covering large buildings or campuses. Second, UTP's lack of electrical shielding makes it a poor choice for networks functioning in locations with high levels of electrical interference. Finally, the Maxwell Smarts and James Bonds of the world find UTP cabling (and copper cabling in general) easy to tap, making it an inappropriate choice for high-security environments. To address these issues, the IEEE 802.3 standard provides for a flavor of 100-megabit Ethernet using fiber-optic cable, called 100BaseFX.

The **100BaseFX** standard saw quite a bit of interest for years, as it combined the high speed of 100-megabit Ethernet with the reliability of fiber optics. Outwardly, 100BaseFX looks exactly like 10BaseFL. Both use the same multimode fiber-optic cabling, and both use SC or ST connectors. 100BaseFX offers improved data speeds over 10BaseFL and equally long cable runs, supporting a maximum cable length of two kilometers.

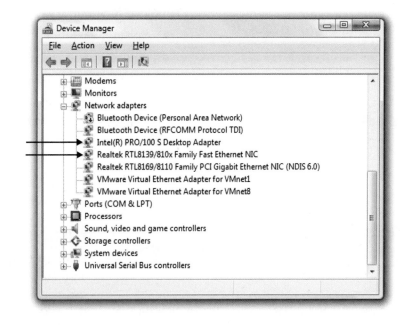

• **Figure 5.3** Typical 100BaseT NIC in Vista

Tech Tip

Shielded Twisted Pair

Installing networks in areas of high electrical interference used to require the use of shielded twisted-pair (STP) cabling rather than UTP. Even though you can still get STP cabling today, its use is rare. Most installations will use fiber-optic cable in situations where UTP won't cut it.

 Just as the old 10BaseFL was often called 10BaseF, 100BaseFX is sometimes called simply 100BaseF.

Try This!

Hub Search

At this point, you've seen different implementations of Ethernet, from 10BaseT (which you read about in Chapter 4) to 100BaseTX and 100BaseFX. If you planned a network today, what kind of equipment could you buy? Don't look at me for the answer—instead, try this!

Go to your local computer store with pen and paper ready, and jot down the variations you find. Does the store carry 10BaseT hubs? What about 10/100 hubs for easy migration? What about a hub that supports both fiber and UTP, so you can connect 100BaseFX and 100BaseTX networks? Finally, how much do these things cost?

100BaseFX Summary

- **Speed**   100 Mbps
- **Signal type**   Baseband

  - **Distance**   Two kilometers between the hub and the node
  - **Node limit**   No more than 1024 nodes per hub
  - **Topology**   Star-bus topology: physical star, logical bus
  - **Cable type**   Uses multimode fiber cabling with ST or SC connectors

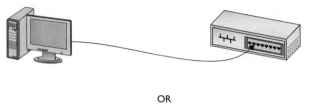

OR

• **Figure 5.4**   Half-duplex; sending at the top, receiving at the bottom

• **Figure 5.5**   Full-duplex

Full-Duplex Ethernet

Early 100BaseT NICs, just like 10BaseT NICs, could send and receive data, but not at the same time—a feature called **half-duplex** (Figure 5.4). The IEEE addressed this characteristic shortly after adopting 100BaseT as a standard. By the late 1990s, most 100BaseT cards could auto-negotiate for full-duplex. With **full-duplex** a NIC can send and receive at the same time, as shown in Figure 5.5.

Almost all NICs today can go full-duplex. The NIC and the attached hub/switch determine full- or half-duplex during the auto-negotiation process. The vast majority of the time you simply let the NIC do its negotiation. Every operating system has some method to force the NIC to a certain speed/duplex, as shown in Figure 5.6.

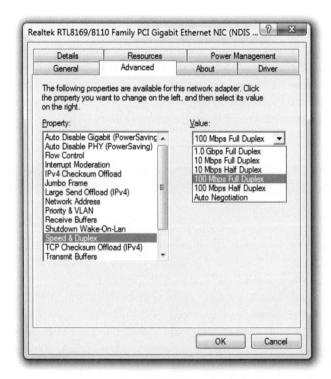

Full-duplex doesn't increase the speed of the network, but it doubles the bandwidth. Image a one-lane road expanded to two lanes while keeping the speed limit the same.

• **Figure 5.6**   Forcing speed and duplex in Windows Vista

■ Gigabit Ethernet

By the end of the 1990s, the true speed junkie needed an even more powerful version of Ethernet. In response, IEEE created **Gigabit Ethernet**, today the most common type of Ethernet found on new NICs.

The IEEE approved two different versions of Gigabit Ethernet. The most widely implemented solution, published under the IEEE **802.3ab** standard, is called **1000BaseT**. The other version, published under the **802.3z** standard and known as **1000BaseX**, is divided into a series of standards, with names such as 1000BaseCX, 1000BaseSX, and 1000BaseLX.

1000BaseT uses four-pair UTP cabling to achieve gigabit performance. Like 10BaseT and 100BaseT, 1000BaseT has a maximum cable length of 100 meters on a segment. 1000BaseT connections and ports look exactly like the ones on a 10BaseT or 100BaseT network. 1000BaseT is the dominant Gigabit Ethernet standard.

The 802.3z standards require a bit more discussion. Let's look at each of these solutions in detail to see how they work.

 The term *Gigabit Ethernet* is more commonly used than *1000BaseT*.

1000BaseCX

1000BaseCX uses a unique cable known as twinaxial cable (Figure 5.7). Twinaxial cables are special shielded 150-Ohm cables with a length limit of only 25 meters. 1000BaseCX has made little progress in the Gigabit Ethernet market.

1000BaseSX

Many networks upgrading to Gigabit Ethernet use the **1000BaseSX** standard. 1000BaseSX uses multimode fiber-optic cabling to connect systems, with a generous maximum cable length of 220 to 500 meters; the exact length is left up to the various manufacturers. 1000BaseSX uses an 850-nm (nanometer) wavelength LED to transmit light on the fiber-optic cable. 1000BaseSX devices look exactly like the 100BaseFX products you read about earlier in this chapter, but they rely exclusively on the SC type of connector.

● **Figure 5.7**   Twinaxial cable

 Cross Check

SC and ST

You saw the common fiber-optic cable SC and ST connectors way back in Chapter 3, so cross-check your knowledge here. What distinguishes the two? Can 100BaseFX NICs use either one? Which do you need to twist, like a bayonet?

1000BaseLX

1000BaseLX is the long-distance carrier for Gigabit Ethernet. 1000BaseLX uses single-mode (laser) cables to shoot data at distances up to 5 kilometers—and some manufacturers use special repeaters to increase that to distances as great as 70 kilometers! The Ethernet folks are trying to position this as the Ethernet backbone of the future, and already some large carriers are beginning to adopt 1000BaseLX. You may live your whole life and never see a 1000BaseLX device, but odds are good that you will encounter connections that use such devices in the near future. 1000BaseLX connectors look like 1000BaseSX connectors.

● **Figure 5.8**   MT-RJ connector

New Fiber Connectors

Around the time that Gigabit Ethernet first started to appear, two problems began to surface with ST and SC connectors. First, ST connectors are relatively large, twist-on connectors, requiring the installer to twist the cable when inserting or removing a cable. Twisting is not a popular action with fiber-optic cables, as the delicate fibers may fracture. Also, big-fingered techs have a problem with ST connectors if the connectors are too closely packed: they can't get their fingers around them. SC connectors snap in and out, making them much more popular than STs. However, SC connectors are also large, and the folks who make fiber networking equipment wanted to pack more connectors onto their boxes. This brought about two new types of fiber connectors, known generically as **Small Form Factor (SFF)** connectors. The first SFF connector—the **Mechanical Transfer Registered Jack (MT-RJ)**, shown in Figure 5.8—gained popularity with important companies like Cisco and is still quite common.

The second type of popular SFF connector is the **Local Connecter (LC)**, shown in Figure 5.9. LC-type connectors are very popular, particularly in the United States, and many fiber experts consider the LC-type connector to be the predominant fiber connector.

● **Figure 5.9**   LC-type connector

LC and MT-RJ are the most popular types of SFF fiber connections, but many others exist, as outlined in Table 5.1. The fiber industry has no standard beyond ST and SC connectors, which means that different makers of fiber equipment may have different connections.

Table 5.1	Gigabit Ethernet Summary			
Standard	**Cabling**	**Cable Details**	**Connectors**	**Length**
1000BaseCX	Copper	Twinax	Twinax	25 m
1000BaseSX	Multimode fiber	850 nm	Variable—LC is common	220–500 m
1000BaseLX	Single-mode fiber	1300 nm	Variable—LC, SC are common	5 km
1000BaseT	CAT 5e/6 UTP	Four-pair/full-duplex	RJ-45	100 m

10-Gigabit Ethernet

The ongoing demand for bandwidth on the Internet means that the networking industry is continually reaching for faster LAN speeds. **10-Gigabit Ethernet (10 GbE)** is showing up in high-level LANs, with the anticipation of trickle-down to the desktops in the near future.

Because 10 GbE is still a new technology, there are a large number of standards in existence. Over time many of these standards will certainly grow in popularity and some will disappear. For now, though, the landscape is in flux. 10 GbE has a number of fiber standards and two copper standards. 10 GbE was first and foremost designed with fiber optics in mind. As a result, it has only been since 2008 that 10-GbE copper products have actually (and very expensively) began to appear for sale.

Fiber-based 10 GbE

When the IEEE members sat down to formalize specifications on Ethernet running at 10 Gbps, they faced an interesting task in several ways. First, they had to maintain the integrity of the Ethernet frame. Data is king, after all, and the goal was to create a network that could interoperate with any other Ethernet network. Second, they had to figure out how to transfer those frames at such blazing speeds. This second challenge had some interesting ramifications because of two factors. They could use the traditional Physical layer mechanisms defined by the Ethernet standard. But, there was already in place a perfectly usable ~10-Gbps fiber network, called **SONET**, used for wide area networking (WAN) transmissions. What to do?

The IEEE created a whole set of 10-GbE standards that could use traditional LAN Physical layer mechanisms, plus a set of standards that could take advantage of the SONET infrastructure and run over the WAN fiber. To make the 10-Gbps jump as easy as possible, the IEEE also recognized the need for different networking situations. Some implementations need data transfers that can run long distances over single-mode fiber, for example, whereas others can make do with short-distance transfers over multimode fiber. This led to a lot of standards for 10 GbE.

The 10-GbE standards are defined by several factors: the type of fiber used, the wavelength of the laser or lasers, and the Physical layer signaling type. These factors also define the maximum signal distance.

There are proposed Ethernet standards that go way beyond 10-Gbps speeds, including a 100-GbE proposal, but nothing is fully standardized as of this writing. 10 GbE is the reigning king of network speeds.

Chapter 14, "Remote Connectivity," covers SONET in great detail. For now just think of it as a data transmission standard that's different from the LAN Ethernet standard.

• Figure 5.10 A 10GBaseSR NIC (photo courtesy of Intel Corporation)

The IEEE uses specific letter codes with the standards to help sort out the differences so that you know what you're implementing or supporting. All the standards have names in the following format: "10GBase" followed by two other characters, what I'll call xy. The x stands for the type of fiber (usually, though not officially) and the wavelength of the laser signal; the y stands for the Physical layer signaling standard. The y code is always either R for LAN-based signaling or W for SONET/WAN-based signaling. The x differs a little more, so let's take a look.

10GBaseSy uses a short-wavelength (850 nm) signal over multimode fiber. The maximum fiber length is 300 meters, although this will vary depending on the type of multimode fiber used. **10GBaseSR** (Figure 5.10) is used for Ethernet LANs and **10GBaseSW** is used to connect to SONET devices.

Standard	Fiber Type	Wavelength	Physical Layer Signaling	Maximum Signal Length
10GBaseSR	Multimode	850 nm	LAN	26–300 m
10GBaseSW	Multimode	850 nm	SONET/WAN	26–300 m

10GBaseLy uses a long-wavelength (1310 nm) signal over single-mode fiber. The maximum fiber length is 10 kilometers, although this will vary depending on the type of single-mode fiber used. **10GBaseLR** is used for Ethernet LANs and **10GBaseLW** is used to connect to SONET equipment. 10GBaseLR is the most popular and cheapest 10-GbE media type.

Standard	Fiber Type	Wavelength	Physical Layer Signaling	Maximum Signal Length
10GBaseLR	Single-mode	1310 nm	LAN	10 km
10GBaseLW	Single-mode	1310 nm	SONET/WAN	10 km

10GBaseEy uses an extra-long-wavelength (1550 nm) signal over single-mode fiber. The maximum fiber length is 40 kilometers, although this will vary depending on the type of single-mode fiber used. **10GBaseER** is used for Ethernet LANs and **10GBaseEW** is used to connect to SONET equipment.

Standard	Fiber Type	Wavelength	Physical Layer Signaling	Maximum Signal Length
10GBaseER	Single-mode	1550 nm	LAN	40 km
10GBaseEW	Single-mode	1550 nm	SONET/WAN	40 km

The 10-GbE fiber standards do not define the type of connector to use and instead leave that to manufacturers (see the upcoming section "10-GbE Physical Connections").

Copper-based 10 GbE

It took until 2006 for IEEE to come up with a standard for 10 GbE running UTP—called, predictably, 10GBaseT. **10GBaseT** looks and works exactly like the slower versions of UTP Ethernet. The only downside is that 10GBaseT running on CAT 6 has a maximum cable length of only 55 meters.

Table 5.2	10-GbE Summary				
Standard	**Cabling**	**Wavelength/ Cable Details**	**Connectors**	**Length**
10GBaseSR /SW	Multimode fiber	850 nm	Not defined	26–300 m
10GBaseLR /LW	Single-mode fiber	1310 nm	Variable—LC is common	10 km
10GBaseER /EW	Single-mode fiber	1550 nm	Variable—LC, SC are common	40 km
10GBaseT	CAT 6/6a UTP	Four-pair/ full-duplex	RJ-45	55/100 m

The updated CAT 6a standard enables 10GBaseT to run at the standard distance of 100 meters. Table 5.2 summarizes the 10-GbE standards.

10-GbE Physical Connections

This hodgepodge of 10-GbE types might have been the ultimate disaster for hardware manufacturers. All types of 10 GbE send and receive the exact same signal; only the physical medium is different. Imagine a single router that had to come out in seven different versions to match all these types! Instead, the 10-GbE industry simply chose not to define the connector types and devised a very clever, very simple concept called **multisource agreements (MSAs)**. An MSA is a modular transceiver that you plug into your 10-GbE equipment, enabling you to convert from one media type to another by inserting the right transceiver. Unfortunately, there have been as many as four different MSA types competing in the past few years. Figure 5.11 shows a typical MSA called XENPAK.

For now, 10-GbE equipment is the exclusive domain of high-bandwidth LANs and WANs, including parts of the big-pipe Internet connections.

Backbones

The beauty and the challenge of the vast selection of Ethernet flavors is deciding which one to use in your network. The goal is to give your users as fast a network response time as possible, combined with keeping costs at a

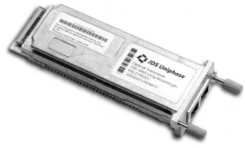

• **Figure 5.11** XENPAK MSA

Tech Tip

The Other 10-Gigabit Ethernet Fiber Standards

Manufacturers have shown in the early days of 10-GbE implementation a lot of creativity and innovation to take advantage of both existing fiber and the most cost-effective equipment. This has led to a variety of standards that are not covered by the CompTIA Network+ competencies, but that you should know about nevertheless. The top three as of this writing are 10GBaseL4, 10GBaseLRM, and 10GBaseZR.

The 10GBaseL4 standard uses four lasers at 1300-nanometer wavelength over legacy fiber. On FDDI-grade multimode cable, 10GBaseL4 can support up to 300-meter transmissions. The range increases to 10 kilometers over single-mode fiber.

The 10GBaseLRM standard uses the long wavelength signal of 10GBaseLR, but over legacy multimode fiber. The standard can achieve a range of up to 220 meters, depending on the grade of fiber cable.

Finally, some manufacturers have adopted the 10GBaseZR "standard," which isn't part of the IEEE standards at all (unlike 10GBaseL4 and 10GBaseLRM). Instead, the manufacturers have created their own set of specifications. 10GBaseZR networks use a 1550-nanometer wavelength over single-mode fiber to achieve a range of a whopping 80 kilometers. The standard can work with both Ethernet LAN and SONET/WAN infrastructure.

Not all 10-GbE manufacturers use MSAs in their equipment.

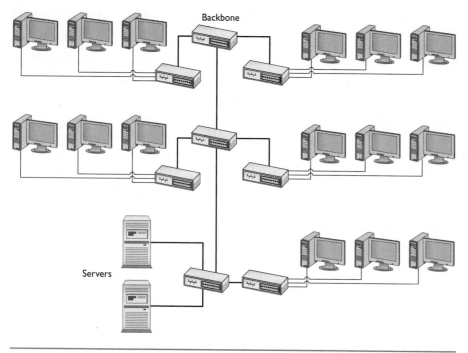

reasonable level. To combine these two issues, most network administrators find that a multispeed Ethernet network works best. In a multispeed network, a series of high-speed (relative to the rest of the network) switches maintain a backbone network. No computers, other than possibly servers, attach directly to this backbone. Figure 5.12 shows a typical backbone network. Each floor has its own switch that connects to every node on the floor. In turn, each of these switches also has a separate high-speed connection to a main switch that resides in the computer room of the office.

In order to make this work, you need switches with separate, dedicated, high-speed ports like the ones shown in Figure 5.13. The add-on ports on the switches run straight to the high-speed backbone switch.

● **Figure 5.12**   Typical network configuration showing backbone

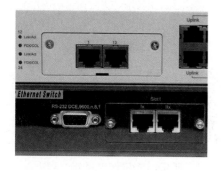

● **Figure 5.13**   Switches with dedicated, high-speed add-on ports

Know Your Ethernets!

This single chapter is little more than a breakdown of the evolution of UTP Ethernet since the old 10BaseT standard. Make sure you know the details of these Ethernet versions and take advantage of the summaries and tables to recognize the important points of each type.

Additionally, keep in mind that you've only just begun to delve into the world of switching. The book has covered thus far only the functions of a basic switch. There is a lot more to see in terms of the capabilities of these powerful devices, but you first need to understand networking a bit deeper.

 Try This!

Shopping for Switches

Cisco, one of the industry leaders for Ethernet switches, has a great Web site for its products. Imagine that you are setting up a network for your school or business (keep it simple and pick a single building if you're in a large organization). Decide what type of switches you'd like to use, including both the backbone and local switches. If you're really motivated, decide where to physically locate the switches. Don't be afraid to try a fiber backbone—almost every Cisco switch comes with special ports to enable you to pick the type of Ethernet you want to use for your backbone.

Chapter 5 Review

■ Chapter Summary

After reading this chapter and completing the exercises, you should understand the following about Ethernet.

Describe the varieties of 100-megabit Ethernet

- Fast Ethernet includes two UTP variations, both arranged in a physical star, but operating in a logical bus—100BaseTX and 100BaseT4.

- In 100BaseTX Ethernet cabling systems, speeds are 100 Mbps, wires are twisted copper pairs, signals are baseband, and distance is limited to 100 meters from the node to the hub, with a limit of 1024 ports per hub. The cabling used must be CAT 5e UTP crimped with RJ-45 connectors.

- In 100BaseT4 Ethernet cabling systems, speeds are 100 Mbps, wires are twisted copper pairs, signals are baseband, and distance is limited to 100 meters from the node to the hub, with a limit of 1024 ports per hub. The cabling used is CAT 3 UTP with RJ-45 connectors. The main difference from 100BaseTX is that all four pairs of wires are used in data transmission.

- Limitations of Fast Ethernet over UTP include distance (only 100 meters), inadequate shielding for some installations, and relative ease of intruder break-ins on the physical cable.

- The fiber-optic variation of Fast Ethernet, 100BaseFX, overcomes these limitations, offering immunity to electrical interference and a range of up to two kilometers from node to hub.

- A half-duplex NIC can only send or receive at any one time. Full-duplex NICs can send and receive at the same time, thereby doubling the bandwidth (but not the speed).

Discuss copper- and fiber-based Gigabit Ethernet

- There are two Gigabit Ethernet standards approved by the IEEE: 802.z (1000BaseX) and 802.3ab (1000BaseT).

- 1000BaseT uses four-pair UTP cabling and has a maximum length of 100 meters.

- 1000BaseX is divided into a number of standards: 1000BaseCX, 1000BaseSX, and 1000BaseLX.

- 1000BaseCX uses twinaxial cable with a maximum length of 25 meters.

- 1000BaseSX uses multimode fiber-optic cable with a maximum length between 220 and 500 meters, depending on the manufacturer.

- 1000BaseLX uses single-mode fiber-optic cable with a maximum length of 5 kilometers. Some manufacturers use repeaters to extend the maximum length to 70 kilometers.

- The Small Form Factor (SFF) fiber connector includes the Mechanical Transfer Registered Jack (MT-RJ) and the Local Connector (LC), both of which were created to overcome problems with the ST and SC connectors.

Compare the competing varieties of 10-Gigabit Ethernet

- 10-Gigabit Ethernet (10 GbE) has several fiber standards and two copper standards. Copper products have only recently become available.

- SONET is the networking standard for long-distance optical connections that serve as the main backbone for the Internet.

- 10 GbE is organized into six different standards: 10GBaseSR, 10GBaseSW, 10GBaseLR, 10GBaseLW, 10GBaseER, and 10GBaseEW.

- 10GBaseS*y* uses multimode fiber with a maximum length of 300 meters. 10GBaseLR is used for Ethernet LANs while 10GBaseSW is used to connect to SONET devices.

- 10GBaseL*y* uses single-mode fiber with a maximum length of 10 kilometers. 10GBaseLR is for Ethernet LANs while 10GBaseLW is used to connect to SONET devices. 10GBaseLR is the most popular and cheapest 10-GbE media type.

- 10GBaseE*y* uses single-mode fiber with a maximum length of 40 kilometers. 10GBaseER is used for Ethernet LANs while 10GBaseEW is used to connect to SONET devices.

- 10GBaseT defines 10-Gigabit Ethernet over UTP cable. It is capable of a maximum distance of 55 meters with CAT 6, while using CAT 6a can achieve 100 meters.

- All types of 10 GbE send and receive the exact same signal. Network devices, such as routers, that need to support different 10-GbE cable types use multisource agreements to enable different cable types to connect.

Key Terms

10GBaseER *(88)*	1000BaseSX *(85)*
10GBaseEW *(88)*	1000BaseT *(85)*
10GBaseLR *(88)*	1000BaseX *(85)*
10GBaseLW *(88)*	802.3ab *(85)*
10GBaseSR *(88)*	802.3z *(85)*
10GBaseSW *(88)*	Fast Ethernet *(81)*
10GBaseT *(88)*	full-duplex *(84)*
10-Gigabit Ethernet (10 GbE) *(87)*	Gigabit Ethernet *(85)*
100BaseFX *(83)*	half-duplex *(84)*
100BaseT *(81)*	Local Connector (LC) *(86)*
100BaseT4 *(81)*	Mechanical Transfer Registered Jack (MT-RJ) *(86)*
100BaseTX *(81)*	multisource agreement (MSA) *(89)*
1000BaseCX *(85)*	Small Form Factor (SFF) *(86)*
1000BaseLX *(85)*	SONET *(87)*

Key Term Quiz

Use the Key Terms list to complete the sentences that follow. Not all terms will be used.

1. When a network device can both send and receive data at the same time, it is said to be _____.

2. _____ has a maximum cable length of two kilometers and uses multimode fiber with ST or SC connectors.

3. 100BaseT is also known as _____.

4. _____ can use CAT 3 but _____ must use CAT 5 or better.

5. 802.3z and 802.3ab are both _____ standards.

6. _____ supports the longest maximum distance for Gigabit Ethernet.

7. The _____ and _____ IEEE standards support the longest maximum distance for 10-Gigabit Ethernet.

8. Many fiber experts consider the _____ connector to be the predominant fiber connector.

9. _____ is the cheapest and most popular 10-GbE media type.

10. Routers with _____ can accept a variety of 10-GbE media types.

Multiple-Choice Quiz

1. Which of the following are 100BaseT cable types? (Select three)
   A. CAT 3
   B. CAT 5
   C. CAT 5e
   D. 10BaseFL

2. What is the physical limit for the number of ports on an Ethernet hub?
   A. 24
   B. 256
   C. 512
   D. 1024

3. When a network device can only send data or receive data, but not both at the same time, it is operating in what mode?

   A. Duplex

   B. Full-duplex

   C. Half-duplex

   D. Halfplex

4. What important backbone technology is also known as Gigabit Ethernet?

   A. 100BaseT

   B. 100BaseFL

   C. 100BaseFX

   D. 1000BaseT

5. What are the two major UTP variations of Fast Ethernet?

   A. 100BaseTL

   B. 100BaseTX

   C. 100BaseFL

   D. 100BaseT4

6. What are three limitations of Fast Ethernet over UTP?

   A. Distance is restricted to 100 meters from node to hub.

   B. Shielding may be inadequate for some installations.

   C. Intrusion from outsiders may be possible without detection.

   D. The obsolete technology is insufficient for most networks.

7. Which standard defines Fast Ethernet using fiber cabling?

   A. 10BaseFL

   B. 100BaseFX

   C. 100BaseT4

   D. 100BaseTX

8. Which of the following are fiber connector types? (Select three)

   A. LC

   B. LS

   C. MT-RJ

   D. ST

9. What do you need to connect varying 10-GbE cable types to the same router?

   A. SFF connectors on all cables

   B. SC connectors on all cables

   C. Multisource agreements on the router

   D. This is not possible.

10. Which standard defines Gigabit Ethernet over UTP copper wire?

   A. 802.3ab

   B. 802.3e

   C. 802.3GbUTP

   D. 802.3z

11. You've lost the manual to your router. How can you tell the difference between a 1000BaseT port and a 100BaseT port on a router just by looking?

   A. The 1000BaseT ports are noticeably larger.

   B. The 100BaseT ports are green while the 1000BaseT ports are gray.

   C. 1000BaseT ports are reversed with the clip on the top.

   D. You can't tell the difference by looking. They look exactly the same.

12. Which statement about Ethernet is correct?

   A. Only 10- and 100-megabit Ethernet may use a hub. Gigabit Ethernet must use a switch.

   B. 10- and 100-megabit Ethernet has a limit of 1024 nodes. Gigabit Ethernet has no limit.

   C. Gigabit Ethernet that uses UTP cabling has a maximum distance between the node and switch of 250–400 meters, depending on the manufacturer.

   D. All versions of 10-Gigabit Ethernet use the same cabling.

13. What will happen if you connect a 10BaseT NIC to an auto-sensing switch?

   A. The switch will operate in hub mode.

   B. The entire switch will operate at 10 megabits, even if there are 100-megabit devices attached.

   C. The 10BaseT NIC will operate at 10 megabits while connected 100-megabit devices will operate at their full speed of 100 megabits.

   D. The 10BaseT NIC will overclock to run at 100 megabits.

14. What benefit does full-duplex offer?

    A. It allows all NICs on a hub to send signals at the same time without collisions.

    B. It doubles the bandwidth of the network.

    C. It doubles the speed of the network.

    D. It doubles both the bandwidth and the speed of the network.

15. What is the difference between the *R* and *W* designations in 10GBase standards? For example, 10GBaseLR and 10GBaseLW, or 10GBaseER and 10GBaseEW?

    A. The *R* indicates "regular," or half-duplex. The *W* indicates "wide mode," the 10-Gigabit Ethernet version of full-duplex.

    B. The *R* indicates "read," or the ability to receive signals, while the *W* indicates "write," or the ability to send signals.

    C. The *R* and *W* indicate differences in the circuitry, with the *W* versions used to connect to SONET equipment.

    D. The *R* indicates the use of UTP while the *W* indicates the use of fiber optics.

■ Essay Quiz

1. Which types of computer network cable connections are you familiar with already? Write a short paragraph describing your experience.

2. Your manager has just informed you that several departments at your company will be switching over to fiber-optic NICs. How many and what type of connectors will be needed for each node on the new segment? Document your recommendations.

3. Compose a letter to the network administrator of a nearby telecommunications company or ISP (Internet service provider). Introduce yourself in the top part of the letter as a networking student. Then ask if the company ever gives tours or holds open houses for the public. Close the letter by thanking the person reading it for their time. Spell-check and have others proofread your letter. Consider mailing the letter if you are serious about your visit and your instructor approves your final copy.

4. Prepare a list of questions you would ask a large organization's network administrator regarding cabling, connections, hubs, switches, and even routers. Use the situation described in Essay 3 to help you create your list of questions.

5. Prepare a thank-you note in advance for having been allowed to participate in a tour, as described in Essay 3. Mention some of the items you observed during the visit. If you would be interested in seeking employment at their facility, consider mentioning that and asking about the steps you would need to take to prepare for such a position. Sometimes a simple thank-you note can help land a job!

Lab Projects

• Lab Project 5.1

Find a hub or switch at your school or company. Examine the wiring closely to determine what cable connections it uses. Try to determine whether the cabling was placed neatly and in an organized manner, whether the ports are clearly labeled, and whether all the ends were crimped well. Be prepared to discuss your findings with the rest of the class.

• Lab Project 5.2

Use the Internet to research prices to order 100 each of the connectors from the following list. Don't forget to include basic shipping and handling to your organization's location, as these would be a price factor in real life.

- RJ-45 connectors
- SC connectors
- ST connectors
- MT-RJ connectors
- LC connectors

From your research, which connectors would be the least costly?

• Lab Project 5.3

All these standards! How can you remember them?

Make a chart that compares the features (cabling, connectors, data throughput, and so on) of the following Ethernet technologies:

- 10BaseT
- 10BaseFL
- 100BaseTX
- 100BaseFX
- 1000BaseT
- 1000BaseCX
- 1000BaseLX
- 1000BaseSX
- 10GBaseSR/10GBaseSW
- 10GBaseLR/10GBaseLW
- 10GBaseER/10GBaseEW

Installing a Physical Network

In this chapter, you will learn how to

- Recognize and describe the functions of basic components in a structured cabling system
- Explain the process of installing structured cable
- Install a network interface card
- Perform basic troubleshooting on a structured cable network

Armed with the knowledge of previous chapters, it's time to start going about the business of actually plugging a physical network together. This might seem easy, because the most basic network is nothing more than a switch with a number of cables snaking out to all of the PCs on the network (Figure 6.1).

On the surface, such a network setup is absolutely correct, but if you tried to run a network using only a switch and cables running to each system, you'd have some serious practical issues. In the real world, you need to deal with physical obstacles like walls and ceilings. You also need to deal with those annoying things called *people*. People are incredibly adept at destroying physical networks. They unplug switches, trip over cables, and rip connectors out of NICs with incredible consistency unless you protect the network from their destructive ways. Although the simplified switch-and-a-bunch-of-cables type of network can function in the real world, the network clearly has some problems that need addressing before it can work safely and efficiently (Figure 6.2).

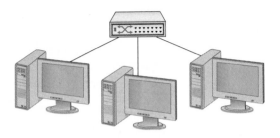

• **Figure 6.1**   What an orderly looking network!

This chapter takes the abstract discussion of network technologies from previous chapters into the concrete reality of real networks. To achieve this goal, it marches you through the process of installing an entire network system from the beginning. The chapter starts by introducing you to the magical world of structured cabling: the critical set of standards used all over the world to install physical cabling in a safe and orderly fashion. It then delves into the world of larger networks—those with more than a single switch—and shows you some typical methods used to organize them for peak efficiency and reliability. Next, you'll take a quick tour of the most common NICs used in PCs, and see what it takes to install them. Finally, you'll look at how to troubleshoot cabling and other network devices, including an introduction to some fun diagnostic tools.

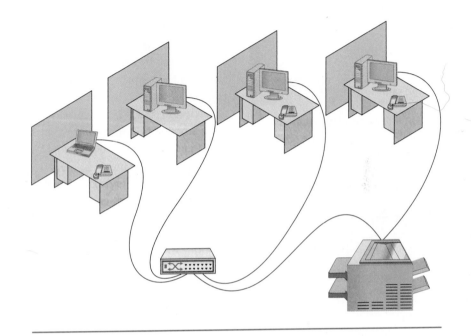

• **Figure 6.2**   A real-world network

Historical/Conceptual

■ Understanding Structured Cabling

If you want a functioning, dependable, real-world network, you need a solid understanding of a set of standards, collectively called **structured cabling**. These standards, defined by the Telecommunications Industry Association/Electronic Industries Alliance (TIA/EIA)—yup, the same folks who tell you how to crimp an RJ-45 onto the end of a UTP cable—give professional cable installers detailed standards on every aspect of a cabled network, from the type of cabling to use to the position of wall outlets.

The CompTIA Network+ exam requires you to understand the basic concepts involved in designing a network and installing network cabling, and to recognize the components used in a real network. The CompTIA Network+ exam does not, however, expect you to be as knowledgeable as a professional network designer or cable installer. Your goal is to understand enough about real-world cabling systems to communicate knowledgeably with cable installers and to perform basic troubleshooting. Granted, by the end of this chapter, you'll have enough of an understanding to try running your own cable (I certainly run my own cable), but consider that knowledge a handy bit of extra credit.

The idea of structured cabling is to create a safe, reliable cabling infrastructure for all of the devices that may need interconnection. Certainly this applies to computer networks, but also to telephone, video—anything that might need low-power, distributed cabling.

You should understand three issues with structured cabling. Cable basics start the picture, with switches, cabling, and PCs. You'll then look at the components of a network, such as how the cable runs through the walls and where it ends up. This section wraps up with an assessment of connections leading outside your network.

Cable Basics—A Star Is Born

This exploration of the world of connectivity hardware starts with the most basic of all networks: a switch, some UTP cable, and a few PCs—in other words, a typical physical star network (Figure 6.3).

No law of physics prevents you from installing a switch in the middle of your office and running cables on the floor to all the computers in your network. This setup will work, but it falls apart spectacularly when applied to the real-world environment. Three problems present themselves to the real-world network tech. First, the exposed cables running along the floor are just waiting for someone to trip over them, causing damage to the network and giving that person a wonderful lawsuit opportunity. Possible accidents aside, simply moving and stepping on the cabling will, over time, cause a cable to fail due to wires breaking or RJ-45 connectors ripping off cable ends. Second, the presence of other electrical devices close to the cable can create interference that confuses the signals going through the wire. Third, this type of setup limits your ability to make any changes to the network. Before you can change anything, you have to figure out which cables in the huge rat's nest of cables connected to the hub go to which machines. Imagine *that* troubleshooting nightmare!

A structured cabling system is useful for more than just computer networks.

Tech Tip

The Big Wireless Lie

Anyone who makes a trip to a local computer store sees plenty of devices that adhere to the 802.11 (wireless networking) standard. There's little doubt about the popularity of wireless. This popularity, however, gives people the impression that 802.11 is pushing wired networks into oblivion. While this may take place one day in the future, a wireless network's unreliability and relatively slow speed (as compared to Gigabit Ethernet) make it challenging to use in a network that requires high reliability and speed. Wireless makes great sense in homes, your local coffeehouse, and offices that don't need high speed or reliability, but any network that can't afford downtime or slow speeds still uses wires.

• **Figure 6.3**   A switch connected by UTP cable to two PCs

Cross Check

TIA/EIA Standards

You should remember the TIA/EIA 568 standards from Chapter 4, "Ethernet Basics," but do you remember how to tell the difference between 568A and 568B? Why were the standards considered necessary?

Tech Tip

Professional Cabling Certifications with BICSI

Installing structured cabling properly takes a startlingly high degree of skill. Thousands of pitfalls await inexperienced network people who think they can install their own network cabling. Pulling cable requires expensive equipment, a lot of hands, and the ability to react to problems quickly. Network techs can lose millions of dollars—not to mention their good jobs—by imagining they can do it themselves without the proper knowledge. If you are interested in learning more details about structured cabling, an organization called BICSI (www.bicsi.org) provides a series of widely recognized certifications for the cabling industry.

"Gosh," you're thinking (okay, I'm thinking it, but you should be), "there must be a better way to install a physical network." A better installation would provide safety, protecting the star from vacuum cleaners, clumsy co-workers, and electrical interference. It would have extra hardware to organize and protect the cabling. Finally, the new and improved star network installation would feature a cabling standard with the flexibility to enable the network to grow according to its needs, and then to upgrade when the next great network technology comes along.

As you have no doubt guessed, I'm not just theorizing here. In the real world, the people who most wanted improved installation standards were the ones who installed cable for a living. In response to this demand for standards, the TIA/EIA developed standards for cable installation. The TIA/EIA 568 standards you saw in earlier chapters are only part of a larger set of TIA/EIA standards, all lumped together under the umbrella of structured cabling.

Test Specific

Structured Cable Network Components

Successful implementation of a basic structured cabling network requires three essential ingredients: a telecommunications room, horizontal cabling, and a work area. Let's zero in on one floor of Figure 5.12 from the previous chapter. All the cabling runs from individual PCs to a central location, the **telecommunications room** (Figure 6.4). What equipment goes in there—a switch or a telephone system—is not the important thing. What matters is that all the cables concentrate in this one area.

All cables run horizontally (for the most part) from the telecommunications room to the PCs. This cabling is called, appropriately, **horizontal cabling**. A single piece of installed horizontal cabling is called a **run**. At the opposite end of the horizontal cabling from the telecommunications room is the work area. The **work area** is often simply an office or cubicle that potentially contains a PC and a telephone. Figure 6.5 shows both the horizontal cabling and work areas.

Each of the three parts of a basic star network—the telecommunications room, the horizontal cabling, and the work area(s)—must follow a series of strict standards designed to ensure that the cabling system is reliable and easy to manage. The cabling standards set by TIA/EIA enable techs to make sensible decisions on equipment installed in the telecommunications room, so let's tackle horizontal cabling first, and then return to the telecommunications room. We'll finish up with the work area.

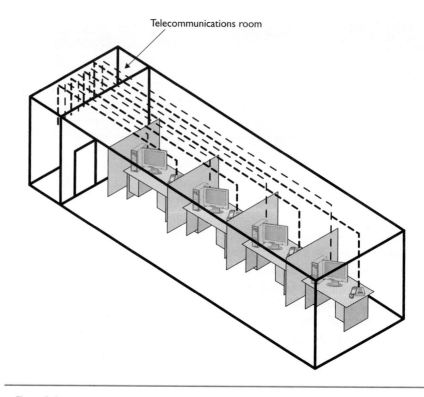

Telecommunications room

• **Figure 6.4**   Telecommunications room

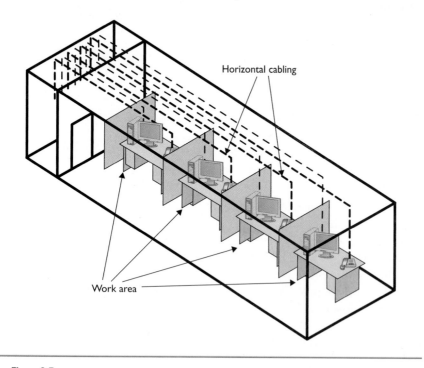

Horizontal cabling

Work area

• **Figure 6.5**   Horizontal cabling and work area

A single piece of cable that runs from a work area to a tele-communications room is called a run.

Horizontal Cabling

A horizontal cabling run is the cabling that goes more or less horizontally from a work area to the telecommunications room. In most networks, this is a CAT 5e or better UTP cable, but when we move into the world of structured cabling, the TIA/EIA standards define a number of other aspects to the cable, such as the type of wires, number of pairs of wires, and fire ratings.

Solid Core vs. Stranded Core   All UTP cables come in one of two types: solid core or stranded core. Each wire in **solid core** UTP uses a single solid wire. With **stranded core**, each wire is actually a bundle of tiny wire strands. Each of these cable types has its benefits and downsides. Solid core is a better conductor, but it is stiff and will break if handled too often or too roughly. Stranded core is not quite as good a conductor, but it will stand up to substantial handling without breaking. Figure 6.6 shows a close-up of solid and stranded core UTP.

TIA/EIA specifies that horizontal cabling should always be solid core. Remember, this cabling is going into your walls and ceilings, safe from the harmful effects of shoes and vacuum cleaners. The ceilings and walls enable us to take advantage of the better conductivity of solid core without risk of cable damage. Stranded cable also has an important function in a structured cabling network, but we need to discuss a few more parts of the network before we see where to use stranded UTP cable.

Number of Pairs Pulling horizontal cables into your walls and ceilings is a time-consuming and messy business, and not a process you want to repeat, if at all possible. For this reason, most cable installers recommend using the highest CAT rating you can afford. A few years ago, I would also mention that you should use four-pair UTP, but today, four-pair is assumed. Four-pair UTP is so common that it's difficult, if not impossible, to find two-pair UTP.

You'll find larger bundled UTP cables in higher-end telephone setups. These cables hold 25 or even 100 pairs of wires (Figure 6.7).

Choosing Your Horizontal Cabling In the real world, network people only install CAT 5e or CAT 6 UTP, although CAT 6a is also starting to show up as 10GBaseT begins to see acceptance. Installing higher-rated cabling is done primarily as a hedge against new network technologies that may require a more advanced cable. Networking *caveat emptor* warning: many network installers take advantage of the fact that a lower CAT level will work on most networks, and bid a network installation using the lowest-grade cable possible.

The Telecommunications Room

The telecommunications room is the heart of the basic star. This room—technically called the **intermediate distribution frame (IDF)**—is where all the horizontal runs from all the work areas come together. The concentration of all this gear in one place makes the telecommunications room potentially one of the messiest parts of the basic star. Even if you do a nice, neat job of organizing the cables when they are first installed, networks change over time. People move computers, new work areas are added, network topologies are added or improved, and so on. Unless you impose some type of organization, this conglomeration of equipment and cables is bound to decay into a nightmarish mess.

Fortunately, the TIA/EIA structured cabling standards define the use of specialized components in the telecommunications room that make organizing

● **Figure 6.6** Solid and stranded core UTP

 Unlike previous CAT standards, TIA/EIA defines CAT 5e and later as four-pair-only cables.

● **Figure 6.7** 25-pair UTP

 The telecommunications room is also known as an intermediate distribution frame (IDF), as opposed to the main distribution frame (MDF), which we will discuss later in the chapter.

 Cross Check

Fire Ratings

You saw another aspect of cabling way back in Chapter 3, "Cabling and Topology," so check your memory here. What are fire ratings? When should you use plenum-grade cabling and when should you use riser-grade cabling? What about PVC? What are the differences?

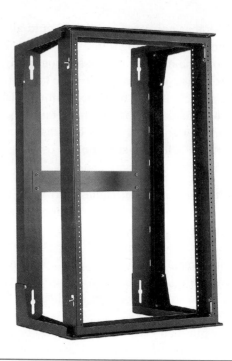

• **Figure 6.8** A short equipment rack

a snap. In fact, it might be fair to say that there are too many options! To keep it simple, we're going to stay with the most common telecommunications room setup, and then take a short peek at some other fairly common options.

Equipment Racks The central component of every telecommunications room is one or more equipment racks. An **equipment rack** provides a safe, stable platform for all the different hardware components. All equipment racks are 19 inches wide, but they vary in height from two- to three-foot-high models that bolt onto a wall (Figure 6.8), to the more popular floor-to-ceiling models (Figure 6.9).

You can mount almost any network hardware component into a rack. All manufacturers make rack-mounted switches that mount into a rack with a few screws. These switches are available with a wide assortment of ports and capabilities. There are even rack-mounted servers, complete with slide-out keyboards, and rack-mounted uninterruptible power supplies (UPSs) to power the equipment (Figure 6.10).

All rack-mounted equipment uses a height measurement known simply as a **U**. A U is 1.75 inches. A device that fits in a 1.75-inch space is called a 1U; a device designed for a 3.5-inch space is a 2U. Most rack-mounted devices are 1U, 2U, or 4U. The rack in Figure 6.10 is called a 96U rack to reflect the total number of Us it can hold.

• **Figure 6.9** A floor-to-ceiling rack

Actual rack measurements may vary slightly from manufacturer to manufacturer.

• **Figure 6.10** A rack-mounted UPS

Patch Panels and Cables Ideally, once you install horizontal cabling, it should never be moved. As you know, UTP horizontal cabling has a solid core, making it pretty stiff. Solid core cables can handle some rearranging, but if you insert a wad of solid core cables directly into your switches, every time you move a cable to a different port on the switch, or move the switch itself, you will jostle the cable. You don't have to move a solid core cable many times before one of the solid copper wires breaks, and there goes a network connection! Luckily for you, you can easily avoid this problem by using a patch panel. A **patch panel** is simply a box with a row of female connectors (ports) in the front and permanent connections in the back, to which you connect the horizontal cables (Figure 6.11).

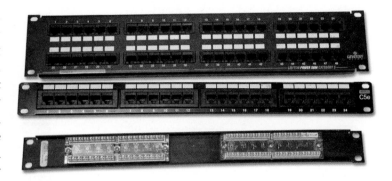

• **Figure 6.11**   Typical patch panels

The most common type of patch panel today uses a special type of connecter called a **110-punchdown block**, or simply a *110 block*. UTP cables connect to a 110-punchdown block using—you guessed it—a **punchdown tool**. Figure 6.12 shows a typical punchdown tool while Figure 6.13 shows the punchdown tool punching down individual strands.

The punchdown block has small metal-lined grooves for the individual wires. The punchdown tool has a blunt end that forces the wire into the groove. The metal in the groove slices the cladding enough to make contact.

At one time the older 66-punchdown block patch panel, found in just about every commercial telephone installation (Figure 6.14), saw some use in the PC network world. Because of its ease and convenience, however, the 110 block is slowly displacing the 66 block for both telephone service and PC LANs. Given their large installed base, it's still very common to find a group of 66-block patch panels in a telecommunications room separate from the PC network's 110-block patch panels.

> The CompTIA Network+ exam uses the terms 110 block and 66 block exclusively to describe the punchdown blocks common in telecommunication. In the field, in contrast, and in manuals and other literature, you'll see the punchdown blocks referred to as 110-punchdown blocks and 66-punchdown blocks as well. Some manufacturers even split punchdown into two words, i.e. punch down. Be prepared to be nimble in the field, but expect 110 block and 66 block on the exam.

• **Figure 6.12**   Punchdown tool

• **Figure 6.13**   Punching down a 110 block

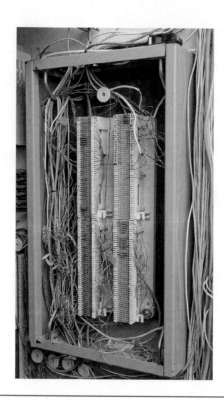

• **Figure 6.14** 66-block patch panels

Not only do patch panels prevent the horizontal cabling from being moved, they are also your first line of defense in organizing the cables. All patch panels have space in the front for labels, and these labels are the network tech's best friend! Simply place a tiny label on the patch panel to identify each cable, and you will never have to experience that sinking feeling of standing in the telecommunications room of your nonfunctioning network, wondering which cable is which. If you want to be a purist, there is an official, and rather confusing, TIA/EIA labeling methodology called **TIA/EIA 606**, but a number of real-world network techs simply use their own internal codes (Figure 6.15).

Tech Tip

Serious Labeling

The TIA/EIA 606 standard covers proper labeling and documentation of cabling, patch panels, and wall outlets. If you want to know how the pros label and document a structured cabling system (and you've got $360 to blow), check out the TIA/EIA 606 standard hardcopy from TIA.

• **Figure 6.15** Typical patch panels

Patch panels are available in a wide variety of configurations that include different types of ports and numbers of ports. You can get UTP, STP, or fiber ports, and some manufacturers combine several different types on the same patch panel. Panels are available with 8, 12, 24, 48, or even more ports. UTP patch panels, like UTP cables, come with CAT ratings, which you should be sure to check. Don't blow a good CAT 6 cable installation by buying a cheap patch panel—get a CAT 6 patch panel! Most manufacturers proudly display the CAT level right on the patch panel (Figure 6.16).

Once you have installed the patch panel, you need to connect the ports to the switch through **patch cables**. Patch cables are short (typically two- to five-foot) UTP cables. Patch cables use stranded rather than solid cable, so they can tolerate much more handling. Even though you can make your own patch cables, most people buy premade ones. Buying patch cables enables you to use different-colored cables to facilitate organization (yellow for accounting, blue for sales, or whatever scheme works for you). Most pre-fabricated patch cables also come with a reinforced (booted) connector specially designed to handle multiple insertions and removals (Figure 6.17).

A telecommunications room doesn't have to be a special room dedicated to computer equipment. You can use specially made cabinets with their own little built-in equipment racks that sit on the floor or attach to a wall, or use a storage room, as long as the equipment can be protected from the other items stored there. Fortunately, the demand for telecommunications rooms has been around for so long that most office spaces have premade telecommunications rooms, even if they are no more than a closet in smaller offices.

At this point, the network is taking shape (Figure 6.18). We've installed the TIA/EIA horizontal cabling and configured the telecommunications room. Now it's time to address the last part of the structured cabling system: the work area.

• **Figure 6.16** CAT level on patch panel

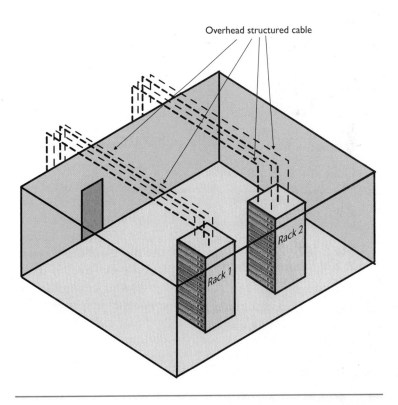

Overhead structured cable

Rack 1

Rack 2

• **Figure 6.17** Typical patch cable

• **Figure 6.18** Network taking shape

● **Figure 6.19** Typical work area outlet

A 320

● **Figure 6.20** Properly labeled outlet

Structured cabling goes beyond a single building and even describes methods for interconnecting multiple buildings. The CompTIA Network+ certification exam does not cover interbuilding connections.

The Work Area

From a cabling standpoint, a work area is nothing more than a wall outlet that serves as the termination point for horizontal network cables: a convenient insertion point for a PC and a telephone. A wall outlet itself consists of one or two female jacks to accept the cable, a mounting bracket, and a faceplate. You connect the PC to the wall outlet with a patch cable (Figure 6.19).

The female RJ-45 jacks in these wall outlets also have CAT ratings. You must buy CAT-rated jacks for wall outlets to go along with the CAT rating of the cabling in your network. In fact, many network connector manufacturers use the same connectors in the wall outlets that they use on the patch panels. These modular outlets significantly increase ease of installation. Make sure you label the outlet to show the job of each connector (Figure 6.20). A good outlet will also have some form of label that identifies its position on the patch panel. Proper documentation of your outlets will save you an incredible amount of work later.

The last step is connecting the PC to the wall outlet. Here again, most folks use a patch cable. Its stranded cabling stands up to the abuse caused by moving PCs, not to mention the occasional kick.

You'll recall from Chapter 5, "Modern Ethernet," that 10/100/1000BaseT networks specify a limit of 100 meters between a hub or switch and a node. Interestingly, though, the TIA/EIA 568 specification allows only UTP cable lengths of 90 meters. What's with the missing 10 meters? Have you figured it out? Hint: the answer lies in the discussion we've just been having. Ding! Time's up! The answer is…the patch cables! Patch cables add extra distance between the hub and the PC, so TIA/EIA compensates by reducing the horizontal cabling length.

The work area may be the simplest part of the structured cabling system, but it is also the source of most network failures. When a user can't access the network and you suspect a broken cable, the first place to look is the work area.

Structured Cable—Beyond the Star

Thus far you've seen structured cabling as a single star topology on a single floor of a building. Let's now expand that concept to an entire building and learn the terms used by the structured cabling folks, such as the demarc and NIU, to describe this much more complex setup.

It's hard to find a building today that isn't connected to both the Internet and the telephone company. In many cases this is a single connection, but for now let's treat them as separate connections.

As you saw in the previous chapter, a typical building-wide network consists of a high-speed backbone that runs vertically through the building, and connects to multispeed switches on each floor that in turn service the individual PCs on that floor. A dedicated telephone cabling backbone that enables the distribution of phone calls to individual telephones runs alongside the network cabling. While every telephone installation varies, most commonly you'll see one or more strands of 25-pair UTP cables running to the 66 block in the telecommunications room on each floor (Figure 6.21).

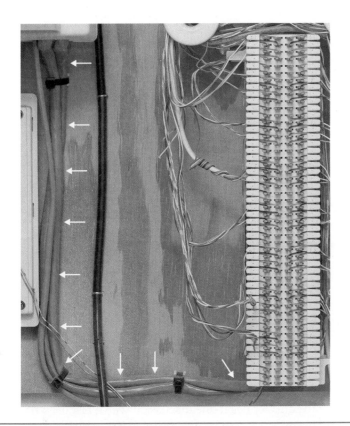

● **Figure 6.21**   25-pair running to local 66-block

Demarc

Connections from the outside world—whether network or telephone—come into a building at a location called a **demarc**, short for *demarcation point*. The term "demarc" refers to the physical location of the connection and marks the dividing line of responsibility for the functioning of the network. You take care of the internal functioning; the person or company that supplies the upstream service to you must support connectivity and function on the far side of the demarc.

In a private home, the DSL or cable modem supplied by your ISP is a **network interface unit (NIU)** that serves as a demarc between your home network and your ISP, and most homes have a network interface box, like the one shown in Figure 6.22, that provides the connection for your telephone.

In an office environment the demarc is usually more complex, given that a typical building simply has to serve a much larger number of telephones and computers. Figure 6.23 shows the demarc for a midsized building, showing both Internet and telephone connections coming in from the outside.

One challenge to companies that supply ISP/telephone services is the need to diagnose faults in the system. Most of today's NIUs come with extra "smarts" that enable the ISP or telephone company to determine if the customer has

● **Figure 6.22**   Typical home network interface box

The best way to think of a demarc is in terms of responsibility. If something breaks on one side of the demarc, it's your problem; on the other side, it's the ISP/phone company's problem.

• **Figure 6.23**   Typical office demarc

disconnected from the NIU. These special (and very common) NIUs are known as **smart jacks**. Smart jacks also have the very handy capability to set up a remote loopback—critical for loopback testing when you're at one end of the connection and the other connection is blocks or even miles away.

Connections Inside the Demarc

After the demarc, network and telephone cables connect to some type of box, owned by the customer, that acts as the primary distribution tool for the building. Any cabling that runs from the NIU to whatever box is used by the customer is the **demarc extension**. For telephones, the cabling might connect to a special box called a **multiplexer**, and on the LAN side almost certainly to a powerful switch. This switch usually connects to a patch panel. This patch panel in turn leads to every telecommunications room in the building. This main patch panel is called a **vertical cross-connect**. Figure 6.24 shows an example of a fiber patch panel acting as a vertical cross-connect for a building.

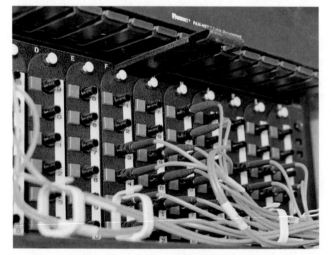

• **Figure 6.24**   LAN vertical cross-connect

Telephone systems also use vertical cross-connects. Figure 6.25 shows a vertical cross-connect for a telephone system. Note the large number of 25-pair UTP cables feeding out of this box. Each 25-pair cable leads to a telecommunications room on a floor of the building.

The combination of demarc, telephone cross-connects, and LAN cross-connects needs a place to live in a building. The room that stores all of this equipment is known as a **main distribution frame (MDF)** to distinguish it from the multiple IDF rooms (a.k.a., telecommuni-cations rooms) that serve individual floors.

The ideal that every building should have a single demarc, a single MDF, and multiple IDFs is only that—an ideal. Every structured cabling installation is unique and must adapt to the physical constraints of the building provided. One building may serve multiple customers, creating the need for multiple NIUs each serving a different customer. A smaller building may combine a demarc, MDF, and IDF into a single room. With structured cabling, the idea is to appreciate the terms while at the same time appreciate that it's the actual building and the needs of the customers that determine the actual design of structured cabling system.

● **Figure 6.25**   Telephone vertical cross-connect

Installing Structured Cabling

A professional installer always begins a structured cabling installation by first assessing your site and planning the installation in detail before pulling a single piece of cable. As the customer, your job is to work closely with the installer. That means locating floor plans, providing access, and even putting on old clothes and crawling along with the installer as he or she combs through your ceilings, walls, and closets. Even though you're not the actual installer, you must understand the installation process, so you can help the installer make the right decisions for your network.

Structured cabling requires a lot of planning. You need to know if the cables from the work areas can reach the telecommunications room—is the distance less than the 90-meter limit dictated by the TIA/EIA standard? How will you route the cable? What path should each run take to get to the wall outlets? Don't forget that just because a cable looks like it will reach, there's no guarantee that it will. Ceilings and walls often include hidden surprises like firewalls—big, thick, concrete walls designed into buildings that require a masonry drill or a jackhammer to punch through. Let's look at the steps that go into proper planning.

Getting a Floor Plan

First, you need a blueprint of the area. If you ever contract an installer and they don't start by asking for a floor plan, fire them immediately and get one who does. The floor plan is the key to proper planning; a good floor plan shows you the location of closets that could serve as telecommunications

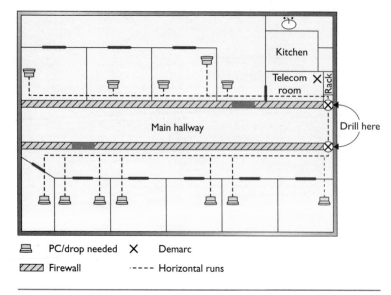

Symbol	Meaning	Symbol	Meaning
PC/drop needed		X	Demarc
Firewall		- - - -	Horizontal runs

Figure 6.26 Hand-drawn network floor plan

Watch out for the word *drop*, as it has more than one meaning. A single run of cable from the telecommunications room to a wall outlet is often referred to as a drop. The word drop is also used to define a new run coming through a wall outlet that does not yet have a jack installed.

rooms, alerts you to any firewalls in your way, and gives you a good overall feel for the scope of the job ahead.

If you don't have a floor plan—and this is often the case with homes or older buildings—you'll need to create your own. Go get a ladder and a flashlight—you'll need them to poke around in ceilings, closets, and crawl spaces as you map out the location of rooms, walls, and anything else of interest to the installation. Figure 6.26 shows a typical do-it-yourself floor plan, drawn out by hand.

Mapping the Runs

Now that you have your floor plan, it's time to map the cable runs. Here's where you run around the work areas, noting the locations of existing or planned systems to determine where to place each cable drop. A **cable drop** is the location where the cable comes out of the wall in the workstation. You should also talk to users, management, and other interested parties to try and understand their plans for the future. It's much easier to install a few extra drops now than to do it a year from now when those two unused offices suddenly find themselves with users who immediately need networked computers!

This is also the point where cost first raises its ugly head. Face it: cables, drops, and the people who install them cost money! The typical price for a network installation is around US $150 per drop. Find out how much you want to spend and make some calls. Most network installers price their network jobs by quoting a per-drop cost.

While you're mapping your runs, you have to make another big decision: Do you want to run the cables in the walls or outside them? Many companies sell wonderful external **raceway** products that adhere to your walls, making for a much simpler, though less neat, installation than running cables in the walls (Figure 6.27). Raceways make good sense in older buildings or when you don't have the guts—or the rights—to go into the walls.

Figure 6.27 A typical raceway

Determining the Location of the Telecommunications Room

While mapping the runs, you should decide on the location of your telecommunications room. When deciding on this location, keep five issues in mind:

- **Distance** The telecommunications room must be located in a spot that won't require cable runs longer than 90 meters. In most locations, keeping runs under 90 meters requires little effort, as long as the telecommunications room is placed in a central location.

- **Power** Many of the components in your telecommunications room need power. Make sure you provide enough! If possible, put the telecommunications room on its own dedicated circuit; that way, when someone blows a circuit in the kitchen, it doesn't take out the entire network.

- **Humidity** Electrical components and water don't mix well. (Remind me to tell you about the time I installed a rack in an abandoned bathroom, and the toilet that later exploded.) Remember that dryness also means low humidity. Avoid areas with the potential for high humidity, such as a closet near a pool or the room where the cleaning people leave mop buckets full of water. Of course, any well air-conditioned room should be fine—which leads to the next big issue…

- **Cooling** Telecommunications rooms tend to get warm, especially if you add a couple of server systems and a UPS. Make sure your telecommunications room has an air-conditioning outlet or some other method of keeping the room cool. Figure 6.28 shows how I installed an air-conditioning duct in my small equipment closet. Of course, I did this only after I discovered that the server was repeatedly rebooting due to overheating!

- **Access** Access involves two different issues. First, it means preventing unauthorized access. Think about the people you do and don't want messing around with your network, and act accordingly. In my small office, the equipment closet literally sits eight feet from me, so I don't concern myself too much with unauthorized access. You, on the other hand, may want to consider placing a lock on the door of your telecommunications room if you're concerned that unscrupulous or unqualified people might try to access it.

• **Figure 6.28** An A/C duct cooling a telecommunications room

One other issue to keep in mind when choosing your telecommunications room is expandability. Will this telecommunications room be able to grow with your network? Is it close enough to be able to service any additional office space your company may acquire nearby? If your company decides to take over the floor above you, can you easily run vertical cabling to another telecommunications room on that floor from this room? While the specific issues will be unique to each installation, keep thinking "expansion" as you design—your network will grow, whether or not you think so now!

So, you've mapped your cable runs and established your telecommunications room—now you're ready to start pulling cable!

Pulling Cable

Pulling cable is easily one of the most thankless and unpleasant jobs in the entire networking world. It may not look that hard from a distance, but the devil is in the details. First of all, pulling cable requires two people if you want to get the job done quickly; having three people is even better. Most pullers like to start from the telecommunications room and pull toward the drops. In an office area with a drop ceiling, pullers will often feed the cabling along the run by opening ceiling tiles and stringing the cable via hooks or **cable trays** that travel above the ceiling (Figure 6.29). Professional cable pullers have an arsenal of interesting tools to help them move the cable horizontally, including telescoping poles, special nylon pull ropes, and even nifty little crossbows and pistols that can fire a pull rope long distances!

Cable trays are standard today, but a previous lack of codes or standards for handling cables led to a nightmare of disorganized cables in drop ceilings all over the world. Any cable puller will tell you that the hardest part of installing cables is the need to work around all the old cable installations in the ceiling (Figure 6.30).

Local codes, TIA/EIA, and the National Electrical Code (NEC) all have strict rules about how you pull cable in a ceiling. A good installer uses either hooks or trays, which provide better cable management, safety, and protection from electrical interference (Figure 6.31). The faster the network, the more critical good cable management becomes. You probably won't have a problem laying UTP directly on top of a drop ceiling if you just want a 10BaseT network, and

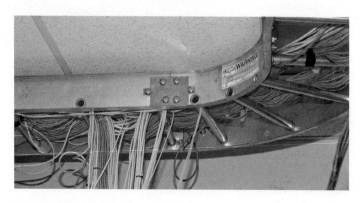

● **Figure 6.30**   Messy cabling nightmare

● **Figure 6.31**   Nicely run cables

you might even get away with this for 100BaseT—but forget about doing this with Gigabit or beyond. Cable installation companies are making a mint from all the CAT 5 and earlier network cabling installations that need to be redone to support Gigabit Ethernet.

Running cable horizontally requires relatively little effort, compared to running the cable down from the ceiling to a pretty faceplate at the work area, which often takes a lot of skill. In a typical office area with sheetrock walls, the installer first decides on the position for the outlet, usually using a stud finder to avoid cutting on top of a stud. Once the worker cuts the hole (Figure 6.32), most installers drop a line to the hole using a weight tied to the end of a nylon pull rope (Figure 6.33). They can then attach the network cable to the pull rope and pull it down to the hole. Once the cable is pulled through the new hole, the installer puts in an outlet box or a low-voltage **mounting bracket** (Figure 6.34). This bracket acts as a holder for the faceplate.

Back in the telecommunications room, the many cables leading to each work area are consolidated and organized in preparation for the next stage: making connections. A truly professional installer takes great care in organizing the equipment closet. Figure 6.35 shows a typical installation using special cable guides to bring the cables down to the equipment rack.

• **Figure 6.32**   Cutting a hole

• **Figure 6.33**   Locating a dropped pull rope

Making Connections

Making connections consists of connecting both ends of each cable to the proper jacks. This step also includes the most important step in the entire process: testing each cable run to ensure that every connection meets the requirements of the network that will use it. Installers also use this step to document and label each cable run—a critical step too often forgotten by inexperienced installers, and one you need to verify takes place!

Connecting the Work Areas

Let's begin by watching an installer connect a cable run. In the work area, that means the cable installer will now crimp a

• **Figure 6.34**   Installing a mounting bracket

• **Figure 6.35**   End of cables guided to rack

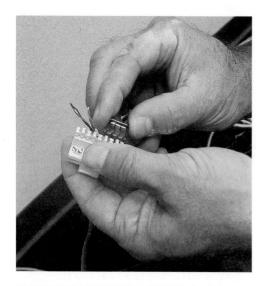

• **Figure 6.36**   Crimping a jack

jack onto the end of the wire and mount the faceplate to complete the installation (Figure 6.36).

Note the back of the jack shown in Figure 6.36. This jack uses the popular 110-punchdown connection just like the one shown earlier in the chapter for patch panels. All 110 connections have a color code that tells you which wire to punch into which connection on the back of the jack.

Rolling Your Own Patch Cables

While most people prefer to simply purchase premade patch cables, it's actually fairly easy to make your own. To make your own, be sure to use stranded UTP cable that matches the CAT level of your horizontal cabling. There are also specific crimps for stranded cable, so don't use crimps designed for solid cable. Crimping is simple enough, although getting it right takes some practice.

Figure 6.37 shows the two main tools of the crimping trade: an RJ-45 crimper with built-in stripper, and a pair of wire snips. Professional cable installers naturally have a wide variety of other tools as well.

Here are the steps for properly crimping an RJ-45 onto a UTP cable. If you have some crimps, cable, and a crimping tool handy, follow along!

1. Cut the cable square using RJ-45 crimpers or scissors.

2. Strip off ½ inch of plastic jacket from the end of the cable (Figure 6.38).

3. Slowly and carefully insert each individual wire into the correct location according to either TIA/EIA 568A or B (Figure 6.39). Unravel as little as possible.

4. Insert the crimp into the crimper and press (Figure 6.40). Don't worry about pressing too hard; the crimper has a stop to prevent you from using too much pressure.

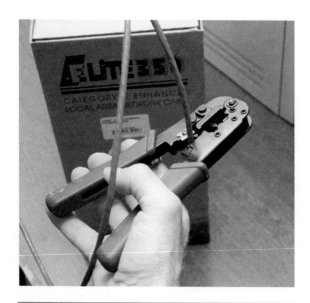

• **Figure 6.37**   Crimper and snips

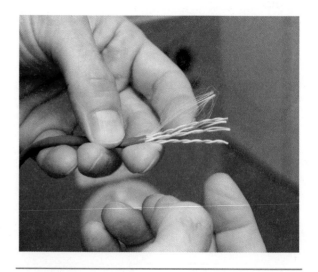

• **Figure 6.38**   Properly stripped cable

● **Figure 6.39**   Inserting the individual strands

● **Figure 6.40**   Crimping the cable

Figure 6.41 shows a nicely crimped cable. Note how the plastic jacket goes into the crimp.

A good patch cable should include a boot. Figure 6.42 shows a boot being slid onto a newly crimped cable. Don't forget to slide each boot onto the patch cable *before* you crimp both ends!

After making a cable you need to test it to make sure it's properly crimped. Read the section on testing cable runs later in this chapter to see how to test them.

> **Try This!**
>
> **Crimping Your Own Cable**
>
> If you've got some spare CAT 5 lying around (and what tech enthusiast doesn't?) as well as a cable crimper and some crimps, go ahead and use the previous section as a guide and crimp your own cable. This is an essential skill for any network technician. Remember, practice makes perfect!

Connecting the Patch Panels

Connecting the cables to patch panels requires you to deal with two issues. The first is patch cable management. Figure 6.43 shows the front of a small network's equipment rack—note the complete lack of cable management!

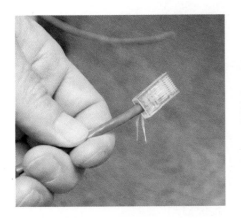

● **Figure 6.41**   Properly crimped cable

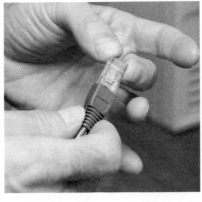

● **Figure 6.42**   Adding a boot

Managing patch cables means using the proper cable management hardware. Plastic D-rings guide the patch cables neatly along the sides and front of the patch panel. Finger boxes are rectangular cylinders with slots in the front; the patch cables run into the open ends of the box, and individual cables are threaded through the fingers on their way to the patch panel, keeping them neatly organized.

Creativity and variety abound in the world of cable-management hardware—there are as many different solutions to cable management as there are ways to screw up organizing them. Figure 6.44 shows a rack using good cable management—these patch cables are well secured using cable-management hardware, making them much less susceptible to damage from mishandling. Plus, it looks much nicer!

The second issue to consider when connecting cables is the overall organization of the patch panel as it relates to the organization of your network. Organize your patch panel so that it mirrors the layout of your network. You can organize according to the physical layout, so the different parts of the patch panel correspond to different parts of your office space—for example, the north and south sides of the hallway. Another popular way to organize patch panels is to make sure they match the logical layout of the network, so the different user groups or company organizations have their own sections of the patch panel.

• **Figure 6.43**   Bad cable management

• **Figure 6.44**   Good cable management

Testing the Cable Runs

Well, in theory, your horizontal cabling system is now installed and ready for a switch and some systems. Before you do this, though, you must test each cable run. Someone new to testing cable might think that all you need to do is verify that each jack has been properly connected. While this is an important and necessary step, the interesting problem comes after that: verifying that your cable run can handle the speed of your network.

Before we go further, let me be clear: a typical network admin/tech cannot properly test a new cable run. TIA/EIA provides a series of incredibly complex and important standards for testing cable, requiring a professional cable installer. The testing equipment alone totally surpasses the cost of most smaller network installations. Advanced network testing tools easily cost over $5,000, and some are well over $10,000! Never fear, though—a number of lower-end tools work just fine for basic network testing.

Most network admin types staring at a potentially bad cable want to know the following:

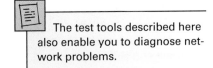

The test tools described here also enable you to diagnose network problems.

- How long is this cable? If it's too long the signal will degrade to the point it's no longer detectable on the other end.

- Are any of the wires broken or not connected in the crimp? If a wire is broken, it no longer has **continuity**.

- If there is a break, where is it? It's much easier to fix if the location is detectable.

- Are all of the wires terminated in the right place in the plug or jack?

- Is there electrical or radio interference from outside sources? UTP is susceptible to electromagnetic interference.

- Is the signal from any of the pairs in the same cable interfering with another pair?

To answer these questions you must verify that both the cable and the terminated ends are correct. Making these verifications requires a **cable tester**. Various models of cable testers can answer some or all of these questions, depending on the amount of money you are willing to pay. At the low end of the cable tester market are devices that only test for continuity. These cheap (under $100) testers are often called **continuity testers** (Figure 6.45). Many of these cheap testers require you to insert both ends of the cable into the tester. Of course, this can be a bit of a problem if the cable is already installed in the wall!

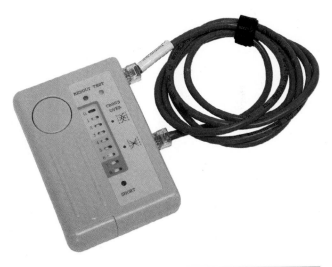

● **Figure 6.45**   Continuity tester

Better testers can run a wire map test that goes beyond mere continuity, testing that all the wires on both ends of the cable connect to the right spot. A wire map test will pick up shorts, crossed wires, and more.

A multimeter works perfectly well to test for continuity, assuming you can place its probes on each end of the cable. Set the multimeter to its continuity setting if it has one (Figure 6.46) or to Ohms. With the latter setting,

Many techs and network testing equipment use the term *wiremap* to refer to the proper connectivity for wires, as in, "Hey Joe, check the wiremap!"

Fat Probes

If you have a multimeter with probes too large to connect to individual contacts on an RJ-45, you can use an old tech trick to finesse the problem. Take a patch cable and cut off about two feet, so you have a short cable with one end bare. Strip an inch of the cladding away from the bare end to expose the wires. Strip a little of the sheath off each wire and plug the cable into the jack. Now you can test continuity by putting the probes directly onto the wire!

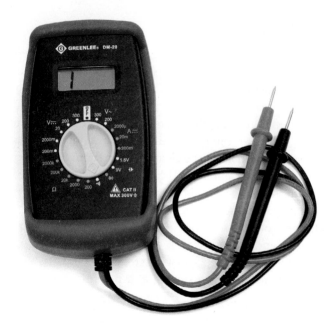

• **Figure 6.46**   Multimeter

if you have a connection, you get zero Ohms, and if you don't have a connection, you get infinite Ohms.

Medium-priced testers (~$400) certainly test continuity and wiremap and include the additional capability to determine the length of a cable, and can even tell you where a break is located on any of the individual wire strands. This type of cable tester (Figure 6.47) is generically called a **time domain reflectometer (TDR)**. Most medium-priced testers come with a small loopback device to insert into the far end of the cable, enabling the tester to

• **Figure 6.47**   A typical medium-priced TDR called a Microscanner

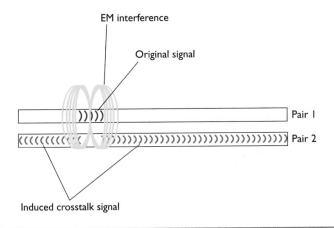

EM interference

Original signal

Pair 1

Pair 2

Induced crosstalk signal

• **Figure 6.48**   Crosstalk

work with installed cables. This is the type of tester you want to have around!

If you want a device that fully tests a cable run to the very complex TIA/EIA standards, the price shoots up fast. These higher-end testers can detect things the lesser testers cannot, such as crosstalk and attenuation.

Crosstalk poses a threat to properly functioning cable runs. Today's UTP cables consist of four pairs of wires, all squished together inside a plastic tube. When you send a signal down one of these pairs, the other pairs pick up some of the signal, as shown in Figure 6.48. This is called **crosstalk**.

Every piece of UTP in existence generates crosstalk. Worse, when you crimp the end of a UTP cable to a jack or plugs, crosstalk increases. A poor-quality crimp creates so much crosstalk that a cable run won't operate at its designed speed. To detect crosstalk, a normal-strength signal is sent down one pair of wires in a cable. An electronic detector, connected on the same end of the cable as the end emanating the signal, listens on the other three pairs and measures the amount of interference, as shown in Figure 6.49. This is called **near-end crosstalk (NEXT)**.

If you repeat this test, sending the signal down one pair of wires, but this time listening on the other pairs on the far end of the connection, you test for **far-end crosstalk (FEXT)**, as shown in Figure 6.50.

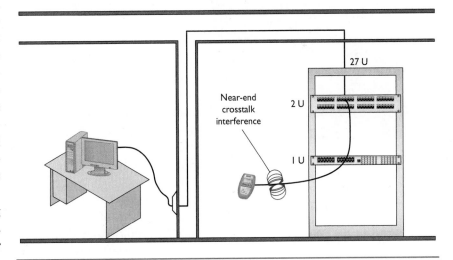

Near-end crosstalk interference

27 U

2 U

1 U

• **Figure 6.49**   Near-end crosstalk

As if that's not bad enough, as a signal progresses down a piece of wire the signal becomes steadily weaker: what's called **attenuation**. As a cable run gets longer, the attenuation increases, and the signal becomes more susceptible to crosstalk. So a tester must send a signal down one end of a wire, test for NEXT and FEXT on the ends of every other pair, and then repeat this process for every pair in the UTP cable.

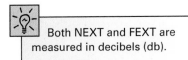

Both NEXT and FEXT are measured in decibels (db).

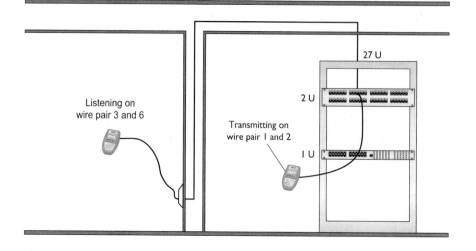

• Figure 6.50   Far-end crosstalk

• **Figure 6.51**   A typical cable certifier—a Microtest OMNIScanner (photo courtesy of Fluke Networks)

This process of verifying that every cable run meets the exacting TIA/EIA standards requires very powerful testing tools, generally known as **cable certifiers** or just certifiers. Cable certifiers can both do the high-end testing and generate a report that a cable installer can print out and hand to a customer to prove that the installed cable runs pass TIA/EIA standards. Figure 6.51 shows an example of this type of scanner made by Fluke (www.fluke.com) in its Microtest line. Most network techs don't need these advanced testers, so unless you have some deep pockets or find yourself doing serious cable testing, stick to the medium-priced testers.

Testing Fiber

Fiber-optic cabling is an entirely different beast in terms of termination and testing. The classic termination method requires very precise stripping, polishing the end of the tiny fiber cable, adding epoxy glue, and inserting the connector. A fiber technician uses a large number of tools (Figure 6.52) and an almost artistic amount of skill. Over the years easier terminations have been developed, but putting an ST, SC, LC, or other connector on the end of a piece of fiber is still very challenging.

A fiber-optic run has problems that are both similar to and different from those of a UTP run. Since most fiber-optic network runs only use two cables, they don't experience crosstalk. Fiber-optic cables do break, so a good tech always keeps an **optical time domain reflectometer (OTDR)** handy (Figure 6.53). OTDRs determine continuity and, if there's a break, tell you exactly how far down the cable to look for the break.

TIA/EIA has very complex requirements for testing fiber runs, and the cabling industry sells fiber certifiers to make sure a fiber will carry its designed signal speed.

The three big issues with fiber are attenuation, light leakage, and modal distortion. The amount of light propagating down the fiber cable diffuses

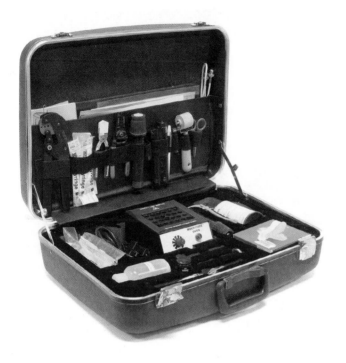

• **Figure 6.52**   Older fiber termination kit

over distance, which causes attenuation or **dispersion** (when the light signal spreads). If you bend a fiber-optic cable too much you get **light leakage**, as shown in Figure 6.54. Every type of fiber cabling has a very specific maximum bend radius. Modal distortion is unique to multimode fiber-optic cable. As the light source illuminates, it sends out light in different modes. Think of a mode as a slightly different direction. Some light shoots straight down the fiber; other modes bounce back and forth at a sharp angle.

The process of installing a structured cabling system is rather involved, requires a great degree of skill, and should be left to professionals. By understanding the process, however, you can tackle most of the problems that come up in an installed structured cabling system. Most importantly, you'll understand the lingo used by the structured cabling installers so you can work with them more efficiently.

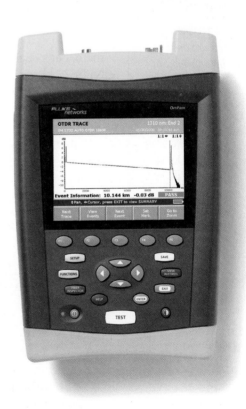

• **Figure 6.53**   An optical time domain reflectometer (photo courtesy of Fluke Networks)

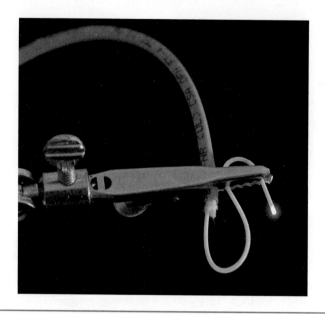

● **Figure 6.54**   Light leakage—note the colored glow at the bends but the dark cable at the straight

■ NICs

Now that the network is completely in place, it's time to turn to the final part of any physical network: the NICs. A good network tech must recognize different types of NICs by sight and know how to install and troubleshoot them. Let's begin by reviewing the differences between UTP and fiber-optic NICs.

All UTP Ethernet NICs use the RJ-45 connector. The cable runs from the NIC to a hub or a switch (Figure 6.55). It is impossible to tell one from the other simply by looking at the connection.

Fiber-optic NICs come in a wide variety; worse, manufacturers will use the same connector types for multiple standards. You'll find a 100BaseFX

Tech Tip

Onboard NICs

It's a rare motherboard these days that doesn't include an onboard NIC. This of course completely destroys the use of the acronym "NIC" for network interface card because there's no card involved. But heck, we're nerds and, just as we'll probably never stop using the term "RJ-45" when the correct term is "8P8C," we'll just keep using the term "NIC." I know! Let's just pretend it stands for network interface connection!

● **Figure 6.55**   Typical UTP NIC

card designed for multimode cable with an SC connector, for example, and an identical card designed for single-mode cable, also with an SC connector. You simply must see the documentation that comes with the two cards to tell them apart. Figure 6.56 shows a typical fiber-optic network card.

Buying NICs

Some folks may disagree with this, but I always purchase name-brand NICs. For NICs, stick with big names, such as 3Com or Intel. The NICs are better made, have extra features, and are easy to return if they turn out to be defective. Plus, it's easy to replace a missing driver on a name-brand NIC, and to be sure that the drivers work well. The type of NIC you purchase de-

• **Figure 6.56**   Typical fiber NIC (photo courtesy of 3Com Corp.)

pends on your network. Try to think about the future and go for multispeed cards if your wallet can handle the extra cost. Also, where possible, try to stick with the same model of NIC. Every different model you buy means another set of driver disks you need to haul around in your tech bag. Using the same model of NIC makes driver updates easier, too.

> Many people order desktop PCs with NICs simply because they don't take the time to ask if the system has a built-in NIC. Take a moment and ask about this!

Physical Connections

I'll state the obvious here: If you don't plug the NIC into the computer, it just isn't going to work! Many users happily assume some sort of quantum magic when it comes to computer communications, but as a tech, you know better. Fortunately, most PCs come with built-in NICs, making physical installation a nonissue. If you're buying a NIC, physically inserting the NIC into one of the PC's expansion slots is the easiest part of the job. Most PCs today have two types of expansion slots. The older, but still common expansion slot is the Peripheral Component Interconnect (PCI) type (Figure 6.57).

The newer PCI Express (PCIe) expansion slots now have some good adoption from NIC suppliers. PCIe NICs usually come in either one-lane (×1) or two-lane (×2) varieties (Figure 6.58).

• **Figure 6.57**   PCI NIC

If you're not willing to open a PC case, you can get NICs with USB or PC Card connections. USB is convenient, but at a maximum speed of 480 Mbps is slower than Gigabit Ethernet; and PC Card is only a laptop solution (Figure 6.59). USB NICs are handy to keep in your toolkit. If you walk up to a machine that might have a bad NIC, test your suspicions by inserting a USB NIC and moving the network cable from the potentially bad NIC to the USB one. (Don't forget to bring your driver disc along!)

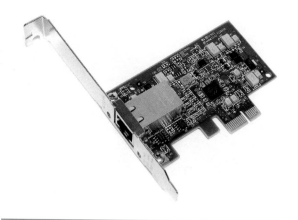

• Figure 6.58   PCIe NIC

• Figure 6.59   USB NIC

Drivers

Installing a NIC's driver into a Windows, Macintosh, or Linux system is easy: just insert the driver CD when prompted by the system. Unless you have a very offbeat NIC, the operating system will probably already have the driver preinstalled, but there are benefits to using the driver on the manufacturer's CD. The CDs that comes with many NICs, especially the higher-end, brand-name ones, include extra goodies such as enhanced drivers and handy utilities, but you'll only be able to access them if you install the driver that comes with the NIC.

Every operating system has some method to verify that the computer recognizes the NIC and is ready to use it. Windows systems have the Device Manager, Ubuntu Linux users can use the Network applet under the Administration menu, and your Macintosh has the Network utility in System Preferences. Actually, most operating systems have multiple methods to show that the NIC is in good working order. Learn the ways to do this for your OS as this is the ultimate test of a good NIC installation.

Bonding

Most switches enable you to use multiple NICs for a single machine, a process called **bonding** or *link aggregation*. Bonding effectively doubles (or more) the speed between a machine and a switch. In preparing for this book, for example, I found that the connection between my graphics development computer and my file server was getting pounded by my constant sending/receiving massive image files, slowing down everyone else's file access. Rather than upgrading the switches and NICs from Gigabit to 10-Gigabit Ethernet—still fairly expensive at this writing—I found that simply doubling the connections among those three machines—graphics computer, switch, and file server—increased performance all around. If you want to add link aggregation to your network to increase performance, try to use identical NICs and switches from the same companies to avoid the hint of incompatibility.

Link Lights

All UTP NICs made today have some type of light-emitting diodes (LEDs) that give information about the state of the NIC's link to whatever's on the other end of the connection. Even though you know the lights are actually LEDs, get used to calling them **link lights**, as that's the term all network techs use. NICs can have between one and four different link lights, and the LEDs can be any color. These lights give you clues about what's happening with the link and are one of the first items to check whenever you think a system is disconnected from the network (Figure 6.60).

A link light tells you that the NIC is connected to a hub or switch. Hubs and switches also have link lights, enabling you to check the connectivity at both ends of the cable. If a PC can't access a network and is acting disconnected, always first check the link lights. Multispeed devices usually have a link light that tells you the speed of the connection. In Figure 6.61, the light for port 2 on the top photo is orange, signifying that the other end of the cable is plugged into either a 10BaseT or 100BaseT NIC. The same port connected to a Gigabit NIC—that's the lower picture—displays a green LED.

A properly functioning link light is steady on when the NIC is connected to another device. No flickering, no on and off, just on. A link light that is off or flickering shows a connection problem.

Another light is the **activity light**. This little guy turns on when the card detects network traffic, so it makes an intermittent flickering when operating properly. The activity light is a lifesaver for detecting problems, because in the real world, the connection light will sometimes lie to you. If the connection light says the connection is good, the next step is to try to copy a file or do something else to create network traffic. If the activity light does not flicker, there's a problem.

You might run into yet another light on some much older NICs, called a collision light. As you might suspect from the name, the **collision light** flickers when it detects collisions on the network. Modern NICs don't have these, but you might run into this phrase on the CompTIA Network+ certification exam.

Keep in mind that the device on the other end of the NIC's connection has link lights too! Figure 6.62 shows the link lights on a modern switch. Most switches have a single LED per port to display connectivity and activity.

No standard governs how NIC manufacturers use their lights and, as a result, they come in an amazing array of colors and layouts. When you encounter a NIC with a number of LEDs, take a moment and try to figure out what each one means. Although different NICs have different ways of arranging and using their LEDs, the functions are always the same: link, activity, and speed.

● **Figure 6.60**   Mmmm, pretty lights!

● **Figure 6.61**   Multispeed lights

● **Figure 6.62**   Link lights on a switch

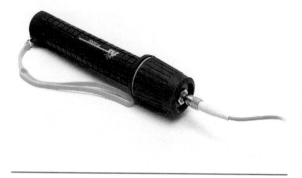

• Figure 6.63 Optical connection tester

Many fiber-optic NICs don't have lights, making diagnosis of problems a bit more challenging. Nevertheless, most physical connection issues for fiber can be traced to the connection on the NIC itself. Fiber-optic cabling is incredibly delicate; the connectors that go into NICs are among the few places that anyone can touch fiber optics, so the connectors are the first thing to check when problems arise. Those who work with fiber always keep around a handy optical tester to enable them to inspect the quality of the connections. Only a trained eye can use such a device to judge a good fiber connection from a bad one—but once you learn how to do it, this kind of tester is extremely handy (Figure 6.63).

■ Diagnostics and Repair of Physical Cabling

"The network's down!" is easily the most terrifying phrase a network tech will ever hear. Networks fail for many reasons, and the first thing to know is that good-quality, professionally installed cabling rarely goes bad. Chapter 15, "Network Troubleshooting," covers principles of network diagnostics and support that apply to all networking situations, but let's take a moment now to discuss what to do when you think you've got a problem with your physical network.

Diagnosing Physical Problems

Look for errors that point to physical disconnection. A key clue that you may have a physical problem is that a user gets a "No server is found" error, or tries to use the operating system's network explorer utility (like Network in Windows Vista) and doesn't see any systems besides his or her own. First try to eliminate software errors: if one particular application fails, try another. If the user can't browse the Internet, but can get his e-mail, odds are good that the problem is with software, not hardware—unless someone unplugged the e-mail server!

Multiple systems failing to access the network often points to hardware problems. This is where knowledge of your network cabling helps. If all the systems connected to one switch suddenly no longer see the network, but all the other systems in your network still function, you not only have a probable hardware problem, you also have a suspect—the switch.

Check Your Lights

If you suspect a hardware problem, first check the link lights on the NIC and switch. If they're not lit, you know the cable isn't connected somewhere. If you're not physically at the system in question (if you're on a tech call, for example), you can have the user check his or her connection status through the link lights or through software. Every operating system has some way to tell you on the screen if it detects the NIC is disconnected. The network status icon in the Notification Area in Windows Vista, for example, will display a little red × when a NIC is disconnected (Figure 6.64). A user who's unfamiliar with link lights (or who may not want to crawl under his or her desk) will have no problem telling you if the icon says "Not connected."

If your problem system is clearly not connecting, eliminate the possibility of a failed switch or other larger problem by checking to make sure other people can access the network, and that other systems can access the shared resource (server) that the problem system can't see. Make a quick visual inspection of the cable running from the back of the PC to the outlet. Finally, if you can, plug the system into a known good outlet and see if it works. A good network tech always keeps a long patch cable for just this purpose. If you get connectivity with the second outlet, you should begin to suspect the structured cable running from the first outlet to the switch. Assuming the cable was installed properly and had been working correctly before this event, a simple continuity test will confirm your suspicion in most cases.

● **Figure 6.64** Disconnected NIC in Vista

Check the NIC

Be warned that a bad NIC can also generate this "can't see the network" problem. Use whatever utility provided with your OS to verify that the NIC works. If you've got a NIC with diagnostic software, run it—this software will check the NIC's circuitry. The NIC's female connector is a common failure point, so NICs that come with diagnostic software often include a special test called a **loopback test**. A loopback test sends data out of the NIC and checks to see if it comes back. Some NICs perform only an internal loopback, which tests the circuitry that sends and receives, but not the actual connecting pins. A true external loopback requires a **loopback plug** inserted into the NIC's port (Figure 6.65). If a NIC is bad, replace it—preferably with an identical NIC so you don't have to reinstall drivers!

 Onboard NICs on laptops are especially notorious for breaking due to constant plugging/ unplugging. On some laptops the NICs are easy to replace; on others it requires a motherboard replacement.

Cable Testing

The vast majority of the network disconnect problems occur at the work area. If you've tested those connections, though, and the work area seems fine, it's time to consider deeper issues.

With the right equipment, diagnosing a bad horizontal cabling run is easy. Anyone with a network should own a midrange tester with TDR such as the Fluke Microscanner. With a little practice, you can easily determine not only whether a cable is disconnected, but also where the disconnection takes place. Sometimes patience is required, especially if you've failed to label your cable runs, but you will find the problem.

When you're testing a cable run, always include the patch cables as you test. This means unplugging the patch cable from the PC, attaching a tester, then going to the telecommunications room. Here you'll want to unplug the patch cable

● **Figure 6.65** Loopback plug

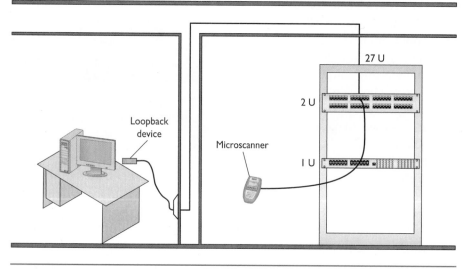

from the switch and plug the tester into that patch cable, making a complete test as shown in Figure 6.66.

Testing in this manner gives you a complete test from the switch to the system. In general, a broken cable must be replaced. A bad patch cable is easy, but what happens if the horizontal cable is to blame? In these cases, I get on the phone and call my local installer. If a cable's bad in one spot, the risk of it being bad in another is simply too great to try anything other than total replacement.

• Figure 6.66   Loopback plug in action

Problems in the Telecommunications Room

Even a well-organized telecommunications room is a complex maze of equipment racks, switches, and patch panels. The most important issue to remember as you work is to keep your diagnostic process organized and documented. For example, if you're testing a series of cable runs along a patch panel, start at one end and don't skip connections. Place a sticker as you work to keep track of where you are on the panel.

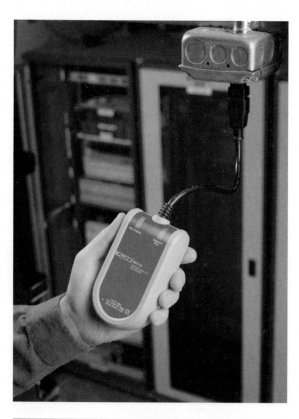

Your biggest concerns in the telecommunications room are power and temperature. All those boxes in the rack need good-quality power. Even the smallest rack should run off of a good UPS, but what if the UPS reports lots of times when it's kicking on? Don't assume the power coming from your physical plant (or power company) is okay. If your UPS comes on too often, it might be time to install a voltage event recorder (Figure 6.67). As its name implies, a **voltage event recorder** plugs into your power outlet and tracks the voltage over time. These devices often reveal interesting issues. A small network was having trouble sending an overnight report to a main branch—the uploading servers reported that they were not able to connect to the Internet. Yet in the morning the report could be run manually with no problems. After placing a voltage event recorder in the telecommunications room, it was discovered that the building management was turning off the power as a power saving measure. This would have been hard to determine without the proper tool.

The temperature in the telecommunications room should be maintained and monitored properly. If you lose the air conditioning, for example, and leave systems running, the equipment will overheat and shut down—sometimes with serious

• Figure 6.67   An excellent voltage event recorder (photo courtesy of Fluke Networks)

damage. To prevent this, all serious telecommunications rooms should have temperature monitors.

Toners

It would be nice to say that all cable installations are perfect, and that over the years they won't grow into horrific piles of spaghetti-like, unlabeled cables. In the real world, though, you might eventually find yourself having to locate or *trace* cables. Even in the best-planned networks, labels fall off ports and outlets, mystery cables appear behind walls, new cable runs are added, and mistakes are made counting rows and columns on patch panels. Sooner or later, most network techs will have to be able to pick out one particular cable or port from a stack.

When the time comes to trace cables, network techs turn to a device called a toner for help. **Toner** is the generic term for two separate devices that are used together: a tone generator and a tone probe. The **tone generator** connects to the cable using alligator clips, tiny hooks, or a network jack, and it sends an electrical signal along the wire at a certain frequency. The **tone probe** emits a sound when it is placed near a cable connected to the tone generator (Figure 6.68). These two devices are often referred to by the brand name Fox and Hound, a popular model of toner made by the Triplett Corporation.

• **Figure 6.68**   Fox and Hound

To trace a cable, connect the tone generator to the known end of the cable in question, and then position the tone probe next to the other end of each of the cables that might be the right one. The tone probe will make a sound when it's placed next to the right cable. Some toners have one tone probe that works with multiple tone generators. Each generator emits a separate frequency, and the probe sounds a different tone for each one. Even good toners are relatively inexpensive ($75); although cheap toners can cost less than $25, they don't tend to work well, so it's worth spending a little more. Just keep in mind that if you have to support a network, you'd do best to own a decent toner.

More advanced toners include phone jacks, enabling the person manipulating the tone generator to communicate with the person manipulating the tone probe: "Jim, move the tone generator to the next port!" These either come with their own headset or work with a *butt set*, the classic tool used by telephone repairmen for years (Figure 6.69).

A good, medium-priced cable tester and a good toner are the most important tools used by folks who must support, but not install, networks. A final tip: be sure to bring along a few extra batteries—there's nothing worse than sitting on the top of a ladder holding a cable tester or toner that has just run out of juice!

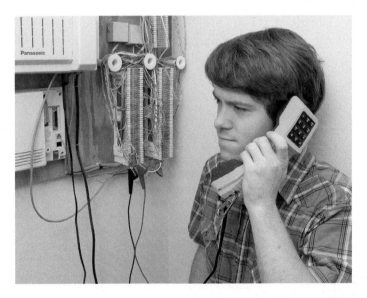

• **Figure 6.69**   Technician with a butt set

Chapter 6 Review

■ Chapter Summary

After reading this chapter and completing the exercises, you should understand the following about installing a physical network.

Recognize and describe the functions of basic components in a structured cabling system

- Structured cabling refers to a set of standards established by the TIA/EIA regarding network cabling. The three basic structured cabling network components are the telecommunications room (a.k.a. server room), the horizontal cabling, and the work area (or the actual workers' office space).

- While wireless networks are popular, they lack the reliability and speed of wired networks.

- All cabling should run from individual PCs to a telecommunications room.

- A telecommunications room should have one or more sturdy equipment racks, used to hold mountable network devices (hubs, switches, and routers); this space also houses server PCs, patch panels, UPSs, monitors, keyboards, mice, tape backup drives, and more.

- Horizontal cabling usually refers to the cabling that runs from the telecommunications room out to the work areas of a single office building floor.

- The work area is where PCs and printers connect to the ends of the horizontal cabling. In other words, the work area is the actual office space where the jacks should be located for connecting to the network.

- UTP cable comes in one of two types: solid core and stranded core. Horizontal cabling should always be solid core.

- Solid core UTP is a better conductor than stranded core, but breaks easily if handled roughly. Stranded core holds up better to substantial handling.

- Equipment racks are 19 inches wide and come in a variety of heights. Rack-mounted equipment is manufactured to fit in the 19-inch width, but they too vary by height.

- Rack-mounted equipment heights are measured in Us, each U being equal to just under 1.75 inches.

- UTP cables can be connected to a 110 block in a patch panel by using a punchdown tool.

- The TIA/EIA 606 labeling standard can help a technician keep track of cables.

- Patch cables are used to connect the ports on a patch panel to a switch. While solid core horizontal runs typically connect to the 110 block, patch cables are usually stranded core.

- Patch cables are also used in the work area to connect a PC to the RJ-45 wall jack.

- TIA/EIA 568 limits horizontal runs to 90 meters, allowing 10 meters for patch cables before the 100-meter limit of UTP cable is reached.

- The demarc location is where the connection is made from the outside world to a private network. An Internet service provider or telephone company provides service through its demarc.

- A network interface unit, such as a cable modem, may sit between the demarc and local network.

- Demarcs and cross-connects typically reside in a room called the main distribution frame.

Explain the process of installing structured cable

- A good installation entails planning the cabling runs with an actual floor plan, as well as poking around in walls and ceilings.

- Raceway products may be used to run cable externally rather than inside walls.

- When planning cable runs, keep five things in mind: distance, power, dryness, temperature, and access.

- Cable trays may be used to aid in pulling cable within a drop ceiling.

- If you make your own patch cables, be sure to use the correct crimp, as they differ for solid core and stranded core UTP.

- A variety of cable testers, including time domain reflectometers and optical time domain reflectometers, can be used to test for continuity, attenuation, and crosstalk.

- Big issues with fiber include attenuation, light leakage, and modal distortion.

Install a network interface card

- All UTP Ethernet NICs use an RJ-45 connector. Fiber-optic NICs use a variety of connectors, depending on the manufacturer.

- Most motherboards now include an onboard NIC.

- Using the same model of NIC for all the PCs on your network makes installing and updating drivers much easier.

- The most common type of expansion card for NICs is PCI, but there are also PCIe × 1 and PCIe × 2 options.

- USB NICs are convenient and you don't have to open the computer case to install one, but their maximum speed of 480 Mbps is slower than Gigabit Ethernet.

- The link lights on a NIC indicate the status of the NIC, such as if it's connected to a network and if there is any network activity. Link lights may include the activity light and collision light.

Perform basic troubleshooting on a structured cable network

- A "no server found" error is likely caused by a physical connection problem. If one program (such as a web browser) works but another (such as e-mail) does not, the problem is likely software related.

- If you suspect a hardware problem, check the link lights on the NIC and the switch. If the lights are not on, the cable is probably disconnected or the port may be faulty.

- A loopback test can check a NIC's circuitry, but not the actual connecting pins.

- When testing cables, be sure to test the entire run, including the patch cable in the work area, the cable leading from the work area wall back to the telecommunications room, and the patch cable from the patch panel to the switch.

- Tools that are helpful for troubleshooting a structured cable network include a voltage event recorder and a toner.

■ Key Terms

110-punchdown block *(103)*
activity light *(125)*
attenuation *(119)*
bonding *(124)*
cable certifier *(120)*
cable drop *(110)*
cable tester *(117)*
cable tray *(112)*
collision light *(125)*
continuity *(117)*
continuity tester *(117)*
crosstalk *(119)*
demarc *(107)*
demarc extension *(108)*
dispersion *(121)*
equipment rack *(102)*
far-end crosstalk (FEXT) *(119)*
horizontal cabling *(99)*
intermediate distribution frame (IDF) *(101)*
light leakage *(121)*
link light *(125)*
loopback plug *(127)*

loopback test *(127)*
main distribution frame (MDF) *(109)*
mounting bracket *(113)*
multiplexer *(108)*
near-end crosstalk (NEXT) *(119)*
network interface unit (NIU) *(107)*
optical time domain reflectometer (OTDR) *(120)*
patch cable *(105)*
patch panel *(103)*
punchdown tool *(103)*
raceway *(110)*
run *(99)*
smart jack *(108)*
solid core *(100)*
stranded core *(100)*
structured cabling *(97)*
telecommunications room *(99)*
TIA/EIA 606 *(104)*
time domain reflectometer (TDR) *(118)*
tone generator *(129)*
tone probe *(129)*
toner *(129)*

Key Term Quiz

Use the Key Terms list to complete the sentences that follow. Not all terms will be used.

1. All the cabling from individual work areas runs via _____ to a central location.

2. The central location that all cabling runs to is called the _____.

3. A single piece of installed horizontal cabling is called a(n) _____.

4. The set of standards established by the EIA/TIA regarding network cabling is called _____.

5. You use a(n) _____ to connect a strand of UTP to a 110 block or 66 block.

6. A short UTP cable that uses stranded, rather than solid, cable is called a(n) _____

and can tolerate much more handling near a patch panel.

7. The type of network interface unit (NUI) that enables an ISP or telephone company to determine if a home DSL box or cable router has been disconnected is called a(n) _____.

8. The spot where a cable comes out of the wall at the workstation is called a(n) _____.

9. The height measurement known as U is used for devices that fit into a(n) _____.

10. The term _____ describes the process of a signal weakening as it progressed down a piece of wire.

Multiple-Choice Quiz

1. Which item describes the length of cable installed within walls from a telecommunications room out to a jack?
   A. Cable drop
   B. Cable run
   C. Cable tester
   D. Cable tray

2. What is the term used to describe where the network hardware and patch panels are kept?
   A. Drop room
   B. Telecommunications room
   C. Routing room
   D. Telecloset room

3. Aside from outright breakage, what's the primary worry with bending a fiber optic cable too much?
   A. Attenuation
   B. Bonding
   C. Light leakage
   D. Near-end crosstalk

4. When connecting a cable run onto a patch panel, which tool should be used?
   A. 110-punchdown tool
   B. Crimper
   C. TDR
   D. Tone generator

5. Which of the following NIC types offers the most versatility?
   A. 10
   B. 10/100
   C. 10/100/1000
   D. Only a nonmultispeed NIC

6. What is the structured cabling name for the end user's office space where network computers will be set up?
   A. Backbone
   B. Building entrance
   C. Cable drop
   D. Work area

7. What type of twisted-pair cabling would work best within ceilings near lighting?

   A. Solid core plenum
   B. Solid core PVC
   C. Stranded core plenum
   D. Stranded core PVC

8. Why would network techs use stranded core cabling from a patch panel's ports to a switch?

   A. Cost
   B. Fire rating
   C. Flexibility
   D. Safety

9. What is the first thing a professional cable installer should do when providing an estimate at a site?

   A. Power on additional lighting.
   B. Put on a grounding wrist strap.
   C. Request a floor plan.
   D. Set up ladders.

10. What component would best allow more servers to be installed in the limited space of a telecommunications room?

   A. Cable tray
   B. Outlet box
   C. Patch panel
   D. Equipment rack

11. How tall is a network router that is 8U?

   A. 8 inches
   B. 8 centimeters
   C. 14 inches
   D. 14 centimeters

12. Your first day on the job, you get a call from the owner complaining that her network connection is down. A quick check of the central switch verifies that it's in good working order, as is the boss's PC. As luck would have it, your supervisor calls at just that time and tells you not to worry; she'll be by in a jiffy with her TDR to help root out the problem. What is she talking about?

   A. Tune domain resonator, her network tone generator
   B. Time detuning resonator, her network tester
   C. Time domain reflectometer, her network tester
   D. Time detail resource, her network schematic

13. Jenny's office building recently had sections renovated, and now some users are complaining that they can't see the network. She suspects that the workers might have inadvertently broken wires when they did ceiling work. George suggests she use a toner to figure out which wires go to the complaining users. Erin disagrees, saying that Jenny should use a Fox and Hound. Who's right?

   A. Only George is right.
   B. Only Erin is right.
   C. Both George and Erin are right.
   D. Neither George nor Erin is right.

14. What is generated by every piece of UTP cable in existence?

   A. Modal distortion
   B. Crosstalk
   C. EMI
   D. ESD

15. Which statement about structured cable is correct?

   A. The term "demarc" refers to a physical location while the phrase "network interface unit" refers to a piece of equipment provided by an ISP.
   B. The term "demarc" refers to a piece of equipment provided by an ISP while the phrase "network interface unit" refers to a piece of equipment provided by the customer.
   C. The terms "demarc" and "network interface unit" refer to pieces of equipment provided by an ISP.
   D. A demarc is used for fiber cabling while a network interface unit is used for UTP.

Essay Quiz

1. Sketch a rough draft of your classroom, office, or the room you are in right now. Indicate any doors, windows, closets, lights, plumbing fixtures, desks or tables, and even any visible electrical wall outlets. Then indicate with a large letter X where you would place a new cable drop. Jot down some notes explaining why you would choose the location you did.

2. Your CompTIA A+ Certified co-worker is listening in on a conversation you are having with your boss, and he thinks he knows what a "demarc" is. Write a quick note to him describing the true meaning of a structured cabling building entrance, so you can leave it on his desk before you leave for the day.

3. The management team at your company wants to network five offices with low-cost PVC stranded core cabling throughout the dropped ceiling in your offices. Compose a memo that justifies the cost of using more expensive cabling. Use any standard memo format that you are already familiar with.

4. The youth group at a local community organization has received funding to help with creating a computer network. They have already purchased the required number of PCI 10/100/1000 NICs. You have been asked by one of the group's leaders to assist with installing the NICs. You want to help, but time doesn't permit you to volunteer any more hours in a week than you already do. It makes better sense to organize a step-by-step fact sheet that describes installing a NIC into an open slot on a computer. When you have finished, e-mail the fact sheet you created to your instructor (or a friend) for comments.

Lab Projects

• Lab Project 6.1

You are a recently hired network technician at a local business. During the interview phase with the company, some questions were raised about installing cable. You made it clear that professional cable installation was the way to go. You justified your statements and impressed the interviewers with your knowledge and honesty, so they hired you.

Now you need to research the company names and "per drop" prices of professional cable installers in your area. Use the Internet to gather research from at least two companies. Prepare a PowerPoint presentation to present your findings to management. Be sure to use color, graphics, and slide transitions (as time permits) to further impress your new bosses!

• Lab Project 6.2

You have become the de facto network administrator for your employer at a nearby tax preparation company. The owner of this small business stays close to all expenses. She realizes that you could use additional tools to help with installing cable for her soon-to-be-expanded office network. You see this as the opportunity to purchase a cable tester and a tone generator. Your boss casually says to check out some prices. You know that well-laid-out numbers could get approval on the toys you'd like!

Prepare a spreadsheet that shows three levels, including prices, for each of these items. Arrange your spreadsheet in a "good/better/best" layout, with "best" listed on top for the most attention. Use the following chart as a guide:

"BEST"	Brand/Model	Price
Cable Tester A		$.
Tone Generator A		$.
Total for A Items		$.
"BETTER"	Brand/Model	Price
Cable Tester B		$.
Tone Generator B		$.
Total for B Items		$.
"GOOD"	Brand/Model	Price
Cable Tester C		$.
Tone Generator C		$.
Total for C Items		$.

TCP/IP Basics

chapter 7

"If it's sent by ship then it's a cargo, if it's sent by road then it's a shipment."

—DAVE ALLEN

In this chapter, you will learn how to

- **Describe how the Internet Protocol works**
- **Explain CIDR and subnetting**
- **Describe the functions of static and dynamic IP addresses**

The mythical MHTechEd network (remember that from Chapter 2?) provided an overview of how networks work. At the bottom of every network, at OSI Layers 1 and 2, resides the network hardware: the wires, switches, network cards, and more that enable data to move physically from one computer to another. Above the Physical and Data Link layers, the "higher" layers of the model—network protocols and applications—work with the hardware to make the network magic happen.

Chapters 3 through 6 provided details of the hardware at the Physical and Data Link layers. You learned about the network protocols, such as Ethernet, that create uniformity within networks, so that the data frame created by one NIC can be read properly by another NIC.

This chapter begins a fun journey into the software side of networking. You'll learn the details about the IP addressing scheme that enables computers in one network to communicate with each other and computers in other networks. You'll get the full story on how TCP/IP networks divide into smaller units—subnets—to make management of a large TCP/IP network easier. And you won't just get it from a conceptual standpoint. This chapter provides the details you've undoubtedly been craving, teaching you how to set up a network properly. The chapter finishes with an in-depth discussion on implementing IP addresses.

Historical/Conceptual

The early days of networking software saw several competing standards that did not work well together. Novell NetWare, Microsoft Windows, and Apple Macintosh ran networking software to share folders and printers, while the UNIX/Linux world did crazy things like sharing terminals—handy for the UNIX/Linux users, but it made no sense to the Windows folks—and there was this new thing called e-mail (like that was ever going to go anywhere). The Internet had just been opened to the public. The World Wide Web was just a plaything for programmers and scientists. All of these folks made their own software, interpreting (or totally ignoring) the OSI model the way they wanted to, and all trying (arguably) to become THE WAY the whole world was going to network. It was an unpleasant, ugly world for guys like me who had the audacity to try to make, for example, a UNIX box work with a Windows computer.

The problem was that no one agreed on how a network should run. Everyone's software had its own set of Rules of What a Network Should Do and How to Do It. These sets of rules—and the software written to follow these rules—were broken down into individual rules called **protocols**. Each set of rules had many protocols lumped together under the term **protocol suite**. Novell NetWare called its protocol suite IPX/SPX, Microsoft called its NetBIOS/NetBEUI, Apple called its AppleTalk, and the UNIX folks used this wacky protocol suite called TCP/IP.

Well, TCP/IP has won. Sure, you may find the occasional network still running one of these other protocol suites, but they're rare these days. To get ahead in today's world, to get on the Internet, and to pass the CompTIA Network+ exam, you only need to worry about TCP/IP. Novell, Microsoft, and Apple no longer actively support anything but TCP/IP. You live in a one-protocol-suite world, the old stuff is forgotten, and you kids don't know how good you got it!

TCP/IP fits nicely into the OSI seven-layer model, occupying Layers 3–5: Network, Transport, and Session, respectively (Figure 7.1). Starting from the bottom up, the **Internet Protocol (IP)**—both version 4 (IPv4), which interests us here, and version 6 (IPv6), which is covered in the chapter of the same name, Chapter 13—stands by itself at Layer 3. IP handles all of the logical addressing issues. The Transmission Control Protocol (TCP), the User Datagram Protocol (UDP), and the Internet Control Message Protocol (ICMP) operate at the Transport and Session layers. These protocols define how the connections take place between two computers. All of these individual protocols work together to make the TCP/IP protocol suite.

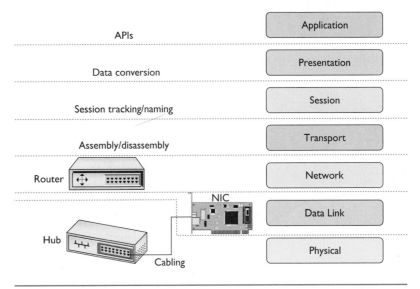

• **Figure 7.1**   OSI redux

Test Specific

■ IP in Depth

TCP/IP supports simple networks and complex networks. You can use the protocol suite to connect a handful of computers to a switch and create a local area network (LAN). TCP/IP also enables you to interconnect multiple LANs into a wide area network (WAN).

At the LAN level, all the computers use Ethernet, and this creates a hurdle for WAN-wide communication. For one computer to send a frame to another computer, the sending computer must know the MAC address of the destination computer. This begs the question: How does the sender get the recipient's MAC address?

 Cross Check

Broadcasting

You first ran into broadcasting way back in Chapter 2, "Building a Network with the OSI Model," so check your memory now. What happens to the broadcast frame? Does it reach all the computers on a LAN? How many computers actually process that broadcast frame?

In a small network this is easy. The sending computer simply *broadcasts* by sending a frame to MAC address FF-FF-FF-FF-FF-FF, the universal MAC address for broadcast. Figure 7.2 shows a computer broadcasting for another computer's MAC address.

Broadcasting takes up some of the network bandwidth, but in a small network it's acceptably small. But what would happen if the entire Internet used broadcasting (Figure 7.3)? In that case the whole Internet would come to a stop.

TCP/IP networks use **IP addressing** to overcome the limitations inherent in Ethernet networks. IP addresses provide several things. First, every machine on a TCP/IP network—small or large—gets a unique IP address that identifies the machine. Second, IP addresses group together sets of computers into logical networks, so you can distinguish one LAN from another, for example. Finally, because TCP/IP network equipment understands the IP

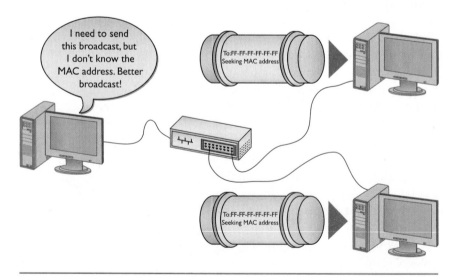

• **Figure 7.2** PC broadcasting for a MAC address

• **Figure 7.3** Broadcasting won't work for the entire Internet.

addressing scheme, computers can communicate with each other *between* LANs, in a WAN, without broadcasting for MAC addresses.

Chapter 2 touched on IP addresses briefly, but network techs need to understand them intimately. Let's dive into the structure and function of the IP addressing scheme.

IP Addresses

The most common type of IP address (officially called IPv4, but usually simplified to just "IP") consists of a 32-bit value. Here's an example of an IP address:

11000000101010000000010000000010

Whoa! IP addresses are just a string of 32 binary digits? Yes they are, but to make IP addresses easier to use for us humans, the 32-bit binary value is broken down into four groups of eight, separated by periods or *dots* like this:

11000000.10101000.00000100.00000010

Each of these 8-bit values is in turn converted into a decimal number between 0 and 255. If you took every possible combination of eight binary values and placed them in a spreadsheet it would look something like the list in the left column. The right column shows the same list with a decimal value assigned to each.

00000000	00000000 = 0
00000001	00000001 = 1
00000010	00000010 = 2

00000011	00000011 = 3
00000100	00000100 = 4
00000101	00000101 = 5
00000110	00000110 = 6
00000111	00000111 = 7
00001000	00001000 = 8
(skip a bunch in the middle)	*(skip a bunch in the middle)*
11111000	11111000 = 248
11111001	11111001 = 249
11111010	11111010 = 250
11111011	11111011 = 251
11111100	11111100 = 252
11111101	11111101 = 253
11111110	11111110 = 254
11111111	11111111 = 255

> When you type an IP address into a computer, the periods are ignored and the decimal numbers are immediately converted into binary. People need dotted decimal, the computers do not.

> Using a calculator utility to convert to and from binary/decimal is a critical skill for a network tech. Later on you'll do this again, but by hand!

Converted, the original value of 11000000.10101000.00000100.00000010 is displayed as 192.168.4.2, IPv4's **dotted decimal notation** (also referred to as the *dotted-octet numbering system*). Note that dotted decimal is simply a shorthand way for people to discuss and configure the binary IP addresses computers use.

People who work on TCP/IP networks must know how to convert dotted decimal to binary and back. It's easy to convert using any operating system's calculator. Every OS has a calculator (Linux/UNIX systems have about 100 different ones to choose from) that has a scientific or programmer mode like the one shown in Figure 7.4.

To convert from decimal to binary, just go into decimal view, type in the value, and then switch to binary view to get the result. To convert to decimal, just go into binary view, enter the binary value, and switch to decimal view to get the result. Figure 7.5 shows the results of Windows Vista's Calculator converting the decimal value 47 into binary. Notice the result is

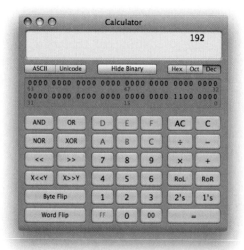

• **Figure 7.4** Macintosh OS X Calculator in Programmer mode

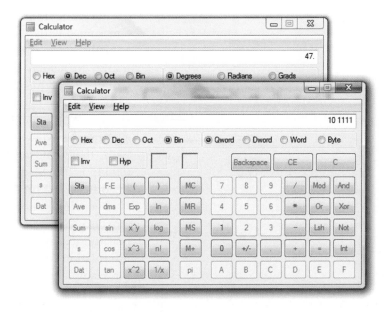

• **Figure 7.5**   Converting decimal to binary with Windows Vista's Calculator

101111—the leading two zeroes do not appear. When you work with IP addresses you must always have eight digits, so just add two more to the left to get 00101111.

Just as every MAC address is unique on a network, every IP address must be unique as well. For logical addressing to work, no two computers on the same network may have the same IP address. In a small network running TCP/IP, every computer has both an IP address and a MAC address (Figure 7.6).

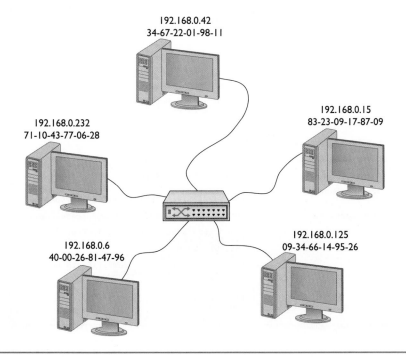

• **Figure 7.6**   Small network with both IP and MAC addresses

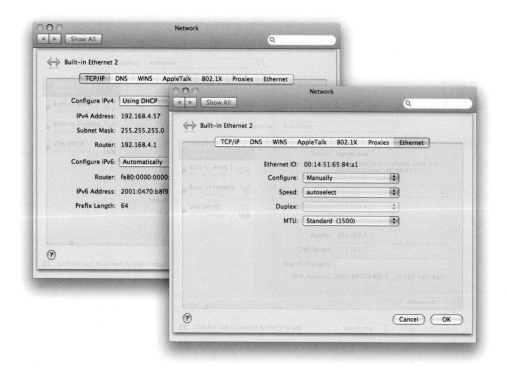

Every operating system comes with a utility (usually more than one utility) to display a system's IP address and MAC address. Figure 7.7 shows a Macintosh OS X system's Network utility. Note the MAC address (00:14:51:65:84:a1) and the IP address (192.168.4.57).

Every operating system also has a command-line utility to give you this information. In Windows, for example, you can use **IPCONFIG** to display the IP and MAC addresses. Run `ipconfig /all` to see the results shown in Figure 7.8.

In the UNIX/Linux/ Mac OS X world, you can run the very similar

• **Figure 7.7**   Macintosh OS X Network utility

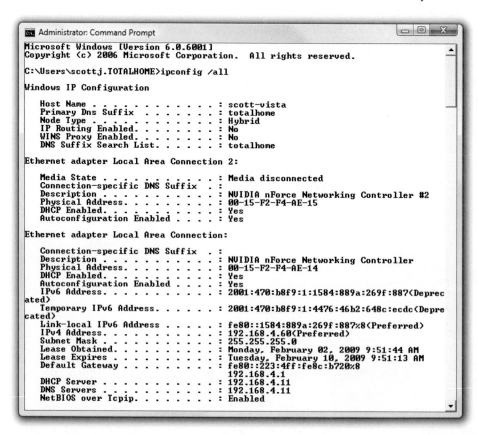

```
Administrator: Command Prompt

Microsoft Windows [Version 6.0.6001]
Copyright (c) 2006 Microsoft Corporation.  All rights reserved.

C:\Users\scottj.TOTALHOME>ipconfig /all

Windows IP Configuration

    Host Name . . . . . . . . . . . . : scott-vista
    Primary Dns Suffix  . . . . . . . : totalhome
    Node Type . . . . . . . . . . . . : Hybrid
    IP Routing Enabled. . . . . . . . : No
    WINS Proxy Enabled. . . . . . . . : No
    DNS Suffix Search List. . . . . . : totalhome

Ethernet adapter Local Area Connection 2:

    Media State . . . . . . . . . . . : Media disconnected
    Connection-specific DNS Suffix  . :
    Description . . . . . . . . . . . : NUIDIA nForce Networking Controller #2
    Physical Address. . . . . . . . . : 00-15-F2-F4-AE-15
    DHCP Enabled. . . . . . . . . . . : Yes
    Autoconfiguration Enabled . . . . : Yes

Ethernet adapter Local Area Connection:

    Connection-specific DNS Suffix  . :
    Description . . . . . . . . . . . : NUIDIA nForce Networking Controller
    Physical Address. . . . . . . . . : 00-15-F2-F4-AE-14
    DHCP Enabled. . . . . . . . . . . : Yes
    Autoconfiguration Enabled . . . . : Yes
    IPv6 Address. . . . . . . . . . . : 2001:470:b8f9:1:1584:889a:269f:887(Deprec
ated)
    Temporary IPv6 Address. . . . . . : 2001:470:b8f9:1:4476:46b2:648c:ecdc(Depre
cated)
    Link-local IPv6 Address . . . . . : fe80::1584:889a:269f:887%8(Preferred)
    IPv4 Address. . . . . . . . . . . : 192.168.4.60(Preferred)
    Subnet Mask . . . . . . . . . . . : 255.255.255.0
    Lease Obtained. . . . . . . . . . : Monday, February 02, 2009 9:51:44 AM
    Lease Expires . . . . . . . . . . : Tuesday, February 10, 2009 9:51:13 AM
    Default Gateway . . . . . . . . . : fe80::223:4ff:fe8c:b720%8
                                        192.168.4.1
    DHCP Server . . . . . . . . . . . : 192.168.4.11
    DNS Servers . . . . . . . . . . . : 192.168.4.11
    NetBIOS over Tcpip. . . . . . . . : Enabled
```

• **Figure 7.8**   IPCONFIG /ALL

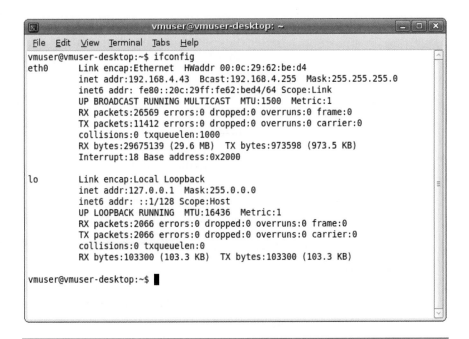

```
                      vmuser@vmuser-desktop: ~
File  Edit  View  Terminal  Tabs  Help
vmuser@vmuser-desktop:~$ ifconfig
eth0      Link encap:Ethernet  HWaddr 00:0c:29:62:be:d4
          inet addr:192.168.4.43  Bcast:192.168.4.255  Mask:255.255.255.0
          inet6 addr: fe80::20c:29ff:fe62:bed4/64 Scope:Link
          UP BROADCAST RUNNING MULTICAST  MTU:1500  Metric:1
          RX packets:26569 errors:0 dropped:0 overruns:0 frame:0
          TX packets:11412 errors:0 dropped:0 overruns:0 carrier:0
          collisions:0 txqueuelen:1000
          RX bytes:29675139 (29.6 MB)  TX bytes:973598 (973.5 KB)
          Interrupt:18 Base address:0x2000

lo        Link encap:Local Loopback
          inet addr:127.0.0.1  Mask:255.0.0.0
          inet6 addr: ::1/128 Scope:Host
          UP LOOPBACK RUNNING  MTU:16436  Metric:1
          RX packets:2066 errors:0 dropped:0 overruns:0 frame:0
          TX packets:2066 errors:0 dropped:0 overruns:0 carrier:0
          collisions:0 txqueuelen:0
          RX bytes:103300 (103.3 KB)  TX bytes:103300 (103.3 KB)

vmuser@vmuser-desktop:~$
```

• **Figure 7.9**   IFCONFIG in Ubuntu

 Make sure you know that IPCONFIG and IFCONFIG provide a tremendous amount of information regarding a system's TCP/IP settings.

IFCONFIG command. Figure 7.9, for example, shows the result of an IFCONFIG ("eth0" is the NIC).

IP Addresses in Action

IP addresses support both LANs and WANs. This can create problems in some circumstances, such as when a computer needs to send data both to computers in its own network and to computers in other networks. How can this be accomplished?

To make all this work, IP must do three things:

1. Create some way to use IP addresses such that each LAN has its own identification.

2. Interconnect all of the LANs together using routers and give those routers some way to use the network identification to send packets to the right network.

3. Give each computer on the network some way to recognize if a packet is for the LAN or for a computer on the WAN so it knows how to handle the packet.

Network IDs

To differentiate LANs from one another, each computer on a single LAN must share a very similar IP address where some of the IP address—reading left to right—matches all the others on the LAN. Figure 7.10 shows a LAN where all of the computers share the first three numbers of the IP address, with only the last number being unique on each system.

In this example, every computer has an IP address of 192.168.5.x. That means the **network ID** is 192.168.5.0. The x part of the IP address is the **host ID**. Combine the network ID (after dropping the ending 0) with the host ID to

The network ID and the host ID are combined to make a system's IP address.

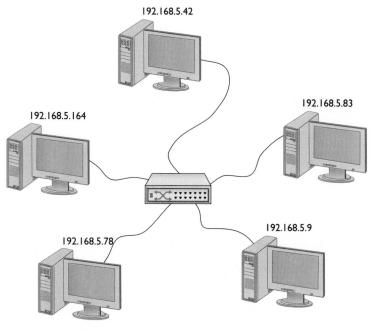

192.168.5.42

192.168.5.164

192.168.5.83

192.168.5.78

192.168.5.9

• **Figure 7.10**   IP addresses for a LAN

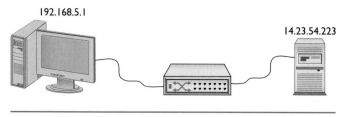

192.168.5.1

14.23.54.223

• **Figure 7.11**   LAN with router

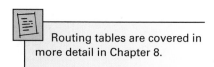
Routing tables are covered in more detail in Chapter 8.

get an individual system's IP address. No individual computer can have an IP address that ends with 0 because that is reserved for network IDs.

Interconnecting

To organize all those individual LANs into a larger network, every TCP/IP LAN that wants to connect to another TCP/IP LAN must have a router connection. There is no exception to this critical rule. A router therefore needs an IP address on the LANs that it serves (Figure 7.11) so that it can correctly route packets.

The IP address of the router's connection to your LAN is known as the **default gateway**. Most network administrators give the LAN-side NIC on the default gateway the lowest host address in the network, usually the host ID of 1.

Routers use network IDs to determine network traffic. Figure 7.12 shows a diagram for a small, two-NIC router similar to the ones you'd see in many homes. Note that one port (192.168.5.1) connects to the LAN and the other port connects to the Internet service provider's network (14.23.54.223). Built into this router is a **routing table**, the actual instructions that tell the router what to do with incoming packets and where to send them.

Now let's add in the LAN and the Internet (Figure 7.13). When discussing networks in terms of network IDs, by the way, especially with illustrations in books, it's common practice to draw circles around stylized networks. It's the IDs you should concentrate on here, not the specifics of the networks.

Network IDs are very flexible, as long as no two interconnected networks share the same network ID. If you wished, you could change the network ID of the 192.168.5.0 network to 192.155.5.0, or 202.21.8.0, just as

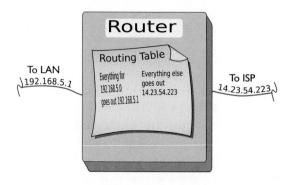

Router

Routing Table

To LAN
192.168.5.1

Everything for 192.168.5.0 goes out 192.168.5.1

Everything else goes out 14.23.54.223

To ISP
14.23.54.223

• **Figure 7.12**   Router diagram

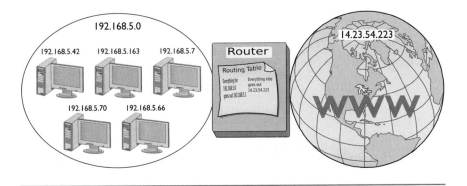

• **Figure 7.13**   LAN, router, and the Internet

long as you guarantee no other LAN on the WAN shares the same network ID. On the Internet, powerful governing bodies make sure no two LANs share the same network ID by carefully allocating the network IDs. I'll talk more about how this works later on in the chapter.

So far you've only seen examples of network IDs where the last value is zero. This is common for small networks, but it creates a limitation. With a network ID of 192.168.5.0, for example, a network is limited to IP addresses from 192.168.5.1 to 192.168.5.254. (192.168.5.255 is a broadcast address used to talk to every computer on the LAN.) This provides only 254 IP addresses: enough for a small network, but many organizations need many more IP addresses. No worries! It's easy enough to simply make a network ID with more zeroes, such as 170.45.0.0 (for a total of 65,534 hosts) or even 12.0.0.0 (for around 16.7 million hosts).

Network IDs enable you to connect multiple LANs into a WAN. Routers connect everything together and use routing tables to keep track of which packets go where. So that handles task number two.

Now that you've seen how IP addressing works with LANs and WANs, let's turn to how IP establishes a way for each computer on the network to recognize if a packet is to a computer on the LAN or to a computer on the WAN so it knows how to handle the packet. The secret to this is something called the subnet mask.

Subnet Mask

Picture this scenario. Three friends sit at their computers—Computers A, B, and C—and want to communicate with each other. Figure 7.14 illustrates the situation. You can tell from the drawing that Computers A and B are in the same LAN, whereas Computer C is on a completely different LAN. The IP addressing scheme can handle this communication, so let's see how it works.

The process to get a packet to a local computer is very different from the process to get a packet to a faraway computer. If one computer

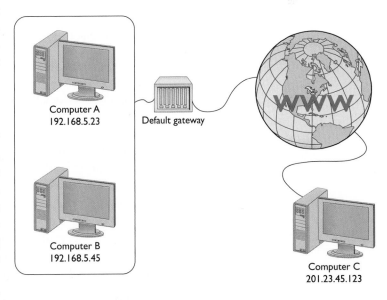

• **Figure 7.14**   The three amigos, separated by walls or miles

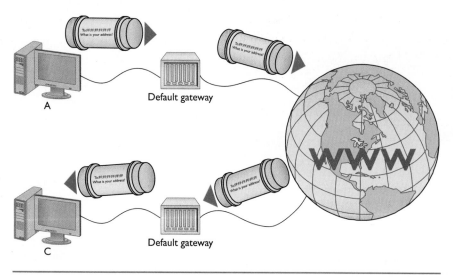

• **Figure 7.15** Sending a packet remotely

wants to send a packet to a local computer, it must send out a broadcast to get the other computer's MAC address, as you'll recall from earlier in the chapter and Figure 7.2. (It's easy to forget about the MAC address, but remember that the network uses Ethernet and *must* have the MAC address to get the packet to the other computer.) If the packet is for some computer on a faraway network, the sending computer must send the packet to the default gateway (Figure 7.15).

In the scenario illustrated in Figure 7.14, Computer A wants to send a packet to Computer B. Computer B is on the same LAN as Computer A, but that begs a question: How does Computer A know this? Every TCP/IP computer needs a tool to tell the sending computer whether the destination IP address is local or long distance. This tool is the subnet mask.

A **subnet mask** is nothing more than a string of ones followed by some number of zeroes, always totaling exactly 32 bits, typed into every TCP/IP host. Here's an example of a typical subnet mask:

11111111111111111111111100000000

For the courtesy of the humans reading this (if there are any computers reading this book, please call me—I'd love to meet you!) let's convert this to dotted decimal. First add some periods:

11111111.11111111.11111111.00000000

Then convert each octet into decimal (use a calculator):

255.255.255.0

When you line an IP address up with a corresponding subnet mask in binary, the portion of the IP address that aligns with the ones of the subnet mask is the network ID portion of the IP address. The portion that aligns with the zeroes is the host ID. With simple IP addresses, you can see this with dotted decimal, but you'll want to see this in binary for a true understanding of how the computers work.

The IP address 192.168.5.23 has a subnet mask of 255.255.255.0. Convert both numbers to binary and then compare the full IP address to the ones and zeroes of the subnet mask:

	Dotted Decimal	**Binary**
IP address	192.168.5.23	11000000.10101000.00000101.00010111
Subnet mask	255.255.255.0	11111111.11111111.11111111.00000000
Network ID	192.168.5.0	11000000.10101000.00000101.x
Host ID	$x.x.x.23$	$x.x.x.$00010111

Before a computer sends out any data, it first compares the destination IP address to its own IP address using the subnet mask. If the destination IP address matches the computer's IP wherever there's a 1 in the subnet mask, then the sending computer knows it's a local destination. The network IDs match. If even 1 bit of the destination IP address where the ones are on the subnet mask is different, then the sending computer knows it's a long-distance call. The network IDs do not match.

Let's head over to Computer A and see how the subnet mask works. Computer A's IP address is 192.168.5.23. Convert that into binary:

11000000.10101000.00000101.00010111

Now drop the periods, because they mean nothing to the computer:

11000000101010000000010100010111

Let's say Computer A wants to send a packet to Computer B. Computer A's subnet mask is 255.255.255.0. Computer B's IP address is 192.168.5.45. Convert this address to binary:

11000000101010000000010100101100

Computer A compares its IP address to Computer B's IP address using the subnet mask, as shown in Figure 7.16. For clarity, I've added a line to show you where the ones end and the zeroes begin in the subnet mask. Computers certainly don't need the pretty red line!

Ah ha! Computer A's and Computer B's network IDs match! It's a local call. Knowing this, Computer A can now send out an ARP broadcast, as shown in Figure 7.17, to determine Computer B's MAC address. The **Address Resolution Protocol (ARP)** is how TCP/IP networks figure out the MAC addresses based on the destination IP address.

The addressing for the ARP packet looks like Figure 7.18. Note that Computer A's IP address and MAC address are included.

Computer B responds to the ARP by sending Computer A an ARP response (Figure 7.19). Once Computer A has Computer B's MAC address, it will now start sending packets.

But what happens when Computer A wants to send a packet to Computer C? First, Computer A compares Computer C's IP address to its own using the subnet mask (Figure 7.20). It sees that the IP addresses do not match in the ones part of the subnet mask—the network IDs don't match—meaning this is a long-distance call.

At this point you should memorize that 0 = 00000000 and 255 = 11111111. You'll find this very helpful throughout the rest of the book.

Computer A's IP: 11000000101010000000010100010111
Subnet mask   11111111111111111111111100000000
Computer B's IP: 11000000101010000000010100101100

These all match! It's a local call.

Figure 7.16   Comparing addresses

Figure 7.17   Sending an ARP

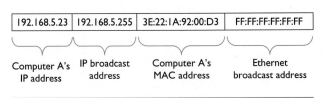

192.168.5.23	192.168.5.255	3E:22:1A:92:00:D3	FF:FF:FF:FF:FF:FF
Computer A's IP address	IP broadcast address	Computer A's MAC address	Ethernet broadcast address

Figure 7.18   ARP packet header showing addresses

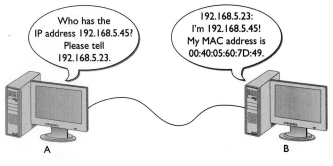

Figure 7.19   Computer B responds

ARP and the OSI Model

Remember the OSI model from way back in Chapter 2? Which layer does IP work on? How about MAC addresses? Where do you think ARP fits into the OSI model?

Computer A's IP: 11000000101010000000010100010111
Subnet mask: 11111111111111111111111100000000
Computer C's IP: 10110110110111010000001100110111

Not a match! It's a long-distance call!

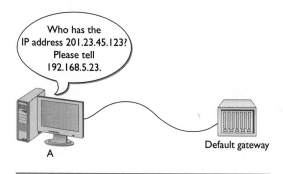

● **Figure 7.20** Comparing addresses again

● **Figure 7.21** Sending an ARP to the gateway

Whenever a computer wants to send to an IP address on another LAN, it knows to send the packet to the default gateway. It still sends out an ARP, but this time to the default gateway (Figure 7.21). Once Computer A gets the default gateway's MAC address, it then begins to send packets.

Subnet masks are represented in dotted decimal just like IP addresses—just remember that both are really 32-bit binary numbers. All of the following (shown in both binary and dotted decimal formats) can be subnet masks:

11111111111111111111111100000000 = 255.255.255.0
11111111111111110000000000000000 = 255.255.0.0
11111111000000000000000000000000 = 255.0.0.0

Most network folks represent subnet masks using special shorthand: a / character followed by a number equal to the number of ones in the subnet mask. Here are a few examples:

11111111111111111111111100000000 = /24 (24 ones)
11111111111111110000000000000000 = /16 (16 ones)
11111111000000000000000000000000 = /8 (8 ones)

Try This!

ARP in Windows

To show Windows' current ARP table, open a command line and type this:

```
arp -a
```

You should see results similar to this:

```
Interface: 192.168.4.71 --- 0x4
  Internet Address      Physical Address      Type
  192.168.4.76          00-1d-e0-78-9c-d5     dynamic
  192.168.4.81          00-1b-77-3f-85-b4     dynamic
```

Now delete one of the entries in the ARP table with the command:

```
arp -d [ip address from the previous results]
```

Run the arp -a command again. The line for the address you specified should be gone. Now try and PING the address you deleted and check the ARP table again. Is the deleted address back?

An IP address followed by the / and number tells you the IP address and the subnet mask in one statement. For example, 201.23.45.123/24 is an IP address of 201.23.45.123, with a subnet mask of 255.255.255.0. Similarly, 184.222.4.36/16 is an IP address of 184.222.4.36, with a subnet mask of 255.255.0.0.

Fortunately, computers do all of this subnet filtering automatically. Network administrators need only to enter the correct IP address and subnet mask when they first set up their systems, and the rest happens without any human intervention.

If you want a computer to work in a routed network (like the Internet), you absolutely must have an IP address that's part of its network ID, a subnet mask, and a default gateway. No exceptions!

> By definition, all computers on the same network will have the same subnet mask and network ID.

Class IDs

The Internet is by far the biggest and the most complex TCP/IP network, numbering over half a billion computers at the beginning of 2009 and growing quickly. The single biggest challenge for the Internet is to make sure no two devices on the Internet share the same IP address. To support the dispersion of IP addresses, an organization called the **Internet Assigned Numbers Authority (IANA)** was formed to track and disperse IP addresses to those who needed them. Initially handled by a single person (the famous Jon Postel) until 1998, the IANA has grown dramatically and now oversees a number of Regional Internet Registries (RIRs) who parcel out IP addresses to large ISPs. The vast majority of end users get their IP addresses from their respective ISPs. The IANA passes out IP addresses in contiguous chunks called **class licenses**, outlined in the following table:

	First Decimal Value	Addresses	Hosts per Network ID
Class A	1–126	1.0.0.0–126.255.255.255	16,277,214
Class B	128–191	128.0.0.0–191.255.255.255	65,534
Class C	192–223	192.0.0.0–223.255.255.255	254
Class D	224–239	224.0.0.0–239.255.255.255	Multicast
Class E	240–255	240.0.0.0–255.255.255.255	Reserved

A typical Class A license, for example, would have a network ID that starts between 1–126; hosts on that network would have only the first octet in common, with any numbers for the other three octets. Having three octets to use for hosts means you can have an enormous number of possible hosts, over 16 million different number combinations. The subnet mask for Class A licenses is 255.0.0.0.

A Class B license, with a subnet mask of 255.255.0.0, uses the first two octets to define the network ID. This leaves two octets to define host IDs, which means each Class B network ID can have up to 65,534 different hosts.

A Class C license uses the first three octets to define only the network ID. All hosts in network 192.168.35.0, for example, would have all three first numbers in common. Only the last octet defines the host IDs, which leaves only 254 possible unique addresses. The subnet mask for Class C licenses is 255.255.255.0.

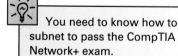
Multicast and reserved class licenses—Classes D and E, respectively—are rather strange and deserve some discussion. There are three types of ways to send a packet: a broadcast, which is where every computer on the LAN hears the message, a **unicast**, where one computer sends a message directly to another user, and **multicast**, where a single computer sends a packet to a group of interested computers. Multicast is uncommon on individual computers, but is often used when routers talk to each other. Reserved addresses are just that—reserved and never used except for occasional experimental reasons.

IP class licenses worked well for the first few years of the Internet, but quickly ran into trouble due to the fact that they didn't quite fit for everyone. Early on IANA gave away IP class licenses rather generously, perhaps too generously. Over time, unallocated IP addresses became scarce. Additionally, the IP class licenses concept didn't scale well. If an organization needed 2000 IP addresses, for example, it either had to take a single Class B license (wasting 63,000 addresses) or eight Class C licenses. As a result, a new method of generating blocks of IP addresses, called **Classless Inter-Domain Routing (CIDR)**, was developed.

■ CIDR and Subnetting

CIDR is based on a concept called **subnetting**: taking a single class of IP addresses and chopping it up into multiple smaller groups. CIDR and subnetting are virtually the same thing. Subnetting is done by an organization—it is given a block of addresses and then breaks the single block of addresses into multiple subnetworks. CIDR is done by an ISP—it is given a block of addresses, subnets the block into multiple subnets, and then passes out the smaller individual subnets to customers. Subnetting and CIDR have been around for quite a long time now and are a critical part of all but the smallest TCP/IP networks. Let's first discuss subnetting and then visit CIDR.

Subnetting

Subnetting enables a much more efficient use of IP addresses than does using class licenses. It also enables you to separate a network for security (separating a bank of public access computers from your more private computers) and for bandwidth control (separating a heavily used LAN from one that's not so heavily used).

The cornerstone to subnetting lies in the subnet mask. You take an existing /8, /16, or /24 subnet and extend the subnet mask by adding more ones (and taking away the same number of zeroes). For example, let's say you have an Internet café with about 50 computers, 40 of which are for public use and 10 of which are used in the back office for accounting and such (Figure 7.22). Your network ID is 192.168.4/24. You want to prevent people using the public systems from accessing your private machines, so you decide to do a subnet. You also have wireless Internet and want to separate wireless clients (never more than 10) on their own subnet.

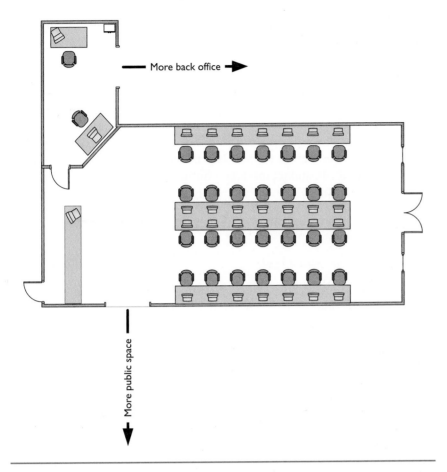

• **Figure 7.22**   Layout of the network

There are two items to note about subnetting. First, start with the given subnet mask and move it to the right until you have the number of subnets you need. Second, forget the dots. Never try to subnet without first converting to binary. Too many techs are what I call "victims of the dots." They are so used to working only with class licenses that they forget there's more to subnets than just /8, /16, and /24 networks. There is no reason network IDs must end on the dots. The computers, at least, think it's perfectly fine to have subnets that end at points between the periods, such as /26, /27, or even /22. The trick here is to stop thinking about network IDs, and subnet masks just in their dotted decimal format, and instead go back to thinking of them as binary numbers.

Let's begin subnetting the café's network of 192.168.4/24. Start by changing a zero to a one on the subnet mask so the /24 becomes a /25 subnet:

```
11111111111111111111111110000000
```

Calculating Hosts

Before we even go one step further you need to answer this question: On a /24 network, how many hosts can you have? Well, if you used dotted decimal notation you might say

192.168.4.1 to 192.168.4.254 = 254 hosts

But do this from the binary instead. In a /24 network you have eight zeroes that can be the host ID:

00000001 to 11111110 = 254

There's a simple piece of math here: $2^{(\text{number of zeroes in the subnet mask})} - 2$

$2^8 - 2 = 254$

If you remember this simple formula, you can always determine the number of hosts for a given subnet. This is critical! Memorize this!

If you have a /16 subnet mask on your network, what is the maximum number of hosts you can have on that network?

1. Since a subnet mask always has 32 digits, a /16 subnet means you have 16 zeroes left after the 16 ones.
2. $2^{16} - 2 = 65,534$ total hosts.

If you have a /26 subnet mask on your network, what is the maximum number of hosts you can have on that network?

1. Since a subnet mask always has 32 digits, a /26 subnet means you have 6 zeroes left after the 26 ones.
2. $2^6 - 2 = 62$ total hosts.

Excellent! Knowing how to determine the number of hosts for a particular subnet mask will help you tremendously in a moment.

Your First Subnet

Let's now make a subnet. All subnetting begins with a single network ID. In this scenario, you need to convert the 192.168.4/24 network ID for the café into three network IDs: one for the public computers, one for the private computers, and one for the wireless clients.

The primary tool to subnet is the existing subnet mask. Write it out in binary. Place a line at the end of the ones as shown in Figure 7.23.

Now draw a second line one digit to the right, as shown in Figure 7.24. You've now separated the subnet mask into three areas that I call (from left to right) the subnet mask (SM), the network ID extension (NE), and the hosts (H). These are not industry terms so you won't see them on the CompTIA Network+ exam, but they're a handy Mike Trick that makes the process of subnetting a lot easier.

You now have a /25 subnet mask. At this point, most people first learning how to subnet start to freak out. They're challenged by the idea that a subnet mask of /25 isn't going to fit into one of the three pretty subnets of 255.0.0.0, 255.255.0.0, or 255.255.255.0. They think, "That can't be right! Subnet masks are made out of only 255s and 0s." That's not correct. A subnet mask is a string of ones followed by a string of zeroes. People only convert it into dotted decimal to enter things into computers. So convert /25 into dotted decimal. First write out 25 ones, followed by seven zeroes. (Remember, subnet masks are *always* 32 binary digits long.)

11111111111111111111111110000000

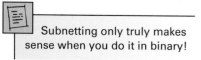

Subnet mask |||||||||||||||||||||||||00000000

• **Figure 7.23**   Step 1 in subnetting

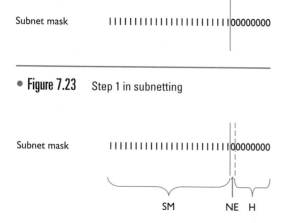

Subnet mask |||||||||||||||||||||||||00000000

SM   NE H

• **Figure 7.24**   Organizing the subnet mask

> Subnetting only truly makes sense when you do it in binary!

Put the periods in between every eight digits:

```
11111111.11111111.11111111.10000000
```

Then convert them to dotted decimal:

```
255.255.255.128
```

Get used to the idea of subnet masks that use more than 255s and 0s. Here are some examples of perfectly legitimate subnet masks. Try converting these to binary to see for yourself.

```
255.255.255.224
255.255.128.0
255.248.0.0
```

Calculating Subnets

When you subnet a network ID, you need to follow the rules and conventions dictated by the good folks who developed TCP/IP to ensure that your new subnets can interact properly with each other and with larger networks. The rules to subnetting are as follows:

1. Starting with a beginning subnet mask, you extend the subnet extension until you have the number of subnets you need.

2. You cannot have an NE of all zeroes or all ones, so you calculate the number of subnets using this formula: new subnets = $2^{\text{(number of network ID extension digits)}} - 2$.

Rule number two can trip up folks new to subnetting, because it seems arbitrary, but it's not. What defines the subnets of a network ID are the different combinations of binary numbers within the NE. All zeroes is by definition a network ID; all ones is used only for broadcasting, so that's not allowed either.

Let's practice this a few times. Figure 7.25 shows a starting subnet of 255.255.255.0. If we move the network ID extension over one, it's only a single digit.

That single digit is only a zero or a one, and you can't have only a zero or a one for a network ID extension! So let's add a third rule:

3. You cannot have a single-character network ID extension. You always start by moving the subnet at least two digits (Figure 7.26).

Back to the first subnet. Let's take /24 and subnet it down to /26. Extending the network ID by two digits creates four new network IDs (two of which you won't be able to use). To see each of these network IDs, first convert the original network ID—192.168.4.0—into binary. Then add the four different network ID extensions to the end, as shown in Figure 7.27.

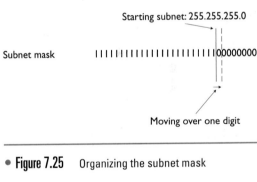

• **Figure 7.25** Organizing the subnet mask

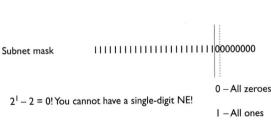

• **Figure 7.26** Single-digit network ID extensions are not allowed.

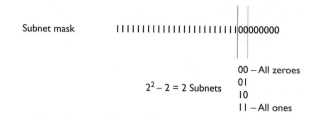

Subnet mask   I I I I I I I I I I I I I I I I I I I I I I I I I I | 00000000

$2^2 - 2 = 2$ Subnets

00 – All zeroes
01
10
11 – All ones

• **Figure 7.27**   Creating the new network IDs

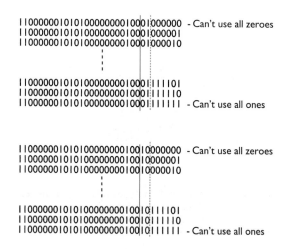

I I 0000000 I 0 I 0 I 0000000000 I 000 | 000000 - Can't use all zeroes
I I 0000000 I 0 I 0 I 0000000000 I 000 | 000001
I I 0000000 I 0 I 0 I 0000000000 I 000 | 000010

I I 0000000 I 0 I 0 I 0000000000 I 000 | I I I 101
I I 0000000 I 0 I 0 I 0000000000 I 000 | I I I 110
I I 0000000 I 0 I 0 I 0000000000 I 000 | I I I 111 - Can't use all ones

I I 0000000 I 0 I 0 I 0000000000 I 00 I | 0000000 - Can't use all zeroes
I I 0000000 I 0 I 0 I 0000000000 I 00 I | 0000001
I I 0000000 I 0 I 0 I 0000000000 I 00 I | 0000010

I I 0000000 I 0 I 0 I 0000000000 I 00 I | 0 I I I 101
I I 0000000 I 0 I 0 I 0000000000 I 00 I | 0 I I I 110
I I 0000000 I 0 I 0 I 0000000000 I 00 I | 0 I I I 111 - Can't use all ones

• **Figure 7.28**   New network ID address ranges

If wasting subnets seems contrary to the goal of efficient use, keep in mind that subnetting has two goals: efficiency and making multiple network IDs from a single network ID. This example is geared more toward the latter goal.

Since the network ID extension can't be all zeroes and all ones, you only get two new network IDs. Figure 7.28 shows all of the IP addresses for each of the two new network IDs.

Now convert these two network IDs back to dotted decimal:

192.168.4.64/26 (192.168.4.65 – 192.168.4.126)
192.168.4.128/26 (192.168.4.129 – 192.168.4.191)

Congratulations! You've just taken a single network ID, 192.168.4.0/24, and subnetted it into two new network IDs! Figure 7.29 shows how you can use these two network IDs in a network.

There's only one problem—the café needs three subnets, not just two! So let's first figure out how large of a network ID extension is needed:

■ Two NE digits = $2^2 - 2 = 2$ network IDs

■ Three NE digits = $2^3 - 2 = 6$ network IDs

Okay, you need to extend the NE three digits to get six network IDs. Because the café only needs three, three are wasted—welcome to subnetting.

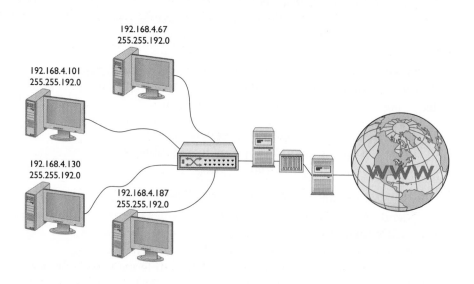

192.168.4.67
255.255.192.0

192.168.4.101
255.255.192.0

192.168.4.130
255.255.192.0

192.168.4.187
255.255.192.0

• **Figure 7.29**   Two networks using the two network IDs

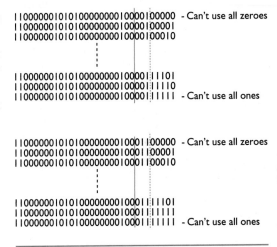

Subnet mask	IIIIIIIIIIIIIIIIIIIIIIIII00000000
192.168.4.0	II000000I0I0I000000000I0000000000
Add 000	II000000I0I0I000000000I0000000000
Add 001	II000000I0I0I000000000I0001000000
Add 010	II000000I0I0I000000000I0010000000
Add 011	II000000I0I0I000000000I0011000000
Add 100	II000000I0I0I000000000I0100000000
Add 101	II000000I0I0I000000000I0101000000
Add 110	II000000I0I0I000000000I0110000000
Add 111	II000000I0I0I000000000I0111000000

• **Figure 7.30**   Moving the network ID extension three digits

First, move the NE over three digits. This creates a /27 subnet for all the new network IDs (Figure 7.30).

To help you visualize the address range, I'll calculate the first two subnets—using 001 and 011 (Figure 7.31). Please do the other four for practice.

Note that in this case you only get $2^5 - 2 = 30$ hosts per network ID! These better be small networks!

Converting these to dotted decimal we get:

192.168.4.32/27 (192.168.4.33 – 192.168.4.62)
192.168.4.64/27 (192.168.4.65 – 192.168.4.94)
192.168.4.96/27 (192.168.4.97 – 192.168.4.126)
192.168.4.128/27 (192.168.4.129 – 192.168.4.158)
192.168.4.160/27 (192.168.4.161 – 192.168.4.190)
192.168.4.192/27 (192.168.4.193 – 192.168.4.222)

These two examples started with a Class C address. There's no reason not to start with any starting network ID. Nothing changes from the process you just learned.

Manual Dotted Decimal to Binary Conversion

The best way to convert from dotted decimal to binary and back is using a calculator. It's easy, fast, and accurate. There's always a chance, however, that you may find yourself in a situation where you need to convert without a calculator. Fortunately, manual conversion, while a bit tedious, is also fairly easy. The secret is to simply remember a single number: 128.

Take a piece of paper and write the number 128 in the top-left corner. Now, what is half of 128? That's right, 64. Write 64 next to 128. Now keep dividing the previous number in half until you get to the number one. The result will look like this:

```
128   64   32   16   8   4   2   1
```

Notice that you have eight numbers. Each of these numbers corresponds to a position of one of the eight binary digits. To convert an 8-bit value to dotted decimal, just take the binary value and put the numbers under the corresponding eight digits. Wherever there's a one, add that decimal value.

II000000I0I0I000000000I0000I00000 - Can't use all zeroes
II000000I0I0I000000000I0000I00001
II000000I0I0I000000000I0000I00010
⋮
II000000I0I0I000000000I0000I11101
II000000I0I0I000000000I0000I11110
II000000I0I0I000000000I0000I11111 - Can't use all ones

II000000I0I0I000000000I0001I00000 - Can't use all zeroes
II000000I0I0I000000000I0001I00001
II000000I0I0I000000000I0001I00010
⋮
II000000I0I0I000000000I0001I11101
II000000I0I0I000000000I0001I11111
II000000I0I0I000000000I0001I11111 - Can't use all ones

• **Figure 7.31**   Two of the six network ID address ranges

Tech Tip

ISPs and Classless Addresses
If you order real, unique, ready-for-the-Internet IP addresses from your local ISP, you'll invariably get a classless set of IP addresses. More importantly, when you order them for clients, you need to be able to explain why their subnet mask is 255.255.255.192, when all the books they read tell them it should be 255.255.255.0!

Let's take the binary value 10010110 into decimal. Write down the numbers as just shown, then write the binary values underneath each corresponding decimal number:

```
128    64    32    16    8    4    2    1
 1      0     0     1    0    1    1    0
```

Add the decimal values that have a 1 underneath:

128+16+4+2 = 150

Converting from decimal to binary is a bit more of a challenge. You still start with a line of decimal numbers starting with 128, but this time place the decimal value above. If the number you're trying to convert is greater than or equal to the number underneath, subtract it and place a 1 underneath that value. If not, then place a 0 underneath and move the number to the next position to the right. Let's give this a try by converting 221 to binary. Begin by placing 221 over the 128:

```
221
128    64    32    16    8    4    2    1
 93
  1
```

Now place the remainder, 93, over the 64:

```
        93
128     64    32    16    8    4    2    1
        29
 1       1
```

Place the remainder, 29, over the 32. The number 29 is less than 32, so place 0 underneath the 32 and move to 16:

```
                     29
128    64    32      16    8    4    2    1
                     13
 1      1     0       1
```

Then move to the 8:

```
                          13
128    64    32    16      8    4    2    1
                           5
 1      1     0     1      1
```

Then the 4:

```
                               5
128    64    32    16    8      4    2    1
                               1
 1      1     0     1    1      1
```

Then the 2. The number 1 is less than 2, so drop a 0 underneath and move to 1:

```
                                         1
128    64    32    16    8    4    2      1

 1      1     0     1    1    1    0      1
```

Finally, the 1; 1 is equal to 1, so put a 1 underneath and you're done. The number 221 in decimal is equal to 11011101 in binary.

Make sure you can manually convert decimal to binary, and binary to decimal.

CIDR: Subnetting in the Real World

I need to let you in on a secret—there's a better than average chance that you'll never have to do subnetting in the real world. That's not to say that subnetting isn't important. It's a critical part of the structure of the Internet. There are two situations in which subnetting most commonly takes place: ISPs who receive class licenses from IANA and then subnet those class licenses for customers, and very large customers who take subnets (sometimes already subnetted class licenses from ISPs) and make their own subnets. Even if you'll never make a working subnet in the real world, there are a number of reasons to learn subnetting.

First and most obvious, the CompTIA Network+ exam expects you to know subnetting. You need to take any existing network ID and break it down into a given number of subnets. You need to know how many hosts the resulting network IDs possess. You need to be able to calculate the IP addresses and the new subnet masks for each of the new network IDs.

Second, even if you never do your own subnetting, there's a pretty good chance that you'll contact an ISP and get CIDR addresses. You can't think about subnet masks in terms of dotted decimal. You need to think of subnets in terms of CIDR values like /8, /22, /26, and so on.

Third, there's a better than average chance you'll look to more advanced IT certifications. Most Cisco, many Microsoft, and a large number of other certifications assume you understand subnetting. It's a competency standard that everyone who's serious about networking understands in detail, a clear separation of those who know networks from those who do not.

You've done well, my little padawan. Subnetting takes a little getting used to. Go take a break. Take a walk outside. Play some World of Warcraft. (You can find me on Blackwater Raiders. My current favorite character is "Polope," undead.) Or fire up your Steam client and see if I'm playing Counter-Strike or Left4Dead (player name "desweds"). After a good mental break, dive back into subnetting and *practice*. Take any old network ID and practice making multiple subnets—lots of subnets!

■ Using IP Addresses

Whew! After all that subnetting, you've reached the point where it's time to start actually using some IP addresses. That is, after all, the goal of going through all that pain. There are two ways to give a computer an IP address, subnet mask, and default gateway: either by typing in all the information (called **static addressing**) or by having some server program running on a system that automatically passes out all the IP information to systems as they boot up on or connect to a network (called **dynamic addressing**). Additionally, you must learn about a number of specialty IP addresses that have unique meanings in the IP world to make this all work.

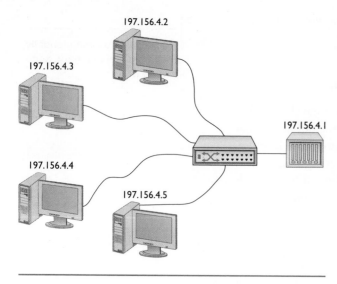

• Figure 7.32 A small network

Static IP Addressing

Static addressing means typing all of the IP information into each of your clients. But before you type in anything, you have to answer two questions: what are you typing in and where do you type it? Let's visualize a four-node network like the one shown in Figure 7.32.

To make this network function, each computer must have an IP address, a subnet mask, and a default gateway. First, decide what network ID to use. In the old days, you were given a block of IP addresses from your ISP to use. Assume that's still the method and you've been allocated a Class C license for 197.156.4/24.

The first rule of Internet addressing is . . . no one talks about Internet addressing. Actually we can maul the *Fight Club* reference and instead say, "The first rule of Internet addressing is that you can do whatever you want with your own network ID." There are no rules other than to make sure every computer gets a legit IP address and subnet mask for your network ID and make sure every IP address is unique. You don't have to use the numbers in order, you don't have to give the default gateway the 192.156.4.1 address—you can do it any way you want. That said, most networks follow a common set of principles:

1. Give the default gateway the first IP address in the network ID.

2. Try to use the IP addresses in some kind of sequential order.

3. Try to separate servers from clients. For example, servers could have the IP addresses 197.156.4.10 to 197.156.4.19, while the clients range from 197.156.4.200 to 197.156.4.254.

4. Write down whatever you choose to do so the person who comes after you understands.

These principles have become unofficial standards for network techs, and following them will make you very popular with whoever has to manage your network in the future.

Now you can give each of the computers an IP address, subnet mask, and default gateway.

Every operating system has some method for you to enter in the static IP information. In Windows, you use the Internet Protocol Version 4 (TCP/IPv4) Properties dialog box, as shown in Figure 7.33.

On a Macintosh OS X, run the Network utility in System Preferences to enter in the IP information (Figure 7.34).

The only universal tool for entering IP information on UNIX/Linux systems is the command-line IFCONFIG command, as shown in Figure 7.35. A warning about setting static IP addresses with IFCONFIG: any address entered will not be permanent and will be lost on reboot. To make the new IP permanent you need to find and edit your network configuration files. Fortunately, modern distributions (distros) make your life a bit easier. Almost every flavor of UNIX/Linux comes with some handy graphical program, such as Network Configuration in the popular Ubuntu Linux distro (Intrepid Ibex 8.10) (Figure 7.36).

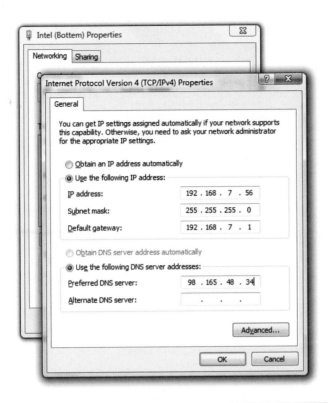

● **Figure 7.33**   Entering static IP information in Windows Internet Protocol Version 4 (TCP/IPv4) Properties

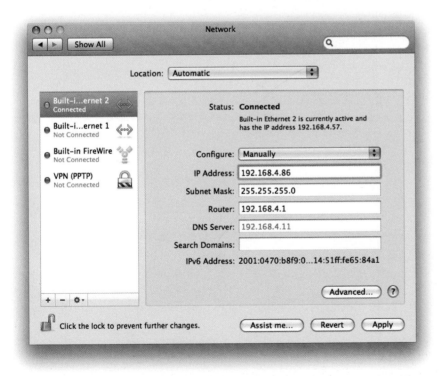

● **Figure 7.34**   Entering static IP information in the OS X Network utility

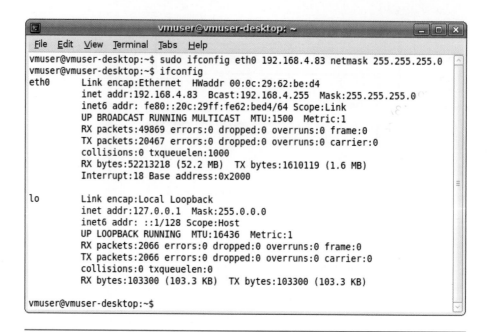

• Figure 7.35   IFCONFIG command to set static IP address

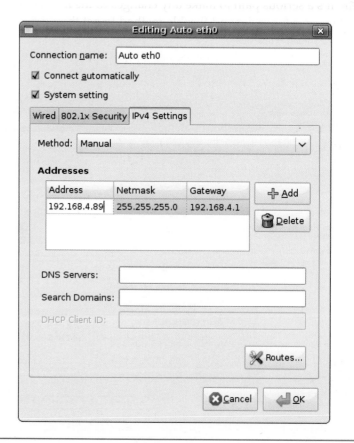

• Figure 7.36   Ubuntu's Network Configuration utility

Once you've added the IP information to at least two systems, you should always verify by using the PING command as shown in Figure 7.37. Always verify with PING—it's too easy to make a typo when you use static IP addresses.

If you set an IP address and your PING is not successful, first check your IP settings. Odds are good you made a typo. Otherwise, check your connections, driver, and so forth.

Static addressing has been around for a long time and is still heavily used for more critical systems on your network, but static addressing poses one big problem: it's a serious pain to make any changes to the network. Most systems today use a far easier and flexible method to get their IP information: dynamic IP addressing.

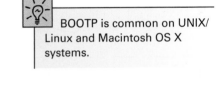

```
Administrator: C:\Windows\system32\cmd.exe

C:\>ping 192.168.4.83

Pinging 192.168.4.83 with 32 bytes of data:
Reply from 192.168.4.83: bytes=32 time=3ms TTL=64
Reply from 192.168.4.83: bytes=32 time<1ms TTL=64
Reply from 192.168.4.83: bytes=32 time<1ms TTL=64
Reply from 192.168.4.83: bytes=32 time<1ms TTL=64

Ping statistics for 192.168.4.83:
    Packets: Sent = 4, Received = 4, Lost = 0 (0% loss),
Approximate round trip times in milli-seconds:
    Minimum = 0ms, Maximum = 3ms, Average = 0ms

C:\>ping 192.168.4.83

Pinging 192.168.4.83 with 32 bytes of data:
Request timed out.
Request timed out.
Request timed out.
Reply from 192.168.4.49: Destination host unreachable.

Ping statistics for 192.168.4.83:
    Packets: Sent = 4, Received = 1, Lost = 3 (75% loss),

C:\>
```

● **Figure 7.37**   Two PINGs (successful PING on top, unsuccessful PING on bottom)

> BOOTP is common on UNIX/Linux and Macintosh OS X systems.

Dynamic IP Addressing

Dynamic IP addressing, better known as **Dynamic Host Configuration Protocol (DHCP)** or the older (and much less popular) **Bootstrap Protocol (BOOTP)**, automatically assigns an IP address whenever a computer connects to the network. DHCP (and BOOTP, but for simplicity I'll just say DHCP) works in a very simple process. First, a computer is configured to use DHCP. Every OS has some method to tell the computer to use DHCP, like the Windows example shown in Figure 7.38.

How DHCP Works

Once a computer is configured to use DHCP, it's called a DHCP client. When a DHCP client boots up it automatically sends out a special DHCP discovery packet using the broadcast address. This DHCP discovery message asks: "Are there any DHCP servers out there?" (See Figure 7.39.)

For DHCP to work, there must be one system on the LAN running special DHCP server software. This server is designed to respond to DHCP discovery requests with a DHCP offer. The DHCP server is configured to pass out IP addresses from a range (called a DHCP scope), a subnet

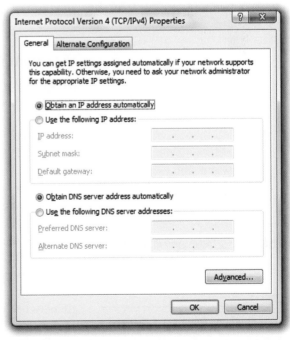

● **Figure 7.38**   Setting up for DHCP

• **Figure 7.39**   Computer sending out a DHCP discovery message

• **Figure 7.40**   DHCP server sending DHCP offer

mask, and a default gateway (Figure 7.40). It also passes out other information that we'll cover in later chapters.

At this point the DHCP client sends out a DHCP request—a poor name choice as it really is accepting the offer. The DHCP server then sends a DHCP acknowledge and lists the MAC address as well as the IP information given to the DHCP client in a database (Figure 7.41).

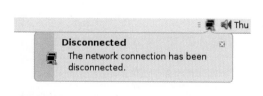

• **Figure 7.41**   DHCP request and DHCP acknowledge

The acceptance from the DHCP client of the DHCP server's data is called a **DHCP lease**. A DHCP lease is set for a fixed amount of time, usually 5 to 8 days. At the end of the lease time, the DHCP client simply makes another DHCP discovery message. The DHCP server looks at the MAC address information and, unless another computer has taken the lease, will always give the DHCP client the same IP information, including the same IP address.

Living with DHCP

DHCP is very convenient and, as such, very popular. So popular that it's very rare to see a user's computer on any network using static addressing.

It's important to know how to deal with the problems that arise with DHCP. The single biggest issue is when a DHCP client tries to get a DHCP address and fails. It's easy to tell when this happens because the operating system will post some form of error telling you there's a problem (Figure 7.42) and the DHCP client will have a rather strange address in the 169.254/16 network ID.

This special IP address is generated by **Automatic Private IP Addressing (APIPA)**. All DHCP clients are designed to generate an APIPA address automatically if there's no response to a DHCP discovery message. The client generates the last two octets of an APIPA address automatically. This will at least allow all the DHCP clients on a single network to continue to communicate with each other because they are on the same network ID. Unfortunately, there's no way for APIPA to give a default gateway, so you'll never get on the Internet using APIPA. That provides a huge clue to a DHCP problem: you can communicate with other computers on your network, but you can't get out to the Internet.

• **Figure 7.42**   DHCP error in Ubuntu Linux

Systems that use static IP addressing can never have DHCP problems.

If you can't get out to the Internet, use whatever tool your OS provides to check your IP address. If it's an APIPA address, you instantly know you have a DHCP problem. First of all, try to reestablish the lease manually. Every OS has some way to do this. In Windows, you can type the following command:

```
ipconfig /renew
```

On a Macintosh, you can go to System Preferences and use the Network utility (Figure 7.43).

Sometimes you might find yourself in a situation where your computer gets confused and won't grab an IP address no matter what you try. In these cases you should first force the computer to release its lease. In Windows, get to a command prompt and type these two commands, each followed by pressing ENTER:

```
ipconfig /release
ipconfig /renew
```

In UNIX/Linux and even Macintosh you can use the IFCONFIG command to release and renew your DHCP address. Here's the syntax to release:

```
sudo ifconfig eth0 down
```

And here is the syntax to renew:

```
sudo ifconfig eth0 up
```

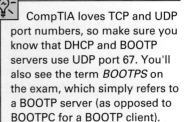

CompTIA loves TCP and UDP port numbers, so make sure you know that DHCP and BOOTP servers use UDP port 67. You'll also see the term *BOOTPS* on the exam, which simply refers to a BOOTP server (as opposed to BOOTPC for a BOOTP client).

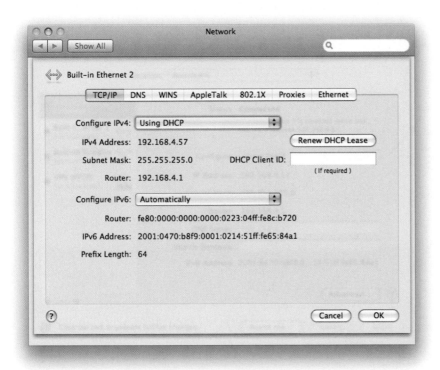

• **Figure 7.43**   Network utility in System Preferences

Tech Tip

Case Matters
With UNIX, Linux, and Macintosh OS X command-line commands, case matters. If you run sudo ifconfig eth0 *down all in lowercase, for example, your Ethernet connection will drop as the DHCP or BOOTP lease is released. If you try running the same command all in upper case, on the other hand, the Linux et al. command prompt will look at you quizzically and then snort with derision. "What's this* SUDO *of which you speak?" it would say. And then give you a prompt for a "real" command. Watch your case with UNIX/Linux/OS X!*

Make sure you know how to configure your computers to use static IP addressing and know that you use PING to ensure they communicate. For dynamic IP addressing, make sure you know it has two names: DHCP and BOOTP. Understand that each client must have some way to "turn on" DHCP. Also understand the concept of a DHCP client and a DHCP server. Last, be comfortable with APIPA and releasing and renewing a lease on a client.

Even though by convention we use 127.0.0.1 as the loopback address, the entire 127.0.0.0/8 subnet is reserved for loopback! You can use any address in the 127.0.0.0/8 subnet as a loopback address.

Make sure you can quickly tell the difference between a private and a public IP address for the CompTIA Network+ exam.

Depending on your distribution, you may not need to type `sudo` first, but you will need to have root privileges to use IFCONFIG. Root privileges are Linux's version of administrative privileges in Windows.

Special IP Addresses

The folks who invented TCP/IP created a number of special IP addresses you need to know about. The first special address is 127.0.0.1, the **loopback address**. When you tell a device to send data to 127.0.0.1, you're telling that device to send the packets to itself. The loopback address has a number of uses. One of the most common is to use it with the PING command. We use the command PING 127.0.0.1 to test a NIC's capability to send and receive packets.

Lots of folks use TCP/IP in networks that either aren't connected to the Internet or want to hide their computers from the rest of Internet. Certain groups of IP addresses, known as private IP addresses, are available to help in these situations. All routers destroy private IP addresses. Those addresses can never be used on the Internet, making them a handy way to hide systems. Anyone can use these private IP addresses, but they're useless for systems that need to access the Internet—unless you use the mysterious and powerful NAT, which we will discuss in the next chapter. (Bet you're dying to learn about NAT now!) For the moment, however, let's just look at the ranges of addresses that are designated private IP addresses:

- 10.0.0.0 through 10.255.255.255 (1 Class A license)
- 172.16.0.0 through 172.31.255.255 (16 Class B licenses)
- 192.168.0.0 through 192.168.255.255 (256 Class C licenses)

All other IP addresses are public IP addresses.

Chapter 7 Review

■ Chapter Summary

After reading this chapter and completing the exercises, you should understand the following about TCP/IP.

Describe how the Internet Protocol works

- While MAC addresses are physical addresses burned into hardware, IP addresses are logical and are assigned via software.

- An IP address consists of 32 binary digits, often written in dotted decimal notation to make it easier for humans to read.

- Every IP address must be unique on its network.

- The utilities IPCONFIG (Windows) and IFCONFIG (UNIX/Linux/Macintosh) can be used to view IP address information.

- Every IP address contains both a network ID and a host ID. Computers on the same network will have the same network ID portion of an IP address while the host ID portion will be unique.

- The IP address of a network's router is called the default gateway. The router uses an internal routing table and network IDs to determine where to send network packets.

- A subnet mask helps to define the network ID of an IP address. All computers on a specific network share the same subnet mask.

- An Address Resolution Protocol (ARP) broadcast is used to determine the MAC address of the destination computer based on its IP address.

- Subnet masks are often written with the IP address in slash notation, such as 201.23.45.123/24. In this example, the IP address is 201.23.45.123 and the subnet mask consists of 24 ones, or 11111111.11111111.11111111.00000000 (255.255.255.0).

- The Internet Assigned Numbers Authority (IANA) is the organization responsible for tracking and dispersing IP addresses to Internet service providers.

- A broadcast is sent to every computer on the network. A unicast is sent from one computer to one other computer. A multicast is sent from one computer to multiple other computers.

Explain CIDR and subnetting

- Subnet masks enable network adapters to determine whether incoming packets are being sent to a local network address or a remote network.

- A subnet mask is similar in form to an IP address. Subnet masks consist of some number of ones, followed by zeroes, to make a total of 32 bits.

- Subnetting is done by organizations when they need to create subnetworks.

- Classless Inter-Domain Routing (CIDR) is when an ISP subnets a block of addresses and passes them out to smaller customers.

- Computers use subnet masks to distinguish (sub)network IDs from host IDs. Any number on the full IP address that corresponds to a 1 on the subnet mask is part of the network ID. Any uncovered (turned off or = "0") bits show the host ID of an IP address.

- IP addresses come in three basic classful address types: Class A, Class B, and Class C.

- The Class A range of addresses has its first octet anywhere from 1 through 126. The standard Class A subnet mask is 255.0.0.0.

- A Class B address has its first octet anywhere from 128 through 191. Class B subnets use mask 255.255.0.0.

- Class C addresses range from 192 through 223, with the standard Class C subnet mask set to 255.255.255.0.

- Classless subnets do away with neat subnet masks. These subnet masks employ other binary representations in the masking process. For example, 255.255.255.0 is a standard Class C subnet mask, allowing for one subnet of 254 systems. Contrast that example with using subnet mask 255.255.255.240, which would allow for 14 subnets with 14 systems each.

Describe the functions of static and dynamic IP addresses

- Static addressing requires the IP address, subnet mask, and default gateway to be entered manually.

- Dynamic addressing uses either Dynamic Host Configuration Protocol (DHCP) or Bootstrap Protocol (BOOTP) to automatically assign an IP address, subnet mask, and default gateway to a network client.

- A network client is assigned an IP address from a DHCP server by exchanging the following packets: DHCP Discovery, DHCP Offer, DHCP Request, and DHCP Acknowledge.

- The data accepted by the DHCP client is called the DHCP lease, which is good for a fixed period of time. The time varies based on how the DHCP server was configured.

- A DHCP client that fails to acquire a DHCP lease from a DHCP server self-generates an IP address and subnet mask via Automatic Private IP Addressing (APIPA).

- The 127.0.0.1 loopback address used in testing is a reserved IP address.

- Private IP addresses include the following ranges: 10.0.0.0–10.255.255.255 (Class A), 172.16.0.0–172.31.255.255 (Class B), and 192.168.0.0–192.168.255.255 (Class C).

■ Key Terms

Address Resolution Protocol (ARP) *(147)*
Automatic Private IP Addressing (APIPA) *(162)*
Bootstrap Protocol (BOOTP) *(161)*
class license *(149)*
Classless Inter-Domain Routing (CIDR) *(150)*
default gateway *(144)*
DHCP lease *(162)*
dotted decimal notation *(140)*
dynamic addressing *(157)*
Dynamic Host Configuration Protocol (DHCP) *(161)*
host ID *(143)*
IFCONFIG *(143)*
Internet Assigned Numbers Authority (IANA) *(149)*

Internet Protocol version 4 (IPv4) *(137)*
IP addressing *(138)*
IPCONFIG *(142)*
loopback address *(164)*
multicast *(150)*
network ID *(143)*
protocol *(137)*
protocol suite *(137)*
routing table *(144)*
static addressing *(157)*
subnet mask *(146)*
subnetting *(150)*
unicast *(150)*

■ Key Term Quiz

Use the Key Terms list to complete the sentences that follow. Not all terms will be used.

1. The _____ portion of an IP address resembles 150.0.0.0.

2. The _____ portion of an IP address consists of from one to three octets, with the final octet between 1 and 254.

3. The single organization that distributes IP addresses is called the _____.

4. The IP address 10.11.12.13 is a valid _____ address.

5. The command _____ is a program that comes with Microsoft Windows to show TCP/IP settings.

6. The command _____ is a program for UNIX/Linux/Macintosh used to show TCP/IP settings.

7. The _____ protocol is used to translate MAC addresses to IP addresses.

8. Computers set for dynamic addressing that cannot locate a DHCP server use _____ to assign themselves an IP address.

9. The _____ is the IP address of the router.

10. The _____ is a 32-bit binary number common to all computers on a network used to determine to which network a computer belongs.

1. What is the result of converting 11110000.10111001.00001000.01100111 to dotted decimal notation?

    A. 4.5.1.5
    B. 240.185.8.103
    C. 15.157.16.230
    D. 103.8.185.240

2. What does IANA stand for?

    A. International Association Numbers Authority
    B. International Association Numbering Authority
    C. Internet Assigned Numbering Authority
    D. Internet Assigned Numbers Authority

3. Which of the following describe IPv4? (Select three.)

    A. Uses decimal, not hexadecimal numbers
    B. Uses periods, not colons, as separators
    C. Uses four octets
    D. Uses eight sets of characters

4. What is the result of converting 192.168.0.1 to binary?

    A. 11000000.10101000.00000000.00000001
    B. 11000000.10101000.00000000.10000000
    C. 11000000.10101000.00000000.1
    D. 11.10101.0.1

5. Which of the following are not valid IP addresses to assign to a Windows-based system? (Select two.)

    A. 1.1.1.1/24
    B. 127.0.0.1/24
    C. 250.250.250.255/24
    D. 192.168.0.1/24

6. Which of the following is a valid Class A IP address?

    A. 22.33.44.55
    B. 127.0.0.1
    C. 250.250.250.250
    D. 192.168.0.1

7. Which of the following is a valid Class B IP address?

    A. 10.10.10.253
    B. 191.254.254.254
    C. 192.168.1.1
    D. 223.250.250.1

8. Which of the following is a valid Class C IP address?

    A. 50.50.50.50
    B. 100.100.100.100
    C. 192.168.0.254
    D. 250.250.250.250

9. Which method sends a packet from a single computer to a group of interested computers?

    A. Broadcast
    B. Unicast
    C. Multicast
    D. Omnicast

10. What is the process used to take a single class of IP addresses and chop it up into multiple smaller groups? (Select two.)

    A. CIDR
    B. PING
    C. Subnetting
    D. Subnitting

11. Which statements about subnet masks are true? (Select two.)

    A. Every network client has a unique subnet mask.
    B. Every client on a network shares the same subnet mask.
    C. A subnet mask consists of a string of zeroes followed by a string of ones.
    D. A subnet mask consists of a string of ones followed by a string of zeroes.

12. In which order are packets created and sent when a client requests an IP address from a DHCP server?

    A. DHCP discovery, DHCP offer, DHCP request, DHCP acknowledge
    B. DHCP discovery, DHCP request, DHCP offer, DHCP acknowledge

C. DHCP request, DHCP offer, DHCP discovery, DHCP acknowledge

D. DHCP request, DHCP offer, DHCP acknowledge, DHCP discovery

13. Which of the following is *not* a valid classful subnet mask?

A. 255.0.0.0

B. 255.255.0.0

C. 255.255.255.0

D. 255.255.255.255

14. Which of the following is a valid classless subnet mask?

A. 255.255.255.240

B. 255.0.0.0

C. 255.255.0.0

D. 255.255.255.0

15. Which of the following IP addresses indicates a computer configured for dynamic addressing was unable to locate a DHCP server?

A. 255.255.255.255

B. 192.168.1.1

C. 127.0.0.1

D. 169.254.1.30

■ Essay Quiz

1. Use your Web browser to go to the www.webopedia.com Web site. Search for the full term TCP/IP. Write down its definition on a piece of paper, being sure to cite the exact Web site link to give credit to where you obtained the information.

2. You and a classmate are trying to calculate the number of possible IPv4 addresses versus IPv6 addresses. (The TCP/IP powers that be created the IPv6 addressing system to replace the IPv4 system discussed in this chapter. Because I feel IPv6 is going to be extremely important for all techs to understand in the future, this book

devotes a full chapter to the subject—Chapter 13, "IPv6.") Research the Internet to discover exactly how many addresses are available for each of these numbering schemes. Document your findings in a short essay.

3. A new intern is confused about the CIDR notation for subnets, such as 192.168.1/24. In your own words, explain to him why the part in front of the slash represents only three of the four octets in an IP address and what the number after the slash is.

Lab Projects

• Lab Project 7.1

Use the Internet to research the components of what an individual TCP packet and an IP packet might look like. You can search on keywords "sample," "TCP," "IP," "session," and "packet." Create a reference document that has links to five sites with

appropriate information. Save the document, so that the links contain hyperlinks that can be clicked on. Then write an additional paragraph describing your overall findings. Print one copy as well.

• Lab Project 7.2

Starting with the IP address 192.42.53.12, create a list of IP address ranges for six subnets.

• Lab Project 7.3

Log in to any available networked Windows 2000 or Windows XP computer. Click Start | Run, and type **cmd** to open a command prompt; from the command prompt, type **ipconfig /all**, and then press ENTER. Fill in as much information as you can from your screen onto a sheet like the following (or create one as directed by your instructor):

Host Name:	
Primary DNS Suffix:	
Node Type:	
IP Routing Enabled:	
WINS Proxy Enabled:	
DNS Suffix Search List:	
Connection-specific DNS Suffix:	
Description:	
Physical Address:	
DHCP Enabled:	
Autoconfiguration Enabled:	
IP Address:	
Subnet Mask:	
Default Gateway:	
DHCP Server:	
DNS Servers:	
Primary WINS Server:	
Lease Obtained:	
Lease Expires:	

The Wonderful World of Routing

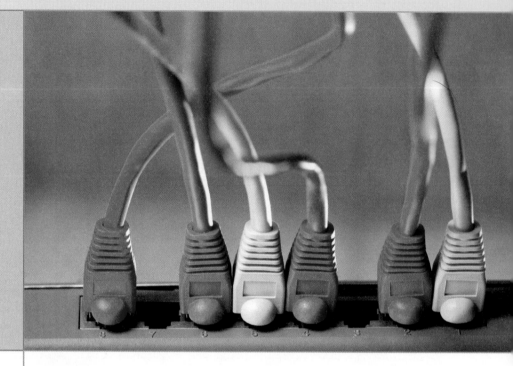

In this chapter, you will learn how to

- **Explain how routers work**
- **Describe dynamic routing technologies**
- **Install and configure a router successfully**

The true beauty, the amazing power of TCP/IP lies in one word: routing. Routing enables us to interconnect individual LANs into WANs. Routers, those magic boxes that act as the interconnection points, have all the built-in smarts to inspect incoming packets and forward them toward their eventual LAN destination. Routers are for the most part automatic. They require very little in terms of maintenance once their initial configuration is complete because of their capability to talk to each other to determine the best way to send IP packets. The goal of this chapter is to take you into the world of routers and show you exactly how they do this.

The chapter discusses how routers work, including an in-depth look at different types of Network Address Translation (NAT), and then dives into an examination of various dynamic routing protocols. You'll learn about distance vector protocols, Routing Information Protocol (RIP), and Border Gateway Protocol (BGP), among others. The chapter finishes with the nitty-gritty of installing and configuring a router successfully. Not only will you understand how routers work, you should be able to set up a basic home router and diagnose common router issues by the end of this chapter.

How Routers Work

A **router** is any piece of hardware or software that forwards packets based on their destination IP address. Routers work, therefore, at Layer 3, the Network layer.

Classically, routers are dedicated boxes that contain at least two connections, although many routers contain many more connections. In a larger business setting, for example, you might see a Cisco 2600 Series device, one of the most popular routers ever made. The 2611 router shown in Figure 8.1 has two connec-

● **Figure 8.1**   Cisco 2611 router

tions (the other connections are used for maintenance and configuration). The two "working" connections are circled. One port leads to one network; the other to another network. The router reads the IP addresses of the packets to determine where to send the packets. (More on how that works in a moment.)

Most techs today get their first exposure to routers with the ubiquitous home routers that enable your PC to connect to a DSL receiver or cable modem (Figure 8.2). The typical home router is more than it appears at first glance, usually combining into that one box a router, a switch, and other features as well, such as a firewall to help protect your network from unwanted intrusion.

● **Figure 8.2**   Business end of a typical home router

Figure 8.3 shows the electronic diagram for a two-port Cisco router, whereas Figure 8.4 shows the diagram for a Linksys home router. Note that both boxes connect two networks. The big difference is that the LAN side of the Linksys home router connects immediately to the built-in switch. That's convenient! You don't have to buy a separate switch to connect multiple computers to the cable modem or DSL receiver. Many new techs look at that router, though, and say "it has five ports," when in reality it can only connect two networks. The extra physical ports belong to the built-in switch.

> See Chapter 17, "Protecting Your Network," for an in-depth look at firewalls and other security options.

All routers, big and small, plain or bundled with a switch, examine packets and then send the packets to the proper destination. Let's take a look at that process in more detail now.

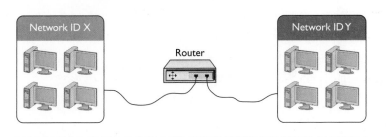

● **Figure 8.3**   Cisco router diagram

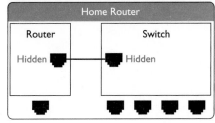

● **Figure 8.4**   Linksys home router diagram

Test Specific

Routing Tables

Routing begins as packets come into the router for handling (Figure 8.5). The router immediately strips off any of the Layer 2 information and drops the resulting IP packet into a queue (Figure 8.6). The important point to make here is that the router doesn't care where the packet came *from*. Everything is dropped into the same queue based on the time it arrived.

The router inspects each packet's destination IP address and then sends the IP packet out the correct port. Each router comes with a **routing table** that tells the router exactly where to send the packets. Figure 8.7 shows the routing table for a typical home router. This router has only two ports internally: one that connects to whichever service provider you use to bring the Internet into your home (cable/DSL/fiber or whatever)—labeled as Interface WAN in the table—and another one that connects to a built-in four-port switch—labeled LAN in the table. Figure 8.8 is a diagram for the router. The routing table is the key to the process of forwarding packets to their proper destination.

• **Figure 8.5**   Incoming packets

• **Figure 8.6**   All incoming packets stripped of Layer 2 data and dropped into a common queue

Cross Check

What's Up with Layer 2?

You first read about routers roughing up packets and relieving them of all their Layer 2 change way back in Chapter 2, "Building a Network with the OSI Model," so check your memory now. What defines the Layer 2 information? How is it assigned? How does it interact with Layer 1?

Each row in the routing table defines a single route. Each column identifies specific criteria. Reading Figure 8.7 from left to right shows the following:

■ **Destination LAN IP** A defined network ID. Every network ID directly connected to one of the router's ports is always listed here.

■ **Subnet Mask** To define a network ID, you need a subnet mask (described in Chapter 7).

Your router uses the combination of the destination LAN IP and subnet mask to see if a packet matches that route. For example, if you had a packet with the destination 10.12.14.26 coming into the router, the router would check the network ID and subnet mask. It would quickly determine that the packet matches the first route shown in Figure 8.7. The other two columns in the routing table then tell the router what to do with the packet.

■ **Gateway** The IP address for the **next hop** router; in other words, where the packet should go. If the outgoing packet is for a network ID that's not directly connected to the router, the Gateway column tells the router the IP address of a router to which to send this packet. That router then handles the packet and your router is done (you count on well-configured routers to make sure your packet will get to where it needs to go!). If the network ID is directly connected, then you don't need a gateway. So this is set to 0.0.0.0 or to the IP address of the directly connected port.

■ **Interface** Tells the router which of its ports to use. On this router it uses the terms "LAN" and "WAN." Other routing tables will use the port's IP address or some other type of abbreviation.

The router compares the destination IP address on a packet to every listing in the routing table and then sends the packet out. There is no top-down or bottom-up to this comparison process; every line is read and then the router decides what to do. The most important trick to reading a routing table is to remember that a zero (0) means "anything." For example, in Figure 8.7 the first route's destination LAN IP is 10.12.14.0. You can compare that to the subnet mask (255.255.255.0) to confirm that this is a /24 network.

Routing Table Entry List Refresh

Destination LAN IP	Subnet Mask	Gateway	Interface
10.12.14.0	255.255.255.0	0.0.0.0	LAN
76.30.4.0	255.255.254.0	0.0.0.0	WAN
0.0.0.0	0.0.0.0	76.30.4.1	WAN

Close

• **Figure 8.7**   Routing table from a home router

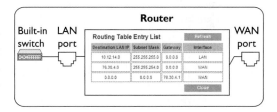

• **Figure 8.8**   Electronic diagram of the router

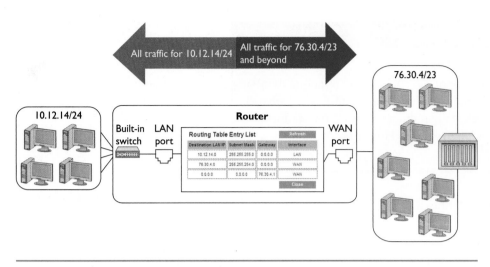

This tells you that any value (between 1 and 254) is acceptable for the last value in the 10.12.14/24 network ID.

Routing tables tell you a lot about how the network connects. From just this single routing table, for example, the diagram in Figure 8.9 can be drawn.

So how do I know the 76.30.4.1 port connects to another network? The third line of the routing table shows the default route for this router, and every router has one. (There's one exception to this. See the Tech Tip "Top o' the Internet.") This line says (Any destination address) (with any subnet mask) (forward it to 76.30.4.1) (using my WAN port).

● **Figure 8.9**　The network based on the routing table

Tech Tip

Top o' the Internet

There are two places where you'll find routers that do not have default routes: private (as in not on the Internet) networks where every router knows every other router, and the monstrous "Tier One" backbone, where you'll find routers that make the main connections of the Internet. Every other router has a default route.

```
Destination LAN IP    Subnet Mask        Gateway        Interface
0.0.0.0               0.0.0.0            76.30.4.1         WAN
```

The default route is very important because this tells the router exactly what to do with every incoming packet *unless* another line in the routing table gives another route. Excellent! Interpret the other two lines of the routing table in Figure 8.7 in the same fashion: (Any packet for the 10.12.14.0) (/24 network ID) (don't use a gateway) (just ARP on the LAN interface to get the MAC address and send it directly to the recipient).

```
Destination LAN IP    Subnet Mask        Gateway        Interface
10.12.14.0            255.255.255.0      0.0.0.0           LAN
```

(Any packet for the 76.30.4.0) (/23 network ID) (don't use a gateway) (just ARP on the WAN interface to get the MAC address and send it directly to the recipient).

```
Destination LAN IP    Subnet Mask        Gateway        Interface
76.30.4.0            255.255.254.0       0.0.0.0           WAN
```

I'll let you in on a little secret. Routers aren't the only devices that use routing tables. In fact, every node (computer, printer, TCP/IP-capable soda dispenser, whatever) on the network also has a routing table.

At first this may seem silly—doesn't every computer only have a single Ethernet connection and therefore all data traffic has to go out that port? First of all, many computers have more than one NIC. (These are called multihomed computers. See the Tech Tip "Multihoming" for more details.) But even if your computer has only a single NIC, how does it know what to do with an IP address like 127.0.01? Secondly, every packet sent out of your computer uses the routing table to figure out where the packet should go, whether directly to a computer or to your gateway. Here's an example of a routing table in Windows. This machine connects to the home router described earlier, so you'll recognize the IP addresses it uses.

```
C:\>route print
===========================================================================
Interface List
0x1 ......................... MS TCP Loopback interface
0x2 ...00 11 d8 30 16 c0 ...... NVIDIA nForce Networking Controller
===========================================================================
===========================================================================
Active Routes:
Network Destination        Netmask          Gateway       Interface  Metric
        0.0.0.0          0.0.0.0      10.12.14.1    10.12.14.201      1
     10.12.14.0    255.255.255.0   10.12.14.201    10.12.14.201      1
   10.12.14.201  255.255.255.255      127.0.0.1       127.0.0.1      1

      127.0.0.0        255.0.0.0      127.0.0.1       127.0.0.1      1
    169.254.0.0      255.255.0.0   10.12.14.201    10.12.14.201     20
      224.0.0.0        240.0.0.0   10.12.14.201    10.12.14.201      1
255.255.255.255  255.255.255.255   10.12.14.201    10.12.14.201      1
Default Gateway:       10.12.14.1
===========================================================================
Persistent Routes:
  None
C:\>
```

Unlike the routing table for the typical home router you saw in Figure 8.7, this one seems a bit more complicated, if for no other reason than it has a lot more routes. My PC has only a single NIC, though, so it's not quite as complicated as it might seem at first glance. Take a look at the details. First note that my computer has an IP address of 10.12.14.201, /24 subnet, and 10.12.14.1 as the default gateway.

You should note two differences in the columns from what you saw in the previous routing table. First, the interface has an actual IP address—10.12.14.201, plus the loopback of 127.0.0.1—instead of the word "LAN." Second—and this is part of the magic of routing—is something called the metric.

A **metric** is just a relative value that defines the "cost" of using this route. The power of TCP/IP is that a packet can take more than one route to get to the same place. Figure 8.10 shows a networked router with two routes to the same place. The router has a route to network X with a metric of 1 using router X, and a second route to network X using router Y with a metric of 10.

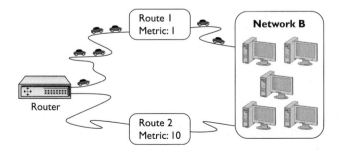

• **Figure 8.10** Two routes to the same network

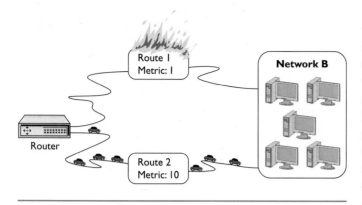

• **Figure 8.11** When a route no longer works, the router automatically switches.

Lowest routes always win. In this case the router will always use the route with the metric of 1, unless that route suddenly stopped working. In that case, the router would automatically switch to the route with the 10 metric (Figure 8.11). This is the cornerstone of how the Internet works! The entire Internet is nothing more than a whole bunch of big, powerful routers connected to lots of other big, powerful routers. Connections go up and down all the time and routers (with multiple routes) constantly talk to each other, detecting when a connection goes down and automatically switching to alternate routes.

I'll go through this routing table one line at a time. Remember, every address is compared to every line in the routing table before it goes out, so it's no big deal if the default route is at the beginning or the end.

This line defines the default route. (Any destination address) (with any subnet mask) (forward it to my default gateway) (using my NIC) (Cost of 1 to use this route).

```
Network Destination      Netmask        Gateway       Interface      Metric
        0.0.0.0          0.0.0.0       10.12.14.1    10.12.14.201        1
```

The next line defines the local connection. (Any packet for the 10.12.14.0) (/24 network ID) (don't use a gateway) (just ARP on the LAN interface to get the MAC address and send it directly to the recipient) (Cost of 1 to use this route).

```
Network Destination      Netmask        Gateway       Interface      Metric
       10.12.14.0    255.255.255.0    10.12.14.201   10.12.14.201        1
```

So, if a gateway of 10.12.14.201 here means "don't use a gateway," why put a number in here at all? Local connections don't use a default gateway, though every routing table has a gateway column. The Microsoft folks had to put *something* there, thus they put the IP address of the NIC. That's why the gateway address is the same as the interface address. Personally, I've always found this confusing. Wouldn't calling the gateway 0.0.0.0, as you saw in the previous routing table, make more sense? Better yet, wouldn't it be even better if we just said, "This is a local call so no gateway is needed"? Well, this is Windows XP. In Windows Vista the gateway value for local connections just says "on-link"—a much more accurate description! Part of the joy of learning routing tables is getting used to how different operating systems deal with issues like these.

Okay, on to the third line. This one's easy. Anything addressed to this machine should go right back to it through the loopback (127.0.0.1).

```
Network Destination      Netmask        Gateway       Interface      Metric
     10.12.14.201    255.255.255.255   127.0.0.1     127.0.0.1          1
```

This next line is another loopback, but look carefully. Earlier you learned that only 127.0.0.1 is the loopback, but according to this route, any 127/8 address is the loopback.

Network Destination	Netmask	Gateway	Interface	Metric
127.0.0.0	255.0.0.0	127.0.0.1	127.0.0.1	1

The next route says that any addresses in the 169.254/16 network ID are part of the LAN (remember, whenever the gateway and interface are the same it's a local connection). If your computer uses Dynamic Host Configuration Protocol (DHCP) and can't get an

Try This!

Getting Looped

Try pinging any 127/8 address to see if they loop back like 127.0.0.1. What happens?

IP address, this route would enable you to communicate with other computers on the network who hopefully are also having the same DHCP problem. Note the high metric.

Network Destination	Netmask	Gateway	Interface	Metric
169.254.0.0	255.255.0.0	10.12.14.201	10.12.14.201	20

This is the multicast address range. Odds are good you'll never need it, but most operating systems put it in automatically.

Network Destination	Netmask	Gateway	Interface	Metric
224.0.0.0	240.0.0.0	10.12.14.201	10.12.14.201	1

This line defines the default IP broadcast. If you send out an IP broadcast (255.255.255.255), your NIC knows to send it out to the local network.

Network Destination	Netmask	Gateway	Interface	Metric
255.255.255.255	255.255.255.255	10.12.14.201	10.12.14.201	1

Freedom from Layer 2

Routers enable you to connect different types of network technologies. You now know that routers strip off all of the Layer 2 data from the incoming packets, but thus far you've only seen routers that connect to different Ethernet networks—and that's just fine with routers. But routers can connect almost anything that stores IP packets. Not to take away from some very exciting upcoming chapters, but Ethernet is not the only networking technology out there. Once you want to start making long-distance connections, Ethernet disappears and technologies with names like Data Over Cable Service Interface Specification (DOCSIS) (cable modems), Frame Relay, and Asynchronous Transfer Mode (ATM) take over. These technologies are not Ethernet. Their frames don't use MAC addresses, although just like Ethernet frames they do store IP packets.

Most serious (that is, not home) routers enable you to add ports. You buy the router and then you snap in different types of ports depending on your needs. Note the Cisco router in Figure 8.12. Like most Cisco routers, it comes with removable modules. If you're connecting Ethernet to ATM, you buy an Ethernet module and an ATM module. If you're connecting Ethernet to a DOCSIS (cable) network, you buy an Ethernet module and a DOCSIS module.

• **Figure 8.12**   Modular Cisco router

Network Address Translation

The ease of connecting computers together using TCP/IP and routers creates a rather glaring security risk. If every computer on a network must have an unique IP address and TCP/IP applications enable you to do something on a remote computer, what's to stop a malicious programmer from writing a program that does things on your computer that you don't want done? All he'd need is the IP address for your computer and he could target you from anywhere on the network. Now expand this concept to the Internet. A computer sitting in Peoria can be attacked by a program run from Bangkok as long as both computers connect directly to the Internet. And this happens all the time.

Security is one problem; two other problems are the finite number of IP addresses available and their cost. IP addresses, once thought limitless, are quickly running out. Most of the available IP numbers have already been allocated, making public IP addresses more and more rare. Anything that's rare costs more money. Legitimate, public IP addresses are therefore more expensive to come by. Wouldn't it be great to lease only one public IP address instead of tens or even hundreds for every computer on your network?

Routers running some form of **Network Address Translation (NAT)** hide the IP addresses of computers on the LAN, but still enable those computers to communicate with the broader Internet. NAT addresses the problems of IP addressing on the Internet. NAT has become extremely common and is heavily in use, so it's important to learn how it works. Note that many routers offer NAT as a feature *in addition to* the core capability of routing. NAT is not routing, but a separate technology. With that said, you are ready to dive into how NAT works to protect computers connected by router technology and conserve IP addresses as well.

The Setup

Here's the situation. You have a LAN with eight computers that need access to the Internet. With classic TCP/IP and routing, several things have to happen. First, you would need to get a block of legitimate, unique, expensive IP addresses from an Internet service provider (ISP). You could call up an ISP and purchase a network ID, say 1.2.3.136/29. Second, you would assign an IP address to each computer and to the LAN connection on the router. Third, you'd assign the IP address for the ISP's router to the WAN connection on the local router, such as 1.2.4.1. After everything was configured, the network would look like Figure 8.13. All of the clients on the network have the same default gateway (1.2.3.137). This router, called a **gateway router** (or simply a *gateway*), acts as the default gateway for a number of client computers.

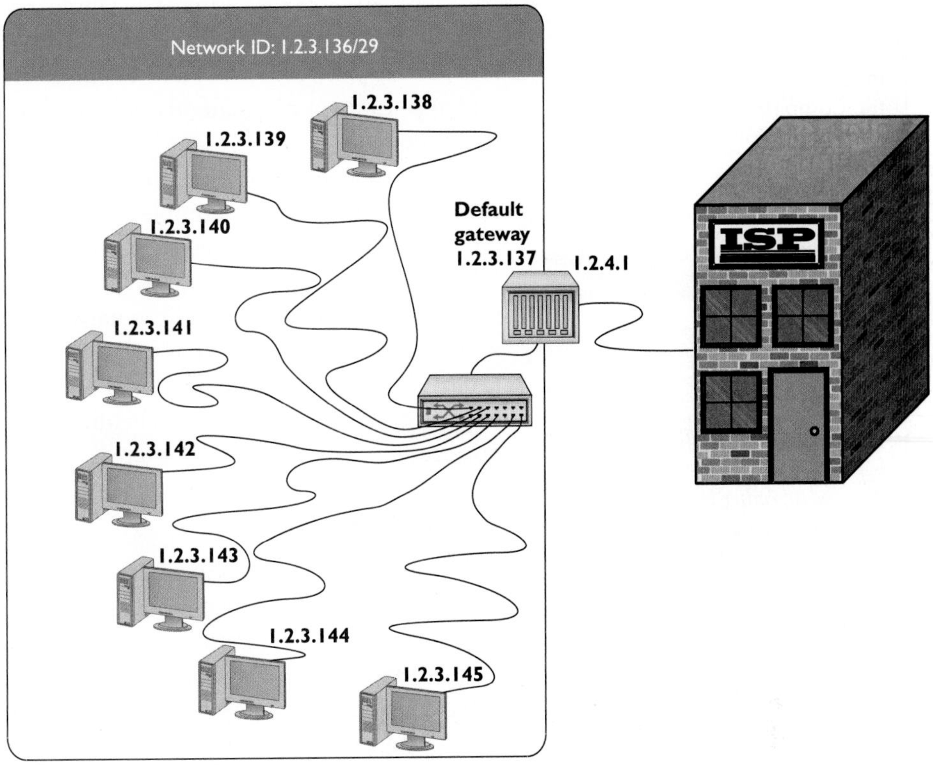

This style of network mirrors how computers in LANs throughout the world connected to the Internet for the first 20 years of the Internet, but the three major problems of security, running out of IP addresses, and the expense of leasing more than one address worsened as more and more computers connected.

• **Figure 8.13**   Network setup

NAT solves all these issues. NAT is a simple concept: you replace the source IP address of a computer with the source IP address from the router on outgoing packets. More complex NAT methods use TCP/IP port numbers to increase the number of computers using a single routable IP address.

> NAT replaces the source IP address of a computer with the source IP address from the router on outgoing packets. NAT is performed by NAT-capable routers.

Translating IP Addresses

With basic NAT, you tell your NAT-capable router to replace the source IP address of a computer with the source IP address from the router on outgoing packets. The outside world never sees the IP addresses used by the internal network, which enables you to use any network ID you wish for the internal network. In most cases, you use a private IP address range, such as 192.168.1.0/24.

The traditional IP address–translating NAT comes in a variety of flavors, with names like Source NAT, Destination NAT, Static NAT, and Dynamic NAT. Not surprisingly, these names get shortened to acronyms that add to the confusion: SNAT, DNAT, SNAT, and DNAT. Ugh! Here's the scoop.

With **Source NAT** and **Destination NAT**, the source or destination IP addresses, respectively, get translated by the NAT-capable router. Many NAT-capable routers can do both.

Static NAT (SNAT) maps a single routable (that is, not private) IP address to a single machine, enabling you to access that machine from outside the network. The NAT keeps track of the IP address or addresses and applies them permanently on a one-to-one basis with computers on the network.

With **Dynamic NAT**, in contrast, many computers can share a pool of routable IP addresses that number fewer than the computers. The NAT might have 10 routable IP addresses, for example, to serve 40 computers on the LAN. LAN traffic uses the internal, private IP addresses. When a computer requests information beyond the network, the NAT doles out a routable IP address from its pool for that communication. Dynamic NAT is also called *Pooled NAT*. This works well enough—unless you're the unlucky 11th person to try to access the Internet from behind the company NAT—but has the obvious limitation of still needing many true, expensive, routable IP addresses.

Adding Ports to the Mix

Translating IP addresses in one or more of the ways just described makes NAT useful, but still doesn't quite solve the inherent problems with TCP/IP addressing. TCP/IP communication involves more than just IP addresses, though; using TCP/IP port numbers in conjunction with IP addresses solves the dual problems of security and limited IP addresses handily. Let's look at port numbers first, and then turn to the implementations of using ports with NAT with overloaded NAT and port forwarding.

A New Kind of Port   The term "port" has several meanings in the computer world. Commonly, "port" defines the connector socket on an Ethernet NIC, where you insert an RJ-45 jack. That's how I've used the term for the most part in this book. It's now time to see another use of the word "ports."

In TCP/IP, **ports** are 16-bit numbers between 0 and 65,535, assigned to a particular TCP/IP session. All TCP/IP packets (except for some really low-level maintenance packets) contain port numbers that the two communicating computers use to determine not only the kind of session—and thus what software protocol—to use to handle the data in the packet, but also how to get the packet or response back to the sending computer.

Each packet has two ports assigned, a destination port and an ephemeral port. The **destination port** is a fixed, predetermined number that defines the function or session type. Common TCP/IP session types use destination port numbers in the range 0–1023. The **ephemeral port** is an arbitrary number generated by the sending computer; the receiving computer uses the ephemeral port as a destination address so that the sending computer knows which application to use for the returning packet. Ephemeral ports usually fall in the 1024–5000 range, but this varies slightly among the different operating systems.

Figure 8.14 shows two packets from a conversation between a Web client and a Web server. The top shows a TCP packet with the client requesting a Web page from the Web server. Note the destination port of 80 and the ephemeral port of 1024. The bottom packet shows the Web server starting to send back the Web page using port 1024 as the destination port and port 80 as the source port. Note that this is not called an ephemeral port for the return trip, because the server does not generate it. The server simply uses the ephemeral port given to it by the client system.

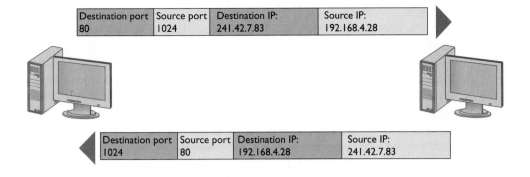

Destination port	Source port	Destination IP:	Source IP:
80	1024	241.42.7.83	192.168.4.28

Destination port	Source port	Destination IP:	Source IP:
1024	80	192.168.4.28	241.42.7.83

• **Figure 8.14**   Ports at work

You'll learn quite a bit more about ports in the next chapter, but you now know enough of the concept to go back to NAT and appreciate the importance of port numbers in this process.

NAT, Overloaded   In the most popular type of NAT, called **overloaded NAT**, a single public IP address is shared by a number of computers that, in most cases, share a private network ID. To set up a small, eight-port LAN connected to a router, like you did earlier, you'd use private IP addresses rather than public ones for each of the computers on the network. But you'd only need one public address, the one assigned to the router's Internet connection. Figure 8.15 changes Figure 8.13 slightly, this time using the network

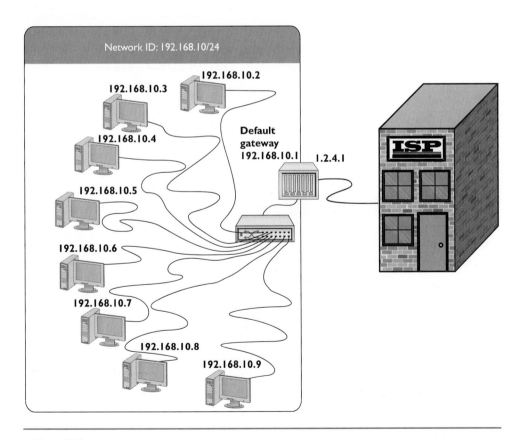

• **Figure 8.15**   Redone network IDs; nodes in the LAN use private IP addresses internally

ID range of 192.168.10/24 for the LAN. By noting the source ephemeral port of each computer making connections, the number of possible connections goes up tremendously.

Let's zero in on what happens inside the gateway router when a computer on the LAN needs information from beyond the LAN. This router has overloaded NAT capability enabled. One of the computers inside the network, 192.168.10.202, needs to send a packet to a faraway computer, 12.43.65.223. The 12.43.65.223 address is clearly not a part of the 192.168.10.0 network, so this packet will be going out the gateway and into the Internet.

As the outgoing IP packet enters the router, the router replaces the sending computer's source IP address with its own public IP address. It then adds the destination IP address and the source ephemeral port to a special database called the **NAT translation table** (Figure 8.16).

When the receiving system sends the packet back, it reverses the IP addresses and ports. The overloaded NAT router compares the incoming destination port and source IP address to the entry in the NAT translation table to determine which IP address to put back on the packet (Figure 8.17). It then sends the packet to the correct computer on the network.

Overloaded NAT takes care of all of the problems facing a network exposed to the Internet. You don't have to use legitimate Internet IP addresses on the LAN and the IP addresses of the computers behind the routers are invisible and protected from the outside world.

> Overloaded NAT is so common that the term NAT almost always means overloaded NAT.

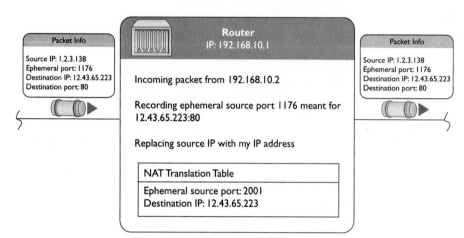

• **Figure 8.16**   NATing a packet

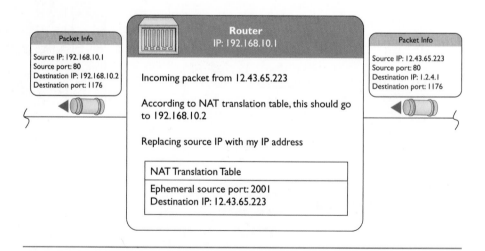

• **Figure 8.17**   Updating the packet

Since the router is revising the packets and recording the IP address and port information already, why not enable it to handle ports more aggressively? Enter port forwarding, stage left.

Port Forwarding **Port forwarding** hides a port number from the wilds of the Internet, enabling public servers to work behind a NAT router. Port forwarding gives servers the protection of NAT while still allowing access to that server. Suppose you have a Web server behind a NAT router. You know from earlier in the book that Web servers look for incoming port 80 addresses. A port-forwarding router recognizes all incoming requests for a particular port and then forwards those requests to an internal IP address. To support an internal Web server, the router is configured to forward all port 8080 packets to the internal Web server at port 80, as shown in Figure 8.18.

Port Address Translation Different manufacturers use the term **Port Address Translation (PAT)** to refer to both overloaded NAT and port forwarding, though not at the same time. The Cisco router in Figure 8.19, for example, calls overloaded NAT Port Address Translation (PAT).

> The CompTIA Network+ exam follows the Cisco definition of Port Address Translation, making the term synonymous with overloaded NAT.

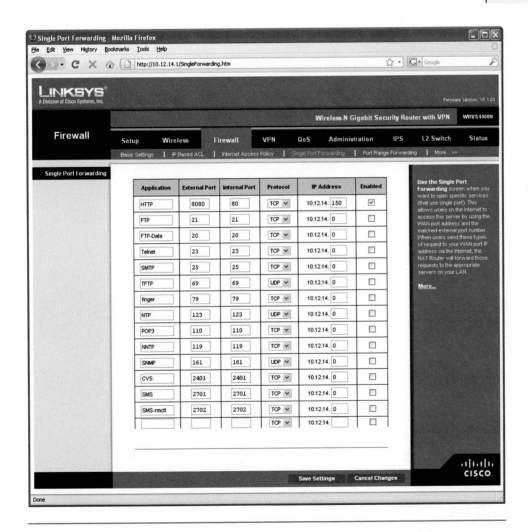

● **Figure 8.18**   Setting up port forwarding on a home router

Chapter 8: The Wonderful World of Routing

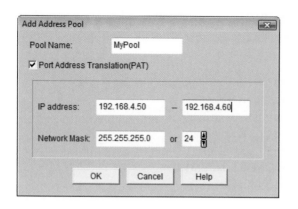

● **Figure 8.20**   NAT setup on home router

● **Figure 8.19**   Configuring Port Address Translation on a Cisco router

Configuring NAT

Configuring NAT on home routers is a no-brainer as these boxes invariably have NAT turned on automatically. Figure 8.20 shows the screen on my home router for NAT. Note the radio buttons that say Gateway and Router.

By default the router is set to Gateway, which is Linksys-speak for "NAT is turned on." If I wanted to turn off NAT, I would set the radio button to Router.

Commercial-grade routers use NAT more explicitly, enabling you to do Static NAT, Pooled NAT, port forwarding, and more. Figure 8.21 shows a router configuration screen on a Cisco router.

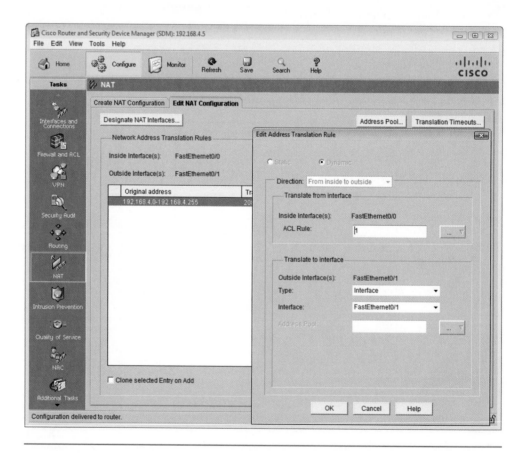

● **Figure 8.21**   Configuring NAT on a commercial-grade router

■ Dynamic Routing

Based on what you've read up to this point, it would seem that routes in your routing tables come from two sources: either they are manually entered or they are detected at setup by the router. In either case, a route seems to be a static beast, just sitting there and never changing. And based on what you've seen so far, that is absolutely true. Routers have **static routes**. But most routers also have the capability to update their routes *dynamically*, assuming they're provided with the extra smarts in the form of **dynamic routing** protocols.

If you've been reading carefully you might be tempted at this point to say: "Why do I need this dynamic routing stuff? Don't routers use metrics so I can add two or more routes to another network ID in case I lose one of my routes?" Yes, but metrics really only help when you have direct connections to other network IDs. What if your routers look like Figure 8.22?

Do you really want to try to set up all these routes statically? What happens when something changes? Can you imagine the administrative nightmare? Why not just give routers the brainpower to talk to each other so that they know what's happening not only to the other directly connected routers but also to routers two or three or more routers away? Each time a packet goes through a router is defined as a **hop**. Let's talk about hops for a

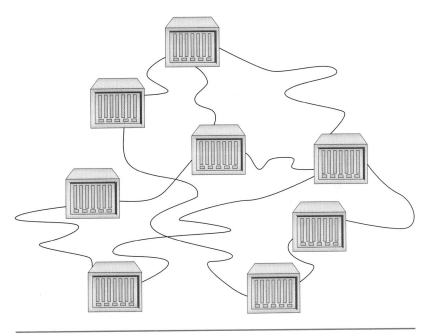

● **Figure 8.22** Lots of routers

moment. Figure 8.23 shows a series of routers. If you're on a computer in Network ID X and you PING a computer in Network ID Y, you go one hop. If you PING a computer in Network ID Z, you go two hops.

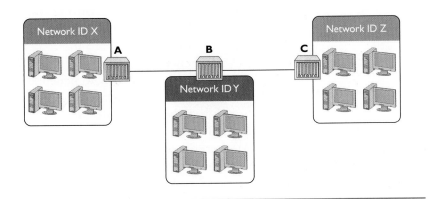

● **Figure 8.23** Hopping through a WAN

Routing protocols have been around for a long time and, like any technology, there have been a number of different choices and variants over those years. CompTIA Network+ competencies break these many types of routing protocols into three distinct groups: distance vector, link state, and hybrid. CompTIA obsesses over these different types of routing protocols, so this chapter does too!

Distance Vector

Distance vector routing protocols were the first to appear in the TCP/IP routing world. The cornerstone of all distance vector routing protocols is some form of total cost. The simplest total cost adds up the hops (the hop count) between a router and a network, so if you had a router one hop away from a network, the cost for that route would be 1; if two hops away, the cost would be 2.

All network connections are not equal. A router might have two one-hop routes to a network—one using a fast connection and the other using a slow connection. Administrators set the metric of the routes in the routing table to reflect the speed. So the slow single-hop route, for example, might be given the metric of 10 rather than the default of 1 to reflect the fact that it's slow. So the total cost for this one-hop route is 10, even though it's only one hop. Don't assume a one-hop route always has a cost of 1.

Distance vector routing protocols calculate the total cost to get to a particular network ID and compare that cost to the total cost of all the other routes to get to that same network ID. The router then chooses the route with the lowest cost.

For this to work, routers using a distance vector routing protocol transfer their entire routing table to other routers in the WAN. Each distance vector routing protocol has a maximum number of hops that a router will send its routing table to keep traffic down.

Assume that you have four routers connected as shown in Figure 8.24. All of the routers have static routes set up between each other with the metrics as shown. You add two new networks, one that connects to Router A and the other to Router D. For simplicity, call them Network ID X and Network ID Y. A computer on one network wants to send packets to a computer on the other network, but the routers in between Routers A and D don't yet know the two new network IDs. That's when distance vector routing protocols work their magic.

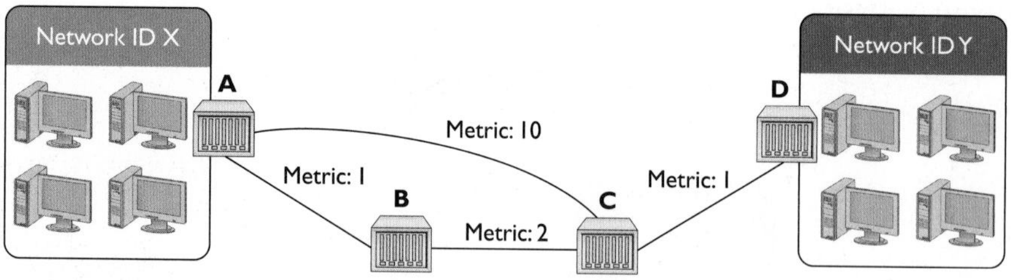

• **Figure 8.24**   Getting a packet from Network ID X to Network ID Y? No clue!

Because all of the routers use a distance vector routing protocol, the problem gets solved quickly. At a certain defined time interval (usually 30 seconds or less) the routers begin sending each other their routing tables (the routers each send their entire routing table, but for simplicity just concentrate on the two network IDs in question). On the first iteration, Router A sends its route to Network ID X to Routers B and C. Router D sends its route to Network ID Y to Router C (Figure 8.25).

This is great—Routers B and C now know how to get to Network ID X and Router C can get to Network ID Y; but there's still no complete path between Network ID X and Network ID Y. That's going to take another interval. After another set amount of time, the routers again send their now updated routing tables to each other, as shown in Figure 8.26.

Router A knows a path now to Network ID Y, and Router D knows a path to Network ID X. As a side effect, Router B and Router C have two routes to Network ID X. Router B can get to Network ID X through Router A and through Router C. Similarly, Router C can get to Network ID X through Router A and through Router B. What to do? In cases where the router discovers multiple routes to the same network ID, the distance vector routing protocol deletes all but the route with the lowest total cost (Figure 8.27).

On the next iteration, Routers A and D get updated information about the lower-total-cost hops to connect to Network IDs X and Y (Figure 8.28).

Just as Routers B and C only kept the routes with the lowest cost, Routers A and D keep only the lowest-cost routes to the networks (Figure 8.29).

Now Routers A and D have a lower-cost route to Network IDs X and Y. They've removed the higher-cost routes and begin sending data.

At this point if routers were human they'd realize that each router has all the information about the network and stop sending each other routing tables. Routers using distance vector routing protocols, however, aren't that smart. The routers continue to

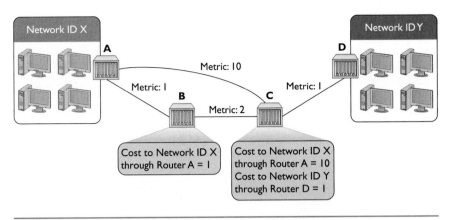

● **Figure 8.25**   Routes updated

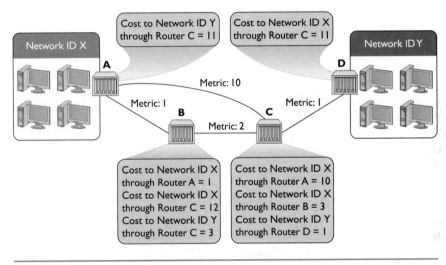

● **Figure 8.26**   Updated routing tables

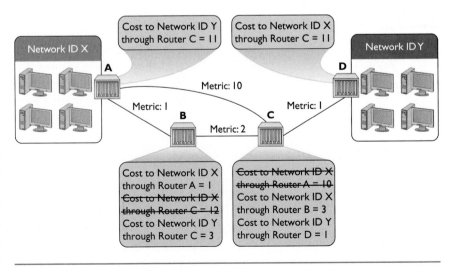

● **Figure 8.27**   Deleting higher-cost routes

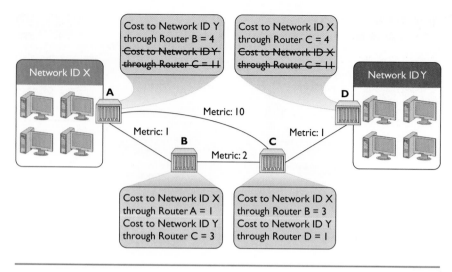

Figure 8.28   Argh! Multiple routes!

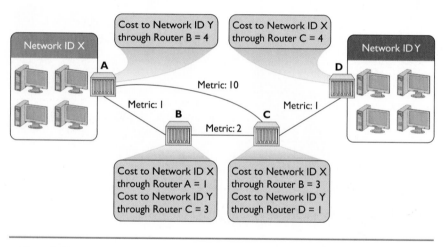

Figure 8.29   Last iteration

send their complete routing tables to each other, but because there's no new information, the routing tables stay the same.

At this point the routers are in **convergence** (also called *steady state*), meaning the updating of the routing tables for all the routers has completed. Assuming nothing changes in terms of connections, the routing tables will not change. In this example, it takes three iterations to reach convergence.

So what happens if the route between Routers B and C breaks? The routers have deleted the higher-cost routes, only keeping the lower-cost route that goes between Routers B and C. Does this mean Router A can no longer connect to Network ID Y and Router D can no longer connect to Network ID X? Yikes! Yes it does. At least for a while.

Routers that use distance vector routing protocols continue to send to each other their entire routing table at regular intervals. After a few iterations, Routers A and D will once again know how to reach each other, though through the once-rejected slower connection.

Distance vector routing protocols work fine in a scenario such as the previous one that has only four routers. Even if you lose a router, a few minutes later the network returns to convergence. But imagine if you had tens of thousands of routers (the Internet). Convergence could take a very long time indeed. As a result, a pure distance vector routing protocol works fine for a network with a few (<10) routers, but isn't good for large networks.

Routers can use one of three distance vector routing protocols: RIPv1, RIPv2, or BGP.

RIPv1

The granddaddy of all distance vector routing protocols is the **Routing Information Protocol (RIP)**. The first version of RIP—called **RIPv1**—dates from the 1980s, although its predecessors go back all the way to the beginnings of the Internet in the 1960s. RIP has a maximum hop count of 15 so your router will not talk to another router more than 15 routers away.

This ended up being a problem because a routing table request could literally loop all the way around back to the initial router.

RIPv1 sent out an update every 30 seconds. This also turned into a big problem because every router on the network would send its routing table at the same time, causing huge network overloads.

As if these issues weren't bad enough, RIPv1 didn't know how to use Classless Inter-Domain Routing (CIDR) subnets and could only route classful subnets. Plus RIPv1 routers had no authorization, leaving them open to hackers sending false routing table information. RIP needed an update.

RIPv2

RIPv2 is the current version of RIP, adopted in 1994. It works the same way as RIPv1, but fixes many of the problems. CIDR support has been added, updates are set at random intervals, and authentication is built into the protocol. (The maximum hop count of 15 continues to apply to RIPv2.)

Most routers still support RIPv2, but RIP's many problems, especially the time to convergence for large WANs, makes it obsolete for all but small, private WANs that consist of a few routers. The growth of the Internet demanded a far more robust dynamic routing protocol. That doesn't mean RIP rests in peace! RIP is both easy to use and easy for manufacturers to implement in their routers, so most routers, even home routers, have the ability to use RIP (Figure 8.30).

BGP

The explosive growth of the Internet in the 1980s required a fundamental reorganization in the structure of the Internet itself. The entities that govern how the Internet works do so in a highly decentralized fashion. Even the organized groups, such as the Internet Society (ISOC) and its better known committees—Internet Assigned Numbers Authority (IANA) and Internet Engineering Task Force (IETF)— are made up of many different individuals, companies, and government organizations from across the globe. The reorganization process took time and many meetings.

What came out of the reorganization eventually was a multitiered structure. At the top of the structure sits many Autonomous Systems. An **Autonomous System (AS)** is one or more networks that are governed by a single protocol within that AS. Figure 8.31 illustrates the central structure of the Internet.

Dynamic Routing			
RIP:	⦿ Enabled	○ Disabled	
RIP Send Packet Version:	RIPv2		
RIP Recv Packet Version:	RIPv2		

• **Figure 8.30**   Setting RIP in a home router

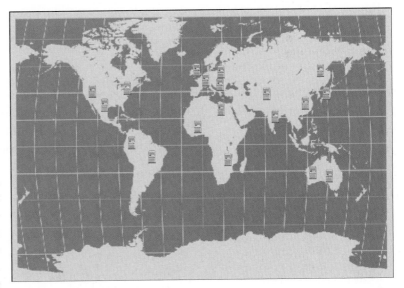

• **Figure 8.31**   The Internet

```
Router2811(config)#router bgp ?
  <1-65535>  Autonomous system number

Router2811(config)#router bgp 1902
```

● **Figure 8.32**   Configuring a Cisco router to use an ASN

Try This!

Discovering the Autonomous System Numbers

You can see the AS for most Web sites by using this handy little Firefox add-on: www.asnumber.networx.ch. It doesn't work for every Web site but it's still interesting.

There's no reason you can't use BGP within an AS to connect networks. So you can and do run into situations where BGP is both the interior and exterior protocol for an AS. To distinguish between the two uses of the protocol, network folks refer to the BGP on the interior as the *internal BGP* (iBGP); the exterior connection then becomes the *exterior BGP* (eBGP).

Please remember that in the earlier general distance vector routing example, I chose not to show that every update was an entire routing table! I only showed the changes, but trust me, the entire routing table is transmitted roughly every 30 seconds (with some randomization).

Autonomous Systems do not use IP addresses, but rather use a special globally unique Autonomous System Number (ASN) assigned by the IANA. Originally a 16-bit number, the current ASNs are 32 bits, displayed as two 16-bit numbers separated by a dot. So, 1.33457 would be a typical ASN. Just as you would assign an IP address to a router, you would configure the router to use or be the ASN assigned by the IANA. See Figure 8.32.

Autonomous Systems communicate with each other using a protocol, called generically an Exterior Gateway Protocol (EGP). The network or networks within an AS communicate with protocols as well, called generically Interior Gateway Protocols (IGPs).

Many protocols are used *within* Autonomous Systems, such as RIP, but the Internet has settled on one protocol for communication between each AS: the **Border Gateway Protocol (BGP)**. BGP is the glue of the Internet, connecting all of the Autonomous Systems. The current version of BGP is BGP-4.

The CompTIA Network+ Exam Objectives list BGP as a distance vector routing protocol, but it's really somewhat different. BGP doesn't have the same type of routing table as you've seen so far. Instead, BGP routers are manually configured (these types of connections aren't the type that go down very often!) and advertise information passed to them from different Autonomous Systems' **edge routers**—that's what the AS-to-AS routers are called. BGP forwards these advertisements that include the ASN and other very non-IP items.

BGP also knows how to handle a number of situations unique to the Internet. If a router advertises a new route but that route isn't reliable, most BGP routers ignore it. BGP also supports policies that ISPs can use to limit who and how other routers may access them.

BGP is an amazing and powerful dynamic routing protocol, but unless you're working deep in the router room of an AS, odds are good you'll never see it in action. Those who need to connect a few routers together usually turn to a family of dynamic routing protocols that work very differently from distance vector routing protocols.

Link State

The limitations of RIP motivated the demand for a faster protocol that took up less bandwidth on a WAN. The basic idea was to come up with a dynamic routing protocol that was more efficient than routers that simply sent out their entire routing table at regular intervals. Why not instead simply announce and forward individual route changes as they appeared? That is the basic idea of a **link state** dynamic routing protocol. There are only two link state dynamic routing protocols: OSPF and IS-IS.

OSPF

Open Shortest Path First (OSPF) is the most commonly used IGP in the entire Internet. Most large Internet users (as opposed to ISPs) use OSPF on their internal networks. Even an AS, while still using BGP on its edge routers, will use OSPF internally because OSPF was designed from the ground up to work within a single AS. OSPF converges dramatically faster and is much more efficient than RIP. Odds are good that if you are using dynamic routing protocols, you're using OSPF.

Before you see OSPF in action, I need to warn you that OSPF is a complex protocol for routers. You won't find OSPF on cheap home routers because making it work takes a lot of computational firepower. But OSPF's popularity and CompTIA's coverage make this an important area for you to understand. The description here, while more than enough to get you through the CompTIA Network+ exam, is still only a light touch on the fascinating world of OSPF.

> Even though OSPF takes serious router firepower, it's usually embarrassingly easy to implement. In many cases you just tell your router to use it and it works perfectly.

Let's head back to the four-router setup used to explain RIP, but this time replace RIP with OSPF. Since OSPF is designed to work with the Internet, let's give Router B an upstream connection to the organization's ISP. When you first start up OSPF-capable routers, they send out *link state advertisements* (LSAs), called *Hello packets*, looking for other OSPF routers (Figure 8.33).

A new router sends out a lot of LSAs when it first starts up. This is called *flooding* and it normally only happens at the first boot.

One of the big differences between OSPF and RIP is the hop cost.

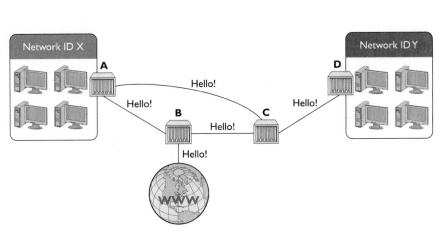

• **Figure 8.33**   Hello!

While single hops in RIP have a cost of 1 unless manually changed, in OSPF the cost is based on the speed of the link. The formula is

```
100,000,000/bandwidth in bps
```

So a 10BaseT link's OSPF cost is 100,000,000/10,000,000 = 10. The faster the bandwidth, the lower the cost. You can override this manually if you wish.

To appreciate the power of OSPF, Figure 8.34 makes Figure 8.33 a bit more complex, adding speeds to each connection. When OSPF routers send LSA Hellos, they exchange this information and update their link state databases.

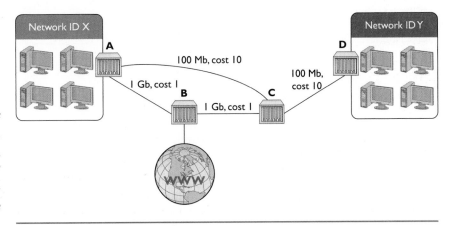

• **Figure 8.34**   Link states

These LSA Hellos are forwarded on to every OSPF router in the network. Every router knows the link state for every other router. This happens in a few seconds.

Even though OSPF Area IDs look like IP addresses, they have nothing to do with IP!

You don't want the routers to flood anywhere beyond your own routers, so every router is assigned an **Area ID**. Area IDs (unfortunately in my opinion) look exactly like IP addresses. Every OSPF router is designed to accept an Area ID that you enter into the routers. In this case all of the routers are given the Area ID of 0.0.0.0. This is commonly called Area 0.

• **Figure 8.35** Area defined

• **Figure 8.36** DR and BDR

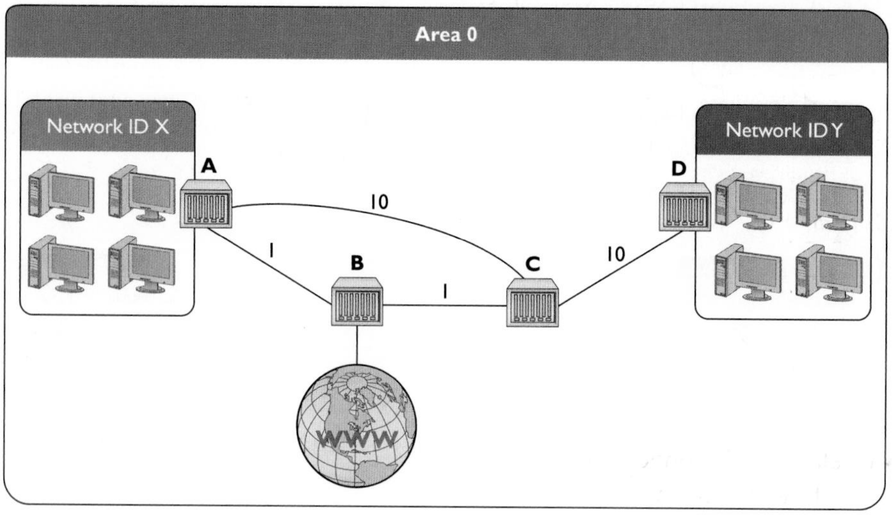

Area 0 is rather important in the world of OSPF. If your network gets more complex, you can make multiple areas. Area 0 is the most important area, however, and thus is called the backbone. In this example, all of the routers are part of Area 0 (Figure 8.35).

Areas are very important for OSPF. To minimize router traffic, every area has one "El Supremo" router that relays information to all of the other routers in the area. This router is called the **designated router (DR)**. A second router is called the **backup designated router (BDR)** in case the DR isn't available. As the routers first begin to communicate, a DR and BDR election automatically begins. The router with the lowest total priority wins. In this case Router B becomes the DR and Router A becomes the BDR. This actually takes place during the initial Hello packet exchange (Figure 8.36). In most cases you simply let the routers decide, but you can manually set a router as the DR and BDR if you desire (which is rare).

Once the elections take place, it's finally time to get some routes distributed across the area. This part is actually almost boring. Routers A and B send a separate LSA telling all routers in the area that they are connected to Network IDs X and Y, respectively. These are *not* the entire routing tables, but rather only a single route that is almost instantly dispersed across the routers in the OSPF area (Figure 8.37).

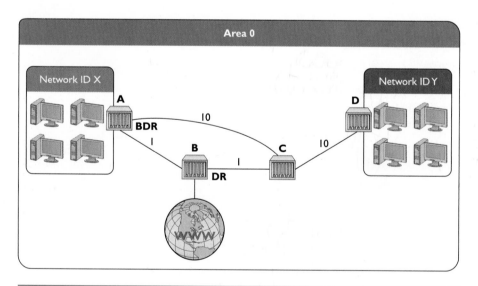

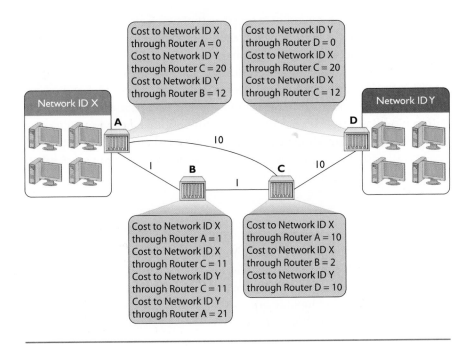

Cost to Network ID X
through Router A = 0
Cost to Network ID Y
through Router C = 20
Cost to Network ID Y
through Router B = 12

Cost to Network ID Y
through Router D = 0
Cost to Network ID X
through Router C = 20
Cost to Network ID X
through Router C = 12

Network ID X

Network ID Y

10

10

Cost to Network ID X
through Router A = 1
Cost to Network ID X
through Router C = 11
Cost to Network ID Y
through Router C = 11
Cost to Network ID Y
through Router A = 21

Cost to Network ID X
through Router A = 10
Cost to Network ID X
through Router B = 2
Cost to Network ID Y
through Router D = 10

• **Figure 8.37**   All routers updated

As you can see, OSPF areas almost instantly gain convergence compared to RIP. Once convergence is reached, all of the routers in the area send each other Hello LSAs every 30 minutes or so unless they detect a break in the link state. Also notice that OSPF routers keep alternate routes to the same network ID.

So what happens when something changes? For example, what if the connection between Routers A and B were to disconnect? In that case both Routers A and B would almost instantly detect the break (as traffic between the two would suddenly stop). Each router would first attempt to reconnect. If this was unsuccessful (over a few seconds), the routers would then send out an LSA announcing the connection between the two was broken (Figure 8.38). Again, this is a single route, not the entire routing table. Each router updates its routing table to remove the route that no longer works.

OSPF isn't popular by accident. It's easy to use, scales to large networks quite well, and is supported by all but the most basic

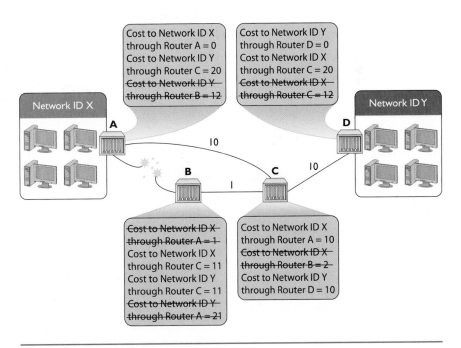

Cost to Network ID X
through Router A = 0
Cost to Network ID Y
through Router C = 20
~~Cost to Network ID Y~~
~~through Router B = 12~~

Cost to Network ID Y
through Router D = 0
Cost to Network ID X
through Router C = 20
~~Cost to Network ID X~~
~~through Router C = 12~~

Network ID X

Network ID Y

10

10

~~Cost to Network ID X~~
~~through Router A = 1~~
Cost to Network ID X
through Router C = 11
Cost to Network ID Y
through Router C = 11
~~Cost to Network ID Y~~
~~through Router A = 21~~

Cost to Network ID X
through Router A = 10
~~Cost to Network ID X~~
~~through Router B = 2~~
Cost to Network ID Y
through Router D = 10

• **Figure 8.38**   Announcing a disconnect

routers. By the way, did I forget to mention that OSPF also supports authentication and that the shortest-path-first method by definition prevents loops? Why would anyone use anything else? Well, OSPF had one problem that wasn't repaired until fairly recently: support for something called IPv6 (see Chapter 13 for details on IPv6). Not to preempt Chapter 13, but IPv6 is a new addressing system for IP that dumps the old 32-bit address, replacing it with a 128-bit address. IPv6 is quickly gaining popularity and will one day replace 32-bit IP addressing. Just for the record, I've been predicting the end of 32-bit IP addressing for so long I'm now afraid to predict anymore when it's going to happen—but it will eventually.

IS-IS

If you want to use a link state dynamic routing protocol and you don't want to use OSPF, your only other option is **Intermediate System to Intermediate System (IS-IS)**. IS-IS is extremely similar to OSPF. It uses the concept of areas and send-only updates to routing tables. IS-IS was developed at roughly the same time as OSPF and had the one major advantage of working with IPv6 from the start. IS-IS has some adoption with ISPs, but for the most part plays a distant second to the popularity of OSPF. Make sure you know that IS-IS is a link state dynamic routing protocol and if you ever see two routers using it call me as I've never seen IS-IS in action.

EIGRP—the Lone Hybrid

There is exactly one protocol that doesn't really fit into either the distance vector or link state camp: Cisco's proprietary **Enhanced Interior Gateway Routing Protocol (EIGRP)**. Back in the days when RIP was dominant, there was a huge outcry for an improvement to RIP, but OSPF wasn't yet out. Cisco, being the dominant router company in the world (a crown it still wears to this day), came out with the Interior Gateway Routing Protocol (IGRP), quickly replaced with EIGRP.

EIGRP has aspects of both distance vector and link state protocols, placing it uniquely into its own "hybrid" category. EIGRP is (arguably) fading away in the face of nonproprietary IGP protocols, especially OSPF.

Dynamic Routing Makes the Internet

Without dynamic routing, the complex, self-healing Internet we enjoy today couldn't exist. So many routes come up and go down so often that manually updating static routes simply couldn't keep up. Review Table 8.1 to help you familiarize with the differences between the different types of dynamic routing protocols.

Table 8.1	Dynamic Routing Protocols		
Protocol	**Type**	**IGP or BGP?**	**Notes**
RIPv1	Distance vector	IGP	Old; only used classful subnets
RIPv2	Distance vector	IGP	Supports CIDR
BGP-4	Distance vector	BGP	Used on the Internet, connects Autonomous Systems
OSPF	Link state	IGP	Fast, popular, uses Area IDs (Area 0/backbone)
IS-IS	Link state	IGP	Alternative to OSPF
EIGRP	Hybrid	IGP	Cisco proprietary

■ Working with Routers

Understanding the different ways routers work is one thing. Actually walking up to a router and making it work is a different animal altogether. This section examines practical router installation. Physical installation isn't very complicated. With a home router, you give it power and then plug in connections. With a business-class router, you insert it into a rack, give it power, and plug in connections.

The complex part of installation comes with the specialized equipment and steps to connect to the router and configure it for your network needs. This section, therefore, focuses on the many methods and procedures used to access and configure a router.

The single biggest item to keep in mind here is that while there are a large number of different methods to connect, hundreds of interfaces, and probably millions of different configurations for different routers, the functions are still the same. It doesn't matter if you're using an inexpensive home router or a hyper-powerful Internet backbone router, you always are working to do one main job: connect different network IDs.

Also keep in mind that routers, especially gateway routers, often have a large number of other features that have nothing to do with routing. Gateway routers, since they act as a separator between the computers and "The Big Scary Rest of the Network," are a convenient place for all kinds of handy features like DHCP, protecting the network from intrusion (better known as firewalls), and NAT.

Connecting to Routers

When a new router comes out of the box, it's not good for very much. You need to somehow plug into that shiny new router and start telling it what you want to do. There are a number of different methods, but one of the oldest (yet still very common) ways is using a special serial connection. This type of connection is almost completely unique to Cisco-brand routers, but Cisco's massive market share makes understanding this type of connection a requirement for anyone who wants to know how to configure routers. Figure 8.39 shows the classic Cisco console cable, more commonly called a *rollover* or **Yost cable**.

At this point I need to add an important point: switches as well as routers often have some form of configuration interface. Granted, there's nothing for you to configure on a basic switch, but in later chapters you'll discover a number of network features that more advanced

The term Yost cable comes from its creator's name, Dave Yost. For more information visit http://yost.com/computers/RJ45-serial.

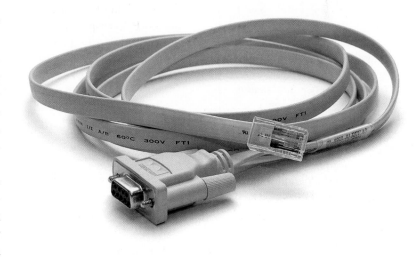

● **Figure 8.39**   Cisco console cable

• **Figure 8.40**   Console port

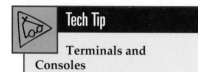
IOS used to stand for *Internetwork Operating System*, but it's just IOS now with a little trademark symbol.

switches need to be configured to use. Both routers and these advanced switches are called **managed devices**. While in this section I use the term *router*, it's important for you to appreciate that all routers and many better switches are all managed devices. The techniques shown here work for both!

When you first unwrap a new Cisco router, you plug the rollover cable into the console port on the router (Figure 8.40) and a serial port on a PC. If you don't have a serial port, then buy a USB-to-serial adapter.

Once you've made this connection, you need to use a terminal emulation program to talk to the router. The two most popular programs are PuTTY (www.chiark.greenend.org.uk/~sgtatham/putty) and HyperTerminal (www.hilgraeve.com/htpe/download.html). Using these programs requires you to know a little about serial ports but these basic settings should get you connected: 9600 baud, 8 data bits, 1 stop bit, and no parity. Every terminal emulator has some way for you to configure these settings. Figure 8.41 shows these settings using PuTTY.

Now it's time to connect. Most Cisco products run **Cisco IOS**, Cisco's proprietary operating system. If you want to configure Cisco routers you must learn IOS. Learning IOS in detail is a massive job and outside the scope of this book. No worries, Cisco provides a series of certifications to support those who wish to become "Cisco People." While CompTIA Network+ won't challenge you in terms of IOS, it's important to get a taste of how this amazing operating system works.

Once you've connected to the router and started a terminal emulator, you should see the initial router prompt, as shown in Figure 8.42. (If you plugged in and then started the router, you can actually watch the router boot up first.)

• **Figure 8.41**   Configuring PuTTY

Mike Meyers' CompTIA Network+ Guide to Managing and Troubleshooting Networks

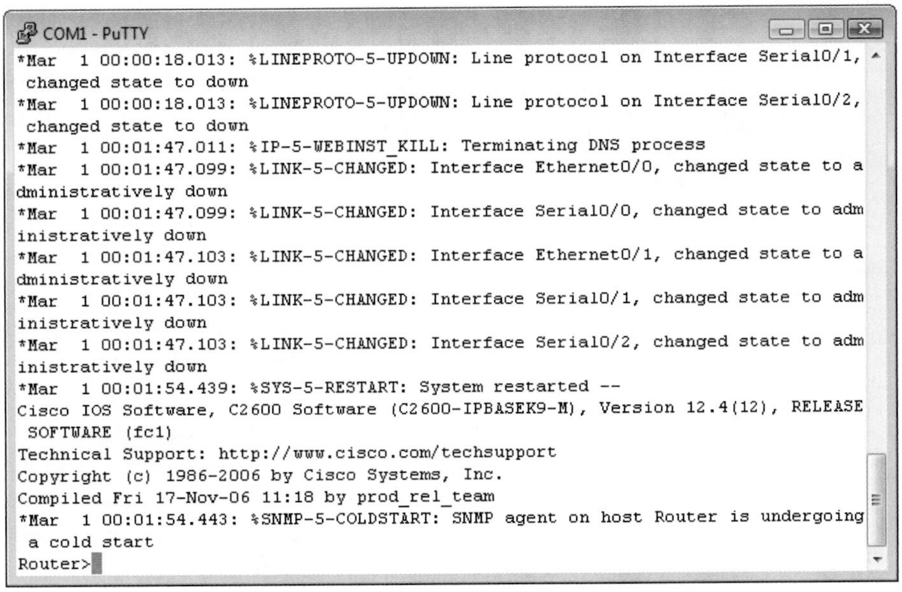

```
COM1 - PuTTY

*Mar  1 00:00:18.013: %LINEPROTO-5-UPDOWN: Line protocol on Interface Serial0/1,
 changed state to down
*Mar  1 00:00:18.013: %LINEPROTO-5-UPDOWN: Line protocol on Interface Serial0/2,
 changed state to down
*Mar  1 00:01:47.011: %IP-5-WEBINST_KILL: Terminating DNS process
*Mar  1 00:01:47.099: %LINK-5-CHANGED: Interface Ethernet0/0, changed state to a
dministratively down
*Mar  1 00:01:47.099: %LINK-5-CHANGED: Interface Serial0/0, changed state to adm
inistratively down
*Mar  1 00:01:47.103: %LINK-5-CHANGED: Interface Ethernet0/1, changed state to a
dministratively down
*Mar  1 00:01:47.103: %LINK-5-CHANGED: Interface Serial0/1, changed state to adm
inistratively down
*Mar  1 00:01:47.103: %LINK-5-CHANGED: Interface Serial0/2, changed state to adm
inistratively down
*Mar  1 00:01:54.439: %SYS-5-RESTART: System restarted --
Cisco IOS Software, C2600 Software (C2600-IPBASEK9-M), Version 12.4(12), RELEASE
 SOFTWARE (fc1)
Technical Support: http://www.cisco.com/techsupport
Copyright (c) 1986-2006 by Cisco Systems, Inc.
Compiled Fri 17-Nov-06 11:18 by prod_rel_team
*Mar  1 00:01:54.443: %SNMP-5-COLDSTART: SNMP agent on host Router is undergoing
 a cold start
Router>
```

• **Figure 8.42**   Initial router prompt

This is the IOS user mode prompt—you can't do too much here. To get to the fun you need to enter exec mode. Type **enable**, press ENTER, and the prompt changes to

```
Router#
```

From here IOS gets very complex. For example, the commands to set the IP address for one of the router's ports look like this:

```
Router#configure terminal
Router(config)#interface Ethernet 0/0
Router(config-if)#ip address 192.168.4.10 255.255.255.0
Router(config-if)#^Z
Router#write memory
```

Cisco has long appreciated that initial setup is a bit of a challenge, so a brand-new router will show you the following prompt:

```
Would you like to enter the initial configuration dialog?
[yes/no]?
```

Just follow the prompts and the most basic setup is handled for you.

You will run into Cisco equipment as a network tech, and you will need to know how to use the console from time to time. For the most part, though, you'll access a router—especially one that's already configured—through Web access or network management software.

> A new Cisco router won't have a password, but all good Cisco people know to add one. Once a router has a password you'll get a prompt to enter that password after you type in **enable**.

Web Access

Most routers come with a built-in Web server. These Web interfaces enable you to do everything you need on your router and are much easier to use than Cisco's command-line IOS. For a Web interface to work, however, the router must have a built-in IP address from the factory or you have to

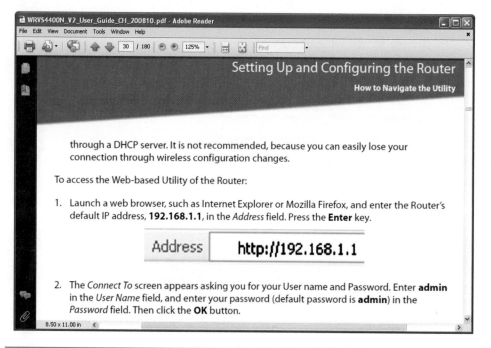

Setting Up and Configuring the Router

How to Navigate the Utility

through a DHCP server. It is not recommended, because you can easily lose your connection through wireless configuration changes.

To access the Web-based Utility of the Router:

1. Launch a web browser, such as Internet Explorer or Mozilla Firefox, and enter the Router's default IP address, **192.168.1.1**, in the *Address* field. Press the **Enter** key.

Address   http://192.168.1.1

2. The *Connect To* screen appears asking you for your User name and Password. Enter **admin** in the *User Name* field, and enter your password (default password is **admin**) in the *Password* field. Then click the **OK** button.

8.50 x 11.00 in

● **Figure 8.43**   Default IP address

Many routers are also DHCP servers, making the initial connection much easier. Check the documentation to see if you can just plug in without setting an IP address on your PC.

● **Figure 8.44**   Entering the IP address

Tech Tip

Default Names and Passwords

Every brand of router tends to use the same default user names and password. Just about every Linksys router, for example, uses a blank user name and the password "admin." An admin who fails to change the default password is asking to get hacked!

enable the Web interface after you've given the router an IP address. Bottom line? If you want to use a Web interface, you have to know the router's IP address. If a router has a default IP address, you will find it in the documentation, as shown in Figure 8.43.

Never plug a new router into an existing network! Most router people use a laptop and a crossover cable to connect to the new router. To get to the Web interface, first set a static address for your computer that will place your PC on the same network ID as the router. If, for example, the router is set to 192.168.1.1/24 from the factory, set your computer's IP address to 192.168.1.2/24. Then connect to the router (some routers tell you exactly where to connect, so read the documentation first) and check the link lights to verify you're properly connected. Open up your Web browser and type in the IP address, as shown in Figure 8.44.

Assuming you've done everything correctly, you'll almost always need to enter a default user name and password, as shown in Figure 8.45.

The default user name and password come with the router's documentation. If you don't have that information, there are plenty of Web sites that list this data. Do a Web search on **"default user name password"** to find one.

Once you've accessed the Web interface, you're on your own to poke around to find the settings you need. There's no standard interface, even between different versions of the same router make and model. When you encounter a new interface, take some time and inspect every tab and menu to learn about the router's capabilities. You'll almost always find some really cool features!

● **Figure 8.45**   User name and password

Network Management Software

The idea of a "Web-server-in-a-router" works well for single routers, but as a network grows into lots of routers, administrators need more advanced tools that describe, visualize, and configure their entire network. These tools, known as **Network Management Software (NMS)**, know how to talk to your routers, switches, and even your computers to give you an overall view of your network. In most cases NMS manifests as a Web site where administrators may inspect the status of the network and make adjustments as needed.

I divide NMS into two camps: proprietary tools made by the folks who make managed devices (OEM), and third-party tools. OEM tools are usually very powerful and easy to use, but only work on that OEM's devices. Figure 8.46 shows an example of Cisco Network Assistant, one of Cisco's NMS applications. Others include the Security Device Manager and CiscoWorks, their enterprise-level tool.

There are a number of third-party NMS tools, even some pretty good freeware NMS options. These tools are invariably harder to configure and must constantly be updated to try to work with as many devices as possible. They usually lack the amount of detail you see with OEM

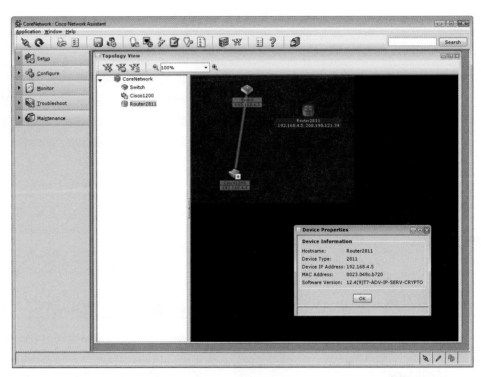

• **Figure 8.46**   Cisco Network Assistant

NMS and lack interactive graphical user interfaces. For example, CiscoWorks enables you to change the IP address of a port, whereas third-party tools will only let you see the current IP settings for that port. Figure 8.47 shows OpenNMS, a popular open source NMS.

There is no single NMS tool that works perfectly. Network administrators are constantly playing with this or that NMS tool in an attempt to give themselves some kind of overall picture of their networks.

Other Connection Methods

Be aware that most routers have even more ways to connect. Many home routers come with USB ports and configuration software. More powerful routers may enable you to connect using the ancient Telnet protocol or its newer and safer equivalent Secure Shell (SSH). These are terminal emulation protocols that look exactly like the terminal emulators seen earlier in this chapter but use the network instead of a serial cable to connect (see Chapter 9, "TCP/IP Applications," for details on these protocols).

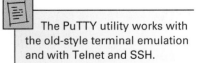

The PuTTY utility works with the old-style terminal emulation and with Telnet and SSH.

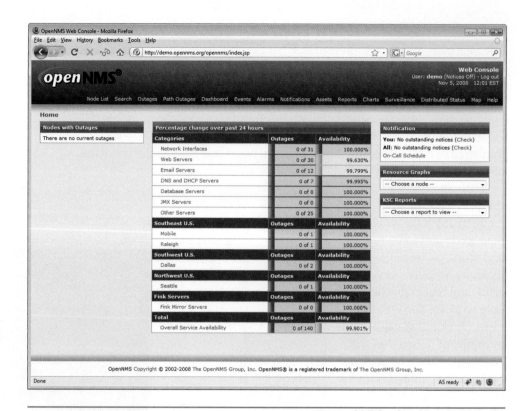

● Figure 8.47   OpenNMS

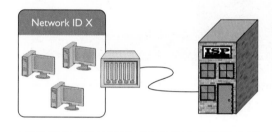

● Figure 8.48   The setup

Basic Router Configuration

A router by definition must have at least two connections. When you set up a router, you must configure every port on the router properly to talk to its connected network IDs and you must make sure the routing table sends packets to where you want them to go. As a demonstration, Figure 8.48 uses an incredibly common setup: a single gateway router used in a home or small office that's connected to an ISP.

Step 1: Set Up the WAN Side

There are a number of other settings here that I'm simply ignoring for the moment. In later chapters most of these will be revisited.

To start, you need to know the network IDs for each side of your router. The WAN side invariably connects to an ISP, so you need to know what the ISP wants you to do. If you bought a static IP address, it's time to type it in now. However—brace for a crazy fact—most home Internet connections use DHCP! That's right, DHCP isn't just for your PC. You can set up your router's WAN connection to use it too. DHCP is by far the most common connection to use for home routers. Access your router and locate the WAN connection setup. Figure 8.49 shows the setup for my home router—set to DHCP.

But what if I called my ISP and bought a single static IP address? This is rarely done anymore, but virtually every ISP will gladly do this for you (although you will pay three to four times as much for the connection). If you use a static IP, your ISP will tell

● Figure 8.49   WAN router setup

you what to enter, usually in the form of an e-mail message like the following:

```
Dear Mr. Meyers,
Thank you for requesting a static IP address from
totalsem.com!
Here's your new static IP information:
IP address: 1.151.35.55
Default Gateway: 1.151.32.132
Subnet Mask: 255.255.128.0

Installation instructions can be found at:
http://totalsem.com/setup/

Support is available at:
http://helpdesk.totalsem.com or by calling (281)922-4166.
```

In such a case, I would need to change the router setting to Static IP (Figure 8.50). Note how changing the drop-down menu to Static IP enables me to enter the information needed.

Once you've set up the WAN side, it's time to head over to set up the LAN side of the router.

Step 2: Set Up the LAN

Unlike the WAN side, you usually have total control on the LAN side of the router. You need to choose a network ID, almost always some arbitrarily chosen private range unless you do not want to use NAT. This is why so many home networks have network IDs of 192.168.1/24, 192.168.0/24, and so forth. Once you decide on your LAN-side network ID, you need to assign the correct IP information to the LAN-side NIC. Figure 8.51 shows the configuration for a LAN NIC on my home router.

Step 3: Establish Routes

Most routers are pretty smart and use the information you provided for the two interfaces to build a routing table automatically. If you need to add more routes, every router provides some method to add routes. The following shows the command line entered on a Cisco router to add a router to one of its NICs. The term "eth0/0" is how Cisco describes Ethernet NICs in its device software (although the full "Ethernet" label often graces their hardware, as you saw way back in Figure 8.1).

```
ip route 192.168.100.0 255.255.255.0 eth0/0 192.168.1.10
```

Step 4 (Optional): Configure a Dynamic Protocol

The rules to using any dynamic routing protocol are fairly straightforward. First, dynamic routing protocols are tied to individual NICs, not the entire router. Second, when you connect two routers together, make sure that

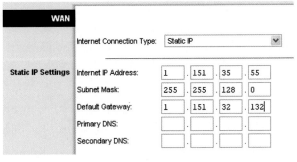

● **Figure 8.50** Entering a static IP

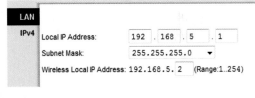

● **Figure 8.51** Setting up an IP address for LAN side

those two NICs are configured to use the same dynamic routing protocol. Third, unless you're in charge of two or more routers, you're probably not going to use any dynamic routing protocol.

The amazing part of a dynamic routing protocol is how easy it is to set up. In most cases you just figure out how to turn it on and that's about it. It just starts working.

Document and Back Up

Once you have your routes configured, take some time to document what you've done. A good router works for years without interaction, so by that time in the future when they do go down, odds are good you've forgotten why you added the routes. Last, take some time to back up the configuration. If a router goes down there's a chance it will forget everything and require you to set it up all over again. But every router has some method to back up the configuration so that you can restore it later.

Router Problems

The CompTIA Network+ exam will challenge you on some basic router problems. All of these questions should be straightforward for you as long as you do the following:

- Consider other issues first, because routers don't fail very often.
- Keep in mind what your router is supposed to do.
- Know how to use a few basic tools that can help you check the router.

Any router problem starts with someone not connecting to someone else. Even in a small network, there are a number of NICs, computers, switches, and routers between you and to whatever it is you're not connecting. Compared to most of these, a router is a pretty robust device and shouldn't be considered as the problem until you've checked out just about everything else first.

In their most basic forms, routers route traffic. Yet you've seen in this chapter that routers can do more than just plain routing—for example, NAT. As this book progresses you'll find that the typical router often handles a large number of duties beyond just routing. Know what your router is doing and appreciate that you may find yourself checking a router for problems that don't really have anything to do with routing at all.

When it comes to tools, the networking world comes with so many utilities and magic devices that it staggers the imagination. Some, like good old PING and route, you've already seen, but let's add two more tools: TRACEROUTE and MTR.

TRACEROUTE, as its name implies, records the route between any two hosts on a network. TRACEROUTE is something like PING in that it sends a single packet to another host, but as it progresses it returns information about every router between them.

Every operating system comes with TRACEROUTE, but the actual command varies among them. In Windows the command is TRACERT and looks like this (I'm running a TRACEROUTE to the router connected to my router—a short trip):

```
C:\>tracert 96.165.24.1

Tracing route to 96.165.24.1 over a maximum of 30 hops:
  1    1 ms     1 ms     1 ms  10.12.14.1
  2   10 ms    10 ms     8 ms  96.165.24.1
Trace complete.
```

The UNIX/Linux command is TRACEROUTE and looks like this:

```
michaelm@ubuntu:~$ traceroute 96.165.24.1
traceroute to 96.165.24.1 (96.165.24.1), 30 hops max, 40 byte
packets
1   10.12.14.1 (10.12.14.1)  0.763 ms 0.432 ms  0.233 ms
2   96.165.24.1 (96.165.24.1) 12.233 ms 11.255 ms 14.112 ms
michaelm@ubuntu:~$
```

TRACEROUTE is a handy tool not so much for what it tells you when everything's working well, but for what it tells you when things are not working. Take a look at the following:

```
 C:\>tracert 96.165.24.1

Tracing route to 96.165.24.1 over a maximum of 30 hops
  1    1 ms     1 ms     1 ms  10.12.14.1
  2    *        *        *        Request timed out
  3  96.165.24.1   reports: Destination host unreachable.
```

If this TRACEROUTE worked in the past but now it no longer works, you know that there's something wrong between your router and the next router upstream. You don't know what's wrong exactly. The connection may be down, the router may not be working; but at least TRACEROUTE gives you an idea where to look for the problem and where not to look.

My TRACEROUTE (MTR) is very similar to TRACEROUTE, but it's dynamic, continually updating the route that you've selected (Figure 8.52). MTR is a Linux tool; you won't find it in Windows.

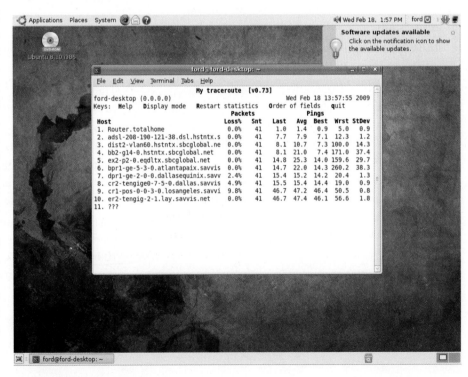

• **Figure 8.52** MTR in action

Chapter 8 Review

■ Chapter Summary

After reading this chapter and completing the exercises, you should understand the following about routing.

Explain how routers work

- A router is any piece of hardware that forwards network packets based on their destination IP addresses.

- A routing table is the chart of information kept on a router to aid in directing the flow of packets through computer networks.

- Some routers have only two ports—one to connect to the Internet and another to connect to a LAN switch. However, some routers have an integrated switch and thus have more than two ports.

- Routers learn new routes as they go, interacting with each other by exchanging the routing table information. The routing tables are checked and can be updated dynamically as data flows across a network, with routers chatting with each other for the latest network and IP address information periodically.

- Routers can connect dissimilar networks, such as Ethernet, Frame Relay, ATM, and DOCSIS networks.

- The acronym NAT stands for Network Address Translation. NAT is a method that allows an internal network (LAN) to use only one outgoing connection to access the Internet.

- NAT saves a table of information, so it knows which system is communicating with which external site. NAT solutions can be software based, or included as part of a hardware device such as a router.

- There are many varieties of NAT, including Source NAT, Destination NAT, Static NAT, Dynamic NAT, Pooled NAT, SecureNAT, Stateful NAT, and overloaded NAT.

- Static NAT maps a single IP address to a single machine, enabling you to access that machine from outside the network.

- Dynamic NAT can share a pool of routable IP addresses with multiple computers.

- All TCP/IP packets include two port numbers—a destination port and an ephemeral port—which aid in determining what software protocol to use.

- The destination port is a fixed, predetermined number that defines the function or session type while the ephemeral port is an arbitrary number generated by the sending computer.

- Port forwarding hides port numbers from the public side of a network. The router simply forwards packets from one port number to another as the packet passes from the public to the private side of the router.

Describe dynamic routing technologies

- Routing table entries are entered manually on static routers and do not change. Dynamic routers, in contrast, automatically update their routing table. This is accomplished by using special routing protocols.

- There are three distinct groups of routing protocols: distance vector, link state, and hybrid.

- Distance vector routing protocols calculate the total cost to get to a particular network ID over differing routes. Routing tables are shared with other routers, and the route with the lowest cost is automatically chosen.

- Distance vector routing protocols are not recommended for networks with more than 10 routers because of the time it takes for the routers to reach convergence.

- Distance vector routing protocols include RIPv1, RIPv2, and BGP.

- RIPv1 has a maximum hop count of 15, with routing table updates sent every 30 seconds. Because RIPv1 was limited to routing classful subnets only, lacked authorization, and experienced network overloads as every router sent its routing table at the same time, the RIPv2 update was developed.

- RIPv2 supports CIDR subnets in addition to classful subnets, sends routing tables at random intervals to lessen network overhead, and provides authentication to prevent hackers from sending false routing table information. RIPv2's lengthy time to convergence for large networks led to the development of Border Gateway Protocol (BGP).

- An Autonomous System (AS) consists of one or more networks that are governed by a single protocol. Autonomous Systems do not use IP addresses, but instead use a special globally unique Autonomous System Number assigned by the IANA.

- The protocol used by Autonomous Systems to communicate with each other is generically called an Exterior Gateway Protocol. Networks within an Autonomous System use an Interior Gateway Protocol. Edge routers connect an AS network to another AS network.

- Interior Gateway Protocols include RIP or other protocols. At this time, the Border Gateway Protocol is the only Exterior Gateway Protocol used on the Internet. It connects all of the Autonomous Systems.

- Link state protocols include OSPF and IS-IS. Link state protocols overcome the slow and bandwidth-heavy usage of RIP.

- OSPF stands for the Open Shortest Path First routing protocol. It is the most commonly used Interior Gateway Protocol in the Internet. It is more efficient than RIP, converges dramatically faster than RIP, and supports IPv6 as of OSPF Version 3.

- OSPF broadcasts link state advertisements (Hello packets) when an OSPF-enabled router first boots up. Routers are assigned an Area ID to prevent LSAs from flooding routers on other networks. An Area ID looks like an IP address but has nothing to do with IP.

- The most important area is called Area 0, or the backbone, and has an Area ID of 0.0.0.0.

- The designated router (DR) relays information to all other routers in the area while the backup designated router (BDR) takes over if the designated router is unavailable.

- Intermediate System to Intermediate System (IS-IS) is another link state dynamic routing protocol similar to OSPF. It has supported IPv6 from the start, but is far behind OSPF in popularity and usage.

- Enhanced Interior Gateway Routing Protocol (EIGRP) is a hybrid protocol, proprietary to Cisco, that has aspects of both distance vector and link state protocols.

Install and configure a router successfully

- A Yost cable (rollover cable) is a special serial cable used to connect directly to a Cisco router for configuration purposes.

- Once a direct connection has been made to a router, use a terminal emulation program such as PuTTY or HyperTerminal to communicate.

- Most Cisco products run Cisco's proprietary operating system, Cisco IOS. While not covered on the CompTIA Network+ certification exam, understanding IOS is a must for anyone who wants to become Cisco Certified.

- Most routers include a built-in Web server for configuration. You must know the router's IP address to make this type of connection.

- Many techs use a laptop and a crossover cable to connect to a Web server–enabled router for the initial configuration. This also requires setting a static IP address on the connected laptop, unless the router includes a DHCP server.

- Network Management Software (NMS) is used to describe, visualize, and configure an entire network. NMS is made both by the companies that make managed devices and by third-party companies.

- In general, NMS made by the companies that make managed devices is easy to use, but only works on specific hardware. Much third-party NMS is available as freeware, but is typically harder to use and must be constantly updated to work with as many devices as possible.

- Some routers may be connected to via USB, Telnet, or SSH.

- When you set up a router, you must configure every port on the router properly to talk to its connected network IDs and to make sure the routing table sends packets to where you want them to go.

- Setting up a router can be broken down into five steps: set up the WAN side, set up the LAN, establish routes, optionally configure a dynamic routing protocol, and finally document and back up your settings.

- The TRACEROUTE utility records the route between any two hosts on a network and can be used to troubleshoot routing problems.

Key Terms

Area ID *(192)*
Autonomous System (AS) *(189)*
backup designated router (BDR) *(192)*
Border Gateway Protocol (BGP-4) *(190)*
Cisco IOS *(196)*
convergence *(188)*
designated router (DR) *(192)*
Destination NAT *(179)*
destination port *(180)*
distance vector *(186)*
Dynamic NAT *(180)*
dynamic routing *(185)*
edge router *(190)*
Enhanced Interior Gateway Routing Protocol (EIGRP) *(194)*
ephemeral port *(180)*
gateway router *(179)*
hop *(185)*
Intermediate System to Intermediate System (IS-IS) *(194)*
link state *(190)*
managed device *(196)*

metric *(175)*
My TRACEROUTE (MTR) *(203)*
NAT translation table *(182)*
Network Address Translation (NAT) *(178)*
Network Management Software (NMS) *(199)*
next hop *(173)*
Open Shortest Path First (OSPF) *(191)*
overloaded NAT *(181)*
port *(180)*
Port Address Translation (PAT) *(183)*
port forwarding *(183)*
RIPv1 *(188)*
RIPv2 *(189)*
router *(171)*
Routing Information Protocol (RIP) *(188)*
routing table *(172)*
Source NAT *(179)*
Static NAT (SNAT) *(180)*
static route *(185)*
TRACEROUTE *(202)*
Yost cable *(195)*

Key Term Quiz

Use the Key Terms list to complete the sentences that follow. Not all the terms will be used.

1. A device called a(n) _____ is also called a Layer 3 switch.

2. The external routing protocol used on the Internet is _____.

3. The variety of _____ methods would include RIP, OSPF, BGP, and IGRP.

4. A(n) _____ is normally entered manually into a router.

5. A(n) _____ connects one Autonomous System to another Autonomous System.

6. _____ is a routing protocol that updates routing tables about every 30 seconds, resulting in overloaded network traffic.

7. When all routers can communicate with each other efficiently, they are said to have reached _____.

8. Multiple networks that do not use IP addresses and are governed by a single protocol are known as _____.

9. You can use the _____ utility to troubleshoot routing problems.

10. A(n) _____ is an arbitrary number generated by the sending computer that enables the receiving computer to know what application to use for the returning packet.

■ Multiple-Choice Quiz

1. How many IP addresses should a router have?
   A. One
   B. One or more
   C. Two
   D. Two or more

2. Choose the Cisco Systems proprietary routing protocols from the following items. (Select two.)
   A. BGP-4
   B. EIGRP
   C. IGRP
   D. OSPF

3. If specialty accounting software being used at your company requires that packet headers remain unchanged, which item cannot be used on your network?
   A. RIP
   B. NAT
   C. OSPF
   D. TRACEROUTE

4. How does a router uses a routing table to determine over which path to send a packet?
   A. The first line in the routing table is used if the path is available; otherwise the router tries the next line down, and so on.
   B. The last line in the routing table is used if the path is available; otherwise the router tries the next line up, and so on.

   C. After examining all rows in the routing table, the router sends the packet along the path with the highest metric.
   D. After examining all rows in the routing table, the router sends the packet along the path with the lowest metric.

5. Which version of NAT maps a single routable IP address to a single network node?
   A. Static NAT
   B. Dynamic NAT
   C. Pooled NAT
   D. SecureNAT

6. Which is not a valid port number?
   A. 0
   B. 255
   C. 1024
   D. 65,536

7. How is the distance between routers measured?
   A. In meters
   B. In hops
   C. In routes
   D. In segments

8. Distance vector routing protocols include which of the following? (Select two.)
   A. RIP
   B. OSPF

C. BGP

D. ASN

9. Which of the following are benefits of RIPv2 over RIPv1? (Select two.)

    A. Longer convergence times

    B. Support for authentication

    C. Support for CIDR subnets

    D. Support for metrics

10. What is one way Autonomous Systems differ from typical Ethernet networks?

    A. They require a minimum of 10 nodes.

    B. They cannot exceed a maximum of 255 nodes.

    C. They are not able to interact with the Internet.

    D. They do not use IP addresses.

11. Why are link state protocols more efficient than RIP?

    A. Entire routing tables are updated on a stricter schedule.

    B. They forward only changes to individual routes instead of forwarding entire routing tables.

    C. Packets can be sent along multiple routes at the same time.

    D. Link state can send larger packets.

12. What happens when you first connect and turn on an OSPF router?

    A. It floods the network with Hello packets as it looks for other OSPF routers.

B. It floods the network by requesting routing tables from every computer on the network.

C. It is unavailable for several hours as it builds its default routing table.

D. It runs a self-test to determine if it should run in hybrid mode (RIP and OSPF) or native mode (OSPF only).

13. Which of the following is a valid Area ID for an Area 0 backbone?

    A. 0

    B. 0.0.0.0

    C. 1.0

    D. 255

14. How can you connect directly to a router for configuration purposes? (Select three.)

    A. Parallel cable

    B. USB cable

    C. Crossover cable

    D. Rollover cable

15. Once you have made a physical direct connection to a router, what utility/program can you use to issue commands and instructions to it? (Select three.)

    A. PuTTY

    B. HyperTerminal

    C. IOS

    D. Internet Explorer

■ Essay Quiz

1. You have been introduced to a lot more "alphabet soup" in this chapter. Quickly jot down what each of the following stands for: BGP-4, NAT, RIP, OSPF, NMS, PAT, EIGRP, IS-IS, AS, ASN, EGP, IGP, DR, and BDR.

2. Explain why a router is sometimes called a Layer 3 switch.

3. Write a short essay about OSPF and its uses, as well as its benefits over using RIPv2.

4. Briefly explain the difference between a destination port and an ephemeral port.

Lab Projects

• Lab Project 8.1

A classmate of yours is all excited about some upcoming classes available at your school that will cover Cisco routing. He keeps talking about EIGRP and its importance in the workplace, as well as how much cash can be earned if you know EIGRP. Use the Internet to research EIGRP—its history, its uses, what devices run using EIGRP, and what salaries can be earned by Cisco Certified professionals—possibly your next certification after passing the CompTIA Network+ exam. Then share this information with your instructor and your classmate to compare your findings. What does EIGRP do for corporate networks? What salaries are realistically possible? What were your sources?

• Lab Project 8.2

Start a command prompt at your computer and enter **netstat –nr** to view its routing table. Create a screenshot of the output and paste it into a word processing document. Under the pasted screenshot, briefly explain what each column is for. Compare your routing table to your classmates' routing tables and explain to each other what the differences are and why there are differences.

TCP/IP Applications

"The World Wide Web is the only thing I know of whose shortened form—www—takes three times longer to say than what it's short for."

—DOUGLAS ADAMS

In this chapter, you will learn how to

- **Describe common Transport layer protocols**
- **Explain the power of port numbers**
- **Define common TCP/IP applications such as HTTP, HTTPS, Telnet, e-mail (SMTP, POP3, and IMAP4), and FTP**

We network to get work done. Okay, sometimes that "work" involves a mad gaming session in which I lay some smack down on my editors, but you know what I mean. Thus far in the book, everything you've read about networking involves connecting computers together. This chapter moves further up the OSI seven-layer model to look at applications such as Web browsers, e-mail messaging, and more.

To understand the applications that use TCP/IP networks, a tech needs to know the structures *below* those applications that make them work. Have you ever opened multiple Web pages on a single computer? Have you ever run multiple Internet programs, such as a Web browser, an e-mail client, and a chat program, all at the same time? Clearly, lots of data is moving back and forth between your computer and many other computers. If you have packets coming in from two, three, or more other computers, there has to be a mechanism, a process, something that knows where to send and receive that data.

In this chapter, you'll discover the process used by TCP/IP networks to make sure the right data gets to the right applications on your computer. This process works through the use of some very important Transport layer protocols, TCP, UDP, and ICMP, as well as something lightly touched on in the previous chapter, the magic of port numbering. When used together, TCP and UDP along with port numbers enable work to get done on a network.

Historical/Conceptual

Transport Layer Protocols

I hate to tell you this, but you've been lied to. Not by me. Even though thus far I've gone along with this Big Lie, it's time to stand up and tell you the truth.

There is no such thing as TCP/IP. *TCP over IP* is really many other things, such as *HTTP, DHCP, POP, and about 500 more terms over TCP; plus UDP and ICMP over IP*. Given that this overly complex but much more correct term is too hard to use, the people who invented this network protocol stack way back when decided to call it *TCP/IP*, even though that term is way too simplistic to cover all the functionality involved.

 There is a strong movement out there that prefers the term "Internet Protocol" instead of the term "TCP/IP." This movement has not yet reached the CompTIA Network+ certification.

To enable you to appreciate how TCP/IP applications work, this chapter breaks down the many unmentioned protocols and shows how they help make applications work. To start this process, let's consider how human beings communicate and you'll see some very interesting commonalities between computers and people.

How People Communicate

Imagine you walk into a school cafeteria to get some lunch. You first walk up to the guy making custom deli sandwiches (this is a great cafeteria!) and say, "Hello!" He says, "How may I help you?" You say, "I'd like a sandwich please." He says, "What kind of sandwich would you like?" and you order your sandwich. After you get your sandwich you say, "Thanks!" and he says, "You're welcome." What a nice guy! In the networking world we would call this a **connection-oriented** communication. Both you and the lunch guy first acknowledge each other. You then conduct your communication; last, you close the communication.

While you're in line you see your friend Janet sitting at your usual table. The line is moving fast so you yell out, "Janet, save me a seat!" before you rush along in the line. In this case you're not waiting for her to answer; you just yell to her and hope she hears you. We call this a **connectionless** communication. There is no acknowledgment or any closing. You just yell out your communication and hope she hears it.

In the networking world any single communication between a computer and another computer is called a **session**. When you open a Web page, you make a session. When you text chat with your buddy, you make a session. All sessions must begin and eventually end.

TCP

The **Transmission Control Protocol (TCP)** is how TCP/IP does connection-oriented communication. TCP is by far the most common type of session on a typical TCP/IP network. Figure 9.1 shows two computers. One computer (Server) runs a Web server and the other (Client) runs a Web browser. When you enter a computer's address in the browser running on Client, it sends a single SYN (synchronize) packet to the Web server. If Server gets that packet, it sends back a single SYN, ACK (synchronize, acknowledge) packet. Client then sends Server a single ACK packet, and immediately requests that Server begin sending the Web page.

Once Server completes sending the Web page, it sends a FIN (finished) packet. Client responds with an RST, ACK (reset, acknowledge) packet and the session is over (Figure 9.2).

Most TCP/IP applications use TCP because connection-oriented sessions are designed to check for errors. If a receiving computer detects a missing packet, it just asks for a repeat as needed.

UDP

User Datagram Protocol (UDP) runs a distant second place to TCP in terms of the number of applications that use it, but don't let that make you think UDP is not important. UDP is perfect for the types of sessions that don't require the overhead of all that connection-oriented stuff. Probably the best example of an application that uses UDP is the Dynamic Host Configuration Protocol (DHCP). DHCP can't assume there's another computer ready on either side of the session, so each step of a DHCP session just sends the information for that step without any confirmation (Figure 9.3).

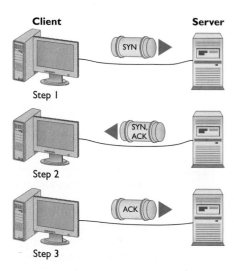

• **Figure 9.1** A connection-oriented session starting

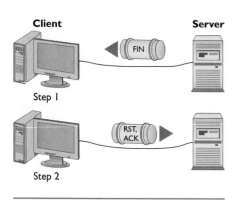

• **Figure 9.2** A connection-oriented session ending

• **Figure 9.3** DHCP steps

You might also be tempted to think that UDP wouldn't work for any situation in which critical data transfer takes place—untrue! **Trivial File Transfer Protocol (TFTP)** is one example of a protocol with which you can transfer files from one machine to another. But TFTP, using UDP, doesn't have any data protection, so you would never use TFTP between computers across the Internet. TFTP is popular for moving files between computers on the same LAN, where the chances of losing packets is very small.

ICMP

While TCP and UDP differ dramatically—the former connection-oriented and the latter connectionless—both manage and modify packets in the classic sense with destination IP address, source IP address, destination port numbers, and source port numbers. A single session might be one packet or a series of packets.

On the other hand, sometimes applications are so simple that they're always connectionless and never need more than a single packet. These are called **Internet Control Message Protocol (ICMP)** applications. Although you won't see ICMP too often in configuration files and such, you do see the results. ICMP handles mundane issues such as disconnect messages (host unreachable) that applications use to let the other side of a session know what's happening.

Good old PING is one place where you'll see ICMP in action. PING is an ICMP application that works by sending a single ICMP packet called an echo request to an IP address you specify. All computers running TCP/IP (assuming there is no firewall involved) respond to echo requests with an echo reply, as shown in Figure 9.4.

 A *firewall* is a device or software that filters all the packets between two computers (or groups of computers) and acts like a club bouncer deciding who gets in and who gets blocked. Firewalls are vital for securing modern networks and will be discussed in Chapter 17.

IGMP

The **Internet Group Management Protocol (IGMP)** is another little-seen but important Transport layer protocol. Do you remember the idea of IP

```
Administrator: C:\Windows\system32\cmd.exe

C:\>ping www.google.com

Pinging www.l.google.com [74.125.95.147] with 32 bytes of data:
Reply from 74.125.95.147: bytes=32 time=70ms TTL=242
Reply from 74.125.95.147: bytes=32 time=70ms TTL=242
Reply from 74.125.95.147: bytes=32 time=70ms TTL=242
Reply from 74.125.95.147: bytes=32 time=70ms TTL=242

Ping statistics for 74.125.95.147:
    Packets: Sent = 4, Received = 4, Lost = 0 (0% loss),
Approximate round trip times in milli-seconds:
    Minimum = 70ms, Maximum = 70ms, Average = 70ms

C:\>
```

• **Figure 9.4**   PING in action

There is some argument over where ICMP and IGMP fit in the OSI seven-layer model. Both of these protocols lack port numbers, so for many people that makes ICMP and IGMP fit more into the Network layer than the Transport layer. When in doubt, place TCP and UDP in the Transport layer and ICMP and IGMP in the Network layer.

 Cross Check

Multicast

You first saw multicast back in Chapter 7, "TCP/IP Basics," when you learned about classful IP addressing. Refer back to that chapter and see if you can answer these questions. What IP numbers are reserved for multicast? What Class is that? What is the difference between unicast and multicast?

multicast addresses, described in Chapter 7? The challenge to multicasting is determining who wants to receive the multicast and who does not. IGMP is the glue that routers use to communicate with hosts to determine a "group" membership. As you might remember from Chapter 7, the multicast Class D licenses are assigned the network ID of 224/8. However, multicast doesn't assign IP addresses to individual hosts in the same manner as you've seen thus far. Instead, a particular multicast (called an *IGMP group*) is assigned to a certain 224/8 address and those who wish to receive this multicast must tell their upstream router or switch (which must be configured to handle multicasts) that they wish to receive it. To do so, they join the IGMP group and then the router or switch knows to send that multicast data stream to that client (Figure 9.5).

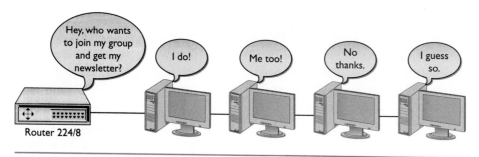

• **Figure 9.5** IGMP in action

■ The Power of Port Numbers

If you want to understand the power of TCP/IP, you have to get seriously into port numbers. If you want to pass the CompTIA Network+ exam, you need to know how TCP/IP uses port numbers and you have to memorize a substantial number of common port numbers. As you saw in the previous chapter, the port numbers make NAT work. As you progress through this book, you'll see a number of places where knowledge of port numbers is critical to protect your network, to make routers work better, and to address a zillion other issues. There is no such thing as a network administrator who isn't deeply into the magic of port numbers and who cannot manipulate them for his or her network's needs.

 TCP/IP port numbers between 0 and 1023 are the well-known port numbers. You'll find them at *every* party.

Let's review and expand on what you learned about port numbers in the previous chapter. Thus far, you know that every TCP/IP application requires a server and a client. There are very clearly defined port numbers for every popular or *well-known* TCP/IP application. A port number is a 16-bit value between 0 and 65,535. Web servers, for example, use port number 80. Port numbers from 0 to 1023 are called **well-known port numbers** and are reserved for specific TCP/IP applications.

When a Web client (let's say your computer running Firefox) sends an HTTP ACK to a Web server to request the Web page, your computer's IP packet looks like Figure 9.6.

As you can see, the destination port number is 80. The computer running the Web server reads the destination port number, telling it to send the incoming packet to the Web server program (Figure 9.7).

The Web client's source port number is generated pseudo-randomly by the Web client computer. This value varies by operating system, but generally falls within the values 1024–5000—the port numbers classically assigned as **ephemeral port numbers**—and 49152–65535—the **dynamic** or **private port numbers**. In the early days of the Internet, only ports 1024–5000 were used, but modern computers can use up all of those. More port numbers were added later. The Internet Assigned Numbers Authority (IANA) today recommends using only ports 49152–65535 as ephemeral port numbers. Let's redraw Figure 9.6 to show the more complete packet (Figure 9.8).

When the serving system responds to the Web client, it uses the ephemeral port number as the destination port to get the information back to the Web client running on the client computer (Figure 9.9).

Registered Ports

The port numbers from 1024 to 49151 are called **registered ports**. Less-common TCP/IP applications can register their ports with the IANA. Unlike well-known ports, anyone can use these port numbers for their servers or for ephemeral numbers on clients. Most operating systems steer away (or are in the

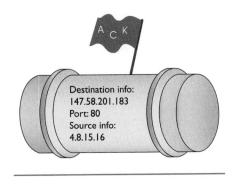

• **Figure 9.6** HTTP ACK packet

• **Figure 9.7** Dealing with the incoming packet

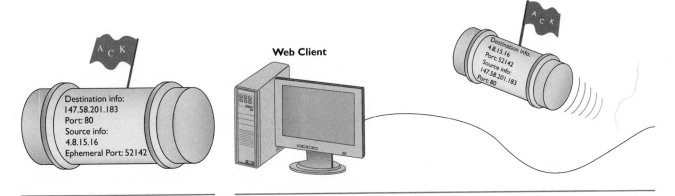

• **Figure 9.8** A more complete IP packet   • **Figure 9.9** Returning the packet

process of steering away) from using these port numbers for ephemeral ports, opting instead for the dynamic/private port numbers. Here's the full list of ports:

0–1023	Well-known port numbers
1024–49151	Registered ports
49152–65535	Dynamic or private ports

Each computer on each side of a session must keep track of the status of the communication. In the TCP/IP world, the session information stored in RAM is called a **socket** or **endpoint**. When discussing the data each computer stores about the connection between two computers' TCP/IP applications, the term to use is **socket pairs** or **endpoints**. A *session* or **connection** refers to the connection in general, rather than specific to TCP/IP. Many people still use the term *session*.

- Terms for the connection data stored on a single computer: socket or endpoint

- Terms for the connection data stored on two computers about the same connection: socket pairs or endpoints

- Terms for the whole interconnection: connection or session

As two computers begin to communicate, they store the information about the session—the endpoints—so that they know where to send and receive data. At any given point in time your computer probably has a large number of communications going on. If you want to know whom your computer is communicating with, you need to see this list of endpoints. As you'll recall from Chapter 8, "The Wonderful World of Routing," Windows, Linux, and Macintosh OS X come with **NETSTAT**, the universal "show me the endpoint" utility. NETSTAT works at the command line, so open one up and type `netstat -n` to see something like this:

```
C:\>netstat -n
Active Connections
  Proto  Local Address          Foreign Address        State
  TCP    192.168.4.27:57913     209.29.33.25:80        ESTABLISHED
  TCP    192.168.4.27:61707     192.168.4.10:445       ESTABLISHED
C:\>
```

Even though almost all operating systems use NETSTAT, there are subtle differences in options and output.

When you run `netstat -n` on a typical computer, you'll see many more than just two connections! The preceding example is simplified for purposes of discussing the details. It shows two connections. My computer's IP address is 192.168.4.27. The top connection is an open Web page (port 80) to a server at 209.29.33.25. The second connection is an open Windows Network browser (port 445) to my file server (192.168.4.10). Looking on my Windows Desktop, you would certainly see at least these two windows open (Figure 9.10).

Don't think that a single open application always means a single connection. The following example shows what `netstat -n` looks like when I open the well-known www.microsoft.com Web site (I took out the

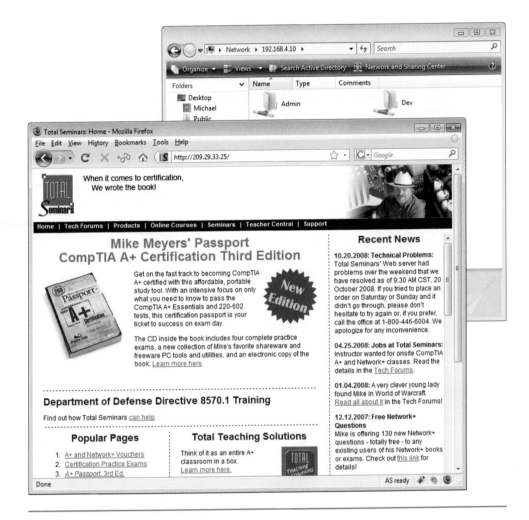

● Figure 9.10 Two open windows

connections that were not involved with the Web browser's connections to www.microsoft.com):

```
C:\>netstat -n
Active Connections
   Proto   Local Address          Foreign Address        State
   TCP     192.168.4.27:50015     80.12.192.40:80        ESTABLISHED
   TCP     192.168.4.27:50016     80.12.192.40:80        ESTABLISHED
   TCP     192.168.4.27:50017     80.12.192.40:80        ESTABLISHED
   TCP     192.168.4.27:50018     80.12.192.40:80        ESTABLISHED
   TCP     192.168.4.27:50019     80.12.192.40:80        ESTABLISHED
   TCP     192.168.4.27:50020     80.12.192.51:80        ESTABLISHED
   TCP     192.168.4.27:50021     80.12.192.40:80        ESTABLISHED
   TCP     192.168.4.27:50022     80.12.192.40:80        ESTABLISHED
   TCP     192.168.4.27:50023     80.12.192.40:80        ESTABLISHED
   TCP     192.168.4.27:50024     80.12.192.40:80        ESTABLISHED
   TCP     192.168.4.27:50025     80.12.192.51:80        ESTABLISHED
   TCP     192.168.4.27:50027     80.12.192.40:80        ESTABLISHED
   TCP     192.168.4.27:50028     80.12.192.40:80        ESTABLISHED
   TCP     192.168.4.27:50036     80.12.192.75:80        ESTABLISHED
```

A single simple Web page needs only a single connection, but this is a very complex Web page. Different elements in the Web page, such as advertisements, each have their own connection.

NETSTAT enables you to see active TCP/IP connections at a glance.

NETSTAT is a powerful tool and you will see it used throughout this book. The CompTIA Network+ exam will also test your NETSTAT skills. On the other hand, connections come and go constantly on your computer and NETSTAT, being a command-line utility, can't update to reflect changes automatically. All of the cool, hip, network techs use graphical end-point tools. Take a moment right now and download the popular, powerful, and completely free TCPView, written by Mark Russinovich, the Guru of Windows utilities. Just type **TCPView** into your search engine to find it or try going here:

http://technet.microsoft.com/en-us/sysinternals/default.aspx

Click the **Networking Utilities** icon to get the latest copy. Figure 9.11 shows TCPView in action. Note the red and green bars: red is for closing connections and green shows new connections as they appear.

TCPView won't work on anything but Windows, but other operating systems have equivalent programs. Linux folks often use the popular Net Activity Viewer (Figure 9.12). You can grab a copy of this program at http://netactview.sourceforge.net.

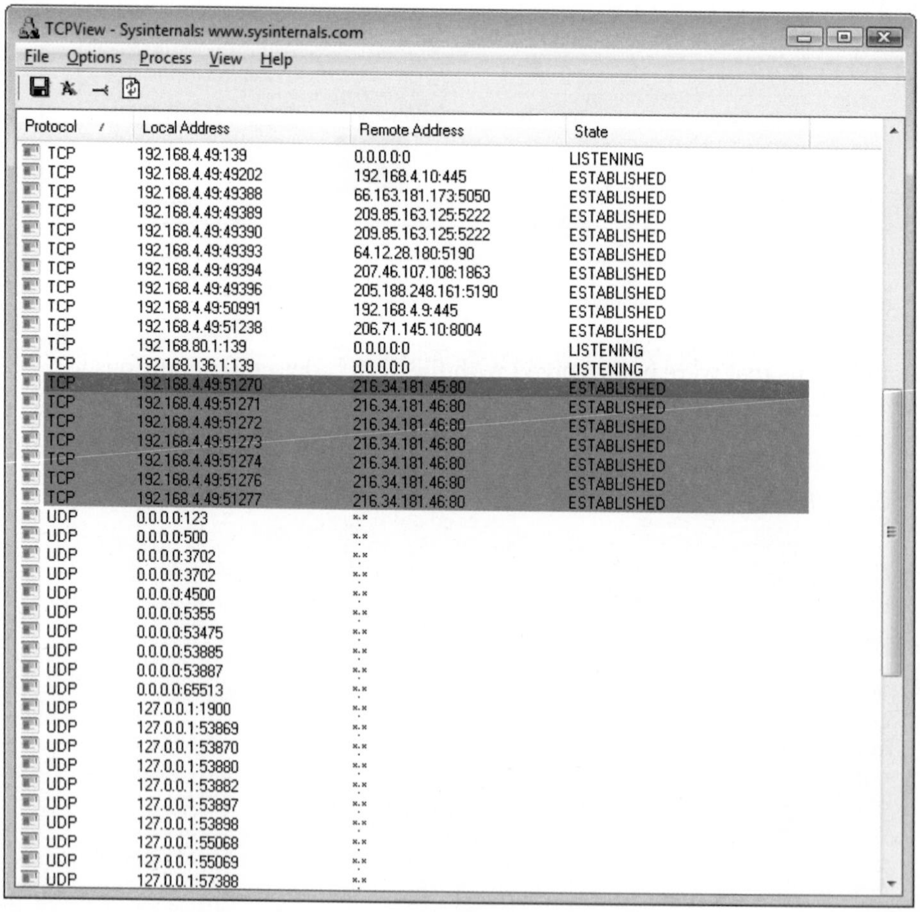

• **Figure 9.11**   TCPView in action

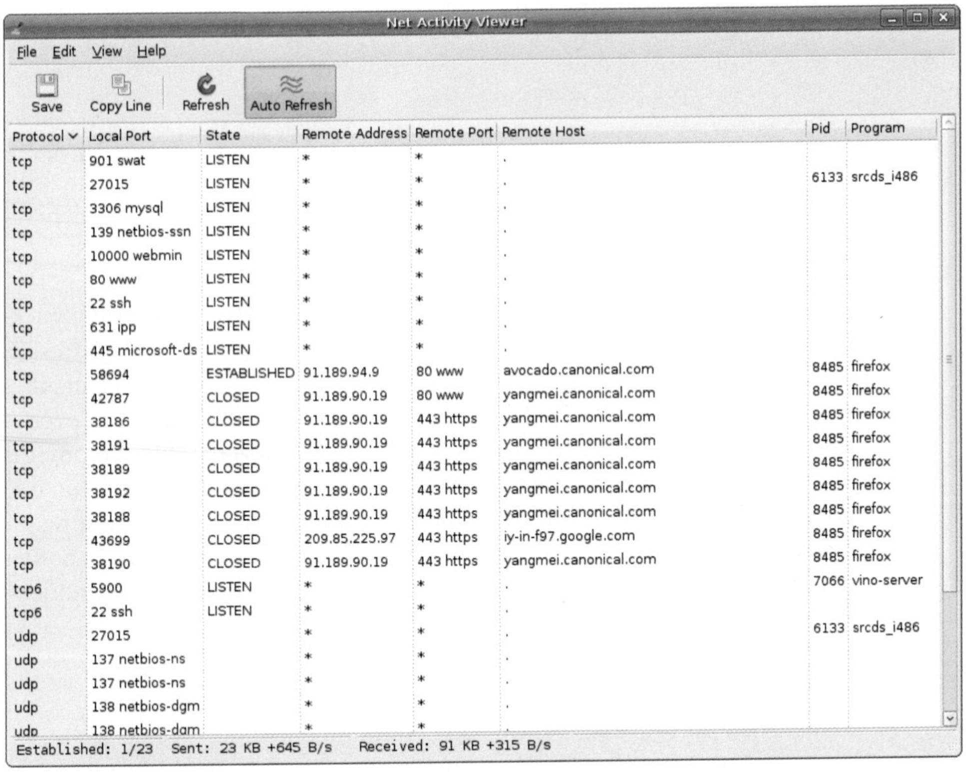

● **Figure 9.12** Net Activity Viewer

Connection Status

Connection states change continually and it's helpful when using tools such as NETSTAT or TCPView to understand their status at any given moment. Let's look at the status of connections so you understand what each means—this information is useful for determining what's happening on networked computers.

A socket that is prepared to respond to any IP packets destined for that socket's port number is called an **open port** or **listening port**. Every serving application has an open port. If you're running a Web server on a computer, for example, it will have an open port 80. That's easy enough to appreciate but you'll be amazed at the number of open ports on just about *any* computer. Fire up a copy of NETSTAT and type `netstat -an` to see all of your listening ports. Running `netstat -an` gives a lot of information, so let's just look at a small amount:

```
C:\>netstat -an
Active Connections
   Proto  Local Address          Foreign Address        State
   TCP    0.0.0.0:7              0.0.0.0:0              LISTENING
   TCP    0.0.0.0:135            0.0.0.0:0              LISTENING
   TCP    0.0.0.0:445            0.0.0.0:0              LISTENING
   TCP    0.0.0.0:912            0.0.0.0:0              LISTENING
   TCP    0.0.0.0:990            0.0.0.0:0              LISTENING
   TCP    127.0.0.1:27015        0.0.0.0:0              LISTENING
   TCP    127.0.0.1:52144        127.0.0.1:52145        ESTABLISHED
   TCP    127.0.0.1:52145        127.0.0.1:52144        ESTABLISHED
```

```
TCP     127.0.0.1:52146         127.0.0.1:52147         ESTABLISHED
TCP     127.0.0.1:52147         127.0.0.1:52146         ESTABLISHED
TCP     192.168.4.27:139        0.0.0.0:0               LISTENING
TCP     192.168.4.27:52312      74.125.47.108:80        TIME_WAIT
TCP     192.168.4.27:57913      63.246.140.18:80        CLOSE_WAIT
TCP     192.168.4.27:61707      192.168.4.10:445        ESTABLISHED
```

The –a switch tells NETSTAT to show all used ports. –n instructs NETSTAT to show raw port numbers and IP addresses.

First look at this line:

```
TCP     0.0.0.0:445             0.0.0.0:0               LISTENING
```

This line shows a listening port, listening and ready for incoming packets that have a destination port number of 445. Notice the local address is 0.0.0.0. This is how Windows tells you that the open port works on all NICs on this PC. In this case my PC has only one NIC (192.168.4.27), but even if you have only one NIC, NETSTAT still shows it this way. This computer is sharing some folders on the network. Since at this moment there's no one connected, NETSTAT shows the Foreign Address as 0.0.0.0. Incoming requests use port number 445 to connect to those shared folders. If another computer on my network (192.168.4.83) was accessing the shared folders, this line would look like

```
TCP     192.168.4.27:445        192.168.4.83:1073       ESTABLISHED
```

Established ports are active, working endpoint pairs.

Over time all connections eventually close like this one:

```
TCP     192.168.4.27:57913      63.246.140.18:80        CLOSE_WAIT
```

This line shows a Web browser making a graceful closure, meaning that each side of the conversation sees the session closing normally.

Not all connections close gracefully. The following line shows a Web browser that has lost the connection to the other side and is waiting a defined amount of time:

```
TCP     192.168.4.27:52312      74.125.47.108:80        TIME_WAIT
```

This is called a timeout period. Most Web browsers time out in around two minutes.

If data's going to move back and forth between computers, there always must be some program that's doing the sending and/or receiving. Take a look at this line from `netstat -an`:

```
TCP     192.168.4.27:52312      74.125.47.108:80        ESTABLISHED
```

You see the 80 and might assume the connection is going out to a Web server. But what program on the computer is sending it? Enter the command `netstat -ano` (the –o switch tells NETSTAT to show the process ID). While you'll see many lines, the one for this connection looks like this:

```
Proto   Local Address       Foreign Address       State          PID
TCP     192.168.4.27:52312  74.125.47.108:80      ESTABLISHED    112092
```

Every running program on your computer gets a process ID (PID), a number used by the operating system to track all the running programs. Numbers aren't very helpful to you, though, because you want to know the name of the running program. In most operating systems, finding this out is fairly easy to do. In Linux you can use the `ps` command:

```
michaelm@ubuntu:~$ ps
PID TTY          TIME CMD
3225 pts/1   00:00:00 bash
3227 pts/1   00:00:00 ps
```

Windows doesn't come with an easy tool to determine what programs are using a certain PID, so once again we turn to Mark Russinovich. His Process Explorer is a perfect tool for this (Figure 9.13). The figure shows Process Explorer scrolled down to the bottom so that you can see the program using PID 112092—good old Firefox!

To get Process Explorer, enter **"Process Explorer"** in your search engine to find it or try going here:

http://technet.microsoft.com/en-us/sysinternals/default.aspx

Click the **Process Utilities** icon to get the latest copy.

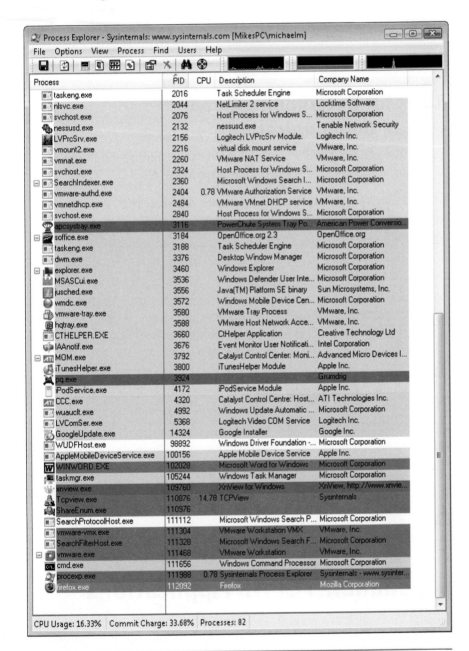

● **Figure 9.13**   Process Explorer

You might be tempted to say "Big whoop, Mike—what else would use port 80?" Then consider the possibility that you run NETSTAT and see a line like the one just shown, but *you don't have a browser open*! You determine the PID and discover that the name of the process is "Evil_Overlord.exe." This is something running on your computer that should not be there.

Understanding how TCP/IP uses ports is a base skill for any network tech. To pass the CompTIA Network+ exam, you need to memorize a number of different well-known ports and even a few of the more popular registered ports. You must appreciate how the ports fit into the process of TCP/IP communications and know how to use NETSTAT and other tools to see what's going on inside your computer.

The biggest challenge is learning what's supposed to be running and what's not. No one on Earth can run a NETSTAT command and instantly recognize every connection and why it's running, but a good network tech should know most of them. For those connections that a tech doesn't recognize, he or she should know how to research them to determine what they are.

Rules for Determining Good vs. Bad Communications

Here is the general list of rules I follow for determining good versus bad communications (as far as networking goes, at least!):

1. Memorize a bunch of known ports for common TCP/IP applications. The next section in this chapter will get you started.

2. Learn how to use NETSTAT to see what's happening on your computer. Learn to use switches such as –a, –n, and –o to help you define what you're looking for.

3. Take the time to learn the ports that normally run on your operating system. When you see a connection using ports you don't recognize, figure out the process running the connection using a utility such as Linux's **ps** or Process Explorer for Windows.

4. Take the time to learn the processes that normally run on your operating system. Most operating systems have their own internal programs (such as Windows SVCHOST.EXE) that are normal and important processes.

5. When you see a process you don't recognize, just enter the filename of the process in a Web search. There are hundreds of Web sites dedicated to researching mystery processes that will tell you what the process does.

6. Get rid of bad processes.

■ Common TCP/IP Applications

Finally! You now know enough about the Transport layer, port numbering, and sockets to get into some of the gritty details of common TCP/IP applications. There's no pretty way to do this, so let's start with the big daddy of them all, the Web.

The World Wide Web

Where would we be without the World Wide Web? If you go up to a non-nerd and say "Get on the Internet," most of them will automatically open a Web browser, because to them the Web *is* the Internet. I think it's safe to assume you've used the Web, firing up your Web browser to surf to one cool site after another, learning new things, clicking links, often ending up somewhere completely unexpected . . . it's all fun! This section looks at the Web and the tools that make it function, specifically the protocols that enable communication over the Internet.

The Web is composed of servers that store specially formatted documents using a language called Hypertext Markup Language (HTML). Figure 9.14 shows the Web page built into my router.

HTML has been around for a long time and as a result has gone through many versions. Today many pages are being written in an updated HTML version called eXtensible HTML (XHTML), which is HTML with an XML syntax. Figure 9.15 shows a small part of the XHTML code for the Web page shown in Figure 9.14.

Web browsers are designed to request HTML pages from Web servers and then open them. To access a Web page, you enter "http://" plus the IP address of the Web server. When you type the address of a Web server, such as http://192.168.4.1, you tell the browser to go to 192.168.4.1 and ask for a Web page. All Web servers have a default Web page that they open unless you enter something more complex like http://192.168.4.1/status.

> XML is a markup language similar to HTML, but it provides more flexibility in how the data is described while being much more strict in its syntax.

> Most Web browsers are pretty forgiving. If you only type in 192.168.4.1, forgetting the "http:" part, they usually just add it for you.

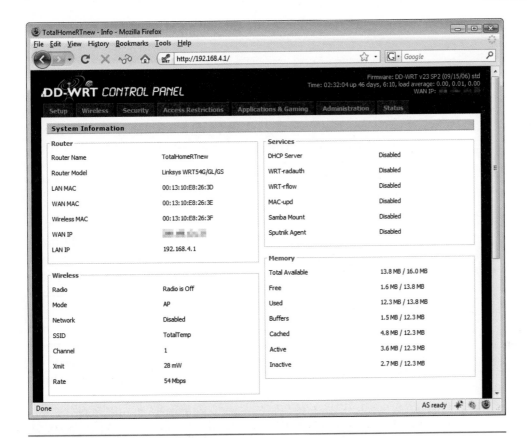

● **Figure 9.14** My router's Web page

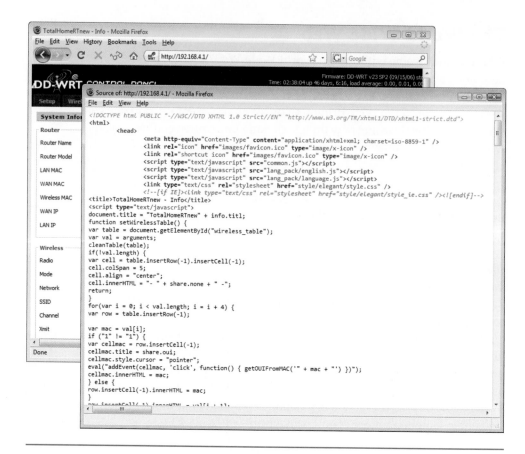

● **Figure 9.15**   XHTML source code

Granted, most people don't enter IP addresses into browsers, but rather enter text like www.totalsem.com or www.google.com. Memorizing text addresses is much easier than memorizing IP addresses. Web site text addresses use a naming protocol called Dynamic Naming System (DNS), which you will learn about in the next chapter. For now, just enter the IP address as shown.

HTTP

The **Hypertext Transfer Protocol (HTTP)** is the underlying protocol used by the Web, and it runs by default on TCP port 80. When you enter "http://" at the beginning of a Web server's IP address, you are identifying how messages are formatted and transmitted, requesting and responding to the transfer of HTML-formatted files. HTTP defines what actions Web servers and browsers should take in response to various commands.

HTTP has a general weakness in its handling of Web pages: it relays commands executed by users without reference to any commands previously executed. The problem with this is that Web designers continue to design more complex and truly interactive Web pages. HTTP is pretty dumb when it comes to remembering what people have done on a Web site. Luckily for Web designers everywhere, other technologies exist to help HTTP relay commands and thus support more-interactive, intelligent Web sites. These technologies include JavaScript/AJAX, server-side scripting, Adobe Flash, and cookies.

Publishing Web Pages

Once you've designed and created an HTML document, you can share it with the rest of the world. To do so, you find a Web server that will "host" the page. You most certainly can install a Web server on a computer, acquire a legitimate IP address for that computer, and host the Web page yourself. Self-hosting is a time-consuming and challenging project, though, so most people use other methods. Most Internet service providers (ISPs) provide Web servers of their own, or you can find relatively inexpensive Web hosting service companies. The price of Web hosting usually depends on the services and drive space offered. You can typically find a good Web host for around $10 a month for simple Web sites.

One option that has been available for a while is free Web hosting. Usually the services are not too bad, but you will run across a few limitations. Nearly all free Web hosts will insist on the right to place ads on your Web page. This is not as much of an issue if you are posting a basic blog or fan Web page, but if you do any sort of business with your Web site, this can be most annoying to your customers. The worst sort of free Web host services place pop-up ads over your Web page. Beyond annoying!

Once you have uploaded your HTML pages to your Web host, the Web server takes over. What's a Web server? I'm glad you asked!

Web Servers and Web Clients

A Web server is a computer that delivers (or *serves up*) Web pages. Web servers listen on port 80, fetching requested HTML pages and sending them to browsers. You can turn any computer into a Web server by installing server software and connecting the machine to the Internet, but you need to consider the operating system and Web server program you'll use to serve your Web site. Microsoft pushes **Internet Information Services (IIS)**, shown in Figure 9.16.

IIS enables you to set a maximum connection limit on your Web server based on available bandwidth and memory. This enables you to protect your network against an overwhelming number of requests due to a particularly popular page or a type of malicious attack called a Denial of Service (DoS) attack. (More on the latter in Chapter 17, "Protecting Your Network.")

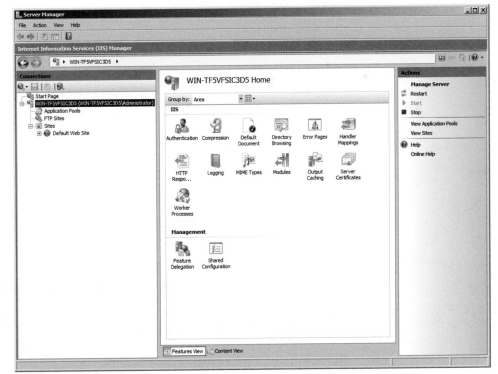

• **Figure 9.16**   IIS in action

Microsoft builds an artificial 20-connection limit into Windows 2000 Professional, Windows XP, and Windows Vista so you should only run IIS on Server versions of Windows (unless you don't expect too many people to visit your Web site at one time).

UNIX/Linux-based operating systems run **Apache HTTP Server**. As of this writing, Apache serves well over 50 percent of the Web sites on the Internet. Apache is incredibly popular, runs on multiple operating systems (including Windows), and, best of all, is *free!* Apache is nothing more than an executable program and a bunch of text files, so it isn't much to look at. To ease configuration, most Web administrators use add-on graphical user interfaces (GUIs) such as Webmin that make administering Apache a breeze. Figure 9.17 illustrates the wonderful simplicity that is Webmin.

IIS and Apache are by far the most common Web servers used on the Internet. In third place is Google Web Server (GWS). GWS, used only by Google's servers, has about 5 percent of the total Web server market! After those three there are literally hundreds of other Web servers, but outside of small personal Web sites you'll rarely see them.

Web clients are the programs used to surf the Web. A client program (a Web browser) reads Web pages supplied by the Web server. Most browsers handle multiple functions, from reading HTML documents to offering FTP services, and even serving as an e-mail or newsgroup reader. (You'll learn all about these functions later in the chapter.) The most popular Web browsers are Microsoft Internet Explorer, Mozilla Firefox, Apple Safari, Opera, and Google Chrome.

In early 2009, China released numbers for a Chinese-only Web server called QZHTTP server and, as with anything to do with China and population, the numbers for hosted sites are staggeringly large. If accurate and sustained, QZHTTP would supplant GWS as the third most popular Web server software.

• **Figure 9.17**   Webmin Apache module

Secure Sockets Layer and HTTPS

HTTP is not a secure protocol. Any nosy person who can plug into a network can see and read the HTTP packets moving between a Web server and a Web client. Less than nice people can easily create a fake Web site to get people to think it's a legitimate Web site and steal their user names and passwords. For an Internet application to be secure it must have authentication (user names and passwords), encryption (stirring up the data so others can't read it), and nonrepudiation (verifying that you are who you really are on both sides of the conversation). While all of Chapter 11, "Securing TCP/IP," is dedicated to these concepts, we can't mention HTTP without at least touching on its secure counterpart, HTTPS. The Web has blossomed into a major economic player, requiring serious security for those who wish to do online transactions (e-commerce). In the early days of e-commerce, people feared that a simple credit card transaction on a less-than-secure Web site could transform their dreams of easy online buying into a nightmare of being robbed blind and ending up living in a refrigerator box.

I can safely say that it was *never* as bad as all that. And nowadays, there are a number of safeguards on the Internet that can protect your purchases *and* your anonymity. One such safeguard is called **Secure Sockets Layer (SSL)**.

SSL is a protocol developed by Netscape for transmitting private documents over the Internet. SSL works by using a public key to encrypt sensitive data. This encrypted data is sent over an SSL connection, and then decrypted at the receiving end using a private key. All the popular Web browsers and Web servers support SSL, and many Web sites use the protocol to obtain confidential user information, such as credit card numbers. One way to tell if a site is using SSL is by looking at the Web page address. By convention, Web pages that use an SSL connection start with *https* instead of *http*. **HTTPS** stands for **Hypertext Transfer Protocol over SSL**. HTTPS uses TCP port 443. You can also look for a small lock icon in the lower-right corner. Figure 9.18 shows a typical secure Web page. The https: in the address and the lock icon are circled.

> Most Windows users just use Internet Explorer since it comes on Windows by default.

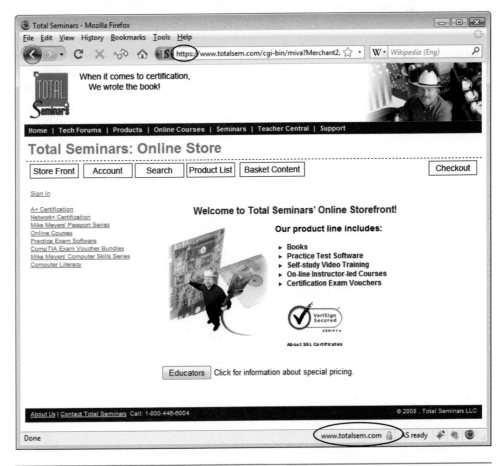

• **Figure 9.18** Secure Web page

The last few years have seen SSL replaced with the more powerful *Transport Layer Security (TLS)*. Your secure Web page still looks the same as with SSL, so only the folks setting this up really care. Just make sure you know that SSL and TLS are functionally the same with Web pages. Read Chapter 11 for more details on SSL and TLS.

Telnet

Roughly one billion years ago there was no such thing as the Internet or even networks . . . Well, maybe it was only about 40 years ago, but as far as nerds like me are concerned, a world before the Internet was filled with brontosauruses and palm fronds. The only computers were huge monsters called mainframes and to access them required a dumb terminal like the one shown in Figure 9.19.

Operating systems didn't have windows and pretty icons. The interface to the mainframe was a command line, but it worked just fine for the time. The cavemen who first lifted their heads up from the computer ooze known as mainframes said to themselves, "Wouldn't it be great if we could access each other's computers from the comfort of our own caves?" That was what started the entire concept of a network. Back then the idea of sharing folders or printers or Web pages wasn't even yet considered. The entire motivation for networking was so people could sit at their dumb terminals and, instead of accessing only their local mainframes, access totally different mainframes. The protocol to do this was called the *Telnet Protocol* or simply **Telnet**.

• **Figure 9.19**   Dumb terminal (photo courtesy of DVQ)

Even though PCs have replaced mainframes for the most part, Telnet still exists as the way to connect remotely to another computer via the command line (Figure 9.20). Telnet runs on TCP port 23, enabling you to connect to a Telnet server and run commands on that server as if you were sitting right in front of it.

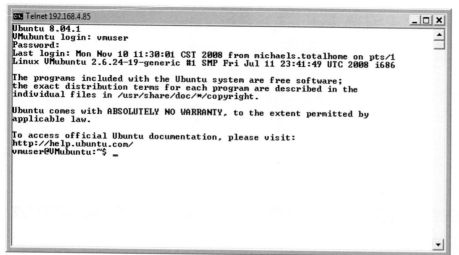

• **Figure 9.20**   Telnet client

This way, you can remotely administer a server and communicate with other servers on your network. As you can imagine, this is sort of risky. If you can remotely control a computer, what is to stop others from doing the same? Thankfully, Telnet does not just allow *anyone* to log on and wreak havoc with your network. You must enter a user name and password to access a Telnet server. Unfortunately, Telnet does not have any form of encryption. If someone intercepted the conversation between a Telnet client and

Telnet server, he or she would see all of the commands you type as well as the results from the Telnet server. As a result, Telnet is rarely used on the Internet and has been replaced with **Secure Shell (SSH)**, a terminal emulation program that looks exactly like Telnet but encrypts the data.

Even though Telnet is less common than SSH, Telnet is a popular second option to connect to almost anything on a trusted TCP/IP network. Most routers have Telnet access capability (although many router admins turn it off for security). Almost every operating system has a built-in Telnet client and most operating systems—though not all Windows operating systems—come with built-in Telnet servers. Almost every type of server application has some way for you to access it with Telnet. It was once quite common, for example, to administer Apache-based Web servers through Telnet.

Telnet Servers and Clients

The oldest Telnet server, found on UNIX and Linux systems, is the venerable telnetd. Like most UNIX/Linux servers, telnetd isn't much to look at, so let's move over to the Windows world. Since Windows itself doesn't have a built-in Telnet server, we lean toward third-party server programs like freeSSHd (Figure 9.21). Note the name—freeSSHd, not "freeTelnet." As Telnet fades away and SSH becomes more dominant, it's hard to find a Telnet-only server these days. All of the popular Telnet servers are also SSH servers.

A Telnet client is the computer from which you log onto the remote server. Most operating systems have a built-in Telnet client that you run from a command prompt. Figure 9.22 shows the Telnet client built into

Telnet only enables command-line remote access, not from a GUI. If you want to access another computer's desktop remotely, you need another type of program.

By default, Windows Server 2008 does not have Telnet Server or Telnet Client installed, though you can install both through Server Manager | Features | Add Features. Windows Vista likewise does not have Telnet Client installed. It is available for quick installation in Programs and Features.

Some versions of Windows Server came with a rather poor Telnet server that only allowed a maximum of two client connections.

● **Figure 9.21** freeSSHd

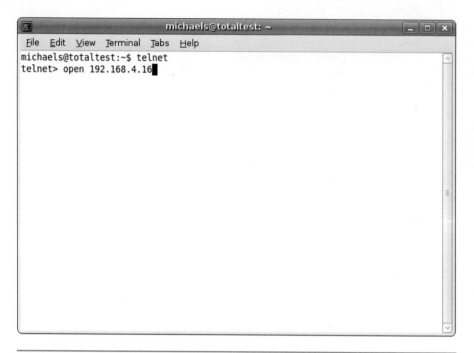

• **Figure 9.22**   Ubuntu Telnet

Ubuntu Linux. Just open a terminal window and type `telnet` and the IP address of the Telnet server.

Command-prompt Telnet clients lack a number of handy features. They can't, for example, remember the IP addresses, user names, or passwords for Telnet servers, so every time you use Telnet, you have to enter all that information again. Third-party Telnet clients, such as the very popular PuTTY you saw in Chapter 8, store all this information and much more (Figure 9.23).

Configuring a Telnet Client

When you configure a Telnet client, you must provide the host name, your user login name, and the password. As I mentioned previously, you must have permission to access the server to use Telnet. A *host name* is the name or IP address of the computer to which you want to connect. For instance, you might connect to a Web server with the host name websrv.mhteched.com. The user *login name* you give Telnet should be the same login name you'd use if you logged into the server at its location. Some computers, usually university libraries with online catalogs, have open systems that enable you to log in with Telnet. These sites will

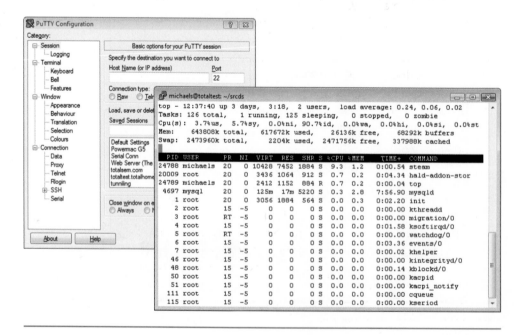

• **Figure 9.23**   PuTTY

Mike Meyers' CompTIA Network+ Guide to Managing and Troubleshooting Networks

either display a banner before the login prompt that tells you what login name to use, or they'll require no login name at all. As with the login name, you use the same password for a Telnet login that you'd use to log into the server directly. It's that simple. Computers with open access will either tell you what password to use when they tell you what login name to use, or they'll require no login name/password at all.

Telnet enables you to control a remote computer from a local computer over a network.

Rlogin, RSH, and RCP

The CompTIA Network+ exam tests you on **rlogin**, **RSH**, and **RCP**. These are three old-school programs in the UNIX world. The *R* stands for *remote* and, like Telnet and SSH, these programs provide remote access and control of servers. Also like Telnet, they do not encrypt data and thus should not be used across the Internet. Here is a quick breakdown of the suite:

- **Rlogin**   Remote login works very similarly to Telnet. You simply run the program with the host name of the server and you can connect and run commands just like with Telnet. It has one very nice advantage over Telnet in that it can be configured to log in automatically without the need to enter a user name and password. Rlogin works over TCP port 513.

- **RSH**   Remote Shell allows you to send single commands to the remote server. Whereas rlogin is designed to be used interactively, RSH can be easily integrated into a script. RSH runs over TCP port 514 by default.

- **RCP**   Remote Copy provides the capability to copy files to and from the remote server without the need to resort to FTP or NFS (Network File System, the UNIX form of folder sharing). RCP can also be used in scripts and shares TCP port 514 with RSH.

SSH and the Death of Telnet

Telnet has seen long and heavy use in the TCP world from the earliest days of the Internet, but it suffers from lack of any security. Telnet passwords as well as data are transmitted in cleartext and are thus easily hacked. To that end, SSH has now replaced Telnet for any serious terminal emulation. In terms of what it does, SSH is extremely similar to Telnet in that it creates a terminal connection to a remote host. Every aspect of SSH, however, including both login and data transmittal, is encrypted. SSH also uses TCP port 22 instead of Telnet's port 23.

SSH enables you to control a remote computer from a local computer over a network, just like Telnet. Unlike Telnet, SSH enables you to do it securely!

E-mail

Electronic mail (e-mail) has been a major part of the Internet revolution, and not just because it has streamlined the junk mail industry. E-mail provides an extremely quick way for people to communicate with one another, letting you send messages and attachments (like documents and pictures) over the Internet. It's normally offered as a free service by ISPs. Most e-mail client programs provide a rudimentary text editor for composing messages, but many can be configured to let you edit your messages using more sophisticated editors.

E-mail consists of e-mail clients and e-mail servers. When a message is sent to your e-mail address, it is normally stored in an electronic mailbox on your e-mail server until you tell the e-mail client to download the message. Most e-mail client programs can be configured to signal you in some way when a new message has arrived or to automatically download e-mails as they come to you. Once you read an e-mail message, you can archive it, forward it, print it, or delete it. Most e-mail programs are configured to automatically delete messages from the e-mail server when you download them to your local machine, but you can usually change this configuration option to suit your circumstances.

E-mail programs use a number of application-level protocols to send and receive information. Specifically, the e-mail you find on the Internet uses SMTP to send e-mail, and either POP3 or IMAP4 to receive e-mail.

SMTP, POP3, and IMAP4, Oh My!

The following is a list of the different protocols that the Internet uses to transfer and receive mail:

SMTP   The **Simple Mail Transfer Protocol (SMTP)** is used to send e-mail. SMTP travels over TCP port 25, and is used by clients to send messages.

POP3   **Post Office Protocol version 3 (POP3)** is one of the two protocols that receive e-mail from SMTP servers. POP3 uses TCP port 110. Most e-mail clients use this protocol, although some use IMAP4.

IMAP4   **Internet Message Access Protocol version 4 (IMAP4)** is an alternative to POP3. Like POP3, IMAP4 retrieves e-mail from an e-mail server. IMAP4 uses TCP port 143 and supports some features that are not supported in POP3. For example, IMAP4 enables you to search through messages on the mail server to find specific keywords, and select the messages you want to download onto your machine. IMAP4 also supports the concept of folders that you can place on the IMAP4 server to organize your e-mail. Some POP3 e-mail clients have folders, but that's not a part of POP3, just a nice feature added to the client.

Alternatives to SMTP, POP3, and IMAP4

While SMTP and POP3 or IMAP4 are by far the most common and most traditional tools for doing e-mail, two other options have wide popularity: Web-based e-mail and proprietary solutions. Web-based mail, as the name implies, requires a Web interface. From a Web browser, you simply surf to the Web-mail server, log in, and access your e-mail. The cool part is that you can do it from anywhere in the world where you find a Web browser and an Internet hookup! You get the benefit of e-mail without even needing to own a computer. Some of the more popular Web-based services are Google's Gmail (Figure 9.24), Microsoft's MSN Hotmail, and Yahoo! Mail.

The key benefits of Web-based e-mail services are as follows:

- You can access your e-mail from anywhere.
- They're free.
- They're handy for throw-away accounts (like when you're required to give an e-mail address to download something, but you know you're going to get spammed if you do).

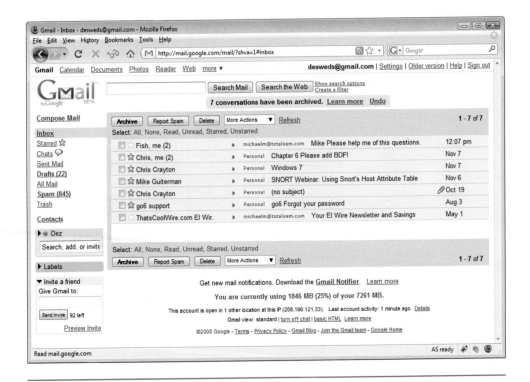

● **Figure 9.24**   Gmail in action

Many traditional SMTP/POP/IMAP accounts also provide Web interfaces, but you should not confuse them with Web mail services. Web-based e-mail services are only available through the Web (although some will also give you SMTP/POP access).

E-mail Servers

The e-mail server world is much more fragmented than the Web server world. The current leader is **sendmail** used on Linux and UNIX operating systems. Like Apache, sendmail doesn't really have an interface, but there are many different third-party interfaces to help configure sendmail, such as Webmin shown in Figure 9.25.

Sendmail controls about 20 percent of all e-mail servers, but only uses SMTP. You must run a POP3 or IMAP4

● **Figure 9.25**   Webmin with the sendmail module

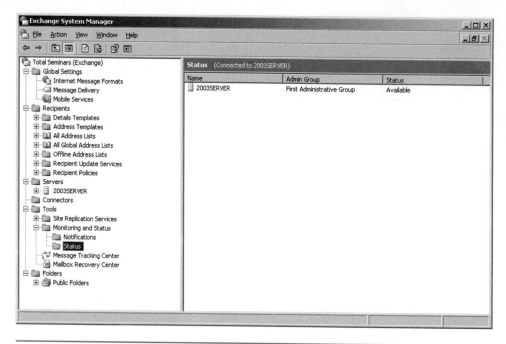

server program to support e-mail clients. Programs like Eudora's Qpopper handle sending mail to POP3 e-mail clients. Microsoft of course has its own e-mail server, Microsoft Exchange Server, and like IIS it only runs on Windows (Figure 9.26). Exchange Server is both an SMTP and a POP3 server in one package.

E-mail servers accept incoming mail and sort out the mail for recipients into individual storage areas mailboxes. These **mailboxes** are special separate holding areas for each user's e-mail. An e-mail server works much like a post office, sorting and arranging incoming messages, and kicking back those messages that have no known recipient.

Perhaps one reason e-mail servers are so little understood is that they're difficult to manage. E-mail servers store user lists, user rights, and messages, and are constantly involved in Internet traffic and resources. Setting up and administering an e-mail server takes a lot of planning, although it's getting easier. Most e-mail server software runs in a GUI, but even the command-line-based interface of e-mail servers is becoming more intuitive.

E-mail Client An **e-mail client** is a program that runs on a computer and enables you to send, receive, and organize e-mail. The e-mail client program communicates with the SMTP e-mail server to send mail and communicates with the IMAP or POP e-mail server to download the messages from the e-mail server to the client computer. There are hundreds of e-mail programs, some of the most popular of which are Microsoft's Windows Mail (Figure 9.27), Microsoft Outlook, Mozilla Thunderbird, and Qualcomm's Eudora.

• **Figure 9.26**   Microsoft Exchange Server

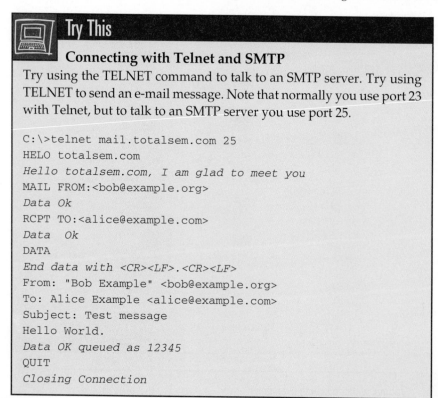

Try This

Connecting with Telnet and SMTP

Try using the TELNET command to talk to an SMTP server. Try using TELNET to send an e-mail message. Note that normally you use port 23 with Telnet, but to talk to an SMTP server you use port 25.

```
C:\>telnet mail.totalsem.com 25
HELO totalsem.com
Hello totalsem.com, I am glad to meet you
MAIL FROM:<bob@example.org>
Data Ok
RCPT TO:<alice@example.com>
Data  Ok
DATA
End data with <CR><LF>.<CR><LF>
From: "Bob Example" <bob@example.org>
To: Alice Example <alice@example.com>
Subject: Test message
Hello World.
Data OK queued as 12345
QUIT
Closing Connection
```

Configuring an E-mail Client

Configuring a client is an easy matter. Your mail administrator will give you the server's addresses and your mailbox's user name and password. You need to enter the POP3 or IMAP4 server's IP address and the SMTP server's address to the e-mail client (Figure 9.28). Every e-mail client has a different way to add the server IP addresses, so you may have to poke around but you'll find the option there somewhere! In many cases this may be the same IP address for both the incoming and outgoing servers—the folks administering the mail servers will tell you. Besides the e-mail server addresses, you must also enter the user name and password of the e-mail account the client will be managing.

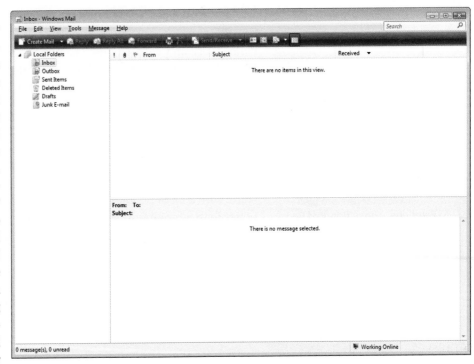

● **Figure 9.27**   Windows Mail

FTP

File Transfer Protocol (FTP) is the original protocol used on the Internet for transferring files. Although HTTP can be used to transfer files as well, the transfer is often not as reliable or as fast as with FTP. In addition, FTP can do the transfer with security and data integrity. FTP uses TCP ports 21 and 20 by default.

FTP sites are either anonymous sites, meaning that anyone can log on, or secured sites, meaning that you must have a user name and password to be able to access the site and transfer files. A single FTP site can offer both anonymous access and protected access, but you'll see different resources depending on which way you log in.

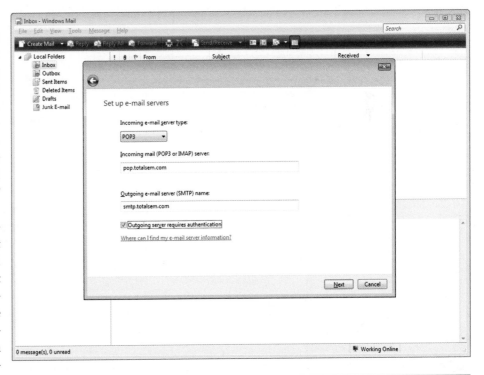

● **Figure 9.28**   Entering server information in Windows Mail

FTP Servers and FTP Clients

The FTP server does all the real work of storing the files, accepting incoming connections and verifying user names and passwords, and transferring the files. The client logs onto the FTP server (either from a Web site, a command line, or a special FTP application) and downloads the requested files onto the local hard drive.

FTP Servers We don't set up servers for Internet applications nearly as often as we set up clients. I've set up only a few Web servers over the years whereas I've set up thousands of Web browsers. FTP servers are the one exception, as we nerds like to exchange files. If you have a file you wish to share with a lot of people (but not the entire Internet), there are few options better than whipping up a quick FTP server. Most versions of Linux/UNIX have built-in FTP servers, but many third-party applications offer better solutions. One of the best, especially for those "let me put up an FTP server so you guys can get a copy" type of situations is Mozilla's FileZilla Server (Figure 9.29).

FTP is not very secure so you don't want to use FTP for sensitive data. But you can add user names and passwords to prevent all but the most serious hackers from accessing your FTP server. I avoid using the anonymous login unless I'm not worried about who gets a hold of the files I'm offering on my FTP server.

Another thing to check when deciding on an FTP server setup is the number of clients you want to support. Most anonymous FTP sites limit the number of users who may download at any one time to around 500. This protects you from a sudden influx of users flooding your server and eating up all your Internet bandwidth.

> Most Web servers are also FTP servers. These bundled versions of FTP servers are robust, but do not provide all the options one might want.

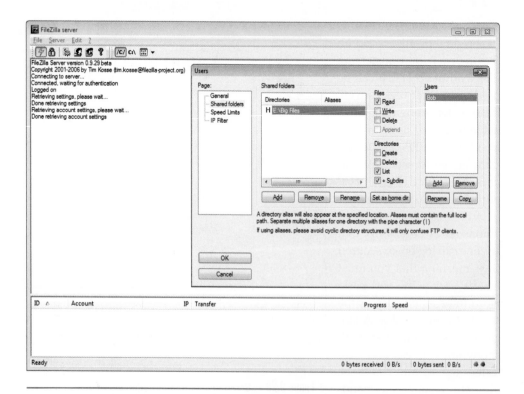

• **Figure 9.29** FileZilla Server

FTP Clients   FTP clients, as noted before, can access an FTP server through a Web site, a command line, or a special FTP application. Usually special FTP applications offer the most choices for accessing and using an FTP site.

You have a lot of choices when it comes to FTP clients. For starters, most Web browsers handle FTP as well as HTTP, although they lack a few features. For example, Firefox only supports an anonymous login. To use your Web browser as an FTP client, type **ftp://** followed by the IP address of the FTP server (Figure 9.30).

The best way to use FTP is to use a dedicated FTP client. There are so many good ones that I find myself using a different one all the time. FileZilla comes in a client version, but these days I'm using an add-on to Firefox called FireFTP (Figure 9.31).

Passive vs. Active FTP

FTP has two ways to transfer data, called active and passive FTP. Traditionally, FTP uses the active process—let's see how this works. Remember that FTP uses TCP ports 20 and 21? Well, when your client sends an FTP request, it goes out on port 21. However, when your FTP server responds, it

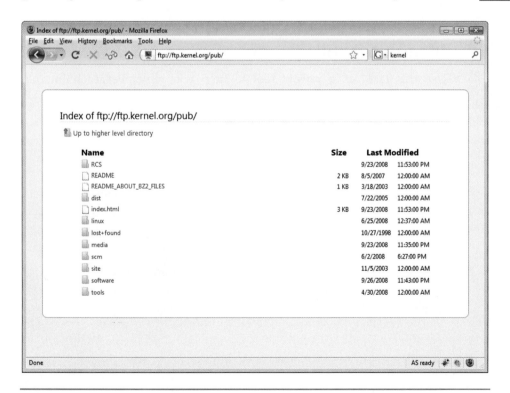

• **Figure 9.30**   FTP in a Web browser

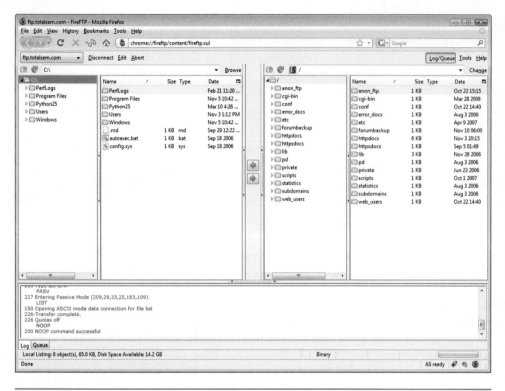

● **Figure 9.31**   Author's FireFTP hard at work

sends the data back using an ephemeral destination port and port 20 as a source port.

Active FTP works great unless your client uses NAT. Since your client didn't initiate the incoming port 20, your NAT router has no idea where to send this incoming packet. No problem! Good FTP clients all support passive FTP. With passive FTP, the server doesn't use port 20. Instead, it sends back the packet using the ephemeral source port used by the client as the destination port and uses another ephemeral port for the source port. This way the NAT router knows where to send the packet.

The only trick to passive FTP is that the client needs to expect this other incoming data. When you configure an FTP client for passive, you're telling it to expect these packets.

> TFTP is used for transferring files and has a similar-sounding name to FTP, but beyond that it is very different. TFTP uses UDP port 69 and does not use user names and passwords, although you can usually put some restriction based on the client's IP address. TFTP is not at all secure, so never use it on any network that's less than trustworthy.

Internet Applications

Use this table as a review tool to help you remember each Internet application:

Application	TCP/UDP	Port	Notes
HTTP	TCP	80	The Web
HTTPS	TCP	443	The Web, securely
Telnet	TCP	23	Terminal emulation
SSH	TCP	22	Secure terminal emulation
SMTP	TCP	25	Sending e-mail
POP3	TCP	110	E-mail delivery
IMAP4	TCP	143	E-mail delivery
FTP	TCP	20/21	File transfer
TFTP	UDP	69	File transfer

Chapter 9 Review

■ Chapter Summary

After reading this chapter and completing the exercises, you should understand the following about the basics of TCP/IP.

Describe common Transport layer protocols

- TCP/IP involves many more protocols other than just TCP over IP. HTTP, DHCP, POP, UDP, and ICMP are just a few of the hundreds of other protocols that operate over IP.

- Connections between computers are called sessions. If every communication requires an acknowledgment from the receiving computer, the session is said to be connection-oriented. Otherwise, the session is connectionless.

- TCP is a connection-oriented protocol while UDP is connectionless. TCP packets must create a connection between systems to ensure that each packet reached its destination intact. UDP packets do not have a built-in checking mechanism to make sure they were received correctly.

- Applications that use ICMP, such as PING, are always connectionless and never need more than a single packet.

- IGMP allows routers to forward multicast IP packets to IGMP groups.

Explain the power of port numbers

- Well-known port numbers fall within the range 0–1023. Web servers use port 80.

- Ephemeral port numbers fall within the range 1024–5000—the classic ephemeral ports—and 49152–65535—the dynamic or private ports.

- Registered ports are those that have been registered with the Internet Assigned Numbers Authority and fall within the range 1024–49151.

- Information about a session is stored in RAM and is called a socket. The sockets stored by two computers in a session with each other are called socket pairs or endpoints.

- The NETSTAT command-line utility, with the –n switch, is used to view a list of endpoints.

However, it can't automatically update to display real-time information.

- An open port, or listening port, is a socket prepared to respond to incoming IP packets. You can type `netstat –an` to see all of your listening ports.

- You can use the `netstat –ano` command to identify which application is using a specific port, allowing techs to identify malicious software.

- The NETSTAT switches –a, –n, and –o are important for any tech to know.

Define common TCP/IP applications, such as HTTP, HTTPS, Telnet, e-mail (SMTP, POP3, and IMAP4), and FTP

- HTTP stands for the Hypertext Transfer Protocol. HTTP uses port 80 to transmit the common data used in Web pages.

- To make Web pages available to the public, the Web pages must reside on a computer with Web server software installed and configured. Microsoft's Internet Information Services and Apache HTTP Server are the most common Web server software.

- A Web client is a program, such as a Web browser, that displays or reads Web pages.

- HTTPS stands for Hypertext Transfer Protocol over Secure Sockets Layer (SSL), which uses port 443. HTTPS protects sensitive data, like credit card numbers and personal information, by encrypting it.

- Telnet is a protocol that enables a user with the proper permissions to log onto a host computer, acting as a Telnet client. The user could then perform tasks on a remote computer, called a Telnet server, as if he or she were sitting at the remote computer itself.

- Telnet sends passwords and data in easily detected cleartext, so most servers use Secure Shell (SSH) now.

- The UNIX utilities rlogin, RSH, and RCP enable a user to issue commands to a server remotely. They should not be used across the Internet because none of them encrypt data.

- The term e-mail stands for electronic mail. E-mail is sent using the SMTP protocol on port 25, and is received using either POP3 (on port 110) or IMAP4 (on port 143).

- E-mail servers are needed to help forward, store, and retrieve e-mail messages for end users, who need a valid user name and password to gain access. E-mail can also contain attachments of limited size, like pictures or small programs or data files.

- Sendmail is the leading e-mail server for Linux and UNIX, but it only supports SMTP. Exchange Server is the e-mail server software from Microsoft and it supports both SMTP and POP.

- A mailbox is a storage area with an e-mail server that holds all the e-mail for a specific user.

- An e-mail client allows you to send, receive, and organize e-mail. Popular e-mail clients include Microsoft Outlook, Windows Mail, Mozilla Thunderbird, and Qualcomm's Eudora.

- FTP stands for the File Transfer Protocol, which uses ports 20 and 21, and efficiently transmits large files. Many FTP sites allow anonymous access to avoid end users sending their passwords in clear-text format.

- Active FTP uses both ports 20 and 21 and can be problematic if you are using NAT. Passive FTP uses only port 20 and works fine with NAT.

- Trivial FTP (TFTP) uses UDP port 69 and does not use user names or passwords, making it very insecure.

- A good network tech knows the port numbers for popular Internet applications and protocols such as HTTP, Telnet, SSH, SMTP, POP3, IMAP4, FTP, and TFTP.

■ Key Terms

Apache HTTP Server *(226)*
connection *(216)*
connectionless *(211)*
connection-oriented *(211)*
dynamic port number *(215)*
electronic mail (e-mail) *(231)*
e-mail client *(234)*
endpoint *(216)*
endpoints *(216)*
ephemeral port number *(215)*
File Transfer Protocol (FTP) *(235)*
Hypertext Transfer Protocol (HTTP) *(224)*
Hypertext Transfer Protocol over SSL (HTTPS) *(227)*
Internet Control Message Protocol (ICMP) *(213)*
Internet Group Management Protocol (IGMP) *(213)*
Internet Information Services (IIS) *(225)*
Internet Message Access Protocol version 4 (IMAP4) *(232)*
listening port *(219)*
mailbox *(234)*

NETSTAT *(216)*
open port *(219)*
Post Office Protocol version 3 (POP3) *(232)*
private port number *(215)*
RCP *(231)*
registered port *(215)*
rlogin *(231)*
RSH *(231)*
Secure Shell (SSH) *(229)*
Secure Sockets Layer (SSL) *(227)*
sendmail *(233)*
session *(211)*
Simple Mail Transfer Protocol (SMTP) *(232)*
socket *(216)*
socket pairs *(216)*
Telnet *(228)*
Transmission Control Protocol (TCP) *(212)*
Trivial File Transfer Protocol (TFTP) *(213)*
User Datagram Protocol (UDP) *(212)*
well-known port number *(214)*

■ Key Term Quiz

Use the Key Terms list to complete the sentences that follow. Not all terms will be used.

1. The TCP port numbers ranging from 0–1023 are called _____.

2. The TCP port numbers ranging from 1024–49151 are called _____.

3. The protocol used to transmit large files over the Web using both ports 20 and 21 is called _____.

4. The protocol that is not as popular as POP3 for receiving e-mail is _____.

5. Port 23 is used by _____ to emulate terminals on TCP/IP networks.

6. When you send out an e-mail message it uses _____.

7. The quickest way to send to a few co-workers information about an upcoming meeting would be to send a(n) _____.

8. The _____ utility can be used to view the endpoints of your computer's sessions.

9. Telnet has largely been replaced by _____, which provides better security through data encryption.

10. TCP is _____ in that it requires computers to acknowledge each other; while UDP is _____ in that it provides no guarantee packets were successfully received.

■ Multiple-Choice Quiz

1. What port number is the well-known port used by Web servers to distribute Web pages to Web browsers?

   A. Port 20

   B. Port 21

   C. Port 25

   D. Port 80

2. What protocol handles large file transfers between Internet users?

   A. FTP

   B. IMAP

   C. POP3

   D. SMTP

3. How can you tell that a secure Web page transaction is taking place?

   A. The URL in the address bar starts with https

   B. The URL in the address bar starts with http/ssl

   C. The URL in the address bar starts with ssl

   D. The URL in the address bar starts with tls

4. Jane has been tasked to find and implement an application that will enable her boss to log into and control a server remotely and securely. Which of the following applications would work best?

   A. E-mail

   B. FTP

   C. Telnet

   D. SSH

5. How do Web pages get created on the Internet?

   A. By ICANN

   B. By InterNIC

   C. By publishing them

   D. By the FCC

6. Which of the following Microsoft operating systems limit Web site access from other systems when using Internet Information Services software? (Select three.)

   A. Windows 2000

   B. Windows XP

   C. Windows Vista

   D. Windows 2003 server

7. Which of the following are names of Web server software? (Select two.)

   A. Apache

   B. Exchange

   C. IIS

   D. Proxy server

8. Which of the following are names of Internet browser software? (Select two.)

A. Internet Surfware

B. Internet Explorer

C. Firefox

D. WS_FTP

9. Which of the following items does the *S* in HTTPS represent?

A. Proxy server

B. Secure Sockets Layer

C. Subnet mask

D. Switch

10. When using Windows, which command will show all used ports and the IP addresses using them?

A. `telnet localhost 25`

B. `telnet -ano`

C. `netstat -an`

D. `netstat -ao`

11. What is the main difference between TCP and UDP?

A. TCP is connection-oriented while UDP is connectionless.

B. TCP supports HTTPS while UDP supports SSL.

C. TCP sessions can be encrypted while UDP sessions cannot.

D. TCP is used on Windows while UDP is used on Linux/UNIX/Mac OS X.

12. What protocol is used by applications requiring a single packet over a connectionless session?

A. TCP

B. UDP

C. ICMP

D. IGMP

13. Which of the following provide Web services? (Select three.)

A. Apache

B. IIS

C. GWS

D. Exchange

14. Which UNIX utility enables you to connect to a server automatically and run commands without entering a user name and password every time?

A. Telnet

B. rlogin

C. RSH

D. RCP

15. What should you do if you are having difficulty transferring files with your FTP client when your router supports NAT?

A. Configure your FTP client to use active FTP.

B. Configure your FTP client to use passive FTP.

C. Use SSH to transfer your files instead.

D. Use Telnet to connect to the server, then use NETSTAT to transfer the files.

■ Essay Quiz

1. Your company is interested in setting up secure Web pages for credit card transactions. The company currently does have a Web presence. Write two short paragraphs describing the two different port numbers that would be used on the company's improved Web site.

2. After checking various e-mail settings, a colleague of yours mentions port numbers. Write down some quick notes about which TCP ports would handle e-mail.

3. Write down a few notes explaining why some Web pages have an extra *s* after the http in their Web addresses. Be prepared to discuss your findings in class.

4. Write on a sheet of paper a paragraph that describes what a Web server does. Write a second paragraph that describes what an e-mail server does.

Lab Projects

• Lab Project 9.1

Start some Internet programs, like a Web browser, e-mail or FTP client, or an instant messenger. Open a command prompt and type `netstat -ano`. Make a list of the well-known ports in use and the process ID using the port. Then write the actual name of the application identified by the process ID. Linux users can type `ps` to learn the application name of a process ID, but Windows users have to use a third-party tool like Process Explorer.

• Lab Project 9.2

Using a word processing program or a spreadsheet program, create a chart that lists all the port numbers mentioned in this chapter, similar to the following list. Use the Internet to look up other commonly used port numbers as well. Fill in the Abbreviation column, the Full Name column, and the Brief Description column. Repeat this lab exercise several times until you have memorized it fully. This activity will help you pass the CompTIA Network+ exam!

Port #	Abbreviation	Full Name	Brief Description of What This Port Does...
20			
21			
22			
23			
25			
80			
110			
143			
443			

Network Naming

chapter

10

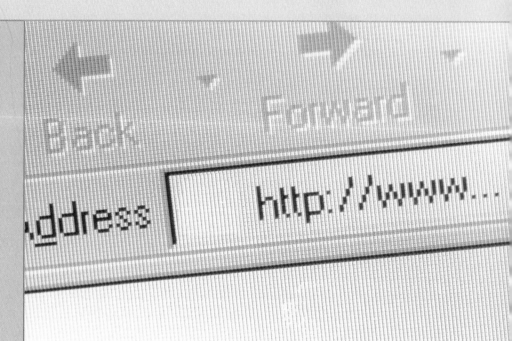

"What's in a name? That which we call a rose
By any other name would smell as sweet."

—WILLIAM SHAKESPEARE

In this chapter, you will learn how to

- **Describe the function and capabilities of DNS**
- **Configure and troubleshoot WINS**
- **Use common TCP/IP utilities to diagnose problems with DNS and WINS**

Did the last chapter seem a bit IP address heavy to you? When you open a Web page, for example, do you normally type something like http://192.168.4.1 or do you usually type something like www.totalsem.com? Odds are good you normally do the latter and only rarely the former. There's a good reason for this: people are terrible at memorizing numbers but are pretty good at memorizing words. This creates an interesting dilemma.

Although computers use IP addresses to communicate with each other over a TCP/IP network, people prefer easy-to-remember names over IP addresses. To solve this problem, TCP/IP developers created a process called **name resolution** to convert names to IP addresses (and *vice versa*) to make it easier for people to communicate with the computers (Figure 10.1).

Like any process that's been around for a long time, name resolution has gone through a number of evolutions over the years: some dramatic and some subtle. Entire TCP/IP applications have been written, only to be supplanted (but never totally abandoned) by newer name resolution protocols.

The end result is that today we have a single major name resolution protocol called **Domain Name System (DNS)**, but your brand new system running the latest version of whatever operating system you prefer still fully supports a number of much older name resolution protocols! Name resolution in today's networking world is like a well-run home that's also full of ghosts that can do very strange things if you don't understand how those ghosts think.

In this chapter, you'll take an in-depth tour of name resolution, starting with an in-depth discovery of DNS. After DNS, the chapter looks at one of the scariest ghosts running around inside your computer: an ancient and theoretically abandoned name resolution protocol invented by Microsoft called **Windows Internet Name Service (WINS)**. Despite what Microsoft claims, the ghost of WINS still lingers, not only on Windows computers, but even on most Linux and Macintosh OS X systems too, as these folks discovered that if you don't respect these ghosts, you won't be able to do name resolution when you connect to a Windows computer.

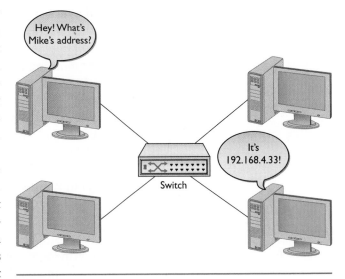

• **Figure 10.1**   Turning names into numbers

Odds are good you have a system that is connected—or at least can connect—to the Internet. If I were you, I'd fire that system up, because the vast majority of the programs you're going to learn about here come free with every operating system made. Finding them may be a challenge on some systems, but don't worry—I'll show you where they all hang out.

Historical/Conceptual

▣ DNS

When the Internet was very young and populated with only a few hundred computers, name resolution was pretty simple. The original TCP/IP specification implemented name resolution using a special text file called HOSTS. A copy of this file was stored on every computer system on the Internet. The **HOSTS file** contained a list of IP addresses for every computer on the Internet, matched to the corresponding system names. Remember, not only was the Internet a lot smaller then, there weren't yet rules about how to compose Internet names, such as that they must end in .com or .org, or start with www or ftp. Anyone could name their computer pretty much anything they wanted (there were a few restrictions on length and allowable characters) as long as nobody else had snagged the name first. Part of an old HOSTS file might look something like this:

```
192.168.2.1     fred
201.32.16.4     school2
123.21.44.16    server
```

If your system wanted to access the system called fred, it looked up the name fred in its HOSTS file, and then used the corresponding IP address to contact fred. Every HOSTS file on every system on the Internet was updated every morning at 2 A.M. This worked fine when the Internet was still the province of a few university geeks and some military guys, but when the Internet grew to about 5000 systems, it became impractical to make every system use and update a HOSTS file. This created the motivation for a more scalable name resolution process, but the HOSTS file did not go away.

Believe it or not, the HOSTS file is still alive and well in every computer. You can find the HOSTS file in the \WINNT\SYSTEM32\DRIVERS\ETC folder in Windows 2000, and in \WINDOWS\SYSTEM32\DRIVERS\ETC in Windows XP/2003/Vista/Windows 7. On OS X and Linux systems, it's usually found in the /etc/ folder. It's just a text file that you can open with any text editor. Below are a few lines from the default HOSTS file that comes with Windows. See the # signs? Those are remark symbols that designate lines as comments (for humans to read) rather than code. Windows ignores any line that begins with #. Remove the # and Windows will read the line and try to act on it. While all operating systems continue to support the

 Try This

Editing the HOSTS File

Every Windows computer has a HOSTS file that you can edit, so try this!

1. Go to a command prompt and type `ping www.totalsem .com`. You may or may not be successful with the PING, but you will get the IP address for my Web site. (You may get a different IP address from the one shown in this example.)

```
C:\>ping www.totalsem.com
Pinging www.totalsem.com [209.29.33.25] with 32 bytes of data:
Reply from 209.29.33.25: bytes=32 time=60ms TTL=51
Reply from 209.29.33.25: bytes=32 time=60ms TTL=51
Reply from 209.29.33.25: bytes=32 time=60ms TTL=51
Reply from 209.29.33.25: bytes=32 time=60ms TTL=51
Ping statistics for 209.29.33.25:
    Packets: Sent = 4, Received = 4, Lost = 0 (0% loss),
Approximate round trip times in milli-seconds:
    Minimum = 60ms, Maximum = 60ms, Average = 60ms
```

2. Open your HOSTS file using any text editor and add this line (keep in mind you may have a different IP address from the one shown in this example). Just press the SPACEBAR a few times to separate the IP address from the word "timmy."

```
209.29.33.25     timmy
```

3. Save the HOSTS file and close the text editor.

4. Open your Web browser and type **timmy**. You can also type **http://timmy** if you'd like. What happens?

HOSTS file, it is rarely used in the day-to-day workings of most TCP/IP systems.

```
# Additionally, comments (such as these) may be inserted on individual
# lines or following the machine name denoted by a '#' symbol.
#
# For example:
#
#      102.54.94.97       rhino.acme.com          # source server
#       38.25.63.10       x.acme.com              # x client host
127.0.0.1           localhost
```

Even though the HOSTS file is rarely used, *every* operating system will always first look in the HOSTS file before anything else when attempting to resolve a name. To see the power of the HOSTS file, do the first Try This! sidebar in this chapter.

The Try This! sidebar example uses a Web browser, but keep in mind that a name in a HOSTS file resolves names for *every* TCP/IP application on that system. Go to a command prompt and type `ping timmy`. It works for PING too.

HOSTS files still have their place in today's world. Lots of people place shortcut names in a HOSTS file to avoid typing long names in some TCP/IP applications. Yet even though HOSTS still has some use, for the most part we use the vastly more powerful DNS.

Test Specific

How DNS Works

The Internet folks, faced with the task of replacing HOSTS, first came up with the idea of creating one supercomputer that did nothing but resolve names for all the other computers on the Internet. Problem: even now, no computer is big enough or powerful enough to handle the job alone. So, they fell back on that time-tested bureaucratic solution: delegation! The top-dog DNS system would delegate parts of the job to subsidiary DNS systems, who, in turn, would delegate part of their work to other systems, and so on, potentially without end. These systems run a special DNS server program, and are called, amazingly enough, **DNS servers**.

This is all peachy, but it raises another issue: you need some way to decide how to divvy up the work. Toward this end, they created a naming system designed to facilitate delegation. The top-dog DNS server is actually a bunch of powerful computers dispersed around the world and working as a team, known collectively as the **DNS root servers** (or simply as the *DNS root*). The Internet name of this computer team is "."—that's right, just "dot." Sure, it's weird, but it's quick to type, and they had to start somewhere.

DNS root has the complete definitive name resolution table, but most name resolution work is delegated to other DNS servers. Just below the DNS root in the hierarchy is a set of DNS servers—called the **top-level domain servers**—that handle what are known as the top-level domain names. These are the famous COM, ORG, NET, EDU, GOV, MIL, and INT. The top-level DNS servers delegate to thousands of second-level DNS servers; they

The DNS root for the entire Internet consists of 13 powerful DNS server clusters scattered all over the world. Go to http://www.root-servers.org to see exactly where all the root servers are located.

DNS servers use TCP and UDP port 53.

handle the millions of names like totalsem.com and whitehouse.gov that have been created within each of the top-level domains. Second-level DNS servers support individual computers. For example, stored on the DNS server controlling the totalsem.com domain is a listing that looks like this:

www   209.29.33.25

This means the totalsem.com domain has a computer called *www* with the IP address of 209.29.33.25. Only the DNS server controlling the totalsem.com domain stores the actual IP address for *www*.totalsem.com. The DNS servers above this one have a hierarchical system that enables any other computer to find the DNS server that controls the totalsem.com domain.

Name Spaces

What does *hierarchical* mean in terms of DNS? Well, the DNS **hierarchical name space** is an imaginary tree structure of all possible names that could be used within a single system. By contrast, a HOSTS file uses a **flat name space**—basically just one big undivided list containing all names, with no grouping whatsoever. In a flat name space, all names must be absolutely unique—no two machines can ever share the same name under any circumstances. A flat name space works fine on a small, isolated network, but not so well for a large organization with many interconnected networks. To avoid naming conflicts, all its administrators would need to keep track of all the names used throughout the entire corporate network.

A hierarchical name space offers a better solution, permitting a great deal more flexibility by enabling administrators to give networked systems longer, more fully descriptive names. The personal names people use every day are an example of a hierarchical name space. Most people address our town postman, Ron Samuels, simply as Ron. When his name comes up in conversation, people usually refer to him as Ron. The town troublemaker, Ron Falwell, and Mayor Jones's son, Ron, who went off to Toledo, obviously share first names with the postman. In some conversations, people need to distinguish between the good Ron, the bad Ron, and the Ron in Toledo (who may or may not be the ugly Ron). They could use a medieval style of address, and refer to the Rons as Ron the Postman, Ron the Blackguard, and Ron of Toledo, or they could use the modern Western style of address and add their surnames: "That Ron Samuels—he is such a card!" "That Ron Falwell is one bad apple." "That Ron Jones was the homeliest child I ever saw." You might visualize this as the People name space, illustrated in Figure 10.2. Adding the surname creates what you might fancifully call a *Fully Qualified Person Name*—enough information to prevent confusion among the various people named Ron.

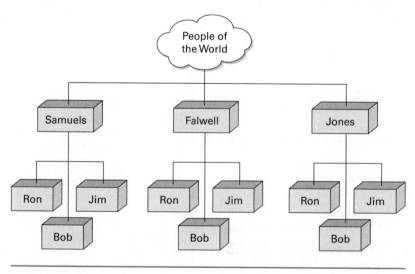

• **Figure 10.2**   Our People name space

A name space most of you are already familiar with is the hierarchical file name space used
by hard drive volumes. Hard drives formatted
using one of the popular file formats, like Window's NTFS or Linux's EXT3, use a hierarchical
name space; you can create as many files named
DATA.TXT as you want, as long as you store
them in different parts of the file tree. In the example shown in Figure 10.3, two different files
named DATA.TXT can exist simultaneously on
the same system, but only if they are placed in
different directories, such as C:\PROGRAM1\
CURRENT\DATA.TXT and C:\PROGRAM1\
BACKUP\DATA.TXT. Although both files
have the same basic filename—DATA.TXT—
their fully qualified names are different: C:\
PROGRAM1\CURRENT\DATA.TXT and C:\
PROGRAM1\BACKUP\DATA.TXT. Additionally, multiple subfolders can use the same
name. There's no problem with having two
subfolders using the name DATA, as long as
they reside in different folders. Any Windows

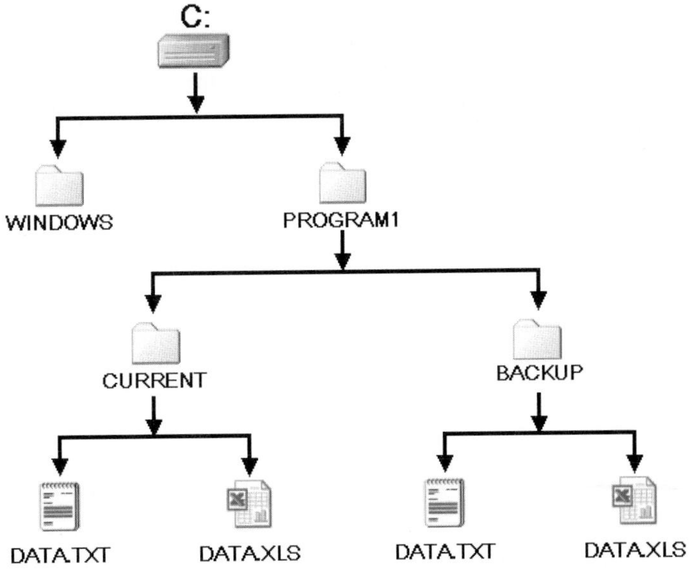

• **Figure 10.3** Two DATA.TXT files in different directories on the same system

file system will happily let you create both C:\PROGRAM1\DATA and C:\
PROGRAM2\DATA folders. We like this because we often want to give the
same name to multiple folders doing the same job for different applications.

In contrast, imagine what would happen if your computer's file system
didn't support folders/directories. It would be as if Windows had to store
all the files on your hard drive in the root directory! This is a classic example
of a flat name space. Because all your files would be living together in one
directory, each one would have to have a unique name. Naming files would
be a nightmare! Software vendors would have to avoid sensible descriptive
names like README.TXT, because they would almost certainly have been
used already. You'd probably have to do what the Internet does for IP addresses: An organization of some sort would assign names out of the limited
pool of possible filenames. With a hierarchical name space, on the other
hand, which is what all file systems use (thank goodness!), naming is much
simpler. Lots of programs can have files called README.TXT, because each
program can have its own folder and subfolders.

As hard as this may be to believe, some early file systems
used a flat name space. Back in
the late 1970s and early 1980s,
operating systems such as CPM
and the early versions of DOS
did not have the capability to
use directories, creating a flat
name space where all files re-
sided on a single drive.

The DNS name space works in a manner extremely similar to how your
computer's file system works. The DNS name space is a hierarchy of *DNS
domains* and individual computer names organized into a tree-like structure
that we call, rather appropriately, a *tree*. Each domain is like a folder—a
domain is not a single computer, but rather a holding space into which you
can add computer names. At the top of a **DNS tree** is the root. The *root* is the
holding area to which all domains connect, just as the root directory in your
file system is the holding area for all your folders. Individual computer
names—more commonly called **host names** in the DNS naming
convention—fit into domains. In the PC, you can place files directly into the
root directory. The DNS world also enables us to add computer names to the
root, but with the exception of a few special computers (described in a
moment), this is rarely done. Each domain can have subdomains, just as the

folders on your PC's file system can have subfolders. You separate each domain from its subdomains with a period. Characters for DNS domain names and host names are limited to uppercase and lowercase letters (A–Z, a–z), numbers (0–9), and the hyphen (-). No other characters may be used.

Don't think DNS is only for computers on the Internet. If you want to make your own little TCP/IP network using DNS, that's fine, although you will have to set up at least one DNS server as the root server for your little private *intranet*. Every DNS server program can be configured as a root server; just don't connect that DNS server to the Internet, because it won't work outside your little network. Figure 10.4 shows a sample DNS tree for a small TCP/IP network that is not attached to the Internet. In this case, there is only one domain: ABCDEF. Each computer on the network has a host name, as shown in the figure.

When you write out the complete path to a file stored on your PC, the naming convention starts with the root directory on the left, followed by the first folder, then any subfolders (in order), and finally the name of the file—for example, c:\sounds\thunder\mynewcobra.wav. The DNS naming convention is *exactly the opposite*. A complete DNS name, including the host name and all of its domains (in order), is called a **fully qualified domain name (FQDN)**, and it's written out with the root on the far right, followed by the names of the domains (in order) added to the left of the root, and the host name on the far left. Figure 10.4 shows the FQDNs for two systems in the ABCDEF domain. Note the period for the root is on the far *right* of each FQDN!

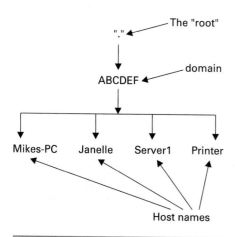

• **Figure 10.4**   Private DNS network

Mikes-PC.ABCDEF.
Janelle.ABCDEF.

Given that every FQDN will always have a period on the end to signify the root, it is commonplace to drop the final period when writing out FQDNs. To make the two example FQDNs fit into common parlance, therefore, you'd skip the last period:

Mikes-PC.ABCDEF
Janelle.ABCDEF

If you're used to seeing DNS names on the Internet, you're probably wondering about the lack of ".com," ".net," or other common DNS domain names. Those conventions are needed for computers that are visible on the Internet, such as Web servers, but they're not required on a private TCP/IP network. As long as you make a point never to make these computers visible on the Internet, you can use any naming convention you want!

Let's look at another DNS name space example, but make it a bit more complex. This network is not on the Internet, so I can use any domain I want. The network has two domains, Houston and Dallas, as shown in Figure 10.5. Note that each domain has a computer called Server1.

Because the network has two different domains, it can have two systems (one on each domain) with the same host name, just as you can have two files with the same name in

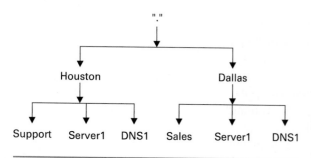

• **Figure 10.5**   Two DNS domains

different folders on your PC. Now, let's add some subdomains to the DNS tree, so that it looks like Figure 10.6.

You write out the FQDN from left to right, starting with the host name and moving up to the top of the DNS tree, adding all domains until you get to the top of the DNS tree:

Mikes-PC.Support.Houston
Tom.Server1.Houston
Janelle.Sales.Dallas
Server1.Dallas

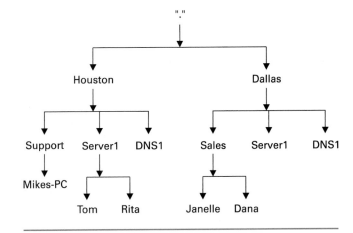

Name Servers

So where does this naming convention reside and how does it work? Here's where the analogy to the

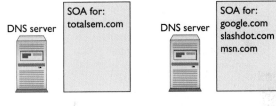

• **Figure 10.6**   Subdomains added

PC's file system breaks down completely. DNS does not have a single hard drive in which to store a directory structure, like you have on a PC. Rather, systems running DNS server software store the DNS information. When a system needs to know the IP address for a specific FQDN, it queries the DNS server listed in its TCP/IP configuration. On a simple network, there is usually one DNS server for the entire network. This single DNS server has a list of all the host names on the domain and their corresponding IP addresses. It's known as the **authoritative DNS server** for the domain (also called Start of Authority, or SOA).

Folks who administer complex networks assign different domains to different DNS servers to keep a single server from being swamped by DNS requests. A single DNS server acts as the authoritative DNS server for one domain or many domains (Figure 10.7).

Equally, a single DNS domain may have a single authoritative DNS server but a number of other DNS servers, known simply as **name servers** (we use the abbreviation "NS"), that are subordinate to the authoritative DNS server but all support the same domain, as shown in Figure 10.8. The SOA is a name server as well.

Note that every DNS server, whether it's the SOA or just an NS, knows the name and address of the SOA as well as every other NS server in the domain. It's the SOA's job to make sure that all the other name servers are

> The DNS naming convention allows for DNS names up to 255 characters, including the separating periods.

• **Figure 10.7**   A single SOA can support one or more domains.

• **Figure 10.8**   DNS flexibility

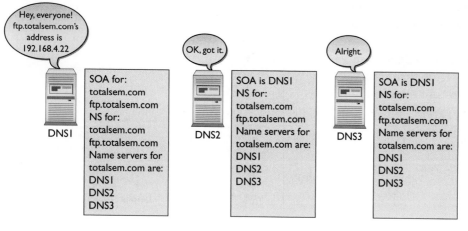

• **Figure 10.9**   New information passed out

In the early days of DNS, you were required to enter manually into your DNS server the host name and IP address of every system on the network. While you can still do that if you want, today most DNS servers take advantage of Dynamic DNS (DDNS). DDNS enables systems to register their host names with their DNS server automatically, eliminating the need to enter them manually.

updated for changes. Let's say you add to the totalsem.com domain a new computer called ftp.totalsem.com with the IP address 192.168.4.22. As an administrator, you typically add this data to the SOA DNS server. The SOA will then automatically distribute this information to the other name servers in the domain (Figure 10.9). This is a critically important feature of DNS—you'll see more of this in detail later in this chapter. For now just appreciate that you can have multiple DNS servers for a single domain.

Now let's see how root servers work in DNS. What if Mikes-PC.Support.Houston needed the IP address of Server1.Dallas? Refer to Figure 10.10 for the answer. The network has two DNS servers: DNS1.Houston and DNS1.Dallas. DNS1.Dallas is the authoritative DNS server for all of the Dallas domains and DNS1.Houston is in charge of all the Houston domains. DNS1.Houston is also the root server for the entire network. (DNS servers may act as both a root server and an SOA at the same time—a very common practice in private networks.) As a root server, the Houston server has a listing for the SOA in the Dallas domain. This does *not* mean it knows the IP address for every system in the Dallas network. As a root server, it only knows

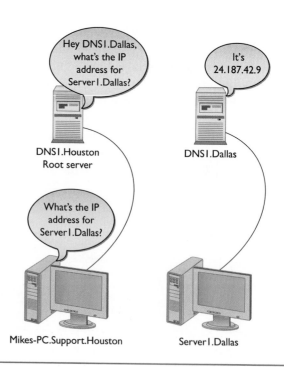

• **Figure 10.10**   Root server in action

that if any system asks for an IP address from the Dallas side, it will tell that system the IP address of the Dallas server. The requesting system will then ask the Dallas DNS server (DNS1.Dallas) for the IP address of the system it needs. That's the beauty of DNS root servers—they don't know the IP addresses for all of the computers, but they know where to send the requests!

The hierarchical aspect of DNS has a number of benefits. For example, the vast majority of Web servers are called www. If DNS used a flat name space, only the first organization that created a server with the name www could use it. Because DNS naming appends domain names to the server names, however, the servers www.totalsem.com and www.microsoft.com can both exist simultaneously. DNS names like www.microsoft.com must fit within a worldwide hierarchical name space, meaning that no two machines should ever have the same FQDN.

Figure 10.11 shows the host named accounting with an FQDN of accounting.texas.totalsem.com.

These domain names must be registered for Internet use with an organization called the Internet Corporation for Assigned Names and Numbers, or ICANN (www.icann.org). They are arranged in the familiar "second level.top level" domain name format, where the top level is COM, ORG, NET, and so on, and the second level is the name of the individual entity registering the domain name.

Just because most Web servers are named www doesn't mean they must be named www! Naming a Web server www is etiquette, not a requirement.

Technically, the texas .totalsem.com domain shown in Figure 10.11 is a subdomain of totalsem.com. Don't be surprised to see the terms "domain" and "subdomain" used interchangeably, as it's a common practice.

Name Resolution

You don't have to use DNS to access the Internet, but it sure makes life a lot easier! Programs like Internet Explorer accept names such as www.microsoft.com as a convenience to the end user, but utilize the IP address that corresponds to that name to create a connection. If you know the IP address of the system you want to talk to, you don't need DNS at all. Figure 10.12 shows Internet Explorer displaying the same Web page when given the straight IP address as it does when given the DNS name www .microsoft.com. In theory, if you knew the IP addresses of all the systems you wanted to access, you could turn off DNS completely. I guess you could also start a fire using a bow and drill too, but most people wouldn't make a habit of it if there were a more efficient alternative, which in this case, DNS definitely is! I

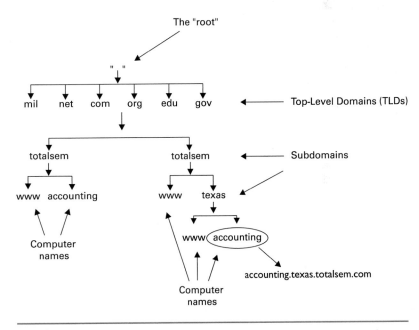

• **Figure 10.11**   DNS domain

have no trouble keeping hundreds of DNS names in my head, but IP addresses? Forget it! Without DNS, I might as well not even try to use the Internet, and I'd wager that's true of most people.

When you type in a Web address, Internet Explorer must resolve that name to the Web server's IP address to make a connection to that Web server. It can resolve the name in three ways: by broadcasting, by consulting the locally stored HOSTS text file, or by contacting a DNS server.

● **Figure 10.12** Any TCP/IP-savvy program accepts either an IP address or an FQDN.

To *broadcast* for name resolution, the host sends a message to all the machines on the network, saying something like, "Hey! If your name is JOESCOMPUTER, please respond with your IP address." All the networked hosts receive that packet, but only JOESCOMPUTER responds with an IP address. Broadcasting works fine for small networks, but it is limited because it cannot provide name resolution across routers. Routers do not forward broadcast messages to other networks, as illustrated in Figure 10.13.

As discussed earlier, a HOSTS file functions like a little black book, listing the names and addresses of machines on a network, just like a little black book lists the names and phone numbers of people. A typical HOSTS file would look like this:

```
109.54.94.197      stephen.totalsem.com
138.125.163.17     roger.totalsem.com
127.0.0.1          localhost
```

> Notice that the name "localhost" appears in the HOSTS file as an alias for the loopback address, 127.0.0.1.

The final way to resolve a name to an IP address is to use DNS. Let's say you type "www.microsoft.com" in your Web browser. To resolve the name www.microsoft.com, the host contacts its DNS server and requests the IP address, as shown in Figure 10.14.

To request the IP address of www.microsoft.com, your PC needs the IP address of its DNS server. You must enter DNS information into your system. DNS server data is part of the critical basic IP information such as your IP address, subnet mask, and default gateway, so it's usually entered at the same time as the other IP information. You configure DNS in Windows Vista using the Internet Protocol Version 4 (TCP/IPv4) Properties dialog

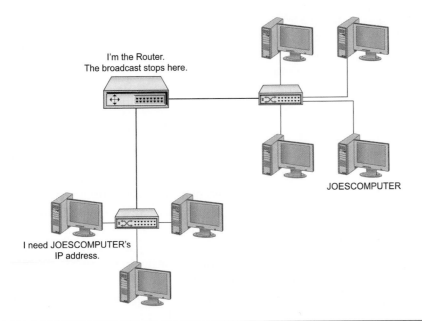

I'm the Router.
The broadcast stops here.

JOESCOMPUTER

I need JOESCOMPUTER's
IP address.

• **Figure 10.13** Routers don't forward broadcasts!

Client

Client's DNS server

1. The client asks its DNS server for the www.microsoft.com IP address.

2. The DNS server doesn't know the IP address, so it asks the root DNS server.

• **Figure 10.14** A host contacts its local DNS server.

box. Figure 10.15 shows the DNS settings for my system. Note that I have more than one DNS server setting; the second one is a backup in case the first one isn't working. Two DNS settings is not a rule, however, so don't worry if your system shows only one DNS server setting, or perhaps more than two.

Every operating system has a way for you to enter DNS server information. In Linux you can directly edit the /etc/resolv.conf file

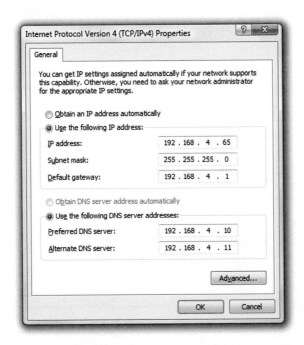

• **Figure 10.15** DNS information in Windows

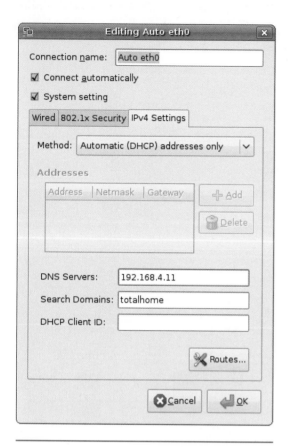

• **Figure 10.16** Entering DNS information in Ubuntu

using a text editor. Just about every version of Linux has some form of graphical editor as well to make this an easy process. Figure 10.16 shows Ubuntu's Network Configuration utility.

Every operating system also comes with a utility you can use to verify the DNS server settings. You can see your current DNS server settings in Windows by typing `ipconfig /all` at the command prompt (Figure 10.17). In UNIX/Linux type `cat /etc/ resolv.conf`.

Now that you know how your system knows the DNS server's IP address, let's return to the DNS process.

The DNS server receives the request for the IP address of www.microsoft.com from your client computer. At this point, your DNS server checks a cache of previously resolved FQDNs to see if www.microsoft.com is there (Figure 10.18). In this case, www.microsoft.com is not in the cache.

It's now time for your DNS server to get to work. The local DNS server may not know the address for www.microsoft .com, but it does know the addresses of the DNS root servers. The root servers, maintained by InterNIC, know all the addresses of the top-level domain DNS servers. The root servers don't know the address of www.microsoft.com, but they do know the address of the DNS servers in charge of all .com addresses. The root servers send your DNS server an IP address for a .com server (Figure 10.19).

The .com DNS server also doesn't know the address of www.microsoft.com, but it knows the IP address of the microsoft.com DNS server. It sends that IP address to your root server (Figure 10.20).

The microsoft.com server does know the IP address of www .microsoft.com, and can send that information back to the local DNS server. Figure 10.21 shows the process of resolving an FQDN into an IP address.

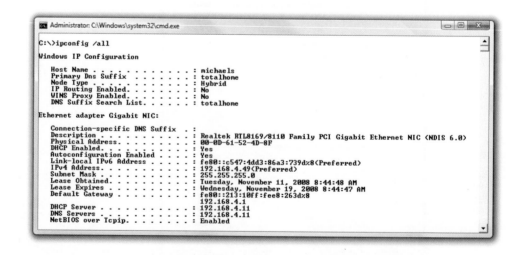

• **Figure 10.17** IPCONFIG /ALL showing DNS information in Windows

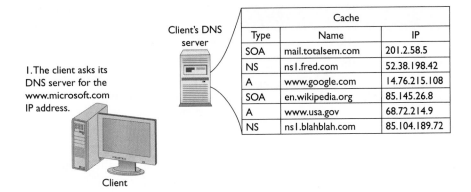

Figure 10.18 Checking the DNS cache

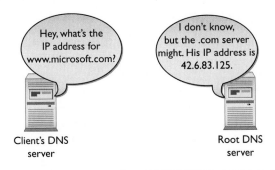

Figure 10.19 Talking to a root server

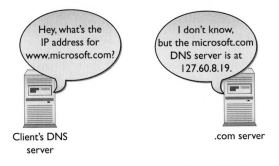

Figure 10.20 Talking to .com server

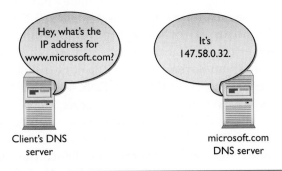

Figure 10.21 Talking to microsoft.com DNS server

Now that your DNS server has the IP address for www.microsoft .com, it stores a copy in its cache and sends the IP information to your PC. Your Web browser then begins the HTTP request to get the Web page.

Your computer also keeps a cache of recently resolved FQDNs. In Windows, for example, open a command prompt and type `ipconfig /displaydns` to see them. Here's a small part of the results of IPCONFIG /DISPLAYDNS:

```
gizmodo.com
----------------------------------------
Record Name . . . . . : gizmodo.com
Record Type . . . . . : 1
Time To Live  . . . . : 70639
Data Length . . . . . : 4
Section . . . . . . . : Answer
A (Host) Record . . . : 69.60.7.199
ftp.totalsem.com
----------------------------------------
Record Name . . . . . : ftp.totalsem.com
Record Type . . . . . : 1
Time To Live  . . . . : 83733
Data Length . . . . . : 4
Section . . . . . . . : Answer
A (Host) Record . . . : 209.29.33.25
C:\>
```

DNS Servers

We've been talking about DNS servers for so long, I feel I'd be untrue to my vision of an All-in-One book unless we took at least a quick peek at a DNS server in action. Lots of operating systems come with built-in DNS server software, including Windows Server and just about every version of UNIX/ Linux. There are also a number of third-party DNS server programs for virtually any operating system. I'm going to use the DNS server program that comes with Microsoft Windows Server 2003 primarily because (1) it takes the prettiest screen snapshots and (2) it's the one I use here at the office. You access the Windows DNS server by selecting **Start | Administrative Tools | DNS**. When you first open the DNS server, there's not much to see other than the name of the server itself. In this case, Figure 10.22 shows a server, imaginatively named TOTALHOMEDC1.

 The most popular DNS server tool used in UNIX/Linux systems is called BIND.

The DNS server has three folder icons visible: Cached Lookups, Forward Lookup Zones, and Reverse Lookup Zones. Let's look at all three.

When you open the tree on a Windows DNS server, the first folder you see is called Cached Lookups. Every DNS server keeps a list of **cached lookups**—that is, all the IP addresses it has already resolved—so it won't have to re-resolve an FQDN it has already checked. There is a limit to the size of the cache, of course, and you can also set a limit on how long the DNS server holds cache entries. Windows does a nice job of separating these

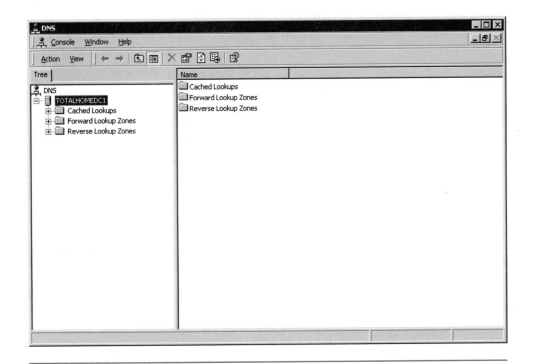

• **Figure 10.22** DNS server main screen

cached addresses by placing all cached lookups in little folders that share the first name of the top-level domain with subfolders that use the second-level domain (Figure 10.23). This sure makes it easy to see where folks have been Web browsing!

Now let's watch an actual DNS server at work. Basically, you choose to configure a DNS server to work in one of two ways: as an authoritative DNS server or as a cache-only DNS server. Authoritative DNS servers store

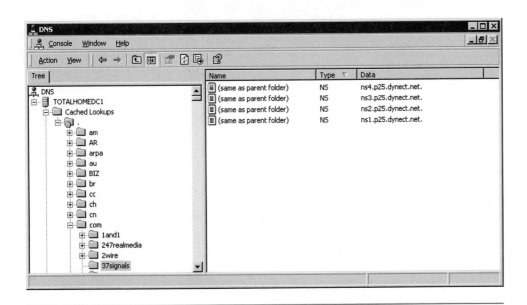

• **Figure 10.23** Inspecting the DNS cache

Cache		
Type	Name	IP
SOA	mail.totalsem.com	201.2.58.5
NS	ns1.fred.com	52.38.198.42
A	www.google.com	14.76.215.108
SOA	en.wikipedia.org	85.145.26.8
A	www.usa.gov	68.72.214.9
NS	ns1.blahblah.com	85.104.189.72

Authoritative   Cache-only

• **Figure 10.24**   Authoritative vs. cache-only DNS server

Microsoft DNS servers use a folder analogy to show lookup zones even though they are not true folders.

IP addresses and FQDNs of systems for a particular domain or domains. **Cache-only DNS servers** do not store any FQDNs and are only used to talk to other DNS servers to resolve IP addresses for DNS clients (Figure 10.24).

The IP addresses and FQDNs for the computers in a domain are stored in special storage areas called **forward lookup zones**. Forward lookup zones are the most important part of any DNS server. Figure 10.25 shows the DNS server for my small corporate network. My domain is called "totalhome." I can get away with a domain name that's not Internet legal because none of these computers are visible on the Internet. The totalhome domain only works on my local network for local computers to find each other. I have created a forward lookup zone called totalhome.

Let's look at the contents of the totalhome domain. First, notice a number of folders: _msdcs, _sites, _tcp, and _udp. These folders are unique to Microsoft DNS servers and you'll see what they do in a moment. For now ignore them and concentrate on the individual computer listings. Every forward lookup zone requires a Start of Authority, the single DNS server in charge. The record called SOA (Start of Authority) in the folder totalhome indicates that my server is the authoritative DNS server for a domain called totalhome. You can even see a few of the systems in that domain (note to hackers: these are fake, so don't bother). A tech looking at this would know that totalhomedc1.totalhome is the authoritative DNS server for the totalhome domain. The **NS records** are all of the DNS servers for totalhome. Note that totalhome has two DNS servers: totalhomedc1.totalhome and tera. Tera is not a member of the totalhome domain. In fact, tera isn't a member of *any* domain. A DNS server does not have to be a member of a domain to be a name server for that domain.

Having two DNS servers insures that if one fails, the totalhome domain will continue to have a DNS server. The **A records** in the folder are the IP addresses and names of all the systems on the totalhome domain.

Every DNS forward lookup zone will have one SOA and at least one NS record. In the vast majority of cases, a forward lookup zone will have some

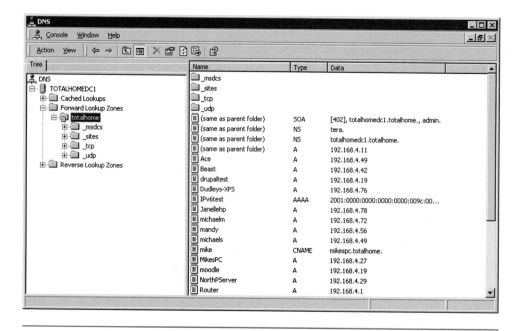

• **Figure 10.25**   Forward lookup zone totalhome

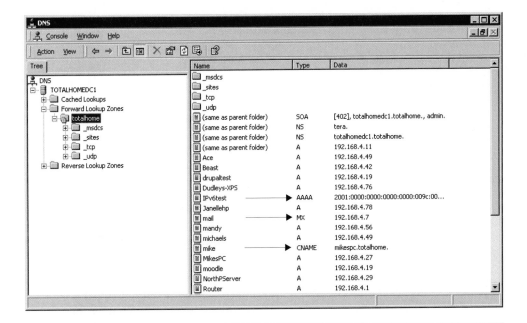

● **Figure 10.26**   Less common DNS record types

number of A records. But there are a number of other records you may or may not see in your standard DNS server. Look at Figure 10.26 for these less common types of DNS records: CNAME, MX, and AAAA.

A **canonical name (CNAME)** record acts like an alias. My computer's name is mikespc.totalhome, but you can also now use mike.totalhome to reference that computer. A PING of mike.totalhome returns the following:

```
C:\>ping mike.totalhome
Pinging mikespc.totalhome [192.168.4.27] with 32 bytes of data:
Reply from 192.168.4.27: bytes=32 time=2ms TTL=128
Reply from 192.168.4.27: bytes=32 time<1ms TTL=128
```
(rest of PING results deleted)

If your computer is a member of a domain and you are trying to access another computer in that domain, you can even skip the domain name because your PC will simply add it back:

```
C:\>ping mike
Pinging mikespc.totalhome [192.168.4.27] with 32 bytes of data:
Reply from 192.168.4.27: bytes=32 time<1ms TTL=128
Reply from 192.168.4.27: bytes=32 time<1ms TTL=128
```
(rest of PING results deleted)

MX records are used exclusively by SMTP servers to determine where to send mail. I have an in-house SMTP server on a computer I cleverly called mail. If other SMTP servers wanted to send mail to mail.totalhome (they can't because the SMTP server isn't connected to the Internet and lacks a legal FQDN), they would use DNS to locate the mail server.

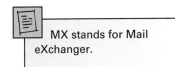

MX stands for Mail eXchanger.

AAAA records are for a newer type of IP addressing called IPv6. You'll learn a lot more about IPv6 in Chapter 13.

There are two common types of forward lookup zones: a primary zone and a secondary zone. **Primary zones** are created on the DNS server that will act as the SOA for that zone. **Secondary zones** are created on other DNS

TOTALDNSI TOTALDNS2

● **Figure 10.27** Two DNS servers with updating taking place

If you're looking at a Windows server and adding a new forward lookup zone, you'll see a third type called an Active Directory–integrated forward lookup zone. I'll cover those in just a moment.

Reverse lookup zone

● **Figure 10.28** Reverse lookup zone

● **Figure 10.29** NetBIOS broadcast

servers to act as backups to the primary zone. It's standard practice to have at least two DNS servers for any forward lookup zone: one primary and one secondary. Even in my small network I have two DNS servers: TOTALDNS1, which runs the primary zone, and TOTALDNS2, which runs a secondary zone (Figure 10.27). Any time a change is placed on TOTALDNS1, TOTALDNS2 is quickly updated.

A **reverse lookup zone** (Figure 10.28) enables a system to determine an FQDN by knowing the IP address; that is, it does the exact reverse of what DNS normally does! Reverse lookup zones take a network ID, reverse it, and add the term "in-addr-arpa" to create the zone. A few low-level functions (like mail) and some security programs use reverse lookup zones, so DNS servers provide them. In most cases the DNS server will ask you if you want to make a reverse lookup zone when you make a new forward lookup zone. When in doubt, make one. If you don't need it, it won't cause any trouble.

Microsoft added some wrinkles to DNS servers with the introduction of Windows 2000 Server, and each subsequent version of Windows Server retains the wrinkles. Windows Server can do cached lookups, primary and secondary forward lookup zones, and reverse lookup zones, just like UNIX/Linux DNS servers. But it also has a Windows-only type of forward lookup zone called an Active Directory–integrated zone.

Enter Windows

DNS works beautifully for any TCP/IP application that needs an IP address of another computer, but it has one glaring weakness: you need to add A records to the DNS server manually. This can be a problem, especially in a world where you have many DHCP clients whose IP addresses may change from time to time. Interestingly, it was a throwback to an old Microsoft Windows protocol that fixed this and a few other problems all at the same time.

Even though TCP/IP was available, back in the 1980s Microsoft popularized another networking protocol called **NetBIOS/NetBEUI**. NetBIOS/NetBEUI was pretty simplistic compared to TCP/IP. It had a very simple naming convention (the NetBIOS part) that used broadcasts. When a computer booted up, it just told the world its name (Figure 10.29).

NetBIOS/NetBEUI was suitable only for small networks. It provided no logical addressing like IP addresses; you just had to remember the NetBIOS name and the MAC address. NetBIOS/NetBEUI was almost exclusively used to share folders and printers. There was no such thing as Telnet or the Web with NetBIOS/NetBEUI, but it worked well for what it did at the time.

By the mid-1990s Microsoft realized that the world was going to TCP/IP and it needed to switch too. Instead of dumping NetBIOS/NetBEUI entirely, Microsoft designed a new TCP/IP protocol that enabled it to keep using the NetBIOS names but dump the ancient NetBEUI protocol and instead run NetBIOS on top of IP. In essence Microsoft created its own name resolution protocol that had nothing to do with DNS!

Microsoft managed to crowbar the NetBIOS naming system into DNS basically by making the NetBIOS name the DNS name. Technically, NetBIOS no longer exists, but the overlying protocol that used it to share folders and printers is still very much alive. This protocol was originally called Server Message Block (SMB); the current version is called **Common Internet File System (CIFS)**.

Microsoft has used DNS names with the SMB/CIFS protocol to provide folder and printer sharing in small TCP/IP networks. SMB/CIFS is so popular that other operating systems have adopted support for SMB/CIFS. UNIX/Linux systems (including Mac OS X) come with the very popular Samba, the most popular tool for making non-Windows systems act like Windows computers (Figure 10.30).

Living with the Legacy of CIFS CIFS makes most small networks live in a two-world name resolution system. When your computer wants to access another computer's folders or files, it uses a simple CIFS broadcast to get the name. If that same computer wants to do anything "Internety," it uses its DNS server. Both CIFS and DNS live together perfectly well and, while there are many alternatives to this dual name resolution world, the vast majority of us are happy with this relationship.

Well, almost happy, except for one little item: CIFS organizes your computers into groups. There are three types of groups: workgroup, Windows domain, and Active Directory. A **workgroup** is just a name that organizes a group of computers. A computer running Windows (or another operating system running Samba) joins a workgroup, as shown in Figure 10.31. Once a computer joins a workgroup, this does little more than organize all the computers in the Network/My Network Places folder, as shown in Figure 10.32.

A **Windows domain** is a group of computers controlled by a computer running Windows Server. This Windows Server computer is configured as a domain controller. You would then have your computers join the domain.

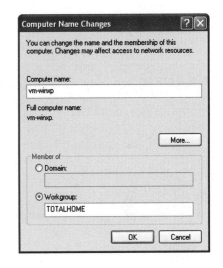

• **Figure 10.30**   Samba on Ubuntu (it's so common that the OS doesn't even use the term in the dialog box)

• **Figure 10.31**   Joining a workgroup

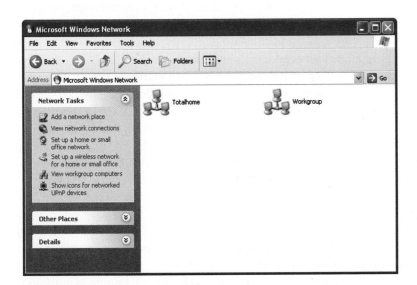

• **Figure 10.32**   Two workgroups in Network folder

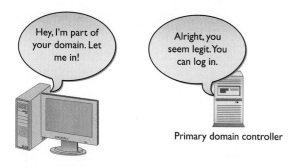

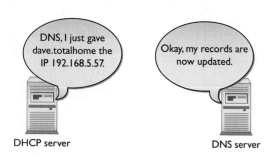

• **Figure 10.33** Logging into the domain

• **Figure 10.34** If one domain controller goes down, another automatically takes over.

• **Figure 10.35** Updating DNS information in Windows

All the computers within a domain authenticate to the domain controller when they log in. This is a very powerful part of the control Windows gives you over who can access what on your network (Figure 10.33).

Note that a Windows domain is not the same as a DNS domain. In the early days, a Windows domain didn't even have a naming structure that resembled the DNS hierarchically organized structure.

Microsoft eventually revamped its domain controllers to work as part of DNS, and Windows domains now use DNS for their names. A Windows domain must have a true DNS name. DNS domains that are not on the Internet should use the top-level name .local (although you can cheat, as I do on my totalhome network, and not use it).

On a bigger scale, a Windows network can get complicated, with multiple domains connecting over long distances. To help organize this, Windows uses a type of super domain called Active Directory. An **Active Directory** is an organization of related computers that shares one or more Windows domains. Windows domain controllers are also DNS servers. The beauty of Active Directory is that there's no single domain controller: all of the domain controllers are equal partners and any domain controller can take over if one domain controller fails (Figure 10.34).

Active Directory–Integrated Zones Now that you have an understanding of Windows domains and Active Directory, let's return to forward lookup zones and DNS. You have enough information to understand an Active Directory–integrated zone.

A standard primary zone stores the DNS information in text files. You then need secondary zones on other DNS servers to back up that server. If the primary DNS server goes down, the secondary servers can resolve FQDNs, but you can't add any new records. Nothing can be updated until the primary DNS server comes back up. In an Active Directory–integrated zone, all of the domain controllers (which are all also DNS servers) are equal and the whole DNS system is not reliant on a single DNS server.

Last, Windows DHCP servers will automatically update all the client information in the Active Directory–integrated zone. If a computer gets a DHCP lease, the DHCP server (or, in the latest versions of Windows, the client itself) tells the DNS server that it has new DNS information (Figure 10.35). Non-Windows systems can only do this using Windows clients (like Samba).

Troubleshooting DNS

As I mentioned earlier, most DNS problems result from a problem with the client systems. This is because DNS servers rarely go down, and if they do, most clients have a secondary DNS server setting that enables them to continue to resolve DNS names. DNS servers have been known to fail, however, so it's important to know when the problem is the client system, and when you can complain to the person in charge of your DNS server. All of the tools you're about to see come with every operating system that supports TCP/IP, with the exception of the IPCONFIG commands, which I'll mention when we get to them.

So how do you know when to suspect DNS as a problem on your network? Well, just about everything you do on an IP network depends on DNS to find the right system to talk to for whatever job the application does. E-mail clients use DNS to find their e-mail servers, FTP clients use DNS for their servers, Web browsers use DNS to find Web servers, and so on. The first clue is usually a user calling you and saying he's getting a "server not found" error. Server not found errors look different on different applications, but you can count on something in there that says in effect "server not found." Figure 10.36 shows how this error appears in an FTP client.

Before you start testing, you need to eliminate any DNS caches on the local system. If you're running Windows, run the `ipconfig /flushdns` command now. In addition, most Web browsers also have caches, so you can't use a Web browser for any testing. In such cases, it's time to turn to the **PING** command.

PING is your best friend when you're testing DNS. Run `ping` from a command prompt, followed by the name of a well-known Web site, such as www .microsoft.com. Watch the output carefully to see if you get an IP address. You may get a "request timed out" message, but that's fine; you just want to see if DNS is resolving FQDNs into IP addresses (Figure 10.37).

If you get a "server not found" error, you need to ping again using just an IP address. Most network techs keep the IP address of a known server in their heads. If you don't have one memorized, try 74.125.95.99. If PING works with the IP address but not with the Web site name, you know you have a DNS problem.

Once you've determined that there's a DNS problem, check to make sure your system has the correct DNS server entry. Again, this information is something you should keep around. I can tell you the DNS server IP address for every Internet link I own—two in the office, one at the house, plus two dial-ups I use on the road. You don't have to memorize the IP addresses, but you should have all the critical IP information written down. If that isn't the problem, run **IPCONFIG** and the /ALL switch to see if those DNS settings are the same as the ones in the server; if they aren't, you may need to refresh your DHCP settings. I'll show you how to do that next.

If you have the correct DNS settings for your DNS server and the DNS settings in IPCONFIG /ALL match those settings, you

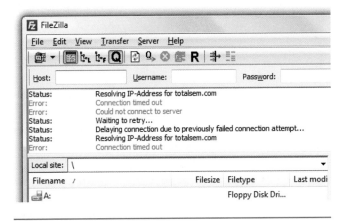

• **Figure 10.36**   DNS error

PING is your friend. If you can PING an IP address but not the name associated with that address, check DNS.

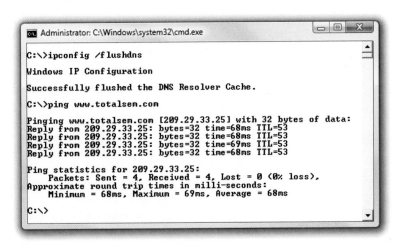

• **Figure 10.37**   Using PING to check DNS

can assume the problem is with the DNS server itself. There's a popular command for working with DNS servers called **NSLOOKUP** (name server lookup). NSLOOKUP comes with all operating systems. It's a handy tool that advanced techs use to query the functions of DNS servers.

NSLOOKUP is an amazingly complex program that you run from a command prompt. With NSLOOKUP, you can (assuming you have the permission) query all types of information from a DNS server and change how your system uses DNS. While most of these commands are far outside the scope of the CompTIA Network+ exam, there are a few places where NSLOOKUP makes for a great basic tool. For instance, just running nslookup alone from a command prompt shows you some output similar to the following:

```
C:\>nslookup
Default Server:  totalhomedc2.totalhome
Address:  192.168.4.155

>
```

Make sure you know how to use NSLOOKUP to determine if a DNS server is active!

Running NSLOOKUP gives me the IP address and the name of my default DNS server. If I got an error at this point, perhaps a "server not found" error, I would know that either my primary DNS server is down or I might not have the correct DNS server information in my DNS settings. I can attach to any DNS server by typing server, followed by the IP address or the domain name of the DNS server:

```
> server totalhomedc1
Default Server:  totalhomedc1.totalhome
Addresses:  192.168.4.157, 192.168.4.156
```

This new server has two IP addresses; it probably has two multihomed NICs to ensure that there's a backup in case one NIC fails. If I get an error on one DNS server, I use NSLOOKUP to check for another DNS server. I can then switch to that server in my TCP/IP settings as a temporary fix until my DNS server comes back up.

Those using UNIX/Linux have an extra DNS tool called **domain information grouper (DIG)**. DIG is very similar to NSLOOKUP, but it runs noninteractively. In NSLOOKUP, you're in the command until you type exit; NSLOOKUP even has its own prompt. The DIG tool, on the other hand, is not interactive—you ask it a question, it answers the question, and it puts you back at a command prompt, with nothing to exit. When you run DIG, you tend to get a large amount of information. The following is a sample of a dig command run from a Linux prompt:

```
[mike@localhost]$dig -x 13.65.14.4
; <<>> DiG 8.2 <<>> -x
;; res options: init recurs defnam dnsrch
;; got answer:
;; ->>HEADER<<- opcode: QUERY, status: NOERROR, id: 4
;; flags: qr aa rd ra; QUERY: 1, ANSWER: 1, AUTHORITY: 2,
ADDITIONAL: 2
;; QUERY SECTION:
;;      4.14.65.13.in-addr.arpa, type = ANY, class = IN
;; ANSWER SECTION:
```

```
  4.14.65.13.in-addr.arpa.   4H IN PTR
server3.houston.totalsem.com.
  ;; AUTHORITY SECTION:
  65.14.4.in-addr.arpa.   4H IN NS   kernel.risc.uni-linz.ac.at.
  65.14.4.in-addr.arpa.   4H IN NS   kludge.risc.uni-linz.ac.at.
  ;; ADDITIONAL SECTION:
  kernel.risc.uni-linz.ac.at.   4H IN A   193.170.37.225
  kludge.risc.uni-linz.ac.at.   4H IN A   193.170.37.224
  ;; Total query time: 1 msec
  ;; FROM: kernel to SERVER: default -- 127.0.0.1
  ;; WHEN: Thu Feb 10 18:03:41 2000
  ;; MSG SIZE  sent: 44  rcvd: 180
[mike@localhost]$
```

■ WINS

Even though current versions of Windows use either DNS or CIFS names, NetBIOS names can still appear in older versions of Windows like Windows 9*x* or some versions of Windows 2000. A Windows NetBIOS system claims a NetBIOS name for itself simply by broadcasting out to the rest of the network. As long as no other system is already using that name, it works just fine. Of course, broadcasting can be a bit of a problem for routers and such, but this example presumes a single network on the same wire, so it's okay in this context.

NetBIOS was invented way back in the early 1980s. Microsoft had a big investment in NetBIOS, and had to support a large installed base of systems, so even after NetBEUI began to lose market share to TCP/IP, Microsoft had to continue to support NetBIOS or incur the wrath of millions of customers. What happened next seems in retrospect more a comedy than the machinations of the most powerful software company in the world. Microsoft did something that should not have been possible: it redesigned NetBIOS to work with TCP/IP. Let's look at some of the strategies and techniques Microsoft used to make NetBIOS and TCP/IP coexist on the same network.

Eventually, Microsoft came up with CIFS, as you know from earlier in the chapter, and made NetBIOS DNS-compatible. But it tried a couple of things first.

One early strategy Microsoft came up with to reduce the overhead from NetBIOS broadcasts was to use a special text file called LMHOSTS. **LMHOSTS** contains a list of the NetBIOS names and corresponding IP addresses of the host systems on the network. Sound familiar? Well, it should—the LMHOSTS file works exactly the same way as the DNS HOSTS file. Although Microsoft still supports LMHOSTS file usage, and every Windows system has an LMHOSTS file for backward compatibility, networks that still need NetBIOS support will usually run Windows Internet Name Service (WINS) servers for name resolution. WINS servers let NetBIOS hosts register their names with just the one server, eliminating the need for broadcasting and thereby reducing NetBIOS overhead substantially. Figure 10.38 shows the copy of the WINS server that comes with Windows 2000 Server. Note that some of the PCs on this network have registered their names with the WINS server.

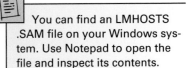
You can find an LMHOSTS .SAM file on your Windows system. Use Notepad to open the file and inspect its contents.

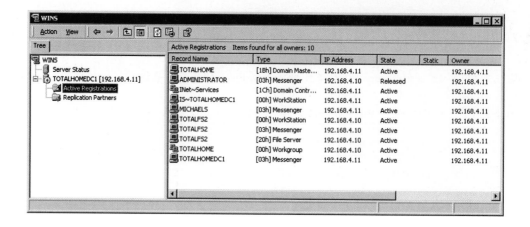

• **Figure 10.38** WINS server

• **Figure 10.38** WINS server

There are only two good reasons to use a WINS server: (1) to reduce over-head from broadcasts; and (2) to enable NetBIOS name resolution across rout-ers. What does a WINS server have to do with routers, you ask? Just this: the WINS server enables NetBIOS to function in a routed network. IP routers are programmed to *kill* all broadcasts, remember? While newer Windows clients will just register directly with the WINS server, older (pre-Win95) Windows systems will still try to broadcast. To get around this problem, you can config-ure a system to act as a **WINS proxy agent**, forwarding WINS broadcasts to a WINS server on the other side of the router (Figure 10.39).

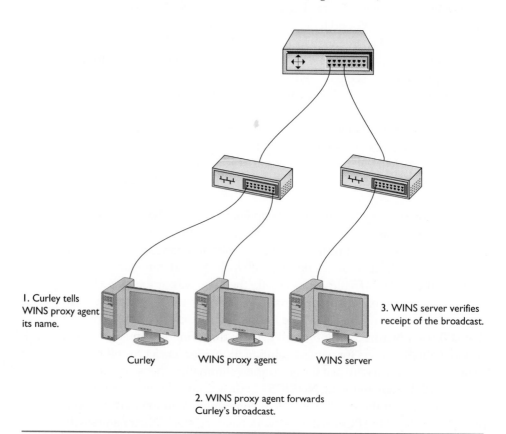

• **Figure 10.39** WINS server

The bottom line with WINS servers is this: larger or routed networks that run NetBIOS still need them. As long as Windows NT and Windows 9*x* systems are out there running NetBIOS, don't be surprised to find that some system somewhere is running a WINS server.

Configuring WINS Clients

You don't need to do much to get a Windows client to use WINS. In fact, you only need to configure the IP address of a WINS server in its WINS settings under Network Properties. From now on, the Windows system will look for a WINS server to register its NetBIOS name. If it finds a WINS server, it will register its NetBIOS name to the WINS server; if it doesn't, it will automatically start broadcasting its NetBIOS name. You can add WINS information to DHCP if necessary, so unless you're running static IP addresses, you may never have to enter anything into your Windows clients to get WINS to work.

 Think WINS is dead? Open **Manage network connections** in your Network and Sharing Center. There's still a WINS setting for backward compatibility with older computers on the network.

Troubleshooting WINS

Most WINS problems are not WINS problems at all. They are NetBIOS problems. By far, the most common problem is having two systems share the same name. In that case, you get a pretty clear error. It looks different in different versions of Windows, but it usually says about the same thing: another system has this name. How do you fix it? Change the name of the system!

You can use the **NBTSTAT** program to help deal with NetBIOS problems. NBTSTAT will do a number of jobs, depending on the switches you add to the end of the command. The –c switch, for example, tells NBTSTAT to check the current NetBIOS name cache (yup, NetBIOS caches names just like some systems cache DNS names). The NetBIOS name cache contains the NetBIOS names and corresponding IP addresses that have been resolved by a particular host. You can use NBTSTAT to see if the WINS server has supplied inaccurate addresses to a WINS client. Here's an example of the nbtstat -c command and its results:

```
C:\ >nbtstat -c

Node IpAddress: [192.168.43.5] Scope Id: []
              NetBIOS Remote Cache Name Table

    Name            Type     Host Address    Life [sec]
    ---------------------------------------------------------
    WRITERS    <1B>  UNIQUE   192.168.43.13      420
    SCOTT      <20>  UNIQUE   192.168.43.3       420
    VENUSPDC   <00>  UNIQUE   192.168.43.13      120
    MIKE       <20>  UNIQUE   192.168.43.2       420
    NOTES01    <20>  UNIQUE   192.168.43.4       420
```

◼ Diagnosing TCP/IP Networks

I've dedicated the entire Chapter 15 to network diagnostic procedures, but TCP/IP has a few little extras that I want to talk about here. TCP/IP is a pretty tough protocol, and in good networks, it runs like a top for years without problems. Most of the TCP/IP problems you'll see come from improper configuration, so I'm going to assume you've run into problems with a new TCP/IP install, and we'll look at some classic screw-ups common in this situation. I want to concentrate on making sure you can PING anyone you want to PING.

I've done thousands of IP installations over the years, and I'm proud to say that, in most cases, they worked right the first time. My users jumped on the newly configured systems, fired up their My Network Places/Network, e-mail software, and Web browsers, and were last seen typing away, smiling from ear to ear. But I'd be a liar if I didn't also admit that plenty of setups didn't work so well. Let's start with the hypothetical case of a user who can't see something on the network. You get a call: "Help!" he cries. The first troubleshooting point to remember here: it doesn't matter *what* he can't see. It doesn't matter if he can't see other systems in his network, or can't see the home page on his browser, because you go through the same steps in any event.

Remember to use common sense wherever possible. If the problem system can't ping by DNS name, but all the other systems can, is the DNS server down? Of course not! If something—*anything*—doesn't work on one system, *always* try it on another one to determine whether the problem is specific to one system or affects the entire network.

One thing I always do is check the network connections and protocols. We're going to cover those topics in greater detail later in the book, so, for now, we'll assume our problem systems are properly connected and have good protocols installed. Here are some steps to take:

1. *Diagnose the NIC.* First, use PING with the loopback address to determine if the system can send and receive packets. Specifically, type `ping 127.0.0.1` or `ping localhost` (remember the HOSTS file?). If you're not getting a good response, your NIC has a problem! Check your NIC's driver and replace it if necessary.

2. *Diagnose locally.* If the NIC's okay, diagnose locally by pinging a few neighboring systems, both by IP address and DNS name. If you're using NetBIOS, use the `net view` command to see if the other local systems are visible (Figure 10.40). If you can't ping by DNS, check your DNS settings. If you can't see the network using NET VIEW, you may have a problem with your NetBIOS settings.

3. *Check IP address and subnet mask.* If you're having a problem pinging locally, make sure you have the right IP address and subnet mask. Oh, if I had a nickel for every time I entered those incorrectly! If you're on DHCP, try renewing the lease—sometimes that will do the trick. If DHCP fails, call the person in charge of the server.

4. *Run NETSTAT.* At this point, another little handy program comes into play called **NETSTAT**. NETSTAT offers a number of options. The two handiest ways to run NETSTAT are with no options at all, and with the –s option. Running `netstat` with no options shows you all the current connections to your system. Look for a connection here that isn't working with an application—that's often a clue to an application problem, such as a broken application or a sneaky application running in the background. Figure 10.41 shows a NETSTAT program running.

A good testing trick is to use the NET SEND command to try sending messages to other systems. Not all versions of Windows support NET SEND, however.

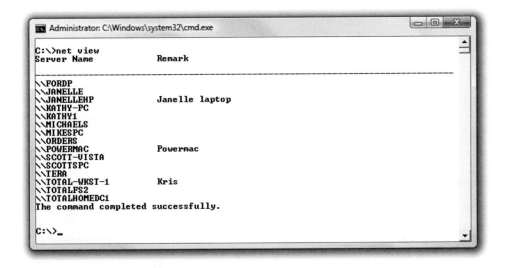

• **Figure 10.40**   NET VIEW in action

5. *Run* `netstat -s`. Running NETSTAT with the **–s** option displays several statistics that can help you diagnose problems. For example, if the display shows you are sending but not receiving, you almost certainly have a bad cable with a broken receive wire.

6. *Diagnose to the gateway.* If you can't get out to the Internet, check to see if you can PING the router. Remember, the router has two interfaces, so try both: first the local interface (the one on your subnet), and then the one to the Internet. You *do* have both of those IP addresses memorized, don't you? You should! If you can't PING the router, either it's down or you're not connected to it. If you can only PING the near side, something in the router itself is messed up.

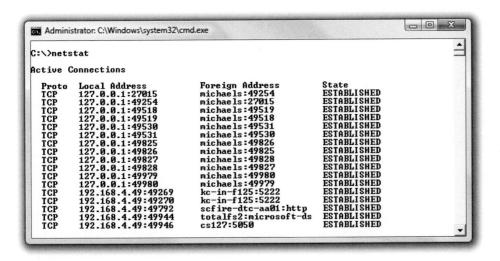

• **Figure 10.41**   NETSTAT in action

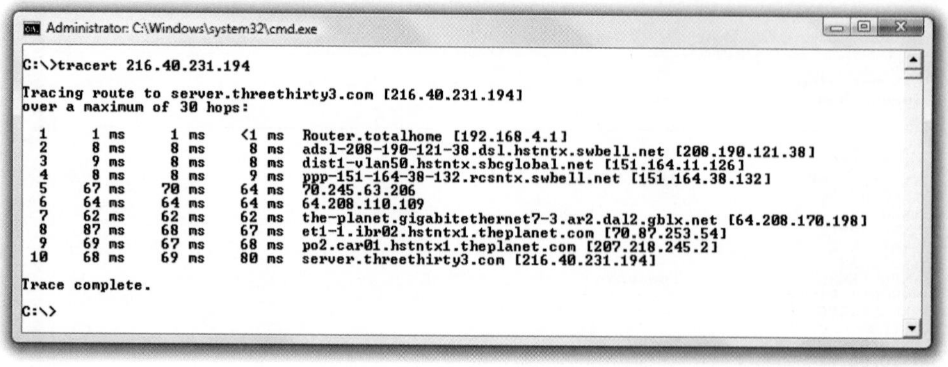

```
Administrator: C:\Windows\system32\cmd.exe

C:\>tracert 216.40.231.194

Tracing route to server.threethirty3.com [216.40.231.194]
over a maximum of 30 hops:

  1    1 ms    1 ms   <1 ms  Router.totalhome [192.168.4.1]
  2    8 ms    8 ms    8 ms  adsl-208-190-121-38.dsl.hstntx.swbell.net [208.190.121.38]
  3    9 ms    8 ms    8 ms  dist1-vlan50.hstntx.sbcglobal.net [151.164.11.126]
  4    8 ms    8 ms    9 ms  ppp-151-164-38-132.rcsntx.swbell.net [151.164.38.132]
  5   67 ms   70 ms   64 ms  70.245.63.206
  6   64 ms   64 ms   64 ms  64.208.110.109
  7   62 ms   62 ms   62 ms  the-planet.gigabitethernet7-3.ar2.dal2.gblx.net [64.208.170.198]
  8   87 ms   68 ms   67 ms  et1-1.ibr02.hstntx1.theplanet.com [70.87.253.54]
  9   69 ms   67 ms   68 ms  po2.car01.hstntx1.theplanet.com [207.218.245.2]
 10   68 ms   69 ms   80 ms  server.threethirty3.com [216.40.231.194]

Trace complete.

C:\>
```

• **Figure 10.42**   Using TRACERT

7. *Diagnose to the Internet.* If you can PING the router, it's time to try to PING something on the Internet. If you can't PING one address, try another—it's always possible that the first place you try to PING is down. If you still can't get through, you can try to locate the problem using the **TRACERT** (trace route) command. TRACERT will mark out the entire route the PING packet traveled between you and whatever you were trying to PING and, even better, will tell you where the problem lies (see Figure 10.42).

Chapter 10 Review

■ Chapter Summary

After reading this chapter and completing the exercises, you should able to do the following.

Describe the function and capabilities of DNS

- A HOSTS file maps a computer name to an IP address. When the Internet was in its infancy, every Internet-connected computer had a copy of the same HOSTS file. Today, computers have their own unique HOSTS file, which is always checked before a computer tries to resolve a name using another method.

- DNS is vital to IP networking, whether on the Internet or within the smallest of networks. DNS stands for Domain Name System, which functions as a hierarchical naming system for computers on a network. A DNS server resolves FQDNs (fully qualified domain names) to IP addresses.

- The 13 DNS root servers for the Internet are logical servers composed of many DNS servers acting as a single monstrous server.

- If one DNS domain name space cannot find out (resolve) the IP address of a computer, the request gets passed along further to another DNS server. The process continues until the request reaches the destination computer.

- Note that because not all computers are connected to the Internet, computer networks are not required to belong to a DNS domain. However, administrators can set up their own DNS domain name spaces without ever connecting to the Internet. These isolated internal intranets can be given elaborate naming structures of their own as well.

- DNS is a convenience, not a requirement. You can connect to a Web site by typing the correct IP address, bypassing the need to resolve an FQDN.

- Name resolution can be accomplished through broadcasting, by consulting the local HOSTS file, or by contacting a DNS server.

- IPCONFIG /ALL can be used to view your DNS server settings. IPCONFIG /DISPLAYDNS displays a cache of recently resolved FQDNs.

- DNS servers store a list of cached lookups—all IP addresses the server has already resolved.

- An authoritative DNS server stores IP addresses and FQDNs of all systems for a particular domain while a cache-only DNS server is used to communicate with other DNS servers.

- Forward lookup zones are the most important part of any DNS server because they contain the IP addresses and FQDNs.

- Of the two types of forward lookup zones, primary zones are created on authoritative DNS servers while secondary zones are created on other DNS servers to act as a backup to the primary zone.

- A records, CNAME records, and MX records must be properly configured on any DNS server.

- Reverse lookup zones resolve an IP address to an FQDN.

- Microsoft's Common Internet File System (CIFS), which began as Server Message Block (SMB), originated when NetBIOS/NetBEUI dropped NetBEUI in favor of IP and used the NetBIOS name as the DNS name. It was used primarily to share files and printers in small TCP/IP networks.

- CIFS organizes computers into one of three types of groups: workgroup, Windows domain, or Active Directory.

- A Windows domain provides centralized management and user authentication via a computer acting as a domain controller.

- An Active Directory is an organization of related computers that shares one or more Windows domains. There is no single domain controller in Active Directory because all domain controllers operate equally.

- Under Active Directory, all domain controllers are also DNS servers. Because Active Directory domain controllers operate equally, there is no single point of failure throughout Active Directory's DNS system. All domain controllers hold primary zones.

- The command IPCONFIG is useful for troubleshooting TCP/IP settings. Running `ipconfig /flushdns` will clear the local cache of DNS entries.

- The PING command is essential in establishing connectivity to a destination PC. If you can PING a host computer by IP address (for example, `ping 192.168.4.55`), but not by name (`ping acctngpc2`), then you have a DNS resolution issue. Check cables, check the DNS servers listed under each network adapter card's settings, and finally, check to see that the DNS server is truly up and operational.

- The NSLOOKUP command enables you to research what name servers are being used by a particular computer. Advanced variations of the NSLOOKUP command can query information from a DNS server and even change how your system uses DNS.

- UNIX/Linux users have an additional DNS tool called DIG, which is different from NSLOOKUP in that DIG runs noninteractively.

Configure and troubleshoot WINS

- An LMHOSTS file works almost the same as a HOSTS file, except it correlates NetBIOS names to IP addresses.

- WINS stands for Windows Internet Name Service, which is an older name resolution method. WINS servers help Windows systems (in place of the even older LMHOSTS files) with resolving NetBIOS computer names (like SALESPC7) to IP addresses (like 192.168.10.7) on a Windows network.

- WINS clients virtually configure themselves by using broadcasts to find WINS servers. A WINS proxy agent forwards WINS broadcasts across routers that would normally block such broadcasts.

- WINS problems relate directly to NetBIOS problems. The most common problem by far is having two systems share the same name. The resulting error message clearly indicates that another system is trying to use the same name. Simply change the computer's system name to fix this common problem.

- Using the NBTSTAT –c command will check the current NetBIOS name cache. This NetBIOS name cache contains the NetBIOS names (along with their corresponding IP addresses) that have been resolved already by a particular host.

- Use the NBTSTAT command alone to see whether the WINS server has supplied inaccurate addresses to a particular WINS client.

Use common TCP/IP utilities to diagnose problems with DNS and WINS

- Always try to connect from another system to determine the extent of the problem. You can then begin the steps in diagnosing TCP/IP errors on a single system.

- Remember to work "from the inside out"—that is, check for connectivity problems on the local system before moving on to check the larger network structure. First, type `ping 127.0.0.1` (or `ping localhost`) to ensure that the local NIC is seated properly and TCP/IP is installed.

- On Windows systems, the NET VIEW command is worth trying. If you can't see the network using NET VIEW, you may have a problem with your NetBIOS settings.

- Running `netstat` shows all the current connections on your system. Running `netstat -s` displays useful statistical information.

- The TRACERT command allows you to mark the entire route a ping packet travels, telling you exactly where a problem lies.

■ Key Terms

A record *(260)*
Active Directory *(264)*
authoritative DNS server *(251)*
cached lookup *(258)*
cache-only DNS server *(260)*
canonical name (CNAME) *(261)*
Common Internet File System (CIFS) *(263)*
DNS root server *(247)*
DNS server *(247)*

DNS tree *(249)*
domain information grouper (DIG) *(266)*
Domain Name System (DNS) *(245)*
flat name space *(248)*
forward lookup zone *(260)*
fully qualified domain name (FQDN) *(250)*
hierarchical name space *(248)*
host name *(249)*
HOSTS file *(245)*

IPCONFIG *(265)*
LMHOSTS *(267)*
MX record *(261)*
name resolution *(244)*
name server *(251)*
NetBIOS/NetBEUI *(262)*
NETSTAT *(270)*
NBTSTAT *(269)*
NSLOOKUP *(266)*
NS record *(260)*

PING *(265)*
primary zone *(261)*
reverse lookup zone *(262)*
secondary zone *(261)*
TRACERT *(272)*
top-level domain server *(247)*
Windows domain *(263)*
Windows Internet Name Service (WINS) *(245)*
WINS proxy agent *(268)*
workgroup *(263)*

■ Key Term Quiz

Use the Key Terms list to complete the sentences that follow. Not all the terms will be used.

1. The _____ command is used to establish connectivity.

2. Using _____ alone can help determine whether a WINS server has supplied inaccurate addresses to a particular WINS client.

3. The term _____ refers to networks that use DNS belonging to the same DNS system.

4. A helpful command that displays TCP/IP naming information is _____.

5. _____ is responsible for resolving NetBIOS names to IP addresses on predominately Windows networks.

6. To connect to systems on the Internet, your network needs the name of at least one _____.

7. To forward WINS broadcasts to a WINS server on the other side of the router, you need to set up a(n) _____.

8. You can use the diagnostic utility called _____ to trace the progress of a ping packet between your system and a remote computer.

9. To avoid having to re-resolve an FQDN that it has already checked, a Windows DNS server keeps a list of IP addresses it has already resolved, called _____.

10. This single DNS server that has a list of all the host names on the domain and their corresponding IP addresses is the _____.

■ Multiple-Choice Quiz

1. Which of the following are needed for e-mail clients to find their e-mail servers, FTP clients to find their file servers, and Web browsers to find Web servers?

   A. DHCP servers

   B. DNS servers

   C. E-mail servers

   D. WINS servers

2. What do DNS servers use to help resolve IP addresses to DNS names?

   A. Authentication

   B. Authorization

   C. Backward lookup zones

   D. Reverse lookup zones

3. What do DNS servers use to help resolve DNS names to IP addresses?

   A. Accounting

   B. Administration

   C. Backward lookup zones

   D. Forward lookup zones

4. What type of DNS servers do not have any forward lookup zones, and will resolve names of systems on the Internet for a network, but are not responsible for telling other DNS servers the names of any clients?

   A. Cache-only servers

   B. Primary servers

   C. Secondary servers

   D. WINS servers

5. What single command gives you the IP address and the name of your system's default DNS server?

   A. `nbtstat`

   B. `nslookup`

   C. `ping`

   D. `winword`

6. What file can be replaced when a network has a WINS server?

   A. HOSTS

   B. LMHOSTS

   C. SAM

   D. WINS

7. What file can be replaced when a network has a DNS server?

   A. HOSTS

   B. LMHOSTS

   C. SAM

   D. WINS

8. What will adding a WINS proxy agent enable you to accomplish on your network?

   A. Cross a hub

   B. Cross a server

   C. Cross a switch

   D. Cross a router

9. Folders with subfolders on a system, like domain names with subdomains, are said to have a structure resembling what?

   A. Branch

   B. Forest

   C. Root

   D. Tree

10. Which of the following commands clears the local cache of DNS entries?

   A. `ipconfig /clear`

   B. `ipconfig /cls`

   C. `ipconfig /flushdns`

   D. `ipconfig /renew`

11. Which variation of the NBTSTAT command will check the current NetBIOS name cache?

   A. `nbtstat`

   B. `nbtstat -c`

   C. `nbtstat /checkupgradeonly`

   D. `nbtstat /status`

12. Which of these terms are frequently used interchangeably? (Select two.)

   A. Domain

   B. Folder

   C. Subdomain

   D. Zone

13. Which of the following are valid DNS record entry types? (Select three.)

   A. A

   B. M

   C. NS

   D. SOA

14. Which of the following is an example of a top-level domain?

   A. .com

   B. totalsem.com

   C. support.totalsem.com

   D. houston.support.totalsem.com

15. How do authoritative DNS servers and cache-only DNS servers differ?

   A. Authoritative DNS servers contain forward lookup zones while cache-only DNS servers contain only reverse lookup zones.

   B. Authoritative DNS servers store IP addresses and FQDNs of systems for a particular domain or domains while cache-only DNS servers do not store any FQDNs because they are only used to talk to other DNS servers to resolve IP addresses.

   C. Authoritative DNS servers service requests for top-level domains while cache-only DNS servers service requests for down-level domains.

   D. Authoritative DNS servers are found only in Windows Active Directory networks while cache-only DNS servers are found universally throughout the Internet.

■ Essay Quiz

1. Some classmates at school have been playing with (and giggling over) the NET SEND command during class time. The instructor notices what's going on, and hoping to turn the experience into something useful, asks each student to write down a valid use of the NET SEND command. Write down your answer.

2. Your boss comes into your office in a panic. He can't reach the company's internal Web server from his office. It worked yesterday. Write an essay describing what you'd do to troubleshoot the situation. Which tool or tools would you use? Why?

3. After discussing flat versus hierarchical naming schemes in class, a feisty classmate proclaims that flat names should be used on individual systems as well as on the Internet for simplification. Write a brief reason or two why he is wrong in his oversimplification.

4. Jot down some brief notes about how you would troubleshoot and diagnose a TCP/IP issue on one of the systems on your network. You can list the actual commands if you like, too. Choose an interesting Web site that you would ping out on the Internet as your final step.

Lab Projects

• Lab Project 10.1

This chapter has presented a lot of variations of common network troubleshooting commands. You have decided it would be beneficial to create an alphabetized chart of these commands, including their variations and what they do. Using either a word processing program or spreadsheet program, create a chart like the following—you fill in the rightmost column:

Command	Variation	What It Does . . .
IPCONFIG	(blank)	
IPCONFIG	/ALL	
IPCONFIG	/RELEASE	
IPCONFIG	/RENEW	
IPCONFIG	/FLUSHDNS	
NBTSTAT	(blank)	
NBTSTAT	–c	
NET	SEND	
NET	VIEW	
PING	127.0.0.1	
PING	disney.com	
PING	localhost	

• Lab Project 10.2

There are potentially many trips a request must make when trying to resolve a fully qualified domain name to an IP address. Aside from the HOSTS file, there are primary DNS servers, secondary DNS servers, authoritative DNS servers, cache-only DNS servers, DNS root servers, top-level DNS servers, and second-level domain servers. On a piece of paper, sketch a diagram/flowchart showing how a request for www.example.com gets resolved to an IP address.

Securing TCP/IP

"Better to be despised for too anxious apprehensions than ruined by too confident a security."

—EDMUND BURKE

In this chapter, you will learn how to

- **Discuss the standard methods for securing TCP/IP networks**
- **Compare TCP/IP security standards**
- **Implement secure TCP/IP applications**

If you really want to get into the minds of the folks who invented TCP/IP, you merely have to look at TCP/IP from the aspect of security. While today the first creators of TCP/IP are now lauded professors and leaders in our field, at the time they were for the most part pretty much just a bunch of hippies who never seriously considered the idea that evil people would get on their beloved networks and do naughty things. No part of TCP/IP has any real security. Oh sure, you can put user names and passwords on FTP, Telnet, and the like; but everything else is wide open. Those hippies must have thought that the intent of the Internet was openness.

Sadly, today's world shows a totally different perspective. Every device with a public IP address on the Internet is constantly bombarded with malicious code trying to gain some level of access to our precious data. Even data moving between two hosts is relatively easily intercepted and read. Bad guys are making millions stealing our data in any of a thousand different ways, and TCP/IP in its original form is all but powerless to stop them.

This chapter takes you on a tour of the many ways smart people have improved TCP/IP to protect our data from those who wish to do evil things to it. It's an interesting story of good intentions, knee-jerk reactions, dead ends, and failed attempts that luckily ends with a promise of easy-to-use protocols that protect our data.

This chapter examines the ways to make TCP/IP data and networks secure. I'll first give you a look at concepts of security, then turn to specific standards and protocols used to implement security. The chapter wraps with a discussion on secure TCP/IP applications and their methods.

Test Specific

■ Making TCP/IP Secure

I break down TCP/IP security into four areas: encryption, nonrepudiation, authentication, and authorization. **Encryption** means to scramble, to mix up, to change the data in such a way that bad guys can't read the data. Of course, this scrambled-up data must also be descrambled by the person receiving the data.

Nonrepudiation is the process that guarantees that the data is as originally sent and that it came from the source you think it should have come from. Nonrepudiation is designed to cover situations in which someone intercepts your data on-the-fly and makes changes, or someone pretends to be someone they are not.

Authentication means to verify that whoever accesses the data is the person you want accessing that data. The most classic form of authentication is the user name and password combination, but there are plenty more ways to authenticate.

Authorization defines what a person accessing the data can do with that data. Different operating systems provide different schemes for authorization, but the classic scheme for Windows is to assign permissions to a user account. An administrator, for example, can do a lot more after being authenticated than a limited user can do.

Encryption, nonrepudiation, authentication, and authorization may be separate issues, but in the real world of TCP/IP security they overlap a lot. If you send a user name and password over the Internet, wouldn't it be a good idea to encrypt the user name and password so others can't read it? Equally, if you send someone a "secret decoder ring" over the Internet so he or she can unscramble the encryption, wouldn't it be a good idea for the recipient to know that the decoder ring actually came from you? In TCP/IP security, you have complete protocols that combine encryption, (sometimes) nonrepudiation, authentication, and authorization to create complete security solutions for one TCP/IP application or another.

Encryption

All data on your network is nothing more than ones and zeroes. Identifying what type of data the strings of ones and zeroes in a packet represent usually

● Figure 11.1　Plaintext

is easy. A packet of data on the network always comes with a port number, for example, so a bad guy knows what type of data he's reading.

All data starts as **plaintext**, a somewhat misleading term that simply means the data is in an easily read or viewed industry-wide standard format. Plaintext, often also referred to as **cleartext**, implies that all data starts off as text—untrue! Data often is text, but it also might be a binary file such as a photograph or an executable program. Regardless of the type of data, it all starts as plaintext. I'll use the image in Figure 11.1 as a universal figure for a piece of plaintext.

If you want to take some data and make figuring out what it means difficult for other people, you need a cipher. A **cipher** is a series of complex and hard-to-reverse mathematics—called an **algorithm**—you run on a string of ones and zeroes to make a new set of seemingly meaningless ones and zeroes. A cipher and the methods used to implement that cipher is commonly called the **complete algorithm**. (I know that's a mouthful of new terms— check the sidebar for details.)

Let's say we have a string of ones and zeroes that looks like this:

```
01001101010010010100101101000101
```

This string may not mean much to you, but if it was part of an HTTP packet, your Web browser would instantly know that this is Unicode—that is, numbers representing letters and other characters—and convert it into text:

```
01001101 01001001 01001011 01000101
M        I        K        E
```

So let's create a cipher to encrypt this cleartext. All binary encryption requires some interesting binary math. You could do something really simple such as add 1 to every value (and ignore carrying the 1):

$0 + 1 = 1$ and $1 + 1 = 0$
```
10110010101101101011010010111010
```

No big deal; that just reversed the values. Any decent hacker would see the pattern and break this code in about three seconds. Let's try something harder to break by bringing in a second value (a key) of any eight binary numbers (let's use 10101010 for this example) and doing some math to every eight binary values using this algorithm:

If cleartext is...	And key value is...	Then the result is...
0	0	0
0	1	1
1	0	1
1	1	0

This is known as a binary XOR (eXclusive OR). Line up the key against the first eight values in the cleartext:

```
10101010
01001101010010010100101101000101
11100111
```

Then do the next eight binary values:

```
10101010
010011010100100101000101101000101
1110011111100011
```

Then the next eight:

```
1010101010101010101010
010011010100100101001011010001011
11001111110001111100001
```

Then the final eight:

```
10101010101010101010101010101010
010011010100100101001011001000101
11100111111000111110000111101111
```

If you want to decrypt the data, you need to know the algorithm and the key. This is a very simple example of how to encrypt binary data. At first glance you might say this is good encryption, but the math is simple, and a simple XOR is easy for someone to decrypt.

An XOR works with letters as well as numbers. See if you can crack the following code:

```
WKH TXLFN EURZQ IRA MXPSV RYHU WKH ODCB GRJ
```

This is a classic example of what's known as the Caesar cipher. You just take the letters of the alphabet and transpose them:

```
Real Letter: ABCDEFGHIJKLMNOPQRSTUVWXYZ
Code letter: DEFGHIJKLMNOPQRSTUVWXYZABC
```

Caesar ciphers are very easy to crack by using word patterns, frequency analysis, or brute force. The code "WKH" shows up twice, which means it's the same word (word patterns). We also see the letters *W* and *H* show up fairly often. Certain letters of the alphabet are used more than others, so a code-breaker can use that to help decrypt the code (frequency analysis). Assuming that you know this is a Caesar cipher, a computer can quickly go through every different code possibility and determine the answer (brute force). Incredibly, even though it's not as obvious, binary code also suffers from the same problem.

In computing you need to make a cipher hard for anyone to break except the people you want to read the data. Luckily, computers do more complex algorithms very quickly (it's just math) and you can use longer keys to make the code much harder to crack.

Okay, let's take the information above and generate some more symbols to show this process. When you run cleartext through a cipher algorithm using a key, you get what's called **ciphertext** (Figure 11.2).

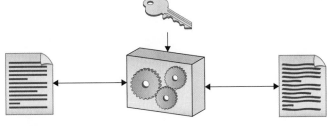

• **Figure 11.2** Encryption process

Over the years, computing people have developed hundreds of different complete algorithms for use in encrypting binary data. Of these, only a few were or still are commonly used in the TCP/IP world. The math behind all of these complete algorithms is incredibly complex, and way outside the scope of the CompTIA Network+ exam, but all of them have two items in common: a complex algorithm underlying the cipher, and a key or keys used to encrypt and decrypt the text.

Any encryption that uses the same key for both encryption and decryption is called symmetric-key encryption or a **symmetric-key algorithm**. If you want someone to decrypt what you encrypt, you have to make sure they have some tool that can handle the algorithm and you have to give them the key. This is a potential problem I will address later in this chapter.

Any encryption that uses different keys for encryption and decryption is called asymmetric-key encryption or an **asymmetric-key algorithm**. Let's look at symmetric-key encryption first, then turn to asymmetric-key encryption.

Symmetric-Key Algorithm Standards

There is one difference among symmetric-key algorithms. Most algorithms we use are called **block ciphers** because they encrypt data in single "chunks" of a certain length at a time. Let's say you have a 100,000-byte Microsoft Word document you want to encrypt. One type of encryption will take 128-bit chunks and encrypt each one separately (Figure 11.3). Block ciphers work well when data comes in clearly discrete chunks. Most data crossing wired networks comes in IP packets, for example, so block ciphers are very popular with these sorts of packets.

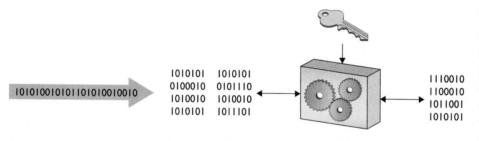

● **Figure 11.3**   Block cipher

The alternative is a **stream cipher**, which takes a single bit at a time and encrypts on-the-fly (Figure 11.4). Stream ciphers are very popular whenever your data comes in long streams (such as with older wireless networks or cell phones).

The granddaddy of all TCP/IP symmetric-key algorithms is the **Data Encryption Standard (DES)**. DES was developed by the United States

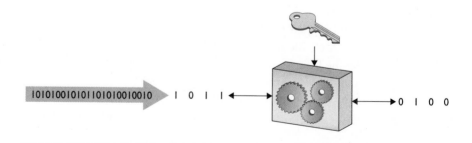

● **Figure 11.4**   Stream cipher

government in the late 1970s and was in widespread use in a variety of TCP/IP applications. DES used a 64-bit block and a 56-bit key. Over time, the 56-bit key made DES susceptible to brute-force attacks. The computing world came up with a number of derivatives of DES to try to address this issue, with names such as 3DES, International Data Encryption Algorithm (IDEA), and Blowfish.

On the streaming side the only symmetric-key algorithm you'll probably ever see is **Rivest Cipher 4 (RC4)** stream cipher. RC4 was invented in the late 1980s by Ron Rivest, cryptographer and arguably the most famous of all inventors of TCP/IP security algorithms. RC4 is used in a number of TCP/IP applications.

Over the years improvements in computing power made both DES and RC4 vulnerable to attacks in certain circumstances. As a result almost all TCP/IP applications have moved to **Advanced Encryption Standard (AES)**. AES is a block cipher, created in the late 1990s. It uses a 128-bit block size and 128-, 192-, or 256-bit key size. AES is incredibly secure, practically uncrackable (for now at least), and is so fast that even applications that traditionally used stream ciphers are switching to AES.

Not at all limited to just TCP/IP, you'll find AES used from file encryption to wireless networking to some Web sites. Given that AES is still somewhat new, many TCP/IP applications are still in the process of moving toward adoption.

> When in doubt on a question about encryption algorithms, always pick AES. You'll be right most of the time.

Asymmetric-Key Algorithm Standards

Symmetric-key encryption has one serious weakness: anyone who gets ahold of the key can encrypt or decrypt data with it. The nature of symmetric-key encryption forces us to send the key to the other person in one way or another, making it a challenge to use symmetric-key encryption safely. As a result, there's been a strong motivation to create a methodology that allows the encryptor to send a key to the decryptor without fear of interception (Figure 11.5).

The answer to the problem of key sharing came in the form of using two different keys, one to encrypt and one to decrypt, an asymmetric-key algorithm. Three men in the late 1970s—Whitfield Diffie, Martin Hellman, and Ralph Merkle—introduced what became known as **public-key cryptography**, with which keys could be exchanged securely.

Ron Rivest (along with Adi Shamir and Leonard Adleman) came up with some improvements to the Diffie-Hellman method of public-key cryptography by introducing a fully functional algorithm called **Rivest Shamir Adleman (RSA)** that enabled secure digital signatures. Here's how public-key cryptography works.

Say we have two people, Mike and Melissa, who wish to send each other encrypted e-mail (Figure 11.6). SMTP doesn't have any (popular) form of encryption, so Mike and Melissa must come up with some program that

Sending...

• **Figure 11.5**　How do we safely deliver the key?

> The public-key cryptography introduced by Diffie, Hellman, and Merkle became known as the *Diffie-Hellman key exchange*. Hellman, on the other hand, has insisted that if the scheme needs a name, it should be called the *Diffie-Hellman-Merkle key exchange*.

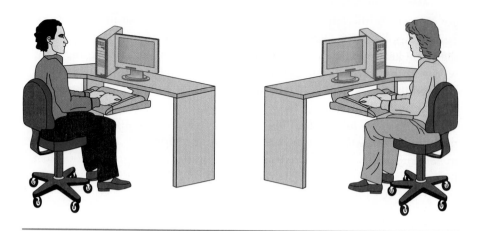

● **Figure 11.6** Mike and Melissa, wanting to send encrypted e-mail messages

encrypts their messages. They will then send the encrypted messages as regular e-mail.

Before Melissa can send an encrypted e-mail to Mike, he first generates *two* keys. One of these keys is kept on his computer (the private key) and the other key is sent to anyone from whom he wants to receive encrypted e-mail (the public key). These two keys—called a **key pair**—are generated at the same time and are designed to work together. He sends a copy of the public key to Melissa (Figure 11.7).

A public-key cryptography algorithm works by encrypting data with a public key and then decrypting data with a private key. The public key of the key pair encrypts the data, and only the associated private key of the key pair can decrypt the data. Since Melissa has Mike's public key, Melissa can encrypt and send a message to Mike that only Mike's private key can decrypt. Mike can then decrypt the message (Figure 11.8).

If Melissa wants Mike to send encrypted e-mail to her, she must generate her own key pair and send Mike the public key. In a typical public-key

● **Figure 11.7** Sending a public key

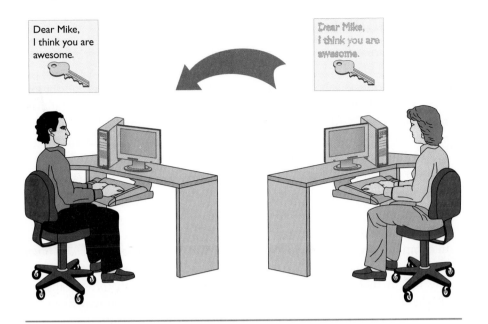

• **Figure 11.8**   Decrypting a message

cryptography setup, everyone has their own private key plus a copy of the public keys for anyone with whom they wish to communicate securely (Figure 11.9).

The only problem with all these keys is the chance that someone pretending to be someone else might pass out a public key. Thus, there's a strong desire by the recipients to know who is passing out a key. This issue falls under the banner of nonrepudiation.

• **Figure 11.9**   Lots of keys

Nonrepudiation

Within networking, nonrepudiation simply means that the receiver of information has a very high degree of confidence that the sender of a piece of information truly is who the receiver thinks it should be. Nonrepudiation takes place all over a network. Is this truly the person who sent in the user name and password to log into my Windows domain? Is this really the eBay.com Web site I'm entering my credit card number into? Did this public key really come from Mike Meyers? As a result, nonrepudiation comes in a number of forms, but most of them use a very clever little bit of mathematical magic called a hash.

Hash

In computer security, a **hash** (or more accurately, a *cryptographic hash function*) is a mathematical function that you run on a string of binary digits of any length that results in a value of some fixed length (often called a checksum or a digest). A cryptographic hash function is a one-way function.

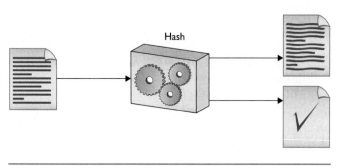

One-way means the hash is practically irreversible. You should not be able to re-create the data even if you know the hashing algorithm and the checksum. A cryptographic hash function should also have a unique checksum for any two different input streams (Figure 11.10).

Cryptographic hash functions have a huge number of uses, but one of the most common is for files. Let's say I'm sharing a file on my Web site. I'm worried that an evil hacker might alter that file, so I run a hash on the file and supply you with both the file and the checksum. Message-Digest algorithm version 5—everybody just calls it **MD5**—is arguably the most popular hashing function for this type of work. Figure 11.11 shows an example of this, a program called Net.MD5.

• **Figure 11.10**   A hash at work

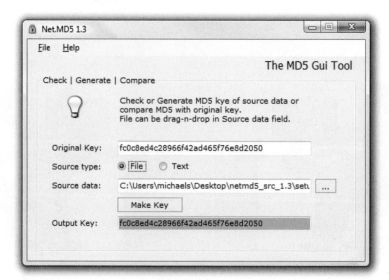

• **Figure 11.11**   File and MD5

This is only one example of how to use hashes. It's also about the only example in which you actually see hashes at work.

MD5 is a very popular cryptographic hash, but it's not the only one. The other hash you'll see from time to time is called **Secure Hash Algorithm (SHA)**. There are two versions of SHA: SHA-1 and SHA-2. Many encryption and authentication schemes also use hashes. Granted, you won't actually see the hashes as they're used, but trust me: hashes are everywhere. For example, some SMTP servers use a special form of MD5, called Challenge-Response Authentication Mechanism-Message Digest 5 (CRAM-MD5), as a tool for server authentication. (See the discussion of CHAP later in this chapter for details on how challenge-response works.) Now that you understand hashes, let's return to public-key cryptography and see how digital signatures make public-key cryptography even more secure.

Try This!

Doing the MD5 Thang!

Net.MD5 is a Windows program. Every operating system has lots of MD5 digest creators and checkers. If you use Linux try the popular MD5Sum utility. The following instructions are for Net.MD5:

1. Download the program from the Web site http://sourceforge.net/project/platformdownload.php?group_id=190760 and install it.

2. Download the setup_netmd5.exe.md5 file and open it in Notepad to see the MD5 digest. Copy it to the clipboard.

3. Start the Net.MD5 program.

4. Next to the **Source Data** field, browse to the Download_setup_netmd5.exe file and click **OK**.

5. Paste in the MD5 digest under the **Original Key** field.

6. Click the **Make Key** button.

Are the MD5 digests the same? Then you know you have a legit copy of Net.MD5!

> Look for CRAM-MD5 to show up on the CompTIA Network+ exam as a tool for server authentication.

Digital Signatures

As mentioned earlier, public-key cryptography suffers from the risk that you might be getting a message or a public key from someone who isn't who they say they are. To avoid this problem we add a digital signature. A **digital signature** is another string of ones and zeroes that can only be generated by the sender, usually by doing something mathematically complex (part of the algorithms always includes some hashing) to the message and the private key. The person with the matching public key does something to the digital signature using the public key to verify it came from the intended sender. Digital signatures are very popular with e-mail users. Figure 11.12 shows an e-mail message being both encrypted and digitally signed in Mozilla Thunderbird using a special Thunderbird add-on called OpenPGP. You'll read more about the PGP family of authentication/encryption tools later in this chapter.

PKI

Digital signatures are great, but what happens when you want to do business with someone you do not know? Before you enter a credit card number to buy that new USB3 Blu-ray Disc player, wouldn't you like to know that the Web site you are doing business with truly is eBay? To address that need the industry came up with the idea of certificates. A **certificate** is a standardized type of digital signature that usually includes the digital signature of a third party, a person or a company that guarantees that who is passing out this certificate truly is who they say they are. As you might imagine, certificates are

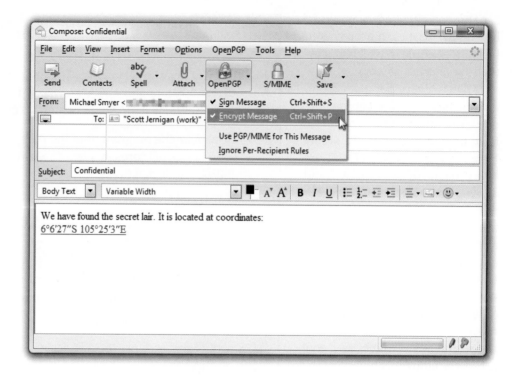

• Figure 11.12   Digitally signed

If you see https:// or a small lock icon, you are most likely on a secure Web site.

incredibly common with secure Web pages. When you go to eBay to sign in, your browser redirects to a secure Web page. These are easy to identify by the lock icon at the bottom of the screen or in the address bar (Figure 11.13) or the https:// used (instead of http://) in the address bar.

• Figure 11.13   Secure Web page

In the background, several items take place (all before the secure Web page loads). First, the Web server automatically sends down a copy of its certificate. Built into that certificate is the Web server's digital signature and a signature from the third party who guarantees this is really eBay. Go to your national version of eBay (I'm in the United States, so I'll use eBay.com) and click **Sign In** (you don't even need an eBay account to do this). Now look at the certificate for the current session. Depending on the Web browser you use, there are different ways to see it. Try clicking the little lock icon at the bottom of the page or in the address bar as this usually works. Figure 11.14 shows the certificate for this session.

So there's a company called VeriSign that issued this certificate. That's great, but how does your computer check all this? Simple, VeriSign is a certificate authority. Every Web browser keeps a list of certificate authority certificates that it checks against when it receives a digital certificate. Figure 11.15 shows the certificate authority certificates stored on my system.

When someone wants to create a secure Web site, he or she buys a certificate signed by a certificate authority, such as VeriSign (the biggest player in the market and the one I'll use for this example). VeriSign acts as the root,

It is very difficult to become a root certificate authority with enough respect to have Web browsers install your certificate!

● **Figure 11.14**   eBay sign-in certificate

- **Figure 11.15**   Certificate authority certificates on system

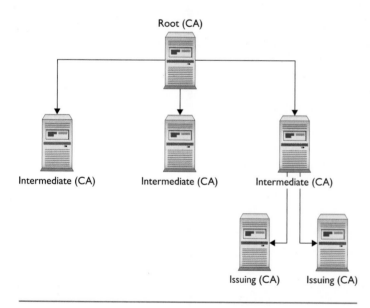

- **Figure 11.16**   VeriSign's PKI tree

and the new Web site's certificate contains VeriSign's signature. For more advanced situations, VeriSign includes an intermediate certificate authority between VeriSign's root certificate authority and the user's certificate. This creates a tree of certificate authorization, with the root authorities at the top and issued certificates at the bottom. You can also have intermediate authorities, although these are not as heavily used. Together, this organization is called a **public-key infrastructure (PKI)** (Figure 11.16).

You don't have to use PKI to use certificates. First, you can create your own, unsigned, certificates. These are perfectly fine for lower-security situations (e-mail among friends, personal Web page, and so forth), but don't expect anyone to buy products on a Web site or send highly sensitive e-mail without a signed certificate from a well-known certificate authority like VeriSign, thawte, or GoDaddy.

Last, many certificate providers, primarily for e-mail, provide a Web-of-trust option. In this case, someone else who is already part of a trust group signs your certificate. There is no certificate authority, just a group of peers who trust each other. The popular Pretty Good Privacy (PGP) encryption program, among many others, uses such a trust model.

Digital certificates and asymmetric cryptography are closely linked because digital certificates are almost always used to verify the exchange of public keys. In many cases this takes place behind the scenes of e-mail, Web pages, and even in some very secure wireless networks. Though you may not see certificates in action very often, do know they are there.

Authentication

You most likely have dealt with authentication at some level. Odds are good you've at least had to type in a user name and password on a Web site. Maybe your computer at work or school requires you to log onto the network. Whatever the case, the first exposure to authentication for most users is a request to enter a user name and password. A network technician should understand not only how different authentication methods control user names and passwords, but also some of the authentication standards used in today's TCP/IP networks.

Passwords offer significant security challenges. What happens after you type in a user name and password? How is this data transferred? Who or what reads this? What is the data compared to? A series of TCP/IP security standards that use combinations of user names, passwords, and sometimes certificates, all handled in a usually secure manner, address these issues, as described in the upcoming section "TCP/IP Security Standards."

Authorization

A large part of the entire networking process involves one computer requesting something from another computer. A Web client might ask for a Web page, for example, or a Common Internet File System (CIFS) client might ask a file server for access to a folder. A computer far away might ask another computer for access to a private network. Whatever the case, you should carefully assign levels of access to your resources. This is authorization. To help define how to assign levels of access, you use an access control list.

An **access control list (ACL)** is nothing more than a clearly defined list of permissions that specify what an authenticated user may perform on a shared resource. Over the years the way to assign access to resources has changed dramatically. To help you to understand these changes, the security industry likes to use the idea of *ACL access models*. There are three types of ACL access models: mandatory, discretionary, and role based.

In a **mandatory access control (MAC)** security model, every resource is assigned a label that defines its security level. If the user lacks that security level, he or she does not get access. MAC is used in many operating systems to define what privileges programs have to other programs stored in RAM. The MAC security model is the oldest and least common of the three.

Discretionary access control (DAC) is based on the idea that there is an owner of a resource who may at his or her discretion assign access to that resource. DAC is considered much more flexible than MAC.

Role-based access control (RBAC) is the most popular model used in file sharing. RBAC defines a user's access to a resource based on the roles the user plays in the network environment. This leads to the idea of creation of groups. A group in most networks is nothing more than a name that has clearly defined accesses to different resources. User accounts are placed into various groups. A network might have a group called "Sales" on a Web server that gives any user account that is a member of the Sales group access to a special Web page that no other groups can see.

Keep in mind that these three types of access control are models. Every TCP/IP application and operating system has its own set of rules that sometimes follows one of these models, but in many cases does not. But do make sure you understand these three models for the CompTIA Network+ exam!

■ TCP/IP Security Standards

Now that you have a conceptual understanding of encryption, nonrepudiation, authentication, and authorization, it's time to see how the TCP/IP folks have put it all together to create standards so that you can secure just about anything in TCP/IP networks.

TCP/IP security standards are a rather strange mess. Some are authentication standards, some are encryption standards, and some are so unique to a single application that I'm not even going to talk about them in this section and instead will wait until the "Secure TCP/IP Applications" discussion at the end of this chapter. There's a reason for all this confusion: TCP/IP was never really designed for security. As you read through this section, you'll discover that almost all of these standards either predate the whole Internet, are slapped-together standards that have some serious issues, or, in the case of the most recent standards, are designed to combine a bunch of old, confusing standards. So hang tight—it's going to be a bumpy ride!

Authentication Standards

Authentication standards are some of the oldest standards used in TCP/IP. Many are so old they predate the Internet itself. There was a time when nobody had fiber-optic, cable modem, or DSL connections to their ISPs. For the most part, if you wanted to connect to the Internet you had a choice: go to the computer center or use dial-up.

Dial-up, using for the most part telephone lines, predates the Internet, but the nerds of their day didn't want just anybody dialing into their computers. To prevent unauthorized access, they developed some excellent authentication methods that TCP/IP adopted for itself. A number of authentication methods were used back in these early days, but for the most part TCP/IP authentication started with something called the Point-to-Point Protocol.

PPP

The **Point-to-Point Protocol (PPP)** enables two point-to-point devices to connect, authenticate with a user name and password, and negotiate the network protocol the two devices will use. Today that network protocol is almost always TCP/IP.

Note that point-to-point and dial-up are not Ethernet, but still can support TCP/IP. Many network technologies don't need Ethernet, such as telephone, cable modem, microwave, and wireless (plus a bunch more you won't even see until Chapter 14, "Remote Connectivity"). In fact, once you leave a LAN, most of the Internet is just a series of point-to-point connections.

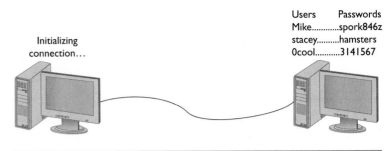

● **Figure 11.17**   A point-to-point connection

PPP provided the first common method to get a server to request a user name and password. In such a point-to-point connection, the side asking for the connection is called the initiator while the other side, which has a list of user names and passwords, is called the authenticator (Figure 11.17).

PPP came with two methods to authenticate a user name and password. The original way—called **Password Authentication Protocol (PAP)**—simply transmits the user name and password over the connection in plaintext. Unfortunately, that means that anyone who could tap the connection could learn the user name and password (Figure 11.18).

Fortunately, with PPP you also have the choice of the safer **Challenge Handshake Authentication Protocol (CHAP)** to provide a more secure authentication routine. CHAP relies on hashes based on a shared secret, usually a password that both ends of the connection know. When the initiator of the connection makes the initial connection request, the authenticator creates some form of challenge message. The initiator then makes a hash using the password and sends that to the authenticator. The authenticator in turn compares that value to its own hash calculation based on the password. If they match, the initiator is authenticated (Figure 11.19).

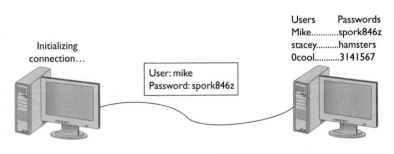

● **Figure 11.18**   PAP in action

CHAP works nicely because it never sends the actual password over the link. The CHAP standard leaves a number of issues undefined, however, like "If the hash doesn't match, what do I do?" The boom in dial-up connections to the Internet in the 1990s led Microsoft to invent a more detailed version of CHAP called **MS-CHAP**. The current version of MS-CHAP is called MS-CHAPv2. MS-CHAPv2 is still the most common authentication method for the few of us using dial-up connections. Dial-up is still being used out there and even the latest operating systems support it. Figure 11.20 shows the dial-up connection options for Vista.

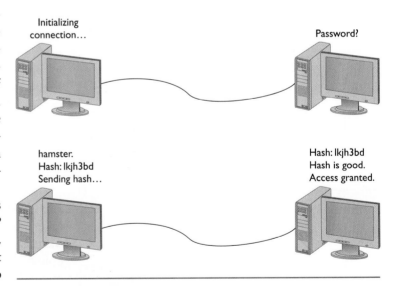

● **Figure 11.19**   CHAP in action

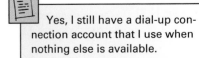

Yes, I still have a dial-up connection account that I use when nothing else is available.

If you get a question on PAP, CHAP, and MS-CHAP on the CompTIA Network+ exam, remember that MS-CHAP offers the most security.

• **Figure 11.20**   MS-CHAP is alive and well

AAA

PPP does a great job of handling authentication for point-to-point connections, but it has some limitations. The biggest problem is that, in many cases, a network might have more than one point for an initiator to enter. PPP assumes that the authenticator at the endpoint has all the user name and password information, but that's not necessarily true. In traditional modem communication, for example, an Internet service provider (ISP) has a large bank of modems to support any number of users. When a user dials in, the modem bank provides the first available connection, but that means that any modem in the bank has to support any of the users. You can't put the database containing all user names and passwords on every modem (Figure 11.21).

In this case you need a central database of user names and passwords. That's simple enough, but it creates another problem—anyone accessing the network can see the passwords (Figure 11.22). PPP is good at the endpoints, but once the data gets on the network it's unencrypted.

Thus the folks overseeing central databases full of user names and passwords needed to come up with standards to follow to protect that data. They first agreed upon a philosophy called **Authentication, Authorization, and Accounting (AAA)**. AAA is designed for the idea of

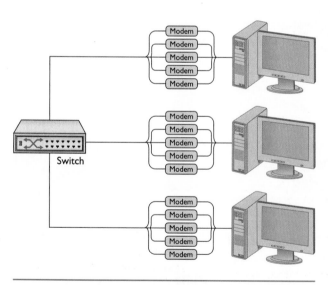

• **Figure 11.21**   Where do you put the user names and passwords?

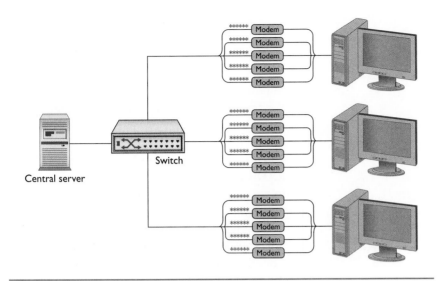

● **Figure 11.22**   Central servers are prone to attack.

port authentication—the concept of allowing remote users authentication to a particular point-of-entry (a port) to another network.

- **Authentication**   A computer that is trying to connect to the network must present some form of credential for access to the network. This credential is most commonly a user name and password, but it might also be a security token such as a smart card, retinal scan, or digital certificate. It might even be a combination of some of these. The authentication gives the computer the right to access the network.

- **Authorization**   Once authenticated, the computer determines what it can or cannot do on the network. It might only be allowed to use a certain amount of bandwidth. It might be limited to working only certain times of day or might be limited to using only a certain set of applications.

- **Accounting**   The authenticating server should do some form of accounting such as recording the number of times a user logs on and logs off. It might track unsuccessful logon attempts. It may track what services or resources the client system accessed. The number of items to be accounted is massive.

Once the idea of AAA took shape, those smart Internet folks got to work developing two standards: RADIUS and TACACS+. Both standards offer authentication, authorization, and accounting.

RADIUS   Remote Authentication Dial-In User Service (RADIUS) is the better known of the two AAA standards and, as its name implies, was created to support ISPs with hundreds if not thousands of modems in hundreds of computers to connect to a single central database. RADIUS consists of three devices: the RADIUS server that has access to a database of user names and passwords, a number of **Network Access Servers (NASs)** that control the modems, and a group of systems that dial into the network (Figure 11.23).

 NAS stands for either Network Access Server or Network Attached Storage. Make sure you read the question to see which NAS it's looking for!

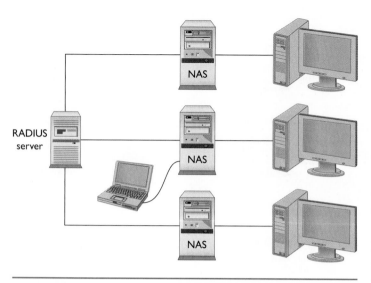

To use RADIUS you need a RADIUS server. The most popular choice for Microsoft environments is **Internet Authentication Service (IAS)**. IAS comes built in with most versions of Microsoft Windows Server operating systems. For the UNIX/Linux crowd, the popular (yet in my opinion hard to set up) **FreeRADIUS** is the best choice. If you prefer a more prepackaged server, you might look at Juniper Network's Steel-Belted RADIUS—a very powerful and somewhat easy to set up option that many people feel is well worth the roughly $3000 price tag.

A single RADIUS server can support multiple NASs and provide a complete PPP connection from the requesting system, through the NAS, all the way to the RADIUS server. Like any PPP connection, the RADIUS server supports PAP, CHAP, and MS-CHAP. Even if you use PAP, RADIUS hashes the password so that at no time is the user name/password exposed. Newer versions of RADIUS support even more authentication methods, as you will soon see. RADIUS performs all this authentication on either UDP ports 1812 and 1813 or UDP ports 1645 and 1646.

TACACS+   Routers and switches need administration. In a simple network, you can access the administration screen for each router and switch by entering a user name and password for each device. When a network becomes complex, with many routers and switches, logging into each device separately starts to become administratively messy. The answer is to make a single server store the ACL for all the devices in the network. To make this secure, you need to follow the AAA principles.

Terminal Access Controller Access Control System Plus (TACACS+) is a proprietary protocol developed by Cisco to support AAA in a network with many routers and switches. TACACS+ is very similar to RADIUS in function, but uses TCP port 49 by default and separates authorization, authentication, and accounting into different parts. TACACS+ uses PAP, CHAP, and MD5 hashes, but can also use something called Kerberos as part of the authentication scheme.

Kerberos

Up to this point almost all the authentication schemes we've discussed either are based on PPP or at least take the idea of PPP and expand upon it. Of course, every rule needs an exception and Kerberos is the exception here.

Kerberos is an authentication protocol that has no connection to PPP. Twenty years ago some Internet folks began to appreciate that TCP/IP was not secure and thus designed Kerberos. Kerberos is an authentication protocol for TCP/IP networks with many clients all connected to a single authenticating server—no point-to-point here! Kerberos works nicely in a network, so nicely that Microsoft adopted it as the authentication protocol for all Windows networks using a domain controller.

The cornerstone of Kerberos is the **Key Distribution Center (KDC)**, which has two processes: the **Authentication Server (AS)** and the Ticket-Granting Service (TGS). In Windows server environments, the KDC is installed on the domain controller (Figure 11.24).

When your client logs onto the domain, it sends to the AS a request that includes a hash of the user name and password. The AS compares the results of that hash to its own hash (as it also stores the user name and password) and, if they match, sends a **Ticket-Granting Ticket (TGT)** and a timestamp (Figure 11.25). The ticket has a default lifespan in Windows of eight hours. The client is now authenticated, but not yet authorized.

The client then sends the timestamped TGT to the TGS for authorization. The TGS sends a timestamped service ticket (also called a token or access token) back to the client (Figure 11.26).

This token is the key that the client uses to access any resource on the entire domain. This is where authorization takes place. The token authorizes the user to access resources without "reauthenticating." Any time the client attempts to access a folder, printer, or service anywhere in the domain, the server sharing that resource uses the token to see exactly what access the client may have to that resource.

Timestamping is important for Kerberos because it forces the client to request a new token every eight hours. This prevents third parties from intercepting the tokens and attempting to crack them. Kerberos tokens can be cracked, but it's doubtful this can be done in under eight hours.

Kerberos is very popular, but has some serious weaknesses. First, if the KDC goes down, no one has access. That's why Microsoft and other operating systems that use Kerberos always stress the importance of maintaining a backup KDC. In Windows it is standard practice to have at least two domain controllers. Second, timestamping requires that all the clients and servers synchronize their clocks. This is fairly easy to do in a wired network (such as a Windows domain or even a bunch of connected routers using TACACS+), but adds an extra level of challenge in dispersed networks (such as those connected across the country).

• **Figure 11.24**   Windows Kerberos setup

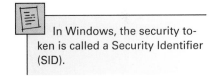

• **Figure 11.25**   AS sending a TGT back to client

In Windows, the security token is called a Security Identifier (SID).

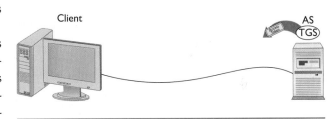

• **Figure 11.26**   TGS sending token to client

EAP

One of the great challenges to authentication is getting the two ends of the authentication process to handle the many different types of authentication options. The **Extensible Authentication Protocol (EAP)** was developed to help two devices negotiate. Despite the name, EAP is not a protocol in the classic sense, but rather it is a wrapper that EAP-compliant applications can use to accept one of many types of authentication. While EAP is a general-purpose authentication wrapper, its only substantial use is in wireless networks. (See Chapter 16, "Wireless Networking," to see where EAP is

Wireless client   Wireless Access Point

Password: Eggs

• **Figure 11.27**   EAP-PSK in action

used.) EAP comes in various types, but currently only six types are in common use:

- **EAP-PSK**   Easily the most popular form of authentication used in wireless networks today, EAP-PSK (Personal Shared Key) is nothing more than a shared secret code that's stored on both the Wireless Access Point (WAP) and the wireless client, encrypted using the powerful AES encryption (Figure 11.27). See Chapter 16 for the scoop on WAPs and EAP.

- **EAP-TLS**   EAP with Transport Layer Security (TLS) defines the use of a RADIUS server as well as mutual authentication, requiring certificates on both the server and every client. On the client side, a smart card may be used in lieu of a certificate. EAP-TLS is very robust, but the requirement of having certificates on the client side is an administrative challenge. Even though it's a challenge, the most secure wireless networks all use EAP-TLS. EAP-TLS is only used on wireless networks, but TLS is used heavily on secure Web sites (see the section "SSL/TLS" later in this chapter). Figure 11.28 shows a typical EAP-TLS setup for a wireless network.

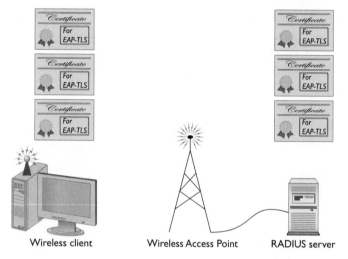

Wireless client   Wireless Access Point   RADIUS server

• **Figure 11.28**   EAP-TLS

- **EAP-TTLS**   EAP-TTLS (Tunneled TLS) is similar to EAP-TLS but only uses a single server-side certificate. EAP-TTLS is very common for more secure wireless networks (Figure 11.29).

- **EAP-MS-CHAPv2, more commonly known as PEAP**   **Protected Extensible Authentication Protocol (PEAP)** uses a password function based on MS-CHAPv2 with the addition of an encrypted TLS tunnel similar to EAP-TLS.

- **EAP-MD5**   This is a very simple version of EAP that uses only MD5 hashes for transfer of authentication credentials. EAP-MD5 is weak and the least used of all the versions of EAP described.

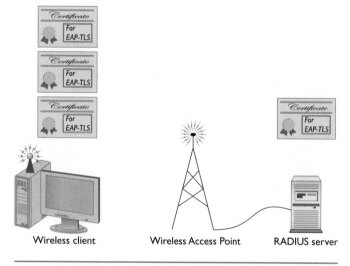

Wireless client   Wireless Access Point   RADIUS server

• **Figure 11.29**   EAP-TTLS

- **LEAP**   **Lightweight Extensible Authentication Protocol (LEAP)** is a proprietary EAP authentication used almost exclusively by Cisco wireless products. LEAP is an interesting combination of MS-CHAP authentication between a wireless client and a RADIUS server.

802.1X

When wireless networks first came out many years ago, they lacked any form of authentication. After many fits and starts the wireless community grabbed a preexisting authentication standard called 802.1X to use in their wireless networks.

802.1X is a port-authentication network access control mechanism for networks. In other words, it's a complete authentication standard designed to force devices to go through a full AAA process to get anywhere past the interface on a gateway system. Before 802.1X, a system on a wired network could always access another system's port. Granted, an attacker wouldn't be able to do much until he gave a user name/password or certificate, but he could still send packets to any computer on the network. This wasn't good, because it enabled attackers to get to the systems to try to do evil things. 802.1X prevented them from even getting in the door until they were authenticated and authorized.

The interesting part is that you already know about most of the parts of 802.1X, because the standard worked hard to use existing technologies. From a distance, 802.1X looks a lot like a RADIUS AAA setup. 802.1X changes the names of some of the components, as shown in Figure 11.30. Compare this to Figure 11.23 to get the new names (the jobs don't change).

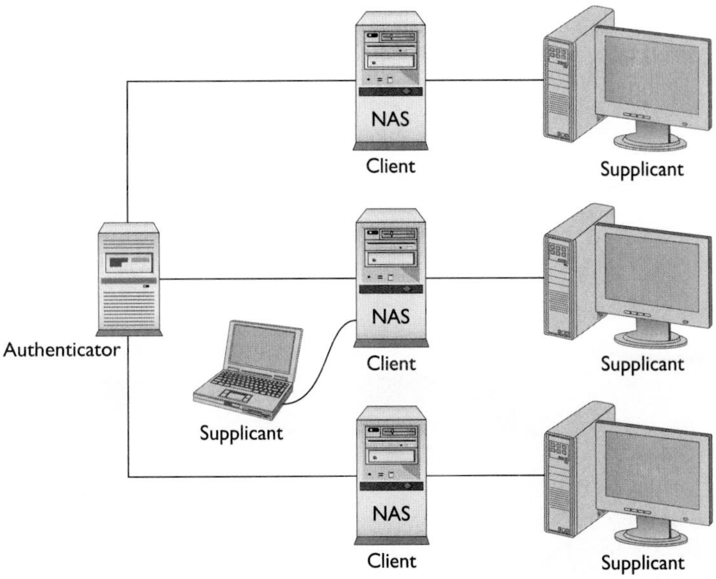

802.1X combines the RADIUS-style AAA with EAP versions to make a complete authentication solution. The folks who developed 802.1X saw it as a total replacement for every other form of authentication (even Kerberos), but the reality is that most people don't like changing something that already works. To that end, only wireless networking broadly adopted 802.1X.

We're not done with authentication and authorization, but at least you now understand the basics of the popular authentication and authorization protocols and standards. There are more protocols to learn, but all of them are rather specialized for specific uses and thus are covered at various places throughout the book.

• **Figure 11.30**   802.1X components

Technically, wireless networks don't use EAP. They use 802.1X, which in turn uses EAP.

Encryption Standards

The Internet had authentication long before it had encryption. As a result, almost all encryption came out as a knee-jerk reaction to somebody realizing that his or her TCP/IP application wasn't secure. For years there were new secure versions of just about every protocol in existence. New versions of all the classics started to appear, almost all starting with the word "Secure": Secure FTP, Secure SMTP, and even Secure POP were developed. They worked, but there were still hundreds of not-yet-secured protocols and the specter of redoing all of them was daunting. Fortunately, some new, all-purpose encryption protocols were developed that enabled a client to connect to a server in a secure way while still using their older, unsecure protocols—and it all started because of Telnet.

SSH

The broad adoption of the Internet by the early 1990s motivated programmers to start securing their applications. Telnet had a big problem. It was

incredibly useful and popular, but it was completely insecure. If any one TCP application needed fixing then the world was behind anyone who could fix Telnet. As the story goes, Tatu Ylonen of the Helsinki University of Technology, reacting to an attack that intercepted Telnet user names and passwords on his network, invented a new secure replacement for Telnet called **Secure Shell (SSH)**. You've already seen SSH in action (in Chapter 9, "TCP/IP Applications") as a secure version of Telnet, but now that you know more about security, let's look at SSH in detail.

SSH servers use PKI in the form of an RSA key. The first time a client tries to log into an SSH server, the server sends its public key to the client (Figure 11.31).

● **Figure 11.31**   PuTTY getting an RSA key

After the client receives this key, it creates a session ID, encrypts it using the public key, and sends it back to the server. The server decrypts this session ID and uses it in all data transfers going forward. Only the client and the server know this session ID. Next, the client and server negotiate the type of encryption to use for the session. These days AES is popular, but older symmetric-key ciphers such as 3DES may still be used. The negotiation for the cipher is automatic and invisible to the user.

Using RSA and a cipher makes a very safe connection, but the combination doesn't tell the server who is using the client. All SSH servers, therefore, add user names and passwords to authenticate the client (Figure 11.32). Once a user logs in with a user name and password, he or she has access to the system.

In addition to using a password for authentication, SSH also can use public keys to identify clients. This opens up some interesting possibilities such as no-interaction logins. You can also turn off password login altogether, hardening your server even further. To use public/private keys for authentication, you must first generate a pair of RSA or Digital Signature Algorithm (DSA) keys with a tool such as PuTTYgen (Figure 11.33). The public key is then copied to the server and the private key is kept safe on the client.

User: Mike
Password: Eggs

User: Sarah
Password: Bacon

User: Mike
Password: Eggs
User: Sarah
Password: Bacon

● **Figure 11.32**   Users on an SSH server

When you connect to the server, your client generates a signature using its private key and sends it to the server. The server then checks the signature with its copy of the public key, and if everything checks out, you will be authenticated with the server.

If SSH stopped here as a secure replacement for Telnet, that would be fantastic, but SSH has another trick up its sleeve: the capability to act as a *tunnel* for *any* TCP/IP application. Let's see what tunnels are and how they work for us.

Tunneling

Simply, a **tunnel** is an encrypted link between two programs on two separate computers. Let's take a look at an SSH link between a server and a client. Once established, anything you enter into the client application is encrypted, sent to the server, decrypted, and then acted upon (Figure 11.34).

The nature of SSH is such that it took very little to extend the idea of SSH to accept input from any source, even another program (Figure 11.35). As long as the program could redirect to the SSH client and then the SSH server redirect to the server application, anything can go through an SSH connection encrypted. This is an SSH tunnel.

SSH tunnels are wildly popular and fairly easy to set up. Equally, all of the popular SSH clients and servers are designed to go into tunnel mode, usually with no more than the simple click of a check box (Figure 11.36).

There are many tunneling protocols and standards used in TCP/IP. SSH is one of the simplest types of tunnels so it's a great first exposure to tunneling. As the book progresses, you'll see more tunneling protocols, but you have the basics of tunneling. For now, make sure you understand that a tunnel is an encrypted connection between two endpoints. Any packet that enters the encrypted tunnel, including a packet with unencrypted data, is automatically encrypted, goes through the tunnel, and is decrypted on the other endpoint.

• **Figure 11.33** Generated keys in PuTTYgen

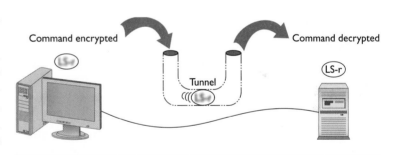

• **Figure 11.34** SSH in action

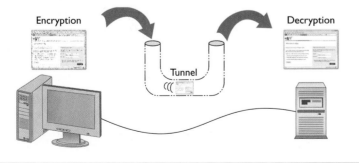

• **Figure 11.35** Encrypting a Web client

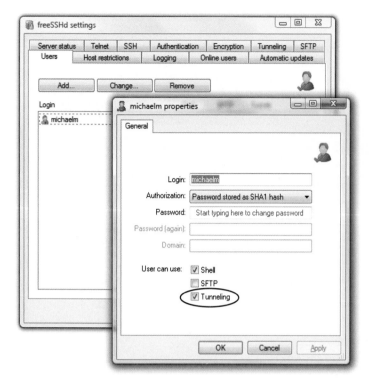

Hey, can I have access to you?

First take a look at this.

• **Figure 11.37**   SSL at work

SSL/TLS also supports mutual authentication, but this is relatively rare.

SSH may be popular, but it's not the only option for encryption. All of the other encryption standards are built into combined authentication/encryption standards, as covered in the next section.

Combining Authentication and Encryption

The rest of the popular authentication and encryption standards are combined to include both authentication and encryption in a single standard. Lumping together authentication and encryption into the same standard does not make it weaker than the standards already discussed. These are some of the most popular standards used on the Internet today, because they offer excellent security.

SSL/TLS

The introduction and rapid growth of e-commerce on the World Wide Web in the mid 1990s made it painfully obvious that some form of authentication and encryption was needed. Netscape Corporation took the first shot at a new standard. At the time, the dominant Web browser was Netscape Navigator. Netscape created a standard called **Secure Sockets Layer (SSL)**. SSL requires a server with a certificate. When a client requests access to an SSL-secured server, the server sends to the client a copy of the certificate. The SSL client checks this certificate (all Web browsers come with an exhaustive list of CA root certificates preloaded), and if the certificate checks out, the server is authenticated and the client negotiates a symmetric-key cipher for use in the session (Figure 11.37). The session is now in a very secure encrypted tunnel between the SSL server and the SSL client.

SSL has now been greatly updated to a new standard called **Transport Layer Security (TLS)**. TLS is very similar to SSL, working in almost the same way. TLS is more robust and flexible and works with just about any TCP application. SSL is limited to HTML, FTP, SMTP, and a few older TCP applications. TLS has no such restrictions and is used in securing Voice over IP (VoIP) and virtual private networks (VPNs), but it is still most heavily used in securing Web pages. Every Web browser today uses TLS for HTTPS-secured Web sites, and EAP-TLS is common for more-secure wireless networks.

IPSec

Every authentication and encryption protocol and standard you've learned about so far works *above* the Network layer of the OSI seven-layer model. **Internet Protocol Security (IPSec)** is an encryption protocol that works at the Network layer and, while not very popular currently, will soon become the dominant encryption protocol as IPv6 begins to roll out in the next few years. (See Chapter 13, "IPv6," for details on the upcoming IPv6.)

IPSec works in two different modes: Transport mode and Tunnel mode. In Transport mode, only the actual payload of the IP packet is encrypted: the destination and source IP addresses, port numbers, and other IP header information are still readable. In Tunnel mode, the entire IP packet is encrypted and then placed into an IPSec endpoint where it is encapsulated inside another IP packet. The mode you use depends on the application (Figure 11.38). IPv6 will use the IPSec Transport mode by default.

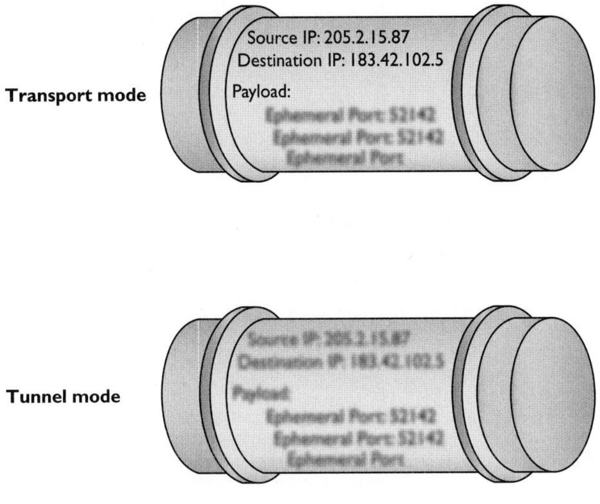

IPSec has a strong authentication. Not only does IPSec support Internet Key Exchange (IKE, the standard for exchanging keys on the Internet), it aggressively protects against attacks by adding an authentication header (AH) to every IP packet that use IPSec. While a full discussion of the AH is way beyond the scope of the CompTIA Network+ exam, you should understand that the AH's two different hash values ensure the integrity of every packet.

IPSec is an incredibly powerful authentication/encryption protocol, but until IPv6 is widely implemented its only common current use is creating secure tunnels between two computers: a job it performs very well. Keep an eye out for IPSec!

• **Figure 11.38**   IPSec's two modes

Secure TCP/IP Applications

We've covered quite a few TCP/IP security standards and protocols thus far in the chapter, but we really haven't put anything to work yet. It's now time to talk about actual applications that use these tools to make secure connections. As mentioned earlier, this is in no way a complete list, as there are thousands of secure TCP applications; we'll stick to ones you will see on the CompTIA Network+ exam. Even within that group, I've saved discussion of some of the applications for other chapters that deal more directly with certain security aspects (such as remote connections).

Of all the protocols and standard discussed so far, only SSH is also an application.

HTTPS

You've already seen HTTPS back in Chapter 9 so let's do a quick review and then take the coverage a bit deeper. You know that HTTPS documents are unique pages that traditionally start with https:// and that most browsers also show a small lock icon in the lower-right corner or in the address bar. You also know that HTTPS uses SSL/TLS for the actual authentication and encryption process. In most cases, all of this works very well, but what do you do when HTTPS has trouble?

Since you won't get an HTTPS connection without a good certificate exchange, the most common problems are caused by bad certificates. When a certificate comes in from an HTTPS Web site, your computer checks the expiration date to verify the certificate is still valid and checks the Web site's

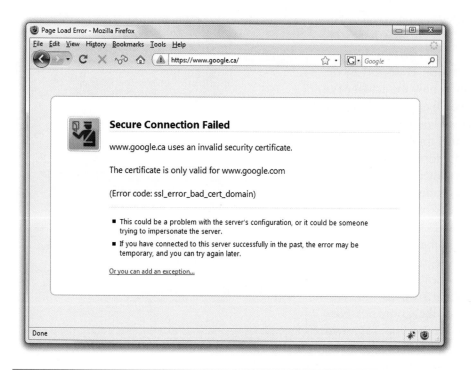

URL to make sure it's the same as the site you are on. If either of these is not correct, you get an error such as shown in Figure 11.39.

If you get one of these errors, you need to decide what to do. Good certificates do go bad (this even happened on my own Web site once) and sometimes the URLs on the certificates are not exactly the same as the site using them. When in doubt, stop. On the other hand, if the risk is low (for example, you're not entering a credit card number or other sensitive information) and you know and trust the site, proceeding is safe in most cases. A courtesy e-mail or phone call to the Web site administrator notifying him or her about the invalid certificate is usually greatly appreciated.

- **Figure 11.39**   Certificate problem

Invalid certificates aren't the only potential problems. After this basic check, the browser checks to see if the certificate has been revoked. Root authorities, like VeriSign, generate Certificate Revocation Lists (CRLs) that a Web browser can check against. Certificates are revoked for a number of reasons, but most of the time the reasons are serious, such as a hacked certificate. If you get a revoked certificate error, it's better to stay away from the site until they fix the problem.

SCP

One of the first SSH-enabled programs to appear after the introduction of SSH was **Secure Copy Protocol (SCP)**. SCP was one of the first protocols used to transfer data securely between two hosts and thus might have replaced FTP. SCP works well but lacks features such as a directory listing. SCP still exists, especially with the well-known UNIX SCP command-line utility, but has for the most part been replaced by the more powerful SFTP.

SFTP

Secure FTP (SFTP), also called SSH FTP, was designed as a replacement for FTP after many of the inadequacies of SCP (such as the inability to see the files on the other computer) were discovered. Although SFTP and FTP have similar

Cross Check

FTP and TFTP

You saw FTP and TFTP back in Chapter 9, "TCP/IP Applications," so check your memory now. How do they differ from SFTP? Do they use the same ports? Would you use FTP and TFTP in the same circumstances? Finally, what's the difference between active and passive FTP?

names and perform the same job of transferring files, the way in which they do that job differs greatly.

The introduction of SSH made it easy to secure most TCP applications just by running them in an SSH tunnel. But FTP was a different case. FTP uses two ports, 20 and 21, creating a two-session communication. This makes FTP a challenge to run in its original form over SSH, because SSH can only handle one session per tunnel. To fix this, a group of programmers from the OpenBSD organization developed a series of secure programs known collectively as **OpenSSH**. SFTP was one of those programs. SFTP looks like FTP, with servers and clients, but relies on an SSH tunnel. If you are on Windows and would like to connect with an SFTP server, WinSCP and FileZilla are two great client options.

SNMP

Simple Network Management Protocol (SNMP) is a very popular method for querying the state of SNMP-capable devices. SNMP can tell you a number of settings like CPU usage, network utilization, and detailed firewall hits. SNMP uses *agents* (special client programs) to collect network information from a **Management Information Base (MIB)**, SNMP's version of a server. To use SNMP you need SNMP-capable devices and some tool to query them. One tool is Cacti (www.cacti.net), shown in Figure 11.40. Cacti, like most good SNMP tools, enables you to query an SNMP-capable device for hundreds of different types of information.

SNMP is a useful tool for network administrators, but the first version, SNMPv1, sent all data, including the passwords, unencrypted over the net-

SNMP runs on UDP port 161.

work. SNMPv2 had good encryption, but was rather challenging to use. SNMPv3 is the standard version used today and combines solid, fairly easy-to-use authentication and encryption.

NTP

The **Network Time Protocol (NTP)** does one thing: it gives you the current time. NTP is an old protocol and isn't in and of itself much of a security risk unless you're using some timestamping protocol like Kerberos. Windows is by far the most common Kerberos user, so just make sure all of your computers have access to an NTP server so that users don't run into problems when logging in. NTP uses UDP port 123.

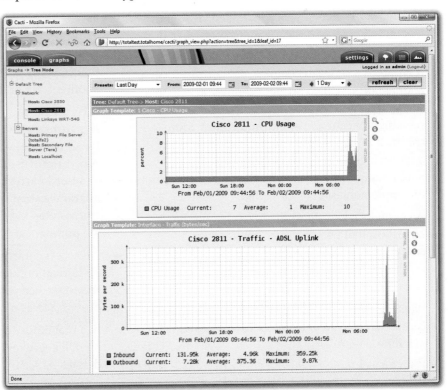

● **Figure 11.40** Cacti at work

Chapter 11 Review

■ Chapter Summary

After reading this chapter and completing the exercises, you should understand the following about securing TCP/IP.

Discuss the standard methods for securing TCP/IP networks

- TCP/IP security can be broken down into four areas: encryption, nonrepudiation, authentication, and authorization.

- Encryption means to scramble, to mix up, to change the data in such a way that bad guys can't read the data.

- Nonrepudiation is the process that guarantees that the data is as originally sent and that it came from the source you think it should have come from.

- Authentication means to verify that whoever accesses the data is the person you want accessing that data.

- Authorization defines what a person accessing the data can do with that data.

- All data starts as plaintext (also called cleartext), meaning the data is in an easily read or viewed industry-wide standard format.

- A cipher is a series of complex and hard-to-reverse mathematics—called an algorithm—you run on a string of ones and zeroes to make a new set of seemingly meaningless ones and zeroes. More specifically, a cipher is a general way to encrypt data, an algorithm is the cipher's underlying mathematical formula, and a complete algorithm is the implementation of the cipher.

- A symmetric-key algorithm is any encryption algorithm that uses the same key for both encryption and decryption. There are two types of symmetric-key algorithms: block ciphers and stream ciphers.

- Block ciphers encrypt data in single chunks of a certain length. Stream ciphers encrypt a single bit at a time.

- Data Encryption Standard (DES) is the oldest TCP/IP symmetric-key algorithm and uses a 64-bit block with a 56-bit key. DES is susceptible to brute-force attacks.

- Advanced Encryption Standard (AES) is the most secure TCP/IP symmetric-key algorithm and uses a 128-bit block with a 128-, 192-, or 256-bit key. AES is practically uncrackable.

- Symmetric-key encryption has one serious weakness: anyone who gets ahold of the key can encrypt or decrypt.

- Public-key cryptography is an implementation of asymmetric-key encryption, which uses one key to encrypt and a different key to decrypt.

- A key pair consists of a public key, which is shared and distributed to senders to use to encrypt data, and a private key, which is kept only by the recipient and used to decrypt data.

- A hash is a mathematical function that you run on a string of binary digits of any length that results in a value of some fixed length, often called a checksum or a digest.

- A cryptographic hash function is a one-way function that produces a unique checksum that can be used to verify nonrepudiation. MD5 and SHA are popular hashes for this type of work.

- A digital signature is a string of ones and zeroes that can only be generated by the sender and is another form of nonrepudiation.

- A certificate is a standardized type of digital signature used to verify the identity of someone (or something) you do not know, like a Web site. A certificate usually includes the digital signature of a third party, a person or a company that guarantees that who is passing out this certificate truly is who they say they are. VeriSign and thawte are popular certificate authorities.

- An access control list (ACL) is used to control authorization, or what a user is allowed to do once they have been authenticated. There are three types of ACL access modes: MAC, DAC, and RBAC.

- In a mandatory access control (MAC) security model, every resource is assigned a label that defines its security level. If the user lacks that security level, they do not get access.

- Discretionary access control (DAC) is based on the idea that there is an owner of a resource who may at his or her discretion assign access to that resource.

- Role-based access control (RBAC) is the most popular model used in file sharing and defines a user's access to a resource based on the user's group membership.

Compare TCP/IP security standards

- The Point-to-Point Protocol (PPP) enables two point-to-point devices to connect, authenticate with a user name and password, and negotiate the network protocol the two devices will use.

- PPP includes two methods to authenticate a user name and password: PAP and CHAP.

- Password Authentication Protocol (PAP) transmits the user name and password over the connection in plaintext, which is not secure.

- Challenge Handshake Authentication Protocol (CHAP) provides a more secure authentication routine because it relies on hashes based on a shared secret, usually a password that both ends of the connection know. Microsoft created its own version called MS-CHAP.

- Authentication, Authorization, and Accounting (AAA) is a philosophy applied to computer security. RADIUS and TACACS+ are standard implementations of AAA.

- Remote Authentication Dial-In User Service (RADIUS) is the better known of the two AAA standards and was created to support ISPs with hundreds if not thousands of modems in hundreds of computers to connect to a single central database.

- Microsoft's RADIUS server is called Internet Authentication Service (IAS) and comes built in with most versions of Microsoft Windows Server. FreeRADIUS is a popular RADIUS server for UNIX/Linux.

- Terminal Access Controller Access Control System Plus (TACACS+) is a proprietary protocol developed by Cisco to support AAA in a network with many routers and switches.

- Kerberos is an authentication protocol for TCP/IP networks with many clients all connected to a single authenticating server, unlike PPP.

- Kerberos, which is the authentication protocol for all Windows networks using a domain controller, uses a Key Distribution Center (KDC) that has two

processes: the Authentication Server (AS) and the Ticket-Granting Service (TGS).

- The Authentication Server authenticates users at login and, if successful, sends a Ticket-Granting Ticket (TGT) (good for eight hours by default) allowing the user to access network resources without having to reauthenticate.

- The timestamped TGT is sent to the TGS, which returns an access token used by the client for authorization to network resources.

- The Extensible Authentication Protocol (EAP) was developed to help two devices negotiate the authentication process. It is used primarily in wireless networks. There are six commonly used types of EAP: EAP-PSK, EAP-TLS, EAP-TTLS, EAP-MS-CHAPv2 (PEAP), EAP-MD5, and LEAP.

- EAP Personal Shared Key (EAP-PSK) is the most popular form of authentication used in wireless networks today.

- Early wireless networks lacked any form of authentication, so the wireless community grabbed a preexisting authentication standard called 802.1X to use in their wireless networks. 802.1X combines the RADIUS-style AAA with EAP versions to make a complete authentication solution.

- Secure Shell (SSH) is a secure replacement for Telnet. SSH uses PKI in the form of an RSA key. At login, the SSH server sends its public key to the client. The client then encrypts data using the public key and transmits the data, which is subsequently decrypted on the server with the private key.

- Netscape created the Secure Sockets Layer (SSL) standard, which requires a server with a certificate. SSL has been updated to the Transport Layer Security (TLS) standard and is used for secure Web transactions, such as online credit card purchases.

- SSL is limited to HTML, FTP, SMTP, and a few older TCP applications while TLS is less restrictive and is used for everything SSL does in addition to VoIP and VPNs.

- IPSec is an encryption protocol and is destined to become the dominant encryption protocol under IPv6. IPSec works in two different modes: Transport mode and Tunnel mode. IPv6 uses the IPSec Transport mode by default.

- In Transport mode, only the actual payload of the IP packet is encrypted; the destination and source

IP addresses, port numbers, and other IP header information is still readable.

- In Tunnel mode, the entire IP packet is encrypted and then placed into an IPSec endpoint where it is encapsulated inside another IP packet.

Implement secure TCP/IP applications

- HTTPS uses SSL/TLS for the actual authentication and encryption process. Most browsers show a small lock icon in the lower right corner or in the address bar when an HTTPS connection is established.

- The most common problems with HTTPS connections are caused by bad or outdated certificates.

- Secure Copy Protocol (SCP) is an SSH-enabled program or protocol used to securely copy files between a client and a server. It has been replaced by Secure FTP (SFTP).

- Simple Network Management Protocol (SNMP) is a method for querying the state of SNMP-capable devices. SNMP can tell you a number of settings like CPU usage, network utilization, and detailed firewall hits. SNMP uses agents and MIBs to capture and monitor network usage.

- SNMPv1 sent all data, including the passwords, unencrypted over the network. SNMPv2 had good encryption but was rather challenging to use. SNMPv3 is the standard version used today and combines solid, fairly easy-to-use authentication and encryption.

- Network Time Protocol (NTP) gives you the current time. It isn't much of a security risk unless you're using some timestamping protocol like Kerberos.

■ Key Terms

802.1X *(299)*
access control list (ACL) *(291)*
Advanced Encryption Standard (AES) *(283)*
algorithm *(280)*
asymmetric-key algorithm *(282)*
authentication *(279)*
Authentication Server (AS) *(297)*
Authentication, Authorization, and Accounting (AAA) *(294)*
authorization *(279)*
block cipher *(282)*
certificate *(287)*
Challenge Handshake Authentication Protocol (CHAP) *(293)*
cipher *(280)*
ciphertext *(281)*
cleartext *(280)*
complete algorithm *(280)*
Data Encryption Standard (DES) *(282)*
digital signature *(287)*
discretionary access control (DAC) *(291)*
encryption *(279)*
Extensible Authentication Protocol (EAP) *(297)*
FreeRADIUS *(296)*
hash *(286)*

Internet Authentication Service (IAS) *(296)*
Internet Protocol Security (IPSec) *(302)*
Kerberos *(296)*
Key Distribution Center (KDC) *(297)*
key pair *(284)*
Lightweight Extensible Authentication Protocol (LEAP) *(298)*
Management Information Base (MIB) *(305)*
mandatory access control (MAC) *(291)*
MD5 *(286)*
MS-CHAP *(293)*
Network Access Server (NAS) *(295)*
Network Time Protocol (NTP) *(305)*
nonrepudiation *(279)*
OpenSSH *(305)*
Password Authentication Protocol (PAP) *(293)*
plaintext *(280)*
Point-to-Point Protocol (PPP) *(292)*
Protected Extensible Authentication Protocol (PEAP) *(298)*
public-key cryptography *(283)*
public-key infrastructure (PKI) *(290)*
Remote Authentication Dial-In User Service (RADIUS) *(295)*
Rivest Cipher 4 (RC4) *(283)*

Rivest Shamir Adleman (RSA) *(283)*
role-based access control (RBAC) *(291)*
Secure Copy Protocol (SCP) *(304)*
Secure FTP (SFTP) *(304)*
Secure Hash Algorithm (SHA) *(287)*
Secure Shell (SSH) *(300)*
Secure Sockets Layer (SSL) *(302)*

Simple Network Management Protocol (SNMP) *(305)*
stream cipher *(282)*
symmetric-key algorithm *(282)*
Terminal Access Controller Access Control System Plus (TACACS+) *(296)*
Ticket-Granting Ticket (TGT) *(297)*
Transport Layer Security (TLS) *(302)*
tunnel *(301)*

■ Key Term Quiz

Use the Key Terms list to complete the sentences that follow. Not all the terms will be used.

1. _____ defines what a person accessing data can do with that data.

2. _____ is the act of verifying you are who you say you are.

3. _____ is the process of guaranteeing that data is as originally sent and that it came from the source from which you think it should have come.

4. A(n) _____ encrypts data in fixed-length chunks at a time.

5. _____ is a secure replacement for Telnet.

6. A(n) _____ uses one key to encrypt data and a different key to decrypt the same data.

7. SSL has been replaced by the more robust _____.

8. SCP has been replaced by _____, a secure protocol for copying files to a server.

9. _____ is the default authentication protocol for Windows domains and is extremely time sensitive.

10. _____ uses a 128-bit block, up to a 256-bit key, and is a virtually uncrackable encryption algorithm.

■ Multiple-Choice Quiz

1. Justin wants his team to be able to send him encrypted e-mails. What should he do?

    A. Send to each team member his private key.

    B. Send to each team member his public key.

    C. Ask each team member for their private key.

    D. Ask each team member for their public key.

2. Which of the following are popular cryptographic hashing functions? (Select two.)

    A. MD5

    B. SHA

    C. RADIUS

    D. TACACS+

3. A public and private key pair is an example of what?

    A. Symmetric-key algorithm

    B. Asymmetric-key algorithm

    C. Certificate

    D. RADIUS

4. Which authentication protocol is time sensitive and is the default authentication protocol on Windows domains?

    A. PPP

    B. MS-CHAP

    C. IPSec

    D. Kerberos

5. What helps to protect credit card numbers during online purchases? (Select two.)

    A. Certificates

    B. TLS

    C. SCP

    D. NTP

6. Emily wants to remotely and securely enter commands to be run at a remote server. What application should she use?

   A. Telnet

   B. SSH

   C. SFTP

   D. RSA

7. A hash function is by definition:

   A. A complex function

   B. A PKI function

   C. A one-way function

   D. A systematic function

8. In order to have a PKI infrastructure you must have a(n):

   A. Web server

   B. Web of trust

   C. Root authority

   D. Unsigned certificate

9. Which term describes the process of guaranteeing that data that is received is in fact the data that was sent—and that it came from the presumed source?

   A. Authentication

   B. Authorization

   C. Encryption

   D. Nonrepudiation

10. If you saw some traffic running on TCP port 49, what AAA standard would you know was running?

    A. PPP

    B. RADIUS

    C. MS-CHAP

    D. TACACS+

11. What is the difference between RADIUS and TACACS+?

A. RADIUS is authentication control for Windows networks while TACACS+ is authentication control for UNIX/Linux networks.

B. RADIUS is an implementation of authentication control while TACACS+ is an implementation of authorization control.

C. RADIUS is a generic name for authentication control, and there are implementations for Windows, UNIX, and Linux servers. TACACS+ is authentication control for Cisco routers and switches.

D. RADIUS supports encryption, TACACS+ does not and is therefore less desirable in a network.

12. AES is a(n) _____ cipher.

    A. Block

    B. Forwarding

    C. Stream

    D. Asymmetric

13. Which authentication protocol is broadly used on wireless networks?

    A. 802.1X

    B. PPP

    C. PAP

    D. MS-CHAP

14. Digital signatures and certificates help which aspect of computer security?

    A. Accounting

    B. Authentication

    C. Authorization

    D. Nonrepudiation

15. Which authorization model grants privileges based on the group membership of network users?

    A. MAC

    B. DAC

    C. RBAC

    D. GAC

■ Essay Quiz

1. Explain the difference between symmetric-key and asymmetric-key algorithms and give examples of each. Which is more secure? Why?

2. Access control lists help to control the authorization of network resources. Explain the differences between the three ACL access models.

3. You receive a call from a distressed user telling you they were in the middle of an online purchase (just entering their credit card number) when they noticed a certificate warning on the screen saying the Web site's certificate has expired. What advice would you give the user?

Lab Projects

• Lab Project 11.1

Download a copy of GnuPG from www.gnupg.org and one of the frontends from www.gnupg.org/related_software/frontends.en.html. Generate a key pair and share your public key with a classmate.

Have your classmate encrypt a file using your public key and e-mail it to you. Decrypt your file with your private key.

• Lab Project 11.2

You have learned many acronyms in this chapter! Make a list of the following acronyms, state what they stand for, and briefly describe them. Use this as a study sheet for the CompTIA Network+ certification exam: DES, AES, RSA, MD5, SHA, PKI, CRAM-MD5, ACL, MAC, DAC, RBAC, PPP, PAP, CHAP, MS-CHAP, AAA, RADIUS, TACACS+, KDC, AS, TGT, SID, EAP, EAP-TLS, EAP-PSK, EAP-TTLS, EAP-MS-CHAPv2, PEAP, EAP-MD5, LEAP, SSH, SSL, TLS, HTTPS, SCP, SFTP, SNMP, and NTP.

Advanced Networking Devices

"It followed from the special theory of relativity that mass and energy are both but different manifestations of the same thing. A somewhat unfamiliar conception for the average mind."

—ALBERT EINSTEIN

In this chapter, you will learn how to

- **Discuss the four logical topologies as defined by CompTIA**
- **Configure and deploy VLANs**
- **Implement advanced switch features**

As we delve deeper into the world of networking in this book, the protocols and standards get more complex, but all of the hardware has stayed pretty much constant. Up to this point, we've dealt with nothing more than hubs, switches, and routers. The beauty of these three devices is that you can look at any one of them and instantly say at what layer of the OSI seven-layer model it operates. Hubs work at Layer 1, switches work at Layer 2, and routers work at Layer 3. Life is good, but a bit simplistic, because most of today's networking boxes take on more than one OSI layer.

Historical/Conceptual

Let's take a typical home router as an example. My router at home is really two devices in one: a four-port switch and a router. When you combine these features into a single box, you have more than just a switch and a router. By working together as a single piece of hardware, these features can do some truly amazing things that a single, separate switch connected to a single, separate router simply cannot do. This combination of features transforms a little home router into an advanced device that works at multiple layers of the OSI seven-layer model. It's not truly accurate to even call my little home router a router. Calling it a **multilayer switch** at least gives people a clue that it's more than just a router and a switch in the same box.

The world is filled with multilayer switches. These switches do hundreds of different jobs, and this chapter is designed to show you some examples of the jobs multilayer switches do so you can appreciate how and why we use them in the majority of networks.

To learn about these devices, you need to understand first the concept of what CompTIA calls *logical network topologies*—the way in which the many systems on a network are organized to send data to each other. Then I'll go into great detail about one of the four logical network topologies, VLAN, to demonstrate why many serious networks use this powerful feature (with the help of advanced switches) to administer a network. Last, I will give you a tour of a number of unique advanced devices, using the OSI seven-layer model as a tool to organize them.

Logical Network Topologies

Recall from Chapter 3, "Cabling and Topology," that the term "physical topology" describes the physical layout of the cabling and the term "signaling topology" refers to how the signals actually progress through the network. A star-bus topology, for example, has a physical star but a logical bus. These two terms work well for describing how data moves about a network—as long as you're working with a single broadcast domain. Just in case you don't remember your broadcast domains, let's do a quick review. Imagine a simple network with some number of computers connected to a single switch. When you send a piece of data to another single computer (a unicast), the switch creates a direct connection. When you send a broadcast message, every computer on the network receives the message (Figure 12.1).

Cross Check

Broadcast Domains and CSMA/CD

You learned about broadcast domains and the trouble with CSMA/CD back in Chapter 4, "Ethernet Basics," so check your memory now—or glance back at that chapter—to answer these questions. What function does CSMA/CD serve in an Ethernet network? How do collisions manifest within a single broadcast domain? What about between two broadcast domains? How does a switch affect things?

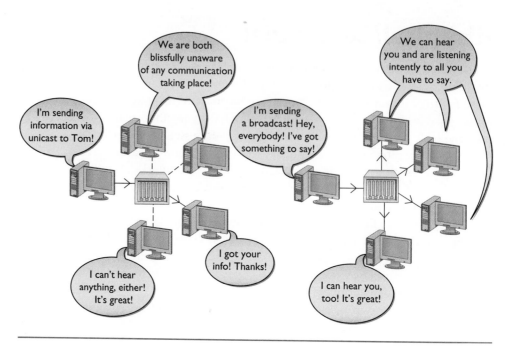

● **Figure 12.1**   Unicast (left) and broadcast (right)

Tech Tip

CompTIA Terminology

While your humble author loves CompTIA, I need to warn you: outside of the CompTIA Network+ exam objectives, I don't think you'll ever see or hear these four terms lumped together: client/server, peer-to-peer, VPN, and VLAN. For the most part, the CompTIA Network+ exam objectives follow real-world terminology and examples, but lumping together this terminology is just a touch off the mark.

Routers block broadcasts and are used to connect broadcast domains. Figure 12.2 shows two broadcast domains separated by a single router.

But we're about to add some really interesting advanced features to your routers and switches, giving them the power to do things that go beyond the types of topologies thus far discussed. So we now need to talk about four topologies that go beyond the description of either physical or signaling topologies: peer-to-peer, client/server, VPN, and VLAN. CompTIA uses the name "logical network topologies" for these topologies.

CompTIA may like to use the term "logical network topologies" but the more common term heard out in the real world, at least to describe client/server and peer-to-peer, is "software architecture model." In common use, the terms refer to the role computers play in a network, as in which computers act as servers and which computers act as clients. I have some strong feelings about these terms—read on and see.

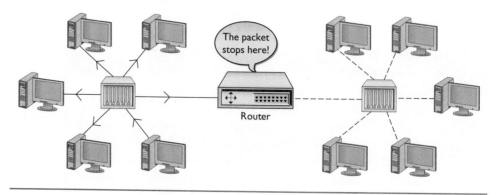

● **Figure 12.2**   Two broadcast domains

Test Specific

Client/Server

The earliest networks used a **client/server** model. In that model, certain systems acted as dedicated servers. Dedicated servers were called "dedicated" because that's all they did. You couldn't go up to a dedicated server and run Word or Solitaire. Dedicated servers ran powerful server network operating systems that offered up files, folders, Web pages, and so on to the network's client systems. Client systems on a client/server network never functioned as servers. One client system couldn't access shared resources on another client system. Servers serve and clients access, and never the twain shall . . . cross over . . . in the old days of client/server! Figure 12.3 shows a typical client/server network. As far as the clients are concerned, the only system on the network is the server system. The clients cannot see each other nor can they share data with each other directly. They must save the data on the server so that other systems can access it.

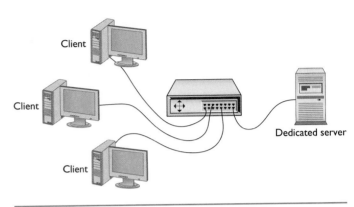

• **Figure 12.3**   A simple client/server network

Back in the old days there was an operating system called Novell NetWare. Novell NetWare servers were true dedicated servers. You couldn't go up to a Novell NetWare server and write yourself a resume; there was no Windows, there were no user applications. The only thing Novell NetWare servers knew how to do was share their own resources, but they shared those resources extremely well! The Novell NetWare operating system was unique. It wasn't Windows, Macintosh, or Linux. It required you to learn an entirely different set of installation, configuration, and administration commands. Figure 12.4 shows a screen from Novell NetWare. Don't let the

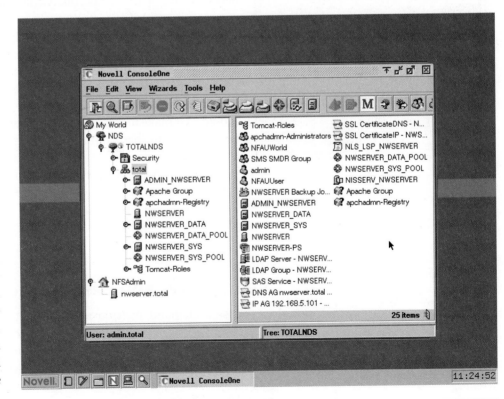

• **Figure 12.4**   Novell NetWare in action

passing resemblance to Windows fool you—it was a completely different operating system!

Dedicated servers enabled Novell to create an entire feature set not seen before on personal computers. Each dedicated server had its own database of user names and passwords. You couldn't access any of the resources on the server without logging in. The server's administrator would assign "permissions" to a specific user account, such as Write (add files to a directory), File Scan (see the contents of a directory), and Erase (delete files).

By keeping the server functionality separate from the client systems, the Novell folks made very powerful, dedicated servers without overwhelming the client computers with tons of software. (This was, after all, in the early days of personal computers and they didn't have anything near the power of a modern PC!) NetWare servers had tremendous power and great security because the only thing they did was run serving software. In the early days of networking, client/server was king!

Peer-to-Peer

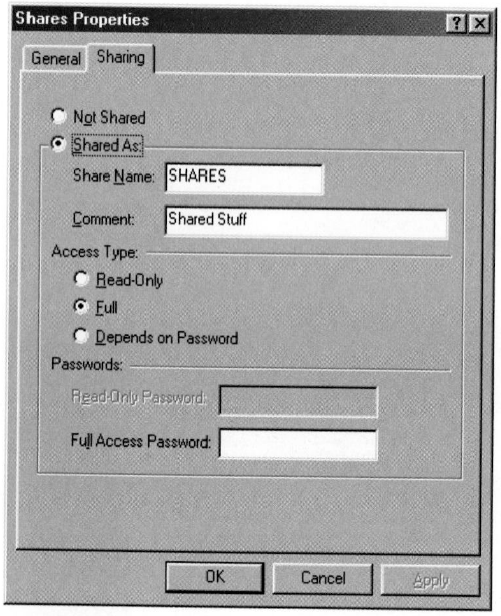

Novell NetWare was the first popular way to network PCs, but it wasn't too many years later that Microsoft introduced the first versions of network-capable Windows. The way in which these versions of Windows looked at networking, called peer-to-peer, was completely different from the client/server view of networking. In a **peer-to-peer** network, any system acts as a server, a client, or both, depending on how you configure that system. PCs on peer-to-peer networks frequently act as both clients and servers. One of the most common examples of a peer-to-peer network is the venerable Windows 9*x* series of operating systems. Figure 12.5 shows the sharing options for the ancient Windows 98 operating system, providing options to share a folder and thus turn that computer into a server.

At first glance, it would seem that peer-to-peer is the way to go— why create a network that doesn't allow the clients to see each other? Wouldn't it make more sense to give users the freedom to allow their systems both to share and access any resource? The problem was a lack of security.

The early Windows systems did not have user accounts and the only permissions were Read Only and Full Control. So they made it easy to share, but hard to control access to the shared resources. People wanted the freedom of peer-to-peer with the security of client/server.

● **Figure 12.5**   Sharing options in Windows 98

The "old school" client/server model means dedicated servers with strong security. Clients only see the server. In the peer-to-peer model, any system is a client, server, or both, but at the cost of lower security and additional demands on the system resources of each peer.

Client/Server and Peer-to-Peer Today

In response to demand, every modern operating system has dumped the classic client/server or peer-to-peer label. Windows, Linux, and Macintosh all have the capability to act as a server or a client while also providing robust security through user accounts and permissions and the like.

So why learn about classic client/server and peer-to-peer? Because CompTIA wants you to. Since the widespread adoption of TCP/IP and the Internet, however, client/server and peer-to-peer have taken on new or updated definitions, and refer more to applications than to network operating systems. Consider e-mail for a moment. For traditional e-mail to work, you need an e-mail client like Microsoft Outlook. But you also need an e-mail server program like Microsoft Exchange to handle the e-mail requests from your e-mail client. Outlook is a *dedicated client*—you cannot use the Outlook client as a mail-serving program. Likewise, you cannot use Microsoft Exchange as an e-mail client. Exchange is a *dedicated server* program.

Peer-to-peer applications, often referred to simply as P2P, act as both client and server. The best examples of these applications are the now infamous file-sharing applications based on special TCP/IP protocols. The applications, with names like BitTorrent, LimeWire, and DC++, act as both clients and servers, enabling a user both to share files and access shared files. BitTorrent is actually an entire protocol, not just a particular application. There are many different applications that use the BitTorrent standard. Figure 12.6 shows one such program, µTorrent, in the process of simultaneously uploading and downloading files.

Talking about client/ server or peer-to-peer when discussing classic networks or modern networking applications is great, but we can extend the idea of logical network topologies beyond the simple notions of client/server and peer-to-peer. Advanced networking devices enable the development of networks of amazing complexity, security, and power: virtual private networks and virtual LANs.

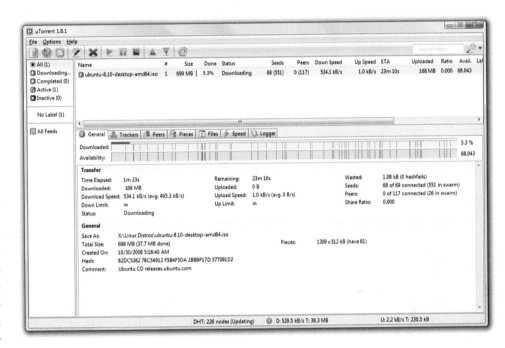

● **Figure 12.6**   µTorrent downloading an Ubuntu release

VPN

Remote connections have been around for a long time, long before the Internet existed. The biggest drawback about remote connections was the cost to connect. If you were on one side of the continent and had to connect to your LAN on the other side of the continent, the only connection option was a telephone. Or, if you needed to connect two LANs across the continent, you ended up paying outrageous monthly charges for a private connection. The introduction of the Internet gave people wishing to connect to their home networks a very cheap connection option, but there was one problem—the whole Internet is open to the public. People wanted to stop using dial-up and expensive private connections and use the Internet instead, but they wanted to be able to do it securely.

If you read the previous chapter, you might think we could use some of the tools for securing TCP/IP to help: and you would be correct. Several standards, many based on the Point-to-Point Protocol (PPP), have been

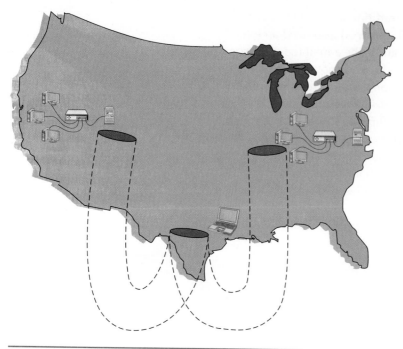

Figure 12.7 VPN connecting computers across the United States

created that use encrypted tunnels between a computer (or a remote network) and a private network through the Internet (Figure 12.7), resulting in what is called a **Virtual Private Network (VPN)**.

As you saw in the previous chapter, an encrypted tunnel requires endpoints—the ends of the tunnel where the data is encrypted and decrypted. In the tunnels you've seen thus far, the client for the application sits on one end and the server sits on the other. VPNs do exactly the same thing. Either some software running on a computer or, in some cases, a dedicated box must act as an endpoint for a VPN (Figure 12.8).

The key with the VPN is that all of the computers should be on the same network—and that means they must all have the same network ID. For example, you would want the laptop that you are using in an airport lounge to have the same network ID as all of your computers in your LAN back at the office. But there's no simple way to do this. If it's a single client trying to access a network, that client is going to take on the IP address from its local DHCP server. In the case of your laptop in the airport, your network ID and IP address come from the DHCP server in the airport, not the DHCP server back at the office.

If we are trying to connect two networks, we could make them each take on a subnet from a single network ID, but that creates all kinds of administrative issues (Figure 12.9).

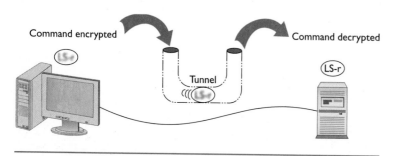

Figure 12.8 Typical tunnel

To make the VPN work, we need a protocol that will use one of the many tunneling protocols available but add the ability to query for an IP address from a local DHCP server to give the tunnel an IP address that matches the subnet of the local LAN. The connection will keep the IP address to connect

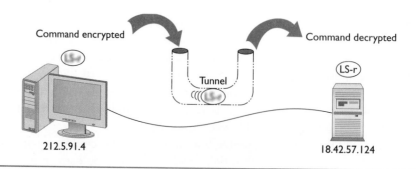

212.5.91.4   18.42.57.124

Figure 12.9 How do we get the same network IDs?

to the Internet, but the tunnel endpoints must act like they are NICs (Figure 12.10). Two protocols fit our needs, PPTP and L2TP.

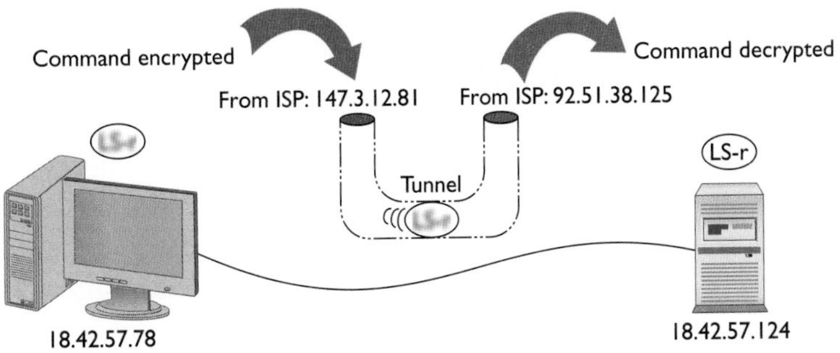

PPTP VPNs

So how do we make IP addresses appear out of thin air? What tunneling protocol have we learned about that has the smarts to query for an IP address? That's right! Good old PPP! Microsoft got the ball rolling with the **Point-to-Point Tunneling Protocol (PPTP)**, an advanced version of PPP that handles all this right out of the box. The only trick is the endpoints. In Microsoft's view, a VPN is intended for individual clients to connect to a private network, so Microsoft places the PPTP endpoints on the client and a special remote access server program, originally only available on Windows Server, called **Routing and Remote Access Service (RRAS)** on the server—see Figure 12.11.

On the Windows client side, you run Create a New Connection. This creates a virtual NIC that, like any other NIC, does a DHCP query and gets an IP address from the DHCP server on the private network (Figure 12.12).

When your computer connects to the RRAS server on the private network, PPTP creates a secure tunnel through the Internet back to the private LAN. Your client takes on an IP address of that network, as if your computer is directly connected to the LAN back at the office, even down to the default

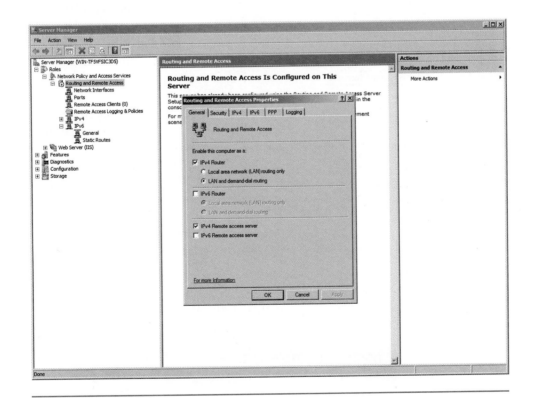

• **Figure 12.10**   Endpoints must have their own IP addresses.

A system connected to a VPN looks as though it's on the local network, but performs much slower than if the system was connected directly back at the office.

• **Figure 12.11**   RRAS in action

Chapter 12: Advanced Networking Devices

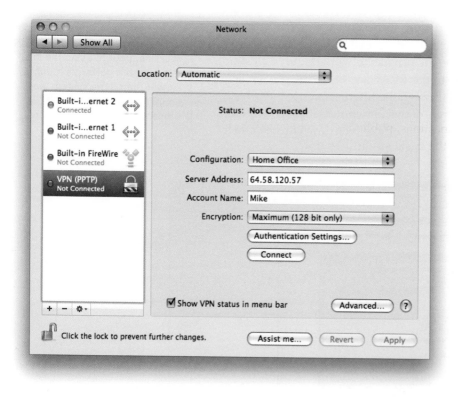

• Figure 12.13   VPN on a Macintosh OS X system

gateway. If you open your Web browser, your client will go across the Internet to the local LAN and then use the LAN's default gateway to get to the Internet! Using a Web browser will be much slower when you are on a VPN.

PPTP VPNs are very popular. Every operating system comes with some type of built-in VPN client that supports PPTP (among others). Figure 12.13 shows Network, the Macintosh OS X VPN connection tool.

L2TP VPNs

Microsoft pushed the idea of a single client tunneling into a private LAN using software. Cisco, being the router king that it is, came up with its own VPN protocol called **Layer 2 Tunneling Protocol (L2TP)**. L2TP took all the good features of PPTP and added support to run on almost any type of connection possible, from telephones to Ethernet to ultra-high-speed optical connections. Cisco also moved the endpoint on the local LAN from a server program to a VPN-capable router, called a **VPN concentrator**, such as the Cisco 2811 Integrated Services Router shown in Figure 12.14.

Cisco provides free client software to connect a single faraway PC to a Cisco VPN. Network people often directly connect two Cisco VPN concentrators to permanently connect two separate LANs. It's slow, but it's cheap compared to a dedicated high-speed connection between two faraway LANs.

L2TP differs from PPTP in that it has no authentication or encryption. L2TP usually uses IPSec for all the security needs. Technically, you should call an L2TP VPN an "L2TP/IPSec" VPN.

• Figure 12.14   Cisco 2811 Integrated Services Router

L2TP works perfectly well in the single-client-connecting-to-a-LAN world, too. Every operating system's VPN client fully supports L2TP/IPSec VPNs.

Alternatives to PPTP and L2TP

The majority of VPNs use either PPTP or L2TP. There are other options, some of them quite popular. First is OpenVPN, which, like the rest of what I call "OpenXXX" applications, uses Secure Shell (SSH) for the VPN tunnel. Second is IPSec. We are now seeing some pure (no L2TP) IPSec solutions that use IPSec tunneling for VPNs.

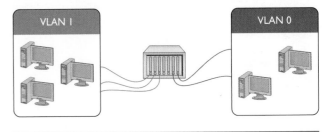

Over the years there's been plenty of crossover between Microsoft and Cisco. Microsoft RRAS supports L2TP and Cisco routers support PPTP.

VLAN

The last of CompTIA's logical network topologies is known as a **Virtual Local Area Network (VLAN)**. It's hard to find anything but the smallest of LANs today that do not use VLANs. VLANs are so important and so common that we need to spend a serious amount of time discussing them and how they work. Let's take some time to dive deeply into VLANs.

■ VLAN in Depth

Today's LANs are complex places. It's rare to see any serious network that doesn't have remote incoming connections, public Web or e-mail servers, and wireless networks, as well as the basic string of connected switches. Leaving all of these different features on a single broadcast domain creates a tremendous amount of broadcast traffic and creates a security nightmare. You could separate the networks with multiple switches and put routers in between, but that's very inflexible and hard to manage. What if you could segment the network using the switches you already own? You can, and that's what a VLAN enables you to do.

Creating a VLAN means to take a single physical broadcast domain and chop it up into multiple virtual broadcast domains. VLANs require special switches loaded with extra programming to create the virtual networks.

Imagine a single switch with a number of computers connected to it. Up to this point a single switch is always a single collision domain, but that's about to change. We've decided to take this single switch and turn it into two VLANs. VLANs typically get the name "VLAN" plus a number, like VLAN1 or VLAN275. We usually start at 0, though there's no law or rules on the numbering. We'll configure the ports on our single switch to be in one of two VLANs, VLAN0 or VLAN1 (Figure 12.15). I promise to show you how to configure ports for different VLANs shortly, but we've got a couple of other concepts to hit first.

• **Figure 12.15**   Switch with two VLANs

Figure 12-15 shows a switch configured to assign individual ports to VLANs, but VLANs use more than just ports to define different VLANs. A VLAN might use the computers' MAC addresses to determine VLAN membership. A computer in this type of VLAN is always a member of the same VLAN no matter what port on the switch into which you plug the computer.

A single switch configured into two VLANs is the simplest form of VLAN possible. More serious networks usually have more than one switch. Let's say you added a switch to our simple network. You'd like to keep VLAN0 and VLAN1 but use both switches. You can configure the new switch to use VLAN0 and VLAN1, but you've got to enable data to flow between the two switches, regardless of VLAN. That's where trunking comes into play.

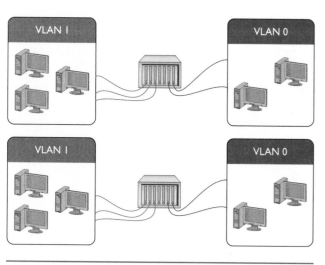

• Figure 12.16 Two switches, each with a VLAN0 and a VLAN1

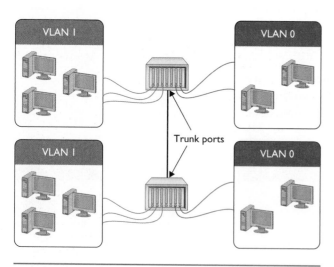

• Figure 12.17 Trunk ports

Trunking

Trunking is the process of transferring VLAN data between two or more switches. Imagine two switches, each configured with a VLAN0 and a VLAN1, as shown in Figure 12.16.

We want all of the computers connected to VLAN0 on one switch to talk to all of the computers connected to VLAN0 on the other switch. Of course we want to do this with VLAN1 also. To do this, a port on each switch must be configured as a **trunk port**. A trunk port is a port on a switch configured to carry all data, regardless of VLAN number, between all switches in a LAN (Figure 12.17).

In the early days of VLANs, every switch manufacturer had its own way to make VLANs work. Cisco, for example, had a proprietary form of trunking called Inter-Switch Link (ISL), which most Cisco switches still support. Today, every Ethernet switch prefers the IEEE 802.1Q trunk standard, enabling you to connect switches from different manufacturers.

Configuring a VLAN-capable Switch

If you want to configure a VLAN-capable switch, you must have a method to do that configuration. One method used to configure some switches is to use a serial port like the one described earlier in the book, but the most common method is to make the switch a Web server, like the one shown in Figure 12.18. Catalyst is a model name for a series of popular Cisco routers with advanced switching features. Any switch that you can access and configure is called a *managed switch*.

So if you're giving the switch a Web page, that means the switch needs an IP address—but don't switches use MAC addresses? They do, but managed switches also come with an IP address for configuration. A brand-new managed switch out of the box invariably has a preset IP address similar to the preset, private IP addresses you see on routers. This IP address isn't for any of the individual ports, but rather is for the whole switch. That means no matter where

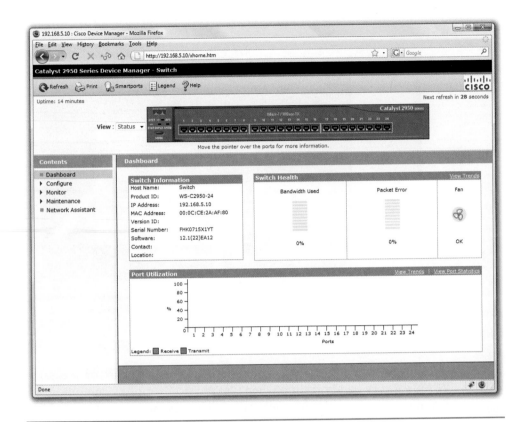

● **Figure 12.18** Catalyst 2950 Series Device Manager

you physically connect to the switch, the IP address to get to the configuration screen is the same.

Every switch manufacturer has its own interface for configuring VLANs, but the interface shown in Figure 12.19 is a classic example. This is Cisco Network Assistant, a very popular tool that enables you to configure multiple devices through the same interface. Note that you first must define your VLANs.

After you create the VLANs, you usually either assign computers' MAC addresses to VLANs or assign ports to VLANs. Assigning MAC addresses means that no

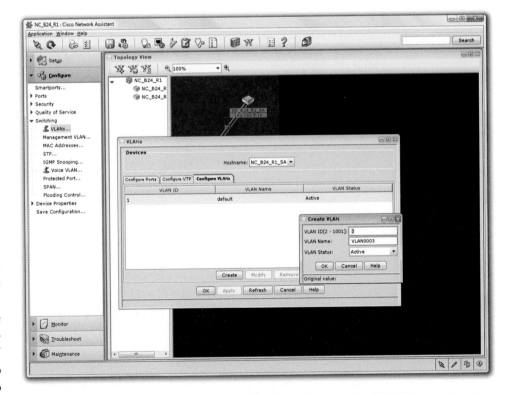

● **Figure 12.19** Defining VLANs in Cisco Network Assistant

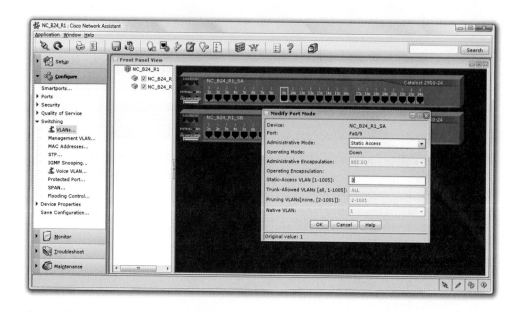

● **Figure 12.20** Assigning a port to a VLAN

VLANs based on ports are the most common type of VLAN and are commonly known as static VLANs. VLANs based on MAC addresses are called dynamic VLANs.

matter where you plug in a computer, it is always part of the same VLAN—a very handy feature when you physically move a computer! Assigning each port to a VLAN means that whatever computer plugs into that port, it will always be a member of that port's VLAN. Figure 12.20 shows a port being assigned to a particular VLAN.

InterVLAN Routing

Once you've configured a switch to support multiple VLANs, each VLAN is its own broadcast domain, just as if the two VLANs were on two completely separate switches. There is no way for data to get from one VLAN to another unless you use a router. In the early days of VLANs it was common to use a router with multiple ports as a backbone for the network. Figure 12.21 shows one possible way to connect two VLANs with a single router.

Adding a physical router like this isn't a very elegant way to connect

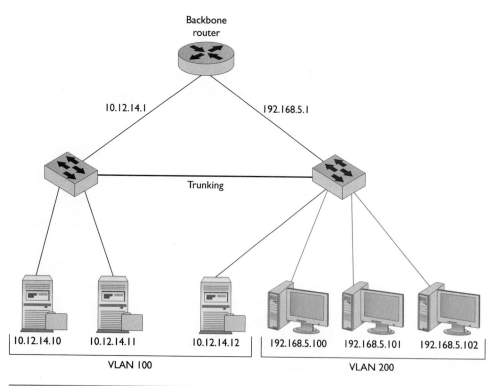

● **Figure 12.21** One router connecting multiple VLANs

VLANs. This forces almost all traffic to go through the router, and it's not a very flexible solution if you want to add more VLANs in the future. As a result, all but the simplest VLANs have at least one very special switch that has the ability to make virtual routers. Cisco calls this feature **interVLAN routing**. Figure 12.22 shows an older but very popular interVLAN routing–capable switch, the Cisco 3550.

● **Figure 12.22**   Cisco 3550

From the outside, the Cisco 3550 looks like any other switch. On the inside, it's an incredibly powerful and flexible device that not only supports VLANs, but also enables you to create virtual routers to interconnect these VLANs. Figure 12.23 shows the configuration screen for the 3550's interVLAN routing between two VLANs.

If the Cisco 3550 is a switch but also has built-in routers, on what layer of the OSI seven-layer model does it operate? If it's a switch, then it works at Layer 2. But it also has the capability to create virtual routers, and routers work at Layer 3. This isn't an ordinary switch. The Cisco 3550 works at both Layers 2 and 3 at the same time.

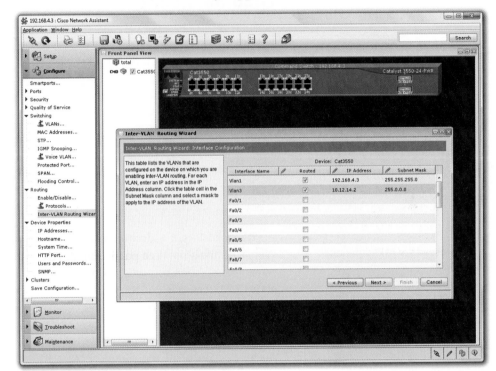

● **Figure 12.23**   Setting up interVLAN routing

■ Multilayer Switches

The Cisco 3550 is an amazing box in that it seems to utterly defy the entire concept of a switch because of its support of interVLAN routing. Up to this point we always said a switch works at Layer 2 of the OSI model, but now you've just seen a very powerful (and expensive) switch that clearly also works at Layer 3. The Cisco 3550 is one example of what we call a *multilayer switch*.

At this point you must stop thinking that a switch is always Layer 2. Instead, think of the idea that any device that forwards traffic based on anything inside a given packet is a switch. A Layer 2 switch forwards traffic based on MAC addresses, whereas a Layer 3 switch (also called a router) forwards traffic based on IP addresses. From here on out, we will carefully address at what layer of the OSI seven-layer model a switch operates.

Multilayer switches are incredibly common and support a number of interesting features, clearly making them part of what I call advanced

Any device that works at multiple layers of the OSI seven-layer model, providing more than a single service, is called a *multifunction network device*.

networking devices and what CompTIA calls specialized network devices. We are going to look at three areas where multilayer switches are very helpful: load balancing, quality of service, and network protection (each term is defined in its respective section). These three areas aren't the only places where multiplayer switches solve problems but they are the most popular and the ones that the CompTIA Network+ exam covers. Let's look at these areas that are common to more advanced networks and see how more advanced network devices help in these situations.

Load Balancing

Popular Internet servers are exactly that—popular. So popular that it's impossible for a single system to support the thousands if not millions of requests per day that bombard them. But from what we've learned thus far about servers, we know that a single server has a single IP address. Put this to the test. Go to a command prompt and type ping www.google.com.

```
C:\>ping www.google.com

Pinging www.1.google.com [74.125.95.147] with 32 bytes of data:
Reply from 74.125.95.147: bytes=32 time=71ms TTL=242
Reply from 74.125.95.147: bytes=32 time=71ms TTL=242
Reply from 74.125.95.147: bytes=32 time=70ms TTL=242
Reply from 74.125.95.147: bytes=32 time=70ms TTL=242
```

It's difficult to come up with a consensus on statistics like the number of requests/day or how many requests a single server can handle. Just concentrate on the concept. If some nerdy type says my numbers are way off, nicely agree and walk away. Just don't invite them to any parties.

It's hard to get a definite number but poking around on a few online Web site analysis Web sites like Alexa (www.alexa.com), it seems that www.google.com receives around 130 to 140 million requests per day; about 1600 requests per second. Each request might require the Web server to deliver thousands of HTTP packets. A single, powerful, dedicated Web server (arguably) handles at best 2000 requests/second. Even though www.google.com is a single IP address, there has to be more than one Web server to handle all the requests. Actually there are thousands of Google Web servers stretched across multiple locations around the world. So how does www.google.com use a single IP address and lots and lots of servers? The answer is in something called load balancing.

Load balancing means to take a bunch of servers and make them look like a single server, creating a *server cluster*. Not only do you need to make them look like one server, you need to make sure that requests to these servers are distributed evenly so no one server is bogged down while another is idle. There are a few ways to do this, as you are about to see. Be warned, not all of these methods require an advanced network device, but it's very common to use one. A device designed to do one thing really well is always much faster than using a general-purpose computer and slapping on software.

DNS Load Balancing

Using DNS for load balancing is one of the oldest and still very common ways to support multiple Web servers. In this case, each Web server gets its own (usually) public IP address. Each DNS server for the domain has multiple "A" DNS records, each with the same fully qualified domain name (FQDN), for each DNS server. The DNS server then cycles around these

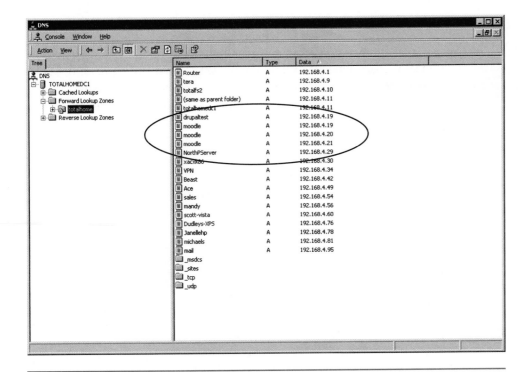

• **Figure 12.24**   Multiple IP addresses, same name

records so the same domain name resolves to different IP addresses. Figure 12.24 shows a Windows DNS server with multiple A records for the same FQDN.

Now that the A records are added, you need to tell the DNS server to cycle around these names. With Windows DNS Server, there's a check box to do so, as shown in Figure 12.25.

When a computer comes to the DNS server for resolution, the server cycles through the DNS A records, giving out first one and then the next in a cyclic (round robin) fashion.

The popular BIND DNS server has a very similar process, but adds even more power and features such as weighting one or more servers more than others or randomizing the DNS response.

Using a Multilayer or Content Switch

DNS is an easy way to load balance, but it still relies on multiple DNS servers each with its own IP address. As Web clients access one DNS server or another, they cache that DNS server's IP address. The next time they access the server, they go directly to the cached DNS server and skip the round robin, reducing its effectiveness.

To hide all of your Web servers behind a single IP, there are two popular choices. First is to use a special multilayer switch that works at Layers 3 and 4. This switch is really just a router that performs NAT and port forwarding, but also has the capability to query the hidden Web servers continually and send HTTP requests to a server that has a lower workload than the other servers.

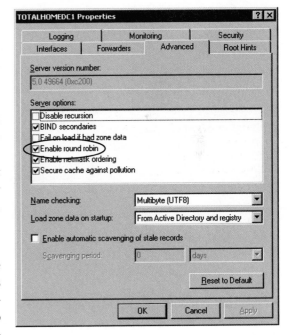

• **Figure 12.25**   Enabling round robin

Your other option is to use a **content switch**. Content switches must always work at least at Layer 7 (Application layer). Content switches designed to work with Web servers therefore are able to read the incoming HTTP and HTTPS requests. This gives you the capability to do very advanced actions, such as handling SSL certificates and cookies, on the content switch, taking the workload off the Web servers. Not only can these devices load balance in the ways previously described, but their HTTP savvy can actually pass a cookie to HTTP requesters— Web browsers—so the next time that client returns, they are sent to the same server (Figure 12.26).

• **Figure 12.26**   Layer 7 content switch

> Content switches are incredibly powerful—and incredibly expensive.

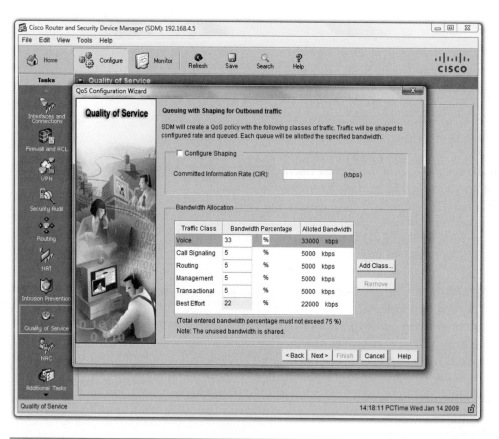

• **Figure 12.27**   QoS configuration on a router

> The term *bandwidth shaping* is synonymous with traffic shaping. The routers and switches that can implement traffic shaping are commonly referred to as *shapers*. The CompTIA Network+ exam refers to such devices as *bandwidth shapers*.

QoS and Traffic Shaping

Just about any router you buy today has the capability to block packets based on port number or IP address, but these are simple mechanisms mainly designed to protect an internal network. What if you need to control how much of your bandwidth is used for certain devices or applications? In that case you need **quality of service (QoS)**, policies to prioritize traffic based on certain rules. These rules control how much bandwidth a protocol, PC, user, VLAN, or IP address may use (Figure 12.27).

On many advanced routers and switches, you can implement QoS through bandwidth management such as **traffic shaping**, controlling the flow of packets into or out from the network according to the type of packet or other rules. Traffic shaping is very important when you must guarantee a device or application a certain amount of bandwidth and/or latency, such as with VoIP or video. Traffic shaping is also very popular in places such as schools, where IT professionals need to be able to control user activities, such as limiting HTTP usage or blocking certain risky applications such as peer-to-peer file sharing.

Network Protection

The last area where you're likely to encounter advanced networking devices is network protection. *Network protection* is my term to describe four different areas that CompTIA feels fits under the term specialized network devices:

- Intrusion protection/intrusion detection
- Port mirroring
- Proxy serving
- Port authentication

Intrusion Detection/Intrusion Prevention

Intrusion detection/intrusion prevention are very similar to the processes used to protect networks from intrusion and to detect that something has intruded into a network. Odds are good you've heard the term firewall. Firewalls are hardware or software tools that block traffic based on port number or IP address. A traditional firewall is a static tool: it cannot actually detect an attack. An *intrusion detection system (IDS)* is an application (often running on a dedicated IDS box) that inspects incoming packets, looking for active intrusions. A good IDS knows how to find attacks that no firewall can find, such as viruses, illegal logon attempts, and other well-known attacks. An IDS will always have some way to let the network administrators know if an attack is taking place: at the very least the attack is logged, but some IDSs offer a pop-up message, an e-mail, or even a text message to your phone.

Third-party IDS tools, on the other hand, tend to act in a much more complex and powerful way. You have two choices with a real IDS: network based or host based. A *network-based IDS (NIDS)* consists of multiple sensors placed around the network, often on one or both sides of the gateway router. These sensors report to a central application that in turn reads a signature file to detect anything out of the ordinary (Figure 12.28).

A *host-based IDS (HIDS)* is software running on individual systems that monitors for events such as system file modification or registry changes (Figure 12.29). More expensive third-party system IDSs do all this and add the ability to provide a single reporting source—very handy when one person is in charge of anything that goes on throughout a network.

A well-protected network uses both a NIDS and a HIDS. A NIDS monitors the incoming and outgoing traffic from the Internet while the HIDS monitors the individual computers.

An *intrusion prevention system (IPS)* is very similar to an IDS, but an IPS adds the capability to react to an attack. Depending on what IPS product you choose, an IPS can block incoming packets on-the-fly based on IP address, port number, or application type. An IPS might go even further, literally fixing certain packets on-the-fly.

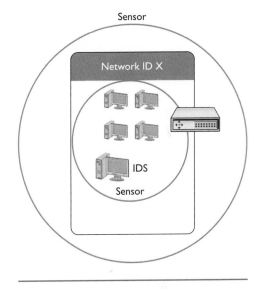

• **Figure 12.28**   Diagram of network-based IDS

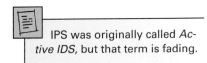

IPS was originally called *Active IDS*, but that term is fading.

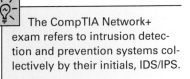

The CompTIA Network+ exam refers to intrusion detection and prevention systems collectively by their initials, IDS/IPS.

• **Figure 12.29** OSSEC HIDS

Port Mirroring

IDS/IPS often take advantage of something called **port mirroring**. Many advanced switches have the capability to mirror data from any or all physical ports on a switch to a single physical port. It's as though you make a customized, fully-configurable promiscuous port. Port mirroring is incredibly useful for any type of situation where an administrator needs to inspect packets coming to or from certain computers.

Proxy Serving

A **proxy server** sits in between clients and external servers, essentially pocketing the requests from the clients for server resources and making those requests itself. The client computers never touch the outside servers and thus stay protected from any unwanted activity A proxy server usually *does something* to those requests as well. Let's see how proxy servers work using HTTP—one of the oldest uses of proxy servers.

Since proxy serving works by redirecting client requests to a proxy server, you first must tell the Web client not to use the usual DNS resolution to determine the Web server and instead to use a proxy. Every Web client comes with a program that enables you to set the IP address of the proxy server, as shown in the example in Figure 12.30.

Once the proxy server is configured, HTTP requests move from the client directly to the proxy server. Built into every HTTP request is the URL of the target Web server, so the Web proxy knows where to get the requested data once it gets the request. In the simplest format, the proxy server simply forwards the requests using its own IP address and then forwards the returning packets to the client (Figure 12.31).

This simple version of proxy prevents the Web server from knowing where the client is located. This is a pretty handy trick for those who wish to keep people from knowing where they are coming from, assuming you can find a public proxy server that accepts your HTTP requests (there are plenty!). There are many other good reasons to use a proxy server. One big benefit is caching. A proxy server keeps a copy of the served resource, giving clients a much faster response. A proxy server might inspect the contents of the resource, looking for inappropriate content, viruses/malware, or just about anything else the creators of the proxy might desire it to identify.

HTTP proxy servers are the most common type of proxy server, but any TCP application can take advantage of proxy servers. Numerous proxy serving programs are available, such as Squid, shown in Figure 12.32. Proxy serving takes some substantial processing, so many vendors sell proxy servers in a box, such as the Blue Coat ProxySG 510.

Port Authentication

The last place where you see advanced networking devices is in port authentication. We've already covered the concept in the previous chapter: **port authentication** is a critical component for any AAA authentication method, in particular RADIUS, TACACS+, and 802.1X. When you make a connection, you must have something at the point of connection to make the authentication, and that's where advanced networking devices come into play. Many switches, and almost every wireless access point, come with feature sets to support port authentication. A superb example is my own Cisco 2811 router. It supports RADIUS and 802.1X port authentication, as shown in Figure 12.33.

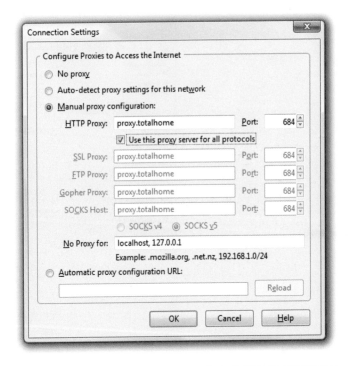

• **Figure 12.30**   Setting a proxy server in Mozilla Firefox

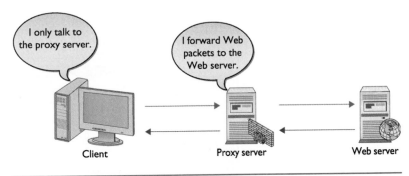

• **Figure 12.31**   Web proxy at work

Try This!

Exploring Switch Capabilities

If you have access to a managed switch of any kind, now would be a great time to explore its capabilities. Use a Web browser of choice and navigate to the switch. What can you configure? Do you see any options for proxy serving, load balancing, or other fancy capability? How could you optimize your network by using some of these more advanced capabilities?

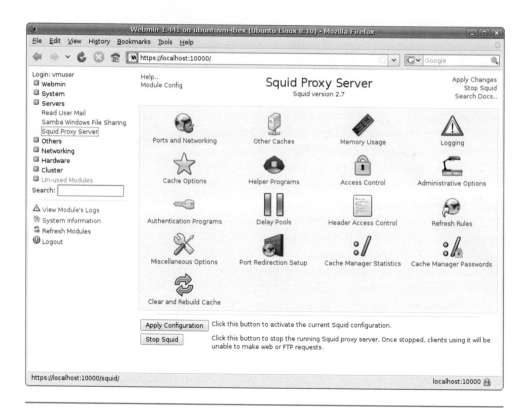

● Figure 12.32   Squid proxy software

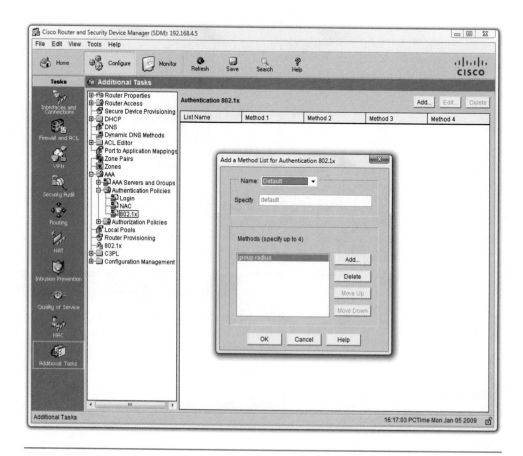

● Figure 12.33   802.1X configuration on a Cisco 2811

Chapter 12 Review

■ Chapter Summary

After reading this chapter and completing the exercises, you should understand the following about networking devices.

Discuss the four logical topologies as defined by CompTIA

■ A physical topology describes the physical layout of cabling, while a signaling topology refers to how the signals actually progress through a network.

■ Logical network topologies include peer-to-peer, client/server, VPN, and VLAN. Client/server and peer-to-peer are more commonly referred to as software architecture models.

■ In a client/server model, certain systems act as dedicated servers. A client never acts as a server, so one client can never access shared resources on another client.

■ In a peer-to-peer network, any system can act as a client, server, or both. This model first became popular in the 1990s with Microsoft Windows.

■ Today, the terms client/server and peer-to-peer refer more to applications than to network operating systems.

■ A VPN creates a tunnel that enables users to connect to remote LANs across the Internet.

■ RRAS, a program available only on Windows servers, allows VPN connections using PPTP. PPTP creates the secure tunnel through the Internet to your private LAN.

■ L2TP is a Cisco VPN protocol that was built upon the best features of Microsoft's PPTP. Rather than requiring special server software (such as Microsoft's RRAS), L2TP places a tunnel endpoint directly on a VPN-capable router.

■ L2TP provides no authentication or encryption. It usually relies on IPSec for this.

■ The majority of PPTP and L2TP VPNs use either PPTP or L2TP. However, some use other options such as OpenVPN or IPSec.

Configure and deploy VLANs

■ A VLAN takes a single physical broadcast domain and splits it into multiple virtual broadcast domains, thereby reducing broadcast traffic.

■ Trunking allows multiple switches to assign individual ports to specific VLANs. This allows multiple computers on the same LAN, but connected to different physical switches, to be members of the same VLAN.

■ A trunk port carries all data, regardless of VLAN number, between all switches on a LAN. Today, every Ethernet switch prefers the 802.1Q trunk standard, enabling you to connect switches from different manufactures.

■ Many switches can be configured for VLANs via a serial port connection, but the most common method is via a Web server built into the switch.

■ Once the VLANs have been created on the switches, the next steps include assigning computers' MAC addresses to VLANs (dynamic VLANs) or assigning switch ports to VLANs (static VLANs).

■ A switch that has the ability to do interVLAN routing can act as a virtual router, connecting different VLANs.

Implement advanced switch features

■ A multilayer switch is one that operates at multiple levels of the OSI model, such as the Cisco 3550 switch that functions at both Layer 2 and Layer 3.

■ Any device that forwards traffic based on packet contents is a switch. Layer 2 switches forward packets based on MAC addresses while Layer 3 switches (also called routers) forward packets based on IP addresses.

■ Load balancing involves configuring multiple servers to look like a single server, allowing multiple servers to handle requests sent to a single IP address. Additionally, load balancing spreads the requests evenly across all the servers so that no one system is bogged down.

- With DNS load balancing, each Web server receives a unique IP address because the DNS servers hold multiple A records, each with the same domain name, for each Web server. The DNS server then cycles around these records so that the same domain name resolves to different IP addresses.

- DNS load balancing loses effectiveness when client computers cache the resolved IP address, bypassing the DNS server when connecting to a Web server.

- A content switch provides load balancing by reading the HTTP and HTTPS requests and acting upon them, taking the workload off the Web servers.

- Quality of service (QoS) sets priorities for how much bandwidth is used for certain protocols, PCs, users, VLANs, IP addresses, or other devices or applications. This is often implemented through traffic shaping.

- Intrusion detection systems (IDSs) inspect incoming packets and actively monitor for attacks. A network-based IDS (NIDS) typically consists of sensors on one or both sides of the gateway router while a host-based IDS (HIDS) consists of monitoring software installed on individual computers.

- Intrusion prevention systems (IPSs) can react to attacks. An IPS proactively monitors for attacks, then reacts if an attack is identified.

- Port mirroring mirrors data from any or all physical ports on a switch to a single physical port, making it easy for administrators to inspect packets to or from certain computers.

- A proxy server intercepts client requests and acts upon them, usually by blocking the request or forwarding the request to other servers.

- Many switches support port authentication, a feature that requires network devices to authenticate themselves, protecting your network from rogue devices.

■ Key Terms

client/server *(315)*

content switch *(328)*

interVLAN routing *(325)*

intrusion detection/intrusion prevention *(329)*

Layer 2 Tunneling Protocol (L2TP) *(320)*

load balancing *(326)*

multilayer switch *(313)*

peer-to-peer *(316)*

Point-to-Point Tunneling Protocol (PPTP) *(319)*

port authentication *(331)*

port mirroring *(330)*

proxy server *(330)*

quality of service (QoS) *(328)*

Routing and Remote Access Service (RRAS) *(319)*

traffic shaping *(328)*

trunk port *(322)*

trunking *(322)*

Virtual Local Area Network (VLAN) *(321)*

Virtual Private Network (VPN) *(318)*

VPN concentrator *(320)*

■ Key Term Quiz

Use the Key Terms list to complete the sentences that follow. Not all terms will be used.

1. _____ is Cisco's VPN protocol that relies on IPSec for all its security needs.

2. In a(n) _____ network, all computers can act in dual roles as clients or servers.

3. A(n) _____ services client requests and forwards them to the appropriate server.

4. In a(n) _____ network, client computers cannot share resources with each other or see each other. They can only connect to a server.

5. _____ allows a VLAN to be defined across multiple switches.

6. Routers that enable you to set QoS often use _____ to limit the amount of bandwidth used by certain devices or applications.

7. Creating a(n) _____ helps to reduce broadcast traffic on any one network by separating the one large network into smaller ones, but requires the use of a special switch.

8. A(n) _____ is a network created by a secure tunnel from one network to another remote network.

9. _____ is a special program running on Microsoft servers that enables remote users to connect to a local Microsoft network.

10. Microsoft's _____ enables computers on one end of a VPN to receive an IP address on the subnet of the remote network.

■ Multiple-Choice Quiz

1. Which network model uses only truly dedicated servers?

   A. Client/server

   B. Peer-to-peer

   C. Virtual Private Network

   D. Virtual Local Area Network

2. Marcy is home sick, but uses a VPN to connect to her network at work and is able to access files stored on the remote network just as if she were physically in the office. Which protocols make it possible for Marcy to receive an IP address from the DHCP server at work? (Select two.)

   A. PPTP

   B. IDS

   C. L2TP

   D. IPS

3. What is one benefit of a VLAN?

   A. It allows remote users to connect to a local network via the Internet.

   B. It reduces broadcast traffic on a LAN.

   C. It can create a WAN from multiple disjointed LANs.

   D. It provides encryption services on networks that have no default encryption protocol.

4. Rashan's company has multiple FTP servers, allowing remote users to download files. What should Rashan implement on his FTP servers so that they appear as a single server with a guarantee that no single FTP server is receiving more requests than any other?

   A. Load balancing

   B. Port authentication

   C. Port mirroring

   D. Trunking

5. Raul sits down at his computer, checks his e-mail, edits a document on the server, and shares a folder with other users on the network. What kind of network is Raul on?

   A. Client/server

   B. Peer-to-peer

   C. PPTP

   D. Trunked

6. Which of the following describes a VPN?

   A. A remote connection using a secure tunnel across the Internet

   B. Segmenting a local network into smaller networks without subnetting

   C. A network that is protected from viruses

   D. A protocol used to encrypt L2TP traffic

7. To enable computers connected to different switches to be members of the same VLAN, what do the switches have to support?

   A. Content switching

   B. Port authentication

   C. Port mirroring

   D. Trunking

8. What is true of a multilayer switch?

   A. It can work at multiple OSI layers at the same time.

   B. It can work with one of several OSI layers at a time, depending on its configuration mode. Working at a different layer requires making a configuration change and resetting the switch.

   C. It can communicate with other switches that work at different OSI layers.

   D. It has twice the ports of a standard switch because it contains two regular switches, one stacked on top of the other.

9. Which statement about L2TP is true?

   A. It is more secure than PPTP.

   B. It was developed by Microsoft and is available by default on all Microsoft servers.

   C. It lacks security features and therefore relies on other protocols or services to handle authentication and encryption.

   D. It ensures router tables are kept synchronized across VLANs.

10. What are the benefits of caching on a Web proxy? (Select two.)

   A. Response time

   B. Virus detection

   C. Tracking

   D. Authentication

11. Which are effective methods of implementing load balancing? (Select two.)

   A. Content switching

   B. DNS round robin

   C. Traffic shaping

   D. Proxy serving

12. Employees in the sales department complain that the network runs slowly when employees in the art department copy large graphics files across the network. What solution might increase network speed for the sales department?

   A. DNS load balancing

   B. Content switching

   C. Traffic shaping

   D. 802.1z

13. How does an IPS compare to an IDS?

   A. An IPS is more secure because it uses IPSec.

   B. An IDS is more secure because it uses L2TP.

   C. An IPS is more robust because it can react to attacks.

   D. An IDS is more robust because it can react to attacks.

14. A dynamic VLAN assigns VLANs to:

   A. IP addresses

   B. MAC addresses

   C. Ports

   D. Trunks

15. Novell NetWare is an example of what?

   A. A dedicated client

   B. A dedicated server

   C. A multilayer VLAN switch

   D. Intrusion detection system software

■ Essay Quiz

1. Your boss is becoming increasingly worried about hacking attempts on the company Web server. Write a letter explaining the various options for protecting against, and reacting to, attacks.

2. A co-worker is constantly talking about VLANs and VPNs, but rarely uses the terms correctly. Educate your co-worker as to what VPNs and VLANs are, what they are for, and how they differ.

Lab Projects

• Lab Project 12.1

You have read quite a bit in this chapter about securing networks against attacks. Research at least three intrusion prevention systems and create a matrix comparing them. Include comparisons of features, cost, reliability, network/operating system support, and general user reviews.

• Lab Project 12.2

Your boss wants to reduce broadcast traffic and asks you to segment the network into multiple VLANs. Use your favorite e-commerce Web site for purchasing computer and networking devices and find at least three switches that support VLANs. Create a matrix comparing features and cost. Based on your research, which VLAN switch would you recommend to your employer and why?

IPv6

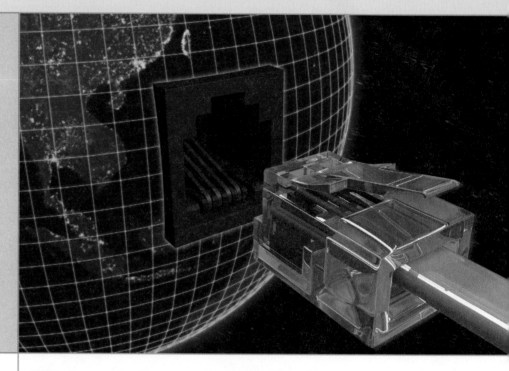

In this chapter, you will learn how to

- **Discuss the fundamental concepts of IPv6**
- **Describe IPv6 practices**
- **Implement IPv6 in a TCP/IP network**

The Internet developers wanted to make a networking protocol that had serious longevity, so they had to define a large enough IP address space to last well beyond the foreseeable future. They had to determine how many computers might exist in the future, then make the IP address space even bigger. But how many computers would exist in the future? Keep in mind that TCP/IP development took place back in the early 1970s. There were less than 1000 computers in the entire world at the time, but that didn't keep the IP framers from thinking big! They decided to go absolutely crazy (as many people considered at the time) and around 1979 created the **Internet Protocol version 4 (IPv4)** 32-bit IP address space, creating up to about 4 billion IP addresses. That should hold us for the foreseeable future!

It hasn't. First, the TCP/IP folks wasted huge chunks of IP addresses due to classful addressing and a generally easygoing, wasteful method of parceling out IP addresses. Second, the Internet reached a level of popularity way beyond the original framers' imagination. By the mid-1980s the rate of consumption for IP addresses started to worry the Internet people and the writing was on the wall for IPv4's 32-bit addressing. As a result, the Internet Engineering Task Force (IETF) developed a new IP addressing scheme, called **Internet Protocol version 6 (IPv6)**, that is slowly replacing IPv4. IPv6 extends the 32-bit IP address space to 128 bits, allowing up to 2^{128} (that's close to 3.4×10^{38}) addresses! That should hold us for the foreseeable future! 3.4×10^{38} addresses is something like all the grains of sand on Earth or 1/8 of all the molecules in the atmosphere.

 If you really want to know how many IP addresses IPv6 provides, here's your number: 340,282,366,920,938,463,463,374, 607,431,768,211,456.

But IPv6 isn't just about expanding the IP address space. IPv6 also improves security by making the Internet Protocol Security (IPSec) protocol support a standard part of every IPv6 stack. That doesn't mean you actually have to use IPSec, just that manufacturers must support it. If you use IPSec, every packet sent from your system is encrypted, opening the possibility that IPv6 would eliminate most (but not all) of the many encryption methods currently in use today.

IPv6 also provides a more efficient routing scheme. Taking advantage of aggregation (see the section "Aggregation" later in this chapter), routing tables should shrink dramatically, enabling fast routing.

It's taking a while, but IPv6 is finally gaining traction. You must learn and use IPv6, both for the CompTIA Network+ exam and for the real world. This chapter breaks the process into three parts for you. First, you need the basic concepts, such as how the numbers work. Second, you need to learn how to enable or apply IPv6 in a variety of technologies, such as NAT and DHCP. Finally, you need answers on how to deploy IPv6 in an IPv4 world.

IPv6 Basics

Although they achieve the same function—enabling computers on IP networks to send packets to each other—IPv6 and IPv4 differ a lot when it comes to implementation. The addressing numbers work differently, for example, and don't look alike. IPv6 uses link-local addressing, a concept not present in IPv4. Subnetting works differently as well. You also need to understand the concepts of global addresses and aggregation, both topics uniquely IPv6. Let's look at all five topics.

Test Specific

IPv6 Address Notation

The 32-bit IPv4 addresses are written as 197.169.94.82, using four octets. Well, IPv6 has 128 bits, so octets are gone. IPv6 addresses are written like this:

```
2001:0000:0000:3210:0800:200C:00CF:1234
```

For those who don't play with hex regularly, one hexadecimal character (for example, *F*) represents 4 bits, so four hexadecimal characters make a 16-bit group.

IPv6 uses a colon as a separator, instead of the period used in IPv4's dotted decimal format. Each group is a hexadecimal number between 0000 and FFFF.

A complete IPv6 address always has eight groups of four hexadecimal characters. If this sounds like you're going to type in really long IP addresses, don't worry, IPv6 offers a number of shortcuts.

First, leading zeroes can be dropped from any group, so 00CF becomes CF and 0000 becomes 0. Let's rewrite that IPv6 address using this shortcut:

```
2001:0:0:3210:800:200C:CF:1234
```

To write IPv6 addresses containing strings of zeroes, you can use a pair of colons (::) to represent a string of consecutive groups with a value of zero. For example, using the :: rule you can write the IPv6 address:

```
2001:0:0:3210:800:200C:CF:1234
```

as

```
2001::3210:800:200C:CF:1234
```

Double colons are very handy, but you have to be careful when you use them. Take a look at this IPv6 address:

```
FEDC:0000:0000:0000:00CF:0000:BA98:1234
```

If I convert it to

```
FEDC::CF:0:BA98:1234
```

I may not use a second :: to represent the third-to-last group of four zeroes—only one :: is allowed per address! There's a good reason for this rule. If more than one :: was used, how could you tell how many sets of zeroes were in each group? Answer: you couldn't.

Here's an example of a very special IPv6 address that takes full advantage of the double colon, the IPv6 loopback address:

```
::1
```

The unspecified address (all zeroes) can never be used, and neither can an address that contains all ones (all *F*s in IPv6 notation).

Without using the double-colon nomenclature, the IPv6 address would look like this:

```
0000:0000:0000:0000:0000:0000:0001
```

 Cross Check

Loopback

You learned about the IPv4 loopback address in Chapter 7, "TCP/IP Basics," so check your memory as you read about the IPv6 loopback address here. What IP address or addresses could you use for a loopback address? When might you PING the loopback address? How would this differ from loopback testing discussed in Chapter 6, "Installing a Physical Network"?

IPv6 still uses subnets, but you won't find a place to type in 255s anywhere. IPv6 uses the "/X" Classless Inter-Domain Routing (CIDR) nomenclature. Here's how to write an IP address and subnet for a typical IPv6 host:

```
FEDC::CF:0:BA98:1234/64
```

Link-Local Address

The folks who created IPv6 worked hard to make it powerful and easy to use, but you pretty much have to forget all the rules you learned about IPv4 addressing. The biggest item to wrap your mind around is that you no longer have a single IP address unless your network isn't connected to a router. When a computer running IPv6 first boots up, it gives itself a **link-local address**. Think of a link-local address as IPv6's equivalent to IPv4's APIPA address. The first 64 bits of a link-local address are always FE80::/64. That means every address always begins with FE80:0000:0000:0000. If your operating system supports IPv6 and IPv6 is enabled, you can see this address. Figure 13.1 is a screenshot of Linux's IFCONFIG command, showing the link-local address.

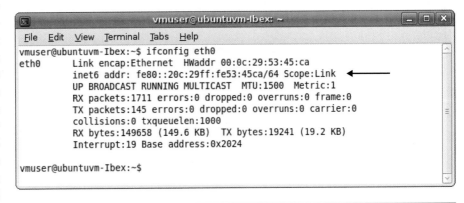

● **Figure 13.1**   Link-local address

Take a close look at the IP address and compare it to the MAC address. The last 64 bits of the IPv6 address, collectively called the **Extended Unique Identifier, 64-bit (EUI-64)**, are taken from the MAC address. MAC addresses only contain 48 bits, so your system creates the EUI-64 as follows:

1. Remove the dashes from the MAC address and split it in half:

   ```
   000C29    5345CA
   ```

2. Add "FFFE" in the middle:

   ```
   000C29FFFE5345CA
   ```

3. This step requires a little binary knowledge. You convert the second hexadecimal digit, in this example the second 0, into binary: 0 in hex = 0000 in binary. You take the third binary digit and complement it, which means that if it's a 0, as in this example, you make it a 1, and if it's a 1, you make it a 0. Then convert it back to hexadecimal: 0010 = 2 in hexadecimal.

4. Put that value back in the second position:

   ```
   020C29FFFE5345CA
   ```

5. Break it into standard IPv6 format:

   ```
   020C:29FF:FE53:45CA
   ```

You can reconfigure Vista to use EUI-64 for link-local addresses by typing this at a command prompt:

```
netsh interface ipv6
set global
randomizeidentifiers=
disabled
```

6. Add it to the first 64 bits and drop leading zeroes:

```
FE80::20C:29FF:FE53:45CA
```

Don't worry about exactly how to make your own EUI-64: just understand how your system comes up with this value. Every operating system, with the exception of Windows Vista and Windows 7, creates link-local addresses using EUI-64 by default. Microsoft adds a lot of extra steps in Vista but the big difference is that the last 64 bits of the link-local addresses are generated randomly. I think Microsoft does this as a privacy issue. If someone's link-local address ties directly to a real MAC address, in theory some bad guy might use this against them. No other operating system, not even Windows XP or Windows Server, does this randomized link-local numbering (Figure 13.2).

The link-local address does all the hard work in IPv6 and, as long as you don't need an Internet connection, it's all you need.

● **Figure 13.2** Link-local address in Windows Vista

The old concepts of static and DHCP addressing don't really make much sense in IPv6 unless you have dedicated servers (even in IPv6 servers usually still have static IP addresses). Link-local addressing takes care of all your local network needs!

IPv6 Subnet Masks

IPv6 subnets function the same as IPv4 subnets in that systems use them to determine whether to ARP for a MAC address or send packets to a default gateway. But there are two new rules you need to know:

- The last 64 bits of an IPv6 address are generated by the NIC, leaving a maximum of 64 bits for the subnet. Therefore, no subnet is ever longer than /64.

- The IANA passes out /32 subnets to big ISPs and end users who need large allotments. ISPs and others may pass out /48 and /64 subnets to end users. Therefore, the vast majority of IPv6 subnets are between /48 and /64.

You will never type in a subnet mask. With link-local addressing the subnet mask is defined as /64. Other types of IPv6 addresses get the subnet information automatically from their routers (described next).

The End of Broadcast

A system's IPv6 link-local address is a **unicast address**, a unique address that is exclusive to that system. IPv4 also relies on unicast addresses. But IPv6 completely drops the idea of broadcast addressing and replaces it with the idea of *multicast*. An IPv6 **multicast address** is a set of reserved addresses designed to go only to certain systems. For example, if a system sends out a multicast to the address FF02::2, only routers read the message, while everyone else ignores it (Figure 13.3).

Technically, a multicast is a broadcast in that every computer gets the packet, but while every computer reads an IPv4 broadcast (like 255.255.255.255), only the computers defined by the IPv6 address read an IPv6 multicast. The difference is subtle but important. Table 13.1 shows some of the more useful IPv6 multicast addresses. You've just seen FF02::2; you'll see the rest explained later in this chapter.

Looking at the first listing, FF02::1, you might ask: "How is that different from a broadcast?" The answer lies more in the definition of multicast than in what really takes place. A computer must be a member of a particular group to read a particular multicast. In this case if a computer is a member of "All Nodes" then it will read the message. Granted, it looks and acts exactly like an IPv4 broadcast, but it is a multicast.

Beyond unicast and multicast, IPv6 uses a third type of addressing called **anycast**. An anycast address is a bit a of strange animal, so it's very helpful to see why you need an anycast address before you try to understand what one is. The best place to look to understand how anycast works and why it is needed is the one place where its use is very common: DNS.

You learned in Chapter 10, "Network Naming," that the top of the DNS root structure consists of a number of root DNS servers. Every DNS server on the Internet keeps the IP addresses of the root servers in a file called *root hints*. Here's one part of the root hints file from my own DNS server:

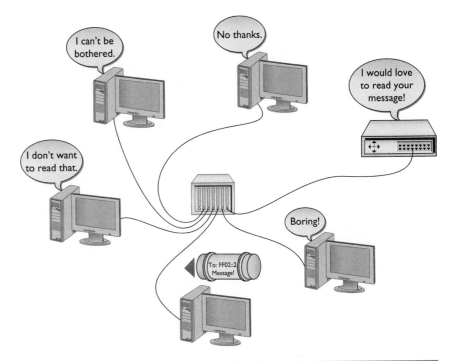

● **Figure 13.3**   Multicast to routers

Table 13.1	IPv6 Multicast Addresses
Address	**Function**
FF02::1	All Nodes Address
FF02::2	All Routers Address
FF02::1:FFXX:XXXX	Solicited-Node Address

```
.                        NS    F.ROOT-SERVERS.NET.
F.ROOT-SERVERS.NET.      A     192.5.5.241
F.ROOT-SERVERS.NET.      AAAA  2001:500:2f::f
```

At first glance, you might think that this root server is a single physical box because it only has a single IPv4 address and a single IP v6 address. It's not. It is roughly 20 groups of server clusters strategically placed all over the world. Back in Chapter 12 you saw how DNS can make a cluster of computers (by *cluster* I mean the computers are all in the same building, behind a common box of some sort) act as a single server, but none of those solutions can make a bunch of clusters all over the world act as a single server. To do this we need anycasting.

Anycasting starts by giving a number of computers (or clusters of computers) the same IP address. We then give routers (in the case of DNS only the biggest, tier-one Internet routers) the smarts to determine which of the many computers with the same IP address are closest. When that router gets a packet addressed to that IP address, it sends it only to the closest root DNS server, even though it may know where others are located. That is an anycast address.

An anycast address looks like a unicast address and, in most cases, the computer sending the packet doesn't know or care to know that the address is anycast and not unicast. The only device that knows (and cares) is the top-tier router that has the smarts to send the packet only to the closest root DNS server.

Global Address

To get on the Internet, your system needs a second IPv6 address called a **global unicast address**, usually shortened to "global address." The only way to get a global address is from your default gateway router, which must be configured to pass out global IPv6 addresses. When your computer boots up, it sends out a router solicitation message on multicast address FF02::2 looking for a router. Your router hears this message and tells your computer your network ID and subnet (together called the prefix). See Figure 13.4.

Once you have your prefix, your computer generates the rest of the global address. It uses the MAC address to create the last 64 bits just like it does to create the last 64 bits of a link-local address. You now have a legitimate, public IP address as well as your link-local address. Figure 13.5 shows the IPv6 information on a Macintosh running OS X 10.5.

Let's look at this process in detail with an example:

• **Figure 13.4**   Getting a global address

1. An IPv6-capable computer boots up. As it boots it sends out a router solicitation message (FF02::2).

2. An IPv6-configured router hears the request and then sends the prefix to the computer. In this example let's say it is 2001:470:b8f9:1/64.

3. The computer takes the prefix and adds the EUI-64 address to the end of the prefix. If the MAC address is 00-0C-29-53-45-CA, then the EUI-64 address is 20C:29FF:FE53:45CA.

4. Putting the prefix with the EUI-64 address, you get the global address: 2001:470:b8f9:1:20C:29FF:FE53:45CA.

At the moment, IANA only passes out global addresses that begin with the number 2 (for example, 2001::, 2002::, and so on). As demand increases this will certainly change, but for now it sure makes it easy to know a global address when you see one.

   Computers using IPv6 need a global address to access the Internet.

A global address is a true Internet address. If another computer is running IPv6 and also has a global address, it can access your system unless you have some form of firewall.

Aggregation

Routers need to know where to send every packet they encounter. Most routers have a default path on which they send packets that aren't specifically defined to go on any other route. As you get to the top of the Internet, the tier-one routers that connect to the other tier-one routers can't have any default route (Figure 13.6). We call these the no-default routers.

The current state of the upper tiers of the Internet is rather messy. A typical nondefault router has somewhere around 30,000 to 50,000 routes in its routing table, requiring a router with massive firepower. But what would happen if the Internet was organized as shown in Figure 13.7? Note how every router underneath one router always uses a subnet of that router's existing routes. This is called **aggregation**.

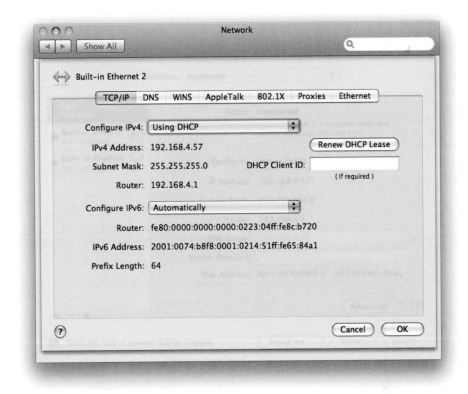

• **Figure 13.5**   IPv6 configuration on Macintosh OS X

Aggregation would drastically reduce the size and complexity of routing tables and make the Internet faster. Aggregation would also give a more detailed, geographic picture of how the Internet is organized—you could get a strong idea of where a person is physically located just by looking at their IP address.

It's way too late for IPv4 to use aggregation. Many organizations who received class licenses 20 to 30 years ago simply will not relinquish them, and

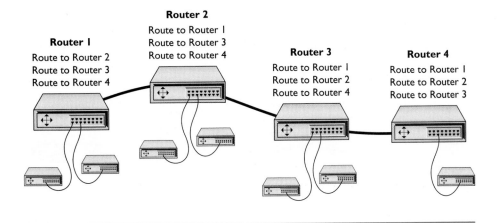

Router 1
Route to Router 2
Route to Router 3
Route to Router 4

Router 2
Route to Router 1
Route to Router 3
Route to Router 4

Router 3
Route to Router 1
Route to Router 2
Route to Router 4

Router 4
Route to Router 1
Route to Router 2
Route to Router 3

• **Figure 13.6**   No-default routers

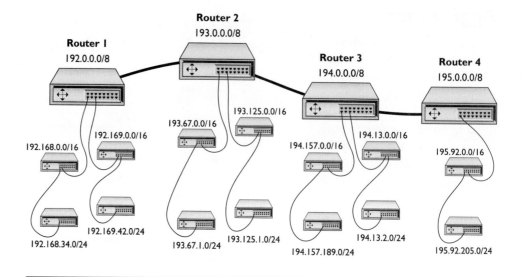

Router 1
192.0.0.0/8

Router 2
193.0.0.0/8

Router 3
194.0.0.0/8

Router 4
195.0.0.0/8

192.168.0.0/16

192.169.0.0/16

193.67.0.0/16

193.125.0.0/16

194.157.0.0/16

194.13.0.0/16

195.92.0.0/16

192.168.34.0/24

192.169.42.0/24

193.67.1.0/24

193.125.1.0/24

194.157.189.0/24

194.13.2.0/24

195.92.205.0/24

• **Figure 13.7** Aggregation

the amount of work necessary to make aggregation work would require a level of synchronization that would bring the entire Internet to its knees for days if not weeks.

But aggregation is part and parcel with IPv6. Remember that your computer gets the first 64 bits of its Internet address from your gateway router. The router in turn gets a (usually) 48-bit prefix from its upstream router and adds its own 16-bit subnet.

This method allows the entire IPv6 network to change IP addresses on-the-fly to keep aggregation working. Imagine you have your gateway router connected to an upstream router from your ISP as shown in Figure 13.8.

Your PC's IPv6 address is: 2001:d0be:7922:1:fc2d:aeb2:99d2:e2b4. Let's cut out the last 64 bits and look at the prefix and see where this comes from:

Your network's prefix: 2001:d0be:7922:1/64

IPv6 addresses begin at the very top of the Internet from the no-default servers. We'll assume your ISP's ISP is one of those routers. Your ISP gets (usually) a 32-bit prefix from IANA or from its ISP if it is small.

In this case the prefix is 2001:d0be/32. This prefix comes from the upstream router, and your ISP has no control over it. However, the person setting up the ISP's router will add a 16-bit subnet to the prefix as shown in Figure 13.9.

A 48-bit prefix from upstream router + 16-bit subnet from gateway router + 64-bit unique number = 128-bit IPv6 address.

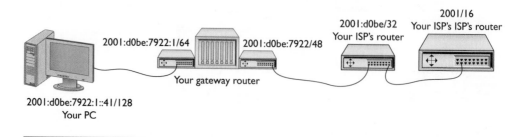

2001:d0be:7922:1/64

2001:d0be:7922:48

2001:d0be/32
Your ISP's router

2001/16
Your ISP's ISP's router

Your gateway router

2001:d0be:7922:1::41/128
Your PC

• **Figure 13.8** An IPv6 group of routers

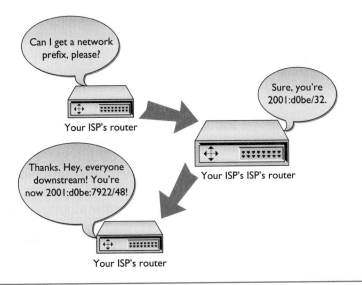

• **Figure 13.9**   Adding the first prefix

Your gateway router receives a 48-bit prefix (in this case 2001:d0be:7922/48) from your ISP's router. Your gateway router has no control over that prefix. However, the person setting up your gateway router adds your own 16-bit subnet (in this case :0001 or :1) to the 48-bit prefix to make the 64-bit prefix for your network (Figure 13.10).

What makes all this particularly interesting is that any router upstream of anyone else may change the prefix they send downstream, keeping aggregation intact. To see this in action, let's watch what happens if your ISP decides to change to another upstream ISP (Figure 13.11). In this case, your ISP moves from the old ISP (ISP1) to a new ISP (ISP2). When your ISP makes the new connection, the new ISP passes out a different 32-bit prefix (in this example 2AB0:3C05/32). As quickly as this change takes place, all of the

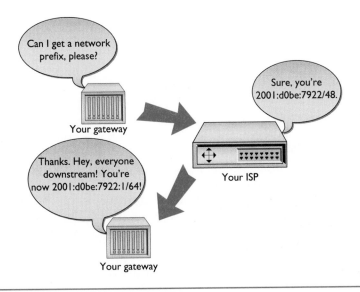

• **Figure 13.10**   Adding the second prefix

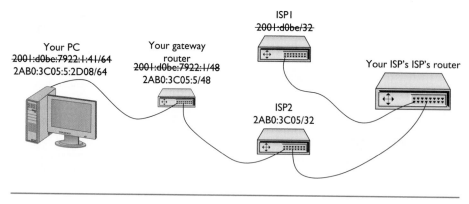

downstream routers make an "all nodes" multicast and all clients get new IP addresses.

Aggregation is an intrinsic but for the most part completely transparent part of IPv6. Know that our IPv6 Internet addresses may suddenly change from time to time and that the address changes are a fairly rare but normal aspect of using IPv6.

• **Figure 13.11**   New IP address updated downstream

Using IPv6

Once IPv6 fully replaces IPv4 we will find ourselves in a very different world from the one we left in terms of configuration. In this section you will see what it takes to turn on IPv6 for your network. This section also assumes you've turned off IPv4—which isn't a realistic option right now because IPv4 is prevalent, but it makes understanding some aspects of using IPv6 much easier. You'll also learn how IPv6 works (or doesn't work, as the case may be) with NAT, DHCP, and DNS. We'll cover the idea of running IPv6 and IPv4 at the same time in the next section.

Enabling IPv6

Enabling IPv6 is very easy because in most cases it is already running on your operating system. Table 13.2 lists the popular operating systems and their IPv6 status.

The fastest way to verify if your system runs IPv6 is to check the IP status for your OS. In Windows, go to a command prompt and type `ipconfig` (Figure 13.12). In Linux or Macintosh OS X, go to a terminal and type `ifconfig` (Figure 13.13). Remember that you will have a link-local address only if your router isn't configured for IPv6.

Table 13.2	IPv6 Adoption by OS
Operating System	**IPv6 Status**
Windows 2000	Windows 2000 came with "developmental" IPv6 support. Microsoft does not recommend using Windows 2000 for IPv6.
Windows XP	Original Windows XP came with a rudimentary but fully functional IPv6 stack that had to be installed from the command prompt. SP1 added the ability to add the same IPv6 stack under the **Install	Protocols** menu.
Windows Vista/Windows 7	Complete IPv6 support. IPv6 is active on default installs.
Windows Server 2003	Complete IPv6 support. IPv6 is not installed by default but is easily installed via the **Install	Protocols** menu.
Windows Server 2008	Complete IPv6 support. IPv6 is active on default installs.
Linux	Complete IPv6 support from kernel 2.6. IPv6 is active on most default installs.
Macintosh OS X	Complete IPv6 support on all versions. IPv6 is active on default installs.

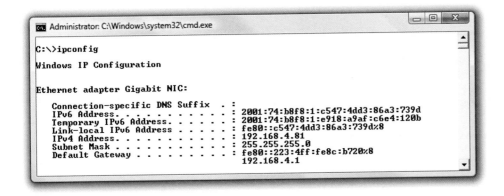

● Figure 13.12   IPv6 enabled in Windows Vista

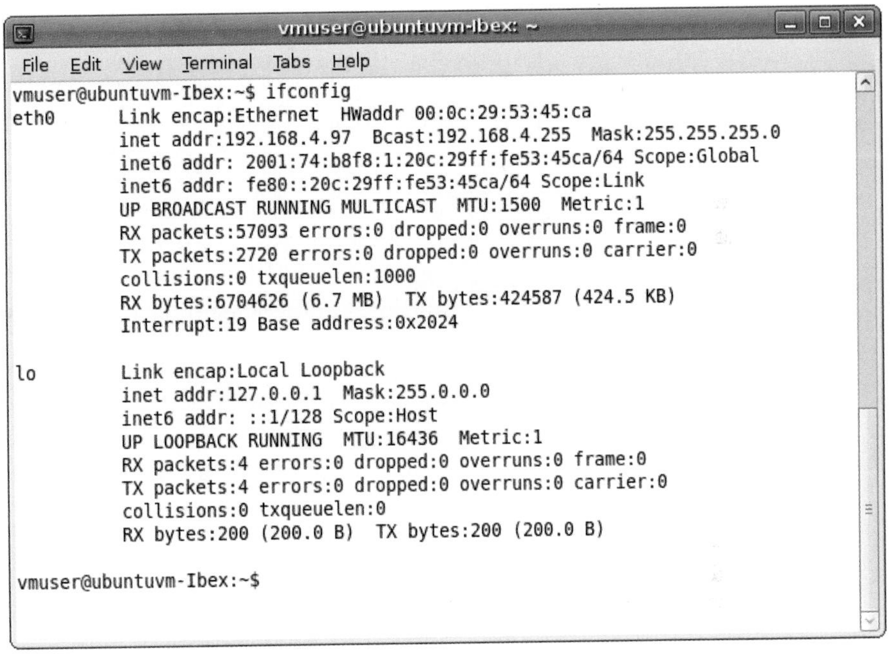

NAT in IPv6

The folks pushing IPv6 forward are a vocal group with some pretty strong feelings about how IPv6 should work. If you want to get some really nasty e-mail, just go to one of the many IPv6 sites and ask this question: "How do I set up NAT on IPv6?" I know they will get mad because I asked that question. Here are some of the answers as I saw them:

> "NAT was developed a long time ago as a way to avoid running out of IP addresses. It was never meant to be a type of firewall."

> "NAT messes up IPSec."

> "Only jerks use NAT!"

● Figure 13.13   IPv6 enabled in Ubuntu 8.10

If you're going to use IPv6, you're not going to use NAT. That means every one of your IP addresses will be exposed to the Internet, and that's not good. The answer is: count on IPv6 to make life hard on hackers and use a good firewall.

One big problem with IPv4 is how easy it is to sniff networks. Using tools like Anton Keks' popular Angry IP Scanner (www.angryziber.com/w/Home), you can scan an entire subnet looking for active IP addresses, as shown in Figure 13.14.

IPv6's huge address space makes such scanning programs obsolete. Let's say you knew my subnet was 2001:d0be:7922:1/64. There are 2^{64}

There is a version of NAT for IPv6 called NAPT-PT (an earlier version was called NAT-PT). This is a solution to get an IPv6 network to use a single IPv4 address and it does not work well.

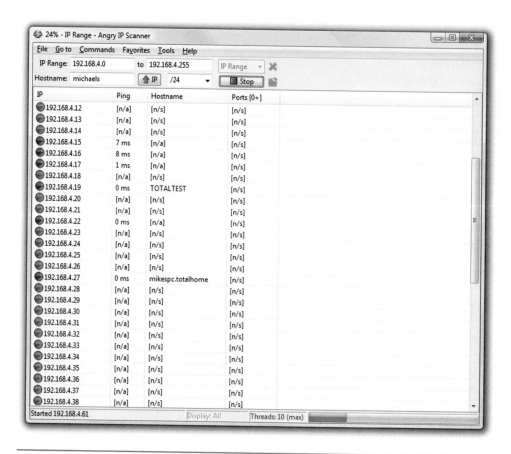

● **Figure 13.14**   Angry IP Scanner at work

different possible IP addresses on this subnet. Assuming a scanner could check one million addresses/second, it would take something like 580,000 years to check them all.

If a bad guy knows your address, the hope is that you'll be using IPSec to prevent other people from reading your information. Otherwise there are a number of other security options that aren't specific to IPv6 that you can use. Some of these, like encryption, you've seen in earlier chapters. Others, like good firewalling, you'll see in Chapter 17, "Protecting Your Network."

DHCP in IPv6

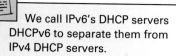

We call IPv6's DHCP servers DHCPv6 to separate them from IPv4 DHCP servers.

DHCP is alive and well in the IPv6 world but works very differently than IPv4's DHCP. At first glance you'd think you wouldn't need DHCP anymore. IPv6 clients get their IP address and subnet from their gateway router's advertisements (so they also know the default gateway). This is true, but IPv6 router advertisements do not pass out a number of other very important bits of information that clients need, such as DNS server information, giving DHCP a very important place in IPv6.

A fully functional DHCPv6 server works in one of two modes: stateful or stateless. A **stateful** DHCPv6 server works very similarly to an IPv4

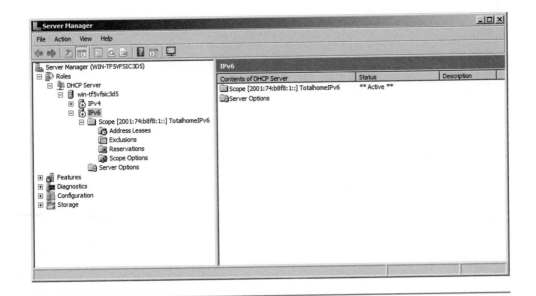

● **Figure 13.15**   DHCPv6 server in action

DHCP server, passing out IPv6 addresses, subnet masks, and default gateways as well as optional items like DNS server addresses. A **stateless** DHCPv6 server only passes out optional information. Figure 13.15 shows the DHCPv6 server on Windows Server 2008.

Cross Check

DHCP with IPv4

You read about the IPv4 version of DHCP way back in Chapter 7, "TCP/IP Basics," so check your memory now. How does DHCP work? What does a DHCP lease do for you? What happens if your computer can't get to a DHCP server but is configured for DHCP?

Most IPv6 installations should take advantage of IPv6's autoconfiguration and only run stateless DHCPv6 servers. But if you really want to skip aggregation you may certainly go stateful. Be careful going stateful: as long as you're using an intranet or your upstream router knows what to do with your non-aggregated network ID, you're okay. Stateful DHCPv6 might be helpful for internal networks that do strange things like try to use subnets greater than /64, but for the most part expect stateless to be the norm.

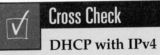 There's a push to get DNS server information added to IPv6 router advertisements. If this happens the need for DHCPv6 might fall dramatically.

DNS in IPv6

DNS with IPv6 is trivial. Just about every DNS server made in the last five to six years or so supports IPv6 addresses. All IPv6 addresses use an AAAA nomenclature. Figure 13.16 shows some IPv6 addresses in Windows Server 2000.

A common trick to get around using DHCPv6 is to manually add DNS server information to IPv6 clients. You do this exactly the same as you do with IPv4, as shown in Figure 13.17. This isn't the best long-term solution but, until all the IPv6 DNS details are worked out, it works well.

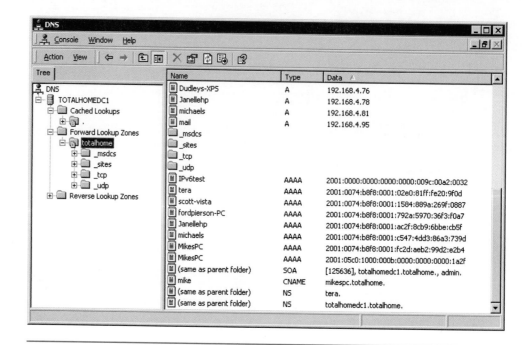

● **Figure 13.16**   IPv6 addresses on DNS server

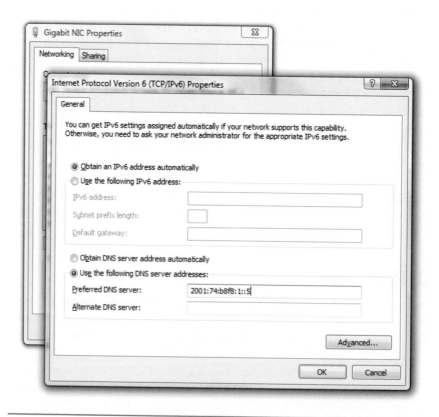

● **Figure 13.17**   Manually adding an IPv6 DNS server in Vista

Moving to IPv6

There's no reason for you *not* to try running IPv6 today—like right now! At the very least there's a whole world of IPv6-only Web sites for you to explore. At the most you may very well become the IPv6 expert in your organization. You almost certainly have an operating system ready to do IPv6; the only trick is to get you connected to the rest of us fun-loving IPv6-capable folks.

This section is designed to help you get connected. If you can, grab an IPv6-capable system, fire up IPv6 as shown earlier, and make sure you're connected to the Internet, because we are going someplace you've never been before, the IPv6 Internet.

IPv4 and IPv6

The first and most important point to make right now is that you can run both IPv4 and IPv6 on your computers and routers at the same time, just as my computer does, as shown in Figure 13.18. This ability is a critical part of the process enabling the world to slowly migrate from IPv4 to IPv6.

Almost all operating systems support IPv6 and almost all serious routers support IPv6, but very few of the small home routers support IPv6. Plus not all routers on the Internet have their IPv6 support turned on.

In order for IPv6 to work we need every router and every computer on the Internet to support IPv6, and we are not yet there. However, two critical parts of the Internet are ready:

- All of the root DNS servers now support IPv6 resolution.

- Almost all of the tier-one ISP routers properly forward IPv6 packets.

The problem is that the routers and DNS servers between your IPv6-capable computer and the other IPv6-capable computers to which you would like to connect are not yet IPv6-ready. How do we get past this IPv6 gap (Figure 13.19)?

Tunnels

To get on the IPv6 network you need to leap over this gap. The folks who developed IPv6 have a number of ways for you to do this using one of many IPv4-to-IPv6 tunneling standards. An IPv4-to-IPv6 tunnel works like any other tunnel, encapsulating one type of data into another. In this case, you will be encapsulating your IPv6 traffic into an IPv4 tunnel to get to an IPv6-capable router, as shown in Figure 13.20.

To make this tunnel, you are going to download a tunneling client and install it on your computer. You will then fire up the client and make the tunnel connection—it's very easy to do. Before you create this tunnel, you need to appreciate that this is only one way to make an IPv6 connection—I'll show you other ways in a moment. There are four popular IPv4-to-IPv6 tunneling standards, described next.

Tech Tip

IPv6 Security
IPv6 is just now gaining wide support so there are issues in connecting to the IPv6 world. There are potential security risks as well as less-than-perfect IPv6 support with operating systems. Don't connect to the IPv6 Internet on a mission-critical computer.

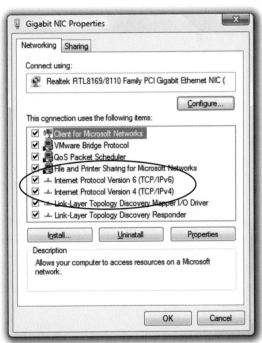

• **Figure 13.18**   IPv4 and IPv6 on one computer

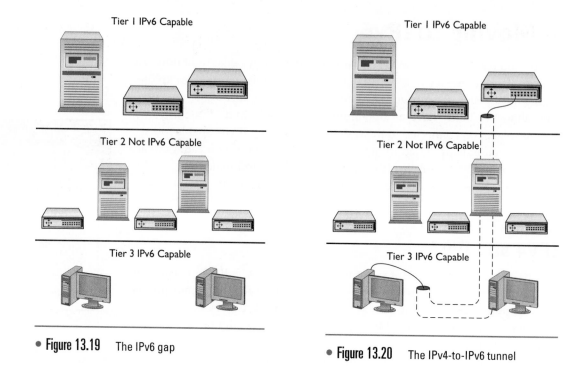

• Figure 13.19   The IPv6 gap

• Figure 13.20   The IPv4-to-IPv6 tunnel

6to4

6to4 is the dominant tunneling protocol because it is the only IPv6 tunnel that doesn't require a tunnel broker (see the section "Tunnel Brokers"). It is usually used to connect two routers directly because it normally requires a public IPv4 address. 6to4 addresses always start with 2002:/16. If you have an IPv6-capable router, or if you have a computer directly connected to the Internet, you can set up a 6to4 tunnel. 6to4 uses public relay routers all around the world. Search the Web for **"public 6to4 relays"** to find one close to you. One IPv4 address, 192.88.99.1, is called the *6to4 anycast address* and works everywhere.

Setting up a 6to4 tunnel can be more challenging than setting up the tunnels that use tunnel brokers. If you're feeling adventurous, just do a Web search on **"6to4 setup"** and the name of your operating system. There are hundreds of Web sites to show you how to set up a 6to4 tunnel.

6in4

6in4 (also called IPv6-in-IPv4) is one of the most popular of all the IPv6 tunneling standards and the one we'll be using in our tunneling example. 6in4 is one of only two IPv6 tunneling protocols that can go through a NAT (called NAT traversal).

Teredo

Teredo is the second NAT-traversal IPv6 tunneling protocol. Teredo is built into Microsoft Windows and as a result sees some adoption. Teredo addresses start with 2001:0000:/32. Most people prefer to skip Windows built-in support and instead get a third-party tool that supports 6to4 or 6in4.

ISATAP

Intra-Site Automatic Tunnel Addressing Protocol (ISATAP) is designed to work within an IPv4 network by actually adding the IPv4 address to an IPv6 prefix to create a rather interesting but nonstandard address for the endpoints. One example of an ISATAP address is 2001:DB8::98CA:200:131. 107.28.9. ISATAP has a strong following, but other tunneling standards are gaining ground because they use a more common IPv6 addressing structure.

Tunnel Brokers

Setting up an IPv6 tunnel can be a chore. You have to find someone willing to act as the far endpoint, you have to connect to them somehow, and then you have to know the tunneling standard they use. To make life easier, those who provide the endpoints have created the idea of the **tunnel broker**. Tunnel brokers create the actual tunnel and (usually) offer a custom-made endpoint client for you to use, although more advanced users can often make a manual connection. Many tunnel brokers take advantage of one of two automatic configuration protocols, called **Tunnel Setup Protocol (TSP)** and **Tunnel Information and Control protocol (TIC)**. These protocols set up the tunnel and handle configuration as well as login. If it wasn't for TSP and TIC, there would be no such thing as automatic third-party tunnel endpoint clients for you to use. Here's a short list of the most popular IPv6 tunnel brokers around the world. For a more complete list, go to www.sixxs.net/tools/aiccu/brokers.

Tunnel Broker	URL
Hexago/Freenet/Go6	www.go6.net
SixXS	www.sixxs.net
Hurricane Electric (no TSP/TIC)	www.tunnelbroker.net
AARNet	http://broker.aarnet.net.au

 You rarely have a choice of tunneling protocol. The tunneling protocol you use is the one your tunnel broker provides and is usually invisible to you.

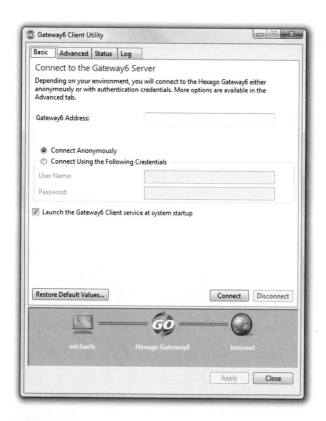

Figure 13.21 Gateway6 Client Utility

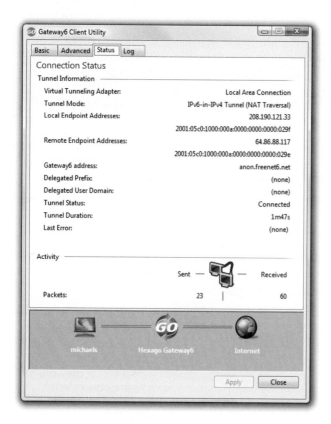

Figure 13.22 Gateway6 Client Utility Status tab

Setting Up a Tunnel

Every tunnel broker has its own setup, so you should always read the instructions carefully. In this example we will install the Hexago client (called the Go6 Gateway6 client) onto Windows Vista. Go to www.go6.net and register for an account (there is currently a "Join go6" link on the page). You'll then be led to a download page where you then download the Gateway6 client. Go6 is always updating this client so be sure to download the latest version. Install the client to see the screen shown in Figure 13.21. Enter the Gateway6 address and your user name and password. You can log on anonymously, but I think it works more reliably if you log in.

Click **Connect** and, assuming you have a good connection, you should be on the IPv6 Internet. Go to the **Status** tab to see your IP information (Figure 13.22).

Excellent! Now let's go check out the Internet. Try these IPv6-only Web pages:

- www.ipv6.sixxs.net (click the **Enter website** hyperlink to see your IPv6 address on the bottom left of the page)

- http://ipv6.google.com

- http://ipv6.sunny.ch (shows your IPv6 address)

IPv6 Is Here, Really!

Depending on who you speak to, IPv6 is going to happen, and when it does happen it's going to happen very quickly. Again depending on who you speak to, IPv4 addresses will run out anywhere between 2011 and 2019. The people who know IPv6 will be in a unique place to leap into the insanity of what will invariably be called "The Big Switchover" and will find themselves making a lot of money. Take some time to learn IPv6. You'll be glad you did.

Chapter 13 Review

Chapter Summary

After reading this chapter and completing the exercises, you should understand the following about IPv6.

Discuss the fundamental concepts of IPv6

- IPv4 supports only about 4 billion addresses, which is no longer enough for the future. IPv6 supports 2^{128} (or ~ 3.4×10^{38}) IP addresses.

- In addition to an expanded address space, IPv6 improves security by supporting IPSec out of the box.

- IPv6 provides a more efficient routing scheme because it uses aggregation.

- IPv6 addresses are composed of 128 bits written in hexadecimal notation. Every 4 bits are separated by a colon. 2001:0000:0000:3210:0800:200C:00CF:1234 is a valid IPv6 address.

- Leading zeroes can be dropped and double colons may be used to represent consecutive groups of zeroes in order to write an IPv6 address with fewer characters. 2001::3210:800:200C:CF:1234 is a valid IPv6 address.

- IPv6 subnet masks are represented with the /X CIDR naming convention. FEDC::CF:0:BA98:1234/64 translates to a 64-bit subnet mask.

- Computers using IPv6 that are on the Internet have two IPv6 addresses: a link-local address and a global address.

- A link-local address is similar to an IPv4 APIPA address in that it is self-generated. The link-local address is guaranteed to be unique because it is partially based on the MAC address of the NIC.

- A link-local address always starts with FE80::. The last 64 bits of the link-local address are generated from the NIC's MAC address.

- Microsoft Windows Vista and Microsoft Windows 7 generate the last 64 bits of a link-local address randomly so as to not reveal the MAC address. This adds security against hackers.

- An IPv6 computer not on the Internet needs only the self-generated link-local address to participate on a local network. However, a server on such a network still needs a static IP address, not a random self-generated link-local address.

- Link-local addresses always use /64 as the subnet mask.

- IPv6 link-local addresses are unicast, or unique to a specific computer or network node.

- IPv6 replaced broadcasts with multicasts. A multicast is a set of reserved addresses designed to go to only certain systems. Packets sent to addresses beginning with FF02::2 are only sent to routers.

- Multicasts, like broadcasts, are still sent to every computer on the network. Unlike broadcasts, though, only the destined systems read the multicast packet.

- An IPv6 global unicast address is required for Internet access.

- Global unicast addresses are distributed by the default gateway router, provided the router is configured to pass out global IPv6 addresses.

- The first half of a global unicast address is called the prefix and consists of the network ID and subnet mask. The prefix is passed out by the default gateway router. The last half of the global address is self-generated by the computer.

- Aggregation reduces the size and complexity of routing tables by allowing downstream routers to use a subset of an upstream router's routes to populate its routing table rather than tens of thousands of disjointed routes.

Describe IPv6 practices

- Not all versions of Windows support IPv6, and some that do enable it by default whereas others require manual installation.

- IPv6 is active by default on Macintosh OS X, and active by default on most Linux installs using at least kernel 2.6.

- IPv6 does not support NAT. Every IPv6 address is exposed to the Internet, so use a good firewall!

- While IPv6 global addresses are passed out by the default gateway router (with a portion self-generated), DHCP servers are still important because they pass out DNS server information.

- Stateful DHCPv6 servers pass out IPv6 addresses, subnet masks, default gateway addresses, and DNS server addresses, as well as other, optional information.

- Stateless DHCPv6 servers pass out only optional information. Stateless DHCPv6 servers are preferred to stateful servers because stateless servers support aggregation.

- DHCPv6 servers may be bypassed by manually entering DNS server information into the IP settings of an IPv6 client.

Implement IPv6 in a TCP/IP network

- Do not connect to the IPv6 Internet on a critical computer! Limited IPv6 support means potential security risks.

- Currently, all root DNS servers support IPv6 resolution and almost all tier-one ISP routers properly forward IPv6 packets. However, the routers between you and these root and tier-one servers may not support IPv6 at the moment.

- An IPv4-to-IPv6 tunnel can be used to bridge the gap created by non-IPv6 routers, allowing you access to the root and tier-one routers that do support IPv6.

- There are four popular tunneling standards: 6to4, 6in4, Teredo, and ISATAP.

- 6to4 is the dominant tunneling protocol and is the only one that doesn't require a tunnel broker. However, it is the most challenging to set up. 6to4 addresses start with 2002:/16.

- Only 6in4 and Teredo can go through NAT.

- Teredo is built into Microsoft Windows. Teredo addresses always start with 2001:0000:/32.

- ISATAP adds an IPv4 address to an IPv6 prefix. For example, 2001:DB8:98CA:200:131.107.28.9.

- A tunnel broker is a service provider that creates the tunnel, acts as the far endpoint, and often provides a tunneling client for easier setup.

- TSP and TIC are two automatic configuration protocols for setting up IPv4-to-IPv6 tunnels.

- It is estimated that IPv4 addresses will run out sometime between the year 2011 and 2019.

■ Key Terms

6in4 *(354)*
6to4 *(354)*
aggregation *(345)*
anycast *(343)*
Extended Unique Identifier, 64-bit (EUI-64) *(341)*
global unicast address *(344)*
Intra-Site Automatic Tunnel Addressing Protocol (ISATAP) *(355)*
Internet Protocol version 4 (IPv4) *(338)*
Internet Protocol version 6 (IPv6) *(339)*

link-local address *(341)*
multicast address *(342)*
stateful *(350)*
stateless *(351)*
Teredo *(354)*
tunnel broker *(355)*
Tunnel Information and Control protocol (TIC) *(355)*
Tunnel Setup Protocol (TSP) *(355)*
unicast address *(342)*

■ Key Term Quiz

Use the Key Terms list to complete the sentences that follow. Not all the terms will be used.

1. A(n) _____ DHCPv6 server passes out only optional information.

2. The _____ tunneling protocol is the only one that doesn't use a tunnel broker.

3. It is the practice of _____ that greatly reduces the size of IPv6 routing tables by reducing them to a subnet of an upstream router.

4. You must have a(n) _____ to connect to the IPv6 Internet.

5. A(n) _____ address contains a total of 32 bits.

6. A packet sent to a(n) _____ is broadcast to all network nodes, but only the target nodes read the packet.

7. The MAC address is used to generate the complete _____, except in Windows Vista and Windows 7.

8. The _____ appends an IPv4 address to the end of the IPv6 prefix.

9. Computers involved in a local network that has no Internet connectivity require only a(n) _____.

10. Employing the services of a(n) _____ automates the process of setting up an IPv6 tunnel.

■ Multiple-Choice Quiz

1. How many bits comprise an IPv6 address?
   A. 32
   B. 48
   C. 64
   D. 128

2. Which of the following is a valid IPv6 address?
   A. 192.168.0.1
   B. 2001:376:BDS:0:3378:BAAF:QR9:223
   C. 2541:FDC::ACDF:2770:23
   D. 0000:0000:0000:0000:0000:0000:0000:0000

3. Which of the following IPv6 addresses are equivalent to ACCB:0876:0000:0000:FD87:0000:0000:0064? (Select two.)
   A. ACCB:876::FD87:0:0:64
   B. ACCB:876::FD87::64
   C. ACCB:876:0:0:FD87::64
   D. ACCB:876:0:FD87:0:64

4. What is the only type of IPv6 address required to communicate with other computers on a local network?
   A. Link-local
   B. Global unicast
   C. EUI-64
   D. Multicast

5. Which of the following is a valid link-local address?
   A. 2001:2323:CCE:34FF:19:DE3:2DBA:52
   B. FE80::1994:33DD:22CE:769B

   C. FEFE:0:0:0:FEFE:0:0:0
   D. FFFF:FFFF:FFFF:FFFF:232D:0:DE44:CB2

6. What is true of link-local addresses?
   A. They are passed out by the default gateway router.
   B. They are completely randomly generated by each computer.
   C. The last 64 bits are always generated from the MAC address, except on Windows Vista and Windows 7.
   D. They always start with 169.254.

7. What is a valid IPv6 subnet mask?
   A. /64
   B. /72
   C. /255
   D. 255.255.255.0

8. How do IPv6 multicasts differ from broadcasts?
   A. Broadcasts are sent to all network nodes. Multicasts are sent only to specific network nodes.
   B. Both broadcasts and multicasts are sent to all network nodes, but in a multicast, only the destination nodes read the incoming packets.
   C. Broadcasts can cross over a router, whereas multicasts cannot.
   D. Broadcasts are used on local networks; multicasts are used on the Internet.

9. What type of address applies to a single unique network node?
   A. Unicast
   B. Unilateral

C. Multicast

D. Omnicast

10. A packet has been sent to the address FF02:0000:0000:0002:0BCD:23DD:3456:0001. What will read the sent packet?

    A. The single computer with the address FF02:0000:0000:0002:0BCD:23DD:3456:0001.

    B. Every network node.

    C. Every router on the network.

    D. Nothing will read the packet because it is an invalid address.

11. What must your computer have to access the IPv6 Internet?

    A. An IPv4 address

    B. A global multicast address

    C. A link-local address

    D. A global unicast address

12. What is true of current global addresses?

    A. They always begin with 2001::, 2002::, 2003::, and so on.

    B. They always begin with FF02::1, FF02::2, FF03::3, and so on.

    C. They are only 64 bits long.

    D. They are only used by root and tier-one routers.

13. What is the main benefit of IPv6 aggregation?

    A. It allows users to combine multiple IPv6 addresses to increase their bandwidth and overall Internet speed exponentially.

    B. It is backward-compatible and can be directly applied to IPv4 networks.

    C. It reduces the size and complexity of routing tables, allowing routers to work more efficiently.

    D. Signals are increased with each router the packet travels through, allowing for greater distances over wireless networks.

14. Which operating systems fully support IPv6? (Select three.)

    A. Windows 2000

    B. Windows XP

    C. Windows Vista

    D. Macintosh OS X

15. As IPv6 clients can get a portion of their IP address from the default gateway server, what purpose does a DHCPv6 server serve?

    A. DHCPv6 servers can still distribute DNS server information.

    B. DHCPv6 servers provide link-local addresses.

    C. DHCPv6 servers provide the other half of the IPv6 address.

    D. There is no such thing as a DHCPv6 server.

■ Essay Quiz

1. Explain to a colleague the difference between link-local and global IPv6 addresses. Be sure to include when each one is necessary.

2. Explain how aggregation reduces the size and complexity of routing tables.

3. NAT is not supported in IPv6, meaning that every computer with a global IPv6 address is exposed to the Internet. Why is this not a big concern?

Lab Projects

• Lab Project 13.1

Any decent network tech can work effectively with binary and hexadecimal notation. Get some practice by taking the following MAC addresses and calculating the EUI-64:

00-14-22-46-8A-77

BC-23-44-AB-A7-21

12-00-CF-C2-44-1A

Now use IPCONFIG /ALL to find your own MAC address and calculate the EUI-64.

• Lab Project 13.2

Choose one of the IPv4-to-IPv6 tunneling methods (6to4, 6in4, Teredo, or ISATAP) and configure a lab computer to connect to the Internet using IPv6. Write down which method you used and the steps you took to get it working. Make your steps clear so that someone else can follow them. Swap your steps with a classmate who used a different tunneling method and follow his or her steps to connect using the alternate method. Which method did you find more difficult? Why?

Remote Connectivity

"Gongs and drums, banners and flags, are means whereby the ears and eyes of the host may be focused on one particular point."

—SUN TZU

In this chapter, you will learn how to

- **Describe WAN telephony technologies, such as SONET, T1, and T3**
- **Compare last-mile connections for connecting homes and businesses to the Internet**
- **Discuss and implement various remote access connections**

Computers connect to other computers locally in a local area network (LAN)—you've read about LAN connections throughout this book—and remotely through a number of different methods. This chapter takes both an historical and a modern look at ways to interconnect a local computer or network with distant computers, what's called *remote connectivity*.

Historical/Conceptual

You must appreciate that remote connections have been around for a long time. Before the Internet, network users and developers developed ways to take a single system or network and connect it to another faraway system or network. This wasn't the Internet! These were private interconnections of private networks. These connections were very expensive and, compared to today's options, pretty slow.

As the Internet developed, most of the same technologies used to make the earlier private remote connections became the way the Internet itself interconnects. The days of private interconnections are quickly fading: today the ultimate remote connection is nothing more than you opening your Web browser and accessing someone's faraway Web page. However, there are hundreds of thousands of organizations that still use their own private interconnections (which may or may not also connect to the Internet) for security or speed.

This chapter shows you all the ways you can make remote connections. You'll see every type of remote connection currently in popular use, from good old telephone lines to advanced fiber-optic carriers, and even satellites. There are so many ways to make remote connections that this chapter is broken into three parts. The first part, "Telephony and Beyond," gives you a tour of the technologies that originally existed for long-distance voice connections that now also support data. The next part, "The Last Mile," goes into how we as individual users connect to those long-distance technologies. Last, "Using Remote Access" shows you the many different ways to use these connections to connect to another, faraway computer.

■ Telephony and Beyond

We've already discussed the tier-one ISPs of the Internet, but let's look at them once again in a different way. Describing the tier-one Internet is always an interesting topic. Those of us in the instruction business invariably start this description by drawing a picture of the United States (we Americans are so conceited sometimes) and then adding lines connecting big cities, as shown in Figure 14.1.

But what are these lines and where did they come from? If the Internet is just a big TCP/IP network, wouldn't one assume that these lines are Ethernet connections? Maybe copper, maybe fiber, but Ethernet? Well, traditionally they're not (with one exception; see the following Note). The vast majority of the long-distance connections that make up the Internet use an unique type of signal called SONET. SONET was originally designed to handle

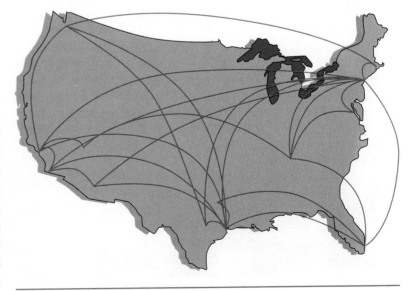

● **Figure 14.1**   The tier-one Internet

special heavy-duty circuits with names like T1. Never heard of SONET or T1? Don't worry—you're about to learn quite a bit.

Most of the connections that make up the high-speed backbone of the Internet use technologies designed at least 20 years ago to support telephone calls. We're not talking about your cool, cell phone–type calls here: we're talking the old-school, wire-runs-up-to-the-house, telephone-connected-to-a-phone-jack connections known lovingly as **Plain Old Telephone Service (POTS)**. If you want to understand how the Internet connects, you have to go way back to the 1970s and 1980s, before the Internet really took off, and learn how the U.S. telephone system developed to support networks.

The Dawn of Long Distance

Have you ever watched one of those old-time movies in which someone makes a phone call by picking up the phone and saying "Operator, get me Mohawk 4, 3-8-2-5!" Suddenly, the scene changes to some person sitting at a switchboard like the one shown in Figure 14.2.

This was the telephone operator. The telephone operator made a physical link between your phone and the other phone, making your connection. This worked pretty well in the first few years of telephones, but it quickly became a problem as more and more phone lines began to fill the skies overhead (Figure 14.3).

These first generations of long-distance telephone systems (think 1930s here) used analog signals because that was how your telephone worked—the louder you spoke, the greater the voltage. If you graphed out a voice signal, it looked something like Figure 14.4. This was a problem, because analog signals over long distances, even if you amplified them, lost sound quality very quickly.

The first problem to take care of was the number of telephone wires. Individual wires were slowly replaced with special boxes called multiplexers. A **multiplexer** took a circuit and combined it with a few hundred other circuits into a single complex circuit on one wire. A second multiplexer on the other end of the connection split the individual connections back out (Figure 14.5).

Even as you read this, more and more of the Internet interconnections are moving toward 1-Gigabit and 10-Gigabit Ethernet. However, telephone technologies continue to dominate.

> **Tech Tip**
>
> **Telephony in Depth**
> *This section is just the lightest of overviews to get you through the CompTIA Network+ exam. The full history of long-distance communication is an incredible story, full of good guys, bad guys, crazy technology, and huge fortunes won and lost.*

• **Figure 14.2**   Old-time telephone operator (photo courtesy of the Richardson Historical and Genealogical Society)

• **Figure 14.3**   Now that's a lot of telephone lines!

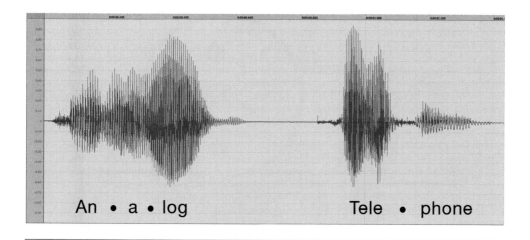

● **Figure 14.4**   Another problem of early long-distance telephone systems

Over time, the entire United States was divided into hundreds, eventually thousands, of local exchanges. Local exchanges were a defined grouping of individual phone circuits served by a single multiplexer (calls within the exchange were handled differently). One or more exchanges were (and still are) housed in a physical building called a **central office** (Figure 14.6) where individual voice circuits all came together. Local calls were still manually connected (although dial-up began to appear in earnest by the 1950s, after which a lot of operators lost their jobs) but any connection between exchanges was carried over these special multiplexed trunk lines. Figure 14.7 shows a very stylized example of how this worked.

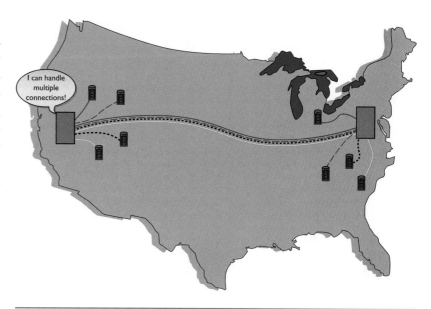

● **Figure 14.5**   Multiplexers combine multiple circuits.

● **Figure 14.6**   A central office building

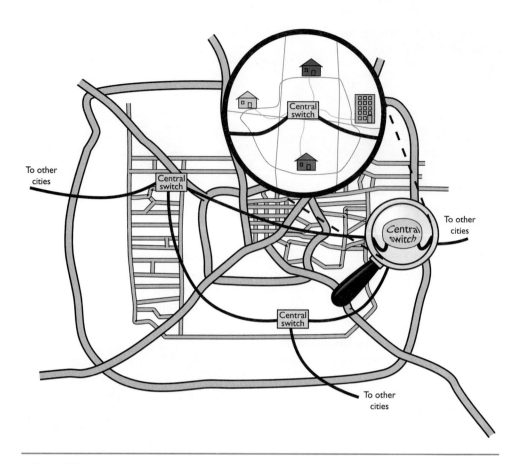

● **Figure 14.7**   Interconnected central offices

These old-style trunk lines were fascinating technology. How did they put a bunch of voice calls on a single piece of cable yet still somehow keep them separate? The trick was appreciating a little bit about frequency. Your typical telephone only detects a fairly limited frequency range—from around 350 Hz to around 4000 Hz. This range covers enough of the human speech range to make a decent phone call. As the individual calls came into the multiplexer, it added a certain frequency multiplier to each call, keeping every separate call in its own unique frequency range (Figure 14.8). We call this process **Frequency Division Multiplexing (FDM)**.

This analog network still required a physical connection from one phone to the other, even if those phones were on opposite sides of the country. Long distance was a series of trunk lines, and at each intersection of those lines an operator had to connect the calls. When you physically connect two phones together on one circuit, you are using something called **circuit switching**. As you might imagine, circuit switching isn't that great for long distance, but it's your only option when you use analog.

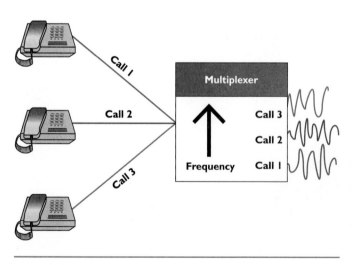

● **Figure 14.8**   Multiplexed FDM

This analog system worked pretty well through the 1930s to the 1950s, but telephones became so common and demand so heavy that the United States needed a new system to handle the load. The folks developing this new system realized that they had to dump analog and replace it with a digital system—and here is where the remote connections that eventually became the Internet were born.

Digital data is much easier to carry long distances than analog data because you can use repeaters (you cannot use repeaters on analog signals). If you remember from earlier chapters, a repeater is not an amplifier. An amplifier just increases the voltage and includes all the pops and hisses created by all kinds of interferences. A repeater takes the entire digital signal and re-creates it out the other end (Figure 14.9).

The downside to digital was that all voice calls were analog. Something, somewhere had to convert the analog voice calls to digital. This was a massive undertaking, but luckily, virtually the entire U.S. phone system at that time was a monopoly run by a company called AT&T. A single company could make all of its own decisions and its own standards—one of the few times in history where a monopoly was probably a good thing. The AT&T folks had a choice here: completely revamp the entire U.S. phone system, including replacing every single telephone in the United States, or just make the trunk lines digital and let the central offices convert from analog to digital. They chose the latter. Even today, a classic POTS line in your home or small office is analog—the rest of the entire telephone system is digital. This is not unique to the United States; POTS is analog, everything else is digital. The telecommunications industry calls the connection from a central office to individual users the **last mile**. The telephone company's decision to keep the last mile analog has had serious repercussions that still challenge us even in the 21st century (Figure 14.10)

There were attempts to convert the entire telephone system, including your telephones, to digital but they never really took off. See "ISDN" later in this chapter.

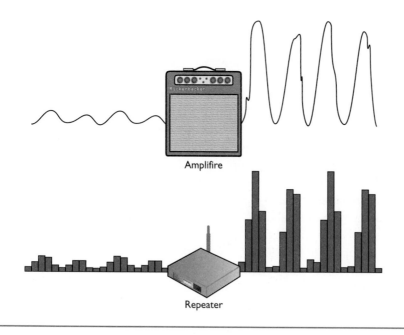

Amplifire

Repeater

• **Figure 14.9**   Repeater vs. amplifier

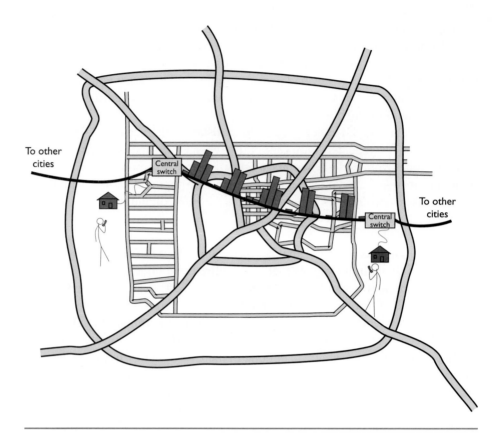

- **Figure 14.10**   Analog and digital

Test Specific

Digital Telephony

The best part about digital telephony is that most of the aspects you've already learned about computer networking work roughly the same way in a telephone network. In fact, most of the concepts that created computer networking came from the telephone industry. For example, the telephone industry was the first technology to heavily adopt the idea of digital packets. It was the first to do what we now call switching. Heck, the telephone industry even made the first working topologies! Let's take advantage of what you already know about how networks work to learn about how the telephone industry invented the idea of digital networks.

When you learned about networks in the first few chapters of this book, you learned about cabling, frame types, speeds, switching, and so on. All of these are important for computer networks. Well, let's do it again (in a much simpler format) to see the cabling, frame types, speed, and switching used in telephone systems. Don't worry, unlike computer networks, in which a certain type of cable might run different types of frames at different speeds, most of the remote connections used in the telephony world tend to have one type of cable that only runs one type of frame at one type of speed.

The only real question is where to start. The best place to begin is with the most basic data chunk you get in the telephone world: DS0.

It All Starts with DS0

When AT&T decided to go digital, it knew all phone calls had to be broken into a digital sample. AT&T chose (some people say "guessed" or "compromised") and decided that if it took an analog signal of a human voice and converted it into 8-bit chunks 8000 times a second, that would be good enough to re-create the sound later. Figure 14.11 shows an example of the analog human voice seen earlier being converted into a digital sample.

Converting analog sound into 8-bit chunks 8000 times a second creates a data stream (called a digital signal) of 64 kilobits per second (Kbps). This digital signal rate is known as **DS0** and is the simplest data stream (and the slowest rate) of the digital part of the telephone system. Each analog voice call is converted into a DS0 signal at the telephone company's central office. From there they are multiplexed into larger circuits.

Now that we have our voice calls converted to digital data, we need to get them to the right telephone. First, we need network technologies to handle the cabling, frames, and speed. Second, we need to come up with a method to switch the digital voice calls across a network. To handle the former, we need to define the types of interconnections, with names like T1 and OC3. To handle the latter, we no longer connect via multiplexed circuit switching, as we did back with analog, but rather are now switching packets. I'll show you what I mean as we learn about the digital lines in use today.

Tech Tip

Modems

A device that takes an analog signal and converts it into a digital signal is a modulator. A device that takes a digital signal and converts it into an analog signal is a demodulator. A device that does both is called a modulator-demodulator, better known as a modem.

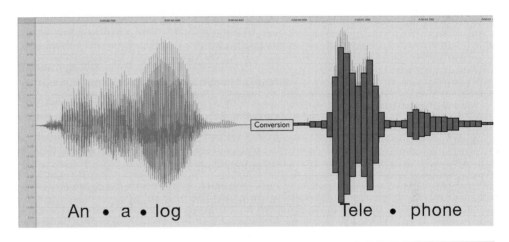

An • a • log   Tele • phone

• **Figure 14.11**   Analog to digital

Copper Carriers: T1 and T3

The first and still popular digital trunk carriers used by the telephone industry are called T-carriers. There are a number of different versions of T-carriers and the CompTIA Network+ exam expects you to know something about them. Let's begin with the most common and most basic, the venerable T1.

T1 has several meanings. First, it refers to a high-speed digital networking technology called a T1 connection. Second, the term **T1 line** refers to the specific, shielded, two-pair cabling that connects the two ends of a T1 connection (Figure 14.12). Two wires are for sending data and two wires are for receiving data. At either end of a T1 line you'll find an unassuming box called a **Channel Service Unit/Digital Service Unit (CSU/DSU)**. The CSU/DSU

• **Figure 14.12**   T1 line

has a second connection that goes from the phone company (where the boxes reside) to a customer's equipment (usually a router). A T1 connection is point-to-point—you cannot have more than two CSU/DSUs on a single T1 line.

T1 uses a special signaling method called **DS1**. DS1 uses a relatively primitive frame—the frame doesn't need to be complex because with point-to-point there's no addressing necessary. Each DS1 frame has 25 pieces: a framing bit and 24 channels. Each DS1 channel holds a single 8-bit DS0 data sample. The framing bit and data channels combine to make 193 bits per DS1 frame. These frames are transmitted 8000 times/sec, making a total throughput of 1.544 Mbps (Figure 14.13). DS1 defines, therefore, a data transfer speed of 1.544 Mbps, split into 24 64-Kbps DS0 channels. This process of having frames that carry a bit of every channel in every frame sent on a regular interval is called **time division multiplexing**.

An analogy I like to use in class for T1 technology is that of a conveyor belt in a milk-bottling factory. At regular intervals, big crates with 24 bottles come rolling down the belt. When they reach the filling machine, the bottles get filled with milk and the crate keeps rolling down to the other end where two machines take over: the labeling and sorting machines. The labeling machine plucks out the bottles and applies a label to each, appropriate to the contents. The sorting machine sorts the bottles into cases of each type.

This is pretty simple if the filling machine uses only one type of milk. All 24 bottles fill with whole milk; all are labeled as whole milk; and all go into the case marked "Whole Milk." Once enough full bottles of milk arrive, the case gets completed, and you have a product.

That's pretty much how an Ethernet packet works, right? The whole packet is used for a single set of data, and then multiple packets get together at the end to make your data transfer complete.

The cool thing about the DS1 frame, though, is that you don't have to use the whole frame for a single set of data. With the right CSU/DSU at either end, you can specify which channels go with a specific thread of data. Sloshing back into the analogy . . . the milk company produces four types of milk: whole milk, lowfat milk, chocolate milk, and strawberry milk. The strawberry milk is seasonal; the whole milk sells the most, followed by chocolate, and then lowfat.

To accommodate the different products, the factory master might designate channels 1–10 for whole milk, 11–18 for chocolate milk, 19–22 for lowfat milk, and 23–24 for strawberry. Now the labeling and sorting machines are going to have to work for a living! When a crate reaches the filling machine, the bottles get filled with the various types of milk, and then the crate trundles on down the belt. The labeling machine knows the numbering system, so it labels bottles 1–10 as whole milk, 11–18 as chocolate, and so on. The sorting machine also knows

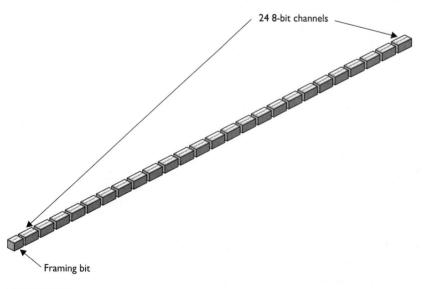

24 8-bit channels

Framing bit

• **Figure 14.13** DS1 frame

the system and has four cases at hand, one for each product. As the bottles arrive, it places them into the appropriate cases. Notice that the cases will fill at different rates of speed. It'll take a while for the strawberry milk case to fill, especially compared to the whole milk, because only two channels in each crate carry strawberry.

What happens if the cows temporarily stop producing chocolate milk? Will the whole factory need to be reordered so the filling machine's eight chocolate dispensers can dispense some other kind of milk? The answer at this factory is no. The crates continue to roll down the conveyor belt at regular intervals. The filling machine fills the bottles in channels 1–10 with whole milk, leaves the bottles in channels 11–18 empty, and puts lowfat and strawberry in channels 19–22 and 23–24, respectively.

DS1/T1 work the same way. The frame just keeps jetting down the line, even if some of the channels contain no data. The CSU/DSU at the other end collects the data streams and keeps them separate. To paraphrase the immortal words of Professor Egon, "Never cross the streams." Otherwise you'd lose data.

To bring the milk bottling factory analogy completely into the realm of networking and T1 connections, keep in mind that there would be two conveyor belts running in opposite directions. Milk flows in; milk flows out. You can both send and receive on T1 connections.

A T1 line is a dedicated phone connection that you lease, usually on a monthly basis, from the telephone company. It has no telephone number and it's always connected. An entire T1 bundle can be expensive, so many telephone companies let you buy just some of these individual channels. This is known as **fractional T1 access**.

A **T3 line** is a dedicated telephone connection supporting a data rate of about 43 Mbps. A T3 line consists of 672 individual DS0 channels. T3 lines (sometimes referred to as DS3 lines) are mainly used by regional telephone companies and ISPs connecting to the Internet.

Similar to the North American T1 line, **E1** is the European format for digital transmission. An E1 line carries signals at 2.048 Mbps (32 channels at 64 Kbps), compared to the T1's 1.544 Mbps (24 channels at 64 Kbps). Both E1 and T1 lines may be interconnected for international use. There are also **E3** lines, which carry 16 E1 lines, with a bandwidth of 34.368 Mbps.

A CSU/DSU, as mentioned earlier, connects a leased T1 or T3 line from the telephone company to a customer's equipment. A CSU/DSU has (at least) two connectors, one that goes to the T1/T3 line running out of your demarc and another connection that goes to your router. It performs line encoding and conditioning functions, and often has a loopback function for testing. Many newer routers have CSU/DSUs built into them. Figure 14.14 shows the front of a Juniper Networks router with two T1 interfaces. Two interfaces on one router is quite common, with the dual links providing redundancy if one link goes down.

Tech Tip

DS1 Gets No Respect!

People rarely use the term "DS1." Since T1 lines only carry DS1 signals, we usually just say T1 when describing the signal, even though the term DS1 is more accurate.

 Each 64-Kbps channel in a DS1 signal is a DS0.

● **Figure 14.14**   CSU/DSU on a Juniper router (photo courtesy of Juniper Networks, Inc.)

The CSU part of a CSU/DSU is designed to protect the T1 or T3 line and the user equipment from lightning strikes and other types of electrical interference. It also stores statistics and has capabilities for loopback testing.

Table 14.1	T-carriers	
Carrier	**Channels**	**Speed**
T1	24	1.544 Mbps
T3	672	44.736 Mbps
E1	32	2.048 Mbps
E3	512	34.368 Mbps

Tech Tip

What's in a Name?

Students often wonder why two separate names exist for the same technology. In reality, SONET and SDH vary a little in their signaling and frame type, but routers and other magic boxes on the Internet handle the interoperability between the standards. The American National Standards Institute (ANSI) publishes the standard as SONET; the International Telecommunications Union (ITU) publishes the standard as SDH, but includes SONET signaling. For simplicity's sake and because SONET is the more common term in the United States, this book uses SONET as the generic term for this technology.

SONET is one of the most important standards for making all of our WAN interconnections—and it's also the least likely standard you'll ever see because it's hidden away from all but the biggest networks.

The DSU part supplies timing to each user port, taking the incoming user data signals and converting the input signal into the specified line code, and then framing the format for transmission over the provided line.

Make sure you know the four T-carriers shown in Table 14.1!

Fiber Carriers: SONET/SDH and OC

T-carriers were a great start into the digital world, but in the early 1980s fiber-optic cabling became the primary tool for long-distance communication all over the world. By now AT&T was gone, replaced by a number of competing carriers. Competition was strong and everyone was making their own fiber transmission standards. In an incredible moment of corporate cooperation, in 1987, all of the primary fiber-optic carriers decided to drop their own standards and move to a new international standard called **Synchronous Optical Network (SONET)** in the United States and **Synchronous Digital Hierarchy (SDH)** in Europe.

All of these carriers, all adopting the same standard, created a world of simple interconnections between competing voice and data carriers. This adoption defined the moment that truly made the Internet a universal network. Before SONET, interconnections happened but they were outlandishly expensive, preventing the Internet from reaching many areas of the world.

SONET is the primary standard for long-distance, high-speed, fiber-optic transmission systems. There is a high level of comparison of SONET to network standards like Ethernet because SONET defines interface standards at the Physical and Data Link layers of the OSI seven-layer model. The physical aspect of SONET is partially covered by the Optical Carrier standards, but it also defines a ring-based topology that most SONET adopters now use. SONET does not require a ring, but a SONET ring has extra survivability in case of line loss. As a result, most of the big, long-distance optical pipes for the world's telecommunications networks are SONET rings.

The real beauty of SONET lies in its multiplexing capabilities. A single SONET ring can combine multiple DS1, DS3, even European E1 signals and package them into single, huge SONET frames for transmission. Clearly, for SONET to handle such large data rates it needs high-capacity fiber optics—and that's where the Optical Carrier standards come into play!

The **Optical Carrier (OC)** specification is used to denote the optical data carrying capacity (in Mbps) of fiber-optic cables in networks conforming to the SONET standard. The OC standard is an escalating series of speeds, designed to meet the needs of medium-to-large corporations. SONET establishes OCs from 51.8 Mbps (OC-1) to 39.8 Gbps (OC-768).

SONET uses the **Synchronous Transport Signal (STS)** signal method. The STS consists of two parts: the **STS payload** (which carries data) and the **STS overhead** (which carries the signaling and protocol information). When we talk about STS, we add a number to the end of "STS" to designate the speed of the signal. For example, STS-1 is the 51.85-Mbps signal that runs on an OC-1 line. STS-3 runs at 155.52 Mbps on OC-3 lines, and so on.

Table 14.2 describes the most common optical carriers.

Table 14.2	Common Optical Carriers	
SONET Optical Level	**Line Speed**	**Signal Method**
OC-1	51.85 Mbps	STS-1
OC-3	155.52 Mbps	STS-3
OC-12	622.08 Mbps	STS-12
OC-24	1.244 Gbps	STS-24
OC-48	2.488 Gbps	STS-48
OC-192	9.955 Gbps	STS-192
OC-256	13.22 Gbps	STS-256
OC-768	39.82 Gbps	STS-768

Packet Switching

All of these impressive connections that start with *T*s and *O*s are powerful, but they are not in and of themselves a complete WAN solution. These WAN connections with their unique packets (DS-0, STS, and so on) make up the entire mesh of long-range connections we call the Internet, carrying both packetized voice data and TCP/IP packets. All of these connections are point-to-point, so we need to add another level of devices to enable us to connect multiple T1s, T3s, or OC connections together to make that mesh. That's where packet switching comes into play.

Packets, as you know from what you've learned about networking, need some form of addressing scheme to get from one location to another. The telephone industry came up with its own types of packets that run on T-carrier and OC lines to get data from one central office to another. These packet-switching protocols are functionally identical to routable network protocols like TCP/IP. Today's WAN connections predominantly use two different forms of packet switching: Frame Relay and ATM.

Frame Relay

Frame Relay is an extremely efficient packet-switching standard, designed for and used primarily with T-carrier lines. It is especially effective for the off-again/on-again traffic typical of most LAN applications. Frame Relay switches packets quickly, but without any guarantee of data integrity at all. You can't even count on it to deliver all the frames, because it will discard frames whenever there is network congestion. In practice, however, a Frame Relay network delivers data quite reliably because T-carrier digital lines that use Frame Relay have very low error rates.

Frame Relay was extremely popular and is still widely available. If you decide to go with a T1 line in the United States, what you're getting is a T1 line running Frame Relay, although many companies use the newer ATM standard as their packet-switching solution with T-carrier lines.

ATM

Don't think automatic teller machine here! **Asynchronous Transfer Mode (ATM)** is a network technology originally designed for high-speed LANs in the early 1990s. ATM only saw limited success in the LAN world, but has become extremely popular in the WAN world. In fact, most of the SONET rings that move voice and data all over the world use ATM for packet switching. ATM integrates voice, video, and data on one connection, using short and fixed-length packets called *cells* to transfer information. Every cell sent with the same source and destination travels over the same route, giving ATM the potential to remove the performance bottlenecks that exist in today's LANs and WANs.

The key problem ATM addresses is that data and audio/video transmissions have different transfer requirements. Data can tolerate a delay in transfer, but not signal loss (if it takes a moment for a Web page to appear, you don't care). Audio and video transmissions, on the other hand, can tolerate signal loss but not delay (it would make the phone calls sound delayed). Because ATM transfers information in cells of one set size (53 bytes long), it is scalable and can handle both types of transfers well. ATM transfer speeds range from 155.52 to 622.08 Mbps and beyond. If your location was big enough to order an OC line from your ISP, odds are good you'd be getting an OC line running ATM.

MPLS

Frame Relay and ATM are both fantastic packet-switching technologies but they're designed to support any type of traffic that might come over the network. Today, TCP/IP is the predominant data technology and has a number of issues that neither Frame Relay nor ATM addresses. To address these issues, many ISPs (and large ISP clients) use an additional technology called **Multi-Protocol Label Switching (MPLS)**.

Frame Relay and ATM networks are the property of the telephone networks. Those of us who use these networks (and all of us do) never actually see exactly where the packets really go—nor do we have to, because the telephone companies are very dependable. Since we neither can see nor do anything with these networks, the network industry likes to represent them using a cloud analogy. Figure 14.15 shows an example of a connection between a Web server and a Web client. We only show routers that we actually control—everything else is "in the clouds."

● **Figure 14.15**   The cloud

In some situations we do want to know what's happening in the clouds. Here's an example: Anyone who can't afford not to be on the Internet has at least two ISP connections. Let's say Company X has two locations. Each location has an ATM OC-1 line with a Frame Relay T-3 line as a backup (Figure 14.16).

Normally, your gateway router decides what to use based on availability and the router table. But what if you have some really critical data (FTP for example) that you only want to send out on the ATM link? There's nothing to force that to happen. The quality of service (QoS) standards that you saw in Chapter 12, "Advanced Networking Devices," only cover the amount of bandwidth to use, not which port to use. MPLS is a router feature that labels certain data to use a desired connection. It works with any type of packet switching (even Ethernet) to force certain types of data to use a certain path. This path in essence is a VPN—just like the VPNs we saw in Chapter 12 (but not encrypted). When you use MPLS, you usually say "MPLS VPN" because it creates a virtualized private tunnel through the cloud of the Internet.

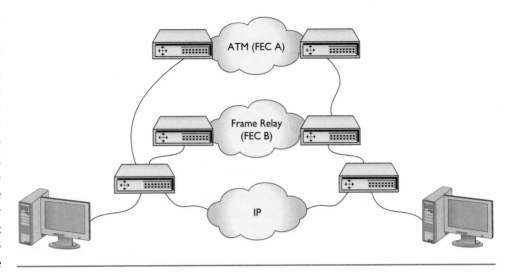

• **Figure 14.16**   Company X's network

Real-World WAN

There are two reasons to use a telephony WAN connection: to get your LAN on the Internet or to make a private connection between two or more of your private LANs. How you go about getting one of these lines changes a bit depending on which you want to do. Let's start with connecting to the Internet.

Traditionally, getting a WAN Internet connection was a two-step process: you talked to the telephone company to get the line physically installed and then talked to an ISP to provide you with Internet access. Today, almost every telephone company is also an ISP so this is usually a simple process. Just go online and do a Web search of ISPs in your area and give them a call. You'll get a price quote and, if you sign up, they will do the installation.

There are a few tricks to reduce the price. If you're in an office building, odds are very good that there's already a T1 or better line installed you can use and that an ISP is already serving people in your building. Talk to the building supervisor to find out. If there isn't, you have to pay for a new line. If there's a nearby interconnect, this might be cheap. If you want the telephone company to run an OC line to your house, brace for a quote of thousands of dollars just to get the line.

The telephone company runs your T-carrier (or bigger) line to a demarc. This demarc is important because this is where the phone company's responsibility ends! Everything on "your" side of the demarc is your responsibility. From there, you or your ISP installs a CSU/DSU (for T-carriers) and that device connects to your router.

There's a tremendous amount of variance here depending on who does this for you. The classic example (sticking with T-carrier here) is a demarc, CSU/DSU, and router setup, as shown in Figure 14.17.

T-carriers have been around so long that many of these parts are combined. It's very common to have a single box that combines the CSU/DSU and the router in one handy device, such as the Juniper router shown earlier in Figure 14.14.

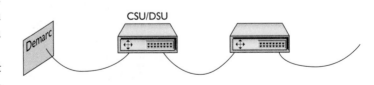

• **Figure 14.17**   Old-school T-carrier setup

WAN telephony carriers are incredibly dependable, far more dependable than cheaper alternatives (like cable modems), and that's one of the main reasons people still use them. But it's critical that you know how to test your end of the connection if you ever suspect a problem. The single most important test is called the **Bit Error Rate Test (BERT)**. A BERT test is an end-to-end test that verifies the T-carrier connection. Every CSU/DSU has a different way to BERT test—just make sure you know how to do it on yours!

Alternative to Telephony WAN

Telephony WANs were the first big connections. They're still the core of what makes up most of the Internet backbone and private connections, but have given way to more advanced technologies. The three biggest newer technologies for Internet connections are Ethernet, DSL, and cable modems. I need to give them a quick mention here.

Many ISPs provide straight Ethernet connections. As you should well appreciate by now, Ethernet has some serious distance limitations, covering no more than a kilometer, except for very expensive single mode fiber solutions. This limits Ethernet to places like large cities where you as a customer are close to your ISP. On the other hand, Ethernet links are extremely easy to set up, because you usually have nothing more than a fiber cable that you connect directly to a router. Many companies are dropping T1 and other slower options for the speed of Ethernet.

DSL and cable have been around for quite a while and deserve some serious discussion. However, you can't install your own DSL or cable modem connection as you can with telephony WANs carriers. For example, you can't have your own private cable modem connection between two of your offices. DSL and cable modems are only for Internet connections and, as a result, are really more of a last-mile issue—let's discuss DSL and cable in the next section.

■ The Last Mile

Speed is the key to the Internet, but historically there's always been one big challenge: getting data from central offices to individual users. This wasn't a problem for larger companies that could afford their own WAN connections, but what about individuals and small companies that couldn't or wouldn't pay hundreds of dollars a month for a T1? This area, the infamous last mile, was a serious challenge early on for both Internet connections and private connections because the only common medium was POTS lines. A number of last-mile solutions have appeared over the years, and the CompTIA Network+ exam tests you on the most popular ones. Let's begin with the granddaddy of them all, the telephone line that runs to your house.

Telephone

There are many different types of telephone lines available, but all the choices break down into two groups: dedicated and dial-up. **Dedicated lines** are always off the hook (that is, they never hang up on each other).

A dedicated line (like a T1) does not have a phone number. In essence, the telephone company creates a permanent, hard-wired connection between the two locations, rendering a phone number superfluous. **Dial-up lines**, by contrast, have phone numbers; they must dial each other up to make a connection. When they're finished communicating, they hang up. Two technologies make up the overwhelming majority of dial-up connections—PSTN and ISDN.

Public Switched Telephone Network

The oldest, slowest, and most common original phone connection is the **Public Switched Telephone Network (PSTN)**. PSTN is also known as Plain Old Telephone Service. PSTN is just a regular phone line, the same line that used to run into everybody's home telephone jacks from the central office of your local exchange carrier (LEC—the telephone company that provides local connections and usually the one who owns your local central office).

Because PSTN was designed long before computers were common, it was designed to work with only one type of data: sound. Here's how it works. The telephone's microphone takes the sound of your voice and translates it into an electrical analog waveform. The telephone then sends that signal through the PSTN line to the phone on the other end of the connection. That phone translates the signal into sound on the other end using its speaker. The important word here is *analog*. The telephone microphone converts the sounds into electrical waveforms that cycle 2400 times a second. An individual cycle is known as a **baud**. The number of bauds per second is called the **baud rate**. Pretty much all phone companies' PSTN lines have a baud rate of 2400. PSTN uses a connector called RJ-11. It's the classic connector you see on all telephones (Figure 14.18).

When you connect your modem to a phone jack, the line then runs to your **network interface unit (NIU)**, or demarc. The term "network interface unit" is more commonly used to describe the small box on the side of a home that accepts the incoming lines from the telephone company and then splits them to the different wall outlets. Demarc is more commonly used to describe large connections used in businesses. The terms are interchangeable and always describe the interface between the lines the telephone company is responsible for and the lines for which you are responsible (Figure 14.19).

Computers, as you know, don't speak analog—only digital (ones and zeroes) will do. In addition, the people who invented the way PCs communicate decided to divide any digital signal going in and out of your computer into 8 bits at a time. To connect over phone lines, they need two devices: one that converts this 8-bit wide (parallel) digital signal from the computer into serial (1-bit wide) digital data, and then another device to convert (modulate) the data into analog waveforms that can travel across PSTN lines. You already know that the device that converts the analog data to digital and back is called a **modulator-demodulator (modem)**. The modem in your PC (assuming you still have one) also contains a device called a **Universal Asynchronous Receiver/Transmitter (UART)**. The UART takes the 8-bit-wide digital data and converts it into 1-bit-wide digital data and hands it to the modem for conversion to analog data. The process is reversed for incoming data. Even though internal modems are actually both a UART and a modem, we just say the word "modem" (Figure 14.20).

● **Figure 14.18**   RJ-11 connectors (top and side views)

Internal modems are both a UART and a modem. External modems use a serial or USB port. The serial or USB port contains the UART and the external modem truly is just a modem.

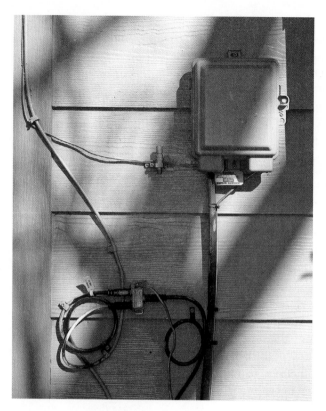

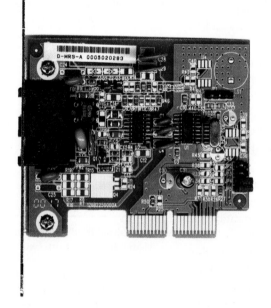

Baud vs. Bits per Second

Modems use phone lines to transmit data at various speeds. These speeds cause a world of confusion and problems for computer people. This is where a little bit of knowledge becomes dangerous. Standard modems you can buy for your home computer normally transmit data at speeds up to 56 Kbps. That's 56 kilobits per second, *not* 56 kilobaud! Many people confuse the terms *baud* and *bits per second*. This confusion arises because the baud rate and bits per second are the same for modems until the data transfer rate surpasses 2400 bps.

A PSTN phone line takes analog samples of sound 2400 times a second. This standard was determined a long time ago as an acceptable rate for sending voice traffic over phone lines. Although 2400-baud analog signals are in fact fine for voice communication, they are a big problem for computers trying to send data because computers only work with digital signals. The job of the modem is to take the digital signals it receives from the computer and send them out over the phone line in an analog form, using the baud cycles from the phone system. A 2400-bps modem—often erroneously called a 2400-baud modem—uses 1 analog baud to send 1 bit of data.

As technology progressed, modems became faster and faster. To get past the 2400-baud limit, modems would modulate the 2400-baud signal multiple times in each cycle. A 4800-bps modem modulated 2 bits per baud, thereby transmitting 4800 bps. All PSTN modem speeds are always a multiple of 2400, with the latest (and last) generation of modems achieving 2400×24 = 57,600 bps (56 Kbps).

V Standards

For two modems to communicate with each other at their fastest rate, they must modulate signals in the same fashion. The two modems must also negotiate with, or *query*, each other to determine the fastest speed they share. The modem manufacturers themselves originally standardized these processes as a set of proprietary protocols. The downside to these protocols was that unless you had two modems from the same manufacturer, modems often would not work together. In response, a European standards body called the **CCITT** established standards for modems. These standards, known generically as the **V standards**, define the speeds at which modems can modulate. The most common of these speed standards are as follows:

- **V.22**   1200 bps
- **V.22bis**   2400 bps
- **V.32**   9600 bps
- **V.32bis**   14,400 bps
- **V.34**   28,000 bps

- **V.90**   57,600 bps
- **V.92**   57,600 bps

The current modem standard now on the market is the **V.92 standard**. V.92 has the same download speed as the V.90, but upstream rates increase to as much as 48 Kbps. If your modem is having trouble getting 56-Kbps rates with V.90 in your area, you will not notice an improvement. V.92 also offers a Quick Connect feature, which implements faster handshaking to cut connection delays. Finally, the V.92 standard offers a Modem On Hold feature, which enables the modem to stay connected while you take an incoming call-waiting call or even initiate an outgoing voice call. This feature only works if the V.92 server modem is configured to enable it.

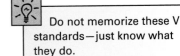 Do not memorize these V standards—just know what they do.

In addition to speed standards, the CCITT, now known simply as ITU, has established standards controlling how modems compress data and perform error checking when they communicate. These standards are as follows:

- **V.42**   Error checking
- **V.42bis**   Data compression
- **V.44**   Data compression
- **MNP5**   Both error checking and data compression

The beauty of these standards is that you don't need to do anything special to enjoy their benefits. If you want 56-Kbps data transfers, for example, you simply need to ensure that the modems in the local system and the remote system both support the V.90 standard. Assuming you have good line quality, the connections will run at or at least close to 56 Kbps.

ISDN

PSTN lines traditionally just aren't that good. While the digital equipment that connects to a PSTN supports a full 64-Kbps DS0 channel, the combination of the lines themselves and the conversion from analog to digital means that most PSTN lines rarely go faster than at most 33 Kbps—and, yes, that includes the 56-Kbps connections.

There are many pieces to a PSTN telephone connection. First, there's the modem in your computer that converts the digital information to analog. Then there's the phone line that runs from your phone out to your NIU and into the central office. The central office stores the modems that convert the analog signal back to digital and the telephone switches that interconnect multiple individual local connections into the larger telephone network. A central office switch connects to long-distance carriers via high-capacity *trunk lines* (at least a T1) and will also connect to other nearby central offices. The analog last mile was an awful way to send data, but it had one huge advantage: most everyone owned a telephone line.

During this upgrade period, customers continued to demand higher throughput from their phone lines. The phone companies were motivated to come up with a way to generate higher capacities. Their answer was fairly straightforward: make the last mile digital. Since everything but the last mile was already digital, by adding special equipment at the central office and the user's location, phone companies felt they could achieve a true, steady, dependable throughput of 64 Kbps per line over the same copper wires already used by PSTN lines. This process of sending telephone transmission across fully digital lines end-to-end is called **Integrated Services Digital Network (ISDN)** service.

ISDN service consists of two types of channels: **Bearer channels (B channels)** carry data and voice information using standard DS0 channels (64 Kbps), while **Delta channels (D channels)** carry setup and configuration information at 16 Kbps. Most providers of ISDN let the user choose either one or two B channels. The more common setup is two B/one D, called a **Basic Rate Interface (BRI)** setup. A BRI setup uses only one physical line, but each B channel sends 64 Kbps, doubling the throughput total to 128 Kbps.

There is also a type of ISDN called **Primary Rate Interface (PRI)**. ISDN PRI is actually just a full T-1 line, carrying 23 B channels.

The physical connections for ISDN bear some similarity to PSTN modems. An ISDN wall socket is usually something that looks like a standard RJ-45 network jack. This line runs to your demarc. In home installations most telephone companies will install a second demarc separate from your PSTN demarc. The most common interface for your computer is a device called a **terminal adapter (TA)**. TAs look like regular modems and, like modems, come in external and internal variants. You can even get TAs that also function as hubs, enabling your system to support a direct LAN connection (Figure 14.21).

You usually need to be within about 18,000 feet of a central office to use ISDN. When you install an ISDN TA, you must configure the other ISDN telephone number you want to call and a special number called the Service Profile ID (SPID). Your ISP provides the telephone number, and the telephone company gives you the SPID. (In many cases the telephone company is also the ISP.) Figure 14.22 shows a typical installation screen for an internal ISDN TA in an old version of Windows. Note that each channel has a phone number in this case.

ISDN continues to soldier on in today's networking world, but has for the most part been replaced by faster and cheaper methods such as DSL and cable modems. Nevertheless, every

● **Figure 14.21** A TeleWell ISDN terminal adapter

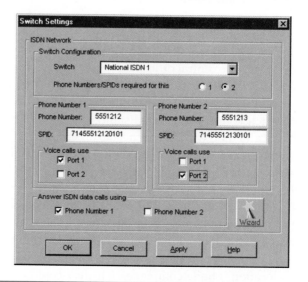

● **Figure 14.22** ISDN settings in an old version of Windows

major telephone company still provides ISDN. ISDN is often the only option for users in locations where other high-speed connection options don't exist.

DSL

Digital Subscriber Line (DSL) is a fully digital, dedicated (no phone number) connection provided by a number of telephone companies. DSL represented the next great leap forward past ISDN for telephone lines. A DSL connection manifests as just another PSTN connection, using the same telephone lines and RJ-11 jacks as any regular phone line. DSL comes in a number of versions, but the three most important to know for the CompTIA Network+ exam are **Symmetric DSL (SDSL)**, **Asymmetric DSL (ADSL)**, and the newer **Very High Bitrate DSL (VDSL)**. SDSL lines provide the same upload and download speeds, making them excellent for those who send as much data as they receive, although SDSL is relatively expensive (VDSL is a new form of SDSL—see "VDSL" in this section). ADSL uses different upload and download speeds. ADSL download speeds are much faster than the upload speeds. Most small office and home office (SOHO) users are primarily concerned with fast *downloads* for things like Web pages, and can tolerate slower upload speeds. ADSL is always much cheaper than SDSL, and VDSL is usually the most expensive.

SDSL

SDSL provides equal upload and download speed and, in theory, provides speeds up to 15 Mbps, although the vast majority of ISPs provide packages ranging from 192 Kbps to 9 Mbps. A recent tour of some major DSL providers in the author's hometown, Houston, Texas, revealed the following SDSL speed options:

- 192 Kbps
- 384 Kbps
- 768 Kbps
- 1.1 Mbps
- 1.5 Mbps

As you might imagine, the pricing for the faster services was higher than for the lower services!

ADSL

ADSL provides theoretical maximum download speeds up to 15 Mbps and upload speeds up to 1 Mbps. However, all ADSL suppliers "throttle" their ADSL speeds and provide different levels of service. Real-world ADSL download speeds vary from 384 Kbps to 15 Mbps, and upload speeds go from as low as 128 Kbps to around 768 Kbps. Touring the same DSL providers in Houston, Texas, here's a few speed options:

- 384 Kbps download/128 Kbps upload
- 1.5 Mbps download/384 Kbps upload
- 6 Mbps download/768 Kbps upload

VDSL

VDSL is the latest version of DSL to appear. Although adoption is fairly low (at least in the United States), its ability to provide speeds up to 100 Mbps in both directions is gaining interest quickly. VDSL achieves these speeds by adding very advanced methods to encode the data. Don't get too excited about these great speed increases. They are very distance dependent: you won't get 100 Mbps unless you're around 300 meters from the DSLAM (see "DSL Features" next). VDSL is designed to run on copper phone lines, but many VDSL suppliers use fiber-optic cabling to increase distances. In the United States, these fiber VDSL services are fiber-to-the-home solutions. The two most popular carriers are AT&T's U-verse and Verizon's Fiber Optic Service (FiOS).

Try This!

Comparing Options in Your Neighborhood

So, what do your local providers offer in terms of higher-speed service, if any? Try this! Call up your local phone company or shop them on the Web (www.dslreports.com is an excellent reference). Does the company offer DSL? What about ISDN? What speed options do you have? If you want to compare with other parts of the United States, check one of the national services, such as Speakeasy (www.speakeasy.net).

Tech Tip

Speed Guarantees

No DSL provider guarantees any particular transmission speed and will only provide service as a "best efforts" contract—a nice way to say that DSL lines are notorious for substantial variations in throughput. This is true even of ISPs that lease the lines from the same telephone service.

Tech Tip

DSL POTS Filters

If you install a telephone onto a line in your home with DSL and you forget to add a filter, don't panic. You won't destroy anything, although you won't get a dial tone either! Just insert a DSL POTS filter and the telephone will work.

DSL Features

One nice aspect of DSL is that you don't have to run new phone lines. The same DSL lines you use for data can simultaneously transmit your voice calls.

All versions of DSL have the same central office–to–end user distance restrictions as ISDN—around 18,000 feet from your demarc to the central office. At the central office your DSL provider has a device called a **DSL Access Multiplexer (DSLAM)** that connects multiple customers to the Internet.

Installing DSL

DSL operates using your pre-existing telephone lines (assuming they are up to specification). This is wonderful, but also presents a technical challenge. For DSL and your run-of-the-mill POTS line to coexist, you need to filter out the DSL signal on the POTS line. A DSL line has three information channels: a high-speed downstream channel, a medium-speed duplex channel, and a POTS channel. Segregating the two DSL channels from the POTS channel guarantees that your POTS line will continue to operate even if the DSL fails. This is accomplished by inserting a filter on each POTS line, or a splitter mechanism that allows all three channels to flow to the DSL modem, but sends only the POTS channel down the POTS line. The DSL company should provide you with a few POTS filters for your telephones. If you need more, most computer/electronics stores stock DSL POTS filters.

The most common DSL installation consists of a **DSL modem** connected to a telephone wall jack and to a standard NIC in your computer (Figure 14.23). A DSL modem is not an actual modem—it's more like an ISDN terminal adapter—but the term stuck, and even the manufacturers of the devices now call them DSL modems.

Many offices use DSL. In my office we use a special DSL line (we use a digital phone system, so the DSL must be separate) that runs directly into our equipment room (Figure 14.24).

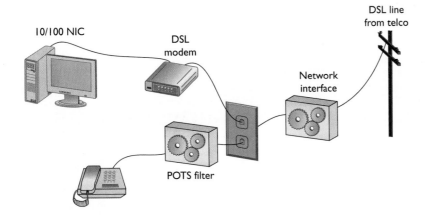

• **Figure 14.23** A DSL modem connection between a PC and telco

This DSL line runs into our DSL modem via a standard phone line with RJ-11 connectors. The DSL modem connects to our gateway router with a CAT 5e patch cable, which in turn connects to the company's hub. Figure 14.25 shows an ADSL modem and a router, giving an idea of the configuration in our office.

Home users often connect the DSL modem directly to their PC's NIC. Either way, there is nothing to do in terms of installing DSL equipment on an individual system—just make sure you have a NIC. The person who installs your DSL will test the DSL line, install the DSL modem, connect it to your system, and verify that it all works. The one issue you may run into with DSL is something called **Point-to-Point Protocol over Ethernet (PPPoE)**.

The first generation of DSL providers used a **bridged connection;** once the DSL line was running it was the same as if you snapped an Ethernet cable into your NIC. You were on the network. Those were good days for DSL. You just plugged your DSL modem into your NIC and, assuming your IP settings were whatever the DSL folks told you to use, you were running.

The DSL providers didn't like that too much. There was no control—no way to monitor who was using the DSL modem. As a result, the DSL folks started to use PPPoE, a protocol that was originally designed to encapsulate PPP frames into Ethernet frames. The DSL people adopted it to make stronger controls over your DSL con-nection. In particular, you could no longer simply connect; you now had to log on with an account and a password to make the DSL connection. PPPoE is now predominant on DSL. If you get a DSL line, your operating system has software to enable you to log onto your DSL network. Most SOHO rout-ers come with built-in PPPoE support, enabling you to enter your user name and password into the router itself (Figure 14.26).

• **Figure 14.24** DSL line into equipment room

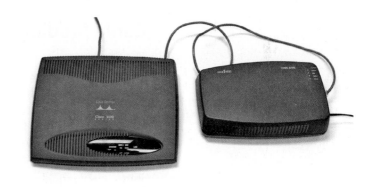

• **Figure 14.25** DSL connection

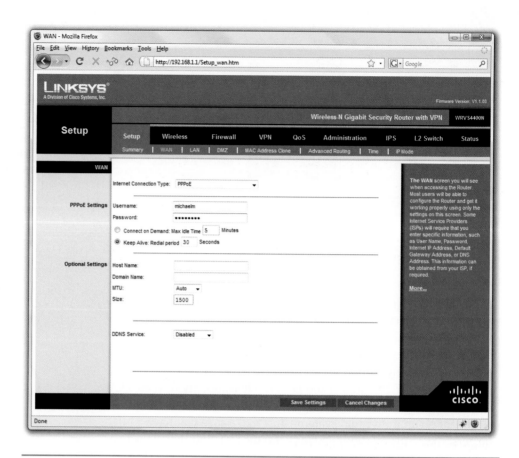

• **Figure 14.26**   PPPoE settings in SOHO router

Cable Modems

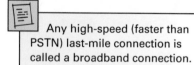

Any high-speed (faster than PSTN) last-mile connection is called a broadband connection.

The first big competition for ADSL came from the cable companies. Almost every house in America has a coax cable running into it for cable TV. In a moment of genius, the cable industry realized that if it could put the Home Shopping Network and the History Channel into every home, why not provide Internet access? The entire infrastructure of the cabling industry had to undergo some major changes to deal with issues like bidirectional communication, but cable modem service is now common in the United States. Cable modems are as common as cable TV boxes.

The single most impressive aspect of cable modems is their phenomenal top speeds. These speeds vary from cable company to cable company, but most advertise speeds in the (are you sitting down?) *10 to 27 megabits per second* range. Most cable modems provide a throughput speed of 1 to 10 Mbps downloading and 500 Kbps to 1 Mbps uploading—there is tremendous variance among different providers.

A cable modem installation consists of a cable modem connected to a cable outlet. The cable modem gets its own cable outlet, separate from the one that goes to the television. It's the same cable line, just split from the main line as if you were adding a second cable outlet for another television. As with ADSL, cable modems connect to PCs using a standard NIC (Figure 14.27).

Cable modems connect using coax cable to a head end, similar to a telephone company's central office. Head ends in turn connect to the cable company's network. This network uses a unique protocol called **Data Over Cable Service Interface Specification (DOCSIS)**. Most recently, the specification was revised (DOCSIS 3.0) to significantly increase transmissions speeds (this time both upstream and downstream) and introduce support for Internet Protocol version 6 (IPv6).

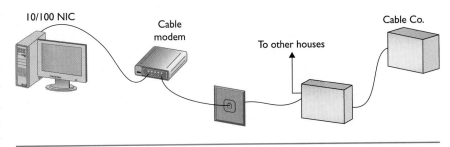

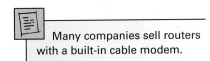

• **Figure 14.27** Cable modem

It's hard to tell a cable modem from a DSL modem. The only difference, other than the fact that one will have "cable modem" printed on it while the other will say "DSL modem," is that the cable modem has a coax and an RJ-45 connecter while the DSL modem has an RJ-11 and an RJ-45 connector.

Cable modems have proven themselves to be reliable and fast and have surpassed DSL as the broadband connection of choice in homes. Cable companies are also aggressively marketing to business customers with high-speed packages, making cable a viable option for businesses.

> Many companies sell routers with a built-in cable modem.

Satellite

Living in the countryside may have its charms, but getting high-speed Internet access is tough. For those too far away to get anything else, satellite may be your only option. Satellite access comes in two types: one-way and two-way. *One-way* means that you download from satellite but you must use a PSTN connection for uploads. *Two-way* means the satellite service handles both the uploading and downloading.

Satellite isn't as fast as DSL or cable modems, but it's still faster than PSTN. Both one-way and two-way satellite connections provide around 500 Kbps download and 50 Kbps upload. Satellite requires a small satellite antenna, identical to the ones used for satellite television. This antenna connects to a satellite modem, which in turn connects to your PC or your network (Figure 14.28).

> Neither cable modems nor satellites use PPP, PPPoE, or anything else that begins with three Ps.

Wireless

Wireless is a big topic for the CompTIA Network+ exam and I've saved an entire chapter (Chapter 16) just to discuss the topic. For now, it's important to appreciate that there are two types of wireless service that people may use for Internet connections: mobile data services (provided by cell phone companies) and 802.11.

Mobile data services have names like GSM, GRPS, EDGE, and HSPDA (there are many more standards). These services use the cellular telephone network to provide access. Mostly used with cell phones and smart phones, most mobile data services have wireless NICs you can use on laptops and desktop computers (Figure 14.29).

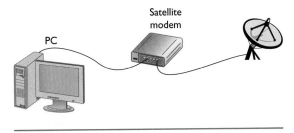

• **Figure 14.28** Satellite connection

802.11 is the main wireless standard, the one used in buildings and installed in just about every laptop. 802.11 isn't a common WAN solution, but is sometimes used in areas where alternatives are not available.

Fiber

DSL was the first popular last-mile WAN option but over the years cable modems have taken the lead. In an attempt to regain market share, telephone providers are now rolling out fiber-to-the-home/fiber-to-the-premises options that are giving the cable companies a scare. In the United States, two companies, AT&T (U-verse) and Verizon (FiOS) are offering very attractive ISP, television, and phone services at speeds that will eventually increase past 100 Mbps. These services are quickly gaining in popularity and giving cable companies a run for the money.

• Figure 14.29 Mobile wireless NIC

Which Connection?

With so many connection options for homes and small offices, making a decision is often a challenge. Your first question is availability: which services are available in your area? The second question is, how much bandwidth do you need? This is a question of great argument. Most services will be more than glad to increase service levels if you find that a certain level is too slow. I usually advise clients to start with a relatively slow level, and then increase if necessary. After all, it's hard to go slower once you've tasted the higher speeds, but relatively painless to go faster!

Try This!

Going Connection Shopping

You've already checked on the availability of DSL and ISDN in your neighborhood, but now you have more choices! Try this! Do you have cable or satellite available? A great Web site to start your search is www.dslreports.com. It has a handy search feature that helps you determine the types of service and the costs for DSL, cable, and other services. Which one makes sense for you?

■ Using Remote Access

Because most businesses are no longer limited to a simple little shop like you would find in a Dickens novel, there is a great need for people to be able to access files and resources over a great distance. Enter remote access. **Remote access** uses WAN and LAN connections to enable a computer user to log onto a network from the other side of a city, a state, or even the globe. As people travel, information has to remain accessible. Remote access enables users to connect a server at the business location and log into the network as if they were in the same building as the company. The only problem with remote access is that there are so many ways to do it! The six most common forms of remote access are as follows:

- **Dial-up to the Internet**   Using a dial-up connection to connect to your ISP

- **Private dial-up**   Using a dial-up connection to connect to your private network

- **Virtual private network** Using an Internet connection to connect to a private network
- **Dedicated connection** Using a non-dial-up connection to another private network or the Internet
- **Remote terminal** Using a terminal emulation program to connect to another computer
- **VoIP** Voice over IP

In this section we look at the issues related to configuring these six types of connections. After seeing how to configure these types of remote connections, we move into observing some security issues common to every type of remote connections.

Extranet is one of those terms that you'll see more in books than in the day-to-day workings of networks and network techs. So, what is an extranet? Whenever you allow authorized remote users to access some part of your private network, you have created an extranet.

Dial-Up to the Internet

Dialing up to the Internet is the oldest and cheapest method to connect to the Internet and is still somewhat common. Even with broadband and wireless so prevalent, every self-respecting network tech (or maybe just old network techs like me) keeps a dial-up account as a backup. You buy a dial-up account from an ISP (many wireless and broadband ISPs give free dial-up— just ask). All operating systems come with dial-up support programs, but you'll need to provide:

- A modem (most operating systems check for a modem before setting up a dial-up connection)
- The telephone number to dial (provided to you by the ISP)
- User name and password (provided to you by the ISP)
- Type of connection (dial-up always uses PPP)
- IP information (provided to you by the ISP—usually just DHCP)

Every operating system comes with the software to help you set up a dial-up connection. In Windows Vista you go to the **Set up a dial-up connection** option in the Network and Sharing Center (Figure 14.30). Whatever the name, this tool is what you use to create dial-up connections.

Private Dial-Up

A private dial-up connection connects a remote system to a private network via a dial-up connection. Private dial-up does not use the Internet! Private dial-up requires two systems. One system acts as a **remote access server (RAS)**. The other system is the client running a connection tool (usually the same tool you just saw in the previous section).

In Windows a RAS is a server running Remote Access Service (RAS) dedicated to handling users who are not directly connected to a LAN but who need to access file and print services on the LAN from a remote location. For example, when a user dials into a network from home using an analog modem connection, she is dialing into a RAS. Once the user is authenticated, she can access shared drives and printers as if her computer were physically connected to the office LAN.

When you run the Microsoft product Remote Access *Service* on a server, you turn that server into a remote access *server*.

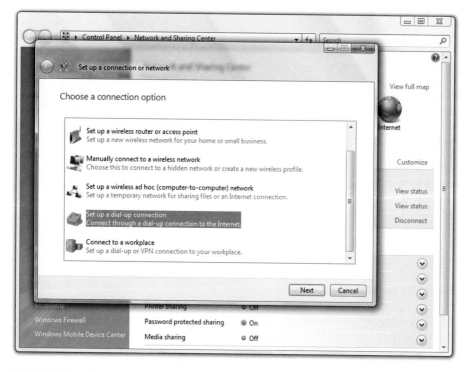

You must set up a server in your LAN as a RAS server. That RAS server, which must have at least one modem, accepts incoming calls and handles password authentication. RAS servers use all the standard authentication methods (PAP, CHAP, EAP, 802.1X, and so on) and have separate sets of permissions for dial-in users and local users. You must also configure the RAS to set the dial-in user's rights and permissions. Configuring a RAS system is outside the scope of this book, because each one is different, but it's something you must do to get RAS to work correctly (Figure 14.31).

Creating the client side of a private dial-up connection is identical to setting up a dial-up connection to the Internet. The only difference is that instead of

● **Figure 14.30**   Dial-up on Windows Vista

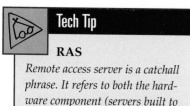

Tech Tip

RAS

Remote access server is a catchall phrase. It refers to both the hardware component (servers built to handle the unique stresses of a large number of clients calling in) and the software component of a remote access solution.

Most techs call RAS "razz," rather than use the initials, "R-A-S." This creates a seemingly redundant phrase used to describe a system running RAS: "RAS server." This helps distinguish servers from clients and makes geeks happier.

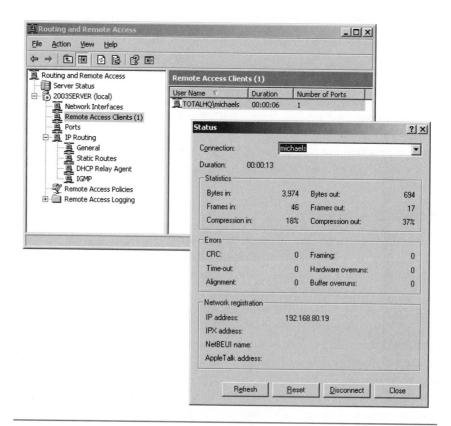

● **Figure 14.31**   Windows RAS in action

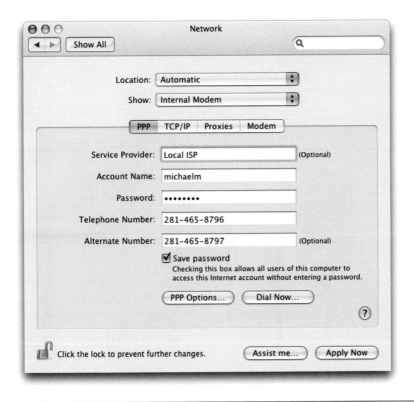

• **Figure 14.32**   Dial-up on Macintosh OS X

having an ISP tell you what IP settings, account name, and password to use, the person who sets up the RAS server tells you this information (Figure 14.32).

VPNs

A VPN enables you to connect through a tunnel from a local computer to a remote network securely, as you'll recall from the in-depth discussion in Chapter 12. Refer back to that chapter for the details.

Dedicated Connection

Dedicated connections are remote connections that are never disconnected. Dedicated connections can be broken into two groups: dedicated private connections between two locations, and dedicated connections to the Internet. Dedicated private connections manifest themselves as two locations interconnected by a (usually high-speed) connection such as a T1 line (Figure 14.33).

Each end of the T1 line goes into a router (after going through a CSU/DSU, of course!). Note that this connection does not use the Internet in any way—it is not a VPN connection. Dedicated connections of this type are expensive and are only used by organizations that need the high bandwidth and high security these connections provide. These connections are invisible to the individual computers on each network. There is no special remote connection configuration of the individual systems, although there may be

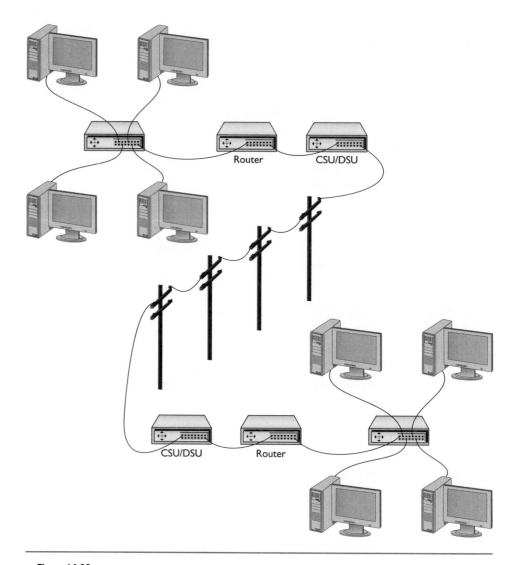

• **Figure 14.33**   Dedicated private connection

some configuration of DHCP, DNS, and WINS servers to insure that the network runs optimally.

Dedicated connections to the Internet are common today. Cable modems and DSL have made dedicated connections to the Internet inexpensive and very popular. In most cases there is nothing to configure in these dedicated connections, but many cable and DSL providers give you a CD-ROM that installs different items, such as testing software, PPPoE login support, and little extras like e-mail clients and software firewalls. Personally, I prefer to not use these (they tend to add a lot of stuff you don't need) and instead use the operating system's tools or a hardware router. Figure 14.34 shows the DSL wizard built into Windows Vista. This program enables you to connect by entering your PPPoE information for your ADSL connection. Once started, these programs usually stay running in the system tray until your next reboot.

Remote Terminal

You can use a terminal emulation program to create a **remote terminal**, a connection on a faraway computer that enables you to control that computer as if you were sitting in front of it, logged in. Terminal emulation has been a part of TCP/IP from its earliest days, in the form of good-old Telnet. Because it dates from pre-GUI days, Telnet is a text-based utility; all modern operating systems are graphical, so there was a strong desire to come up with graphical remote terminal tools. Citrix Corporation made the first (arguably) popular (also arguably) terminal emulation products—the *WinFrame/MetaFrame* products (Figure 14.35).

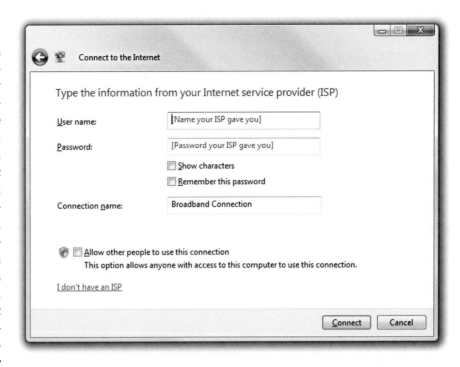

• **Figure 14.34** PPPoE connection

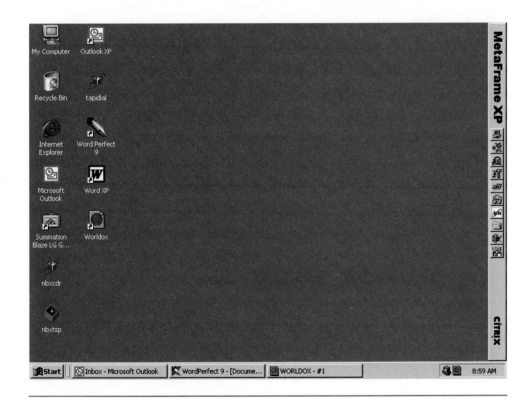

• **Figure 14.35** Citrix MetaFrame

All RDP applications run on port 3389 by default.

Remote terminal programs all require a server and a client. The server is the computer to be controlled. The client is the computer from which you do the controlling. Citrix created a standard called Independent Computing Architecture (ICA) that defined how terminal information was passed between the server and the client. Citrix made a breakthrough product—so powerful that Microsoft licensed the Citrix code and created its own product called Windows Terminal Services. Not wanting to pay Citrix any more money, Microsoft then created its own standard called Remote Desktop Protocol (RDP) and unveiled a new remote terminal called Remote Desktop Connection (RDC) starting with Windows XP. Figure 14.36 shows Windows Remote Desktop Connection running on a Windows Vista system, connecting to a Windows 2000 Server.

Unfortunately, Terminal Services only works in the Windows environment; however, a number of third parties make absolutely amazing terminal emulation programs that run on any operating system. The best of these is *VNC*, which stands for virtual network computing (Figure 14.37). VNC doesn't let you share folders or printers, because it is only a terminal emulator. But it runs on every operating system, is solid as a rock, and even runs from a Web browser. It works nicely in Secure Shell (SSH) tunnels for great security, plus it comes by default with every copy of Macintosh OS X and almost every Linux distro. Why bother sharing if you can literally be at the screen? Oh, and did I mention that VNC is free?

• **Figure 14.36**   RDC in action

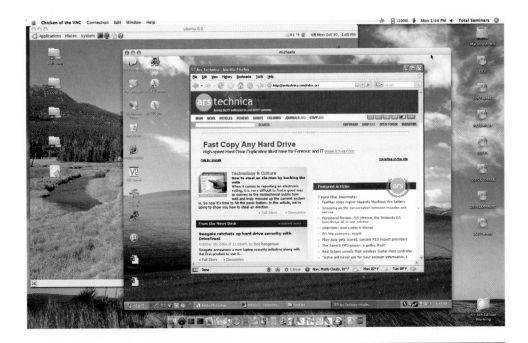

● **Figure 14.37**   VNC in action

VoIP

Voice over IP (VoIP) is simply using an IP network to transfer voice calls. VoIP's biggest benefit is that is uses an existing network you're already paying for (your Internet connection) to replace another network you're also paying for (PSTN lines). The technology to do VoIP isn't very challenging, but making a VoIP system that's standardized so that everyone can use it (and we can still contact those who choose to use PSTN) is quite a bit harder, requiring international standards. VoIP is still a very fractured world, but we're getting closer to universally adopted standards so that one day everyone can contact everyone else, no matter what brand of VoIP they use. To do this, there are three important standards you need to know: RTP, SIP, and H.323.

RTP

The **Real-time Transport Protocol (RTP)** is the bedrock of VoIP standards and is heavily adopted. RTP defines the type of packets used on the Internet to move voice or data from a server to clients. The vast majority of VoIP solutions available today use RTP.

SIP and H.323

Session Initiation Protocol (SIP) and **H.323** are competing VoIP standards that handle the initiation, setup, and delivery of VoIP sessions. VoIP takes a lot of special features that are not very common in many other Internet protocols. The biggest one is multicasting. Multicasting isn't in very high demand unless you want to show a number of people a video or want to make a conference call. SIP and H.323 both have methods for handling multicasting.

> SIP and H.323 both run on top of RTP. Most VoIP solutions are either SIP/RTP or H.323/RTP

Skype

Almost every VoIP solution available today uses SIP or H.323 running on top of RTP, with one huge exception: the very famous and incredibly popular Skype. Skype was unveiled in 2003 by Niklas Zennström, a Swedish computer guy famous for inventing the Kazaa peer-to-peer file-sharing system. Skype is completely different from and completely incompatible with any other type of VoIP solution: Skype doesn't use servers, instead using a peer-to-peer topology identical to the old Kazaa network. Skype calls are also encrypted using a proprietary encryption method. There isn't a standard method for VoIP encryption at this time, although a lot of smart people are working hard on the issue.

Chapter 14 Review

■ Chapter Summary

After reading this chapter and completing the exercises, you should understand the following about remote connections.

Describe WAN telephony technologies, such as SONET, T1, and T3

■ The majority of long-distance connections that make up the Internet use a unique type of signaling called SONET. The Internet backbone uses technologies designed more than 20 years ago to support telephone calls.

■ A multiplexer combines multiple circuits at one end of a connection into a single complex circuit on one wire, then splits the individual connections back out at the other end of the connection.

■ A local telephone exchange is a grouping of individual circuits served by a single multiplexer. Exchanges are housed in physical buildings called central offices.

■ Multiplexers used Frequency Division Multiplexing to keep individual calls separate.

■ Physically connecting two phones on a single circuit is called circuit switching.

■ Analog voice calls had to be converted to digital to accommodate travel over long distances. Central offices convert incoming analog calls to digital, transport the digital signal across trunk lines, and then convert the digital signal back to analog for delivery to the destination phone.

■ The analog connection from the central office to individual users is called the last mile.

■ Converting analog sound into 8-bit chunks 8000 times a second creates a 64-Kbps data stream known as DS0. Every analog voice call is converted to DS0 at the central office, where it is then multiplexed into larger circuits.

■ A device that converts an analog signal to digital is a modulator. A device that converts digital signals to analog is a demodulator. A device that does both is a modulator-demodulator, or modem.

■ T1 refers to a high-speed digital networking technology while T1 line refers to the physical shielded, two-pair cabling that connects the two ends of a T1 connection.

■ A T1 line uses two pairs of wires, one pair to send data and one pair to receive data.

■ A T1 line connects to a CSU/DSU at both ends. The CSU/DSU has a second connection connecting the phone company to a customer's equipment. You cannot have more than one CSU/DSU on a single T1 line because a T1 connection is point-to-point.

■ Many new routers have a CSU/DSU built into them.

■ T1 uses a signaling method called DS1. A DS1 frame is composed of one framing bit and 24 channels. Each DS1 channel holds a single 8-bit DS0, creating 193 bits per DS1 frame. (192 bits from the 24 channels of 8-bit DS0 data samples plus the one framing bit.)

■ DS1 frames are transmitted 8000 times/sec for a T1 data transfer speed of 1.544 Mbps. This is split into 24 64-Kbps DS0 channels.

■ The process of having frames carry a bit of every channel in every frame sent on a regular interval is called time division multiplexing.

■ Because an entire T1 bundle is expensive, many telephone companies allow you to purchase fractional T1 access, or just some of the individual channels.

■ A T3 line supports about 43 Mbps and consists of 672 individual DS0 channels. T3 lines are also known as DS3 lines and are used mainly by regional telephone companies and ISPs connecting to the Internet.

■ An E1 is the European counterpart to a T1, but carries 32 channels at 64 Kbps for a total of 2.048 Mbps—slightly faster than a T1.

■ E1 and T1 lines can be interconnected for international use.

■ An E3 carries 16 E1 lines (512 channels), for a total bandwidth of 34.368 Mbps—a little slower than an American T3.

- The CSU part of a CSU/DSU provides protection to the T1 or T3 lines from lightning strikes and other types of electrical interference. It also stores statistics and has loopback testing capability.

- The DSU part of a CSU/DSU supplies timing to each port, converts incoming signals to line code, and frames the format for transmission over the provided line.

- SONET is the primary standard for long-distance, high-speed, fiber-optic transmission in the United States. It is often implemented as a ring for redundancy. SDH is the European equivalent.

- SONET has extensive multiplexing capabilities, such as combining multiple DS1, DS3, and E1 signals into a single huge frame.

- The Optical Carrier (OC) specification defines speeds from 51.8 Mbps (OC-1) to 39.8 Gbps (OC-768) for fiber-optic cables used in networks conforming to the SONET standard.

- SONET uses the STS signal method where the STS payload carries data and the STS overhead carries signaling and protocol information.

- The number at the end of STS, such as STS-1 or STS-3, indicates signal speed. For example, STS-1 runs on an OC-1 line at 51.85 Mbps while STS-3 runs on an OC-3 line at 155.52 Mbps.

- Frame Relay is a packet-switching standard designed for and used primarily with T-carrier lines. Packets are switched quickly, but with no guarantee of data integrity. Frame Relay actually discards frames whenever there is network congestion; however, T-carrier digital lines using Frame Relay have very low error rates.

- Most SONET rings that move voice and data use ATM for packet switching. ATM integrates voice, video, and data on one connection using short, fixed-length cells to transfer information.

- ATM transfer speeds range from 155.52 to 622.08 Mbps and beyond.

- MPLS is a router feature that labels certain data to use a desired connection. For example, a network administrator can specify that all FTP traffic use the ATM connection rather than a secondary link that might be available on the network.

- There are two reasons to use a telephony WAN connection: to get your LAN on the Internet, and to make a private connection between two or more of your private LANs.

- The first step to getting a WAN Internet connection is to have a line physically installed by the telephone company. The second step is to have an ISP provide Internet access via the line.

- The telephone company runs your line to a demarc. The other side of the demarc is where you (or your ISP) installs a CSU/DSU and your router.

- WAN telephony carriers are more dependable than cheaper alternatives, such as cable modem service. A BERT test, available on every CSU/DSU, can verify your T-carrier connection.

Compare last-mile connections for connecting homes and businesses to the Internet

- Dedicated lines are always off the hook, providing a permanent connection, and do not have an associated phone number. Dial-up lines have phone numbers and must dial to make a connection, hanging up when done.

- PSTN, also called POTS, is a regular phone line designed to work only with analog sound and uses an RJ-11 connector.

- Telephone microphones convert analog sounds into electrical waveforms that cycle 2400 times a second. Each individual cycle is a baud. The number of bauds per second is the baud rate.

- PC communications were designed to transmit data in and out of a computer 8 bits at a time. A UART converts 8-bit-wide parallel bits from the computer into 1-bit-wide serial bits to send to a modem for digital-to-analog conversion. The analog signal can then be sent over phone lines. The process is reversed for incoming signals.

- PSTN phone lines sample analog data 2400 times a second. By modulating the 2400-baud signal multiple times each second, faster transmission speeds are reached—up to 57,600 bps (56 Kbps).

- Modems must query each other to determine a common protocol with which to communicate. The European CCITT developed the V standards, which define modem modulation speed and other features. The current standard is V.92.

- The conversion between analog and digital across the last mile resulted in reduced bandwidth. Making the last mile digital overcomes problems introduced by an analog last mile.

- ISDN lines provide a digital connection across the last mile, achieving dependable throughput of 64 Kbps over the same copper wires used by PSTN.

- ISDN consists of two channels: Bearer (B) and Delta (D) channels. B channels carry voice and data using standard DS0 channels. D channels carry setup and configuration information at 16 Kbps.

- A BRI setup includes two B channels and one D channel, providing a total throughput for voice and data of 128 Kbps.

- A PRI setup includes a full T1 line carrying 23 B channels for a total throughput for voice and data of 1472 Kbps (about 1.5 Mbps).

- A terminal adapter acts as the interface between a computer and the ISDN service.

- DSL provides a fully digital dedicated connection. Three versions of DSL are SDSL, ADSL, and VDSL.

- SDSL supports speeds up to 15 Mbps, but most ISPs only provide SDSL up to 9 Mbps. SDSL provides equal upload and download speeds.

- ADSL provides download speeds up to 15 Mbps and upload speeds up to 1 Mbps, though ISPs offer varying combinations of download/upload speeds.

- VDSL is the newest version of DSL and supports both download and upload speeds up to 100 Mbps. VDSL can also run on fiber-optic lines to increase distances.

- All versions of DSL are limited to a maximum distance of around 18,000 feet between a user's demarc and the central office. The central office houses a DSLAM connecting multiple customers to the Internet.

- Because DSL runs over normal POTS lines, it is necessary to filter out the DSL signal on the POTS line. This guarantees your POTS line will continue to work if the DSL fails.

- A DSL modem connects the telephone jack (with the DSL signal) to your computer. A DSL modem isn't a true modem and is more similar to an ISDN TA.

- RJ-11 connectors connect the telephone jack to the DSL modem while RJ-45 connectors connect the DSL modem to the computer's NIC.

- Early DSL providers used bridged connections, but these connections have been replaced by PPPoE so

that providers can monitor modem usage and require users to log in with a valid account before they gain Internet access.

- Cable Internet providers offer plans ranging in speeds up to 10 or even 27 Mbps. Download speeds are typically much faster than upload speeds.

- Cable modems use coaxial cable to connect to the head end and use regular CAT 5 or better cabling to connect to the PC. The head end connects to the cable company's network using the DOCSIS protocol.

- Satellite access is available as one-way or two-way. With a one-way connection, you download over the satellite connection but upload over PSTN. Two-way satellite service accommodates both downloads and uploads over the satellite connection.

- Satellite access tops out at around 500 Kbps for download and 50 Kbps for upload, making it slower than both DSL and cable. It is sometimes the only option for remote or geographically challenging areas.

- In an attempt to regain their share of the market from cable providers, some phone companies offering DSL are now offering fiber-to-the-home connections in the form of U-verse (AT&T) or FiOS (Verizon).

Discuss and implement various remote access connections

- Remote access allows users to log onto networks remotely, making files and network resources available to users across the city, state, or globe.

- Dialing into the Internet over an analog phone line and modem is the oldest and least expensive means of connecting to the Internet. Many techs keep a dial-up account as a backup.

- A private dial-up connection, which does not use the Internet, connects a remote system to a private network via a dial-up connection. This requires a remote access server on one end and a client running a connection tool at the other end.

- Dedicated connections are remote connections that never disconnect and can be categorized as either dedicated private connections between two locations or dedicated connections to the Internet.

- Dedicated private connections are usually connected by a high-speed line such as a T1. This direct dedicated connection does not use the Internet.

- Remote terminal emulation allows a user to take over a remote computer as if they were sitting in front of it, as opposed to simply accessing remote resources. WinFrame/MetaFrame (made by Citrix) is a popular terminal emulator.

- Microsoft's terminal emulator is called Remote Desktop Connection, which uses its own Remote Desktop Protocol. VNC is a cross-platform terminal emulator that comes with Macintosh OS X and many Linux distributions.

- VoIP uses an IP network to transfer voice calls. It depends on three standards: RTP, SIP, and H.323.

- RTP defines the type of packets used on the Internet to transfer voice or data between servers and clients. Most VoIP networks use RTP.

- SIP and H.323 both support multicasting on VoIP networks, allowing users to show a video to multiple people or hold conference calls.

■ Key Terms

Asymmetric DSL (ADSL) *(381)*
Asynchronous Transfer Mode (ATM) *(373)*
Basic Rate Interface (BRI) *(380)*
baud *(377)*
baud rate *(377)*
Bearer channel (B channel) *(380)*
Bit Error Rate Test (BERT) *(376)*
bridged connection *(383)*
CCITT *(378)*
central office *(365)*
Channel Service Unit/Digital Service Unit (CSU/DSU) *(369)*
circuit switching *(366)*
Data Over Cable Service Interface Specification (DOCSIS) *(385)*
dedicated line *(376)*
Delta channel (D channel) *(380)*
dial-up line *(377)*
Digital Subscriber Line (DSL) *(381)*
DS0 *(369)*
DS1 *(370)*
DSL Access Multiplexer (DSLAM) *(382)*
DSL modem *(382)*
E1 *(371)*
E3 *(371)*
fractional T1 access *(371)*
Frame Relay *(373)*
Frequency Division Multiplexing (FDM) *(366)*
H.323 *(393)*
Integrated Services Digital Network (ISDN) *(380)*
last mile *(367)*
modulator-demodulator (modem) *(377)*

multiplexer *(364)*
Multi-Protocol Label Switching (MPLS) *(374)*
network interface unit (NIU) *(377)*
Optical Carrier (OC) *(372)*
Plain Old Telephone Service (POTS) *(364)*
Point-to-Point Protocol over Ethernet (PPPoE) *(383)*
Primary Rate Interface (PRI) *(380)*
Public Switched Telephone Network (PSTN) *(377)*
Real-time Transport Protocol (RTP) *(393)*
remote access *(386)*
remote access server (RAS) *(387)*
remote terminal *(391)*
Session Initiation Protocol (SIP) *(393)*
Symmetric DSL (SDSL) *(381)*
Synchronous Digital Hierarchy (SDH) *(372)*
Synchronous Optical Network (SONET) *(372)*
Synchronous Transport Signal (STS) *(373)*
STS overhead *(373)*
STS payload *(373)*
T1 *(369)*
T1 line *(369)*
T3 line *(371)*
terminal adapter (TA) *(380)*
time division multiplexing *(370)*
Universal Asynchronous Receiver/Transmitter (UART) *(377)*
V standards *(378)*
V.92 standard *(379)*
Very High Bitrate DSL (VDSL) *(381)*
Voice over IP (VoIP) *(393)*

Key Term Quiz

Use the Key Terms list to complete the sentences that follow. Not all the terms will be used.

1. A(n) _____ line has a maximum throughput of 1.544 Mbps.

2. A(n) _____ is a device that converts signals between analog and digital.

3. It is the job of the _____ to convert between 8-bit-wide digital data and single-bit-wide digital data.

4. A(n) _____ signal is defined as a digital signal of 64 Kbps.

5. A(n) _____ combines individual circuits with hundreds of others, creating a complex circuit on a single wire.

6. _____ is the primary standard in the United States for long-distance, high-speed, fiber-optic transmission systems.

7. In the world of DSL, _____ provides equal upload and download speeds up to 15 Mbps.

8. _____ uses an IP network to transfer voice calls.

9. _____ lines consist of two digital channels over the same copper wire used by regular analog telephones.

10. _____ is a router feature that can help to optimize network traffic by labeling certain data to use a desired connection.

Multiple-Choice Quiz

1. When an analog sound is converted into 8-bit chunks 8000 times a second, this 64 kilobit per second data stream is created.

   A. DS0

   B. DS1

   C. E1

   D. T1

2. What exists at both ends of a T1 connection?

   A. A frame relay

   B. A CSU/DSU

   C. A digital trunk

   D. A multiplexer

3. This frame type consists of a single framing bit and 24 data channels, each holding an 8-bit DS0 sample, for a total of 193 bits.

   A. DS1

   B. T1

   C. T3

   D. SONET

4. Which line consists of 672 DS0 channels for a total throughput of 43 Mbps?

   A. T1

   B. T3

   C. E1

   D. E3

5. Which standard supports a throughput of up to 39.8 Gbps?

   A. ISDN

   B. VDSL

   C. SONET

   D. MPLS

6. If you purchase a T1 line in the United States, how will packets be switched? (Select two.)

   A. OC

   B. Frame Relay

   C. ATM

   D. BERT

7. What describes the problem with "the last mile"?

   A. The connection from a central office to a user's home is analog whereas the rest of the network is digital.

   B. Users must live within a mile of a central office in order to guarantee quality of service (QoS).

C. SONET connections are limited to a maximum distance of one mile, and connecting central offices via multiplexers is expensive and difficult to maintain.

D. Copper wires that carry analog telephone signals are limited to a maximum distance of one mile.

8. What terms describe a common telephone connection? (Select two.)

A. ISDN

B. POTS

C. Fractional T1

D. PSTN

9. What marks where the telephone company's responsibility ends and yours begins?

A. Multiplexer

B. Demarc

C. Primary Rate Interface

D. Bridges connection

10. The CCITT established which set of standards?

A. Optical Carrier (OC)

B. DSL (ADSL, SDSL, VDSL)

C. Data Over Cable Service Interface Specification (DOCSIS)

D. V standards

11. Which is the fastest ISDN connection?

A. BERT

B. BRI

C. PRI

D. ATM

12. Sinjay is 200 meters from his ISP's DSLAM. Which DSL version will provide him with up to 100 Mbps of both download and upload speed?

A. DS3

B. ADSL

C. SDSL

D. VDSL

13. Which protocol is used by cable companies?

A. MPLS

B. DOCSIS

C. PSTN

D. SIP

14. What is the benefit to using a satellite connection?

A. It offers speeds faster than both DSL and cable.

B. The upload and download speeds are always equal.

C. It is often available in remote locations where DSL and cable are not.

D. If offers better security than both DSL and cable.

15. Which protocols support multicasting on VoIP networks? (Select two.)

A. SIP

B. H.323

C. RTP

D. RAS

Essay Quiz

1. Early DSL providers used bridged connections, but now they tend to use PPPoE instead. What is the difference between these connection types and why do you think DSL providers switched?

2. Upon tracing your company's physical T1 line, you find it connected to a box. It appears as though the box has another connection going to your router. What is this box and what does it do?

3. Briefly describe the six types of remote connections that enable users to connect to remote networks.

Lab Projects

• Lab Project 14.1

Many companies, such as Vonage, offer VoIP solutions for home users to replace their analog telephones. Other companies, such as 3Com, offer VoIP solutions for businesses. Research three VoIP solutions and compare them based on the following criteria: Are they targeting home users or businesses? Is long distance included? What is the startup cost? What is the monthly fee? What uptime guarantee is offered? Can emergency calls (911) be made if the network goes down?

• Lab Project 14.2

How much would a T1 cost you? How about a T3? Make a chart listing the provider from whom you could purchase a T1, fractional T1, or T3 and list the services included along with the costs. How do they compare to cable or DSL connections offered in your area?

Network Troubleshooting

"The trouble with doing something right the first time is that nobody appreciates how difficult it was."

—WALT WEST

In this chapter, you will learn how to

- **Describe appropriate troubleshooting tools and their functions**
- **Analyze and discuss the troubleshooting process**
- **Tackle a variety of troubleshooting scenarios**

Have you ever seen a tech walk up to a network and seem to know all the answers, effortlessly typing in a few commands and magically making the system or network work? I've always been intrigued by how they do this. Observing such techs over the years, I've noticed that they tend to follow the same steps for similar problems—looking in the same places, typing the same commands, and so on. When someone performs a task the same way every time, I figure they're probably following a plan. They understand what tools they have to work with, and they know where to start and what to do second and third and fourth until they find the problem. This chapter's lofty goal is to consolidate my observations on how these "übertechs" fix networks. We'll look at the primary troubleshooting tools, formulate a troubleshooting process, and learn where to look for different sorts of problems. At the end of the chapter, we'll apply this knowledge to some common troubleshooting scenarios.

Test Specific

■ Troubleshooting Tools

While working through the process of finding the cause of a problem, you sometimes need tools. These are the software and hardware tools that provide information about your network and enact repairs. We covered a number of tools already: hardware tools like cable testers and crimpers plus software utilities like PING and TRACERT. The trick is knowing when and how to use these tools to solve your network problems.

Almost every new networking person I teach will at some point ask me: "What tools do I need to buy?" My answer shocks them: "None. Don't buy a thing." It's not so much that you don't need tools but more that different networking jobs require wildly different tools. Plenty of network techs never crimp a cable. An equal number never open a system. Some techs do nothing all day but pull cable. The tools you need are defined by your job. You'll know by the end of the first day what you'll need.

This answer is especially true with software tools. Almost all the network problems I encounter in established networks don't require me to use any tools other than the classic ones provided by the operating system. I've fixed more network problems with PING than with any other single tool. As you gain skill in this area you'll find yourself pounded by vendors trying to sell you the latest, greatest networking diagnostic tools. You may like these tools. All I can say is that I've never needed a software diagnostics tool that I had to purchase.

 No matter what the problem, always consider the safety of your data first. Ask yourself this question before you perform any troubleshooting action: "Can what I'm about to do potentially damage my data?"

Hardware Tools

In multiple chapters in this book you've read about a few hardware tools used when configuring a network. These **hardware tools** include cable testers, TDRs, OTDRs, certifiers, voltage event recorders, protocol analyzers, cable strippers, multimeters, tone probes/generators, butt sets, and punchdown tools. Some of these tools can also be used in troubleshooting scenarios to help you eliminate or narrow down the possible causes of certain problems. Let's review the tools as listed in the *CompTIA Network+ Exam Objectives*.

 Read this section! The CompTIA Network+ exam is filled with repair scenarios and you must know what every tool does and when to use it.

Cable Testers, TDRs, and OTDRs

The vast majority of cabling problems occur when the network is first installed or when a change is made. Once a cable has been made, installed, and tested, the chances of it failing are pretty small compared to all of the other network problems that might take place. Imagine what happens when you can't connect to a resource and ask yourself, "Is there a chance the cable is bad?" Broken cables don't make intermittent problems, and they don't slow down data. They make permanent disconnects.

Network techs define a "broken" cable in numerous ways. First, a broken cable might have an *open circuit*, where one or more of the wires in a cable simply don't connect from one end of the cable to the other. The signal lacks *continuity*. Second, a cable might have a *short*, where one or more of the

The CompTIA Network+ objectives use the term "open impedance mismatch (echo)" at the time of this writing. Imagine that there's a comma after "open" so you know you're looking at two different types of broken cable issues.

wires in a cable connect to another wire in the cable. (Within a normal cable, none of the wires connects to another wire.) Third, a cable might have a *wire map problem*, where one or more of the wires in a cable don't connect to the proper location on the jack or plug. This can be caused by improperly crimping a cable, for example. Fourth, the cable might experience *crosstalk*, where the electrical signal bleeds from one wire pair to another, creating interference. Fifth, a broken cable might pick up *noise*, spurious signals usually caused by faulty hardware or poorly crimped jacks. Finally, a broken cable might have *impedance mismatch*. Impedance is the natural electrical resistance of a cable. When cables of different types—think thickness, composition of the metal, and so on—connect and the flow of electrons is not uniform, this can cause a unique type of electrical noise, called an *echo*.

Network technicians use three different devices to deal with broken cables. **Cable testers** can tell you if there's a continuity problem or if a wire map isn't correct (Figure 15.1). Time domain reflectometers (TDRs) and optical time domain reflectometers (OTDRs) can tell you where a break is on the cable (Figure 15.2). A TDR works with copper cables and an OTDR works with fiber optics, but otherwise they share the same function. If a problem shows itself as a disconnect and you've first checked easier issues that would manifest as disconnects, such as loss of permissions, an unplugged cable, or a server shut off, then think about using these tools.

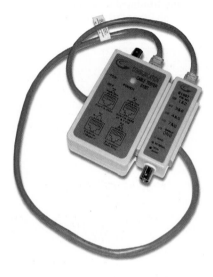

• **Figure 15.1**   Typical cable tester

Certifiers

Certifiers test a cable to ensure that it can handle its rated amount of capacity. When a cable is not broken but it's not moving data the way it should, you turn to a certifier. Look for problems that cause a cable to underperform. A bad installation might increase crosstalk, attenuation, or interference. A certifier can pick up an impedance mismatch as well. Most of these problems show up at installation, but it's never a bad idea to run a certifier to eliminate cabling as a problem. Don't use a certifier for disconnects, only slowdowns. Last, all certifiers need some kind of loopback on the other end of the cable run.

Voltage Event Recorder/Temperature Monitor

Networks need the proper temperature and adequate power, but most network techs tend to view these issues as outside of the normal places to look for problems. That's too bad, because both heat and power problems invariably manifest themselves as intermittent problems. Look for problems that might point to heat or power issues: server rooms that get too hot at certain times of the day, switches that fail whenever an air conditioning system kicks on, and so on. You can use a **voltage event recorder** and a **temperature monitor** to monitor server rooms over time to detect and record issues with electricity or heat, respectively. They're great for those "something happened last night" types of issues.

• **Figure 15.2**   An EXFO AXS-100 OTDR (photo courtesy of EXFO)

Protocol Analyzers

Protocol analyzers monitor the different protocols running at different layers on the network. A good protocol analyzer will give you Application, Session, Network, and Data Link layer information on every frame going through your network. Even though the CompTIA Network+ exam places protocol analyzers in a hardware category, they aren't necessarily always hardware. Some of the best and most useful protocol analyzers are software.

Use a protocol analyzer when being able to see the data on the network will help you answer a question. Is something trying to start a session and not getting an answer? Maybe a DNS server isn't responding. Is some computer on the network placing confusing information on the network? Is a rogue DHCP server sending out responses to DHCP requests? In the same vein, a protocol analyzer helps you determine slowdowns on a network by giving you an idea of excess or unexpected traffic (see the "Packet Sniffer" subsection under "Software Tools" later in this chapter).

Cable Strippers/Snips

A **cable stripper** or **snip** (Figure 15.3) enables you to make UTP cables. Even though the CompTIA Network+ competencies don't mention crimpers, don't forget you'll need them too. You don't need these tools to punch down 66- or 110-blocks. You would use a punchdown tool for that.

• **Figure 15.3** A cable stripping and crimping tool

Multimeters

Multimeters test voltage (both AC and DC), resistance, and continuity. They are the unsung heroes of cabling infrastructures because no other tool can tell you how much voltage is on a line. They are also a great fallback for continuity testing when you don't have a cable tester handy.

Tone Probes and Tone Generators

Tone probes and their partners, **tone generators**, have only one job: to help you locate a particular cable. You'll never use a tone probe without a tone generator.

Butt Sets

Butt sets are the telephone person's best friend. Use a butt set to tap into a 66- or 110-block to see if a particular line is working.

Punchdown Tools

Punchdown tools (Figure 15.4) put UTP wires into 66- and 110-blocks. The only time you would use a punchdown tool in a diagnostic environment is a quick repunch of a connection to make sure all the contacts are properly set.

Try This!

Shopping Spree
As more and more people have networks installed in their homes, the big box hardware stores stock an increasing number of network-specific tools. Everybody loves shopping, right? So try this! Go to your local hardware store—big box, like Home Depot or Lowes, if there's one near you—and check out their tools. What do they offer? Write down prices and features and compare with what your classmates found.

 CompTIA and many techs refer to the probe as a toner probe rather than a tone probe or simply a probe. Don't be surprised on the exam. You always need both a probe and a tone generator to use this tool properly.

● **Figure 15.4**   A punchdown tool in action

The CompTIA Network+ exam tests your ability to recognize the output from all of the built-in tools. Take some time to memorize example outputs on all of these tools.

Software Tools

Make the CompTIA Network+ exam (and real life) easier by separating your software tools into two groups: those that come built into every operating system and those that are third-party tools. Typical built-in tools are TRACERT/TRACEROUTE, IPCONFIG/IFCONFIG, PING, ARP PING, NSLOOKUP/DIG, HOSTNAME, ROUTE, NBTSTAT, and NETSTAT. Third-party tools fall into the categories of packet sniffers and port scanners.

TRACERT/TRACEROUTE

TRACEROUTE (Windows calls it TRACERT) is used to trace all of the routers between two points. Use TRACEROUTE when you have problems reaching a remote system, to diagnose where the problem lies. If a TRACEROUTE stops at a certain router, you know the problem is either the next router or the connections between them. TRACEROUTE isn't perfect, because many routers block TRACEROUTE packets. Try PATHPING when you're not sure whether TRACEROUTE is working properly.

Here's sample TRACEROUTE output:

```
Tracing route to adsl-208-190-121-38.dsl.hstntx.swbell.net
[208.190.121.38] over a maximum of 30 hops:

  1     1 ms    <1 ms     1 ms   Router.totalhome
[192.168.4.1]
  2    38 ms    41 ms    70 ms   adsl-208-190-121-
38.dsl.hstntx.swbell.net [208.190.121.38]
```

Playing Along

This section contains many command-line tools that you've seen earlier in the book in various places. Now is a great time to refresh your memory about how each one works, so try this! After I review each command, run it yourself. Then type `help` followed by the command to see the available switches for that command. Run some to see what they do. It's more fun to do it than just to read about it; plus, it'll help solidify the knowledge you need to master.

IPCONFIG/IFCONFIG

IPCONFIG (Windows) and **IFCONFIG** (everyone else) tells you anything you want to know about a particular computer's IP settings. Make sure you know that typing `ipconfig` alone only gives basic information. Typing `ipconfig /all` gives detailed information (like DNS servers and MAC addresses).

Here's sample IPCONFIG output:

```
Ethernet adapter Main:

   Connection-specific DNS Suffix  . :
   IPv6 Address. . . . . . . . . . . : 2001:470:bf88:1:fc2d:aeb2:99d2:e2b4
   Temporary IPv6 Address. . . . . . : 2001:470:bf88:1:5e4:c1ef:7b30:ddd6
   Link-local IPv6 Address . . . . . : fe80::fc2d:aeb2:99d2:e2b4%8
   IPv4 Address. . . . . . . . . . . : 192.168.4.27
   Subnet Mask . . . . . . . . . . . : 255.255.255.0
   Default Gateway . . . . . . . . . : fe80::223:4ff:fe8c:b720%8
                                       192.168.4.1

Tunnel adapter Local Area Connection* 6:

   Media State . . . . . . . . . . . : Media disconnected
   Connection-specific DNS Suffix  . :
```

And here's sample IFCONFIG output:

```
eth0      Link encap:Ethernet  HWaddr 00:02:b3:8a:7d:ae
          inet addr:192.168.4.19  Bcast:192.168.4.255  Mask:255.255.255.0
          inet6 addr: 2001:470:bf88:1:202:b3ff:fe8a:7dae/64 Scope:Global
          inet6 addr: fe80::202:b3ff:fe8a:7dae/64 Scope:Link
          UP BROADCAST RUNNING MULTICAST  MTU:1500  Metric:1
          RX packets:2206320 errors:0 dropped:0 overruns:0 frame:0
          TX packets:925034 errors:0 dropped:0 overruns:0 carrier:0
          collisions:0 txqueuelen:1000
          RX bytes:292522698 (292.5 MB)  TX bytes:132985596 (132.9 MB)

lo        Link encap:Local Loopback
          inet addr:127.0.0.1  Mask:255.0.0.0
          inet6 addr: ::1/128 Scope:Host
          UP LOOPBACK RUNNING  MTU:16436  Metric:1
          RX packets:15414 errors:0 dropped:0 overruns:0 frame:0
          TX packets:15414 errors:0 dropped:0 overruns:0 carrier:0
          collisions:0 txqueuelen:0
          RX bytes:1006671 (1.0 MB)  TX bytes:1006671 (1.0 MB)
```

PING and ARP PING

PING uses Internet Message Control Protocol (ICMP) packets to query by IP or by name, and works across routers, so it's usually the first tool used to check if a system is reachable. Unfortunately, many devices block ICMP packets, so a failed PING doesn't always point to an off line system.

If PING doesn't work you can try an **ARP PING**, which uses Address Resolution Protocol (ARP) packets instead of ICMP. The only downside to ARP is that ARPs do not cross routers, so you can only use it within a broadcast domain. Windows does not have ARP PING. UNIX and UNIX-like systems use the ARPING utility to perform an ARP PING.

Here's sample PING output:

```
Pinging 192.168.4.19 with 32 bytes of data:
Reply from 192.168.4.19: bytes=32 time<1ms TTL=64
Reply from 192.168.4.19: bytes=32 time<1ms TTL=64
Reply from 192.168.4.19: bytes=32 time<1ms TTL=64
Reply from 192.168.4.19: bytes=32 time<1ms TTL=64

Ping statistics for 192.168.4.19:
    Packets: Sent = 4, Received = 4, Lost = 0 (0% loss),
Approximate round trip times in milli-seconds:
    Minimum = 0ms, Maximum = 0ms, Average = 0ms
```

Next is sample ARPING output:

```
ARPING 192.168.4.27 from 192.168.4.19 eth0
Unicast reply from 192.168.4.27 [00:1D:60:DD:92:C6]   0.875ms
Unicast reply from 192.168.4.27 [00:1D:60:DD:92:C6]   0.897ms
Unicast reply from 192.168.4.27 [00:1D:60:DD:92:C6]   0.924ms
Unicast reply from 192.168.4.27 [00:1D:60:DD:92:C6]   0.977ms
```

The PING command has the word "pinging" in the output. The ARPING command has the word "ARPING." Don't assume that the CompTIA Network+ exam will include those words in its sample outputs.

NSLOOKUP/DIG

NSLOOKUP (all operating systems) and **DIG** (everyone but Windows) are used to diagnose DNS problems. These are very powerful tools, but the CompTIA Network+ exam won't ask you more than basic questions, such as how to use them to see if a DNS server is working. NSLOOKUP is a poor tool that most everyone considers obsolete. DIG is far more powerful. The DIG example below shows the output of this command:

```
dig mx totalsem.com
```

This command says, "Show me all the MX records for the totalsem.com domain."

Here's the output for that DIG command:

```
; <<>> DiG 9.5.0-P2 <<>> mx totalsem.com
;; global options:  printcmd
;; Got answer:
;; ->>HEADER<<- opcode: QUERY, status: NOERROR, id: 6070
;; flags: qr rd ra; QUERY: 1, ANSWER: 3, AUTHORITY: 0, ADDITIONAL: 1
;; QUESTION SECTION:
;totalsem.com.                    IN     MX
;; ANSWER SECTION:
totalsem.com.          86400  IN     MX      10
mx1c1.megamailservers.com.
```

```
totalsem.com.              86400   IN   MX     100
mx2c1.megamailservers.com.
totalsem.com.              86400   IN   MX     110
mx3c1.megamailservers.com.
```

Running the networking commands several times will help you memorize the functions of the commands as well as the syntax. The CompTIA Network+ exam is big on the switches available for various commands, such as `ipconfig /all`.

HOSTNAME

HOSTNAME is the simplest of all the utilities shown here. When you run it, it returns with the host name of the computer you are on. Here's what it looked like when I ran it on my Windows 7 box:

```
C:\>
C:\>hostname
mike-win7beta
```

MTR

My Traceroute (MTR) is a dynamic (keeps running) equivalent to TRACEROUTE. MTR is not available on Windows.

Here's a sample of MTR output:

```
                        My traceroute  [v0.73]
totaltest (0.0.0.0)
Keys:  Help   Display mode   Restart statistics   Order of fields   quit
                                Packets              Pings
Host                            Loss%   Snt   Last   Avg  Best  Wrst StDev
1. Router.totalhome             0.0%     5    0.8   0.8   0.7   0.9   0.1
2. adsl-208-190-121-38.dsl.hstntx.s  0.0%  4   85.7  90.7  69.5 119.2  20.8
```

ROUTE

The **ROUTE** command gives you the capability to display and edit the local system's routing table. To show the routing table, just type `route print`.

Here's a sample of ROUTE PRINT output:

```
===========================================================================
Interface List
  8 ...00 1d 60 dd 92 c6 ...... Marvell 88E8056 PCI-E Ethernet Controller
  1 ........................ Software Loopback Interface 1
===========================================================================
IPv4 Route Table
===========================================================================
Active Routes:
Network Destination        Netmask          Gateway       Interface  Metric
          0.0.0.0          0.0.0.0      192.168.4.1    192.168.4.27      10
        127.0.0.0        255.0.0.0         On-link        127.0.0.1     306
        127.0.0.1  255.255.255.255         On-link        127.0.0.1     306
  127.255.255.255  255.255.255.255         On-link        127.0.0.1     306
      169.254.0.0      255.255.0.0         On-link     192.168.4.27     286
  169.254.214.185  255.255.255.255         On-link  169.254.214.185     276
  169.254.255.255  255.255.255.255         On-link     192.168.4.27     266
      192.168.4.0    255.255.255.0         On-link     192.168.4.27     266
     192.168.4.27  255.255.255.255         On-link     192.168.4.27     266
    192.168.4.255  255.255.255.255         On-link     192.168.4.27     266
        224.0.0.0        240.0.0.0         On-link        127.0.0.1     306
        224.0.0.0        240.0.0.0         On-link  169.254.214.185     276
```

Chapter 15: Network Troubleshooting

```
      224.0.0.0        240.0.0.0        On-link      192.168.4.27    266
255.255.255.255  255.255.255.255        On-link         127.0.0.1    306
255.255.255.255  255.255.255.255        On-link   169.254.214.185    276
255.255.255.255  255.255.255.255        On-link      192.168.4.27    266
===========================================================================
Persistent Routes:
  None
```

NBTSTAT

NBTSTAT is a Windows-only program that can best be described as a command-line equivalent to Window's My Network Places or Network icon. NBTSTAT must run using a switch. The most useful switch is –n, which shows the local NetBIOS names. NBTSTAT is in all versions of Windows through Vista. NBTSTAT is a handy way to see what systems are running on your Windows network. Any systems running SAMBA will also appear here.

Here's an example of running `nbtstat` –n from the command prompt:

```
Main:
Node IpAddress: [192.168.4.27] Scope Id: []
                 NetBIOS Local Name Table

         Name               Type          Status
    ---------------------------------------------------

     MIKESPC          <00>  UNIQUE      Registered
     TOTALHOME        <00>  GROUP       Registered
     MIKESPC          <20>  UNIQUE      Registered
     TOTALHOME        <1E>  GROUP       Registered
```

NETSTAT

NETSTAT is a very handy tool that displays information on the current state of all of your running IP processes. It shows what sessions are active and can also provide statistics based on ports or protocols (TCP, UDP, and so on). Typing `netstat` by itself only shows current sessions. Typing `netstat` –r shows the routing table (virtually identical to ROUTE PRINT). If you want to know about your current sessions, NETSTAT is the tool to use.

Here's sample NETSTAT output:

```
Active Connections

   Proto  Local Address          Foreign Address         State
   TCP    127.0.0.1:27015        MikesPC:51090           ESTABLISHED
   TCP    127.0.0.1:51090        MikesPC:27015           ESTABLISHED
   TCP    127.0.0.1:52500        MikesPC:52501           ESTABLISHED
   TCP    192.168.4.27:54731     72-165-61-141:27039     CLOSE_WAIT
   TCP    192.168.4.27:55080     63-246-140-18:http      CLOSE_WAIT
   TCP    192.168.4.27:56126     acd4129913:https        ESTABLISHED
   TCP    192.168.4.27:62727     TOTALTEST:ssh           ESTABLISHED
   TCP    192.168.4.27:63325     65.54.165.136:https     TIME_WAIT
   TCP    192.168.4.27:63968     209.8.115.129:http      ESTABLISHED
```

Packet Sniffer

Packet sniffer, protocol analyzer, or packet analyzer: all of these names are used to define a tool that intercepts and logs network packets. You have many choices when it comes to packet sniffers. Some sniffers come as programs you run on a computer, while others manifest as dedicated hardware devices. Arguably, the most popular (and also mentioned in the CompTIA Network+ objectives) is **Wireshark** (Figure 15.5). You've already seen Wireshark in the book, but here's a shot to jog your memory.

Port Scanners

A **port scanner** is a program that probes ports on another system, logging the state of the scanned ports. These tools are used to look for unintentionally opened ports that might make a system vulnerable to attack. As you might imagine, they also are used by hackers to break into systems. The most famous of all port scanners is probably the powerful and free NMAP. NMAP is designed to work on UNIX systems, so Windows folks tend to look for alternatives like Angry IP Scanner by Anton Keks (Figure 15.6).

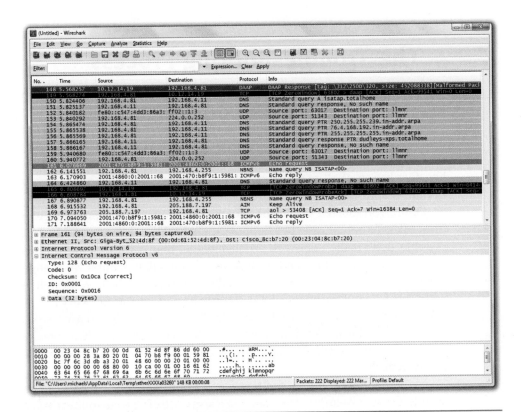

• **Figure 15.5**   Wireshark in action

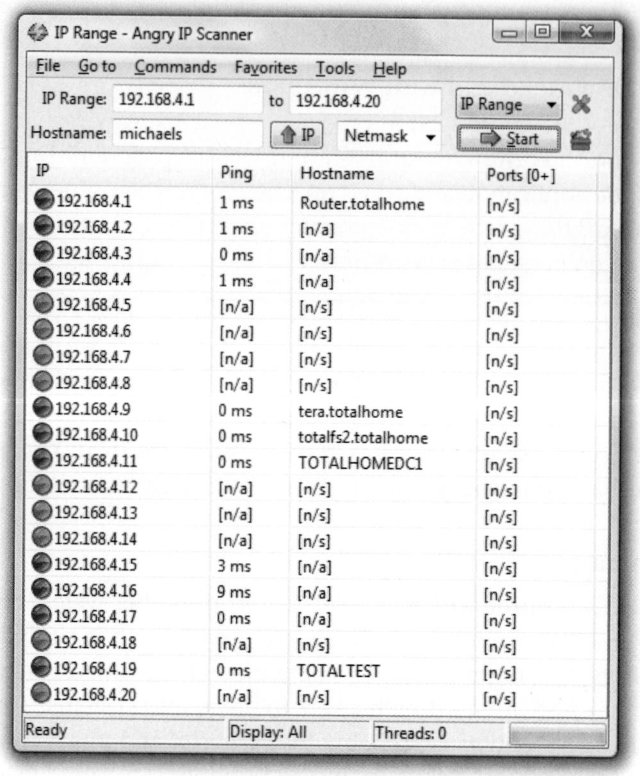
IP Range - Angry IP Scanner
File Go to Commands Favorites Tools Help
IP Range: 192.168.4.1 to 192.168.4.20 IP Range
Hostname: michaels IP Netmask Start
IP Ping Hostname Ports [0+]
192.168.4.1 1 ms Router.totalhome [n/s]
192.168.4.2 1 ms [n/a] [n/s]
192.168.4.3 0 ms [n/a] [n/s]
192.168.4.4 1 ms [n/a] [n/s]
192.168.4.5 [n/a] [n/s] [n/s]
192.168.4.6 [n/a] [n/s] [n/s]
192.168.4.7 [n/a] [n/s] [n/s]
192.168.4.8 [n/a] [n/s] [n/s]
192.168.4.9 0 ms tera.totalhome [n/s]
192.168.4.10 0 ms totalfs2.totalhome [n/s]
192.168.4.11 0 ms TOTALHOMEDC1 [n/s]
192.168.4.12 [n/a] [n/s] [n/s]
192.168.4.13 [n/a] [n/s] [n/s]
192.168.4.14 [n/a] [n/s] [n/s]
192.168.4.15 3 ms [n/a] [n/s]
192.168.4.16 9 ms [n/a] [n/s]
192.168.4.17 0 ms [n/a] [n/s]
192.168.4.18 [n/a] [n/s] [n/s]
192.168.4.19 0 ms TOTALTEST [n/s]
192.168.4.20 [n/a] [n/s] [n/s]
Ready Display: All Threads: 0

• **Figure 15.6** Angry IP Scanner

The Troubleshooting Process

Troubleshooting is a dynamic, fluid process that requires you to make snap judgments and act on them to try and make the network go. Any attempt to cover every possible scenario would be futile at best, and probably also not in your best interests, because any reference that tried to list every troubleshooting problem would be obsolete the moment it was created. If an exhaustive listing of all network problems is impossible, then how do you decide what to do and in what order?

Before you touch a single console or cable, you should remember two basic rules: To paraphrase the Hippocratic Oath, "First, do no harm." If at all possible, don't make a network problem bigger than it was originally. This is a rule I've broken thousands of times, and you will too. But if we change the good doctor's phrase a bit, it's possible to formulate a rule you can live with: "First, do not trash the data!" My gosh, if I had a dollar for every megabyte of irreplaceable data I've destroyed, I'd be rich! I've learned my lesson, and you should learn from my mistakes. The second rule is: Always make good backups! Computers can be replaced; data that is not backed up is gone forever.

No matter how complex and fancy, any troubleshooting process can be broken down into simple steps. Having a sequence of steps to follow makes the entire troubleshooting process simpler and easier, because you have a clear set of goals to achieve in a specific sequence. The most important steps are the first three—they help you narrow down the cause of the problem to a specific item. The reason this matters so much is that figuring out what's wrong will also probably tell you how to fix the problem, and how to prevent it from happening in the future.

The basics of any troubleshooting process should include the following steps:

1. Gather information—identify symptoms and problems.
2. Identify the affected areas of the network.
3. Establish if anything has changed.
4. Establish the most probable cause.
5. Determine if escalation is necessary.
6. Create an action plan and solution identifying potential effects.
7. Implement and test the solution.
8. Identify the results and effects of the solution.
9. Document the solution and the entire process.

Gather Information—Identify Symptoms and Problems

If you are working directly on the affected system and not relying on somebody on the other end of a telephone to guide you, you will establish the symptoms through your observation of what is (or isn't) happening. If you're troubleshooting over the telephone (always a joy, in my experience), you will need to ask questions based on what the user is telling you. These questions can be *close-ended*, which is to say there can only be a yes or no type answer, such as, "Can you see a light on the front of the monitor?" You can also ask *open-ended* questions, such as, "Tell me what you see on the screen." The type of question you use at any given moment will depend on what information you need, and on the knowledge level of the user. If, for example, the user seems to be technically oriented, you will probably be able to ask more close-ended questions, because they will know what you are talking about. If, on the other hand, the user seems to be confused about what's happening, open-ended questions will allow him to explain in his own words what is going on.

Identify the Affected Areas of the Network

One of the first steps in trying to determine the cause of a problem is to understand the extent of the problem—is it specific to one user or is it network-wide? Sometimes this entails trying the task yourself, both from the user's machine and from your own or another machine.

For example, if a user is experiencing problems logging into the network, you might need to go to that user's machine and try to use their user name to log in. This will tell you whether the problem is a user error of some kind, as well as enable you to see the symptoms of the problem yourself. Next, you probably want to try logging in with your own user name from that machine, or have the user try to log in from another machine. In some cases, you can ask other users in the area if they are experiencing the same problem, to see if the problem is affecting more than one user. Depending on the size of your network, you should find out whether the problem is occurring in only one part of your company or across the entire network.

What does all of this tell you? Essentially, it tells you how big the problem is. If nobody in an entire remote office can log in, you may be able to assume that the problem is the network link or router connecting that office to the server. If nobody in any office can log in, you may be able to assume that the server is down or not accepting logins. If only that one user in that one location can't log in, it may be a problem with that user, that machine, or that user's account.

Establish if Anything Has Changed

The goal of this step is to identify if anything has changed that might have caused the problem. You may not have to ask many questions before the people using the problem system can tell you what has changed, but in some cases establishing if anything has changed can sometimes take quite a bit of time and involve further work behind the scenes. Here are some examples of questions to ask:

- "Tell me exactly what was happening when the problem occurred."
- "Has anything been changed on the system recently?"
- "Has the system been moved recently?"

Notice the way I've tactfully avoided the word *you*, as in "Have *you* changed anything on the system recently?" This is a deliberate tactic to avoid any implied blame on the part of the user. Being nice never hurts, and it makes the whole troubleshooting process more friendly.

You should be asking some isolating questions *internally* of yourself, such as, "Was that machine involved in the software push last night?" or "Didn't a tech visit that machine this morning?" Note that you will only be able to answer these questions if *your* documentation is up to scratch. Sometimes, isolating a problem may require you to check system and hardware logs (such as those stored by some routers and other network devices), so make sure you know how to do this.

Establish the Most Probable Cause

This step comes down to experience—or good use of the support tools at your disposal, such as your knowledge base. You need to select the most *probable* cause from all the *possible* causes, so the solution you choose fixes the problem the first time. This may not always happen, but whenever possible, you want to avoid spending a whole day stabbing in the dark while the problem snores softly to itself in some cozy, neglected corner of your network.

Determine if Escalation Is Necessary

Escalation has two meanings: either to inform other parties about a problem for guidance or to pass the job off to another authority who has control over the device/issue that's most probably causing the problem. Let's say you have a server with a bad NIC. This server is used heavily by the accounting department and taking it down may cause problems you don't even know about. You need to inform the boss of accounting to consult with them. Alternatively, there are problems over which you have no control or authority. A badly acting server across the country (hopefully) has another person in charge to whom you need to hand over the job.

Create an Action Plan and Solution
Identifying Potential Effects

By this point you should have some ideas as to what the problem might be. It's time to "look before you leap." An action plan defines how you are going to fix this problem. Most problems are simple, but if the problem is complex you need to write down the steps. As you do this, think about what else might happen as you go about the repair. If you take out a switch, will the users all stop working? Maybe adding the users to a new switch first is a good idea. If you replace a router, can you restore all the old router's settings to the new one or will you have to rebuild from scratch?

Implement and Test a Solution

Once you think you have isolated the cause of the problem, you should decide what you think is the best way to fix it, and then try your solution, whether that's giving advice over the phone to a user, installing a replacement part, or adding a software patch. All the way through this step, try only one likely solution at a time. There's no point in installing several patches at once, because then you can't tell which one fixed the problem. Similarly, there's no point in replacing several items of hardware (such as a hard disk and its controller cable) at the same time, because then you can't tell which part (or parts) was faulty.

As you try each possibility, always *document* what you do and what results you get. This isn't just for a future problem, either—during a lengthy troubleshooting process, it's easy to forget exactly what you tried two hours before, or which thing you tried produced a particular result. Although being methodical may take longer, it will save time the next time—and it may enable you to pinpoint what needs to be done to stop the problem from recurring at all, thereby reducing future call volume to your support team—and as any support person will tell you, that's definitely worth the effort!

Then it's time to test. This is the part everybody hates. Once you think you've fixed a problem, you should try to make it happen again. If you can't, great! But sometimes you will be able to re-create the problem, and then you know you haven't finished the job at hand. Many techs want to slide away quietly as soon as everything seems to be fine, but trust me on this, it won't impress your customer when their problem flares up again 30 seconds after you've left the building—not to mention that you get the joy of another two-hour car trip the next day to fix the same problem, for an even more unhappy client! In the scenario where you are providing support to someone else rather than working directly on the problem, you should make *him* try to re-create the problem. This will confirm whether he understands what

Always test a solution before you walk away from the job!

Memorize these problem analysis steps:

1. Information gathering—identify symptoms and problems.

2. Identify the affected areas of the network.

3. Establish if anything has changed.

4. Establish the most probable cause.

5. Determine if escalation is necessary.

6. Create an action plan and solution identifying potential effects.

7. Implement and test the solution.

8. Identify the results and effects of the solution.

9. Document the solution and the entire process.

you have been telling him, and will educate him at the same time, lessening the chance that he'll call you back later and ask, "Can we just go through that one more time?"

Identify the Results and Effects of the Solution

Okay, now that *you* have changed something on the system in the process of solving one problem, you must think about the wider repercussions of what you have done. If you've replaced a faulty NIC in a server, for instance, will the fact that the MAC address has changed (remember, it's built into the NIC) affect anything else, such as the logon security controls, or your network management and inventory software? If you've installed a patch on a client PC, will this change the default protocol or any other default settings that may affect other functionality? If you've changed a user's security settings, will this affect their ability to access other network resources? This is part of testing your solution to make sure it works properly, but it also makes you think about the impact of your work on the system as a whole.

Document the Solution and the Entire Process

It is *vital* that you document the problem, symptoms, and solutions of all support calls, for two reasons. First, you're creating a support database that will be a knowledge base for future reference, enabling everyone on the support team to identify new problems as they arise, and know how to deal with them quickly, without having to duplicate someone else's research efforts. Second, documentation enables you to track problem trends and anticipate future workloads, or even to identify a particular brand or model of an item, such as a printer or a NIC, that seems to be less reliable or that creates more work for you than others. Don't skip this step—it *really* is essential!

■ Troubleshooting Scenarios

I want to end this chapter with some good troubleshooting scenarios. Take some time and think about these situations and how you would handle them. What questions would you ask? What tests would you do first? The CompTIA Network+ exam absolutely *loves* to ask scenario questions. The knowledge from the previous chapters combined with the methods you've learned in this chapter should enable you to fix any network!

"I Can't Log In!"

One of the most complex troubleshooting issues is that one set of symptoms, in this case a user's inability to log in, can have many causes. Suppose Woody has called complaining that he cannot log into the company's intranet. Tina Tech first tries accessing the intranet site from her system, and finds she has no problem. Tina might also want to have other users try to log

Mike Meyers' CompTIA Network+ Guide to Managing and Troubleshooting Networks

in, or confirm that other users are not having the same problem. Next, Tina should have Woody try to log in from another machine. This will help Tina determine whether the problem lies with Woody's user account's capability to log in, with Woody's system, or with some connectivity issue.

If Woody is unable to log in from another machine, Tina should probably check to be sure Woody is using the correct login ID, password, and procedure when he logs in. On the other hand, if Woody can log in from another user's system, Tina should probably focus on determining whether Woody's system is working properly and connecting to the network. One step she could try here is to PING Woody's system. If Tina can PING Woody's machine successfully, she knows that the machine is up, the TCP/IP protocol is configured correctly, and the system is connected to the network. Tina might then check the configuration of the network client on Woody's system. If Tina is not able to PING the system, however, she might need to test the cables and NIC using cable testers or loopback devices, and verify that TCP/IP was correctly configured using IPCONFIG.

"I Can't Get to This Web Site!"

Reaching external Web sites requires that a variety of components be configured correctly. Some of these components are within your company's internal control; many of them are not. When Fatima calls and tells Tina Tech that she cannot reach www.comptia.org, Tina's first step is to try to reach that site herself. In this case, Tina was also unable to get a response from the comptia.org site. One of her next steps is to PING the site, first by name, and then by IP address. In this case, she gets no response by name, but she does get a normal response when she PINGs the site by IP address. This immediately indicates to her that the problem is name resolution, in this case, DNS.

On the other hand, had Tina been unable to PING successfully using either the IP address or host name, she should consider two possibilities. First, if her company uses a firewall or proxy server to reach the Internet, she should PING that machine. This machine usually has the same IP address as the default gateway TCP/IP setting. If Tina can successfully PING

Cross Check

DNS Settings

You learned about DNS in detail way back in Chapter 10, "Network Naming," so dust off those memories and see if you can answer these questions. What might cause a DNS server to go down? What's a DNS root server? What are the top-level domain servers? Does DNS use a flat name space or a hierarchical name space? What's the difference?

her default gateway, she can be almost certain that the problem is not something she or her company has any control over. To verify this, Tina should attempt to reach some other external sites, both by using PING and a Web browser. If she can reach other sites successfully, the problem is most likely with the comptia.org site or the gateway.

"Our Web Server Is Sluggish!"

Slow response from a server can be related to a variety of things. Usually, however, the problem can be traced to a connection to the server, or to the server itself. When Wanda calls in from working at home and tells Tina Tech that she is getting a slow response from the company's Web site, Tina Tech leaps into action. Tina tries to reach the offending server and is immediately connected; this indicates a connectivity problem for that user. She asks Wanda to execute a `tracert` command from her system to the slow server. This reveals to Tina that the slowdown stems from one of the intermediate steps through which Wanda's system connects to the server. Because of this, the problem is out of Tina's hands, unless she can offer a direct dial-up option for Wanda.

If Tina finds she cannot reach the offending server quickly when she tries from her system, then the problem may lie with the server itself. Tina checks the Change Log for the Web server, to see if anyone has changed anything recently. She discovers that a new antivirus component was recently added, so she checks the vendor's Web site to make sure there are no known problems or patches for that piece of software. She also uses Performance Monitor to compare the server's current responses to the baseline that she previously recorded. This shows her that the bottleneck is related to excessive paging, indicating that the server may need more physical memory, or RAM.

"I Can't See Anything on the Network!"

When a user is completely cut off from the network, the problem is usually limited to that user's system or network connection. When Tina gets a call from Johnny saying his Windows machine is on, but that he can't log in and can't see any other machines on the company's TCP/IP network, Tina goes to Johnny's office to run some tests. The first test Tina runs is to PING an external machine. She doesn't expect it to work, but tests just to be certain. Next, she tries to PING Johnny's machine using either `ping localhost` or `ping 127.0.0.1` (remember the loopback address?). When this PING doesn't work, Tina guesses that the problem is in the TCP/IP configuration. To view the machine's TCP/IP configuration, Tina uses IPCONFIG, and notices the IP address is blank. After checking her network documentation to verify what IP address Johnny's machine should have, she adds the IP address and he is able to connect to the network.

If Tina's `ping 127.0.0.1` had worked, she would have had to assume the TCP/IP and networking configuration of Johnny's machine was correct. She should then check the hardware, using a network card utility to verify that the NIC itself is working correctly, and a cable tester to verify that the cable from Johnny's system is operating properly. In this case, the cable tester shows that the cable is bad, so she replaces the cable between Johnny's system and the patch panel, and he is able to connect.

"It's Time to Escalate!"

No single person is truly in control of an entire Internet-connected network. Large organizations split network support duties into very skill-specific areas: routers, cable infrastructure, user administration, and so on. Even in a tiny network with a single network support person, problems will arise that go beyond the skill level of the tech or that involve equipment they don't own (usually it's their ISP's gear). In these situations it becomes the tech's job to identify a problem and, instead of trying to fix it on his or her own, escalate the issue.

In network troubleshooting, problem escalation should occur when you face a problem that falls outside the scope of your skills and you need help. In large organizations, escalation problems have very clear procedures, such as who to call and what to document. In small organizations, escalation often is nothing more than a technician realizing that he or she needs help. The CompTIA Network+ competencies define some classic networking situations that CompTIA feels should be escalated. Here's how to recognize broadcast storms, switching loops, route problems, routing loops, and proxy ARP.

Broadcast Storms

A **broadcast storm** is the result of one or more devices sending a non-stop flurry of broadcast frames on the network. The first sign of a broadcast storm is when every computer on the broadcast domain suddenly can't connect to the rest of the network. There are usually no clues other than network applications freezing or presenting "can't connect to…" types of error messages. Every activity light on every node is solidly on. Computers on other broadcast domains work perfectly well.

The trick is to isolate; that's where escalation comes in. You need to break down the network quickly by unplugging devices until you can find the one causing trouble. It's usually difficult to get a packet analyzer to work, but at least try. If you can scoop up one packet you'll know what node is causing the trouble. The second the bad node is disconnected, the network returns to normal. But if you have a lot of machines to deal with and a bunch of users who can't get on the network yelling at you, you need help. Call a supervisor to get support to solve the crisis as quickly as possible.

Switching Loops

A **switching loop** is when you connect multiple switches together to cause a loop to appear. Switching loops are rare because most switches use the spanning tree protocol, but they do happen. The symptoms are identical to a broadcast storm: every computer on the broadcast domain can no longer access the network.

The good part about switching loops is that they rarely take place on a well-running network. Someone had to create that loop and that means someone, somewhere is messing with patch cables. Escalate the problem and get the team to help you find the person making changes to the switches.

Route Problems

Improperly configured routers aren't going to send packets to the proper destination. The symptoms are clear: every system that uses the misconfigured router as a default gateway is either not able to get packets out or get packets in, or sometimes both. Web pages don't come up, FTP servers suddenly disappear, and e-mail clients can't access their servers. In these cases you need to verify first that everything under your responsibility works. If that is true, then escalate the problem and find the person responsible for the router.

Routing Loops

A **routing loop** occurs when interconnected routers loop traffic, causing the routers to respond slowly or not respond at all. Dynamic routing protocols sometimes cause routing loops when a router goes down, but most routing loops are caused by static routes. Your big clue is a huge amount of traffic—far more than your usual traffic—on the links between the routers. Router loops never cause individual computers to stop responding (unless they happen to be on the same broadcast domain as the looping packets). Like with any route problem, be able to recognize the symptoms and escalate.

Proxy ARP

Proxy ARP is the process of making remotely connected computers truly act as though they are on the same LAN as local computers. Proxy ARPs are done in a number of different ways, with a Virtual Private Network (VPN) as the classic example. If a laptop in an airport connects to a network through a VPN, that computer takes on the network ID of your local network. In order for all this to work, the VPN concentrator needs to allow some very LAN-type traffic to go through it that would normally never get through a router. ARP is a great example. If your VPN client wants to talk to another computer on the LAN, it has to ARP to get the IP address. Your VPN device is designed to act as a proxy for all that type of data.

Almost all proxy ARP problems take place on the VPN concentrator. With misconfigured proxy ARP settings, the VPN concentrator can send what looks like a Denial of Service (DoS) attack on the LAN. (A DoS attack is usually directed at a server exposed on the Internet, like a Web server. See Chapter 17, "Protecting Your Network," for more details on these and other malicious attacks.) If your clients start receiving a large number of packets from the VPN concentrator, assume it is a proxy ARP problem and escalate by getting the person in charge of the VPN to fix it.

Troubleshooting Is Fun!

The art of network troubleshooting can be a fun, frolicsome, and frequently frustrating feature of your network career. By applying a good troubleshooting methodology and constantly increasing your knowledge of networks, you too can develop into a great troubleshooting artist. This takes time, naturally, but stick with it. Begin the training. Use the Force. Learn new stuff, document problems and fixes, talk to other network techs about similar problems. Every bit of knowledge and experience you gain will make things that much easier for you when crunch time comes and a network disaster occurs—and as any experienced network tech can tell you, it will, even in the most robust network.

Chapter 15 Review

■ Chapter Summary

After reading this chapter and completing the exercises, you should understand the following about network troubleshooting.

Describe appropriate troubleshooting tools and their functions

- Before starting work on any problem, always ask yourself if what you are about to do can potentially harm your data.

- The vast majority of cabling problems take place when the network is first installed or when changes, if any, take place. Cables rarely go bad after they have been made, installed, and tested.

- Broken cables don't create intermittent problems—they make permanent disconnects. A TDR can tell you where a break is on a cable.

- Certifiers test a cable to ensure that it can handle its rated amount of capacity. If a cable isn't broken, yet isn't moving data the way it should, test it with a certifier. Use a certifier for slowdowns, not disconnects.

- Heat and power problems manifest as intermittent network problems. Use a voltage event recorder to measure power, and use a temperature monitor to ensure proper temperature.

- A good protocol analyzer will give you the Application, Session, Network, and Data Link layer information on every frame going through your network. Protocol analyzers can be hardware or software.

- A multimeter tests voltage and can tell you how much voltage is on a line.

- Tone generators and tone probes work as a pair to help you locate a particular cable.

- A butt set is used to tap into a 66- or 110-block to see if a particular line is working.

- A punchdown tool places UTP wires into 66- and 110-blocks. It is useful in a diagnostic environment to repunch a connection to make sure all the contacts are properly set.

- Software tools can be organized in two categories: those that come built into your operating system and those that are provided by a third party.

- TRACEROUTE (called TRACERT in Windows) is used to trace all the routers between two points. Use it to diagnose problems reaching a remote system. Because many routers block TRACERT packets, PATHPING is a viable alternative.

- IPCONFIG (on Windows) and IFCONFIG (on everything else) gives you information about a computer's IP settings. The /all switch gives additional detailed information, including DNS server addresses and MAC addresses.

- PING uses ICMP packets to show you if you can simply reach a remote computer. Because some devices block the ICMP packets, ARPING can be used instead. However, ARPING is available only on UNIX systems—and it can't cross routers.

- NSLOOKUP is used to diagnose DNS problems, but is considered obsolete. DIG is a more powerful alternative, but is not available on Windows.

- The HOSTNAME command simply returns the host name of the local computer.

- MTR, which is not available on Windows, is similar to TRACEROUTE except that it keeps running until shut down.

- The ROUTE command enables you to display and edit the local system's routing table.

- NBTSTAT (Windows only) can show all the local NetBIOS names and is a command-line equivalent to My Network Places. NBTSTAT must be run with a switch.

- NETSTAT displays information on the current state of all the running IP processes on your computer. Use NETSTAT when you want to know about your current sessions.

- A packet sniffer intercepts and logs network packets. Wireshark is a popular packet sniffer.

- A port scanner probes ports on another system, logging the state of scanned ports. It can be used to find an unintentionally open port so that it can be secured. Hackers like to use port scanners to find vulnerabilities in other systems.

Analyze and discuss the troubleshooting process

- There is no reference guide to troubleshooting every possible network problem because such a guide would be obsolete the moment it was created.

- A basic troubleshooting model may include the following nine steps: (1) Gather information—identify symptoms and problems, (2) Identify the affected areas of the network, (3) Establish if anything has changed, (4) Establish the most probable cause, (5) Determine if escalation is necessary, (6) Create an action plan and solution identifying potential effects, (7) Implement and test the solution, (8) Identify the results and effects of the solution, and (9) Document the solution and the entire process.

- When establishing the symptoms, it may be necessary to ask the user reporting the trouble both closed- and open-ended questions.

- Isolating the cause of the problem includes identifying the scope of the problem, such as determining if it affects a single system or the entire network.

- When trying to determine what recent changes may have caused the problem, it is important to recognize things that are not causes. Re-creating the problem yourself removes user error as a possible cause, and experiencing the problem on another computer removes the possibility of changed settings on the first computer as the cause.

- Once you have determined possible causes, you should identify what you feel is the most probable cause. The ability to identify the most probable cause improves with experience.

- When implementing a solution, be sure to try only one thing at a time. If you perform multiple activities or make multiple changes, you won't know which action actually solved the problem—and you won't know which action made things worse.

- Once a solution has been implemented, test it by trying to re-create the problem. If you can re-create the error, you haven't fixed the problem.

- If you have fixed a problem, you need to recognize what potential problems you may have caused. For example, replacing a NIC in a server may get the server back online, but the new NIC has a different MAC address, which may introduce a whole new set of problems.

- Problems, symptoms, and solutions should be documented so the solutions can be used later in a knowledge base. Additionally, the documentation will help you track problem trends.

Tackle a variety of troubleshooting scenarios

- The CompTIA Network+ exam loves to ask scenario questions, so be familiar with as many scenarios as you can!

- Some common scenarios every tech should be familiar with include users not being able to log in, Web sites not loading, servers or networks appearing slow and sluggish, and My Network Places (or Network) not working as expected.

- Various networking problems that fall outside the scope of a tech's skill set should be escalated. These include broadcast storms, switching loops, route problems, routing loops, and proxy ARP.

■ Key Terms

ARP PING *(408)*

broadcast storm *(419)*

butt set *(405)*

cable stripper *(405)*

cable tester *(404)*

certifier *(404)*

DIG *(408)*

hardware tool *(403)*

HOSTNAME *(409)*

IFCONFIG *(407)*

IPCONFIG *(407)*

multimeter *(405)*

My Traceroute (MTR) *(409)*

NBTSTAT *(410)*

NETSTAT *(410)*

NSLOOKUP *(408)*

packet sniffer *(410)*

PING *(408)*

port scanner *(411)*

protocol analyzer *(404)*

proxy ARP *(420)*

punchdown tool *(405)*

ROUTE *(409)*
routing loop *(420)*
snip *(405)*
switching loop *(419)*
temperature monitor *(404)*
tone generator *(405)*

tone probe *(405)*
TRACEROUTE *(406)*
TRACERT *(406)*
voltage event recorder *(404)*
Wireshark *(411)*

■ Key Term Quiz

Use the Key Terms list to complete the sentences that follow. Not all the terms will be used.

1. Use _____ to locate a problem between two routers.

2. Use a(n) _____ to put wires into 66- and 110-blocks.

3. A(n) _____ tests cables to ensure they can handle their rated capacity.

4. If ICMP packets are being blocked, you can use _____ to test connectivity to another system.

5. _____ is a popular packet sniffer/protocol analyzer/packet analyzer.

6. To view IP settings on a UNIX computer, use the _____ command.

7. Use a(n) _____ to test AC/DC voltage, resistance, and continuity.

8. _____ is similar to NSLOOKUP, but much more powerful.

9. _____ uses ICMP packets to test connectivity between two systems.

10. A(n) _____ is used by telephone technicians to tap into a 66- or 110-block to determine if a particular line is working.

■ Multiple-Choice Quiz

1. Jordan says she can't access files on the server any more. No other user has reported this problem and she can PING the server from another computer successfully. Typing `ping 127.0.0.1` from Jordan's computer is also successful. Using PING to try to reach the server or any other computer from Jordan's computer fails. A check of IP settings on Jordan's computer shows that her static IP address and other information is good. What is the most likely cause of the problem?

   A. The router that Jordan's computer connects to is down.

   B. Jordan's network card is bad.

   C. The DHCP server is down.

   D. Jordan's Ethernet cable has become unplugged from her computer.

2. You are trying to locate which patch cable in the main switch traces back to a particular computer. Which tool should you use?

   A. Tone probe

   B. Cable tester

   C. Punchdown tool

   D. Butt set

3. The Windows TRACERT tool fails sometimes because many routers block TRACERT packets. What tool can be used as an alternative?

   A. PING

   B. PATHPING

   C. PATHROUTE

   D. TRACER

4. What is the first step in the troubleshooting model?

   A. Implementing the solution

   B. Testing the solution

   C. Isolating the cause

   D. Establishing the symptoms

5. Kay's computer has lost all network access. Which tool should be used to test for a break on the cable?

    A. Certifier

    B. TDR

    C. Voltage event recorder

    D. Crimper

6. Which command shows you detailed IP information, including DNS server addresses and MAC addresses?

    A. ipconfig

    B. ipconfig -a

    C. ipconfig /all

    D. ipconfig /dns

7. Which tool uses ICMP packets to test connectivity between two systems?

    A. ARP

    B. ARPPING

    C. PATHPING

    D. PING

8. What tools can you (and hackers) use to discover vulnerabilities on your network? (Select three.)

    A. Port scanner

    B. NMAP

    C. Angry IP Scanner

    D. HOSTNAME

9. Asking a user "Can you start your e-mail program?" is what type of question?

    A. Closed-ended

    B. Open-ended

    C. Leading

    D. Unprofessional

10. If you want to see which other computers on your network are currently connected to you, what tool should you use?

    A. PING

    B. NBTSTAT

    C. NETSTAT

    D. TRACERT

11. One of your users calls you with a complaint that they can't reach the site www.yahoo.com. You try and access the site and discover you can't connect either but you can PING the site with its IP address. What is the most probable culprit?

    A. The workgroup switch is down.

    B. Yahoo! is down.

    C. The gateway is down.

    D. The DNS server is down.

12. A brand new employee is complaining on his second day of work that he can't log into his computer. What is the most probable cause?

    A. The server is down.

    B. His network card is bad.

    C. He forgot or is mistyping his password.

    D. A port on the switch is bad.

13. When should you use a cable tester to troubleshoot a network cable?

    A. When you have a host experiencing a very slow connection

    B. When you have an intermittent connection problem

    C. When you have a dead connection and you suspect a broken cable

    D. Never

14. Which tools should you use to diagnose problems with DNS?

    A. NMAP or Wireshark

    B. NSLOOKUP or DIG

    C. PING or PATHPING

    D. TRACERT or PATHPING

15. Which Windows command displays the local system's routing table?

    A. route print

    B. print route

    C. tracert /print

    D. tracert /p

■ Essay Quiz

1. You and a co-worker are working late trying to fix a problem on the server. Your friend suggests applying three hot fixes and swapping out the network card for another. However, he wants to do all these things at the same time to finish the job quicker. Explain to him why that's not a good idea.

2. Because of your outstanding troubleshooting skills, you have been selected by your supervisor to train a new intern. Explain to her the steps of a basic troubleshooting model.

3. You've read in this chapter: "First, do no harm." First, explain in your own words what that means to you. Then, think of a situation in which you were either the technician or the "victim" in a troubleshooting case where harm was done. What happened?

Lab Projects

• Lab Project 15.1

You've learned about many free software tools in this chapter—some available only for Windows, some only for UNIX/Linux/Mac, and some available for all. Make a chart with five columns: tool name, description, useful switches/options, supported operating system(s), built-in or third party. Fill in the chart with the tools from this chapter and use it as a study guide.

• Lab Project 15.2

Using the chart you created in the previous lab activity, run each of the tools to gain some familiarity with the interface, switches, and output. Are there any tools in your chart you already use on a regular (or semi-regular) basis? Which tools are the easiest for you to understand? Which tools do you not completely understand? If there are any that are still unclear, ask your instructor or search the Internet for clarification on the tool's usage. Once you've searched the Internet, compare your findings with classmates or verify with your instructor to make sure your research resulted in correct information!

Wireless Networking

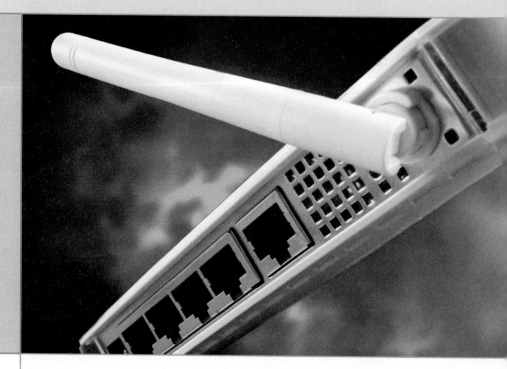

"The wireless telegraph is not difficult to understand. The ordinary telegraph is like a very long cat. You pull the tail in New York, and it meows in Los Angeles. The wireless is the same, only without the cat."

—ALBERT EINSTEIN

In this chapter, you will learn how to

- ■ **Explain wireless networking standards**
- ■ **Describe the process for implementing Wi-Fi networks**
- ■ **Describe troubleshooting techniques for wireless networks**

Every type of network covered thus far in the book assumes that your PCs connect to your network with some kind of physical cabling. Now it's time to cut the cord and look at one of the most exciting developments in network technology: wireless networking.

Historical/Conceptual

Instead of a physical set of wires running among networked PCs, servers, printers, or what-have-you, a **wireless network** uses radio waves to enable these devices to communicate with each other. This offers great promise to the folks who've spent time pulling cable up through ceiling spaces and down behind walls, and therefore know how time consuming that job can be.

But wireless networking is more than just convenient—sometimes it's the only networking solution that works. For example, I have a client whose offices are housed in a building designated as a historic landmark. Guess what? You can't go punching holes in historic landmarks to make room for network cable runs. Wireless networking is the solution.

Wireless networks operate at the same OSI layers and use the same protocols as wired networks. The thing that differs is the type of media—radio waves instead of cables—and the methods for accessing the media. Different wireless networking solutions have come and gone in the past, but the wireless networking market these days is dominated by the most common implementation of the IEEE 802.11 wireless Ethernet standard, **Wi-Fi**.

The chapter looks first at the standards for modern wireless networks, and then turns to implementing those networks. The chapter finishes with a discussion on troubleshooting Wi-Fi.

Because the networking signal is freed from wires, you'll sometimes hear the term "unbounded media" to describe wireless networking.

Test Specific

■ Wi-Fi Standards

Wi-Fi is by far the most widely adopted wireless networking type today. Not only do thousands of private businesses and homes have wireless networks, but many public places, such as coffee shops and libraries, also offer Internet access through wireless networks.

Technically, only wireless devices that conform to the extended versions of the 802.11 standard—802.11a, 802.11b, 802.11g, and 802.11n—are Wi-Fi certified. Wi-Fi certification comes from the Wi-Fi Alliance, a nonprofit industry group made up of over 300 member companies that design and manufacture wireless networking products. Wi-Fi certification ensures compatibility between wireless networking devices made by different vendors. That's the way it's *supposed* to work, anyway, but see the last section of this chapter on troubleshooting for the real-world scoop.

Wi-Fi originally stood for *wireless fidelity* to make it cutely equated with high fidelity or Hi-Fi, but it doesn't really stand for anything anymore.

802.11

The **802.11** standard defines both how wireless devices communicate and how to secure that communication. The communication standards take on the name of the IEEE subcommittee that sets those standards, such as 802.11b and 802.11n. The original 802.11 standard established the baseline features common to all subsequent Wi-Fi standards; we'll examine 802.11 before exploring variations in 802.11b, 802.11a, 802.11g, and 802.11n. The section wraps up with a discussion on security standards, from authentication to encryption.

All Wi-Fi standards share certain features, such as a wireless network card, special configuration software, and the capability to run in multiple styles of networks. In addition, Wi-Fi implementations require a shared network name and channel for communication. Each standard has a certain top speed and range of networking capability. Finally, 802.11 defines how transmissions work, so we'll look at frequencies of radio signals, transmission methods, and collision avoidance.

Hardware

Wireless networking hardware serves the same function as hardware used on wired PCs. Wireless Ethernet NICs take data passed down from the upper OSI layers, encapsulate it into data packets, send the packets out on the network media in strings of ones and zeroes, and receive data packets sent from other PCs. The only difference is that instead of charging up a network cable with electrical current or firing off pulses of light, these devices transmit and receive radio waves.

Wireless networking capabilities of one form or another are built into many modern computing devices. Wireless Ethernet capabilities are increasingly popular as integrated components, or can easily be added using PCI or PC Card add-on cards. In fact, many wireless PCI NICs are simply wireless PC Card NICs that have been permanently housed in a PCI component card. Figure 16.1 shows a wireless PCI Ethernet card.

You can also add wireless network capabilities using external USB wireless network adapters, as shown in Figure 16.2. The USB NICs have the added benefit of being *placeable*—that is, you can move them around to catch the wireless signal as strongly as possible, akin to moving the rabbit ears on old pre-cable television sets.

• **Figure 16.1** Wireless PCI NIC

Tech Tip

USB Extender Cables

Many USB Wi-Fi NICs these days come as little USB sticks, similar in looks to a flash memory thumb drive. You can still position this type of NIC, though, by using a USB extender cable, with a male USB A connector on one end and a female USB A connector on the other.

• **Figure 16.2** External USB wireless NIC

Is the wireless network adapter all the hardware you need to connect wirelessly? Well, if your needs are simple—for example, if you're connecting a small group of computers into a decentralized workgroup—then the answer is yes. However, if you need to extend the capabilities of a wireless Ethernet network—say, connecting a wireless network segment to a wired network—you need additional equipment. This typically means a wireless access point.

A **wireless access point (WAP)** connects wireless network nodes to wireless or wired networks. A basic WAP operates like a hub and works at OSI Layer 1. Many WAP manufacturers combine multiple devices into one box, however, to create a high-speed hub or switch, bridge, and router, all rolled into one and working at many different OSI layers. The Linksys device shown in Figure 16.3 is an example of this type of combo device.

Cross Check

Using Routers

You've seen wired routers before, and wireless routers function similarly, so cross-check your memory. Turn to Chapter 2, "Building a Network with the OSI Model," and see if you can answer these questions. What can a router do for your network? Can you use a router to connect to the Internet? At what layer of the OSI seven-layer model do routers function? How do routers handle addressing?

Software

Every wireless network adapter needs two pieces of software to function with an operating system: a driver and a configuration utility. Installing drivers for wireless networking devices is usually no more difficult than for any other hardware device, but you should always consult your vendor's instructions before popping that card into a slot. Most of the time, you simply have to let Plug and Play (PnP) work its magic and put in the driver disc when prompted, but some devices (particularly USB devices) require that you install the drivers beforehand. All modern operating systems come well equipped for wireless networking. Even so, it's always a good idea to use the manufacturer's drivers and configuration utilities.

You also need a utility for configuring how the wireless hardware connects to other wireless devices. Windows XP, Windows Vista, and Macintosh OS X have built-in tools for configuring these settings, but for previous versions of Windows, you need to rely on wireless client configuration tools provided by the wireless network adapter vendor. Figure 16.4 shows a typical wireless network adapter's client configuration utility. Using this utility, you can determine important things like your **link state** (whether your wireless device is connected) and your **signal strength** (a measurement of how well your wireless device is connecting to other devices); you can also configure items such as your wireless networking *mode*, security encryption, power-saving options, and so on. I'll cover each of these topics in detail later in this chapter.

You configure WAPs and routers through browser-based setup utilities. The section "Implementing Wi-Fi" covers this process in detail a bit later in this chapter. Let's look at the different modes that wireless networks use.

 Some manufacturers drop the word "wireless" from wireless access points and simply call them access points. Further, many sources abbreviate both forms, so you'll see the former written as WAP and the latter as AP.

• **Figure 16.3** Linksys device that acts as wireless access point, switch, and DSL router

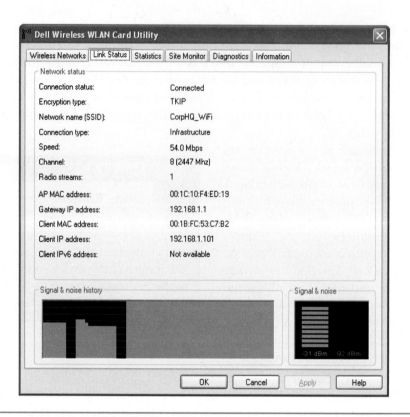

• **Figure 16.4** Wireless client configuration utility

Wireless Network Modes

The simplest wireless network consists of two or more PCs communicating directly with each other without cabling or any other intermediary hardware. More complicated wireless networks use an access point to centralize wireless communication, and to bridge wireless network segments to wired network segments. These two different methods, or *modes*, are called *ad hoc* mode and *infrastructure* mode.

Ad Hoc Mode **Ad hoc mode** is sometimes called **peer-to-peer mode**, with each wireless node in direct contact with each other node in a decentralized free-for-all, as shown in Figure 16.5. Ad hoc mode does not use an access point and instead uses a *mesh* topology, as discussed in Chapter 3, "Cabling and Topology."

Two or more wireless nodes communicating in ad hoc mode form what's called an **Independent Basic Service Set (IBSS)**. This is a basic unit of organization in wireless networks. Think of an IBSS as a wireless workgroup, and you're not far off the mark.

Ad hoc mode networks work well for small groups of computers (fewer than a dozen or so) that need to transfer files or share printers. Ad hoc networks are also good for temporary networks, such as study groups or business meetings.

• **Figure 16.5** Wireless ad hoc mode network

Hardly anyone uses ad hoc networks for day-to-day work, simply because you can't use an ad hoc network to connect to other networks unless one of the machines is running Internet Connection Sharing (ICS) or some equivalent. More commonly, you'll find wireless networks configured in infrastructure mode.

 Infrastructure mode is so much more commonly used than ad hoc mode that most wireless NICs come preconfigured to run on an infrastructure mode network. Getting them to run in ad hoc mode usually requires reconfiguration.

Infrastructure Mode   Wireless networks running in **infrastructure mode** use one or more WAPs to connect the wireless network nodes centrally, as shown in Figure 16.6. This configuration is similar to the *star* topology of a wired network. You also use infrastructure mode to connect wireless network segments to wired segments. If you plan to set up a wireless network for a large number of PCs, or you need to have centralized control over the wireless network, infrastructure mode is what you need.

A single WAP servicing a given area is called a **Basic Service Set (BSS)**. This service area can be extended by adding more access points. This is called, appropriately, an **Extended Service Set (ESS)**.

Wireless networks running in infrastructure mode require a little more planning—such as where you place the WAPs to provide adequate coverage—than ad hoc mode networks, and they provide a stable environment for permanent wireless network installations. Infrastructure mode is better suited to business networks or networks that need to share dedicated resources such as Internet connections and centralized databases. (See "Implementing Wi-Fi" later in this chapter.)

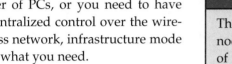

Cross Check

Topologies

The topology of a network represents the physical connectivity between nodes. This seems as good a time as any to cross-check your knowledge of topologies, so recall back to Chapter 3 and answer these questions. What are the four standard topologies? What are the hybrid topologies? If you connect a wireless network in infrastructure mode to a wired Ethernet network, what topology would that combined network have?

Tech Tip

EBSS vs. ESS

A lot of techs have dropped the word "basic" from the Extended Basic Service Set, the early name for an infrastructure-mode wireless network with more than one WAP. Accordingly, you'll see the initials for the Extended Basic Service Set as ESS. Using either EBSS or ESS is correct.

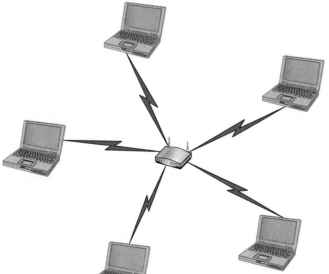

• **Figure 16.6**   Wireless infrastructure mode network

Speed

Wireless networking data throughput speeds depend on a few factors. Foremost is the standard that the wireless devices use. Depending on the standard used, wireless throughput speeds range from a measly 2 Mbps to a quick 300 Mbps. 802.11 topped out at 2 Mbps.

One of the other factors affecting speed is the distance between wireless nodes (or between wireless nodes and centralized access points). Wireless devices dynamically negotiate the top speed at which they can communicate without dropping too many data packets. Speed decreases as distance increases, so the maximum throughput speed is only achieved at extremely close range (less than 25 feet or so). At the outer reaches of a device's effective range, speed may decrease to around 1 Mbps before it drops out altogether.

Finally, speed is affected by interference from other wireless devices operating in the same frequency range—such as cordless phones or baby monitors—and by solid objects. So-called *dead spots* occur when something capable of blocking the radio signal comes between the wireless network nodes. Large electrical appliances, such as refrigerators, *very* effectively block a wireless network signal! Other culprits include electrical fuse boxes, metal plumbing, and air conditioning units.

Range

Wireless networking range is hard to define, and you'll see most descriptions listed with qualifiers such as "*around* 150 feet" and "*about* 300 feet." 802.11 networks fell into the former category. Like throughput speed, wireless range is greatly affected by environmental factors. Interference from other wireless devices and solid objects affect range.

The maximum ranges listed in the sections that follow are those presented by wireless manufacturers as the *theoretical* maximum ranges. In the real world, you'll see these ranges only under the most ideal circumstances. True effective range is probably about half of what you see listed.

BSSID, SSID, and ESSID

Wireless devices connected together into a network, whether ad hoc or infrastructure, require some way to identify that network. Packets bound for computers within the network need to go where they're supposed to go, even when you have more than one Wi-Fi network overlapping. The jargon gets a little crazy here, especially because marketing has come into the mix.

The **Basic Service Set Identifier (BSSID)** defines the most basic infrastructure mode network, a BSS of one WAP and one or more wireless nodes. With such a simple network, the Wi-Fi folks didn't see any reason to create some new numbering or naming scheme, so they made the BSSID the same as the MAC address for the WAP. Simple! Ah, but what to do about ad hoc networks that don't have a WAP? The nodes that connect in an IBSS randomly generate a 48-bit string of numbers that looks and functions just like a MAC address, and that BSSID goes in every packet.

You could, if required, discover the MAC address for the WAP in a BSS and manually type that into the network name field when setting up a wireless computer. But that brings up two problems. First, people don't want to remember strings of 48 digits, even if translated out as six hexadecimal octets, like A9–45–F2–3E–CA–12. People want names. Second, how do you connect two or more computers together into an IBSS when the BSSID has to be randomly generated?

The Wi-Fi folks created another level of naming called a **Service Set Identifier (SSID)**, a standard name applied to the BSS or IBSS to help connection happen. The SSID—sometimes called a **network name**—is a 32-bit identification string that's inserted into the header of each data packet processed by a WAP. Every Wi-Fi device must share the same SSID to communicate in a single network.

So let's take it one step further into a Wi-Fi network that has multiple WAPs, an ESS. How do you determine the network name at this level? You simply repurpose the SSID, only applying it to the ESS as an **Extended Service Set Identifier (ESSID)**.

Unfortunately, most Wi-Fi devices just use the term SSID, not ESSID. When you configure a wireless device to connect to an ESS, you're technically using the ESSID rather than just the SSID, but the manufacturer often has tried to make it simple for you by using only the term SSID.

> The CompTIA Network+ certification exam uses the two terms—SSID and ESSID—interchangeably. Concentrate on these two terms for the exam.

Broadcasting Frequency

One of the biggest issues with wireless communication is the potential for interference from other wireless devices. To solve this, different wireless devices must operate in specific broadcasting frequencies. Knowing these wireless frequency ranges will assist you in troubleshooting interference issues from other devices operating in the same wireless band. The original 802.11 standards use the 2.4-GHz frequency. Later standards use either 2.4-GHz or 5.0-GHz frequencies.

Broadcasting Methods

The original IEEE 802.11 wireless Ethernet standard defined methods by which devices may communicate using *spread-spectrum* radio waves. Spread-spectrum broadcasts data in small, discrete chunks over the different frequencies available within a certain frequency range.

802.11 defines three different spread-spectrum broadcasting methods: **direct-sequence spread-spectrum (DSSS)**, **frequency-hopping spread-spectrum (FHSS)** and **orthogonal frequency-division multiplexing (OFDM)**. DSSS sends data out on different frequencies at the same time, while FHSS sends data on one frequency at a time, constantly shifting (or *hopping*) frequencies. DSSS uses considerably more bandwidth than FHSS—around 22 MHz as opposed to 1 MHz. DSSS is capable of greater data throughput, but it's also more prone to interference than FHSS. OFDM is the latest method and combines the multiple frequencies of DSSS with FHSS's hopping capability. The 802.11 wireless networking implementation used DSSS and later OFDM.

Channels

Every Wi-Fi network communicates on a **channel**, a portion of the spectrum available. The 802.11 standard defined 14 channels, but different countries may limit exactly which channels may be used. In the United States, for example, a WAP may only use channels 1 through 11. These channels have some overlap, so it's not a good idea to have two nearby WAPs to use close channels like 6 and 7. Most WAPs use channel 1, 6, or 11 by default to keep the channels as far apart as possible. You can fine-tune a network by moving WAPs to other channels to avoid overlap with other, nearby WAPs. This is especially important in environments with many wireless networks sharing the same physical space.

CSMA/CA

Because only a single device can use any network at a time, network nodes must have a way to access the network media without stepping on each other's data packets. Wired Ethernet networks use *carrier sense multiple access/collision detection (CSMA/CD)*, as you'll recall from previous chapters, but Wi-Fi networks use **carrier sense multiple access/collision avoidance (CSMA/CA)**. Let's compare both methods.

How do multiple devices share the network media, such as a cable? This is fairly simple: each device listens in on the network media by measuring the level of voltage currently on the wire. If the level is below the threshold, the device knows that it's clear to send data. If the voltage level rises above a preset threshold, the device knows that the line is busy and it must wait before sending data. Typically, the waiting period is the length of the current frame plus a short, predefined silence period called an **interframe space (IFS)**. So far, so good—but what happens when two devices both detect that the wire is free and try to send data simultaneously? As you probably guessed, packets transmitted on the network from two different devices at the same time will corrupt each other, thereby canceling each other out. This is called a *collision*. Collisions are a fact of networking life. So, how do network nodes deal with collisions? They either react to collisions after they happen, or they take steps to avoid collisions in the first place.

CSMA/CD is the reactive method. With CSMA/CD, each sending node detects the collision and responds by generating a random timeout period for itself, during which it doesn't try to send any more data on the network—this is called a *backoff*. Once the backoff period expires (remember that we're only talking about milliseconds here), the node goes through the whole process again. This approach may not be very elegant, but it gets the job done.

CSMA/CD won't work for wireless networking since wireless devices simply can't detect collisions; therefore, wireless networks need another way of dealing with them. The CSMA/CA access method, as the name implies, proactively takes steps to avoid collisions. The 802.11 standard defines two methods of collision avoidance: **Distributed Coordination Function (DCF)** and **Point Coordination Function (PCF)**. Currently, only DCF is implemented.

802.11 was the very oldest wireless standard (see Table 16.1). Over time, more detailed additions to 802.11 came along that improved speed and took advantage of other frequency bands.

Wired Ethernet networks use carrier sense multiple access/collision detection (CSMA/CD). Wi-Fi networks use carrier sense multiple access/collision avoidance (CSMA/CA).

Tech Tip

DCF

DCF specifies much stricter rules for sending data onto the network media. For instance, if a wireless network node detects that the network is busy, DCF defines a backoff period on top of the normal IFS wait period before a node can try to access the network again. DCF also requires that receiving nodes send an acknowledgement *(ACK) for every packet that they process. The ACK also includes a value that tells other wireless nodes to wait a certain duration before trying to access the network media. This period is calculated to be the time that the data packet takes to reach its destination based on the packet's length and data rate. If the sending node doesn't receive an ACK, it retransmits the same data packet until it gets a confirmation that the packet reached its destination.*

Current CSMA/CA devices use the Distributed Coordination Function (DCF) method for collision avoidance.

Table 16.1	802.11 Summary				
Standard	**Frequency**	**Spectrum**	**Speed**	**Range**	**Compatibility**
802.11	2.4 GHz	DSSS	11 Mbps	~300'	802.11

802.11b

The first widely adopted Wi-Fi standard—**802.11b**—supports data throughput of up to 11 Mbps and a range of up to 300 feet under ideal conditions. The main downside to using 802.11b is, in fact, that it's so popular. The 2.4-GHz frequency is already a crowded place, so you're more likely to run into interference from other wireless devices. Table 16.2 gives you the 802.11b summary.

Table 16.2	802.11b Summary				
Standard	**Frequency**	**Spectrum**	**Speed**	**Range**	**Compatibility**
802.11b	2.4 GHz	DSSS	11 Mbps	~300'	802.11b

802.11a

Despite the *a* designation for this extension to the 802.11 standard, **802.11a** was available on the market *after* 802.11b. 802.11a differs from the other 802.11-based standards in significant ways. Foremost is that it operates in a different frequency range, 5 GHz. The 5-GHz range is much less crowded than the 2.4-GHz range, reducing the chance of interference from devices such as telephones and microwave ovens. 802.11a also offers considerably greater throughput than 802.11 and 802.11b, at speeds up to 54 Mbps. Range, however, suffers somewhat, and tops out at about 150 feet. Despite the superior speed of 802.11a, it never enjoyed the popularity of 802.11b.

Although you can get NICs and WAPs that support both 802.11b and 802.11a, the standards are not compatible with each other. A computer with an 802.11b NIC, for example, can't connect to a WAP that's only 802.11a, but could connect to an 802.11a/b WAP. Table 16.3 gives you the 802.11a summary.

Table 16.3	802.11a Summary				
Standard	**Frequency**	**Spectrum**	**Speed**	**Range**	**Compatibility**
802.11a	5.0 GHz	DSSS	54 Mbps	~150'	802.11a

802.11g

The **802.11g** standard offers data transfer speeds equivalent to 802.11a—up to 54 Mbps—and the wider 300-foot range of 802.11b. More importantly, 802.11g is backwardly compatible with 802.11b, so the same 802.11g WAP can service both 802.11b and 802.11g wireless nodes.

If an 802.11g network only has 802.11g devices connected, the network runs in *native mode*—at up to 54 Mbps—whereas when 802.11b devices connect, the network drops down to *mixed mode*—all communication runs only up to 11 Mbps. Table 16.4 gives you the 802.11g summary.

Table 16.4	802.11g Summary				
Standard	**Frequency**	**Spectrum**	**Speed**	**Range**	**Compatibility**
802.11g	2.4 GHz	OFDM	54 Mbps	~300'	802.11b/g

802.11n

The **802.11n** standard brings several improvements to Wi-Fi networking, including faster speeds and new antenna technology implementations.

The 802.11n specification requires all but hand-held devices to use multiple antennae to implement a feature called **multiple in/multiple out (MIMO)**, which enables the devices to make multiple simultaneous connections. With up to four antennae, 802.11n devices can do amazing speeds.

(The official standard supports throughput of up to 600 Mbps, although practical implementation drops that down substantially.)

Many 802.11n WAPs employ **transmit beamforming**, a multiple-antenna technology that helps get rid of dead spots—or at least make them not so bad. The antennae adjust the signal once the WAP discovers a client to optimize the radio signal.

Like 802.11g, 802.11n WAPs can support earlier, slower 802.11b/g devices. The so-called "dual-band" WAPs can run at both 5 GHz and 2.4 GHz simultaneously; some support 802.11a devices as well as 802.11b/g devices. Nice! Table 16.5 gives you the 802.11n summary.

Table 16.5	802.11n Summary				
Standard	**Frequency**	**Spectrum**	**Speed**	**Range**	**Compatibility**
802.11n	2.4 GHz[1]	OFDM	100+ Mbps	~300'	802.11b/g/n[2]

1 Dual-band 802.11n devices can function simultaneously at both 2.4- and 5.0-GHz bands.
2 Many dual-band 802.11n WAPs support 802.11a devices as well as 802.11b/g/n devices. This is not part of the standard, but something manufacturers have implemented.

Tech Tip

802.16

Products that use the 802.16 wireless standard—often called WiMax—are expected on the market any time now. Although speed for 802.16-compliant devices is about the same as 802.11b, manufacturers claim a range of up to 30 miles! This kind of range would be perfect for so-called metropolitan area networks (MANs). Before you get too excited, though, keep in mind that the speed of the network will almost certainly decrease the farther away from the base station (the WAP) the nodes are. Effective range could be as little as three miles, but that still beats 300 feet in my book!

Wireless Networking Security

One of the biggest problems with wireless networking devices is that right out of the box, they provide *no* security. Vendors go out of their way to make it easy to set up their devices, so usually the only thing that you have to do to join a wireless network is turn your wireless devices on and let them find each other. Sure, from a configuration point of view, this is great—but from a security point of view, it's a disaster!

Further, you have to consider that your network's data packets float through the air on radio waves instead of zipping safely along wrapped up inside network cabling. What's to stop an unscrupulous network tech with the right equipment from grabbing those packets out of the air and reading that data?

To address these issues, wireless networks use three methods: MAC address filtering, authentication, and data encryption. The first two methods secure access to the network itself, and the third secures the data that's moving around the network. All three of these methods require you to configure the WAPs and wireless devices. Let's take a look.

MAC Address Filtering

Most WAPs support **MAC address filtering**, a method that enables you to limit access to your network based on the physical addresses of wireless NICs. MAC address filtering creates a type of "accepted users" list to limit access to your wireless network. A table stored in the WAP lists the MAC addresses that are permitted to participate in the wireless network. Any data packets that don't contain the MAC address of a node listed in the table are rejected.

Many WAPs also enable you to deny specific MAC addresses from logging onto the network. This works great in close quarters, such as apartments or office buildings, where your wireless network signal goes beyond your perimeter. You can check the WAP and see the MAC addresses of every node that connects to your network. Check that list against the list of your computers, and you can readily spot any unwanted interloper. Putting an offending MAC address in the "deny" column effectively blocks that system from piggybacking onto your wireless connection.

While both methods work, a hacker can very easily *spoof* a MAC address—make the NIC report a legitimate address rather than its own—and access the network. Worse, a hacker doesn't have to connect to your network to grab your network traffic out of thin air! If you have data so important that a hacker would want to get at it, you should seriously consider using a wired network, or separating the sensitive data from your wireless network in some fashion. MAC address filtering is also a bit of a maintenance nightmare, as every time you replace a NIC, you have to reconfigure your WAP with the new NIC's MAC address.

Wireless Authentication

Implementing authentication enables you to secure a network so that only users with the proper credentials can access network resources. It's not an all-or-nothing deal, of course; you can use authentication to restrict or enable what a specific user can do once inside the network as well.

Authentication in a wired network, as you'll recall from Chapter 11, "Securing TCP/IP," generally takes the form of a centralized security database that contains user names, passwords, and permissions, like the Active Directory in a Windows Server environment. Wireless network clients can use the same security database as wired clients, but it takes a couple of extra steps to get the wireless user authenticated.

The IEEE **802.1X** standard enables you to set up a network with some seriously secure authentication using a RADIUS server and passwords encrypted with **Extensible Authentication Protocol (EAP)**. Let's look at the components and the process.

A **RADIUS server** enables remote users to connect to a network service. It provides authentication through a user name and password, and enables you to set a user's rights once in the network. A RADIUS server functions like a typical server, but the remote aspect of it requires you to learn new jargon. The terms "client" and "server" are so Active Directory, after all.

Here's how it works. The client computer, called a **supplicant**, contacts the WAP, called a **Network Access Server (NAS)**, and requests permission to access the network. The NAS contacts the RADIUS server to see if the supplicant appears in the RADIUS server's security database. If the supplicant appears and the user name and password are correct, then the remote user gets access to the network resources. See Figure 16.7.

Here's where it gets tricky. What are the points of potential failure of security here? All over the place, right? The connection between each of these devices must be secure; several protocols make certain of that security. PPP, for example, provides a secure dial-up connection between the supplicant and the NAS.

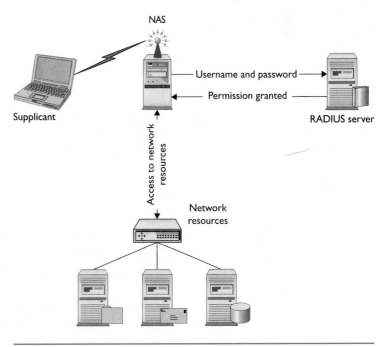

• **Figure 16.7** Authenticating using RADIUS

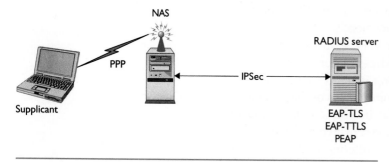

NAS

RADIUS server

PPP

IPSec

Supplicant

EAP-TLS
EAP-TTLS
PEAP

● **Figure 16.8**   Authentication using RADIUS with protocols in place

EAP and RADIUS servers for authentication paint half the picture on 802.1X security implementation. The other half is WPA2, discussed below.

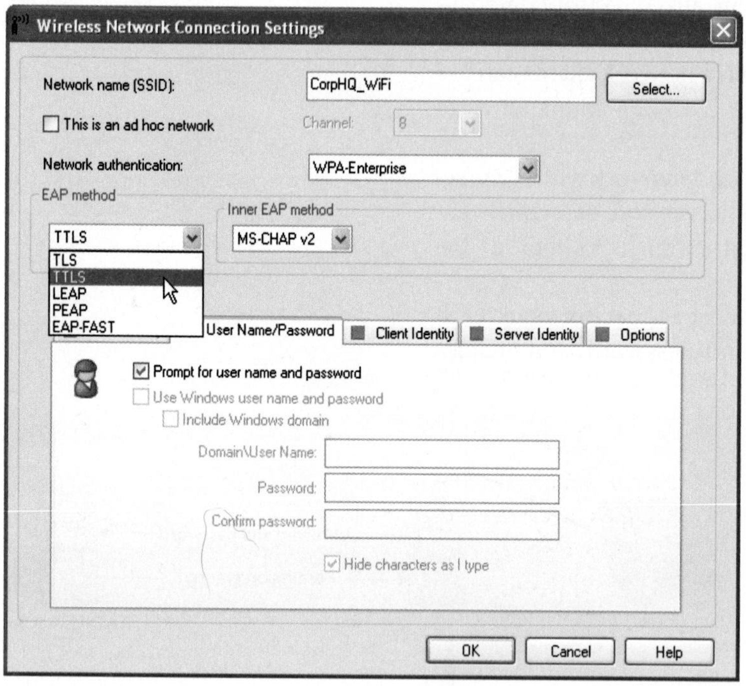

IPSec often provides security between the NAS and the RADIUS server. Finally, the RADIUS server needs to use a protocol, such as one of the many implementations of the Extensible Authentication Protocol (EAP), for the authentication part of the deal. See Figure 16.8.

EAP defines a framework for authentication, but does not specify how the authentication happens. Developers have therefore come up with many ways to handle the specifics, such as EAP-TLS, EAP-TTLS, and PEAP, to name just a few. The differences among the many flavors of EAP cause countless hours of argument among geeks, but from a technician's perspective you simply use the scheme that your network hardware supports. Both the WAP and the wireless NICs have to use the same EAP authentication scheme. You set this in the firmware or software, as you can see in Figure 16.9.

Data Encryption

The final step in securing a wireless network is encrypting the data packets that are floating around. **Encryption** electronically scrambles data packets and locks them with a private encryption key before transmitting them onto the wireless network. The receiving network device has to possess the encryption key to unscramble the packet and process the data. Thus, a hacker who grabs any data packets out of the air can't read those packets unless he or she has the encryption key. Enabling wireless encryption through Wired Equivalent Privacy (WEP), Wi-Fi Protected Access (WPA), or WPA2 provides a good level of security to data packets in transit.

Data Encryption Using WEP   Wired Equivalent Privacy (WEP) encryption uses a 64- or 128-bit encryption algorithm to scramble data packets, though even with the strongest encryption enabled, WEP isn't considered to be a particularly robust security solution. In fact, WEP can be cracked in 60 seconds with just a regular laptop and open source software! WEP doesn't provide complete encryption for data packets. It works only on the two lowest OSI network layers: the Data Link and Physical layers. Encryption is stripped from the data packet before it travels up through the subsequent network layers to the application.

Another problem with WEP is that the encryption key is both static (never changes from session to session) and shared (the same key is used by all network nodes). There is also no mechanism for performing user authentication. That is, network nodes that use WEP encryption are identified by

● **Figure 16.9**   Setting EAP authentication scheme

[Screenshot: Wireless Network Connection Settings dialog]

Wireless Network Connection Settings

Network name (SSID):   CorpHQ_WiFi   Select...

☐ This is an ad hoc network   Channel: 8

Network authentication: WPA-Enterprise

EAP method
TTLS
TLS
TTLS
LEAP
PEAP
EAP-FAST

Inner EAP method
MS-CHAP v2

User Name/Password   ■ Client Identity   ■ Server Identity   ■ Options

☑ Prompt for user name and password
☐ Use Windows user name and password
☐ Include Windows domain
Domain\User Name:
Password:
Confirm password:
☑ Hide characters as I type

OK   Cancel   Help

their MAC address, and no other credentials are offered or required. With just a laptop and some open source software, MAC addresses are very easy to sniff out and duplicate, thus opening up a possible spoofing attack.

Data Encryption Using WPA Wi-Fi Protected Access (WPA) addresses some of the weaknesses of WEP, and acts as a security protocol upgrade to WEP-enabled devices. WPA offers security enhancements such as dynamic encryption key generation (keys are issued on a per-user and per-session basis) and an encryption key integrity-checking feature.

WPA works by using an extra layer of security, called the **Temporal Key Integrity Protocol (TKIP)**, around the WEP encryption scheme. It's not, therefore, a complete replacement protocol for WEP. TKIP added a 128-bit encryption key that seemed unbreakable when first introduced. Within a couple of years of introduction, though, hackers could waltz through WPA security almost as quickly as through WEP security. Another solution had to be found.

Data Encryption Using WPA2 The IEEE **802.11i** standard amended the 802.11 standard to add much-needed security features. One of those features we've discussed already, the 802.1X authentication measure using EAP to provide secure access to Wi-Fi networks. Another key feature, **Wi-Fi Protected Access 2 (WPA2)**, changes the encryption algorithm used in WEP and WPA to the **Advanced Encryption Standard (AES)**, a 128-bit block cipher that's much tougher to crack than the 128-bit TKIP wrapper. WPA2 is not hack proof, but it definitely offers a much tougher encryption standard that stops the casual hacker cold.

Power over Ethernet

Wireless access points need electrical power, but they're invariably placed into strange locations (like ceilings or high up on walls) where it's not convenient to provide electrical power. No worries! Better WAPs now support a standard called **Power over Ethernet (PoE)** where they can get their power from the same Ethernet cables that transfer their data. The switch that connects the WAPs must support PoE, but as long as both the WAP and the switches to which they connect support PoE, there's nothing you have to do other than just plug in Ethernet cables. PoE works automatically. As you might imagine, it costs extra to get WAPs and switches that support PoE, but the convenience of PoE for wireless networks makes it a popular option.

▪ Implementing Wi-Fi

To install and configure a Wi-Fi network requires a number of discrete steps. You should start with a site survey to determine any obstacles you need to overcome. All wireless networks require clients, so that's your next step. That's all the hardware you'll need for an ad hoc network, but an infrastructure network takes a few more pieces, such as installing an access point and configuring both the access point and clients. Unless you have a small, personal network, you need to look at ways to extend the network so you have the coverage you want. Finally, you should put your network to the test, verifying that it works as you intended.

Site Survey

A **site survey** enables you to determine any obstacles to creating the wireless network you want. You should discover any other wireless networks in the area and create a drawing with interference sources clearly marked. This enables you to get the right kind of hardware you need to employ and makes it possible to get the proper network coverage.

What Wireless Is Already There?

Discovering any wireless network signals other than your own in your space enables you to set both the SSID and channel to avoid networks that overlap. Wireless networks send out radio signals along the 2.4- or 5-GHz band and use channels 1–11. If you have an 802.11g WAP and clients, for example, those devices would use the 2.4-GHz band and could be set to channel 1. A quick scan of the Wi-Fi networks in my neighborhood, for instance, shows five Wi-Fi networks, two with the SSID of Linksys, three using Channel 6, and two with both distinctive nondefault names and channels. If my network SSID were set to Linksys, which WAP have I used when I log onto the Linksys network?

Even if you change the SSID, why run on the same channel as other Wi-Fi networks? You'll see better performance if you're on a unique channel.

Interference Sources

It might seem like overkill in a small network, but any network beyond a simple ad hoc one should have a sketched-out site survey with any potential interference sources clearly marked (Figure 16.10). Refrigerators, reinforced walls, metal plumbing, microwave ovens; all of these can create horrible dead spots where your network radio wave can't easily penetrate. With a difficult or high-interference area, you might need to move up to 802.11n equipment with three or four antennae just to get the kind of coverage you want. Or you might need to plan a multiple WAP network to wipe out the dead zones. A proper site survey gives you the first tool for implementing a network that works.

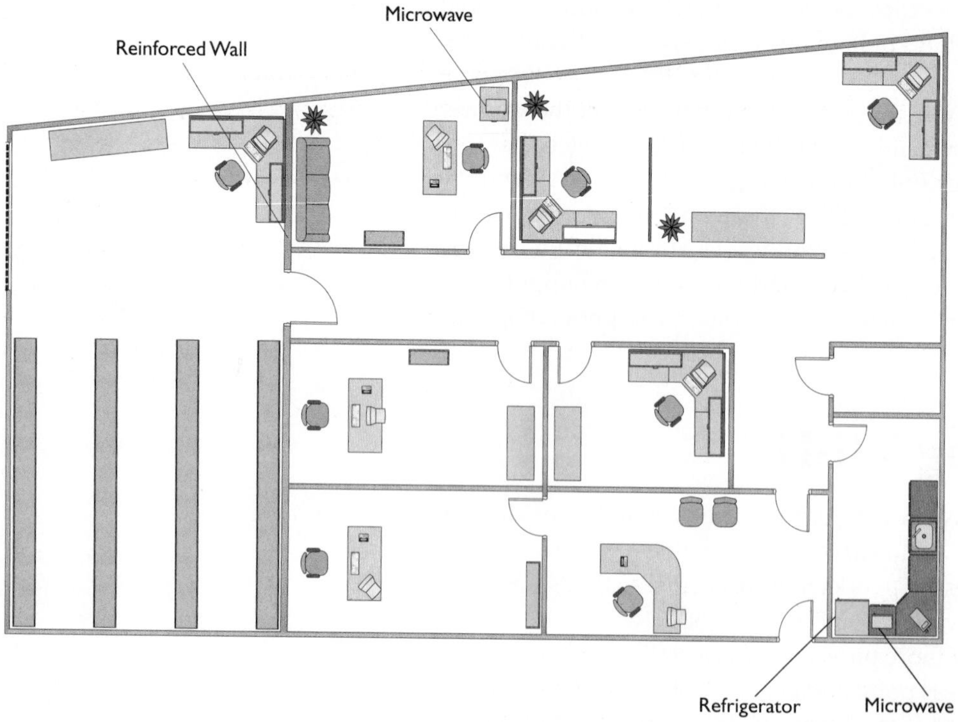

• **Figure 16.10** Site survey with interference sources noted

Installing the Client

Because every Wi-Fi network needs clients (otherwise, what's the point?), you need to install Wi-Fi client hardware and software. With a PCI or PCI Express NIC, power down the PC, disconnect from the AC source, and open the case. Following good CompTIA A+ technician procedures, locate a free slot on the motherboard, remove the slot cover, remove the NIC from its antistatic bag, install the NIC, and affix the retaining screw. See Figure 16.11. Often you'll need to attach the antenna. Button everything up, plug it in, and start the computer. When prompted, put in the disc that came from the manufacturer and install drivers and any other software necessary.

With a USB NIC, you should install the drivers and software before you connect the NIC to the computer. This is standard operating procedure for any USB device, as you most likely recall from your CompTIA A+ certification training (or from personal experience).

● **Figure 16.11**   Wi-Fi PCI NIC installed

Setting Up an Ad Hoc Network

Configuring NICs for ad hoc mode networking requires you to address four things: SSID, IP addresses, channel, and sharing. (Plus, of course, you have to set the NICs to function in ad hoc mode!) Each wireless node must use the same network name (SSID). Also, no two nodes can use the same IP address—although this is unlikely with modern versions of Windows and the Automatic Private IP Addressing (APIPA) feature that automatically selects a Class B IP address for any node not connected to a DHCP server or hard-coded to an IP address. Finally, ensure that the File and Printer Sharing service is running on all nodes. Figure 16.12 shows a wireless network configuration utility with ad hoc mode selected.

 Try This!

Ad Hoc-ing

If you have access to a Wi-Fi-enabled device and a friend or classmate has one as well, try this! Set up your Wi-Fi for ad hoc using the configuration utility, and then try to connect with your partner. Use default settings. Once you connect with the defaults, you can start playing with your ad hoc network! Share a folder—such as Shared Pictures in Windows XP—and then copy the sample images from one machine to another. If you have one, throw a big file into the shared folder and try copying that one, too. Then do it again, but with variations of distance and channels. How far can you separate and still communicate? What happens if you change channels in the configuration utility, such as moving both devices from channel 6 to channel 4?

Setting Up an Infrastructure Network

Site survey in hand and Wi-Fi technology selected, you're ready to set up a wireless network in infrastructure mode. You need to determine the optimal location for your WAP, configure the WAP, and then configure any clients to access that WAP. Seems pretty straightforward, but the devil, they say, is in the details.

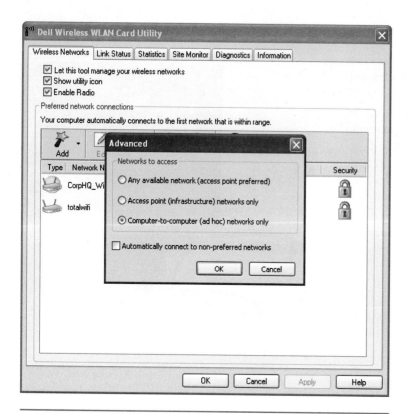

Placing Access Point

The optimal location for an access point depends on the area you want to cover and whether or not you care if the signal bleeds out beyond the borders. You also need to use antennae that provide enough signal and push that signal in the proper direction.

Omni-directional and Centered   For a typical network, you want blanket coverage and would place a WAP with an omni-directional antenna in the center of the area (Figure 16.13). With an omni-directional antenna, the radio wave flows outward from the WAP. This has the advantage of ease of use—anything within the signal radius can potentially access the network. Most wireless networks use this combination, especially in the consumer space. The standard straight-wire antennae that provide most omni-directional function are called **dipole antennae**.

The omni-directional and centered approach does not work for every network, for three reasons. First, if the signal exceeds the size of the network space, that signal bleeds out. The signal can bleed out a lot in some cases, particularly if your specific space doesn't allow you to put the WAP in the center, but rather off-center. This presents a security risk, because someone outside your network

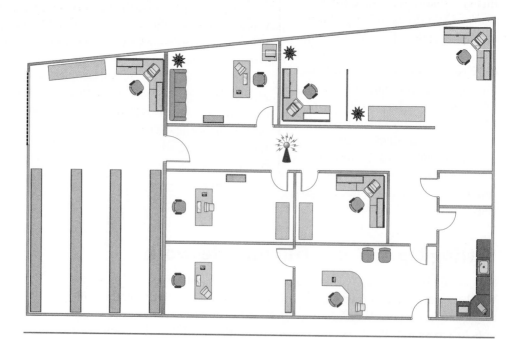

• Figure 16.13   Room layout with WAP in the center

space could lurk, pick up the signal, and run software to try to hack into your network. Or, a hacker might use your wireless signal for purposes that you might not condone. Second, if your network space exceeds the signal of your WAP, you'll need to get some sort of signal booster (see "Gaining Gain," below). Third, any obstacles will produce glaring dead spots in network coverage. Too many dead spots make a less-than-ideal solution. To address these issues you might need to go to other solutions.

Gaining Gain   An antenna strengthens and focuses the radio frequency (RF) output from a WAP. The ratio of increase—what's called **gain**—is measured in decibels (dB). The gain from a typical WAP is 2 dB, enough to cover a reasonable area but not a very large room. To increase that signal requires a bigger antenna. Many WAPs have removable antennae that you can replace. To increase the signal in an omni-directional and centered setup, simply replace the factory antennae with one or more bigger antennae (Figure 16.14). Get a big enough antenna and you can crank it all the way up to 11!

Focusing the Wave   When you don't necessarily want to broadcast to the world, you can use one or more directional antennae to create a nicely focused network. A **directional antenna**, as the name implies, focuses a radio wave into a beam of sorts. Directional antennae come in a variety of flavors, such as parabolic, dish, and Yagi, to name a just a few. A parabolic antenna looks like a satellite dish. A Yagi antenna (named for one of its Japanese inventors) is often called a beam antenna and can enable a focused radio wave to travel a long way, miles even.

• **Figure 16.14**   Replacement antenna on WAP

Tech Tip

Patch Antennae

Patch antennae are flat, plate-shaped antennae that generate a half-sphere beam. Patch antennas are always placed on walls. The half-sphere is perfect for indoor offices where you want to fill the room with a strong signal but not broadcast to the room behind the patch.

Access Point Configuration

Wireless access points have a browser-based setup utility. Typically, you fire up the Web browser on one of your network client workstations and enter the access point's default IP address, such as 192.168.1.1, to bring up the configuration page. You will need to supply an administrative password, included with your access point's documentation, to log in (Figure 16.15).

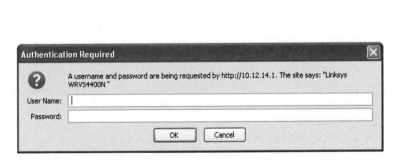

• **Figure 16.15**   Security login for Linksys WAP

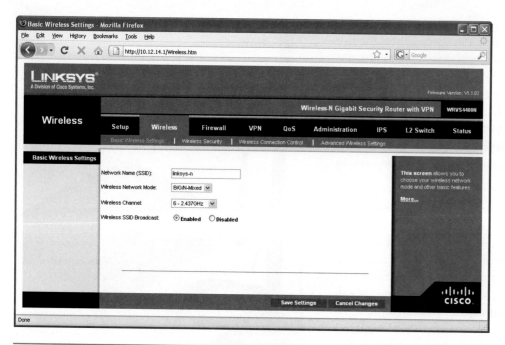

- **Figure 16.16**   Linksys WAP setup screen

Once you've logged in, you'll have configuration screens for changing your basic setup, access point password, security, and so on. Different access points offer different configuration options. Figure 16.16 shows the initial setup screen for a popular Linksys WAP/router.

Configuring the SSID (ESSID) and Beacon

The SSID option is usually located somewhere obvious on the configuration utility. On the Linksys model shown in Figure 16.16, it's on the Setup tab. Set your SSID to something unique. You can choose not to broadcast the SSID, but this only stops casual users— sophisticated wireless intruders have tools to detect networks that do not broadcast their SSIDs.

Aside from the SSID (or ESSID in an extended network), broadcast traffic includes the *beacon*, essentially a timing packet sent from the WAP at regular intervals. The beacon packet enables Wi-Fi networks to function, so this is fairly important. Beacon traffic also makes up a major percentage of network traffic because most WAPs have beacons set to go off every 100 ms! You can adjust the rate of the beacon traffic down and improve your network traffic speeds, but you lower the speed at which devices can negotiate to get on the network, among other things. Figure 16.17 shows the Beacon Interval setting on a Linksys router.

Configuring MAC Address Filtering   Increase security even further by using MAC address filtering. This builds a list of wireless network clients that are permitted or denied access to your wireless network based on their unique MAC addresses.

Figure 16.18 shows the MAC address filtering configuration screen on a Linksys WAP. Simply enter the MAC address of a wireless node that you want to allow (or deny) access to your wireless network.

Configuring Encryption   Enabling encryption ensures that data packets are secured against unauthorized access. To set up encryption, you turn on encryption at the WAP and generate a unique security key. Then you configure all connected wireless nodes on the network with the same key information. Figure 16.19 shows the WEP key configuration dialog box for a Linksys WAP.

You have the option of automatically generating a set of encryption keys or doing it manually. You can save yourself a certain

---

Tech Tip

SSIDs and Overlapping Networks
One of the great benefits of SSIDs in the wild is the ability to configure multiple wireless networks in close proximity, even using the same frequency and channel, and still not conflict. For tight locations, such as dorm rooms, office complexes, and apartments, choose a unique SSID for each wireless network to avoid the potential for overlap problems.

Beacon Interval:	100	(Default: 100 Msec, Range: 20 ~ 1000)
DTIM Interval:	1	(Default: 1, Range: 1 ~ 255)
RTS Threshold:	2346	(Default: 2346, Range: 256 ~ 2346)

- **Figure 16.17**   Setting the beacon interval

amount of effort by using the automatic method. Select an encryption level—the usual choices are either 64-bit or 128-bit—and then enter a unique *passphrase* and click the Generate button (or whatever the equivalent button is called in your WAP's software). Then select a default key and save the settings.

The encryption level, key, and passphrase must match on the wireless client node or communication fails. Many access points have the capability to export the encryption key data onto removable media for easy importing onto a client workstation, or you can configure encryption manually using the vendor-supplied configuration utility, as shown in Figure 16.20.

WPA encryption, if supported by your wireless equipment, is configured in

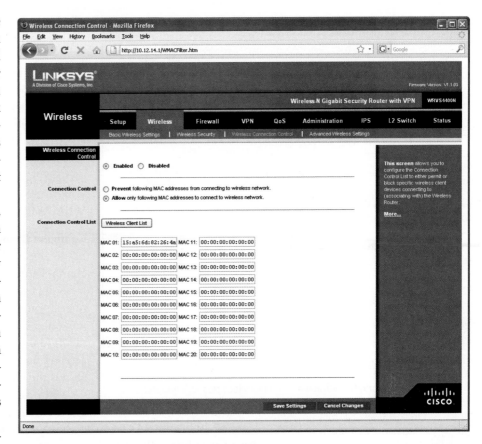

● **Figure 16.18**   MAC address filtering configuration screen for a Linksys WAP

● **Figure 16.19**   Encryption key configuration screen on Linksys WAP

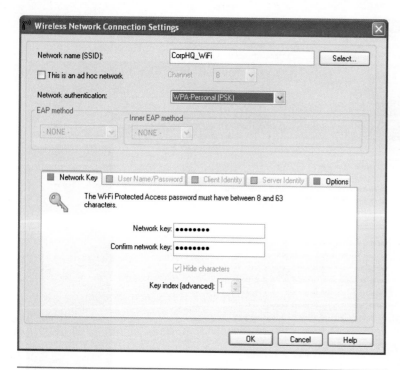

● **Figure 16.20**   Encryption screen on client wireless network adapter configuration utility

much the same way. You may be required to input a valid user name and password to configure encryption using WPA.

If you have the option, choose WPA2 encryption for both the WAP and the NICs in your network. You configure WPA2 the same way you would WPA. Note that the settings such as WPA2 for the Enterprise assume you'll enable authentication using a RADIUS server (Figure 16.21). Use the best encryption you can. If you have WPA2, use it. If not, use WPA. WEP is always a last choice.

Configure Channel and Frequency   With most home networks, you can simply leave the channel and frequency of the WAP at the factory defaults, but in an environment with overlapping Wi-Fi signals, you'll want to adjust one or both features. To adjust the channel, find the option in the WAP configuration screens and simply change it. Figure 16.22 shows the channel option in a Linksys WAP.

With dual-band 802.11n WAPs, you can choose which band to put 802.11n traffic on, either 2.4 GHz or 5 GHz. In an area with overlapping signals, most of the traffic will be on the 2.4-GHz frequency, because most devices are either 802.11b or 802.11g. You can avoid any kind of conflict with your 802.11n devices by using the 5-GHz frequency instead. Figure 16.23 shows the configuration screen for a dual-band 802.11n WAP.

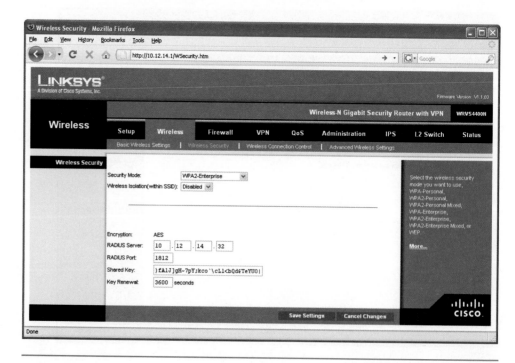

● **Figure 16.21**   Encryption screen with RADIUS option

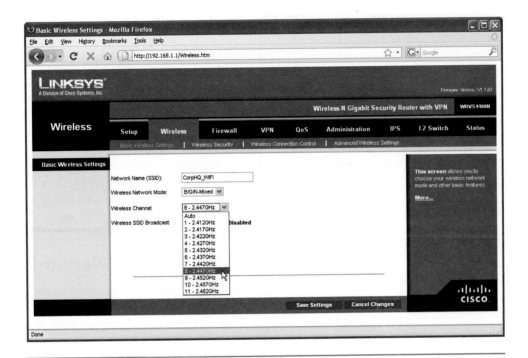

● **Figure 16.22**   Changing the channel

● **Figure 16.23**   Selecting frequency

Chapter 16: Wireless Networking

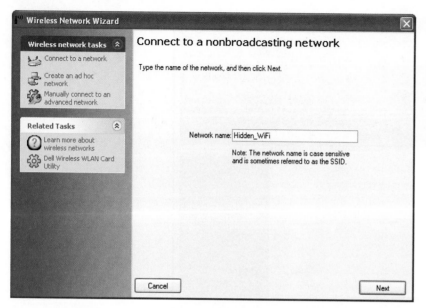

Figure 16.24 Typing in an SSID manually

Configuring the Client

As with ad hoc mode wireless networks, infrastructure mode networks require that the same SSID be configured on all nodes and access points. Normally, the client would pick up a broadcast SSID and all you need to do is type in the security passphrase or encryption key. With nonbroadcasting networks, on the other hand, you need to type in a valid SSID as well as the security information (Figure 16.24).

Extending the Network

Creating a Basic Service Set network with a single WAP and multiple clients works in a relatively small area, but you can extend a Wi-Fi network in a couple of ways if you have difficult spaces—with lots of obstructions, for example—or a need to communicate beyond the ~300-foot range of the typical wireless network. Most commonly, you'd add one or more WAPs to create an Extended Service Set. You can also install a wireless bridge to connect two or more segments.

Adding a WAP

Some manufacturers market special Wi-Fi extenders or repeaters that pick up the Wi-Fi signal wirelessly and repeat it into a wider space.

To add a WAP to a Wi-Fi network generally means to run a UTP cable from the new WAP to the main WAP. So they connect with wires. Configuration is pretty straightforward. Both WAPs require the same ESSID and channel, though the frequency can vary if the two are 802.11n WAPs.

Wireless Bridge

Dedicated **wireless bridges** are used to connect two wireless network segments together, or to join wireless and wired networks together in the same way that wired bridge devices do. You can also use wireless bridges to join wireless networks with other networked devices, such as printers.

Wireless bridges come in two different flavors: point-to-point and point-to-multipoint. **Point-to-point** bridges can only communicate with a single other bridge, and are used to connect two wireless network segments. **Point-to-multipoint** bridges can talk to more than one other bridge at a time, and are used to connect multiple network segments. Some vendors also offer repeating bridges, and bridges with access point and router functions. Figure 16.25 shows a wireless bridge.

Figure 16.25 Linksys wireless bridge device

Verify the Installation

Once you've completed the initial installation of a Wi-Fi network, check it. Move some traffic from one computer to another using the wireless connection. Never leave a job site without verifying the installation.

Troubleshooting Wi-Fi

Wireless networks are a real boon when they work right, but they can also be one of the most vexing things to troubleshoot when they don't. Let's turn to some practical advice on how to detect and correct wireless hardware, software, and configuration problems.

As with any troubleshooting scenario, your first step in troubleshooting a wireless network is to break down your tasks into logical steps. Your first step should be to figure out the scope of your wireless networking problem. Ask yourself *who*, *what*, and *when*:

- Who is affected by the problem?
- What is the nature of their network problem?
- When did the problem start?

The answers to these questions dictate at least the initial direction of your troubleshooting.

So, who's affected? If all machines on your network—wired and wireless—have lost connectivity, you have bigger problems than the wireless machines being unable to access the network. Troubleshoot this situation the way you'd troubleshoot any network failure. Once you determine which wireless nodes are affected, it's easier to pinpoint whether the problem lies in one or more wireless clients or in one or more access points.

After you narrow down the number of affected machines, your next task is to figure out specifically what type of error the users are experiencing. If they can access some, but not all, network services, then it's unlikely that the problem is limited to their wireless equipment. For example, if they can browse the Internet but can't access any shared resources on a server, then they're probably experiencing a permissions-related issue rather than a wireless one.

Finally, determine when the problem started. What has changed that might explain your loss of connectivity? Did you or somebody else change the wireless network configuration? For example, if the network worked fine two minutes ago, and then you changed the WEP key on the access point, and now nobody can see the network, you have your solution—or at least your culprit! Did your office experience a power outage, power sag, or power surge? Any of these might cause a WAP to fail.

Once you figure out the who, what, and when, you can start troubleshooting in earnest. Typically, your problem is going to center on your hardware, software, connectivity, or configuration.

Hardware Troubleshooting

Wireless networking hardware components are subject to the same kind of abuse and faulty installation as any other hardware component. Troubleshooting a suspected hardware problem should bring out the CompTIA A+ certified technician in you.

Open Windows Device Manager and check to see if there's an error or conflict with the wireless adapter. If you see a big yellow exclamation point or a red X next to the device, you have either a driver error or a resource conflict. Reinstall the device driver or manually reset the IRQ resources as needed.

If you don't see the device listed at all, it's possible that the device is not seated properly in its PCI slot, or not plugged all the way into its PC Card or USB slot. These problems are easy to fix. One thing to consider if you're using an older laptop and PC Card combination is that the wireless adapter may be a CardBus type of PC Card device. CardBus cards will not snap into a non-CardBus slot, even though both new and old cards are the same size. If your laptop is older than about five years, it may not support CardBus, meaning you need to get a different PC Card device. Or, if you've been looking for a reason to get a new laptop, now you have one!

Software Troubleshooting

Because you've already checked to confirm that your hardware is using the correct drivers, what kind of software-related problems are left to check? Two things come immediately to mind: the wireless adapter configuration utility and the WAP's firmware version.

As I mentioned earlier, some wireless devices won't work correctly unless you install the vendor-provided drivers and configuration utility before plugging in the device. This is particularly true of wireless USB devices. If you didn't do this, go into Device Manager and uninstall the device, then start again from scratch.

Some WAP manufacturers (I won't name names here, but they're popular) are notorious for shipping devices without the latest firmware installed. This problem often manifests as a device that enables clients to connect, but only at such slow speeds that the devices experience frequent timeout errors. The fix for this is to update the access point's firmware. Go to the manufacturer's Web site and follow the support links until you find the latest version. You'll need your device's exact model and serial number—this is important, because installing the wrong firmware version on your device is a guaranteed way of rendering it unusable!

Again, follow the manufacturer's instructions for updating the firmware to the letter. Typically, you need to download a small executable updating program along with a data file containing the firmware software. The process takes only minutes, and you'll be amazed at the results.

Connectivity Troubleshooting

Properly configured wireless clients should automatically and quickly connect to the desired SSID. If this isn't taking place, it's time for some troubleshooting. Most wireless connectivity problems come down to either an incorrect configuration (like an incorrect password) or low signal strength. Without a strong signal, even a properly configured wireless client isn't going to work. Wireless clients use a multi-bar graph (usually five bars) to give an idea of signal strength: zero bars indicates no signal and five bars indicates maximum signal.

Whether configuration or signal strength, the process to diagnose and repair uses the same methods you use for a wired network. First, check the wireless NIC's link light to see whether it's passing data packets to and from the network. Second, check the wireless NIC's configuration utility. Typically, the utility has an icon in your System Tray that shows the strength of your wireless signal. Figure 16.26 shows Windows XP Professional's built-in wireless configuration utility—called Wireless Zero Configuration (or just Zeroconf)—displaying the link state and signal strength.

The link state defines the wireless NIC's connection status to a wireless network: connected or disconnected. If your link state indicates that your computer is currently disconnected, you may have a problem with your WAP. If your signal is too weak to receive a signal, you may be out of range of your access point, or there may be a device causing interference.

You can fix these problems in a number of ways. Because Wi-Fi signals bounce off objects, you can try small adjustments to your antennae to see if the signal improves. You can swap out the standard antenna for one or more higher-gain antennae. You can relocate the PC or access point, or locate and move the device causing interference.

Other wireless devices that operate in the same frequency range as your wireless nodes can cause interference as well. Look for wireless telephones, intercoms, and so on as possible culprits. One fix for interference caused by other wireless devices is to change the channel your network uses. Another is to change the channel the offending device uses, if possible. If you can't change channels, try moving the interfering device to another area or replacing it with a different device.

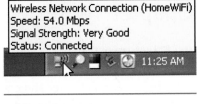

● **Figure 16.26** Windows XP Professional's wireless configuration utility

Configuration Troubleshooting

With all due respect to the fine network techs in the field, the most common type of wireless networking problem is misconfigured hardware or software. That's right—the dreaded *user error*! Given the complexities of wireless networking, this isn't so surprising. All it takes is one slip of the typing finger to throw off your configuration completely. The things that you're most likely to get wrong are the SSID and security configuration.

Verify SSID configuration on your access point first, and then check on the affected wireless nodes. Most wireless devices enable you to use any characters in the SSID, including blank spaces. Be careful not to add blank characters where they don't belong, such as trailing blank spaces behind any other characters typed into the name field.

If you're using MAC address filtering, make sure the MAC address of the client that's attempting to access the wireless network is on the list of accepted users. This is particularly important if you swap out NICs on a PC, or if you introduce a new PC to your wireless network.

Check the security configuration to make sure that all wireless nodes and access points match. Mistyping an encryption key prevents the affected node from talking to the wireless network, even if your signal strength is 100 percent! Remember that many access points have the capability to export encryption keys onto a floppy disk or other removable media. It's then a simple matter to import the encryption key onto the PC using the wireless NIC's configuration utility. Remember that the encryption level must match on access points and wireless nodes. If your WAP is configured for 128-bit encryption, all nodes must also use 128-bit encryption.

Tech Tip

Windows XP and Zeroconf
One trick that works for wireless networks that seem a bit flaky with a Windows XP client is to disable the Wireless Zero Configuration service on the client. To do this, simply open the Services applet in Administrative Tools and change the Startup Type option from Automatic to Disabled. Document your change, of course, so you'll remember to turn Zeroconf back on in case it doesn't provide the fix you want.

Try This!

Breaking Wi-Fi
You've read about it—now it's time to see the movie (or at least the next best thing)! If you have a functional Wi-Fi network set up in infrastructure mode, try breaking it. What happens when you change channels? What if you stop broadcasting the SSID? Be creative here! The goal is to experience typical problems and to understand the specific causes.

Chapter 16 Review

■ Chapter Summary

After reading this chapter and completing the exercises, you should understand the following about wireless networking.

Explain wireless networking standards

- Wireless networks operate much like their wired counterparts, but they eliminate network cabling by using radio waves as a network medium.

- The most common wireless networking standard is IEEE 802.11, also known as Wi-Fi. 802.11 includes extended standards such as 802.11a, 802.11b, 802.11g, and 802.11n.

- Computers that lack a built-in wireless Ethernet NIC can use a PCI expansion card, PC Card, or USB NIC. The benefit of a USB wireless NIC is the ability to use an extender cable, allowing the USB NIC to be placed in the optimum location for signal strength.

- Wireless NICs normally require configuration software supplied by the manufacturer. Microsoft Windows XP systems have wireless NIC configuration software built in.

- A wireless network can operate in one of two modes: ad hoc or infrastructure.

- Ad hoc mode, also known as peer-to-peer, creates an Independent Basic Service Set (IBSS).

- Infrastructure mode is more commonly used than ad hoc mode and allows wireless networks to connect to wired networks. A single wireless access point connecting computers in infrastructure mode is called a Basic Service Set (BSS). If multiple WAPs are used, an Extended Basic Service Set (EBSS) is created, though most techs simply refer to it as an Extended Service Set (ESS).

- Wireless networking speeds range from 2 Mbps to a theoretical limit of 300 Mbps. The speed is affected by the distance between wireless nodes, interference from other wireless devices such as cordless phones or baby monitors, and solid objects such as metal plumbing or air conditioning units.

- Wireless networking ranges are affected by environmental factors, interference from other wireless devices, and solid objects.

- The Basic Service Set Identifier (BSSID) identifies a network so that packets are delivered to the correct computer on the correct network.

- The Service Set Identifier (SSID) configuration parameter enables you to set a basic level of access security. Properly configured SSIDs, or network names, exclude any wireless network device that does not share the same SSID.

- A Wi-Fi network with multiple WAPs applies the SSID to the ESS, creating an Extended Service Set Identifier (ESSID).

- The original 802.11 standards use the 2.4-GHz frequency while later standards use either 2.4-GHz or 5.0-GHz frequencies. These frequencies allow the wireless networks to operate with less chance of interference from other wireless devices that are not part of the network.

- Spread-spectrum radio waves distribute data in small chunks over different frequencies to reduce interference from other wireless devices not part of the network. 802.11 networks use the direct-sequence spread spectrum (DSSS) implementation.

- Wi-Fi channels use a portion of the available frequency spectrum to further tune out potential interference. Most devices are preset to use channel 6.

- Wi-Fi networks use carrier sense media access/collision avoidance (CSMA/CA) to send packets. CSMA/CA is proactive in that it attempts to avoid collisions before they happen rather than simply detecting them when they occur.

- Currently, only the Distributed Coordination Function (DCF) method of CSMA/CA is implemented. DCF uses IFS wait periods, backoff periods, and acknowledgements (ACK) to avoid collisions.

- 802.11b supports data throughput up to 11 Mbps over 300 feet on the 2.4-GHz frequency.

- 802.11a, which was released after 802.11b, supports data throughput up to 54 Mbps over 150 feet on the 5.0-GHz frequency.

- 802.11g supports data throughput up to 54 Mbps over 300 feet on the 2.4-GHz frequency. 802.11g is also backward compatible with 802.11b.

- 802.11n supports data throughput up to 600 Mbps theoretically over 300 feet on the 2.4-GHz frequency. 802.11n requires MIMO and transmit beaming to achieve its greater data throughput. It is also backward compatible with 802.11b and 802.11g.

- 802.16, WiMax, is expected to support ranges up to 30 miles.

- Wireless networks may be secured with MAC address filtering, though this method can be easily hacked by spoofing.

- A RADIUS server allows remote users to connect to a network with a user name and password, providing better security than MAC address filtering. A supplicant contacts a NAS, which in turn contacts the RADIUS server.

- Data should be encrypted when being transferred across a wireless network. WEP offers very little protection because it is easily hacked. WPA is better because it uses the Temporal Key Integrity Protocol (TKIP). WPA2, which uses the Advanced Encryption Standard (AES), is the strongest of the three.

- Better WAPs and switches can use Power over Ethernet (PoE) to provide electrical power to the WAP via the Ethernet cable that connects it with the switch. Both WAP and switch must have this capability built in for it to work.

Describe the process for implementing Wi-Fi networks

- The first step in creating a wireless network is to create a site survey, which identifies other wireless networks or objects that may cause interference.

- Wireless networking hardware must be installed in all the clients. Most laptops have wireless NICs

built in, but a PC Card can be used as an alternative. Desktop computers may use a PCI expansion card. Any computer with a USB port can use a USB wireless NIC.

- Configuring a NIC for ad hoc networking requires the SSID, IP address, channel, and sharing to be configured.

- Configuring a NIC for infrastructure networking requires planning the optimal placement of the WAP. A replacement antenna can strengthen the wireless signal and extend the range. The WAP also needs to be configured with the proper settings for the SSID, security, and encryption options.

- A wireless network's range can be extended by adding multiple WAPs. The additional WAPs typically connect to each other via a hard cable.

- A wireless bridge connects two wireless segments together. A point-to-point bridge can only communicate with a single other bridge while a point-to-multipoint bridge can communicate with more than one other bridge at the same time.

Describe troubleshooting techniques for wireless networks

- As with any troubleshooting scenario, your first step should be to figure out the scope of your wireless networking problem. Ask yourself *who*, *what*, and *when*. This helps you focus your initial troubleshooting on the most likely aspects of the network.

- Hardware troubleshooting for Wi-Fi devices should touch on the usual hardware process. Go to Device Manager and check for obvious conflicts. Check the drivers to make sure you have them installed and up to date. Make certain you have proper connectivity between the device and the PC.

- Software troubleshooting involves checking configuration settings, such as the SSID, WEP, MAC address filtering, and encryption levels. Configuration settings on both the WAP and wireless NIC should be checked.

Key Terms

802.1X *(437)*
802.11 *(427)*
802.11a *(435)*
802.11b *(435)*
802.11g *(435)*
802.11i *(439)*
802.11n *(435)*
802.16 *(436)*
ad hoc mode *(430)*
Advanced Encryption Standard (AES) *(439)*
Basic Service Set (BSS) *(431)*
Basic Service Set Identifier (BSSID) *(432)*
carrier sense multiple access/collision avoidance (CSMA/CA) *(434)*
channel *(433)*
dipole antennae *(442)*
direct-sequence spread-spectrum (DSSS) *(433)*
directional antenna *(443)*
Distributed Coordination Function (DCF) *(434)*
encryption *(438)*
Extended Service Set (ESS) *(431)*
Extended Service Set Identifier (ESSID) *(433)*
Extensible Authentication Protocol (EAP) *(437)*
frequency-hopping spread-spectrum (FHSS) *(433)*
gain *(443)*
Independent Basic Service Set (IBSS) *(430)*
infrastructure mode *(431)*
interframe space (IFS) *(434)*

link state *(429)*
MAC address filtering *(436)*
multiple in/multiple out (MIMO) *(435)*
Network Access Server (NAS) *(437)*
network name *(433)*
orthogonal frequency-division multiplexing (OFDM) *(433)*
peer-to-peer mode *(430)*
Point Coordination Function (PCF) *(434)*
point-to-multipoint *(448)*
point-to-point *(448)*
Power over Ethernet (PoE) *(439)*
RADIUS server *(437)*
Service Set Identifier (SSID) *(433)*
signal strength *(429)*
site survey *(440)*
supplicant *(437)*
Temporal Key Integrity Protocol (TKIP) *(439)*
transmit beamforming *(436)*
Wi-Fi Protected Access (WPA) *(439)*
Wi-Fi Protected Access 2 (WPA2) *(439)*
WiMax *(436)*
wireless access point (WAP) *(429)*
wireless bridge *(448)*
Wired Equivalent Privacy (WEP) *(438)*
Wi-Fi *(427)*
wireless network *(427)*

Key Term Quiz

Use the Key Terms list to complete the sentences that follow. Not all the terms will be used.

1. When a network uses the 802.11 standard, it is said to be a(n) _____.

2. Establishing a unique _____ or network name helps ensure that only wireless network devices configured similarly are permitted access to the network.

3. To connect wireless network segments together, you should use a(n) _____.

4. _____ wireless bridges are used to connect only two wireless network segments together, because they can only communicate with a single other bridge.

5. _____ wireless bridges are used to connect multiple network segments together, because they can talk to more than one other bridge at a time.

6. Of the two wireless encryption protocols, _____ is less secure.

7. Of the two different spread-spectrum broadcasting methods, _____ sends data out on different frequencies at the same time, and therefore uses considerably more bandwidth.

8. WPA uses _____ to encrypt data while WPA2 uses the more secure _____.

9. _____ allows devices on 802.11n networks to make multiple simultaneous connections, allowing for a theoretical throughput of 600 Mbps.

10. 802.11 implements _____, which proactively avoids network packet collisions rather than simply detecting them when they occur.

■ Multiple-Choice Quiz

1. What was the first wireless standard?
   A. 802.11b
   B. 802.11a
   C. 802.11g
   D. 802.11

2. What are currently the most popular wireless standards? (Select two.)
   A. 802.11a
   B. 802.11b
   C. 802.11g
   D. 802.11i

3. Where would wireless access points likely be found? (Select three.)
   A. Airport
   B. Café
   C. Historic buildings
   D. Secure facilities

4. Which of the following statements about SSIDs are true? (Select three.)
   A. All wireless networks use them.
   B. Only one wireless device uses them.
   C. They should be unique to your wireless LAN.
   D. They are broadcast by default by most wireless network devices.

5. What is the best way to connect multiple wireless segments together?
   A. Use an 802.11g network adapter.
   B. Use an 802.11i network adapter.
   C. Use a point-to-multipoint wireless bridge.
   D. Use a point-to-point wireless bridge.

6. What should you use when you want to limit access to your wireless network based on the physical, hard-coded address of each wireless network device?
   A. Bus scheduling
   B. Encoding
   C. Encryption
   D. MAC address filtering

7. What process secures a wireless network by protecting data packets being transmitted?
   A. Data packeting
   B. Pulse encoding
   C. Data encryption
   D. MAC broadcasting

8. What are the two 802.11 standards that define data collision avoidance?
   A. ACF
   B. DCF
   C. ECF
   D. PCF

9. What is the predefined silence period between data transmissions called?
   A. IEEE
   B. IFS
   C. ISM
   D. IPX

10. What is the reactive method used for avoiding collisions on Ethernet networks?

    A. CSMA/CA

    B. CSMA/CD

    C. CSMA/WEP

    D. CSMA/WPA

11. Which of the following networking standards operates at a frequency of 5 GHz?

    A. 802.11a

    B. 802.11b

    C. 802.11g

    D. 802.11i

12. Which of the following is the wireless network encryption method that is most secure?

    A. MAC address filtering

    B. WEP

    C. WPA

    D. WPA2

13. Which of the following is known as a Basic Service Set in infrastructure mode?

    A. A WAP

B. A WPA

C. A RADIUS server

D. A TKIP

14. In an attempt to maximize your wireless throughput while minimizing interference on your brand new 802.11b/g WAP, which setting should you change?

    A. Change the WAP setting to not broadcast the SSID.

    B. Change the channel to 6.

    C. Change the channel to anything other than 6.

    D. Change the frequency to 5.0 GHz.

15. What is true about the 802.16 standard?

    A. It supports about the same speed as 802.11b, but has a range of up to 30 miles.

    B. It supports a speed of about 600 Mbps at a range of about 300 feet.

    C. It supports a speed of about 600 Mbps at a range of up to 30 miles.

    D. There is no such thing as 802.16.

■ Essay Quiz

1. Some friends of yours insist that wireless network standard 802.11a was available before 802.11b. They also say 802.11a is "better" than 802.11b. Find the pages in this chapter that discuss these standards, and jot down some notes to explain the facts.

2. You are enrolled in a writing class at the local community college. This week's assignment is to write on a technical subject. Write a short paragraph about each of the wireless standards that can reach theoretical speeds of 54 Mbps.

3. Prepare a short memo to your instructor (or friend) that outlines the basic differences

between WEP and WPA encryption methods. Use any standard memo format you are familiar with. Include a company or school logo on the top of the page to make the memo appear as if it were printed on company stationery (or "letterhead").

4. Write a few paragraphs describing the pros and cons of both wired and wireless networks. Specifically, compare 100BaseT to the 802.11b standard. Then conclude with a statement of your own personal preference.

Lab Projects

• Lab Project 16.1

You just received a nice tax return and want to expand your home network. Your current wired home network setup consists of two Intel Core 2 Duo-class desktop PCs with 10/100-Mbps NICs, and a relative's older laptop with both an RJ-45 port and 802.11b wireless built in. The main Internet connection coming into your home enters your more powerful desktop system first, and then spreads out to a 10-Mbps hub from there. With your own money to be spent buying equipment, you seek a solution that will satisfy your needs for a long time.

You want to buy your new equipment locally, so you can set it up right away. Use the Internet to explore local stores' prices and equipment. Also check out reviews of the items you are interested in obtaining. After you have done sufficient research, prepare an itemized price list with your choices arranged like the following table:

ITEM	STORE/MODEL	PRICE	QUANTITY	TOTAL
Wireless NICs, PCI				
Wireless NICs, PC Card				
Wireless Access Point				
Other				
TOTALS				

• Lab Project 16.2

You have been tasked with expanding your company's wireless network. Your IT Manager asked you to create a presentation that explains wireless routers and their functions. She specifically said to focus on the 802.11b and 802.11g wireless network standards. Create a brief, yet informative, PowerPoint presentation that includes comparisons of these two technologies. You may include images of actual wireless bridges from vendor Web sites as needed, being sure to cite your sources. Include any up-to-date prices from your research as well.

chapter 17

Protecting Your Network

"The superior man, when resting in safety, does not forget that danger may come."
—CONFUCIUS

In this chapter, you will learn how to

- Discuss the common security threats in network computing

- Describe methods for securing user accounts

- Explain how firewalls, NAT, port filtering, and packet filtering protect a network from threats

The very nature of networking makes networks vulnerable to a dizzying array of threats. By definition, a network must allow multiple users to access serving systems, but at the same time we must protect the network from harm. Who are the people creating this threat?

The news may be full of tales about **hackers** and other malicious people with nothing better to do than lurk around the Internet and trash the peace-loving systems of good folks like us, but in reality hackers are only one of many serious network threats. You will learn how to protect your networks from hackers, but first I want you to appreciate that the average network faces plenty more threats from the folks who are authorized to use it than those who are not authorized. Users with good intentions are far more likely to cause you trouble than any hacker. Additionally, don't think all network threats are people. Let's not forget natural disasters like floods and hurricanes. Even third parties can unintentionally wreak havoc—what will you do if your building suddenly lacks electricity? So a **network threat** can be any number of things that share one essential feature: the potential to damage network data, machines, or users. The first order of business, therefore, is to stop and think about the types of threats that face the average network. As we define the threats, we can discuss the many tools and methods used to protect our precious networks from intentional harm.

Be aware that in some circles, the term "hacker" describes folks who love the challenge of overcoming obstacles and perceived limitations—and that's a positive thing! At least for this chapter we will define a hacker as an unauthorized person who is intentionally trying to access resources on your network.

Test Specific

■ Common Threats

The threats to your network are real and widespread. Here's a list of some of the more common potential threats to your network. The sections that follow give details on those threats and explain how to deal with them.

- System crashes and other hardware failures
- Administrative access control weaknesses
- Malware, such as viruses and worms
- Social engineering
- Denial of Service attacks
- Physical intrusion
- Rogue access points

System Crash/Hardware Failure

Like any technology, computers can and will fail—usually when you can least afford for it to happen. Hard drives crash, servers lock up, the power fails—it's all part of the joy of working in the networking business. We need to create redundancy in areas prone to failure (like installing backup power in case of electrical failure) and performing those all-important data backups. Beyond that, the idea is to deploy redundant hardware to provide **fault tolerance**. Take advantage of technologies like RAID (Redundant Array of Inexpensive Disks) to spread data across multiple drives. Buy a server case with multiple power supplies or add a second NIC.

See Chapter 18, "Network Management," for more information on RAID.

Administrative Access Control

All operating systems and many TCP applications come with some form of access control list (ACL) that defines what users can do with the server's shared resources. An access control might be a file server giving a user read-only privileges to a particular folder, or an FTP server only allowing certain logins to use certain folders. Every operating system—and many Internet applications—are packed with administrative tools and functionality. We need these tools to get all kinds of work done, but by the same token we need to work hard to keep these capabilities out of the reach of those who don't need them.

Make sure you know the "super" accounts native to Windows (administrator) and Linux and Macintosh OS X (root). You must carefully control these accounts. Clearly, giving regular users administrator/root access is a bad idea, but far more subtle problems can arise. I once gave a user Manage Documents permission for a busy laser printer in a Windows network. She quickly realized she could pause other users' print jobs and send her print jobs to the beginning of the print queue—nice for her but not so nice for her co-workers. Protecting administrative programs and functions from access and abuse by users is a real challenge, and one that requires an extensive knowledge of the operating system and of users' motivations.

Malware

The term **malware** defines any program or code (macro, script, and so on) that's designed to do something on a system or network that you don't want to have happen. Malware comes in quite a variety of guises, such as viruses, worms, macros, Trojans, rootkits, and adware and spyware. Let's examine all these malware flavors and then finish with how to deal with them.

Virus

A **virus** is a program that has two jobs: to replicate and to activate. *Replication* means it makes copies of itself, often as code stored in boot sectors or as extra code added to the end of executable programs. *Activation* is when a virus does something like erase the boot sector of a drive. A virus only replicates to other drives, such as thumb drives or optical media. It does not replicate across networks.

Worm

A **worm** is identical in function to a virus except that it replicates exclusively through networks. A worm, unlike a virus, doesn't have to wait for someone to use a removable drive to replicate. If the infected computer is on a network, a worm will immediately start sending copies of itself to any other computers on the network it can locate.

Macro

A **macro** is any type of virus that exploits application macros to replicate and activate. Macros exist in any application that has a built-in macro language, such as Microsoft Excel, that users can program to handle repetitive tasks (among other things).

Trojan

A **Trojan** is a piece of malware that looks or pretends to do one thing while at the same time doing something evil. The more "popular" Trojans turn an infected computer into a server and then open TCP/IP ports so that a remote user can control the infected computer. They can be used to capture keystrokes, passwords, files, credit card information, and more. This type of Trojan is called a *remote administration tool* (*RAT*), though you don't need to know that for the CompTIA Network+ exam. Trojans do not replicate.

Rootkit

For a virus or Trojan to succeed it needs to come up with some method to hide itself. As awareness of malware has grown, anti-malware programs make it harder to find new locations on a computer to hide. A **rootkit** is a Trojan that takes advantage of very low-level operating system functions to hide itself from all but the most aggressive of anti-malware tools.

The most infamous rootkit appeared a few years ago as an antipiracy attempt by Sony on its music CDs. Unfortunately for the media giant, the rootkit software installed when you played a music CD and opened a backdoor to an infected computer that could be used for malicious intent.

Adware/Spyware

There are two types of programs that are similar to malware in that they try to hide themselves to an extent. **Adware** is a program that monitors the types of Web site you frequent and uses that information to generate targeted advertisements, usually pop-up windows. Adware isn't by definition evil, but many adware makers use sneaky methods to get you to use adware, such as using deceptive-looking Web pages ("Your computer is infected with a virus—click here to scan NOW!"). As a result, adware is often considered malware.

Spyware is a function of any program that sends information about your system or your actions over the Internet. The type of information sent depends on the program. An adware program will include your browsing history. A more aggressive malware may send keystrokes or all of the contacts in your e-mail.

Dealing with Malware

We deal with malware in three ways: anti-malware programs, training, and procedures. At the very least, every computer should run an anti-malware program. If possible, add an appliance that runs anti-malware programs against incoming data from your network. Many such appliances exist, but they are most common in proxy servers. Also remember that an anti-malware program is only as good as its updates—keep everyone's definition file up to date! Users must be trained to look for suspicious code and understand that they must not run these programs. Last, your organization should have procedures in place so that everyone knows what to do if they encounter malware.

One of the most important malware mitigation procedures is to keep systems under your control patched and up to date. Microsoft does a very good job putting out bug fixes and patches as soon as problems occur. If your systems aren't set up to update automatically, then schedule manual updates regularly.

Try This!

Scoring Excellent Anti-Malware Programs

You can download many excellent anti-malware programs for free, either for extended trial periods or for indefinite use. Since you need these programs to keep your systems happy, try this! Download one or more anti-malware programs, such as the following:

- **Lavasoft Ad-Aware (www.lavasoft.com)** Ad-Aware is an excellent anti-spyware program. Ad-Aware will root out all sorts of files and programs that can cause your computer to run slowly (or worse).

- **Spybot Search&Destroy (www.safer-networking.org)** Spybot Search&Destroy from Safer Networking Ltd. is another superb anti-spyware program. Many folks use both Ad-Aware and Spybot—though sometimes the two programs detect each other as spyware!

- **AVG Anti-Virus (http://free.avg.com)** AVG offers a free version of their anti-virus software for non-commercial use. Updated regularly to add the latest virus signatures, the software will keep your system clean and bug free.

Social Engineering

The vast majority of attacks against your network come under the heading of social engineering—the process of using or manipulating people inside the networking environment to gain access to that network from the outside. The term "social engineering" covers the many ways humans can use other humans to gain unauthorized information. This unauthorized information may be a network login, a credit card number, company customer data—almost anything you might imagine that one person or organization may not want a person outside of that organization to access.

Social engineering attacks aren't hacking—at least in the classic sense of the word—although the goals are the same. Social engineering is where people attack an organization through the people in the organization or physically access the organization to get the information they need.

The most classic form of social engineering is the telephone scam where someone calls a person and tries to get him to reveal his user name/password combination. In the same vein, someone may physically enter your building under the guise of someone who might have legitimate reason for being there, such as cleaning personnel, repair technicians, or messengers. He then snoops around desks, looking for whatever he has come to find (one of many good reasons not to put passwords on your desk or monitor). They might talk with people inside the organization, gathering names, office numbers, or department names—little things in and of themselves, but powerful tools when combined later with other social engineering attacks.

These old-school social engineering tactics are taking a backseat to a far more nefarious form of social engineering: phishing.

> It's common for these attacks to be used together, so if you discover one of them being used against your organization, it's a good idea to look for others.

Phishing

In a **phishing** attack, the attacker poses as some sort of trusted site, like an on-line version of your bank or credit card company, and solicits you to update your financial information, such as a credit card number. You might get an e-mail message, for example, that purports to be from PayPal telling you that your account needs to be updated and provides a link that looks like it goes to http://billing.paypal.com. Clicking the link http://billing.paypall.com (note the extra "l" in the name), you might end up at a site that resembles the PayPal billing site, but is actually http://www.merchntaccount.com, a phishing site.

Denial of Service

Denial of Service (DoS) attacks are the work of hackers whose only interest is in bringing a network to its knees. This is accomplished by flooding the network with so many requests that it becomes overwhelmed and ceases functioning. These attacks are most commonly performed on Web and e-mail servers, but virtually any part of a network can be attacked via some DoS method.

The secret to a successful DoS attack is to send as many packets as possible against the victim. Not only do you want to send a lot of packets, you want the packets to contain some kind of request that the victim must process as long as possible to force the victim to deal with each attacking packet for as long as possible. There's a number of ways to get a good DoS going, but the CompTIA Network+ objectives expressly mention a **smurf** attack. A *smurf attack* is a form of DoS that sends broadcast PINGs to the victim. Not only that, the source IP of the PINGs is changed from the real system sending the packet to another (often, nonexistent) machine. Smurf attacks are no longer a menace because almost all network devices now know not to forward broadcast PINGs.

 A smurf attack is a form of DoS that sends broadcast PINGs to the victim.

Far more menacing than a simple DoS attack are **Distributed Denial of Service (DDoS) attacks**. A DDoS uses multiple (as in hundreds up to hundreds of thousands) of computers under the control of a single operator to send a devastating attack. DDoS operators don't own these computers, but instead use malware to take control of computers. A single computer under the control of an operator is called a **zombie**. A group of computers under the control of one operator is called a **botnet**.

To take control of your network's computers, someone has to install malware on the computer. Again, anti-malware, training, and procedures will keep you safe from zombification (but feel free to make some joke about eating human brains).

 Zombified computers aren't obvious. DDoS operators often wait weeks or months after a computer's been infected to take control of it.

Physical Intrusion

You can't consider a network secure unless you provide some physical protection to your network. I separate physical protection into two different areas: protection of servers and protection of clients.

Server protection is easy. Lock up your servers to prevent physical access by any unauthorized person. Large organizations have special server rooms, complete with card-key locks and tracking of anyone who enters or exits. Smaller organizations will at least have a locked closet. While you're locking up your servers, don't forget about any network switches! Hackers can access networks by plugging into a switch, so don't leave any switches available to them.

Physical server protection doesn't stop with a locked door. One of the most common mistakes made by techs is walking away from a server while still logged in. Always log off your server when it's not in use! As a backup, add a password-protected screensaver (Figure 17.1).

It's difficult to lock up all of your client systems, but you should have your users performing some physical security. First, all users should use screensaver passwords. Hackers will take advantage of unattended systems to get access to networks. Second, make users aware of the potential for dumpster diving and make paper shredders available. Last, tell users to mind their work areas. It's amazing how many users leave passwords available. I can go into any office, open a few desk drawers, and will invariably find little yellow sticky notes with user names and passwords. If users must write down passwords, tell them to put them in locked drawers!

Rogue Access Points

A **rogue access point** is an unauthorized wireless access point (WAP) installed in a computer network. Rogue access points are a huge problem today. It's easy to purchase an inexpensive WAP and just plug it into a network. To make the issue even worse, almost all WAPs are designed to

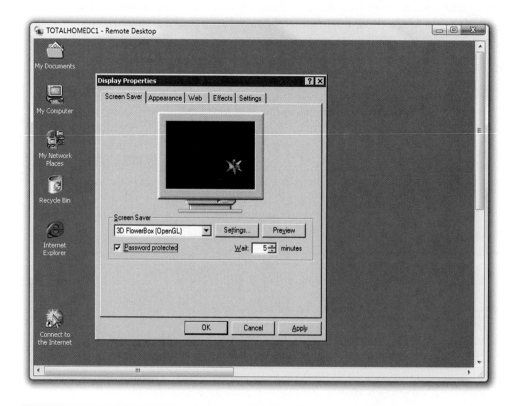

• **Figure 17.1**   Applying a password-protected screensaver

work using the preinstalled configuration, giving bad guys easy access to your network from a location physically outside your network.

The biggest reason rogue access points exist is that members of an organization install them for convenience. Users like their own wireless networks and, due to lack of training, don't appreciate the danger they pose. Bad guys getting into your physical location and installing rogue access points is less common.

Locating rogue access points is a challenge, especially if the person installing the rogue access point is clever enough to turn off SSID broadcasting. There are wireless sniffing programs designed to find any wireless network, but they must be run often.

■ Securing User Accounts

Even the smallest network will have a number of user accounts and groups scattered about with different levels of permissions. Every time you give a user access to a resource, you create potential loopholes that can leave your network vulnerable to unauthorized accesses, data destruction, and other administrative nightmares. We can categorize all of these potential dangers as **internal threats**. To protect your network from these threats, you need to implement the right controls over passwords, user accounts, permissions, and policies. Let's start with probably the most abused of all these areas: passwords.

Passwords

Passwords are the ultimate key to protecting your network. Anyone with access to a user account with a valid password will get into any system. Even if the user account only has limited permissions, you still have a security breach. Remember: for a hacker, just getting into the system is half the battle.

Protect your passwords. Never give out passwords over the phone. If a user loses a password, an administrator should reset the password to a complex combination of letters and numbers, and then allow the user to change the password to something he or she wants. All of the stronger network operating systems have this capability. Windows Server, for example, provides a setting called **User must change password at next logon**, as shown in Figure 17.2.

Make your users choose good passwords. I once attended a network security seminar, and the speaker had everyone stand up. She then began to ask questions about our passwords—if we responded positively to the question we were to sit down. She began to ask questions like "Do you use the name of your spouse as a password?" and "Do you use your pet's name?"

By the time she was done asking about 15 questions, only 6 people out of some 300 were still standing! The reality is that most of us choose passwords that are amazingly easy to hack. Make sure you use strong passwords: at least eight characters in

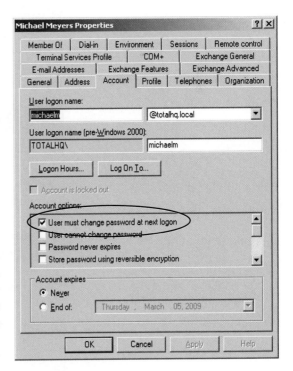

• **Figure 17.2** Windows Server option for requiring a user to change a password

Tech Tip

More Than Letters and Numbers

Using nonalphanumeric characters makes any password much more difficult to crack, for two reasons. First, adding nonalphanumeric characters forces the hacker to consider many more possible characters than just letters and numbers. Second, most password crackers use combinations of common words and numbers to try to hack a password. Because nonalphanumeric characters don't fit into common words or numbers, including a character such as an exclamation point will defeat these common-word hacks. Not all serving systems let you use characters such as @, $, %, or \, however, so you need to experiment to see if a particular server will accept them.

length (more than eight characters is better), including letters, numbers, and punctuation symbols.

Once you've forced your users to choose strong passwords, you should make them change passwords at regular intervals. While this concept sounds good on paper, and for the CompTIA Network+ exam you should remember that regular password changing is a good idea, in the real world it is a hard policy to maintain. For starters, users tend to forget passwords when they change a lot. One way to remember passwords if your organization forces you to change them is to use a numbering system. I worked at a company that required me to change my password at the beginning of each month, so I did something simple. I took a root password—let's say it was "m3y3rs5"—and simply added a number to the end representing the current month. So when June rolled around, for example, I would change my password to "m3y3rs56." It worked pretty well!

No matter how well your password implementation goes, using passwords always creates administrative problems. First, users forget passwords and someone (usually you) has to access their account and reset their passwords. Second, users will write passwords down, giving hackers an easy way into the network if those bits of paper fall into the wrong hands. If you've got the cash, there are two alternatives to passwords: smart devices and biometrics.

Smart devices are credit cards, USB keys, or other small devices that you insert into your PC in lieu of entering a password. They work extremely well and are incredibly difficult to bypass. The downside is that they might be lost or stolen.

If you want to go seriously space-age, then biometrics are the way to go. **Biometric devices** scan fingerprints, retinas, or even the sound of the user's voice to provide a foolproof replacement for both passwords and smart devices. Biometrics have been around for quite a while, but were relegated to extremely high-security networks due to their high cost (thousand of dollars per device). That price has dropped substantially, making biometrics worthy of consideration for some networks.

Try This!

Authentication Factors

You can categorize ways to authenticate into three broad areas: ownership factors, knowledge factors, and inherent factors. An ownership factor is something the user has, like an ID card or security token. A knowledge factor is something the user knows, like a password or personal identification number (PIN). An inherent factor is something that is part of the user, like a fingerprint or retinal pattern.

You can use one or more of these factors to authenticate a user. In fact, *two-factor authentication* is a fairly standard practice in secure facilities, like some government offices. Clearly, passwords are not the only way anymore, so try this!

Either head out to your local computer store or access one of the big ones on the Internet (like Amazon) and see what variety of authentication factors you can find. Make a list that contains at least one for each of the three authentication factors and then compare that list with lists compiled by your classmates. What would work for your network?

Controlling User Accounts

A user account is just information: nothing more than a combination of a user name and password. Like any important information, it's critical to control who has a user account and to track what these accounts can do. Access to user accounts should be restricted to the assigned individuals (no sharing, no stealing), and those accounts should have permission to access only the resources they need, no more. This control over what a legitimate account can do is called the *least privilege* approach to network security and is by far the most common approach used in networks.

Tight control of user accounts is critical to preventing unauthorized access. Disabling unused accounts is an important part of this strategy, but good user account control goes far deeper than that. One of your best tools for user account control is groups. Instead of giving permissions to individual user accounts, give them to groups; this makes keeping track of the permissions assigned to individual user accounts much easier. Figure 17.3 shows an example of giving permissions to a group for a folder in Windows Server. Once a group is created and its permissions set, you can then add user accounts to that group as needed. Any user account that becomes a member of a group automatically gets the permissions assigned to that group. Figure 17.4 shows an example of adding a user to a newly created group in the same Windows Server system.

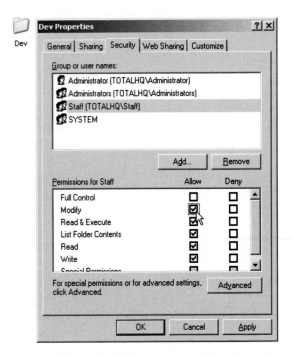

• **Figure 17.3**   Giving a group permissions for a folder in Windows

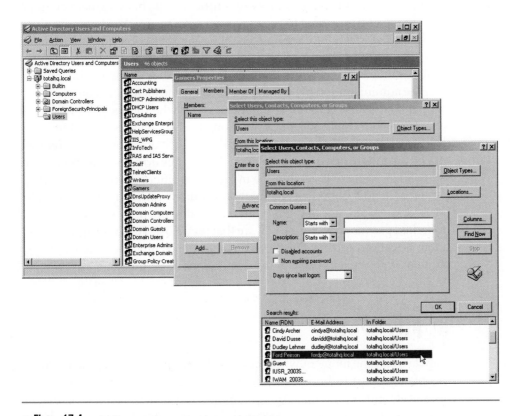

• **Figure 17.4**   Adding a user to a newly created group

Groups are a great way to get increased complexity without increasing the administrative burden on network administrators, because all network operating systems combine permissions. When a user is a member of more than one group, which permissions does he have with respect to any particular resource? In all network operating systems, the permissions of the groups are *combined*, and the result is what we call the **effective permissions** the user has to access the resource. Let's use an example from Windows Server. If Timmy is a member of the Sales group, which has List Folder Contents permission to a folder, and he is also a member of the Managers group, which has Read and Execute permissions to the same folder, Timmy will have List Folder Contents *and* Read and Execute permissions to that folder.

Watch out for *default* user accounts and groups—they can become secret backdoors to your network! All network operating systems have a default Everyone group and it can easily be used to sneak into shared resources. This Everyone group, as its name implies, literally includes anyone who connects to that resource. Some versions of Windows give full control to the Everyone group by default. All of the default groups—Everyone, Guest, Users—define broad groups of users. Never use them unless you intend to permit all those folks to access a resource. If you use one of the default groups, remember to configure it with the proper permissions to prevent users from doing things you don't want them to do with a shared resource!

All of these groups only do one thing for you: they enable you to keep track of your user accounts. That way you know resources are only available for users who need those resources, and users only access the resources you want them to use.

Before we move on, let me add one more tool to your kit: diligence. Managing user accounts is a thankless and difficult task, but one that you must stay on top of if you want to keep your network secure. Most organizations integrate the creation, disabling/enabling, and deletion of user accounts with the work of their human resources folks. Whenever a person joins, quits, or moves, the network admin is always one of the first to know!

The administration of permissions can become incredibly complex even with judicious use of groups. You now know what happens when a user account has multiple sets of permissions to the same resource, but what happens if the user has one set of permissions to a folder, and a different set of permissions to one of its subfolders? This brings up a phenomenon called **inheritance**. We won't get into the many ways different network operating systems handle inherited permissions. Lucky for you, the CompTIA Network+ exam doesn't test you on all the nuances of combined or inherited permissions—just be aware that they exist. Those who go on to get more advanced certifications, on the other hand, must become extremely familiar with the many complex permutations of permissions.

■ Firewalls

I always fear the moment when technical terms move beyond the technical people and start to find use in the nontechnical world. The moment any technical term becomes part of the common vernacular, you can bet that its true meaning will become obscured, because without a technical background people are reduced to simplistic descriptions of what is invariably a far more complex idea. I submit the term *firewall* as a perfect example of this phenomenon. Most people with some level of computer knowledge think of a firewall as some sort of thingamabob that protects an internal network from unauthorized access to and from the Internet at large. That type of definition might work for your VP as you explain why you need to get a firewall, but as techs, we need a deeper understanding.

Firewalls protect networks from **external threats**—potential attacks from outside your network—by using a number of methods, such as hiding IP addresses using NAT, selectively blocking TCP/UDP ports, or even filtering traffic based on MAC addresses. From there, things get much more complex, so for now let's define a firewall as a device that filters IP traffic to protect networks and computers. But a firewall doesn't have to be a dedicated device. There are two very different places where you might run into a firewall. The first place is a device at the edge of your network. Given that there's already a router at the edge of your network, you'd be hard pressed to find a router today that does not also act as a firewall. Since the firewall is in a box on the network, we call these *network-based* firewalls (also called hardware firewalls). The second place is software installed on your computer that does the same job but only firewalls packets coming in and out of your system. We call these *host-based* firewalls (also called software firewalls). In a perfect world, your network has a network-based firewall at the edge of your network and all of your systems run a host-based firewall.

Hiding the IPs

The first and most common technique for protecting a network is to hide the real IP addresses of the internal network systems from the Internet. If a hacker gets a real IP address, he can then begin to probe that system, looking for vulnerabilities. If you can prevent a hacker from getting an IP address to probe, you've stopped most hacking techniques cold. You already know how to hide IP addresses using **Network Address Translation (NAT)**. That's why most routers have built-in NAT capability. Not only does NAT reduce the need for true IANA-supplied public IP addresses, but it also does a great job protecting networks from hackers, because it is difficult to access a network using private IP addresses hidden behind a NAT-enabled router.

 Many sources challenge the idea that NAT is a firewall feature. Granted, NAT wasn't originally designed to act as a firewall, but it sure does protect your network.

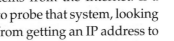 **Cross Check**

NATs Away!

You learned about the many flavors of NAT way back in Chapter 8, "The Wonderful World of Routing," so check your memory. How does overloaded NAT work? What's another name for Port Address Translation (PAT)? What are some of the names represented by the acronym SNAT and how do those technologies work?

Port Filtering

The second most common firewall tool is **port filtering**, also called **port blocking**. Hackers often try less commonly used port numbers to get into a network. Port filtering simply means preventing the passage of any TCP or UDP packets through any ports other than the ones prescribed by the system administrator. Port filtering is effective, but it requires some serious configuration to work properly. The question is always, "Which ports do I allow into the network?"

When you open your browser and access a Web page, your Web browser sends out packets to the Web server with the destination port of 80. Web servers require this and it's how TCP/IP works.

No one has problems with the well-known ports like 80 (HTTP), 20/21 (FTP), 25 (SMTP), and 110 (POP3), but there are a large number of lesser-known ports that networks often want opened.

I recently installed port filtering on my personal firewall and everything worked great—until I decided to play the popular game World of Warcraft on the Internet. (Note to WoW nerds: Blackwater Raiders server, I'm "Pelape" or "Pelope.") I simply could not connect to the Internet servers, until I discovered that World of Warcraft requires TCP port 3724 open to work over the Internet. After reconfiguring my port filter (I reopened port 3724) I was able to play WoW, but when I tried to help one of my friends using Microsoft Remote Desktop, I couldn't access his system! Want to guess where the problem lay? Yup, I needed to open port 3389. How did I figure these out? I didn't know which ports to open, but I suspected that my problem was in the port arena so I fired up my Web browser (thank goodness that worked!) and went to the World of Warcraft and Microsoft Web sites, which told me which ports I needed to open. This constant opening and closing of ports is one of the prices you pay for the protection of port filtering, but it sure stops hackers if they can't use strange ports to gain access.

Most routers that provide port blocking manifest it in one of two ways. The first way is to have port filtering close *all* ports until you open them explicitly. The other port filtering method is to leave all ports open unless you explicitly close them. The gotcha here is that most types of IP sessions require *dynamic port* usage. For example, when my system makes a query for a Web page on HTTP port 80, the Web server and my system establish a session using a *different* port to send the Web pages to my system. Figure 17.5 shows the results of running `netstat -n` switch while I have a number of Web pages open—note the TCP ports used for the incoming Web pages (the Local Address column). Dynamic ports can cause some problems for older (much older) port filtering systems, but almost all of today's port filtering systems are aware of this issue and handle it automatically.

Port filters have many different interfaces. On my little gateway router, the port filtering uses the pretty, Web-based interface shown in Figure 17.6. Linux systems use either IPTABLES or NETFILTER for their firewall work. Like most Linux tools, these programs are rather dull to look at directly and require substantial skill manipulating text files to

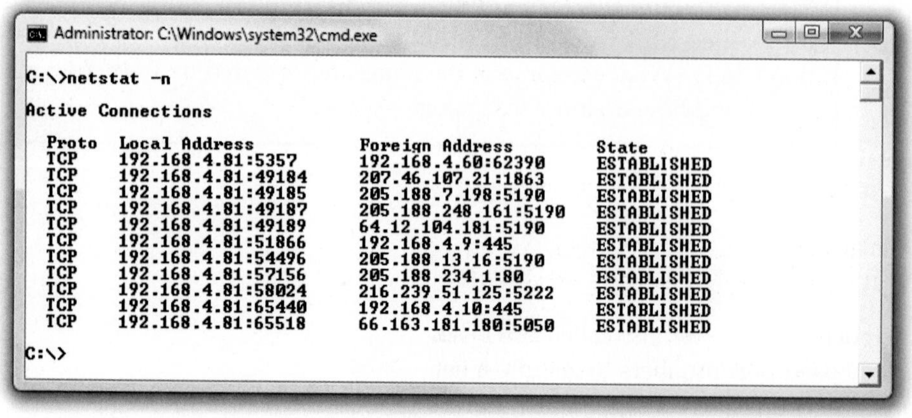

• **Figure 17.5**   The `netstat -n` command showing HTTP connections

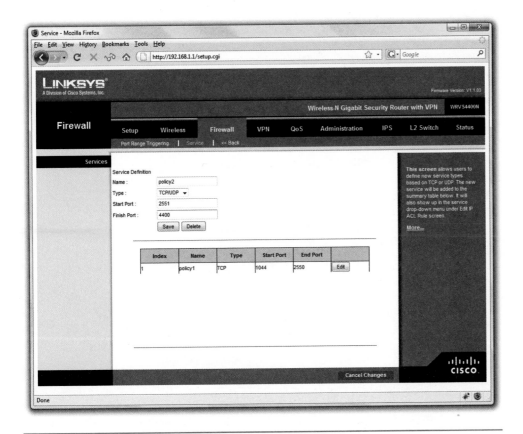

● **Figure 17.6**   Web-based port filtering interface

do your filtering chores. Most Linux distributions come with handy graphical tools, however, to make the job much easier. Figure 17.7 shows the firewall configuration screen from the popular YaST utility, found on the SUSE Linux distribution.

So, can one router have both NAT and port filtering? You bet it can! Most gateway routers come with both—you just need to take the time to configure them and make them work!

The CompTIA Network+ exam expects you to know that NAT, proxy serving, and port filtering are typical firewall functions!

Packet Filtering

Port filtering deals only with port numbers; it completely disregards IP addresses. If an IP packet comes in with a filtered port number, the packet is blocked, regardless of the IP address. **Packet filtering** or **IP filtering** works in the same way, except it blocks packets based on IP addresses. *Packet filters,*

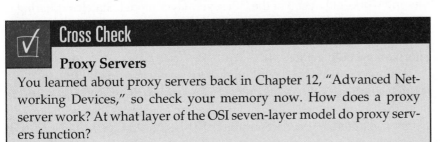

Cross Check

Proxy Servers

You learned about proxy servers back in Chapter 12, "Advanced Networking Devices," so check your memory now. How does a proxy server work? At what layer of the OSI seven-layer model do proxy servers function?

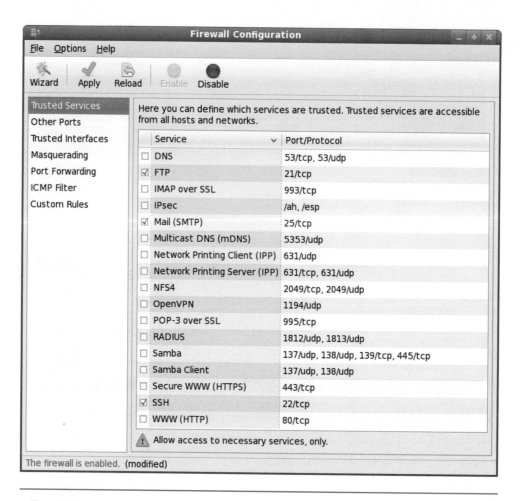

• **Figure 17.7**   YaST configuration program

also known as *IP filters*, will block any incoming or outgoing packet from a particular IP address or range of IP addresses. Packet filters are far better at blocking outgoing IP addresses, because the network administrator knows and can specify the IP addresses of the internal systems. Blocking outgoing packets is a good way to prevent users on certain systems from accessing the Internet. Figure 17.8 shows a configuration page from a router designed to block different ranges of IP addresses and port numbers.

This type of filtering is called **stateless filtering** because the device that does the filtering just checks the packet for IP addresses and port numbers and blocks or allows accordingly. Each packet is judged as an individual entity to determine whether it should be allowed into the network. Stateless filtering works at Layer 3 of the OSI seven-layer model. Stateless filtering is inexpensive and easy to implement, but has one issue: once you've opened a particular path into your network, that path is open. Someone spoofing IP information could get in.

A more secure method of filtering is to use devices that do **stateful filtering**, where all packets are examined as a stream. Stateful devices can do more than allow or block; they can track when a stream is disrupted or packets get corrupted and act accordingly. The best of the stateful filtering devices are application proxies, working at Layer 7 of the OSI seven-layer

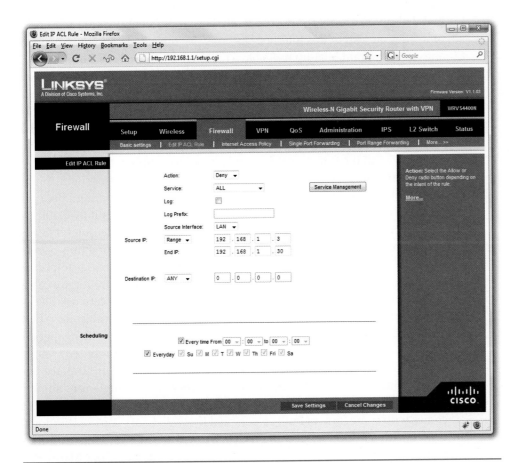

● **Figure 17.8**   Blocking IP addresses

model. The only real problems with application proxies are that they tend to be slower than stateless filters and more expensive.

MAC Filtering

Similar to packet filtering, some firewall devices can allow or deny access to the network according to the MAC address of the client, what's called **MAC filtering**. Because every network device has a unique 48-bit MAC address, this should make for a very secure network. It's often one of the implemented security measures in wireless networks, for example, because it's quick to set up.

Many programs enable you to spoof or mimic a MAC address, though, so MAC filtering is not a strong deterrent for a determined hacker.

Personal Firewalls

Back in the days of dial-up connections, the concept of protection from external threats wasn't very interesting. The concept of dial-up alone was more than enough protection for most users. First, systems using dial-up connections were by definition only periodically on the Internet, making them tough for hackers to detect. Second, all dial-up connections use DHCP-assigned IP addresses, so even if a hacker could access a dial-up user during one session, that dial-up user would almost certainly have a different IP address the next time they accessed the Internet. As long as they have installed a good antivirus program, dial-up users have nothing to fear from hackers.

The onset of high-speed, always-connected Internet links has changed the security picture completely. The user who dumps his or her dial-up connection for ADSL or a cable modem immediately becomes a prime target for hackers. Even though most ADSL and cable modems use DHCP links, the lease time for these addresses is more than long enough to give even the casual hacker all the time he or she needs to poke around in the systems.

One of the first items on the agenda of Windows users with high-bandwidth connections is to turn off File and Print Sharing. Because NetBIOS can run over IP, sharing a folder or printer makes it available to anyone on the Internet unless your ISP helps you out by filtering NetBIOS traffic. Some hacker groups run port scanner programs looking for systems with File and Print Sharing enabled and post these IP addresses to public sites (no, I will not tell you where to find them!). When I first got my cable modem many years ago, I absentmindedly clicked the My Network Places icon on my Desktop and discovered that four of my fellow cable users had their systems shared, and two of them were sharing printers! Being a good neighbor and not a hacker, I made sure they changed their erroneous ways!

Although you can (and should) buy a hardware firewall to place between your system and the Internet, at the very least a single user should employ a personal software firewall program. Every operating system comes with some form of built-in personal firewall. Every copy of Windows comes with Windows Firewall (which we will discuss in detail in a moment). There are also third-party software firewalls like ZoneAlarm Pro (Figure 17.9). These personal firewall programs are quite powerful, and

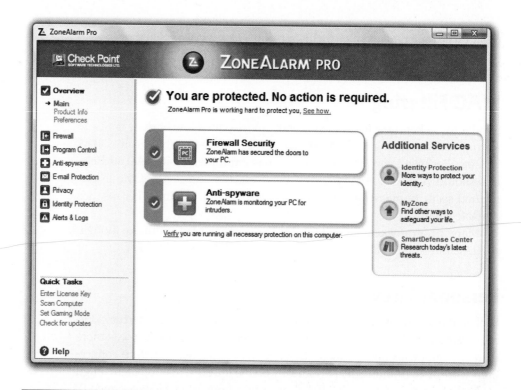

• **Figure 17.9** ZoneAlarm Pro

Mike Meyers' CompTIA Network+ Guide to Managing and Troubleshooting Networks

have the added benefit of being easy to use. These days, there's no excuse for an individual Internet user not to use a personal firewall.

Every version of Windows comes with the handy Internet Connection Sharing (ICS), but ICS alone doesn't provide any level of support other than NAT. Starting with Windows XP, Microsoft included Internet Connection Firewall (ICF), renamed in Windows XP Service Pack 2 as **Windows Firewall**. Windows Firewall works with ICS to provide basic firewall protection for your network. Windows Firewall is often used without ICS to provide protection for single machines connected to the Internet. Figure 17.10 shows the screen where you'd turn on Windows Firewall in Windows Vista.

By default Windows Firewall blocks all incoming IP packets that attempt to initiate a session. This is great for networks that only use the Internet to browse the Web or grab e-mail, but will cause problems in circumstances where you want to provide any type of Internet server on your network. You can manually open ports through the firewall (Figure 17.11).

Products such as ZoneAlarm and Windows Firewall do a fine job protecting a single machine or a small network. But software firewalls run on your system, taking CPU processing away from your system. On an individual system this firewall overhead doesn't strain your system, but once

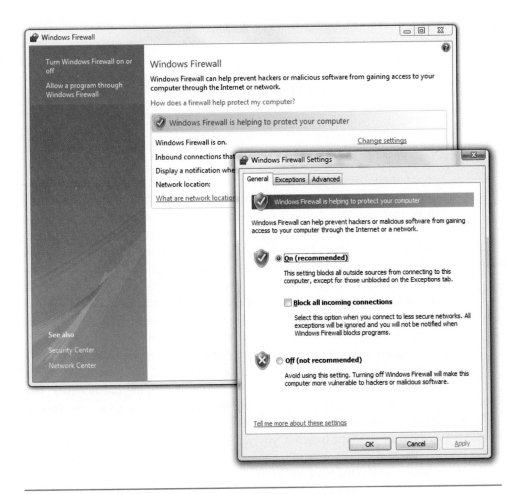

• **Figure 17.10**   Enabling Windows Firewall

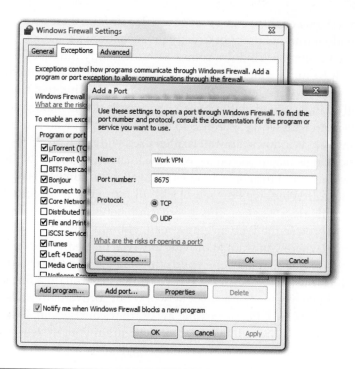

Opening TCP/IP ports in Windows Firewall

you start to add more than three or four systems, or if you need to add advanced functions like a VPN, you'll need a more robust solution. That's where small office and home office (SOHO) connections come into play.

Network Zones

Large networks need heavy-duty protection that not only protects from external threats, but does so without undue restriction on the overall throughput of the network. To do this, large networks will often use dedicated firewall boxes, which usually sit between the gateway router and the protected network. These firewalls are designed to filter IP traffic (including NAT and proxy functions), as well as to provide high-end tools to track and stop incoming threats. Some of the firewall systems even contain a rather interesting feature called a honey pot. A **honey pot** is a device (or a set of functions within a firewall) that creates a fake network, which seems attackable to a hacker. Instead of trying to access the real network, hackers are attracted to the honey pot, which does nothing more than record their actions and keep them away from the true network.

Once you start to add publicly accessible servers to your network, like Web and e-mail servers, you're going to have to step up to a more serious network protection configuration. Because Web and e-mail servers must have exposure to the Internet, you will need to create what's called a **demilitarized zone (DMZ)**, a lightly protected network positioned between your firewall and the Internet. There are a number of ways to configure a DMZ. Figure 17.12 shows one classic example using an external and an internal router.

Look for the CompTIA Network+ exam to refer to network setups where the firewall resides in a dedicated box as a *network-based firewall*. The exam calls firewall programs installed on your computer, such as Windows Firewall, *host-based firewalls*.

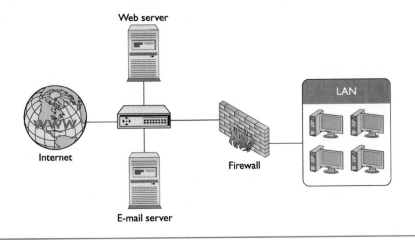

● **Figure 17.12**   A DMZ configuration

The private, protected network is called an **intranet**. Compare this term to the term extranet you learned in Chapter 14, "Remote Connection Basics," and make sure you understand the difference!

Securing Remote Access

The mad proliferation of high-speed Internet connections to most households in the United States has enabled a lot of workers to work partly from home. Although this provides one cost-effective solution to the rising price of gasoline and of physical commuting, from a network security standpoint it opens up a potential can of worms. Network techs and administrators must strike a fine balance between making resources readily available over the Internet and making certain that only authorized users get access to those resources.

Chapter 17 Review

■ Chapter Summary

After reading this chapter and completing the exercises, you should be able to do the following.

Discuss the common security threats in network computing

■ Network threats include system crashes, hardware failure, administrative access control, malware, social engineering, Denial of Service attacks, physical intrusion, and rogue access points.

■ Hard drives crash, servers lock up, and power goes out. It is important to create redundancy as a proactive approach to dealing with these potential hazards before they occur.

■ RAID technology provides fault tolerance for your data stored on hard drives.

■ The administrative account on Windows is "administrator." On Linux and Macintosh OS X, it's "root."

■ Malware describes any program or code that's designed to do something that you don't want to happen. There are many types of malware, including viruses, worms, macros, Trojans, and rootkits.

■ A virus replicates, or makes copies of itself, but only across hard drives, not across networks. It also activates, or does something destructive like erasing files.

■ A worm is identical to a virus except a worm replicates exclusively across networks.

■ A macro is any type of virus that exploits application macros to replicate and activate.

■ A Trojan is malware that looks or pretends to do one thing while at the same time doing something unwanted. Trojans can be used to turn an infected computer into a server and capture keystrokes, passwords, or files. Trojans, unlike viruses, do not replicate.

■ Rootkits are Trojans that hide themselves so that many anti-malware tools can't find them.

■ Malware can be avoided much of the time through user training. If malware infections do occur, they can often be removed with anti-malware software.

However, this software must be kept up to date because new malware threats are discovered often.

■ Social engineering accounts for the vast majority of network attacks. This includes using or manipulating people inside the networking environment in order to gain unauthorized access.

■ Phishing attacks are becoming more common than old-school social engineering. In a phishing scam, an attacker tries to trick users into revealing information by posing as a financial, medical, or other institution or individual in need of help.

■ Phishing attacks can manifest as e-mails, bogus Web sites, or even telephone calls.

■ Flooder hackers perform Denial of Service (DoS) attacks to overwhelm your Web and e-mail servers with so many requests they're forced to cease functioning. DoS attacks include the smurf attack, which repeatedly PINGs an IP address.

■ Distributed Denial of Service (DDoS) attacks are far more menacing than DoS attacks. DDoS attacks use multiple (hundreds) of infected computers (zombies) to perform the attack. A group of zombies under the control of a single operator forms a botnet.

■ Servers should be physically protected by locking them in a room, or at the very least, a locked closet. The same holds true for network switches. A hacker can access your network by simply plugging a laptop into an unsecured switch.

■ Never walk away from a server without logging off or locking the screen. A password-protected screensaver is also a good idea.

■ Papers should be shredded to protect against successful dumpster diving. If you must write your password on a piece of paper, store it in a locked drawer.

■ A rogue access point is an unauthorized wireless access point. These are very common in private homes because wireless routers purchased by novices are often configured to work out of the box with no security, allowing neighbors or anyone parked outside to access the network.

Describe methods for securing user accounts

- Internal threats from employees and users are more successfully subdued through policy implementation than through technology.

- Strong passwords are the ultimate key to protecting your network. A strong password includes upper- and lowercase letters, numbers, and nonalphanumeric characters and is at least eight characters long.

- In a perfect world, the best practice is to change your passwords regularly. However, this practice is difficult to maintain in the real world.

- A smart device, such as a credit card or USB device, can be inserted into a PC in lieu of entering a password. Similarly, biometric devices can be used to scan fingerprints, retinas, or even voice prints to authenticate a user without physically typing a password.

- Unused user accounts should be disabled, such as default accounts like Guest.

- Permissions should not be given to individual user accounts, but rather to groups; then, individual user accounts can be placed in these groups.

- It is possible for a user to be a member of several groups, with each group assigned different permissions. The permissions are combined to create the effective permissions.

- Default groups, such as Everyone, Guest, and Users, should be avoided unless you intend to permit all members of these groups to access a resource.

- When a user has conflicting permissions on a folder and subfolders, inheritance determines the effective permissions.

Explain how firewalls, NAT, port filtering, and packet filtering protect a network from threats

- Firewalls are either hardware or software that use a variety of methods to protect a network from threats. A common way is hiding IP addresses with internal address ranges, like the 192.168.x.y or 10.x.y.z ranges.

- A network-based firewall is integrated into a router, so it is also called a hardware firewall. A host-based firewall is software installed in individual computers. A secure network uses both.

- Network Address Translation hides the real IP addresses of an internal network from the Internet.

- Port filtering (or port blocking) restricts traffic based on port numbers, like allowing port 80 for Web pages (HTTP), but restricting port 23 to block Telnet traffic and hacking attempts.

- Packet filtering (IP filtering) filters signals based on data packets to allow only certain types of packets to flow to and from your network.

- Stateless filtering checks the packet for the IP addresses and port numbers and blocks or allows accordingly. Stateful filtering, which is more secure, examines all packets as a stream and can track when a stream is disrupted or when packets get corrupted.

- MAC filtering filters packets based on MAC addresses rather than IP addresses. MAC addresses can easily be spoofed, however, so this is not secure protection from a determined hacker.

- Dial-up users make poor hacking targets due to the nature of dial-up connections. They are not always connected to the Internet, making them hard to find. And they use DHCP-assigned IP addresses, which change every time they connect to the Internet. Always-on connections, such as cable or DSL, make for easy targets, so they should be protected.

- A personal firewall, such as ZoneAlarm Pro, is powerful enough to protect home computers and often does a better job than the firewall that comes built into Windows.

- A honey pot is a device or set of tools within a firewall that creates a fake network. The fake network directs hacking attacks away from the actual network.

- Larger networks having multiple servers should establish a demilitarized zone (DMZ), which is a network segment on the outer edge of your corporate network between your firewall and the Internet. The DMZ adds a layer of protection around your corporate network and can protect both incoming and outgoing transmissions.

■ Key Terms

adware *(461)*
biometric device *(466)*
botnet *(463)*
demilitarized zone (DMZ) *(476)*
Denial of Service (DoS) attack *(463)*
Distributed Denial of Service (DDoS) attack *(463)*
effective permissions *(468)*
external threat *(469)*
fault tolerance *(459)*
firewall *(469)*
hacker *(459)*
honey pot *(476)*
inheritance *(468)*
intranet *(477)*
internal threat *(465)*
IP filtering *(471)*
MAC filtering *(473)*
macro *(460)*
malware *(460)*
Network Address Translation (NAT) *(469)*

network threat *(459)*
packet filtering *(471)*
password *(465)*
phishing *(463)*
port blocking *(469)*
port filtering *(469)*
rogue access point *(464)*
rootkit *(461)*
smart device *(466)*
smurf *(463)*
social engineering *(462)*
spyware *(461)*
stateful filtering *(472)*
stateless filtering *(472)*
Trojan *(461)*
virus *(460)*
Windows Firewall *(475)*
worm *(460)*
zombie *(463)*

■ Key Term Quiz

Use the Key Terms list to complete the sentences that follow. Not all the terms will be used.

1. Bogus e-mails trying to trick you into revealing information constitute _____ attacks.

2. _____ is when you separate and either allow or deny access based only on the packet type being sent.

3. A(n) _____ is either hardware or software that protects a network from threats by using a variety of methods.

4. When your network blocks out traffic based on port number, you are using _____.

5. The Microsoft Windows XP (Service Pack 2 and later) operating system includes a built-in feature called _____ to protect from network threats.

6. The infamous "smurf attack" is a classic _____.

7. Many IT professionals are surprised when they first learn that the majority of network threats are _____.

8. The _____ is when a network administrator has set up a perimeter defense using two routers on the outer edge of your corporate network between your firewall and the Internet.

9. _____ hides your private network's IP addresses from the Internet.

10. A(n) _____ makes copies of itself across hard drives, but not across a network.

■ Multiple-Choice Quiz

1. Where do most network threats come from?

   A. Internal users

   B. External users

   C. Both internal and external users

   D. Network technicians

2. What aspect of protecting your network involves theft of equipment?

   A. Packet filtering

   B. Physical security

   C. Policies

   D. Port filtering

3. Which of the following items make up the strongest complex passwords? (Select all that apply.)

   A. Lowercase letters

   B. Uppercase letters

   C. Numbers

   D. Special characters

4. What is another name for port filtering?

   A. Port blocking

   B. Port filing

   C. Port folders

   D. Port segments

5. What is the term used to describe when folder permissions flow downward into subfolders?

   A. Flowing

   B. Inheritance

   C. Permissions

   D. Propagation

6. How should user accounts be established? (Select two.)

   A. Open to all company individuals

   B. Only given to specified individuals

   C. Allowed access to needed resources

   D. Allowed access to all resources

7. Where would a DMZ more commonly be found?

   A. On a single PC

   B. On a server

   C. On a SOHO

   D. On a larger network

8. Just after opening a Microsoft Excel spreadsheet, Rowan notices that some of his filenames have changed and that his network connection no longer works. What type of malware has infected his computer?

   A. Worm

   B. Macro

   C. Trojan

   D. Rootkit

9. What problem does a rogue access point introduce?

   A. Unauthorized physical access to a server

   B. Unauthorized access to a wired network

   C. Unauthorized access to a wireless network

   D. Unauthorized physical access to a router or gateway

10. What is the difference between a virus and a worm?

    A. A virus is only distributed via e-mail. A worm is only distributed via infected Web servers.

    B. A worm is only distributed via e-mail. A virus is only distributed via infected Web servers.

    C. A virus replicates across networks. A worm does not.

    D. A worm replicates across networks. A virus does not.

11. Which statements about passwords are true? (Select two.)

    A. You should change your password regularly.

    B. You should use familiar terms, like your pet's name or your birthday, as your password because it will be easy for you to remember.

C. It is okay to write your password on a piece of paper in case you forget it, as long as you keep the paper in a locked drawer.

D. You may not use spaces in a password.

12. Which statement is true?

A. A DoS uses a zombie while a DDoS uses a botnet to attack a single system.

B. A DoS uses a botnet while a DDoS uses a zombie to attack a single system.

C. A DoS attacks a single system while a DDoS attacks multiple systems.

D. A DoS attacks systems on the Internet while a DDoS attacks system in a DMZ.

13. What is a honey pot?

A. It acts as a fake network, luring potential hackers away from the actual network.

B. It is a security measure that slows unauthorized network access to a crawl (as if running in honey), making your network undesirable to hackers.

C. It is what hackers call an easily hacked network.

D. It is a specialized padlock manufactured for the sole purpose of securing computer systems.

14. You receive an e-mail from your credit card company informing you that your card number has been stolen. You click a link in the e-mail and are taken to what looks like your credit card company's Web site, where you are asked to enter your credit card number to determine if it is among those that were recently stolen. What should you do?

A. Enter your credit card number immediately to determine if it is among those stolen, since this is the only way to protect against unauthorized charges to your account.

B. Call the toll-free number listed on the Web site to verify it is legitimate before entering your card number.

C. Call the toll-free number listed on the Web site and read your card number over the phone to the customer service representative.

D. Close your browser without entering your card number, since it is likely a phishing scam, and then call the toll-free number listed on the back of your actual credit card to verify that is the case.

15. Which are examples of a software firewall? (Select two.)

A. The firewall software built into a router

B. Host-based firewalls

C. Network-based firewalls

D. ZoneAlarm Pro

Essay Quiz

1. Many people have said that you don't know something unless you can describe it simply to others. Write down a brief definition of social engineering. Include some examples.

2. Research three software firewall solutions. Compare and contrast the solutions that you find based on cost, reputation (research product reviews), and support provided.

3. Some of the older military veterans in your networking class are surprised to see the term "DMZ" being used. Write a short paragraph defining a DMZ and its uses.

Lab Projects

• Lab Project 17.1

In this lab project you will continue to quench your thirst for knowledge of hacking. Use the Internet to research three hacking tools or techniques. Do not try these techniques on your classroom lab network, but research them as time permits. Document your findings, and be prepared to show off your knowledge with others in your class. Have fun learning even more about hacking!

• Lab Project 17.2

You have been tasked with finding out the cost of a variety of firewalls and other software. Create a spreadsheet similar to the following one. Use the Internet to research prices and Web site locations for each of the following items, as well as current variations/versions of this and other software. Note: some items may be freeware/shareware, or included with an operating system.

Software	Web Site	Cost
AVG Anti-Virus		$
CA Anti-Spyware		$
Cerberus FTP Server		$
Lavasoft Ad-Aware		$
McAfee VirusScan		$
Microsoft ISA Server		$
Norton AntiVirus		$
Norton Internet Security		$
Spybot Search&Destroy		$
Trend Micro HouseCall		$
Windows Firewall		$
ZoneAlarm		$
	Total	$

chapter 18

Network Management

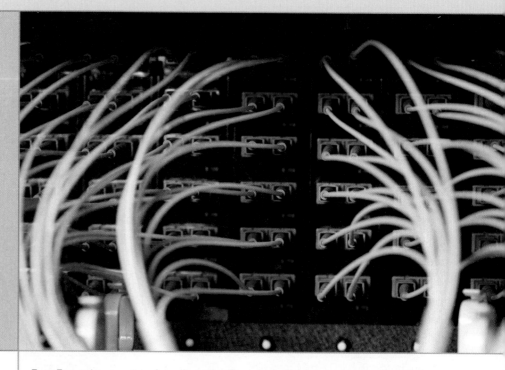

In this chapter, you will learn how to

- **Describe how configuration management documentation enables you to manage and upgrade a network efficiently**
- **Conduct network monitoring to identify performance and connectivity issues**
- **Explain how to optimize network performance**

Managing a network well on-the-fly can challenge even very advanced network techs, so it won't come as any surprise to you that most techs use an array of techniques and tools to make it all . . . well . . . manageable. This chapter looks first at documentation for networks, including how the network is put together and how you go about making changes that don't disrupt the network. We'll then turn to tools and techniques for monitoring performance and connectivity. The chapter concludes with a section on optimizing network performance.

Network Configuration Management

The more complicated a network becomes, the more vulnerable it becomes in terms of security, efficiency, duplication or unnecessary redundancy, and unnecessary cost. Chapter 17 covered many of the security issues, but left a rather major component for coverage here, configuration management. **Configuration management** is a set of documents, policies, and procedures designed to help you maintain and update your network in a logical, orderly fashion so that you may lessen the risks of these vulnerabilities. Your network should standardize on types of NICs, cabling, network operating systems, and network applications to make certain that when upgrades need to happen, they do so with the utmost efficiency.

If you want to upgrade your users from Windows XP to Windows Vista, for example, you don't want to create a huge security risk for your network, nor waste a lot of money, time, and effort by realizing *after the fact* that an important application wasn't compatible with the new OS. That's not the way to do it in the real world!

Configuration Management Documentation

The **configuration management documentation** enables you to see very quickly everything about your network. Good documentation helps you to troubleshoot your network efficiently. You can also determine as efficiently as possible both how to upgrade components of that network and what effects such an upgrade might have. Configuration management documentation covers everything, from the wires used to how the people using the network should be trained. You can think about the configuration management documentation in five broad categories:

- Wiring diagrams
- Network diagrams
- Baselines
- Policies, procedures, and configurations
- Regulations

Wiring Schematics or Diagrams

The **wiring diagram** or **wiring schematic** identifies how the wires in a network connect to various switches and such, plus what standards are used for those wires, such as CAT 5e, CAT 6, 568A, 568B, or various fiber standards. It usually consists of multiple pages, starting with a very detailed overview of every cable run, telecommunications closet, and network outlet, as well as other details such as cross-connects and demarcs (Figure 18.1).

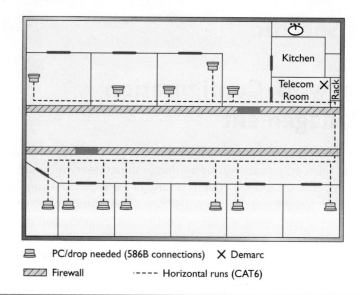

PC/drop needed (586B connections)   ✕ Demarc

Firewall   - - - - Horizontal runs (CAT6)

● Figure 18.1   Wiring diagram overview

The overview is then detailed with diagrams of individual structured cabling connections, mainly cross-connects and patch panels, giving a clear view of the endpoints of each cable. These detailed diagrams will usually include the actual designations for each cable run (Figure 18.2).

It's part of the cabling puller's job to generate the wiring diagram. Depending on the office building, it's very common for telephone runs to show up in the same diagram—although every situation is different. Most wiring diagrams stay with the folks in charge of the building (CompTIA uses the term "building services" to describe those people). A network administrator should at the very least have access to these diagrams and at best have a copy to mark up as he or she plans new runs or other changes to the physical network.

Physical and Logical Network Diagrams

Most of the time network administrators don't need the detail provided by wiring diagrams to deal with the day-to-day issues of network management. In general the problems you run into are more in the vein of "What kind of connection is between these two things" as opposed to "What kind of wiring connects these two things." For that we turn to a physical network diagram. A **physical network diagram** is similar to a wiring diagram in that you see the physical runs, but in this case you define the type of connection: Gigabit Ethernet, T1, and so on. A physical network diagram includes every router, switch, server, CSU/DSU, cable modem, wireless access point, and so on, including the make and model and firmware upgrade. Figure 18.3 shows a typical physical network diagram.

It's the network administrator's job to create the physical network diagram. Lucky for you, there are two critical tools to make your job easier. First are standardized icons. As you look at Figure 18.3, you notice the icons are somewhat cryptic. That's because many years ago Cisco developed this shorthand to represent any type of networking device you might imagine.

All connections must be EIA/TIA 568B. Sample below.

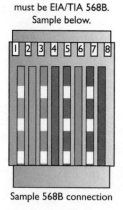

Sample 568B connection

● Figure 18.2   Wiring diagram detail

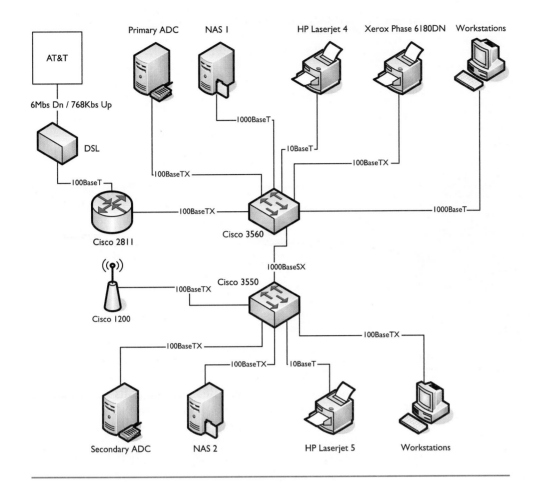

Primary ADC   NAS 1   HP Laserjet 4   Xerox Phase 6180DN   Workstations

AT&T

6Mbs Dn / 768Kbs Up

DSL

—1000BaseT—

—10BaseT—

—100BaseT—   —100BaseTX—   —100BaseTX—

—100BaseTX—   —100BaseTX—   —1000BaseT—

Cisco 2811   Cisco 3560

—1000BaseSX—

((•))   —100BaseTX—   Cisco 3550

Cisco 1200

—100BaseTX—   —100BaseTX—

—100BaseTX—   —10BaseT—

Secondary ADC   NAS 2   HP Laserjet 5   Workstations

• **Figure 18.3**   Physical network diagram

Cisco usually calls these "network topology icons" and they are the accepted standard to use whenever you're drawing a network. Figure 18.4 shows some examples of the more common topology icons.

Your second tool is one of the many drawing programs that support network topology icons. You can use a presentation tool like Microsoft PowerPoint, but Microsoft Visio is the most famous tool for drawing any type of network diagram. Visio adds a number of extras that make putting together any type of diagram a snap. Figure 18.5 shows how I made Figures 18.3 and 18.6: with Visio!

The last paper document you'll find very handy is the logical network diagram. A **logical network diagram** describes the broadcast domains and individual IP addresses for all the devices in your network with static IP addresses. These are at first glance similar to physical network diagrams but in some cases they show the individual computers (if there are not too many) and almost never show connections

New network devices show up all the time, so there's no single place to see every network topology icon available. However, Cisco keeps a fairly complete list at www.cisco.com/web/about/ac50/ac47/2.html.

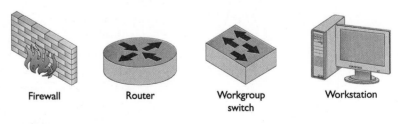

Firewall   Router   Workgroup switch   Workstation

• **Figure 18.4**   Sample network topology icons

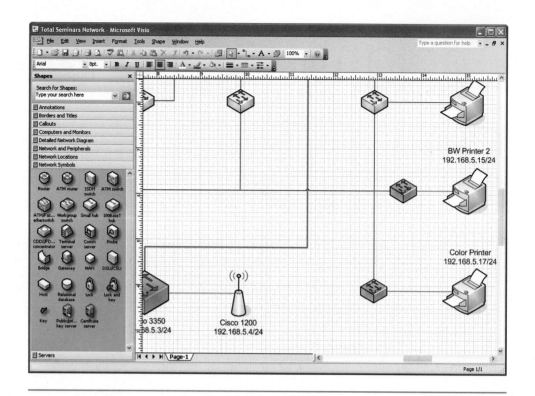

● **Figure 18.5**   Visio in action

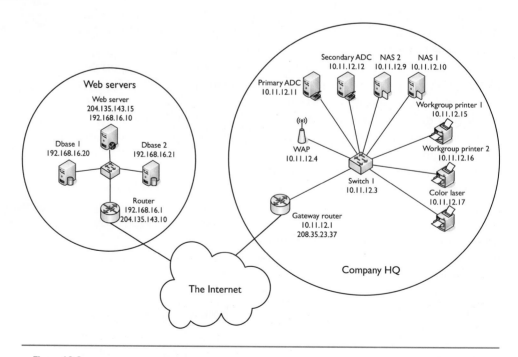

Make updating your network documentation the last step of any changes you make to the network.

to individual computers. Instead, they represent broadcast domains with circles and Internet connections with clouds. Logical network diagrams usually only show a few critical physical switches or routers and only if those devices affect the logical network (gateway routers, VLAN switches). Figure 18.6 show a typical logical network diagram.

● **Figure 18.6**   Logical network diagram

Baselines

The best way to know when a problem is brewing is to know how things perform when all's well with the system. Part of any proper configuration management documentation is a **baseline**: a log of performance indicators such as CPU usage, network utilization, and other values to give you a picture of your network and servers when they are working correctly. A major change in these values can point to problems on a server or the network as a whole.

All operating systems come with some form of baseline tools. A common tool used to create a baseline on Windows systems is the Performance Monitor utility that comes with all versions of Windows. You'll see Performance Monitor at work later in this chapter.

Policies, Procedures, and Configurations

Network security, cost, time, employee and management frustration—all of these things matter when managing a complex network. As part of any good documentation, therefore, you'll find policies about what people can and cannot do with network hardware and software. You'll see procedures outlined for what to do when upgrading components or adding new user accounts. You'll also get down-to-the-user-interface-level information about how software and hardware should be configured.

Much of this stuff should be familiar from a CompTIA A+ certification level. For example, what's a great way to keep a Windows PC from becoming vulnerable to a new piece of malware floating around the Internet? C'mon, one guess! Keep it patched and up to date with Windows Update, right? Exactly.

Properly created configuration management documentation will inform network folks what to do with user training. Who gets it? What departments? What level of access for new employees versus seasoned and trusted veterans?

Many of the polices and procedures help protect your network from harm. In CompTIA terms, they mitigate security risks like those outlined in gory detail in Chapter 17!

Two policies affect most users: acceptable use and security. After explaining these polices, I'll also give you an example of configuration.

Acceptable Use Policy   An **acceptable use policy** defines exactly what you can and cannot do with your computers and network. Some classic areas defined by an acceptable use policy include personal computer use and adding personal software.

Security Policy   An organization's **security policy** defines procedures employees should perform to protect the network's security. Security policies cover a wide gamut. They define password complexity, explain to users how to deal with social engineering, and clarify how to deal with virus attacks. Security policies almost always define action plans to deal with serious events that might threaten your network.

Configuration   **Configurations** are the results of the procedures. It's important to document configurations for critical systems. Imagine if a carefully configured gateway router were to suddenly lose all of its settings and no one had made a backup? Every configurable device in today's networking

```
192.168.4.1 - PuTTY

Welcome to the Cisco 2811 Gateway Router for totalhome!

Gateway#show config
Using 14597 out of 245752 bytes
!
version 12.4
no service pad
service tcp-keepalives-in
service tcp-keepalives-out
service timestamps debug datetime msec localtime show-timezone
service timestamps log datetime msec localtime show-timezone
service password-encryption
service sequence-numbers
!
hostname Gateway
!
boot-start-marker
boot-end-marker
!
security authentication failure rate 3 log
security passwords min-length 6
logging buffered 51200 debugging
logging console critical
███████ ██████ █ ██████████ ██ █████████
!
aaa new-model
--More--
```

• **Figure 18.7** Section of SHOW CONFIG

world comes with some tool to document its configuration. Figure 18.7 shows a part of one of the most famous of all configurations, the infamous SHOW CONFIG command built into almost every device made by Cisco.

Regulations

Very few people profess to liking **regulations**, the rules that govern behavior in the workplace. Nevertheless, regulations help keep networks and people safe and productive. Every decent configuration management documentation talks about the regulations, such as what to do when you have a safety violation or some sort of potentially bad accident.

Change Management Documentation

Although CompTIA seems to separate the detailed overview of the network from how to upgrade it, most networking professionals use the term **change management documentation** to describe the single body of knowledge. An example will make this clear. Let's say you want to change your network by adding a demilitarized zone (DMZ), because you want to add a server that is easily accessible to people outside the network.

> ### ✓ Cross Check
>
> #### DMZ
>
> You read about DMZs in Chapter 17, "Protecting Your Network," so check your memory now. What sorts of servers might be in a DMZ? How does creating a DMZ help protect your internal, private network?

The change management documentation will show you network diagrams, so you can verify where to place the DMZ and what other machines will be potentially affected by the change. Plus, it will give you the detailed information on what to do to get approval from supervisors, get through the budgeting office, and so on.

Change management documentation details the procedures and policies to update the documentation so that after each change in the network, your master documents are accurate. This is an extremely important piece of information! Failure to update the correct document will eventually result in you looking really bad when an otherwise minor troubleshoot turns into a nightmare.

Monitoring Performance and Connectivity

Networking technicians need to know how to use the tools that are available to monitor network performance and connectivity. A network administrator will set up the tools you use, but a tech needs to know how to use those tools to create baselines, monitoring utilities, and logs of various sorts. The tools vary from operating system to operating system, but let's look at the two most commonly in use: Performance Monitor and Event Viewer, both Windows utilities.

Administrators use **Performance Monitor** (also called PerfMon) to view the behavior of hardware and other resources on Windows machines, either locally or remotely. Performance Monitor can monitor both real-time and historical data about the performance of your systems. Figure 18.8 shows the default Performance Monitor in Windows XP.

Once you access Performance Monitor, you need to configure it to display data. To do that accurately, you set objects, counters, and views.

An **object**, in Performance Monitor terms, is a system component that you want to monitor, such as the processor or the memory. Each object has different measurable features, called **counters**. Counters, in other words, are the aspects of an object that you want to track. As you decide which object(s) to monitor, you can also select specific counters for each object. Performance Monitor can organize and display selected counter information using a variety of **views**, each of which provides a different way of presenting information. In addition to showing you real-time information about the system, Performance Monitor can also log so you can store data about your system for later review. This is the view you use to create a baseline.

To create a new log in Windows XP, expand the **Performance Logs and Alerts** tree in the left pane and click **Counter Logs**. Click **Action | New Log Settings** and give the new log a name such as Domain Controller. To add objects to the new log, click the **Add Objects** button in the middle of the dialog box. In the Add Objects dialog box, first select the computer you want to monitor. You can choose either the local machine (the default) or a remote machine. To monitor a remote machine, type the Universal Naming Convention (UNC) name of the computer in question. To monitor a machine named HOUBDC1, for example, you would type **\\HOUBDC1** in the **Select counter objects from computer** field (Figure 18.9).

You must now select the object to monitor. Select one or more objects to monitor from the **Performance objects** list. Note that the Log view is

> Windows Vista calls the tool *Reliability and Performance Monitor*. It functions similarly to the Windows XP tool, though the screens differ a little. Vista calls the log files "Data Collector Sets," though a log file by any other name . . . is still a log file.

> CompTIA Network+ is not going to test you on using Performance Monitor or any other single baselining tool. Just make sure you understand what a baseline does for you.

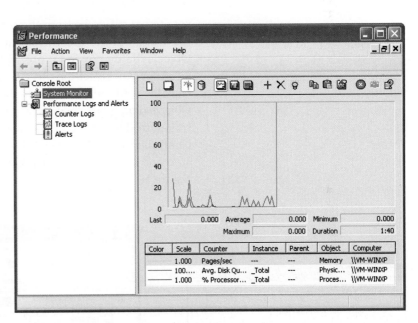

• **Figure 18.8** Performance Monitor in action

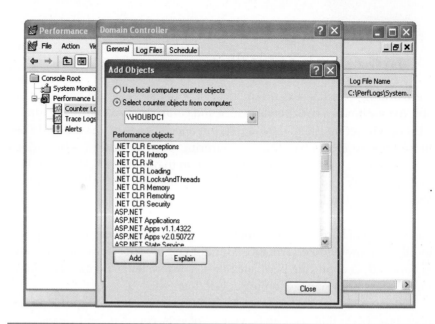

• **Figure 18.9**   Monitoring a remote computer

somewhat different from the other views, in that you only add *objects* to the view, not the specific counters for the objects, as shown in the Add Objects dialog box in Figure 18.10.

After you select the objects for Performance Monitor to track and log, click the **Add** button and then the **Close** button. Click **OK** to close the Add Objects dialog box. Select your new log—in this case labeled Domain Controller. By default, logging will begin immediately upon closing the Domain Controller dialog box. With the newly created log selected, you can easily start and stop logging by clicking the play and pause buttons, as shown in Figure 18.11.

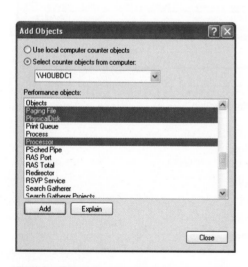

• **Figure 18.10**   Selecting performance objects

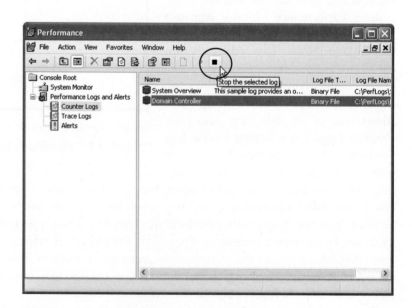

• **Figure 18.11**   Logging data

After you have configured the log settings and captured data for a minute or so, you can then view the results in System Monitor. Click the **System Monitor** item in the console tree on the left. In System Monitor, click the **View Log Data** button and then select the **Log files** radio button on the Source tab of the System Monitor Properties dialog box. From there you can click the **Add** button and select the log file created earlier (Figure 18.12).

When you choose to obtain data from a saved log, you go back to that frozen moment in time and add counters to the other views for the objects you chose to save in the log. In our log options, for

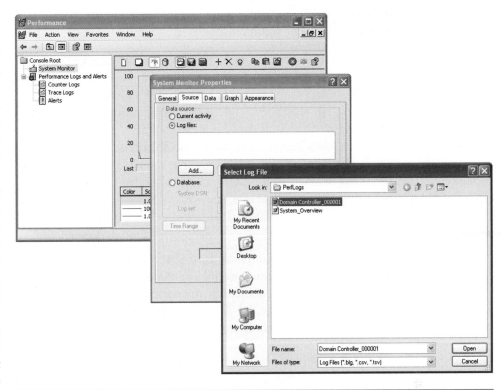

● **Figure 18.12**   Selecting a log file

example, we chose to store data for the paging file, physical disk, and processor objects. After you've loaded a particular log file, you can view a static chart for that moment in time (Figure 18.13).

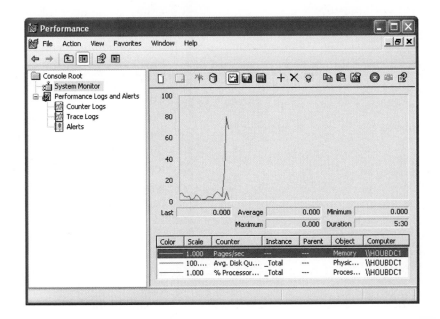

● **Figure 18.13**   Replaying a log file

Using Reliability and Performance Monitor in Windows Vista and Windows 7

The CompTIA Network+ exam won't test you on how to use Performance Monitor in Windows 2000/XP or Reliability and Performance Monitor in Windows Vista and Windows 7, but this stuff is fun. So try this!

If you have a Vista or 7 box handy, open the Control Panel and run Reliability and Performance Monitor. How does it resemble Performance Monitor in Windows XP, as the chapter has described? How does it differ? Go through the steps to create a custom log file—or Data Collector Set—so you get a sense of how to do it.

The Performance Monitor utility described here is specific to Windows 2000 and XP systems, but you should create baselines for whatever types of systems you have, and they should cover all aspects of your network. Be certain to create multiple baselines, to show the systems both at rest and in use, using the baselining tools at your disposal.

Don't limit your thinking to operating system tools when you think about baselining. There are a number of third-party network monitoring tools available that not only generate baselines on almost any criteria you wish but that will also stay online and monitor the network to let you know if any parameters have been exceeded. These network monitors are expensive, but if you want real-time monitoring they are a great option. Since network monitors are always online and always checking for certain items, they also often act as network intrusion detection system (IDS) devices at the same time. Figure 18.14 shows one example, IPSentry by RGE, Inc.

Logs by themselves are a powerful tool because every operating system generates a number of logs outside of the ones you create. Generally you can break up logs into three different types: system, application, and security. In Windows you can see all of these logs in Event Viewer (Figure 18.15). Linux systems tend to have lots of logs, but most versions have a folder called /VAR/LOG where all of your logs (usually) reside. Mac OS X has roughly the same logs as Linux, but has a nice GUI viewer called Console. Whatever the OS, do know

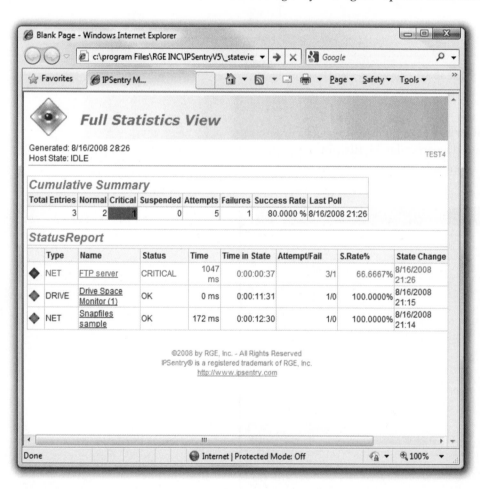

• **Figure 18.14** IPSentry at work

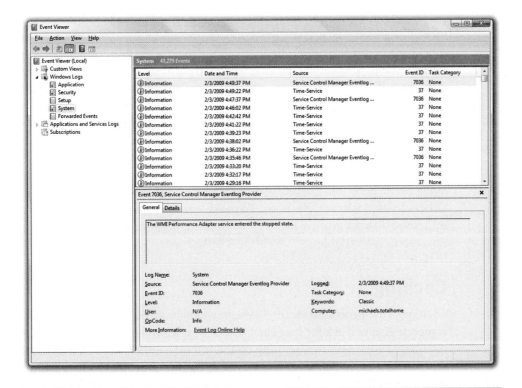

● **Figure 18.15**   Event Viewer in Windows Vista

that the CompTIA Network+ exam takes a Windows bias and assumes there are always at least three logs, Application, Security, and System.

- **Application logs**, as the name implies, deal with events that take place with applications. If an application starts, stops, fails to start, or does anything else an application wishes to report, it shows up here.

- **Security logs** are the place to look for anything that might affect security. The most important counters to look for under Security are successful and failed logons and logoffs.

- **System logs** cover a wide range of issues that deal with the entire system. Anything that has to do with system services, device drivers, or configuration changes tends to show up here.

> Even though the CompTIA Network+ exam lightly touches upon logs and makes some serious simplifications, know that every operating system has a log file for just about any event you might want to know about. Even the default logs are highly customizable, enabling you to choose what types of events you want monitored or not monitored.

■ Network Performance Optimization

It's a tough, ugly world when you're a network administrator. You get very little praise when the network runs well and all the blame when the network isn't running in the fashion the users expect. The situation in which you'll get the most complaints from users is when the network isn't running as fast as they're used to experiencing. We work hard to keep users from contacting us, and the best way to keep them at bay is to make sure the network runs at optimal performance at all times.

Okay, maybe fear of users yelling at you isn't the best rationale. On a more professional basis, we need our networks to deliver their resources as quickly as possible. A Web site that keeps users waiting for long loads or a file server that drags along, leaving users staring at status bars, is contrary to efficiency. It's our duty as network administrators to do everything we can to optimize network performance.

Luckily there are hundreds if not thousands of strategies and technologies designed to optimize network performance. The CompTIA Network+ exam objectives define a short but well-considered list of topics that this section will address. Some of these you've seen in earlier chapters, so I'll not belabor them here, but merely mention and point you to those chapters. Others are topics new to the book. To make learning easier, I've broken them into three distinct groups: caching, controlling data throughput, and keeping resources available.

Caching

Caching is the process of storing data that someone asks for in the hope that someone else will ask for it again. Generally, odds are incredibly good that anytime anyone asks for anything on the Internet, either they or other folks on your LAN will ask for the same thing again—and that's why caching works so well in so many different ways. Caching reduces network workload by eliminating the processes required to reacquire data. Caching reduces network traffic and server workloads.

The challenge to caching is identifying all the diverse places one can cache. Different caching methods and devices have already been discussed in the book. Refer back to Chapter 10, "Network Naming," for DNS caching and Chapter 12, "Advanced Networking Devices," for proxy servers for two examples. To put it simply: when you can cache, do it!

Controlling Data Throughput

Despite the derision aimed at the remarks made by a certain U.S. senator a few years ago to the effect that the Internet is made out of "a series of pipes," there's actually a strong argument for the idea of pipes when discussing the amount of data per second any given Internet connection may need. Unless your budget allows you to buy a "big pipe" connection to the Internet, every network suffers from a limited amount of bandwidth that's rarely truly sufficient for everything your users need. Even if you're lucky enough to have good bandwidth today, ongoing network growth guarantees you'll eventually run into network slowdowns as demand grows.

There's no magic point at which a network goes from working well to working slowly. Most people are used to having to wait a bit for a Web page or a file transfer. Certain applications, called *latency-sensitive* applications, do not perform well when they lack adequate bandwidth. Some latency-sensitive applications require high bandwidth. Streaming video is a great example. Have you ever watched a video on YouTube that constantly stops and starts? At least YouTube enables you to pause the video so it can load more before you continue watching (Figure 18.16).

● **Figure 18.16**   Pausing a video on YouTube

Try watching a video on Hulu.com (Figure 18.17) over an overly busy or slow connection. Hulu, unlike YouTube but like most other video sites, only caches a few seconds (to prevent people from stealing the video) and is all but unwatchable if there are constant stops and starts. Voice over IP (VoIP) applications are another great example. If every conversation is clipped . . . and . . . chopped . . . the beauty of VoIP falls apart.

When the size of your Internet pipe is limited, you need some method to throttle bandwidth so that in high-demand times latency-sensitive applications get more bandwidth at the cost of reducing bandwidth to those applications that don't mind the wait. The CompTIA Network+ exam mentions two of the most common: quality of service (QoS) and traffic shaping, both of which you learned about in Chapter 12, "Advanced Networking Devices." Here's a quick recap and some extra details.

Quality of Service

Quality of service (QoS) is a procedure used almost exclusively on gateway devices to give certain applications priority when a connection reaches a certain amount of utilization. QoS works at Layer 2 of the OSI model and works with 802.1Q trunks to prioritize traffic. QoS applies a Class of Service (CoS) priority (0 to 7) to a certain port. As traffic from that port goes through

> QoS is particularly helpful to reduce jitter on VoIP connections.

• **Figure 18.17**   Hulu.com (I love this site!)

a trunk line, its priority defines how much bandwidth is allocated. The higher the priority of traffic, the more bandwidth it gets. This form of QoS is specialized when you have high-priority file server or VoIP server systems connected to your network.

Traffic Shaping

Traffic shaping (also called bandwidth shaping) prioritizes traffic at Layer 3 and Layer 7 of the OSI seven-layer model. Traffic shaping usually works at the edge routers, placing priority on traffic based usually on TCP/UDP port number. Traffic shaping works in either of two ways: by giving certain packets a priority or by directly assigning a fixed amount of bandwidth (in bits/sec) to packets from a particular application based on port number.

A typical setup of traffic shaping first requires you to tell the router the total upstream and downstream bandwidth of your connection. From there, you assign bandwidth to a particular application, as shown in Figure 18.18

QoS and traffic shaping give you a number of tools to control traffic. You can control or prioritize traffic based on port/MAC address (QoS), IP address, or application. The choice depends on the equipment you choose and the needs of your networks.

> When ISPs limit traffic based on applications to customers, it is called bandwidth throttling.

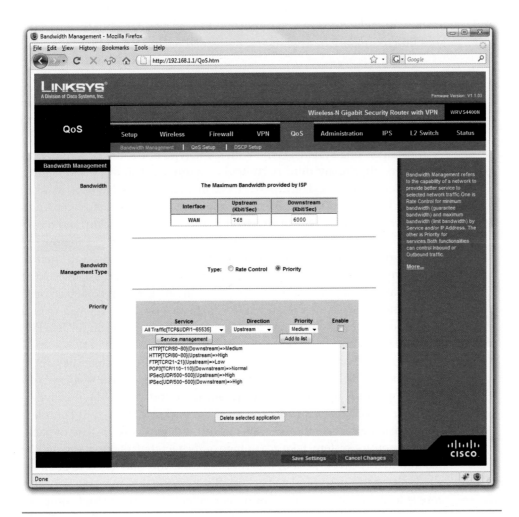

• Figure 18.18   Traffic shaping on a SOHO router

Keeping Resources Available

No throttling or QoS does you a bit of good if the resource itself isn't available due to problems with the hardware. There are two areas where hardware limitations come into play. First is some form of hardware failure. Anyone who has worked on a PC for more than a few months knows one thing: hardware fails. Second, the design of the Internet dictates that a single IP address be given to a resource. Every Web server has a single IP address; every e-mail server eventually goes back to one IP address. This creates a problem when a resource becomes popular, because no single machine could ever handle the demands of a www.yahoo.com or a www.google .com. No worries, though, because there are many techniques to make multiple physical servers look as though they're a single IP address. Collectively, these techniques make sure that a shared resource is available in a timely manner when clients request it: what we call **high availability**.

Proper network management requires **fault tolerance**: systems that can continue to provide network functions even in the face of catastrophic hardware failure. Ensuring fault tolerance begins with a plain old **data backup**, where you make a copy of all important files and folders, but then quickly goes into redundant hardware, real-time load balancing, and more.

Data Backup

Without a solid data backup, you're sunk if too much hardware goes down too quickly. Proper backup routines require both software and hardware to create, preferably, removable or remote backup of all data.

Most operating systems come with some type of backup program, plus developers offer many third-party tools. Figure 18.19 shows the venerable Backup for Windows. Third-party tools include Veritas NetBackup from Symantec and CA ARCserve Backup (from the company formerly known as Computer Associates), both of which offer enterprise-level backup and recovery tools.

Most backup software looks first to tape backup devices and then to hard drive or networked storage for backup. Use of tape drives seemed to be on the wane a few years ago, but they have made a strong comeback as a storage medium. Tape is relatively inexpensive and quite reliable over a long period of time. Some of the big players in tape drives include Dell, HP, IBM, and Qualstar.

The goal of backing up data is to ensure that when a system dies, there will be an available, recent copy you can use to restore the system. You could simply back up the complete system at the end of each day—or whatever interval you feel is prudent to keep the backups fresh—but complete backups can be a tremendous waste of time and materials. Instead of backing up the entire system, take advantage of the fact that all the files won't be changed in any given period; much of the time you only need to back up what's changed since your last backup. Recognizing this, most backup software solutions have a series of options available beyond the old complete (usually called Full or Normal) backup.

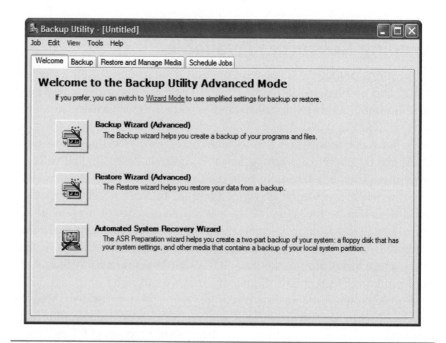

• **Figure 18.19**   Windows Backup

The key to understanding backups other than the full backup is *attributes*, 1-bit storage areas that all files have. The most common attributes are Hidden (don't show the file in Computer or when `dir` is typed at the command line), System (it's a critical file for the system), Read-Only (can't erase it), and Archive. These attributes were first used in FAT-formatted drives in the DOS era, but they are still completely supported today by all file formats. The **archive bit** works basically like this: whenever a file is saved, the archive bit is turned on. Simply opening a file will affect the current state of the archive bit. Backup programs will usually turn off a file's archive bit when the file is backed up. In theory, if a file's archive bit is turned off, it means there's a good backup of that file on some tape. If the archive bit is turned on, it means that the file has been changed since it was last backed up (see Figure 18.20).

Archive bits are used to perform backups that are not full backups. The following backup types are most often supported:

- A **normal backup** is a full backup. Every file selected will be backed up, and the archive bit will be turned off for every file backed up. This is the standard "back it all up" option.

- A **copy backup** is identical to a normal backup, with the important distinction being that the archive bits are *not* changed. This is used (although not often) for making extra copies of a previously completed backup.

- An **incremental backup** includes only files with the archive bit turned on. In other words, it copies only the files that have been changed since the last backup. This backup turns off the archive bits.

- A **differential backup** is identical to an incremental backup, except that it doesn't turn off the archive bits.

- A **daily backup**, also known as a daily copy backup, makes copies of all the files that have been changed that day. It does not change the archive bits.

The motivation for having both the incremental and differential backups may not be clear at first glance—they seem so similar as to be basically the same. Incremental seems the better option at first. If a file is backed up, you would want to turn off the archive bit, right? Well, maybe. But there is one

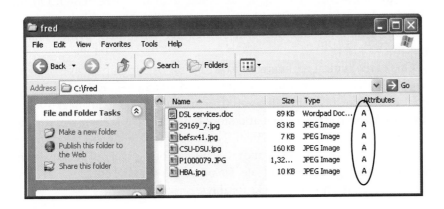

• **Figure 18.20**   The archive bit on these files is on.

Incremental

MON	TUE	WED	THU	FRI
Full Backup	All Tuesday Changes	All Wednesday Changes	All Thursday Changes	All Friday Changes

Differential

MON	TUE	WED	THU	FRI
Full Backup	All Changes Through Tuesday	All Changes Through Wednesday	All Changes Through Thursday	All Changes Through Friday

● **Figure 18.21**   Incremental vs. differential

scenario where that might not be too attractive. Most backups do a big weekly normal backup, followed by daily incremental or differential backups at the end of every business day. Figure 18.21 shows the difference between incremental and differential backups.

Notice that a differential backup is a cumulative backup. Because the archive bits are not set, it keeps backing up all changes since the last normal backup. This means the backup files will get progressively larger throughout the week (assuming a standard weekly normal backup). The incremental backup, by contrast, only backs up files changed since the last backup. Each incremental backup file will be relatively small and also totally different from the previous backup file.

Let's assume that the system is wiped out on a Thursday morning. How can you restore the system to a useful state?

If you're using an incremental backup, you will first have to restore the last weekly backup you ran on Monday, then the Tuesday backup, and then the Wednesday backup before the system is restored to its Thursday morning state. The longer the time between normal backups, the more incremental backups you must restore.

Using the same scenario, but assuming you're doing differential instead of incremental backups, you'll only need the weekly backup, and then the Wednesday backup to restore your system. A differential backup will always require only two backups to restore a system (see Figure 18.22). Suddenly, the differential backup looks better than the incremental! On the other hand, one big benefit of incremental over differential is backup file size. Differential backup files will be massive compared to incremental ones.

One of the typical regimens or rotations for backing up to tape or to external hard drive and rotating media is called **grandfather, father, son (GFS)**, and it works like this. Typically, you'd have a weekly and daily backup. You run a full backup once a week and store the tape offsite. Then you'd run a differential backup each day. The full backup is the father and the differential backups are the son. The grandfather would be the last full backup of the month that then gets stored off site. Using such a strategy enables you to restore by previous months, weeks, or days.

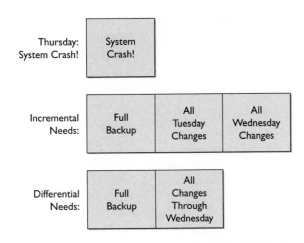

| Thursday: System Crash! | System Crash! | | |

| Incremental Needs: | Full Backup | All Tuesday Changes | All Wednesday Changes |

| Differential Needs: | Full Backup | All Changes Through Wednesday |

• **Figure 18.22**　Restoring from backups

Choosing between incremental backups and differential backups is only one factor in choosing how you back up your data. You must also consider your business, your data, your backup hardware, your operating systems, and other factors to create a backup strategy.

UPS　An **uninterruptible power supply (UPS)** keeps your servers afloat in the event of an electrical brownout or blackout. Without a good UPS, you simply cannot guarantee the proper level of uptime for your server. A UPS enables a computer to function for a short period of time, but for extended outages, there's only one answer: backup generators.

Backup Generators　For extended blackouts, such as when Hurricane Ike took down my office (and much of the Gulf Coast) for several weeks in 2008, you need to have backup generators to guarantee any hope of uninterrupted uptime. A **backup generator** runs on some sort of fuel (often diesel or gasoline) to provide electricity.

RAID and Redundant Hardware　Once you've secured the electricity for your servers, you need to make sure that individual components within the system don't take out your entire server. Most commonly, these redundant pieces of hardware include multiple hard drives, power supplies, and network connections.

As you most likely recall from studying for your CompTIA A+ exam, you can use two or more hard drives to provide fault tolerance through one of the several levels of **Redundant Array of Independent Disks (RAID)**. There are three RAID levels commonly used in networks: RAID 0, RAID 1, and RAID 5.

RAID 0 is known as striping. Requiring at least two drives, RAID 0 breaks files into chunks called stripes and spreads the stripes across each drive in the RAID 0 array. RAID 0 arrays are fast, but if one drive dies you lose everything. There's no fault tolerance with RAID 0.

RAID 1 is mirroring. Again requiring at least two drives, RAID 1 makes a copy of every stripe and places it on each drive. RAID 1 arrays have great fault tolerance, but because every file is copied twice they're slower than RAID 0 arrays.

Tech Tip

Stand By Your UPS

Uninterruptible power supplies differ a lot in how they work and in the quality of electricity they provide. The standard device we call a UPS is actually a standby power supply *as it takes a few milliseconds to bring the power online. These are fine and they are much cheaper than a true UPS.*

Try This!

Shopping for RAID

Many current motherboards support RAID, right out of the box, so here's a shopping trip to see what's out there. If you have a computer store handy in your neighborhood, check out its motherboards. What kind of RAID can you find? What's the price difference between a motherboard with RAID 0 and 1 versus one with RAID 5 as well? What seems to be the sweet spot for price and protection?

The CompTIA Network+ exam doesn't require you to know the different levels of RAID.

You might recall another use for a second network connection—bonding, using multiple NICs to increase your throughput. Bonding provides no fault tolerance but can be very useful if you have an overly busy server!

RAID 5 is disk striping with distributed parity. RAID 5 requires at least three drives. RAID 5 takes stripes, performs a parity calculation, and then stores the stripes and the parity across the drives in the array. If a single drive fails, the RAID array can rebuild the data. RAID 5 is fast and provides good fault tolerance.

Redundant power supplies and network connections provide exactly what their names suggest. The spare power supply should kick on automatically if the main power supply dies for some reason. The spare network connection can do the same for either a dead NIC or a dead connection.

Cluster Servers and Load Balancing   If you're not content with duplicating hardware components inside a server, you're not alone. Many network installations reproduce entire servers or use multiple servers that act as a cluster server, so that if any server goes down, the rest just pick up the slack and keep on chugging. Clustering servers requires cluster-aware operating systems, such as Windows Server for the Enterprise.

Clustered servers can also balance the load when dealing with heavy usage, as you'll recall from the discussion of busy Web servers in Chapter 12. When scaled up and done right, to the end user there's only one identity. Google.com's home page might be balanced on 20 giant servers, for example, but you merely type in www.google.com and away you go.

Chapter 18 Review

■ Chapter Summary

After reading this chapter and completing the exercises, you should understand the following about network management.

Describe how configuration management documentation enables you to manage and upgrade a network efficiently

■ The more complicated a network is, the more vulnerable it is in terms of security, efficiency, and other aspects. Configuration management helps you maintain and update your network in a logical and orderly fashion to lessen these vulnerabilities.

■ Networks should be standardized on the types of NICs, cabling, network operating systems, and network applications to make upgrades to the network as efficient as possible.

■ Configuration management documentation includes wiring diagrams, network diagrams, baselines, policies, procedures, configurations, and regulations.

■ A wiring diagram (or wiring schematic), which usually consists of multiple pages, shows how the wires in a network connect to switches and other nodes, what types of cable are used, and how patch panels are configured, and usually includes details about each and every cable run.

■ It is the cable puller's job to create the wiring schematic. In office buildings, the schematic often includes telephone wires. The schematic itself is usually kept by the people in charge of the building (building services).

■ A physical network diagram is similar to a wiring schematic, but defines the type of connection such as Gigabit Ethernet, T1, and so forth. It also includes every router, switch, server, CSU/DSU, cable modem, wireless access point, and details about each.

■ The network administrator should create the physical network diagram, using standardized icons and one of the many diagramming programs, such as Microsoft Visio.

■ A logical network diagram shows the broadcast domains and individual IP addresses for all devices on the network. Only critical switches and routers are shown.

■ A baseline is a log of performance indicators, such as CPU usage, network utilization, and other values that describe how the network functions when things are working normally. The Performance Monitor utility that comes with Windows is helpful for creating baselines on individual Windows systems.

■ Procedure and policy documentation should state what people can and cannot do with network hardware and software. Acceptable use policies and security policies are two such policies.

■ Configuration settings of routers, switches, and other network devices should be documented in case they lose their settings or have to be replaced. Documenting the configuration helps to ensure that policies and procedures can still be enforced after devices have been replaced or reprogrammed.

■ Regulations govern behavior in the workplace, such as what to do when a particular event occurs. Regulations should be part of your configuration management documentation.

■ Change management documentation details the procedures and policies to update other documentation. For example, if a change was made to the network, the change management documentation would describe which other documents had to be updated to keep track of the change.

Conduct network monitoring to identify performance and connectivity issues

■ Baselines create a benchmark or standard measurement of when everything is working correctly on your network. Consider this to be a snapshot of your systems. On a Windows computer, Performance Monitor (PerfMon) watches itself or other Windows machines, either locally or remotely.

■ Every operating system creates a variety of logs automatically. These can typically be categorized as System, Application, and Security logs. In Windows, use Event Viewer to view these logs.

In Linux, most of these logs reside in the /VAR/ LOG directory. On a Macintosh, use the GUI log viewer called Console.

- The Application log tracks events that take place with individual applications, such as starts, stops, start failures, crashes, and so forth.

- The Security log tracks anything that affects security, such as successful and failed logons and logoffs.

- The System log covers issues dealing with the overall system, such as system services, device drivers, or configuration changes.

Explain how to optimize network performance

- Quality of service is a procedure used almost exclusively on gateway devices to give certain applications priority when a connection reaches a certain amount of utilization.

- Traffic shaping (or bandwidth shaping) prioritizes traffic at Layers 3 and 7 of the OSI model. Usually in effect at the edge routers, certain packets are given priority or a fixed amount of bandwidth is allocated to packets from a particular application based on port number.

- High availability describes a situation in which a resource is available when a client requests it. QoS, bandwidth shaping, and fault tolerance help to increase the potential for high availability.

- A system that is fault tolerant can continue to function even in the face of catastrophic hardware failure. Fault tolerance can be accomplished through data backups, redundant hardware, and real-time load balancing.

- Proper backup routines require both software and hardware, including backup software such as Windows Backup, Veritas NetBackup, or CA ARCserve Backup and appropriate hardware on which to store the data backups. Backup hardware can include hard drives or tape drives.

- In a full backup, every file selected will be backed up, and the archive bit will be turned off for every file backed up. This is the standard "back it all up" option.

- A copy backup is identical to a normal backup, with the important distinction being that the archive bits are not changed. This is used (although not often) for making extra copies of a previously completed backup.

- An incremental backup includes only files with the archive bit turned on. In other words, it copies only the files that have been changed since the last backup. This backup turns off the archive bits.

- A differential backup is identical to an incremental backup, except that it doesn't turn off the archive bits.

- Full backups get everything but require the most space and take the longest. Incremental backups are quick and use very little space; differential backups take longer than incremental backups and use more space, but they potentially offer a much quicker restore time.

- A UPS keeps delivering power to your devices for a short period of time in the event of a power outage. For extended periods of power outages, you need a backup generator.

- Servers using RAID can continue to function and serve data even if a hard drive crashes. RAID 1 and RAID 5 both offer fault tolerance.

- Clustering servers allows multiple servers to appear as a single server. This offers fault tolerance in the event one server goes down. Creating and managing clustered servers requires special operating systems, such as Windows Server for the Enterprise.

- Clustered servers can also implement load balancing to spread out client requests equally among all the clustered servers. This helps to ensure that no single machine is overloaded.

◼ Key Terms

acceptable use policy *(489)*
Application log *(495)*
archive bit *(501)*
backup generator *(503)*
baseline *(489)*
change management documentation *(490)*

configuration management *(485)*
configuration management documentation *(485)*
configuration *(489)*
copy backup *(501)*
counter *(491)*
daily backup *(501)*

data backup *(499)*

differential backup *(501)*

fault tolerance *(499)*

grandfather, father, son (GFS) *(502)*

high availability *(499)*

incremental backup *(501)*

logical network diagram *(487)*

normal backup *(501)*

object *(491)*

Performance Monitor *(491)*

physical network diagram *(486)*

quality of service (QoS) *(497)*

Redundant Array of Independent Disks (RAID) *(503)*

regulations *(490)*

Security log *(495)*

security policy *(489)*

System log *(495)*

traffic shaping *(498)*

uninterruptible power supply (UPS) *(503)*

view *(491)*

wiring diagram *(485)*

wiring schematic *(485)*

■ Key Term Quiz

Use the Key Terms list to complete the sentences that follow. Not all the terms will be used.

1. The best Windows software tool to use when trying to establish baselines is _____.

2. A(n) _____ shows all the wiring in a building, often including the telephone system, and is kept by the people in charge of the building.

3. The _____ tracks successful and failed logons and logoffs.

4. When network resources are always ready whenever a client requests them, they are said to have _____.

5. A(n) _____ provides long-term power in the event of an extended blackout.

6. A(n) _____ shows the broadcast domains and individual IP addresses for all the devices in your network.

7. A(n) _____ shows cabling runs and the type of connection in addition to showing every router, switch, and server and their makes, models, and firmware versions.

8. A(n) _____ provides short-term power in the event of a brownout.

9. A(n) _____ copies only the files that have been changed since the last backup. This backup turns off the archive bits.

10. A(n) _____ defines exactly what you can and cannot do with your computers and network.

■ Multiple-Choice Quiz

1. What should be created to establish normal operating conditions on your network?

   A. Backups

   B. Baselines

   C. Remote access

   D. Troubleshooting

2. Where could you find a list of problems that occurred on a system?

   A. Wiring schematic

   B. Event Viewer

   C. Performance Monitor

   D. RAID

3. Where should backup tapes be kept?

   A. In the server room

   B. On a shelf in the storeroom

   C. In a locked cabinet away from the server room

   D. In the boss's car trunk

4. Your boss asks you for a diagram showing every server on the network. What do you provide to her?

   A. Logical network diagram

   B. Physical network diagram

   C. Wiring schematic

   D. Baseline

5. You are hired as a consultant to troubleshoot a network. Your client reports the network has recently slowed significantly. What should you ask to see first?

   A. Baseline

   B. Security policy

   C. Application logs

   D. PerfMon counters

6. When using Performance Monitor, what do you call the actual component you want to monitor?

   A. Counter

   B. Histogram

   C. Object

   D. View

7. You are using Performance Monitor to monitor the CPU. You need to define what aspects of the CPU to monitor, such as the percentage in use and the percentage free. What must you configure?

   A. Counter

   B. Histogram

   C. Object

   D. View

8. Which types of logs are automatically created? (Select three.)

   A. Application

   B. Login

   C. Security

   D. System

9. What technology ensures data is still immediately available in the event of a hard drive crash?

   A. Backup generator

   B. UPS

   C. GFS

   D. RAID

10. Where can you find the log files on most Linux installations?

    A. /VAR/LOG

    B. /CONFIG/LOG

    C. /ADMIN/LOGS

    D. /LOGFILES

11. How can you connect to another computer named SERVER2 using the Universal Naming Convention?

    A. http://SERVER2

    B. //SERVER2

    C. \\SERVER2

    D. SERVER2/

12. Which program can be used to create baselines?

    A. Event Viewer

    B. Performance Monitor

    C. Microsoft Visio

    D. Veritas NetBackup

13. Which backup type always requires only two backups to restore a system?

    A. Copy backup

    B. Differential backup

    C. Full backup

    D. Incremental backup

14. What is defined in a security policy? (Select two.)

    A. What users can and cannot do with their computers

    B. How complex user passwords should be

    C. How to deal with social engineering hacking attempts

    D. How users should install their own software

15. What can help to maintain high availability? (Select three.)

    A. QoS

    B. RAID

    C. VoIP

    D. UPS

■ Essay Quiz

1. Some students in class are discussing when tape backups should be performed. One student says daily, during nonpeak hours, while another student suggests weekly. A third student says both students are correct. The trio suddenly looks at you for your definitive answer. Write down what you would say.

2. How can you view log files on Windows, Linux, and Macintosh OS X computers?

3. An intern has come to you confused and stressed because he has been asked to review the configuration management documentation. Ease the poor guy's mind and explain the difference between a wiring schematic, physical network diagram, logical network diagram, policy, procedure, configuration, regulation, acceptable use policy, and security policy.

Lab Projects

• Lab Project 18.1

Create a step-by-step guide for using Performance Monitor to create a baseline. Swap guides with a classmate and see if you can follow each other's steps. If either of you has problems, go back and fix your steps to make them clearer.

• Lab Project 18.2

Use the Internet to find Network+ practice questions. Try to locate as many troubleshooting scenario questions in the time allowed. Share your findings with classmates who have done the same.

The more practice questions you cover as a group, the better prepared you will be to handle real questions on the Network+ exam.

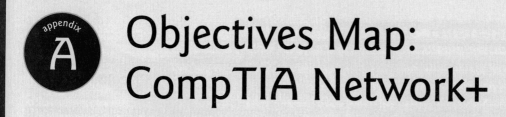

Objectives Map: CompTIA Network+

Topic	Chapter(s)
1.0 Network Technologies	
1.1 Explain the function of common networking protocols	
TCP	2, 7, 8, 9, 10, 11, 12, 13, 17
FTP	9
UDP	9
TCP/IP suite	2, 7, 8, 9
DHCP	7
TFTP	9
DNS	10
HTTP(S)	9
ARP	7
SIP (VoIP)	14
RTP (VoIP)	14
SSH	11
POP3	9
NTP	11
IMAP4	9
Telnet	8, 9
SMTP	9
SNMP2/3	11
ICMP	9
IGMP	9
TLS	9, 11
1.2 Identify commonly used TCP and UDP default ports	
TCP ports:	
FTP – 20, 21	9
SSH – 22	9
TELNET – 23	9
SMTP – 25	9
DNS – 53	10
HTTP – 80	9
POP3 – 110	9
NTP – 123	11

Topic	Chapter(s)
IMAP4 – 143	9
HTTPS – 443	9
UDP ports:	
TFTP – 69	9
DNS – 53	10
BOOTPS/DHCP – 67	7
SNMP – 161	11
1.3 Identify the following address formats	
IPv6	13
IPv4	7
MAC addressing	2, 13
1.4 Given a scenario, evaluate the proper use of the following addressing technologies and addressing schemes	
Addressing Technologies:	
Subnetting	2, 7
Classful vs. classless (e.g. CIDR, Supernetting)	7
NAT	8
PAT	8
SNAT	8
Public vs. private	7
DHCP (static, dynamic APIPA)	7
Addressing schemes:	
Unicast	7
Multicast	7
Broadcast	2, 4, 7
1.5 Identify common IPv4 and IPv6 routing protocols	
Link state:	
OSPF	8
IS-IS	8
Distance vector:	
RIP	8
RIPv2	8
BGP	8
Hybrid:	
EIGRP	8
1.6 Explain the purpose and properties of routing	
IGP vs. EGP	8
Static vs. dynamic	8
Next hop	8
Understanding routing tables and how they pertain to path selection	8
Explain convergence (steady state)	8

Topic	Chapter(s)
1.7 Compare the characteristics of wireless communication standards	
802.11 a/b/g/n:	
Speeds	16
Distance	16
Channels	16
Frequency	16
Authentication and encryption:	
WPA	16
WEP	16
RADIUS	11, 16
TKIP	16
2.0 Network Media and Topologies	
2.1 Categorize standard cable types and their properties	
Type:	
CAT3, CAT5, CAT5e, CAT6	3
STP, UTP	3
Multimode fiber, single-mode fiber	3
Coaxial	3
RG-59	3
RG-6	3
Serial	3
Plenum vs. Non-plenum	3
Properties:	
Transmission speeds	4, 5
Distance	4, 5
Duplex	4, 5
Noise immunity (security, EMI)	3
Frequency	4, 5
2.2 Identify common connector types	
RJ-11	3
RJ-45	3
BNC	3
SC	3
ST	3
LC	3
RS-232	3
RG-59	3
RG-6	3
2.3 Identify common physical network topologies	
Star	3
Mesh	3
Bus	3
Ring	3

Topic	Chapter(s)
Point to point	3
Point to multipoint	3
Hybrid	3
2.4 *Given a scenario, differentiate and implement appropriate wiring standards*	
568A	4
568B	4
Straight vs. cross-over	4
Rollover	8
Loopback	6
2.5 *Categorize WAN technology types and properties*	
Type:	
Frame relay	14
E1/T1	14
ADSL	14
SDSL	14
VDSL	14
Cable modem	14
Satellite	14
E3/T3	14
OC-x	14
Wireless	14
ATM	14
SONET	14
MPLS	14
ISDN BRI	14
ISDN PRI	14
POTS	14
PSTN	14
Properties:	
Circuit switch	14
Packet switch	14
Speed	14
Transmission media	14
Distance	14
2.6 *Categorize LAN technology types and properties*	
Type:	
Ethernet	3, 4, 5
10BaseT	4
100BaseTX	5
100BaseFX	5
1000BaseT	5
1000BaseX	5
10GBaseSR	5

Topic	Chapter(s)
10GBaseLR	5
10GBaseER	5
10GBaseSW	5
10GBaseLW	5
10GBaseEW	5
10GBaseT	5
Properties:	
CSMA/CD	4
Broadcast	3, 4
Collision	4
Bonding	6
Speed	4, 5
Distance	4, 5
2.7 Explain common logical network topologies and their characteristics	
Peer to peer	12
Client/server	12
VPN	12
VLAN	12
2.8 Install components of wiring distribution	
Vertical and horizontal cross-connects	6
Patch panels	6
66 block	6
MDFs	6
IDFs	6
25 pair	6
100 pair	6
110 block	6
Demarc	6
Demarc extension	6
Smart jack	6
Verify wiring installation	6
Verify wiring termination	6
3.0 Network Devices	
3.1 Install, configure, and differentiate between common network devices	
Hub	2, 4
Repeater	4
Modem	11, 14
NIC	2, 4, 6
Media converters	4
Basic switch	4
Bridge	4
Wireless access point	16

Topic	Chapter(s)
Basic router	2, 7, 9
Basic firewall	8, 17
Basic DHCP server	8
3.2 Identify the functions of specialized network devices	
Multilayer switch	12
Content switch	12
IDS/IPS	12
Load balancer	12
Multifunction network devices	12
DNS server	10
Bandwidth shaper	12
Proxy server	12
CSU/DSU	14
3.3 Explain the advanced features of a switch	
PoE	14
Spanning tree	4
VLAN	12
Trunking	12
Port mirroring	12
Port authentication	12
3.4 Implement a basic wireless network	
Install client	16
Access point placement	16
Install access point	16
Configure appropriate encryption	16
Configure channels and frequencies	16
Set ESSID and beacon	16
Verify installation	16
4.0 Network Management	
4.1 Explain the function of each layer of the OSI model	
Layer 1 – Physical	2
Layer 2 – Data Link	2
Layer 3 – Network	2
Layer 4 – Transport	2
Layer 5 – Session	2
Layer 6 – Presentation	2
Layer 7 – Application	2
4.2 Identify types of configuration management documentation	
Wiring schematics	18
Physical and logical network diagrams	18
Baselines	18
Policies, procedures, and configurations	18
Regulations	18

Topic	Chapter(s)
4.3 Given a scenario, evaluate the network based on configuration management documentation	
Compare wiring schematics, physical and logical network diagrams, baselines, policies and procedures, and configurations to network devices and infrastructure	18
Update wiring schematics, physical and logical network diagrams, configurations, and job logs as needed	18
4.4 Conduct network monitoring to identify performance and connectivity issues using the following:	
Network monitoring utilities (e.g. packet sniffers, connectivity software, load testing, throughput testers)	15, 18
System logs, history logs, event logs	18
4.5 Explain different methods and rationales for network performance optimization	
Methods:	
QoS	18
Traffic shaping	18
Load balancing	18
High availability	18
Caching engines	18
Fault tolerance	18
Reasons:	
Latency sensitivity	18
High bandwidth applications	18
VoIP	18
Video applications	18
Uptime	18
4.6 Given a scenario, implement the following network troubleshooting methodology	
Information gathering; identify symptoms and problems	15
Identify the affected areas of the network	15
Determine if anything has changed	15
Establish the most probable cause	15
Determine if escalation is necessary	15
Create an action plan and solution identifying potential effects	15
Implement and test the solution	15
Identify the results and effects of the solution	15
Document the solution and the entire process	15
4.7 Given a scenario, troubleshoot common connectivity issues and select an appropriate solution	
Physical issues:	
Crosstalk	6
Near-end crosstalk	6
Attenuation	6
Collisions	6
Shorts	6
Open impedance mismatch (echo)	15
Interference	6

Topic	Chapter(s)
Logical issues:	
Port speed	5
Port duplex mismatch	5
Incorrect VLAN	12
Incorrect IP address	7, 15
Wrong gateway	7, 15
Wrong DNS	10, 15
Wrong subnet mask	7, 15
Issues that should be identified but escalated:	
Switching loop	15
Routing loop	15
Route problems	15
Proxy arp	15
Broadcast storms	15
Wireless issues:	
Interference (bleed, environmental factors)	16
Incorrect encryption	16
Incorrect channel	16
Incorrect frequency	16
ESSID mismatch	16
Standard mismatch (802.11 a/b/g/n)	16
Distance	16
Bounce	16
Incorrect antenna placement	16

5.0 Network Tools

5.1 Given a scenario, select the appropriate command-line interface tool and interpret the output to verify functionality

Traceroute	8, 15
Ipconfig	15
Ifconfig	15
Ping	7, 8, 9, 15
Arp ping	10, 15
Arp	15
Nslookup	10, 15
Hostname	15
Dig	10, 15
Mtr	8
Route	8, 15
Nbtstat	10, 15
Netstat	8, 9, 10, 15

5.2 Explain the purpose of network scanners

Packet sniffers	15
Intrusion detection software	12
Intrusion prevention software	12
Port scanners	15

Topic	Chapter(s)
5.3 Given a scenario, utilize the appropriate hardware tools	
Cable testers	15
Protocol analyzer	15
Certifiers	15
TDR	15
OTDR	15
Multimeter	15
Toner probe	15
Butt set	15
Punch down tool	15
Cable stripper	15
Snips	15
Voltage event recorder	15
Temperature monitor	15
6.0 Network Security	
6.1 Explain the function of hardware and software security devices	
Network-based firewall	17
Host-based firewall	17
IDS	12
IPS	12
VPN concentrator	12
6.2 Explain common features of a firewall	
Application layer vs. network layer	17
Stateful vs. stateless	17
Scanning services	17
Content filtering	17
Signature identification	17
Zones	17
6.3 Explain the methods of network access security	
Filtering:	
ACL	11
MAC filtering	17
IP filtering	17
Tunneling and encryption	11, 12
SSL VPN	12
VPN	12
L2TP	12
PPTP	12
IPSec	11, 12, 13
Remote access	14
RAS	14
RDP	14
PPPoE	14

Topic	Chapter(s)
PPP	11, 14
VNC	14
ICA	14
6.4 Explain methods of user authentication	
PKI	11
Kerberos	11
AAA	11
RADIUS	11
TACACS+	11
Network access control	11
802.1x	11
CHAP	11
MS-CHAP	11
EAP	11
6.5 Explain issues that affect device security	
Physical security	17
Restricting local and remote access	17
Secure methods vs. unsecure methods	11
SSH, HTTPS, SNMPv3, SFTP, SCP	9, 11
TELNET, HTTP, FTP, RSH, RCP, SNMPv1/2	9, 11
6.6 Identify common security threats and mitigation techniques	
Security threats:	
DoS	17
Viruses	17
Worms	17
Attackers	17
Man in the middle	17
Smurf	17
Rogue access points	17
Social engineering (phishing)	17
Mitigation techniques:	
Policies and procedures	17
User training	17
Patches and updates	17

About the CD-ROM

The CD-ROM included with this book comes with an introduction video from the author, Mike Meyers; a sample of the Total Tester practice exam software; a sample of LearnKey's Network+ video training, starring Mike Meyers; and a useful collection of tools and utilities for network management. The software can be installed on any Windows 98/NT/2000/XP/Vista computer and must be installed to access the Total Tester practice exam and LearnKey video training software.

■ Playing Mike Meyers' Introduction Video

If your computer CD-ROM drive is configured to auto-run, the CD-ROM will automatically start up upon inserting the disc. If the auto-run feature did not launch your CD, browse to the CD and click the **Launch.exe** icon.

From the opening screen you can launch the video message from Mike by clicking the **Mike Meyers Introduction Video** button. This launches the .avi file using your system's default video player.

■ System Requirements

The software requires Windows 98 or higher, Internet Explorer 5.5 or higher or Firefox with Flash Player, and 30 MB of hard disk space for full installation.

You can check your system compatibility at the online site by clicking the **Getting Started** tab and selecting the **Download Detection Utility**. This utility will verify that you have all the standard components on your machine, and if you need any downloads, the site provides directions for downloading them for free.

■ Installing and Running Total Tester

From the opening screen you may install the Total Tester by clicking the **Install Network+ Practice Exam** button. This will begin the installation process, create a program group named **Total Seminars**, and put an icon on your desktop. To run Total Tester, navigate to **Start | Programs | Total Seminars** or double-click the icon on your desktop.

To uninstall the Total Tester software, go to **Start | Settings | Control Panel | Add/Remove Programs**, and then select the **Network+ Total Tester** program. Select **Remove** and Windows will completely uninstall the software.

Total Tester

Total Tester provides you with a simulation of the CompTIA Network+ exam. There is one complete CompTIA Network+ practice exam. The exam can be taken in either Practice or Final mode. Practice mode provides an assistance window with hints, references to the book, an explanation of the answer, and the option to check your answer as you take the test. Both Practice and Final modes provide an overall grade and a grade broken down by certification objective. To take a test, launch the program, select a suite from the menu at the top, and then select an exam from the menu.

LearnKey Video Training

Clicking the **Install LearnKey demo** link will launch your browser and take you to a registration site. A valid e-mail address is required. Complete the registration and proceed to the **Network+ Demo Course**. The first 50 minutes of the training is provided completely free of charge. Additional sessions for this course may be purchased from Total Seminars at www.totalsem.com or by calling 800-446-6004.

Mike's Cool Tools

Mike loves freeware/open source networking tools! Most of the utilities mentioned in the text are right here on the CD in the \CoolTools folder. Please read the CoolTools.rtf file for a description of the utilities. Warning! While all of the tools are "Mike Meyers Approved," there is no guarantee they will work for you. Read any and all documentation that comes with each utility before using it.

Technical Support

For questions regarding the Total Tester software, visit www.totalsem.com, e-mail support@totalsem.com, or e-mail customer.service@mcgraw-hill.com. For customers outside the United States, e-mail international_cs@mcgraw-hill.com.

LearnKey Technical Support

For technical support with the online training, contact techsupport@learnkey.com.

GLOSSARY

6in4 One of the most popular of all the IPv6 tunneling standards, and one of only two IPv6 tunneling protocols that can go through a NAT.

6to4 The dominant IPv6 tunneling protocol because it is the only IPv6 tunnel that doesn't require a tunnel broker. It is usually used to directly connect two routers because it normally requires a public IPv4 address.

10BaseFL Fiber-optic implementation of Ethernet that runs at 10 megabits per second (Mbps) using baseband signaling. Maximum segment length is 2 km.

10BaseT An Ethernet LAN designed to run on UTP cabling. Runs at 10 Mbps and uses baseband signaling. Maximum length for the cabling between the NIC and the hub (or the switch, the repeater, and so forth) is 100 m.

10GBaseER/10GBaseEW A 10-GbE standard using 1550-nm single-mode fiber. Maximum cable length up to 40 km.

10GBaseLR/10GBaseLW A 10-GbE standard using 1310-nm single-mode fiber. Maximum cable length up to 10 km.

10GBaseSR/10GBaseSW A 10-GbE standard using 850-nm multimode fiber. Maximum cable length up to 300 m.

10GBaseT A 10-GbE standard designed to run on CAT 6a UTP cabling. Maximum cable length of 100 m.

10-Gigabit Ethernet (10 GbE) Currently (2009) the fastest Ethernet designation available, with a number of fiber-optic and copper standards.

100BaseFX An Ethernet LAN designed to run on fiber-optic cabling. Runs at 100 Mbps and uses baseband signaling. Maximum cable length is 400 m for half-duplex, and 2 km for full-duplex.

100BaseT An Ethernet LAN designed to run on UTP cabling. Runs at 100 Mbps, uses baseband signaling, and uses two pairs of wires on CAT 5 or better cabling.

100BaseT4 An Ethernet LAN designed to run on UTP cabling. Runs at 100 Mbps and uses four-pair CAT 3 or better cabling. Made obsolete by 100BaseT.

100BaseTX The technically accurate but little-used name for 100BaseT.

110-Punchdown Block The most common connection used on the back of an RJ-45 jack and patch panels.

110-Punchdown Tool *See* Punchdown Tool.

802 Committee The IEEE committee responsible for all Ethernet standards.

802.1X A port-authentication network access control mechanism for networks.

802.3 Ethernet *See* Ethernet.

802.3ab The IEEE standard for 1000BaseT.

802.3z The umbrella IEEE standard for all versions of Gigabit Ethernet other than 1000BaseT.

802.11 *See* IEEE 802.11.

802.11a A wireless standard that operates in the frequency range of 5 GHz and offers throughput of up to 54 Mbps.

802.11b The first popular wireless standard, operates in the frequency range of 2.4 GHz and offers throughput of up to 11 Mbps.

802.11g Currently (2009) the wireless standard with the widest use, 802.11g operates on the 2.4-GHz band with a maximum throughput of 54 Mbps.

802.11i A wireless standard that added security features.

802.11n An updated 802.11 standard that increases transfer speeds and adds support for multiple in/multiple out (MIMO) by using multiple antennae. 802.11n can operate on either the 2.4- or 5-GHz frequency and has a maximum throughput of 400 Mbps.

802.16 An updated wireless standard (also known as WiMax) with a range of up to 30 miles.

1000BaseCX A Gigabit Ethernet standard using unique copper cabling. 25-m maximum cable distance.

1000BaseLX A Gigabit Ethernet standard using single-mode fiber cabling. 220 to 500-m maximum cable distance.

1000BaseSX A Gigabit Ethernet standard using multimode fiber cabling. 5-km maximum cable distance.

1000BaseT A Gigabit Ethernet standard using CAT 5e/6 UTP cabling. 100-m maximum cable distance.

1000BaseX An umbrella Gigabit Ethernet standard. Also known as 802.3z. Comprises all Gigabit standards with the exception of 1000BaseT, which is under the 802.3ab standard.

A Records A list of the IP addresses and names of all the systems on a DNS server domain.

AAA (Authentication, Authorization, and Accounting) *See* Authentication, Authorization, and Accounting (AAA).

Acceptable Use Policy A document that defines what a person may and may not do on an organization's computers and networks.

Access Control List (ACL) A clearly defined list of permissions that specifies what actions an authenticated user may perform on a shared resource.

Active Directory A form of directory service used in networks with Windows servers. Creates an organization of related computers that share one or more Windows domains.

Activity Light An LED on a NIC, hub, or switch that blinks rapidly to show data transfers over the network.

Ad Hoc Mode A wireless networking mode where each node is in direct contact with every other node in a decentralized free-for-all. Ad hoc mode is similar to the *mesh topology*.

Address Resolution Protocol (ARP) A protocol in the TCP/IP suite used with the command-line utility of the same name to determine the MAC address that corresponds to a particular IP address.

ADSL (Asymmetric Digital Subscriber Line) *See* Asymmetric Digital Subscriber Line (ADSL).

Advanced Encryption Standard (AES) A block cipher created in the late 1990s that uses a 128-bit block size and a 128-, 192-, or 256-bit key size. Practically uncrackable.

Adware A program that monitors the types of Web sites you frequent and uses that information to generate targeted advertisements, usually pop-up windows.

Aggregation A router hierarchy in which every router underneath a higher router always uses a subnet of that router's existing routes.

Algorithm A set of rules for solving a problem in a given number of steps.

Anycast A method of addressing groups of computers as though they were a single computer. Anycasting starts by giving a number of computers (or clusters of computers) the same IP address. Advanced routers then send incoming packets to the closest of the computers.

Apache HTTP Server An open-source HTTP server program that runs on a wide variety of operating systems.

Application Layer *See* OSI Seven-Layer Model.

Application Log Tracks application events, such as when an application opens or closes. Different types of application logs record different events.

Archive Bit An attribute of a file that shows whether the file has been backed up since the last change. Each time a file is opened, changed, or saved, the archive bit is turned on. Some types of backups turn off this archive bit to indicate that a good backup of the file exists on tape.

Area ID Address assigned to routers in an OSPF network to prevent flooding beyond the routers in that particular network. *See also* OSPF (Open Shortest Path First).

ARP PING A PING command that uses the ARP command instead of ICMP. ARP PING won't cross any routers, so it will only work within a broadcast domain.

Asymmetric Digital Subscriber Line (ADSL) A fully digital, dedicated connection to the telephone system that provides download speeds of up to 9 Mbps and upload speeds of up to 1 Mbps.

Asymmetric-Key Algorithm An encryption method in which the key used to encrypt a message and the key used to decrypt it are different, or asymmetrical.

Asynchronous Transfer Mode (ATM) A network technology that runs at speeds between 25 and 622 Mbps using fiber-optic cabling or CAT 5 or better UTP.

Attenuation The degradation of signal over distance for a networking cable.

Authentication A process that proves good data traffic truly came from where it says it originated by verifying the sending and receiving users and computers.

Authentication, Authorization, and Accounting (AAA) A security philosophy wherein a computer trying to connect to a network must first present some form of credential in order to be authenticated, and then must have limitable permissions within the network. The authenticating server should also record session information about the client.

Authentication Server (AS) In Kerberos, a system that hands out Ticket-Granting Tickets to clients after comparing the client hash to its own. *See also* Ticket-Granting Ticket (TGT).

Authoritative DNS Servers DNS servers that hold the IP addresses and names of systems for a particular domain or domains in special storage areas called *forward lookup zones*.

Authorization A step in the AAA philosophy during which a client's permissions are decided upon. *See also* Authentication, Authorization, and Accounting (AAA).

Automatic Private IP Addressing (APIPA) A networking feature in operating systems that enables DHCP clients to self-configure an IP address and subnet mask automatically when a DHCP server isn't available.

Autonomous System (AS) One or more networks that are governed by a single protocol within that AS, which provides routing for the Internet backbone.

Back Up To save important data in a secondary location as a safety precaution against the loss of the primary data.

Backup Designated Router A second router set to take over if the designated router fails. *See also* Designated Router (DR).

Backup Generator An onsite generator that provides electricity if the power utility fails.

Bandwidth A piece of the spectrum occupied by some form of signal, whether it is television, voice, fax data, and so forth. Signals require a certain size and location of bandwidth to be transmitted. The higher the bandwidth, the faster the signal transmission, thus allowing for a more complex signal such as audio or video. Because bandwidth is a limited space, when one user is occupying it, others must wait their turn. Bandwidth is also the capacity of a network to transmit a given amount of data during a given period.

Baseband Digital signaling that has only one signal (a single signal) on the cable at a time. The signals must be in one of three states: one, zero, or idle.

Baseline Static image of a system's (or network's) performance when all elements are known to be working properly.

Basic Rate Interface (BRI) The basic ISDN configuration, which consists of two *B* channels (which can carry voice or data at a rate of 64 Kbps) and one *D* channel (which carries setup and configuration information, as well as data, at 16 Kbps).

Basic Service Set (BSS) In wireless networking, a single access point servicing a given area.

Basic Service Set Identifier (BSSID) Naming scheme in wireless networks.

Baud One analog cycle on a telephone line.

Baud Rate The number of bauds per second. In the early days of telephone data transmission, the baud rate was often analogous to bits per second. Due to advanced modulation of baud cycles as well as data compression, this is no longer true.

Bearer Channel (B Channel) A type of ISDN channel that carries data and voice information using standard DS0 channels at 64 Kbps.

Biometric Devices Devices that scan fingerprints, retinas, or even the sound of the user's voice to provide a fool-proof replacement for both passwords and smart devices.

Bit Error Rate Test (BERT) An end-to-end test that verifies a T-carrier connection.

Block Cipher An encryption algorithm in which data is encrypted in "chunks" of a certain length at a time. Popular in wired networks.

BNC Connector A connector used for 10Base2 coaxial cable. All BNC connectors have to be locked into place by turning the locking ring 90 degrees.

Bonding Two or more NICs in a system working together to act as a single NIC to increase performance.

BOOTP (Bootstrap Protocol) A component of TCP/IP that allows computers to discover and receive an IP address from a DHCP server prior to booting the OS. Other items that may be discovered during the BOOTP process are the IP address of the default gateway for the subnet and the IP addresses of any name servers.

Border Gateway Protocol (BGP-4) An exterior gateway routing protocol that enables groups of routers to share routing information so that efficient, loop-free routes can be established.

Botnet A group of computers under the control of one operator, used for malicious purposes.

Bps (Bits Per Second) A measurement of how fast data is moved across a transmission medium. A Gigabit Ethernet connection moves 1,000,000,000 bps.

Bridge A device that connects two networks and passes traffic between them based only on the node address, so that traffic between nodes on one network does not appear on the other network. For example, an Ethernet bridge only looks at the MAC address. Bridges filter and forward packets based on MAC addresses and operate at Level 2 (Data Link layer) of the OSI seven-layer model.

Bridge Loop A negative situation in which bridging devices (usually switches) are installed in a loop configuration, causing packets to loop continuously. Switches using Spanning Tree Protocol (STP) prevent bridge loops by automatically turning off looping ports.

Bridged Connection An early type of DSL connection that made the DSL line function the same as if you snapped an Ethernet cable into your NIC.

Broadband Analog signaling that sends multiple signals over the cable at the same time. The best example of broadband signaling is cable television. The zero, one, and idle states (*see* Baseband) exist on multiple channels on the same cable.

Broadcast A packet addressed to all machines, almost always limited to a broadcast domain.

Broadcast Address The address a NIC attaches to a frame when it wants every other NIC on the network to read it. In TCP/IP, the general broadcast address is 255.255.255.255. In Ethernet, the broadcast MAC address is FF-FF-FF-FF-FF-FF.

Broadcast Domain A network of computers that will hear each other's broadcasts. The older term *collision domain* is the same but rarely used today.

Browser A software program specifically designed to retrieve, interpret, and display Web pages.

Building Entrance Location where all the cables from the outside world (telephone lines, cables from other buildings, and so on) come into a building.

Bus Topology A network topology that uses a single bus cable that connects all of the computers in line. Bus topology networks must be terminated to prevent signal reflection.

Butt Set Device that can tap into a 66- or 110-punchdown block to see if a particular line is working.

Byte Eight contiguous bits, the fundamental data unit of personal computers. Storing the equivalent of one character, the byte is also the basic unit of measurement for computer storage. Bytes are counted in powers of two.

CAB Files Short for "cabinet files." These files are compressed and most commonly used during Microsoft operating system installation to store many smaller files, such as device drivers.

Cable Certifier A very powerful cable testing device used by professional installers to test the electrical characteristics of a cable and then generate a certification report, proving that cable runs pass TIA/EIA standards.

Cable Drop Location where the cable comes out of the wall at the workstation location.

Cable Modem A bridge device that interconnects the cable company's DOCSIS service to the user's Ethernet network. In most locations, the cable modem is the demarc.

Cable Stripper Device that enables the creation of UTP cables.

Cable Tester   A generic name for a device that tests cables. Some common tests are continuity, electrical shorts, crossed wires, or other electrical characteristics.

Cable Tray   A device for organizing cable runs in a drop ceiling.

Cache   A special area of RAM that stores frequently accessed data. In a network there are a number of applications that take advantage of cache in some way.

Cache-Only DNS Servers (Caching-Only DNS Servers) DNS servers that do not have any forward lookup zones. They resolve names of systems on the Internet for the network, but are not responsible for telling other DNS servers the names of any clients.

Cached Lookup   The list kept by a DNS server of IP addresses it has already resolved, so it won't have to re-resolve an FQDN it has already checked.

Canonical Name (CNAME)   Less common type of DNS record that acts as a computer's alias.

Capturing a Printer   A process by which a printer uses a local LPT port that connects to a networked printer. This is usually only done to support older programs that are not smart enough to know how to print directly to a UNC-named printer; it's quite rare today.

Card   Generic term for anything that you can snap into an expansion slot.

Carrier Sense Multiple Access with Collision Avoidance (CSMA/CA)   *See* CSMA/CA.

Carrier Sense Multiple Access with Collision Detection (CSMA/CD)   *See* CSMA/CD.

CAT 3   Category 3 wire, a TIA/EIA standard for UTP wiring that can operate at up to 16 Mbps.

CAT 4   Category 4 wire, a TIA/EIA standard for UTP wiring that can operate at up to 20 Mbps. This is not widely used, except in older Token Ring networks.

CAT 5   Category 5 wire, a TIA/EIA standard for UTP wiring that can operate at up to 100 Mbps.

CAT 5e   Category 5e wire, a TIA/EIA standard for UTP wiring with improved support for 100 Mbps using two pairs, and support for 1000 Mbps using four pairs.

CAT 6   Category 6 wire, a TIA/EIA standard for UTP wiring with improved support for 1000 Mbps.

Category (CAT) Rating   A grade assigned to cable to help network installers get the right cable for the right network technology. CAT ratings are officially rated in megahertz (MHz), indicating the highest-frequency bandwidth the cable can handle.

CCITT   European standards body that established the V standards for modems.

Central Office   Building that houses local exchanges and a location where individual voice circuits come together.

Certificate   A public encryption key signed with the digital signature from a trusted third party called a *certificate authority (CA)*. This key serves to validate the identity of its holder when that person or company sends data to other parties.

Change Management Documentation   A set of documents that defines procedures for changes to the network.

Channel   A portion of the wireless spectrum on which a particular wireless network operates. Setting wireless networks to different channels enables separation of the networks.

Channel Service Unit/Digital Service Unit (CSU/DSU)   *See* CSU/DSU.

CHAP (Challenge Handshake Authentication Protocol) A remote access authentication protocol. It has the serving system challenge the remote client, which must provide an encrypted password.

Chat   A multiparty, real-time text conversation. The Internet's most popular version is known as Internet Relay Chat (IRC), which many groups use to converse in real time with each other.

Checksum   A simple error-detection method that adds a numerical value to each data packet, based on the number of data bits in the packet. The receiving node applies the same formula to the data and verifies that the numerical value is the same; if not, the data has been corrupted and must be re-sent.

CIDR (Classless Inter-Domain Routing)   Method of categorizing IP addresses in order to distribute them. *See also* Subnetting.

Cipher   A series of complex and hard-to-reverse mathematics run on a string of ones and zeroes in order to make a new set of seemingly meaningless ones and zeroes.

Ciphertext   The output when cleartext is run through a cipher algorithm using a key.

Circuit Switching   The process for connecting two phones together on one circuit.

Cisco IOS   Cisco's proprietary operating system.

Cladding   The part of a fiber-optic cable that makes the light reflect down the fiber.

Class License   Contiguous chunk of IP addresses passed out by the Internet Assigned Numbers Authority (IANA).

Classless Subnet   A subnet that does not fall into the common categories such as Class A, Class B, and Class C.

Cleartext   *See* Plaintext.

Client   A computer program that uses the services of another computer program; software that extracts information from a server. Your autodial phone is a client, and the phone company is its server. Also, a machine that accesses shared resources on a server.

Client/Server   A relationship in which client software obtains services from a server on behalf of a user.

Client/Server Application   An application that performs some or all of its processing on an application server rather than on the client. The client usually only receives the result of the processing.

Client/Server Network   A network that has dedicated server machines and client machines.

Coaxial Cable   A type of cable that contains a central conductor wire surrounded by an insulating material, which in turn is surrounded by a braided metal shield. It is called coaxial because the center wire and the braided metal shield share a common axis or centerline.

Collision   The result of two nodes transmitting at the same time on a multiple access network such as the Ethernet. Both packets may be lost or partial packets may result.

Collision Domain   *See* Broadcast Domain.

Collision Light   A light on some older NICs that flickers when a network collision is detected.

Command   A request, typed from a terminal or embedded in a file, to perform an operation or to execute a particular program.

Common Internet File System (CIFS)   The protocol that NetBIOS used to share folders and printers. Still very common, even on UNIX/Linux systems.

Complete Algorithm   A cipher and the methods used to implement that cipher.

Concentrator   A device that brings together at a common center connections to a particular kind of network (such as Ethernet), and implements that network internally.

Configuration Management   A set of documents, policies, and procedures designed to help you maintain and update your network in a logical, orderly fashion.

Configuration Management Documentation
Documents that define the configuration of a network. These would include wiring diagrams, network diagrams, baselines, and policy/procedure/configuration documentation.

Configurations   The settings stored in devices that define how they are to operate.

Connection-Oriented Communication   A protocol that establishes a connection between two hosts before transmitting data and verifies receipt before closing the connection between the hosts. TCP is an example of a connection-oriented protocol.

Connectionless Communication   A protocol that does not establish and verify a connection between the hosts before sending data; it just sends the data and hopes for the best. This is faster than connection-oriented protocols. UDP is an example of a connectionless protocol.

Content Switch   Advanced networking device that works at least at Layer 7 (Application layer) and hides servers behind a single IP.

Continuity   The physical connection of wires in a network.

Continuity Tester   Cheap network tester that can only test for continuity on a line.

Convergence   Point at which the routing tables for all routers in a network are updated.

Copy Backup   A type of backup similar to Normal or Full, in that all selected files on a system are backed up. This type of backup does *not* change the archive bit of the files being backed up.

Core The central glass of the fiber-optic cable that carries the light signal.

Counter A predefined event that is recorded to a log file.

CRC (Cyclic Redundancy Check) A mathematical method that is used to check for errors in long streams of transmitted data with high accuracy. Before data is sent, the main computer uses the data to calculate a CRC value from the data's contents. If the receiver calculates a different CRC value from the received data, the data was corrupted during transmission and is resent. Ethernet packets have a CRC code.

Crimper Also called a *crimping tool*, the tool used to secure a crimp (or an RJ-45 connector) onto the end of a cable.

Crossover Cable A special UTP cable used to interconnect hubs/switches or to connect network cards without a hub/switch. Crossover cables reverse the sending and receiving wire pairs from one end to the other.

Crossover Port Special port in a hub that crosses the sending and receiving wires, thus removing the need for a crossover cable to connect the hubs.

Cross-Platform Support Standards created to enable terminals (and now operating systems) from different companies to interact with one another.

Crosstalk Electrical signal interference between two cables that are in close proximity to each other.

CSMA/CA (Carrier Sense Multiple Access with Collision Avoidance) Access method used mainly on wireless networks. Before hosts send out data, they send out a signal that checks to make sure that the network is free of other signals. If data is detected on the wire, the hosts wait a random time period before trying again. If the wire is free, the data is sent out.

CSMA/CD (Carrier Sense Multiple Access with Collision Detection) Access method that Ethernet systems use in LAN technologies, enabling packets of data to flow through the network and ultimately reach address locations. Known as a *contention* protocol, hosts on CSMA/CD networks send out data without checking to see if the wire is free first. If a collision occurs, then both hosts wait a random time period before retransmitting the data.

CSU/DSU (Channel Service Unit/Data Service Unit) A piece of equipment that connects a T-carrier leased line from the telephone company to a customer's equipment (such as a router). It performs line encoding and conditioning functions, and it often has a loopback function for testing.

Daily Backup Also called a *daily copy backup*, makes a copy of all files that have been changed on that day without changing the archive bits of those files.

Daisy-chain A method of connecting together several devices along a bus and managing the signals for each device.

Data Backup The process of creating extra copies of data to be used in case the primary data source fails.

Data Encryption Standard (DES) A symmetric-key algorithm developed by the U.S. government in the 1970s and formerly in use in a variety of TCP/IP applications. DES used a 64-bit block and a 56-bit key. Over time, the 56-bit key made DES susceptible to brute-force attacks.

Data Link Layer *See* OSI Seven-Layer Model.

Data Over Cable Service Interface Specification (DOCSIS) The unique protocol used by cable modem networks.

Datagram Another term for *network packets* or *frames*. *See both* Packet *and* Frame.

Dedicated Circuit A circuit that runs from a breaker box to specific outlets.

Dedicated Line A telephone line that is an always open, or connected, circuit. Dedicated telephone lines usually do not have telephone numbers.

Dedicated Server A machine that does not use any client functions, only server functions.

Default A software function or operation that occurs automatically unless the user specifies something else.

Default Gateway In a TCP/IP network, the IP address of the router that interconnects the LAN to a wider network, usually the Internet. This router's IP address is part of the necessary TCP/IP configuration for communicating with multiple networks using IP.

Delta Channel (D Channel) A type of ISDN line that transfers data at 16 Kbps.

Demarc   A device that marks the dividing line of responsibility for the functioning of a network between internal users and upstream service providers.

Demarc Extension   Any cabling that runs from the network interface to whatever box is used by the customer as a demarc.

Denial of Service (DoS) Attack   An attack that floods a networked server with so many requests that it becomes overwhelmed and ceases functioning.

Designated Router (DR)   The main router in an OSPF network that relays information to all other routers in the area.

Destination NAT   Type of NAT in which the destination IP addresses get translated by the router.

Destination Port   A fixed, predetermined number that defines the function or session type in a TCP/IP network.

Device Driver   A subprogram to control communications between the computer and some peripheral hardware.

Device ID   The last six digits of a MAC address, identifying the manufacturer's unique serial number for that NIC.

DHCP (Dynamic Host Configuration Protocol)   A protocol that allows a DHCP server to set TCP/IP settings automatically for a DHCP client.

DHCP Lease   Created by the DHCP server to allow a system requesting DHCP IP information to use that information for a certain amount of time.

DHCP Scope   The pool of IP addresses that a DHCP server may allocate to clients requesting IP addresses, or other IP information like DNS server addresses.

Dial-up Lines   Telephone lines with telephone numbers; they must dial to make a connection, as opposed to a dedicated line.

Differential Backup   Similar to an incremental backup in that it backs up the files that have been changed since the last backup. This type of backup does not change the state of the archive bit.

DIG (Domain Information Grouper)   *See* Domain Information Grouper.

Digital Signature   A string of characters, created from a private encryption key, that verifies a sender's identity to those who receive encrypted data or messages.

Digital Subscriber Line (DSL)   A high-speed Internet connection technology that uses a regular telephone line for connectivity. DSL comes in several varieties, including Asymmetric (ADSL) and Symmetric (SDSL), and many speeds. Typical home-user DSL connections are ADSL with a download speed of up to 1.5 Mbps and an upload speed of up to 384 Kbps.

Dipole Antenna   The standard straight-wire antenna that provides most omni-directional function.

Direct Current (DC)   A type of electric circuit where the flow of electrons is in a complete circle.

Direct-Sequence Spread-Spectrum (DSSS)   A spread-spectrum broadcasting method defined in the 802.11 standard that sends data out on different frequencies at the same time.

Discretionary Access Control (DAC)   Authorization method based on the idea that there is an owner of a resource who may at his or her discretion assign access to that resource. DAC is considered much more flexible than MAC.

Disk Mirroring   Process by which data is written simultaneously to two or more disk drives. Read and write speed is decreased but redundancy, in case of catastrophe, is increased. Also known as RAID level 1. *See also* Duplexing.

Disk Striping   Process by which data is spread among multiple (at least two) drives. It increases speed for both reads and writes of data, but provides no fault tolerance. Also known as RAID level 0.

Disk Striping with Parity   Process by which data is spread among multiple (at least three) drives, with parity information as well to provide fault tolerance. The most commonly implemented type is RAID 5, where the data and parity information is spread across three or more drives.

Dispersion   Diffusion over distance of light propagating down fiber cable.

Distance Vector   Set of routing protocols that calculates the total cost to get to a particular network ID and compares that cost to the total cost of all the other routes to get to that same network ID.

Distributed Coordination Function (DCF) One of two methods of collision avoidance defined by the 802.11 standard and the only one currently implemented. DCF specifies strict rules for sending data onto the network media.

Distributed Denial of Service (DDoS) Attack A DoS attack that uses multiple (as in hundreds up to hundreds of thousands) of computers under the control of a single operator to send a devastating attack.

DLL (Dynamic Link Library) A file of executable functions or data that can be used by a Windows application. Typically, a DLL provides one or more particular functions, and a program accesses the functions by creating links to the DLL.

DMZ (Demilitarized Zone) A lightly protected or unprotected subnet network positioned between an outer firewall and an organization's highly protected internal network. DMZs are used mainly to host public address servers (like a Web server).

DNS (Domain Name System) A TCP/IP name resolution system that resolves host names to IP addresses.

DNS Domain A specific branch of the DNS name space. First-level DNS domains include .com, .gov, and .edu.

DNS Resolver Cache A cache used by Windows DNS clients to keep track of DNS information.

DNS Root Servers The highest in the hierarchy of DNS servers running the Internet.

DNS Server A system that runs a special DNS server program.

DNS Tree A hierarchy of DNS domains and individual computer names organized into a tree-like structure, the top of which is the root.

Document A medium and the data recorded on it for human use; for example, a report sheet or book. By extension, any record that has permanence and that can be read by a human or a machine.

Documentation A collection of organized documents or the information recorded in documents. Also, instructional material specifying the inputs, operations, and outputs of a computer program or system.

Domain A term used to describe a grouping of users, computers, and/or networks. In Microsoft networking, a domain is a group of computers and users that shares a common account database and a common security policy. For the Internet, a domain is a group of computers that shares a common element in their DNS hierarchical name.

Domain Controller A Microsoft Windows Server system specifically configured to store user and server account information for its domain. Often abbreviated as "DC." Windows domain controllers store all account and security information in the *Active Directory* directory service.

Domain Information Grouper (DIG) Command-line tool in non-Windows systems used to diagnose DNS problems.

Domain Users and Groups Users and groups that are defined across an entire network domain.

Dotted Decimal Notation Shorthand method for discussing and configuring binary IP addresses.

Download The transfer of information from a remote computer system to the user's system. Opposite of *upload*.

Drive Duplexing *See* Duplexing.

Drive Mirroring The process of writing identical data to two hard drives on the same controller at the same time, to provide data redundancy.

DS0 The digital signal rate created by converting analog sound into 8-bit chunks 8000 times a second, with a data stream of 64 Kbps. This is the simplest data stream (and the slowest rate) of the digital part of the phone system.

DS1 The signaling method used by T1 lines, which uses a relatively simple frame consisting of 25 pieces: a framing bit and 24 channels. Each DS1 channel holds a single 8-bit DS0 data sample. The framing bit and data channels combine to make 193 bits per DS1 frame. These frames are transmitted 8000 times/sec, making a total throughput of 1.544 Mbps.

DSL Access Multiplexer (DSLAM) A device located in a telephone company's central office that connects multiple customers to the Internet.

DSL Modem   A device that enables customers to connect to the Internet using a DSL connection. A DSL modem isn't really a modem—it's more like an ISDN terminal adapter—but the term stuck, and even the manufacturers of the devices now call them DSL modems.

DSP (Digital Signal Processor)   A specialized microprocessor-like device that processes digital signals at the expense of other capabilities, much as the floating-point unit (FPU) is optimized for math functions. DSPs are used in such specialized hardware as high-speed modems, multimedia sound cards, MIDI equipment, and real-time video capture and compression.

Duplexing   Also called *disk duplexing* or *drive duplexing*, similar to mirroring in that data is written to and read from two physical drives for fault tolerance. In addition, separate controllers are used for each drive, for both additional fault tolerance and additional speed. Considered RAID level 1. *See also* Disk Mirroring.

Dynamic Addressing   A way for a computer to receive IP information automatically from a server program. *See* DHCP (Dynamic Host Configuration Protocol).

Dynamic Link Library (DLL)   *See* DLL (Dynamic Link Library).

Dynamic NAT   Type of NAT in which many computers can share a pool of routable IP addresses that number fewer than the computers.

Dynamic Port Numbers   Port numbers 49152–65535, recommended by the IANA to be used as ephemeral port numbers.

Dynamic Routing   Process by which routers in an internetwork automatically exchange information with other routers. Requires a dynamic routing protocol, such as OSPF or RIP.

Dynamic Routing Protocol   A protocol that supports the building of automatic routing tables, such as OSPF or RIP.

E1   The European counterpart of a T1 connection that carries 32 channels at 64 Kbps for a total of 2.048 Mbps—making it slightly faster than a T1.

E3   The European counterpart of a T3 line that carries 16 E1 lines (512 channels), for a total bandwidth of 34.368 Mbps—making it a little bit slower than an American T3.

Edge Router   Router that connects one automated system (AS) to another.

Effective Permissions   The permissions of all groups combined in any network operating system.

E-mail (Electronic Mail)   Messages, usually text, sent from one person to another via computer. E-mail can also be sent automatically to a large number of addresses, known as a mailing list.

E-mail Client   Program that runs on a computer and enables you to send, receive, and organize e-mail.

E-mail Server   Also known as *mail server*, a server that accepts incoming mail, sorts the mail for recipients into mailboxes, and sends mail to other servers using SMTP.

EMI (Electro-Magnetic Interference)   Interference from one device to another, resulting in poor performance in the device's capabilities. This is similar to having static on your TV while running a hair dryer, or placing two monitors too close together and getting a "shaky" screen.

Encapsulation   The process of putting the packets from one protocol inside the packets of another protocol. An example of this is TCP/IP encapsulation in Ethernet, which places TCP/IP packets inside Ethernet frames.

Encryption   A method of securing messages by scrambling and encoding each packet as it is sent across an unsecured medium, such as the Internet. Each encryption level provides multiple standards and options.

Endpoint   In the TCP/IP world, the session information stored in RAM. *See also* Socket.

Endpoints   Correct term to use when discussing the data each computer stores about the connection between two computers' TCP/IP applications. *See also* Socket Pairs.

Enhanced Interior Gateway Routing Protocol (EIGRP)   Cisco's proprietary hybrid protocol that has elements of both distance vector and link state routing.

Ephemeral Port   In TCP/IP communication, an arbitrary number generated by a sending computer that the receiving computer uses as a destination address when sending a return packet.

Ephemeral Port Numbers   *See* Ephemeral Port.

Equipment Rack   A metal structure used in equipment rooms to secure network hardware devices and patch panels. Most racks are 19″ wide. Devices designed to fit in such a rack use a height measurement called *units*, or simply *U*.

ESD (Electro-Static Discharge)   The movement of electrons from one body to another. ESD is a real menace to PCs because it can cause permanent damage to semiconductors.

Ethernet   Name coined by Xerox for the first standard of network cabling and protocols. Ethernet is based on a bus topology. The IEEE 802.3 subcommittee defines the current Ethernet specifications.

Executable Viruses   Viruses that are literally extensions of executables and that are unable to exist by themselves. Once an infected executable file is run, the virus loads into memory, adding copies of itself to other EXEs that are subsequently run.

Extended Service Set (ESS)   A single wireless access point servicing a given area that has been extended by adding more access points.

Extended Service Set ID (ESSID)   An SSID applied to an Extended Service Set as a network naming convention.

Extended Unique Identifier, 64-bit (EUI-64)   The last 64 bits of the IPv6 address, which are determined based off of a device's MAC address.

Extensible Authentication Protocol (EAP)   Authentication wrapper that EAP-compliant applications can use to accept one of many types of authentication. While EAP is a general-purpose authentication wrapper, its only substantial use is in wireless networks.

External Data Bus (EDB)   The primary data highway of all computers. Everything in your computer is tied either directly or indirectly to the EDB.

External Network Address   A number added to the MAC address of every computer on an IPX/SPX network that defines every computer on the network; this is often referred to as a *network number*.

External Threats   Threats to your network through external means; examples include virus attacks and the exploitation of users, security holes in the OS, or the network hardware itself.

FAQ (Frequently Asked Questions)   Common abbreviation coined by BBS users and spread to Usenet and the Internet. This is a list of questions and answers that pertains to a particular topic, maintained so that users new to the group don't all bombard the group with similar questions. Examples are "What is the name of the actor who plays *X* on this show, and was he in anything else?" or "Can anyone list all of the books by this author in the order that they were published so that I can read them in that order?" The common answer to this type of question is "Read the FAQ!"

Fast Ethernet   Nickname for the 100-Mbps Ethernet standards. Originally applied to 100BaseT.

Fault Tolerance   The capability of any system to continue functioning after some part of the system has failed. RAID is an example of a hardware device that provides fault tolerance for hard drives.

Federal Communications Commission (FCC)   In the United States, regulates public airwaves and rates PCs and other equipment according to the amount of radiation emitted.

FEXT (Far-End Crosstalk)   Crosstalk on the opposite end of a cable from the signal's source.

Fiber-Optic Cable   A high-speed physical medium for transmitting data that uses light rather than electricity to transmit data and is made of high-purity glass fibers sealed within a flexible opaque tube. Much faster than conventional copper wire.

File Server   A computer designated to store software, courseware, administrative tools, and other data on a local or wide area network. It "serves" this information to other computers via the network when users enter their personal access codes.

Fire Ratings   Ratings developed by Underwriters Laboratories (UL) and the National Electrical Code (NEC) to define the risk of network cables burning and creating noxious fumes and smoke.

Firewall   A device that restricts traffic between a local network and the Internet.

FireWire   An IEEE 1394 standard to send wide-band signals over a thin connector system that plugs into TVs, VCRs, TV cameras, PCs, and so forth. This serial bus developed by Apple and Texas Instruments enables connection of 60 devices at speeds ranging from 100 to 800 Mbps.

Flat Name Space A naming convention that gives each device only one name that must be unique. NetBIOS used a flat name space. TCP/IP's DNS uses a hierarchical name space.

Forward Lookup Zones The storage areas in DNS servers to store the IP addresses and names of systems for a particular domain or domains.

FQDN (Fully Qualified Domain Name) The complete DNS name of a system, from its host name to the top-level domain name.

Fractional T1 Access A service provided by many telephone companies wherein customers can purchase a number of individual channels in a T1 line in order to save money.

Frame A defined series of binary data that is the basic container for a discrete amount of data moving across a network. Also commonly called a *packet*.

Frame Check Sequence (FCS) A sequence of bits placed in a frame that is used to check the primary data for errors.

Frame Relay An extremely efficient data transmission technique used to send digital information such as voice, data, LAN, and WAN traffic quickly and cost-efficiently to many destinations from one port.

FreeRADIUS Free RADIUS server software for UNIX/Linux systems.

Freeware Software that is distributed for free, with no license fee.

Frequency Division Multiplexing (FDM) A process of keeping individual phone calls separate by adding a different frequency multiplier to each phone call, making it possible to separate phone calls by their unique frequency range.

Frequency-Hopping Spread-Spectrum (FHSS) A spread-spectrum broadcasting method defined in the 802.11 standard that sends data on one frequency at a time, constantly shifting (or *hopping*) frequencies.

FTP (File Transfer Protocol) A set of rules that allows two computers to talk to one another as a file transfer is carried out. This is the protocol used when you transfer a file from one computer to another across the Internet.

FUBAR Fouled Up Beyond All Recognition.

Full-Duplex Any device that can send and receive data simultaneously.

Fully Meshed Topology A mesh network where every node is directly connected to every other node.

Gain The strengthening and focusing of radio frequency output from a wireless access point (WAP).

Gateway Router A router that acts as a default gateway in a TCP/IP network.

Giga- The prefix that generally refers to the quantity 1,073,741,824. One gigabyte is 1,073,741,824 bytes. With frequencies, in contrast, giga- often refers to one billion. One gigahertz is 1,000,000,000 hertz.

Gigabit Ethernet *See* 1000BaseT.

Gigabyte 1024 megabytes.

Global Unicast Address A second IPv6 address that every system needs in order to get on the Internet.

Grandfather, Father, Son (GFS) A tape rotation strategy used in data backups.

Group Policy A feature of Windows Active Directory that allows an administrator to apply policy settings to network users *en masse*.

Group Policy Object (GPO) Enables network administrators to define multiple rights and permissions to entire sets of users all at one time.

Groups Collections of network users who share similar tasks and need similar permissions; defined to make administration tasks easier.

H.323 A VoIP standard that handles the initiation, setup, and delivery of VoIP sessions.

Hackers People who break into computer systems with malicious intent.

Half-Duplex Any device that can only send or receive data at any given moment.

Hardware Tools Tools such as cable testers, TDRs, OTDRs, certifiers, voltage event recorders, protocol analyzers, cable strippers, multimeters, tone probes/generators, butt sets, and punchdown tools used to configure and troubleshoot a network.

Hash A mathematical function used in cryptography that is run on a string of binary digits of any length that results in a value of some fixed length.

Hex (Hexadecimal)　Hex symbols based on a numbering system of 16 (computer shorthand for binary numbers), using ten digits and six letters to condense zeroes and ones to binary numbers. Hex is represented by digits 0 through 9 and alpha *A* through *F*, so that 09h has a value of 9, and 0Ah has a value of 10.

Hierarchical Name Space　A naming scheme where the full name of each object includes its position within the hierarchy. An example of a hierarchical name is www.totalseminars.com, which includes not only the host name, but also the domain name. DNS uses a hierarchical name space scheme for fully qualified domain names (FQDNs).

High Availability　A collection of technologies and procedures that work together to keep an application available at all times.

Home Page　Either the Web page that your browser is set to use when it starts up or the main Web page for a business, organization, or person. Also, the main page in any collection of Web pages.

Honey Pot　An area of a network that an administrator sets up for the express purpose of attracting a computer hacker. If a hacker takes the bait, the network's important resources are unharmed and network personnel can analyze the attack to predict and protect against future attacks, making the network more secure.

Hop　The passage of a packet through a router.

Horizontal Cabling　Cabling that connects the equipment room to the work areas.

Host　A single device (usually a computer) on a TCP/IP network that has an IP address; any device that can be the source or destination of a data packet.

Host ID　The portion of an IP address that defines a specific machine in a subnet.

Host Name　An individual computer name in the DNS naming convention.

HOSTNAME　Command-line tool that returns the host name of the computer it is run on.

HOSTS File　The predecessor to DNS, a static text file that resides on a computer and is used to resolve DNS host names to IP addresses. The HOSTS file is checked before the machine sends a name resolution request to a DNS name server. The HOSTS file has no extension.

HTML (Hypertext Markup Language)　An ASCII-based script-like language for creating hypertext documents like those on the World Wide Web.

HTTP (Hypertext Transfer Protocol)　Extremely fast protocol used for network file transfers in the WWW environment.

HTTP over SSL (HTTPS)　A secure form of HTTP, used commonly for Internet business transactions or any time where a secure connection is required. *See also* HTTP (Hypertext Transfer Protocol) *and* SSL (Secure Sockets Layer).

Hub　An electronic device that sits at the center of a star topology network, providing a common point for the connection of network devices. In a 10BaseT Ethernet network, the hub contains the electronic equivalent of a properly terminated bus cable. Hubs are rare today, replaced by switches.

Hybrid Topology　A mix or blend of two different topologies. A star-bus topology is a hybrid of the star and bus topologies.

Hypertext　A document that has been marked up to enable a user to select words or pictures within the document, click them, and connect to further information. The basis of the World Wide Web.

IANA (Internet Assigned Numbers Authority)　The organization responsible for assigning public IP addresses. IANA no longer directly assigns IP addresses, having delegated this to the five Regional Internet Registries. *See* Regional Internet Registries.

ICF (Internet Connection Firewall)　The software firewall built into Windows XP that protects your system from unauthorized access from the Internet. Microsoft changed the name to the Windows Firewall in Windows Service Pack 2.

ICS (Internet Connection Sharing)　Also known simply as *Internet sharing*, the technique of enabling more than one computer to access the Internet simultaneously using a single Internet connection. When you use Internet sharing, you connect an entire LAN to the Internet using a single public IP address.

IDF (Intermediate Distribution Frame)　The room where all the horizontal runs from all the work areas on a given floor in a building come together.

IEEE (Institute of Electrical and Electronics Engineers) The leading standards-setting group in the United States.

IEEE 802.2 IEEE subcommittee that defined the standards for Logical Link Control (LLC).

IEEE 802.3 IEEE subcommittee that defined the standards for CSMA/CD (a.k.a. *Ethernet*).

IEEE 802.11 IEEE subcommittee that defined the standards for wireless.

IEEE 802.14 IEEE subcommittee that defined the standards for cable modems.

IEEE 1284 The IEEE standard for the now obsolete parallel communication.

IEEE 1394 IEEE standard for FireWire communication.

IETF (Internet Engineering Task Force) The primary standards organization for the Internet.

IFCONFIG A command-line utility for Linux servers and workstations that displays the current TCP/IP configuration of the machine, similar to IPCONFIG for Windows systems.

IMAP (Internet Message Access Protocol) An alternative to POP3. IMAP retrieves e-mail from an e-mail server, like POP3; IMAP uses TCP port 143.

Impedance The amount of resistance to an electrical signal on a wire. It is used as a relative measure of the amount of data a cable can handle.

Incremental Backup Backs up all files that have their archive bits turned on, meaning they have been changed since the last backup. This type of backup turns the archive bits off after the files have been backed up.

Independent Basic Service Set (IBSS) A basic unit of organization in wireless networks formed by two or more wireless nodes communicating in ad hoc mode.

Infrastructure Mode Mode in which wireless networks use one or more wireless access points to connect the wireless network nodes centrally. This configuration is similar to the *star topology* of a wired network.

Inheritance A method of assigning user permissions, in which folder permissions flow downward into subfolders.

Insulating Jacket The external plastic covering of a fiber-optic cable.

Integrated Services Digital Network (ISDN) *See* ISDN (Integrated Services Digital Network).

Interframe Space (IFS) Short, predefined period of silence in CSMA/CA appended to the waiting time when a device detects activity on the line.

Intermediate System to Intermediate System (IS-IS) Protocol similar to, but not as popular as, OSPF, but with support for IPv6 since inception.

Internal Network A private LAN, with a unique network ID, that resides behind a router.

Internal Threats All the things that a network's own users do to create problems on the network. Examples include accidental deletion of files, accidental damage to hardware devices or cabling, and abuse of rights and permissions.

Internet Authentication Service (IAS) Popular RADIUS server for Microsoft environments.

Internet Connection Firewall (ICF) *See* ICF (Internet Connection Firewall).

Internet Connection Sharing (ICS) *See* ICS (Internet Connection Sharing).

Internet Control Message Protocol (ICMP) Protocol in which messages consist of a single packet and are connectionless. ICMP packets determine connectivity between two hosts.

Internet Group Management Protocol (IGMP) Protocol that routers use to communicate with hosts to determine a "group" membership in order to determine which computers want to receive a multicast.

Internet Information Services (IIS) Microsoft's Web server program for managing Web servers.

Internet Message Access Protocol Version 4 (IMAP4) An alternative to POP3 for receiving e-mail from an e-mail server. Supports searching through messages stored on a server and supports using folders to organize e-mail.

Internet Protocol Version 4 (IPv4) Protocol in which addresses consist of four sets of numbers, each number being a value between 0 and 255, using a period to separate the numbers. Often called *dotted decimal* format.

No IPv4 address may be all 0s or all 255s. Examples include 192.168.0.1 and 64.176.19.164.

Internet Protocol Version 6 (IPv6)   Protocol in which addresses consist of eight sets of four hexadecimal numbers, each number being a value between 0000 and FFFF, using a colon to separate the numbers. No IP address may be all 0s or all FFFFs. An example is FEDC:BA98:7654:3210:0800:200C:00CF:1234.

InterNIC   The organization that maintains the DNS services, registrations, and so forth run by Network Solutions, General Atomics, and AT&T.

InterVLAN Routing   A feature on some switches to create virtual routers.

Intra-Site Automatic Tunnel Addressing Protocol
An IPv6 tunneling protocol that adds the IPv4 address to an IPv6 prefix.

Intranet   A private TCP/IP network inside a company or organization.

Intrusion Detection/Intrusion Prevention   A process used to protect networks from intrusion and to detect that something has intruded into a network.

IP (Internet Protocol)   The Internet standard protocol that handles the logical naming for the TCP/IP protocol, using IP addresses.

IP Address   The numeric address of a computer connected to a TCP/IP network, such as the Internet. IPv4 addresses are 32 bits long, written as four octets of 8-bit binary. IPv6 addresses are 128 bits long, written as eight sets of four hexidecimal characters. IP addresses must be matched with a valid subnet mask, which identifies the part of the IP address that is the network ID and the part that is the host ID.

IP Filtering   A method of blocking packets based on IP addresses.

IPCONFIG   A command-line utility for Windows that displays the current TCP/IP configuration of the machine; similar to UNIX/Linux's IFCONFIG.

IPSec (IP Security)   A IP packet encryption protocol. IPSec is the only IP encryption protocol to work at Layer 3 of the OSI seven-layer model. IPSec is most commonly seen on Virtual Private Networks. *See* VPN (Virtual Private Network).

IRC (Internet Relay Chat)   An online group discussion. Also called *chat*.

ISDN (Integrated Services Digital Network)   The CCITT (Comité Consutatif Internationale Téléphonique et Télégraphique) standard that defines a digital method for telephone communications. Originally designed to replace the current analog telephone systems. ISDN lines have telephone numbers and support up to 128-Kbps transfer rates. ISDN also allows data and voice to share a common phone line. Never very popular, ISDN is now relegated to specialized niches.

ISP (Internet Service Provider)   An institution that provides access to the Internet in some form, usually for a fee.

IT (Information Technology)   The business of computers, electronic communications, and electronic commerce.

Java   A network-oriented programming language invented by Sun Microsystems and specifically designed for writing programs that can be safely downloaded to your computer through the Internet and immediately run without fear of viruses or other harm to your computer or files. Using small Java programs (called *applets*), Web pages can include functions such as animations, calculators, and other fancy tricks.

Just a Bunch of Disks (JBOD)   An array of hard drives that are simply connected with no RAID implementations.

K-   Most commonly used as the suffix for the binary quantity 1024. 640 K means 640 × 1024 or 655,360. Just to add some extra confusion to the IT industry, *K* is often misspoken as "kilo," the metric value for 1000. 10 KB, for example, spoken as "10 kilobytes," means 10,240 bytes rather than 10,000 bytes.

Kbps (Kilobits Per Second)   Data transfer rate.

Kerberos   An authentication standard designed to allow different operating systems and applications to authenticate each other.

Key Distribution Center (KDC)   System for granting authentication in Kerberos.

Key Pair   Name for the two keys generated in asymmetric-key algorithm systems.

Kilohertz (KHz)   A unit of measure that equals a frequency of 1000 cycles per second.

LAN (Local Area Network) A group of PCs connected together via cabling, radio, or infrared that use this connectivity to share resources such as printers and mass storage.

Last Mile The connection between a central office and individual users in a telephone system.

Layer A grouping of related tasks involving the transfer of information. Also, a particular level of the OSI seven-layer model; for example, Physical layer, Data Link layer, and so forth.

Layer 2 Switch Any device that filters and forwards data packets based on the MAC addresses of the sending and receiving machines. What we normally call a "switch" is actually a "Layer 2 switch."

Layer 2 Tunneling Protocol (L2TP) A VPN protocol developed by Cisco that can be run on almost any connection imaginable. LT2P has no authentication or encryption, but uses IPSec for all its security needs.

Layer 3 Switch Also known as a *router*, filters and forwards data packets based on the IP addresses of the sending and receiving machines.

LC A duplex type of Small Form Factor (SFF) fiber connector, designed to accept two fiber cables.

LED (Light Emitting Diodes) Solid-state devices that vibrate at luminous frequencies when current is applied.

Light Leakage The type of interference caused by bending a piece of fiber-optic cable past its maximum bend radius. Light bleeds through the cladding, causing signal distortion and loss.

Lightweight Extensible Authentication Protocol (LEAP) A proprietary EAP authentication used almost exclusively by Cisco wireless products. LEAP is an interesting combination of MS-CHAP authentication between a wireless client and a RADIUS server.

Link Light An LED on NICs, hubs, and switches that lights up to show good connection between the devices.

Link-Local Address The address that a computer running IPv6 gives itself after first booting. The first 64 bits of a link-local address is always FE80::/64.

Link Segments Segments that link other segments together but are unpopulated or have no computers directly attached to them.

Link State Type of dynamic routing protocol that announces only changes to routing tables, as opposed to entire routing tables. Compare to distance vector routing protocols.

Linux The popular open source UNIX-clone operating system.

Listening Port A socket that is prepared to respond to any IP packets destined for that socket's port number.

LMHOSTS File A static text file that resides on a computer and is used to resolve NetBIOS names to IP addresses. The LMHOSTS file is checked before the machine sends a name resolution request to a WINS name server. The LMHOSTS file has no extension.

Load Balancing The process of taking several servers and making them look like a single server.

Local Refers to the computer(s), server(s), and/or LAN that a user is physically using or that is in the same room or building.

Local Connector One popular type of Small Form Factor (SFF) connector, considered by many to be the predominant fiber connector.

Local User Accounts The accounts unique to a single Windows system. Stored in the local system's registry.

Localhost The HOSTS file alias for the loopback address of 127.0.0.1, referring to the current machine.

Logical Address A programmable network address, unlike a physical address that is burned into ROM.

Logical Network Diagram A document that shows the broadcast domains and individual IP addresses for all devices on the network. Only critical switches and routers are shown.

Logical Topology A network topology defined by signal paths as opposed to the physical layout of the cables. *See also* Physical Topology.

Loopback Address Sometimes called the localhost, a reserved IP address used for internal testing: 127.0.0.1.

Loopback Plug Network connector that connects back into itself, used to connect loopback tests.

Loopback Test A special test often included in diagnostic software that sends data out of the NIC and checks to see if it comes back.

MAC (Media Access Control) Address Unique 48-bit address assigned to each network card. IEEE assigns blocks of possible addresses to various NIC manufacturers to help ensure that each address is unique. The Data Link layer of the OSI seven-layer model uses MAC addresses for locating machines.

MAC Address Filtering A method of limiting access to a wireless network based on the physical addresses of wireless NICs.

MAC Filtering *See* MAC Address Filtering.

Macro A specially written application macro (collection of commands) that performs the same functions as a virus. These macros normally autostart when the application is run and then make copies of themselves, often propagating across networks.

Mailbox Special holding area on an e-mail server that separates out e-mail for each user.

Malware Any program or code (macro, script, and so on) that's designed to do something on a system or network that you don't want to have happen.

MAN (Metropolitan Area Network) Multiple computers connected via cabling, radio, leased phone lines, or infrared that are within the same city. A typical example of a MAN is a college campus. No firm dividing lines dictate what is considered a WAN, MAN, or LAN.

Managed Device Networking devices, such as routers and advanced switches, that must be configured to use.

Management Information Base (MIB) SNMP's version of a server. *See* SNMP (Simple Network Management Protocol).

Mandatory Access Control (MAC) A security model in which every resource is assigned a label that defines its security level. If the user lacks that security level, they do not get access.

MB (Megabyte) 1,048,576 bytes.

MD5 Arguably the most popular hashing function.

MDF (Main Distribution Frame) The room in a building that stores the demarc, telephone cross-connects, and LAN cross-connects.

Media Converter A device that lets you interconnect different types of Ethernet cable.

Mega- A prefix that usually stands for the binary quantity 1,048,576. One megabyte is 1,048,576 bytes. One megahertz, however, is a million hertz. Sometimes shortened to *meg*, as in "a 286 has an address space of 16 megs."

Mesh Topology Topology in which each computer has a direct or indirect connection to every other computer in a network. Any node on the network can forward traffic to other nodes. Popular in cellular and many wireless networks.

Metric Relative value that defines the "cost" of using a particular route.

MHz (Megahertz) A unit of measure that equals a frequency of 1 million cycles per second.

MIME (Multipurpose Internet Mail Extensions) A standard for attaching binary files, such as executables and images, to the Internet's text-based mail (24-Kbps packet size).

Mirroring Also called *drive mirroring*, reading and writing data at the same time to two drives for fault-tolerance purposes. Considered RAID level 1.

Modal Distortion A light distortion problem unique to multimode fiber-optic cable.

Modem (Modulator-Demodulator) A device that converts both digital bit streams into analog signals (modulation) and incoming analog signals back into digital signals (demodulation). Most commonly used to interconnect telephone lines to computers.

Mounting Bracket Bracket that acts as a holder for a faceplate in cable installations.

MS-CHAP Microsoft's dominant variation of the CHAP protocol, uses a slightly more advanced encryption protocol.

MSA (Multisource Agreement) Interchangeable modular transceivers used in 10-GbE networking devices.

MT-RJ (Mechanical Transfer Registered Jack) The first type of Small Form Factor (SFF) fiber connector, still in common use.

Multi-Protocol Label Switching (MPLS) A router feature that labels certain data to use a desired connection. It works with any type of packet switching (even Ethernet) to force certain types of data to use a certain path.

Multicast   Method of sending a packet in which the sending computer sends it to a group of interested computers.

Multicast Addresses   In IPv6, a set of reserved addresses designed to go only to certain systems.

Multilayer Switch   A switch that has functions that operate at multiple layers of the OSI seven-layer model.

Multimeter   A tool for testing voltage (AC and DC), resistance, and continuity.

Multimode   Type of fiber-optic cable that uses LEDs.

Multiple In/Multiple Out (MIMO)   A feature in 802.11 WAPs that enables them to make multiple simultaneous connections.

Multiplexer   A device that merges information from multiple input channels to a single output channel.

Multispeed Hub   Any hub that supports more than one network speed for otherwise similar cabling systems. Multispeed hubs come in two flavors: one has mostly dedicated slower ports, with a few dedicated faster ports, while the other has only special auto-sensing ports that automatically run at either the faster or the slower speed.

MX Records   Records used by SMTP servers to determine where to send mail.

My Traceroute (MTR)   Terminal command in Linux that dynamically displays the route a packet is taking. Similar to TRACEROUTE.

Name Resolution   A method that enables one computer on the network to locate another to establish a session. All network protocols perform name resolution in one of two ways: *broadcasting* or by providing some form of *name server*.

Name Server   A computer whose job is to know the name of every other computer on the network.

NAT (Network Address Translation)   A means of translating a system's IP address into another IP address before sending it out to a larger network. NAT manifests itself by a NAT program that runs on a system or a router. A network using NAT provides the systems on the network with private IP addresses. The system running the NAT software has two interfaces: one connected to the network and the other connected to the larger network.

The NAT program takes packets from the client systems bound for the larger network and translates their internal private IP addresses to its own public IP address, enabling many systems to share a single IP address.

NAT Translation Table   Special database in a NAT router that stores destination IP addresses and ephemeral source ports from outgoing packets and compares them against returning packets.

NBTSTAT   A command-line utility used to check the current NetBIOS name cache on a particular machine. The utility compares NetBIOS names to their corresponding IP addresses.

NetBEUI (NetBIOS Extended User Interface)
Microsoft's first networking protocol, designed to work with NetBIOS. NetBEUI is long obsolesced by TCP/IP. NetBEUI did not support routing.

NetBIOS (Network Basic Input/Output System)
A protocol that operates at the Session layer of the OSI seven-layer model. This protocol creates and manages connections based on the names of the computers involved.

NetBIOS Name   A computer name that identifies both the specific machine and the functions that machine performs. A NetBIOS name consists of 16 characters: the first 15 are an alphanumeric name, and the 16th is a special suffix that identifies the role the machine plays.

NETSTAT   A universal command-line utility used to examine the TCP/IP connections open on a given host.

Network   A collection of two or more computers interconnected by telephone lines, coaxial cables, satellite links, radio, and/or some other communication technique. A computer *network* is a group of computers that are connected together and communicate with one another for a common purpose. Computer networks support "people and organization" networks, users who also share a common purpose for communicating.

Network Access Server (NAS)   Systems that control the modems in a RADIUS network.

Network ID   A number used in IP networks to identify the network on which a device or machine exists.

Network Interface   A device by which a system accesses a network. In most cases, this is a NIC or a modem.

Network Layer   Layer 3 of the OSI seven-layer model. *See* OSI Seven-Layer Model.

Network Management Software (NMS)   Tools that enable you to describe, visualize, and configure an entire network.

Network Protocol   Special software that exists in every network-capable operating system that acts to create unique identifiers for each system. It also creates a set of communication rules for issues like how to handle data chopped up into multiple packets, and how to deal with routers. TCP/IP is the dominant network protocol today.

Network Share   A shared resource on a network.

Network Threat   Any number of things that share one essential feature: the potential to damage network data, machines, or users.

Network Time Protocol (NTP)   Protocol that gives the current time.

Network Topology   Refers to the way that cables and other pieces of hardware connect to one another.

Newsgroup   The name for a discussion group on USENET.

NEXT (Near-End Crosstalk)   Crosstalk at the same end of a cable as the signal is being generated from.

Next Hop   The next router a packet should go to at any given point.

NFS (Network File System)   A TCP/IP file system–sharing protocol that enables systems to treat files on a remote machine as though they were local files. NFS uses TCP port 2049, but many users choose alternative port numbers. Though still somewhat popular and heavily supported, NFS has been largely replaced by Samba/CIFS. *See both* Samba *and* Common Internet File System (CIFS).

NIC (Network Interface Card)   Traditionally, an expansion card that enables a PC to physically link to a network. Modern computers now use built-in NICs, no longer requiring physical cards, but the term "NIC" is still very common.

NIU (Network Interface Unit)   Another name for a demarc. *See* Demarc.

Node   A member of a network or a point where one or more functional units interconnect transmission lines.

Noise   Undesirable signals bearing no desired information and frequently capable of introducing errors into the communication process.

Non-Discovery Mode   A setting for Bluetooth devices that effectively hides them from other Bluetooth devices.

Nonrepudiation   The process that guarantees that the data is as originally sent and that it came from the source you think it should have come from.

Normal Backup   A full backup of every selected file on a system. This type of backup turns off the archive bit after the backup.

Novell NetWare   A powerful, unique, and once dominant network operating system that operated on a client/server model.

Ns (Nanosecond)   A billionth of a second. Light travels a little over 11 inches in 1 ns.

NS Records   Records that list the DNS servers for a Web site.

NSLOOKUP   A once handy tool that advanced techs used to query the functions of DNS servers. Most DNS servers now ignore all but the most basic NSLOOKUP queries.

NTFS (NT File System)   A file system for hard drives that enables object-level security, long filename support, compression, and encryption. NTFS 4.0 debuted with Windows NT 4.0. Windows 2000/XP/2003 come with NTFS 5.0.

NTFS Permissions   Groupings of what Microsoft calls special permissions that have names like Execute, Read, and Write, and that allow or disallow users certain access to files.

NTLDR   A Windows NT/2000/XP/2003 boot file. Launched by the MBR or MFT, NTLDR looks at the BOOT.INI configuration file for any installed operating systems.

Object   A group of related counters used in Windows logging utilities.

OEM (Original Equipment Manufacturer)   Contrary to the name, does not create original hardware, but rather purchases components from manufacturers and puts them together in systems under its own brand name. Dell, Inc. and Gateway, Inc., for example, are for the most part OEMs. Apple, Inc., which manufactures most of the components for its own Macintosh-branded machines, is not an OEM. Also known as *VARs (value-added resellers)*.

Ohm Rating   Electronic measurement of a cable's or an electronic component's impedance.

Open Port   *See* Listening Port.

Open Source   Applications and operating systems that offer access to their source code; this enables developers to modify applications and operating systems easily to meet their specific needs.

OpenSSH   A series of secure programs developed by the OpenBSD organization to fix SSH's limitation of only being able to handle one session per tunnel.

Optical Carrier (OC)   Specification used to denote the optical data carrying capacity (in Mbps) of fiber-optic cables in networks conforming to the SONET standard. The OC standard is an escalating series of speeds, designed to meet the needs of medium-to-large corporations. SONET establishes OCs from 51.8 Mbps (OC-1) to 39.8 Gbps (OC-768).

Orthogonal Frequency-Division Multiplexing (OFDM)
A spread-spectrum broadcasting method that combines the multiple frequencies of DSSS with FHSS's hopping capability.

OS (Operating System)   The set of programming that enables a program to interact with the computer and provides an interface between the PC and the user. Examples are Microsoft Windows XP, Apple Macintosh OS X, and SUSE Linux.

Oscilloscope   A device that gives a graphical/visual representation of signal levels over a period of time.

OSI (Open Systems Interconnection)   An international standard suite of protocols defined by the International Organization for Standardization (ISO) that implements the OSI seven-layer model for network communications between computers.

OSI Seven-Layer Model   An architecture model based on the OSI protocol suite, which defines and standardizes the flow of data between computers. The following lists the seven layers:

- **Layer 1**   The **Physical layer** defines hardware connections and turns binary into physical pulses (electrical or light). Repeaters and hubs operate at the Physical layer.

- **Layer 2**   The **Data Link layer** identifies devices on the Physical layer. MAC addresses are part of the Data Link layer. Bridges operate at the Data Link layer.

- **Layer 3**   The **Network layer** moves packets between computers on different networks. Routers operate at the Network layer. IP and IPX operate at the Network layer.

- **Layer 4**   The **Transport layer** breaks data down into manageable chunks. TCP, UDP, SPX, and NetBEUI operate at the Transport layer.

- **Layer 5**   The **Session layer** manages connections between machines. NetBIOS and Sockets operate at the Session layer.

- **Layer 6**   The **Presentation layer**, which can also manage data encryption, hides the differences between various types of computer systems.

- **Layer 7**   The **Application layer** provides tools for programs to use to access the network (and the lower layers). HTTP, FTP, SMTP, and POP3 are all examples of protocols that operate at the Application layer.

OSPF (Open Shortest Path First)   An interior gateway routing protocol developed for IP networks based on the *shortest path first* or *link-state algorithm*.

OTDR (Optical Time Domain Reflectometer)   Tester for fiber-optic cable that determines continuity and reports the location of cable breaks.

OUI (Organizationally Unique Identifier)   The first 24 bits of a MAC address, assigned to the NIC manufacturer by the IEEE.

Overloaded NAT   The most popular type of NAT, in which a single public IP is shared by a number of computers that, in most cases, share a private network ID.

Packet   Basic component of communication over a network. A group of bits of fixed maximum size and well-defined format that is switched and transmitted as a complete whole through a network. It contains source and destination address, data, and control information. *See also* Frame.

Packet Filtering   A mechanism that blocks any incoming or outgoing packet from a particular IP address or range of IP addresses. Also known as *IP filtering*.

Packet Sniffer   A tool that intercepts and logs network packets.

Pad   Extra data added to an Ethernet frame to bring the data up to the minimum required size of 64 bytes.

PAP (Password Authentication Protocol)   The oldest and most basic form of authentication, and also the least safe because it sends all passwords in cleartext.

Partially Meshed Topology   A mesh topology in which not all of the nodes are directly connected.

Password   A series of characters that enables a user to gain access to a file, a folder, a PC, or a program.

Patch Cables   Short (2 to 5 foot) UTP cables that connect patch panels to the hubs.

Patch Panel   A panel containing a row of female connectors (ports) that terminate the horizontal cabling in the equipment room. Patch panels facilitate cabling organization and provide protection to horizontal cabling.

PBX (Private Branch Exchange)   A private phone system used within an organization.

PDA (Personal Digital Assistant)   A hand-held computer that blurs the line between the calculator and computer. Earlier PDAs were calculators that enabled the user to program in such information as addresses and appointments. Newer machines, such as the Palm Pilot, are fully programmable computers. Most PDAs use a pen/stylus for input rather than a keyboard. A few of the larger PDAs have a tiny keyboard in addition to the stylus.

Peer-to-Peer   A network in which each machine can act as either a client or a server.

Peer-to-Peer Mode   *See* Ad Hoc Mode.

Performance Monitor (PerfMon)   The Windows XP logging utility.

Permissions   Sets of attributes that network administrators assign to users and groups that define what they can do to resources.

Persistent Connection   A connection to a shared folder or drive that the computer immediately reconnects to at logon.

Personal Area Network (PAN)   The network created among Bluetooth devices such as PDAs, printers, keyboards, mice, and so on.

Phishing   A social engineering technique where the attacker poses as a trusted source in order to obtain sensitive information.

Physical Address   An address burned into a ROM chip on a NIC. A MAC address is an example of a physical address.

Physical Layer   *See* OSI Seven-Layer Model.

Physical Network Diagram   A document that shows all of the physical connections on a network. Cabling type, protocol, and speed are also listed for each connection.

Physical Topology   The manner in which the physical components of a network are arranged.

PING (Packet Internet Groper)   A small network message (ICMP ECHO) sent by a computer to check for the presence and aliveness of another. Also used to verify the presence of another system.

Plain Old Telephone Service (POTS)
See Public Switched Telephone Network (PSTN).

Plaintext   Data that is in an easily read or viewed industry-wide standard format.

Platform   Hardware environment that supports the running of a computer system.

Plenum   Usually a space between a building's false ceiling and the floor above it. Most of the wiring for networks is located in this space. Plenum is also a fire rating for network cabling.

Point Coordination Function (PCF)   A method of collision avoidance defined by the 802.11 standard, which has yet to be implemented.

Point-to-Multipoint   Topology in which one device communicates with more than one other device on a network.

Point-to-Point   A network of two single devices communicating with each other.

Point-to-Point Protocol over Ethernet (PPPoE)   A protocol that was originally designed to encapsulate PPP frames into Ethernet frames. Used by DSL providers to force customers to log into their DSL connections instead of simply connecting automatically.

POP3 (Post Office Protocol Version 3)   One of the two protocols that receive e-mail from SMTP servers. POP3 uses TCP port 110. Most e-mail clients use this protocol, although some use IMAP4.

Port That portion of a computer through which a peripheral device may communicate. Often identified with the various plug-in jacks on the back of your computer. On a network hub, it is the connector that receives the wire link from a node. In TCP/IP, ports are 16-bit numbers between 0 and 65,535 assigned to a particular TCP/IP session.

Port Address Translation (PAT) Term used to refer to either overloaded NAT or port forwarding, but never at the same time.

Port Authentication Function of many advanced networking devices that authenticates a connecting device at the point of connection.

Port Blocking Preventing the passage of any TCP or UDP packets through any ports other than the ones prescribed by the system administrator.

Port Filtering *See* Port Blocking.

Port Forwarding Preventing the passage of any IP packets through any ports other than the ones prescribed by the system administrator.

Port Mirroring The capability of many advanced switches to mirror data from any or all physical ports on a switch to a single physical port. Useful for any type of situation where an administrator needs to inspect packets coming to or from certain computers.

Port Number Number used to identify the requested service (such as SMTP or FTP) when connecting to a TCP/IP host. Some example port numbers include 80 (HTTP), 20 (FTP), 69 (TFTP), 25 (SMTP), and 110 (POP3).

PostScript A language defined by Adobe Systems, Inc. for describing how to create an image on a page. The description is independent of the resolution of the device that will create the image. It includes a technology for defining the shape of a font and creating a raster image at many different resolutions and sizes.

Power Users A user account that has the capability to do many, but not all, of the basic administrator functions.

PPP (Point-to-Point Protocol) A protocol that enables a computer to connect to the Internet through a dial-in connection and to enjoy most of the benefits of a direct connection. PPP is considered to be superior to SLIP because of its error detection and data compression features, which SLIP lacks, and the capability to use dynamic IP addresses.

PPPoE (PPP over Ethernet) *See* Point-to-Point Protocol over Ethernet (PPPoE).

PPTP (Point-to-Point Tunneling Protocol) A protocol that works with PPP to provide a secure data link between computers using encryption.

Preamble A 64-bit series of alternating ones and zeroes ending with 11 that begins every Ethernet frame. The preamble gives a receiving NIC time to realize a frame is coming and to know exactly where the frame starts.

Presentation Layer *See* OSI Seven-Layer Model.

Primary Lookup Zones Forward lookup zones stored in text files. *See* Forward Lookup Zones.

Primary Rate Interface (PRI) A type of ISDN that is actually just a full T1 line carrying 23 B channels.

Private Port Numbers *See* Dynamic Port Numbers.

Program A set of actions or instructions that a machine is capable of interpreting and executing. Used as a verb, it means to design, write, and test such instructions.

Promiscuous Mode A mode of operation for a NIC in which the NIC processes all packets that it sees on the cable.

Prompt A character or message provided by an operating system or program to indicate that it is ready to accept input.

Proprietary Term used to describe technology that is unique to, and owned by, a particular vendor.

Protected Extensible Authentication Protocol (PEAP) An authentication protocol that uses a password function based on MS-CHAPv2 with the addition of an encrypted TLS tunnel similar to EAP-TLS.

Protocol An agreement that governs the procedures used to exchange information between cooperating entities; usually includes how much information is to be sent, how often it is sent, how to recover from transmission errors, and who is to receive the information.

Protocol Analyzer A tool that monitors the different protocols running at different layers on the network, and that can give Application, Session, Network, and Data Link layer information on every frame going through a network.

Protocol Stack The actual software that implements the protocol suite on a particular operating system.

Protocol Suite A set of protocols that are commonly used together and operate at different levels of the OSI seven-layer model.

Proxy Server A device that fetches Internet resources for a client without exposing that client directly to the Internet. Most proxy servers accept requests for HTTP, FTP, POP3, and SMTP resources. The proxy server often caches, or stores, a copy of the requested resource for later use.

PSTN (Public Switched Telephone Network) *See* Public Switched Telephone Network (PSTN).

Public-Key Cryptography A method for exchanging digital keys securely.

Public-Key Infrastructure (PKI) The system for creating and distributing digital certificates using sites like VeriSign, thawte, or GoDaddy.

Public Switched Telephone Network (PSTN) Also known as *POTS (Plain Old Telephone Service)*. Most common type of phone connection, which takes your sounds, translated into an analog waveform by the microphone, and transmits them to another phone.

Punchdown Tool A specialized tool for connecting UTP wires to an RJ-45 jack.

PVC (Polyvinyl Chloride) A material used for the outside insulation and jacketing of most cables. Also a fire rating for a type of cable that has no significant fire protection.

Quality of Service (QoS) Policies that control how much bandwidth a protocol, PC, user, VLAN, or IP address may use.

Raceway Cable organizing device that adheres to walls, making for a much simpler, though less neat, installation than running cables in the walls.

RADIUS Server A system that enables remote users to connect to a network service.

RAID (Redundant Array of Independent [or Inexpensive] Devices [or Disks]) A way of creating a fault-tolerant storage system. There are six levels. Level 0 uses byte-level striping and provides no fault tolerance. Level 1 uses mirroring or duplexing. Level 2 uses bit-level striping. Level 3 stores error-correcting information (such as parity) on a separate disk, and uses data striping on the remaining drives. Level 4 is level 3 with block-level striping. Level 5 uses block-level and parity data striping.

RCP (Remote Copy) Provides the capability to copy files to and from the remote server without the need to resort to FTP or NFS (Network File System, UNIX form of folder sharing). RCP can also be used in scripts and shares TCP port 514 with RSH.

Real-Time Processing The processing of transactions as they occur, rather than batching them. Pertaining to an application, processing in which response to input is fast enough to affect subsequent inputs and guide the process, and in which records are updated immediately. The lag from input time to output time must be sufficiently small for acceptable timeliness. Timeliness is a function of the total system: missile guidance requires output within a few milliseconds of input, whereas scheduling of steamships requires a response time in days. Real-time systems are those with a response time of milliseconds; interactive systems respond in seconds; and batch systems may respond in hours or days.

Real-Time Transport Protocol (RTP) Protocol that defines the type of packets used on the Internet to move voice or data from a server to clients. The vast majority of VoIP solutions available today use RTP.

REGEDIT.EXE A program used to edit the Windows registry.

Regional Internet Registries (RIRs) Entities under the oversight of the Internet Assigned Numbers Authority (IANA), which parcels out IP addresses.

Registered Ports Port numbers from 1024 to 49151. Anyone can use these port numbers for their servers or for ephemeral numbers on clients.

Regulations Rules of law or policy that govern behavior in the workplace, such as what to do when a particular event occurs.

Remote   Refers to the computer(s), server(s), and/or LAN that cannot be physically used due to its distance from the user.

Remote Access   The capability to access a computer from outside a building in which it is housed. Remote access requires communications hardware, software, and actual physical links.

Remote Access Server (RAS)   Refers to both the hardware component (servers built to handle the unique stresses of a large number of clients calling in) and the software component (programs that work with the operating system to allow remote access to the network) of a remote access solution.

Remote Authentication Dial-In User Service (RADIUS) An AAA standard created to support ISPs with hundreds if not thousands of modems in hundreds of computers to connect to a single central database. RADIUS consists of three devices: the RADIUS server that has access to a database of user names and passwords, a number of network access servers (NASs) that control the modems, and a group of systems that dial into the network.

Remote Installation Services (RIS)   A tool introduced with Windows 2000 that can be used to initiate either a scripted installation or an installation of an image of an operating system onto a PC.

Remote Terminal   A connection on a faraway computer that enables you to control that computer as if you were sitting in front of it, logged in. Remote terminal programs all require a server and a client. The server is the computer to be controlled. The client is the computer from which you do the controlling.

Repeater   A device that takes all of the data packets it receives on one Ethernet segment and re-creates them on another Ethernet segment. This allows for longer cables or more computers on a segment. Repeaters operate at Level 1 (Physical) of the OSI seven-layer model.

Replication   A process where multiple computers might share complete copies of a database and constantly update each other.

Resistance   The tendency for a physical medium to impede electron flow. It is classically measured in a unit called *ohms*. *See also* Impedence.

Resource   Anything that exists on another computer that a person wants to use without going to that computer. Also an online information set or an online interactive option. An online library catalog and the local school lunch menu are examples of information sets. Online menus or graphical user interfaces, Internet e-mail, online conferences, Telnet, FTP, and Gopher are examples of interactive options.

Reverse Lookup Zones   A DNS setting that resolves IP addresses to FQDNs. In other words, it does exactly the reverse of what DNS normally accomplishes using forward lookup zones.

RG Ratings   Ratings developed by the U.S. military to provide a quick reference for the different types of coaxial cables.

Ring Topology   A network topology in which all the computers on the network attach to a central ring of cable.

RIP (Routing Information Protocol)   Distance vector routing protocol that dates from the 1980s.

RIPv1   The first version of RIP, which had several shortcomings, such as a maximum hop count of 15 and a routing table update interval of 30 seconds, which was a problem because every router on a network would send out its table at the same time.

RIPv2   The current version of RIP. Fixed many problems of RIP v1, but the maximum hop count of 15 still applies.

Riser   Fire rating that designates the proper cabling to use for vertical runs between floors of a building.

Rivest Cipher 4 (RC4)   A popular streaming symmetric-key algorithm.

Rivest Shamir Adleman (RSA)   An improved public-key cryptography algorithm that enables secure digital signatures.

RJ (Registered Jack)   Connectors used for UTP cable on both telephone and network connections.

RJ-11   Type of connector with four-wire UTP connections; usually found in telephone connections.

RJ-45   Type of connector with eight-wire UTP connections; usually found in network connections and used for 10/100/1000BaseT networking.

Rlogin   Program in UNIX that lets you remotely log into a server. Unlike Telnet, it can be configured to log in automatically.

Rogue Access Point   An unauthorized wireless access point (WAP) installed in a computer network.

Role-Based Access Control (RBAC)   The most popular authentication model used in file sharing, defines a user's access to a resource based on the roles the user plays in the network environment. This leads to the idea of creation of groups. A group in most networks is nothing more than a name that has clearly defined accesses to different resources. User accounts are placed into various groups.

ROM (Read-Only Memory)   The generic term for non-volatile memory that can be read from but not written to. This means that code and data stored in ROM cannot be corrupted by accidental erasure. Additionally, ROM retains its data when power is removed, which makes it the perfect medium for storing BIOS data or information such as scientific constants.

Root Directory   The directory that contains all other directories.

Rootkit   A Trojan that takes advantage of very low-level operating system functions to hide itself from all but the most aggressive of anti-malware tools.

ROUTE   A command that enables a user to display and edit the local system's routing table.

Router   A device that connects separate networks and forwards a packet from one network to another based only on the network address for the protocol being used. For example, an IP router looks only at the IP network number. Routers operate at Layer 3 (Network) of the OSI seven-layer model.

Routing and Remote Access Service (RRAS)   A special remote access server program, originally only available on Windows Server, on which a PPTP endpoint is placed in Microsoft networks.

Routing Table   A list of paths to various networks required by routers. This can be built either manually or automatically.

RS-232   The recommended standard (RS) upon which all serial communication takes place on a PC.

RSH (Remote Shell)   Allows you to send single commands to the remote server. Whereas rlogin is designed to be used interactively, RSH can be easily integrated into a script.

Run   A single piece of installed horizontal cabling.

Samba   An application that enables UNIX systems to communicate using SMBs (Server Message Blocks). This, in turn, enables them to act as Microsoft clients and servers on the network.

Scalability   The capability to support network growth.

Scanner   A device that senses alterations of light and dark. It enables the user to import photographs, other physical images, and text into the computer in digital form.

SC Connector   One of two special types of fiber-optic cable used in 10BaseFL networks.

Secondary Lookup Zone   Backup lookup zones stored on other DNS servers. *See also* Forward Lookup Zones.

Secure Copy Protocol (SCP)   One of the first SSH-enabled programs to appear after the introduction of SSH. SCP was one of the first protocols used to transfer data securely between two hosts and thus might have replaced FTP. SCP works well but lacks features such as a directory listing.

Secure FTP (SFTP)   Designed as a replacement for FTP after many of the inadequacies of SCP (such as the inability to see the files on the other computer) were discovered.

Secure Hash Algorithm (SHA)   A popular cryptographic hash.

Secure Shell (SSH)   A terminal emulation program that looks exactly like Telnet but encrypts the data. SSH has replaced Telnet on the Internet.

Secure Sockets Layer (SSL)   A protocol developed by Netscape for transmitting private documents over the Internet. SSL works by using a public key to encrypt sensitive data. This encrypted data is sent over an SSL connection, and then decrypted at the receiving end using a private key.

Security Log   A log that tracks anything that affects security, such as successful and failed logons and logoffs.

Security Policy   A set of procedures defining actions employees should perform to protect the network's security.

Segment   The bus cable to which the computers on an Ethernet network connect.

Sendmail Currently (2009) the leading e-mail server program.

Sequential A method of storing and retrieving information that requires data to be written and read sequentially. Accessing any portion of the data requires reading all the preceding data.

Server A computer that shares its resources, such as printers and files, with other computers on the network. An example of this is a Network File System Server that shares its disk space with a workstation that has no disk drive of its own.

Server-Based Network A network in which one or more systems function as dedicated file, print, or application servers, but do not function as clients.

Service Set Identification (SSID) A 32-bit identification string, sometimes called a *network name*, that's inserted into the header of each data packet processed by a wireless access point.

Session A networking term used to refer to the logical stream of data flowing between two programs and being communicated over a network. Many different sessions may be emanating from any one node on a network.

Session Initiation Protocol (SIP) VoIP protocol competing with H.323 for VoIP dominance.

Session Layer *See* OSI Seven-Layer Model.

Session Software Handles the process of differentiating between various types of connections on a PC.

SFF (Small Form Factor) A description of later-generation fiber-optic connectors designed to be much smaller than the first iterations of connectors. *See both* LC *and* MT-RJ (Mechanical Transfer Registered Jack).

Share Level Security A security system in which each resource has a password assigned to it; access to the resource is based on knowing the password.

Share Permissions Permissions that only control the access of other users on the network with whom you share your resource. They have no impact on you (or anyone else) sitting at the computer whose resource is being shared.

Shareware Software that is protected by copyright, but the copyright holder allows (encourages!) you to make and distribute copies, under the condition that

those who adopt the software after preview pay a fee. Derivative works are not allowed, and you may make an archival copy.

Shell Generally refers to the user interface of an operating system. A shell is the command processor that is the actual interface between the kernel and the user.

Signaling Topology Another name for logical topology. *See* Logical Topology.

Short Circuit Allows electricity to pass between two conductive elements that weren't designed to interact together. Also called a *short*.

Shortest Path First Networking algorithm for directing router traffic. *See also* OSPF (Open Shortest Path First).

Signal Strength A measurement of how well your wireless device is connecting to other devices.

Single-mode Fiber-optic cables that use lasers.

Site Survey A process that enables you to determine any obstacles to creating the wireless network you want.

Smart Device Devices (such as credit cards, USB keys, etc.) that you insert into your PC in lieu of entering a password.

Smart Jack Type of NIU that enables ISPs or telephone companies to test for faults in a network, such as disconnections and loopbacks.

SMB (Server Message Block) Protocol used by Microsoft clients and servers to share file and print resources.

SMTP (Simple Mail Transfer Protocol) The main protocol used to send electronic mail on the Internet.

Snap-Ins Small utilities that can be used with the Microsoft Management Console.

Sneakernet Saving a file on a portable medium and walking it over to another computer.

Sniffer Diagnostic program that can order a NIC to run in promiscuous mode. *See* Promiscuous Mode.

Snip *See* Cable Stripper.

SNMP (Simple Network Management Protocol) A set of standards for communication with devices connected to a TCP/IP network. Examples of these devices include routers, hubs, and switches.

Social Engineering   The process of using or manipulating people inside the networking environment to gain access to that network from the outside.

Socket   A combination of a port number and an IP address that uniquely identifies a connection.

Socket Pairs   *See* Endpoints.

Software   Programming instructions or data stored on some type of binary storage device.

Solid Core   A cable that uses a single solid wire to transmit signals.

SONET (Synchronous Optical Network)   A standard for connecting fiber-optic transmission systems. SONET was proposed in the mid-1980s, and is now an ANSI standard. SONET defines interface standards at the Physical layer of the OSI seven-layer model.

Source NAT   A type of NAT in which the source IP addresses get translated by the router.

Spanning Tree Protocol (STP)   A protocol that enables switches to detect and repair bridge loops automatically.

Spyware   Any program that sends information about your system or your actions over the Internet.

SQL (Structured Query Language)   A language created by IBM that relies on simple English statements to perform database queries. SQL enables databases from different manufacturers to be queried using a standard syntax.

SSL (Secure Sockets Layer)   *See* Secure Sockets Layer (SSL).

ST Connector   One of two special types of fiber-optic cable used in 10BaseFL networks.

Star-bus Topology   A hybrid of the star and bus topologies that uses a physical star, where all nodes connect to a single wiring point such as a hub, and a logical bus that maintains the Ethernet standards. One benefit of a star-bus topology is fault tolerance.

Star-ring Topology   A hybrid of the Token Ring topology and the physical star.

Star Topology   A network topology in which all computers in the network connect to a central wiring point.

Stateful   Describes a DHCPv6 server that works very similarly to an IPv4 DHCP server, passing out IPv6 addresses, subnet masks, and default gateways as well as optional items like DNS server addresses.

Stateful Filtering   A method of filtering in which all packets are examined as a stream. Stateful devices can do more than allow or block; they can track when a stream is disrupted or packets get corrupted and act accordingly.

Stateless   Describes a DHCPv6 server that only passes out optional information.

Stateless Filtering   A method of filtering where the device that does the filtering just checks the packet for IP addresses and port numbers and blocks or allows accordingly.

Static Addressing   The process of assigning IP addresses by manually typing them into client computers.

Static NAT (SNAT)   A type of NAT that maps a single routable IP address to a single machine, allowing you to access that machine from outside the network.

Static Routing   A process by which routers in an internetwork obtain information about paths to other routers. This information must be supplied manually.

Storage   A device or medium that can retain data for subsequent retrieval.

STP (Shielded Twisted Pair)   A popular cabling for networks composed of pairs of wires twisted around each other at specific intervals. The twists serve to reduce interference (also called *crosstalk*). The more twists, the less interference. The cable has metallic shielding to protect the wires from external interference. Token Ring networks are the only common network technology that uses STP, although Token Ring more often now uses UTP.

STP (Spanning Tree Protocol)   *See* Spanning Tree Protocol (STP).

Stranded Core   A cable that uses a bundle of tiny wire strands to transmit signals. Stranded core is not quite as good a conductor as solid core, but it will stand up to substantial handling without breaking.

Stream Cipher   An encryption method that encrypts a single bit at a time. Popular when data comes in long streams (such as with older wireless networks or cell phones).

Stripe Set   Two or more drives in a group that are used for a striped volume.

Structured Cabling   Standards defined by the Telecommunications Industry Association/Electronic Industries Alliance (TIA/EIA) that define methods of organizing the cables in a network for ease of repair and replacement.

STS Overhead   Carries the signaling and protocol information in Synchronous Transport Signal (STS).

STS Payload   Carries data in STS.

Subnet   Each independent network in a TCP/IP internetwork.

Subnet Mask   The value used in TCP/IP settings to divide the IP address of a host into its component parts: network ID and host ID.

Subnetting   Taking a single class of IP addresses and chopping it into multiple smaller groups.

Supplicant   A client computer in a RADIUS network.

Switch   A device that filters and forwards traffic based on some criteria. A bridge and a router are both examples of switches.

Symmetric DSL (SDSL)   Type of DSL connection that provides equal upload and download speed and, in theory, provides speeds up to 15 Mbps, although the vast majority of ISPs provide packages ranging from 192 Kbps to 9 Mbps.

Symmetric-Key Algorithm   Any encryption method that uses the same key for both encryption and decryption.

Synchronous   Describes a connection between two electronic devices where neither must acknowledge (ACK) when receiving data.

Synchronous Digital Hierarchy (SDH)   European fiber carrier standard equivalent to SONET.

Synchronous Optical Network (SONET)   American fiber carrier standard.

Synchronous Transport Signal (STS)   Signal method used by SONET. It consists of the STS payload and the STS overhead. A number is appended to the end of STS to designate signal speed.

System Log   A log file that records issues dealing with the overall system, such as system services, device drivers, or configuration changes.

System Restore   A Windows utility that enables you to return your PC to a recent working configuration when something goes wrong. System Restore returns your computer's system settings to the way they were the last time you remember your system working correctly—all without affecting your personal files or e-mail.

T1   A leased-line connection capable of carrying data at 1,544,000 bps.

T1 Line   The specific, shielded, two-pair cabling that connects the two ends of a T1 connection.

T3 Line   A leased-line connection capable of carrying data at 44,736,000 bps.

TCP (Transmission Control Protocol)   Part of the TCP/IP protocol suite, operates at Layer 4 (Transport) of the OSI seven-layer model. TCP is a connection-oriented protocol.

TCP/IP (Transmission Control Protocol/Internet Protocol)   A set of communication protocols developed by the U.S. Department of Defense that enables dissimilar computers to share information over a network.

TDR (Time Domain Reflectometer)   Advanced cable tester that tests the length of cables and their continuity or discontinuity, and identifies the location of any discontinuity due to a bend, break, unwanted crimp, and so on.

Telecommunications Room   A central location for computer or telephone equipment and, most importantly, centralized cabling. All cables usually run to the telecommunications room from the rest of the installation.

Telephony   The science of converting sound into electrical signals, moving those signals from one location to another, and then converting those signals back into sounds. This includes modems, telephone lines, the telephone system, and any products used to create a remote access link between a remote access client and server.

Telnet   A program that enables users on the Internet to log onto remote systems from their own host systems.

Terminal Access Controller Access Control System Plus (TACACS+) A proprietary protocol developed by Cisco to support AAA in a network with many routers and switches. It is similar to RADIUS in function, but uses TCP port 49 by default and separates authorization, authentication, and accounting into different parts.

Terminal Adapter (TA) The most common interface used to connect a computer to an ISDN line.

Terminal Emulation Software that enables a PC to communicate with another computer or network as if it were a specific type of hardware terminal.

TIA/EIA (Telecommunications Industry Association/Electronics Industry Association) The standards body that defines most of the standards for computer network cabling. Many of these standards are defined under the TIA/EIA 568 standard.

TIA/EIA 568A One of two four-pair UTP crimping standards for 10/100/1000BaseT networks. The other standard is TIA/EIA 568B.

TIA/EIA 568B One of two four-pair UTP crimping standards for 10/100/1000BaseT networks. The other standard is TIA/EIA 568A.

TIA/EIA 606 Official methodology for labeling patch panels.

Ticket-Granting Ticket (TGT) Sent by an Authentication Server in a Kerberos setup if a client's hash matches its own, signaling that the client is authenticated but not yet authorized.

Time Division Multiplexing The process of having frames that carry a bit of every channel in every frame sent on a regular interval in a T1 connection.

Tone Generator *See* Toners.

Tone Probe *See* Toners.

Toners Generic term for two devices used together—a tone generator and a tone locator (probe)—to trace cables by sending an electrical signal along a wire at a particular frequency. The tone locator then emits a sound when it distinguishes that frequency. Also referred to as *Fox and Hound*.

Top-Level Domain Servers A set of DNS servers—just below the root servers—that handle the top-level domain names, such as .com, .org, .net, and so on.

Topology The pattern of interconnections in a communications system among devices, nodes, and associated input and output stations. Also describes how computers connect to each other without regard to how they actually communicate.

Toredo A NAT-traversal IPv6 tunneling protocol, built into Microsoft Windows.

TRACERT (also TRACEROUTE) A command-line utility used to follow the path a packet takes between two hosts.

Traffic Shaping Controlling the flow of packets into or out from the network according to the type of packet or other rules.

Transceiver The device that transmits and receives signals on a cable.

Transmit Beamforming A multiple-antenna technology in 802.11n WAPs that helps get rid of dead spots.

Transport Layer *See* OSI Seven-Layer Model.

Transport Layer Security A robust update to SSL that works with almost any TCP application.

Trivial File Transfer Protocol (TFTP) A protocol that transfers files between servers and clients. Unlike FTP, TFTP requires no user login. Devices that need an operating system, but have no local hard disk (for example, diskless workstations and routers), often use TFTP to download their operating systems.

Trojan A virus that masquerades as a file with a legitimate purpose, so that a user will run it intentionally. The classic example is a file that runs a game, but also causes some type of damage to the player's system.

Trunk Port A port on a switch configured to carry all data, regardless of VLAN number, between all switches in a LAN.

Trunking The process of transferring VLAN data between two or more switches.

Tunnel An encrypted link between two programs on two separate computers.

Tunnel Broker In IPv6, a service that creates the actual tunnel and (usually) offers a custom-made endpoint client for you to use, although more advanced users can often make a manual connection.

Tunnel Information and Control Protocol (TIC) One of the protocols that set up IPv6 tunnels and handle configuration as well as login.

Tunnel Setup Protocol (TSP) One of the protocols that set up IPv6 tunnels and handle configuration as well as login.

Twisted Pair Twisted pairs of cables, the most overwhelmingly common type of cabling used in networks. The two types of twisted pair cabling are UTP (unshielded twisted pair) and STP (shielded twisted pair). The twists serve to reduce interference, called *crosstalk*; the more twists, the less crosstalk.

U (Units) The unique height measurement used with equipment racks; 1 U equals 1.75 inches.

UART (Universal Asynchronous Receiver/Transmitter) A device that turns serial data into parallel data. The cornerstone of serial ports and modems.

UDP (User Datagram Protocol) Part of the TCP/IP protocol suite, a connectionless protocol that is an alternative to TCP.

UNC (Universal Naming Convention) Describes any shared resource in a network using the convention \\<server name>\<name of shared resource>.

Unicast A message sent from one computer to one other computer.

Unicast Address A unique IPv6 address that is exclusive to a system. Link-local addresses are unicast addresses.

Universal Asynchronous Receiver Transmitter (UART) A device inside a modem that takes the 8-bit-wide digital data and converts it into 1-bit-wide digital data and hands it to the modem for conversion to analog data. The process is reversed for incoming data.

UNIX A popular computer software operating system used on many Internet host systems.

Uplink Port Port on a hub that enables you to connect two hubs together using a straight-through cable.

Upload The transfer of information from a user's system to a remote computer system. Opposite of download.

UPS (Uninterruptible Power Supply) A device that supplies continuous clean power to a computer system the whole time the computer is on. Protects against power outages and sags. The term *UPS* is often used mistakenly when people mean SPS (Stand-by Power Supply or System).

URL (Uniform Resource Locator) An address that defines the type and the location of a resource on the Internet. URLs are used in almost every TCP/IP application. A typical HTTP URL is http://www.totalsem.com.

Usenet The network of UNIX users, generally perceived as informal and made up of loosely coupled nodes, that exchanges mail and messages. Started by Duke University and UNC-Chapel Hill. An information cooperative linking around 16,000 computer sites and millions of people. Usenet provides a series of "news groups" analogous to online conferences.

User Anyone who uses a computer. You.

User Account A container that identifies a user to the application, operating system, or network, including name, password, user name, groups to which the user belongs, and other information based on the user and the OS or NOS being used. Usually defines the rights and roles a user plays on a system.

User Datagram Protocol (UDP) A protocol used by some older applications, most prominently TFTP (Trivial FTP), to transfer files. UDP packets are both simpler and smaller than TCP packets, and they do most of the behind-the-scenes work in a TCP/IP network.

User-Level Security A security system in which each user has an account, and access to resources is based on user identity.

User Profiles A collection of settings that corresponds to a specific user account and may follow the user, regardless of the computer at which he or she logs on. These settings enable the user to have customized environment and security settings.

UTP (Unshielded Twisted Pair) A popular cabling for telephone and networks composed of pairs of wires twisted around each other at specific intervals. The twists serve to reduce interference (also called *crosstalk*). The more twists, the less interference. The cable has *no* metallic shielding to protect the wires from external interference, unlike its cousin, *STP*. 10BaseT uses UTP, as do many other networking technologies. UTP is available in a variety of grades, called categories, as defined in the following:

- **Category 1 UTP**   Regular analog phone lines, not used for data communications

- **Category 2 UTP**   Supports speeds up to 4 Mbps

- **Category 3 UTP**   Supports speeds up to 16 Mbps

- **Category 4 UTP**   Supports speeds up to 20 Mbps

- **Category 5 UTP**   Supports speeds up to 100 Mbps

- **Category 5e UTP**   Supports speeds up to 100 Mbps with two pairs and up to 1000 Mbps with four pairs

- **Category 6 UTP**   Improved support for speeds up to 1000 Mbps

V Standards   Standards established by CCITT for modem manufacturers to follow (voluntarily) to ensure compatible speeds, compression, and error correction.

V.92 Standard   The current modem standard, which has a download speed of 57,600 bps and an upload speed of 48 Kbps. V.92 modems have several interesting features, such as Quick Connect and Modem on Hold.

Vertical Cross-Connect   Main patch panel in a telecommunications room. *See also* Patch Panel.

Very High Bitrate DSL (VDSL)   The latest form of DSL with download and upload speeds of up to 100 Mbps. VDSL was designed to run on copper phone lines, but many VDSL suppliers use fiber-optic cabling to increase effective distances.

Virtual Local Area Network (VLAN)   A LAN that, using VLAN-capable switches, places some (or any on the more expensive VLANs) systems on virtual broadcast domains.

Virus   A program that can make a copy of itself without you necessarily being aware of it. Some viruses can destroy or damage files, and generally the best protection is always to maintain backups of your files.

Virus Definition or Data Files   Enable the virus protection software to recognize the viruses on your system and clean them. These files should be updated often. Also called *signature files*, depending on the virus protection software in use.

Voice over IP (VoIP)   Using an IP network to transfer voice calls.

Voltage   The pressure of the electrons passing through a wire.

Voltage Event Recorder   Tracks voltage over time by plugging into a power outlet.

Volts (V)   Units of measurement for *voltage*.

VPN (Virtual Private Network)   A network configuration that enables a remote user to access a private network via the Internet. VPNs employ an encryption methodology called *tunneling*, which protects the data from interception.

WAN (Wide Area Network)   A geographically dispersed network created by linking various computers and LANs over long distances, generally using leased phone lines. There is no firm dividing line between a WAN and a LAN.

Warm Boot   A system restart performed after the system has been powered and operating. This clears and resets the memory, but does not stop and start the hard drive.

Wattage (Watts or W)   The amount of amps and volts needed by a particular device to function.

Web Server   A server that enables access to HTML documents by remote users.

Well-Known Port Numbers   Port numbers from 0 to 1204 that are used primarily by client applications to talk to server applications in TCP/IP networks.

Wi-Fi   The most widely adopted wireless networking type in use today. Technically, only wireless devices that conform to the extended versions of the 802.11 standard—802.11a, 802.11b, and 802.11g—are Wi-Fi certified.

Wi-Fi Protected Access (WPA)   A wireless security protocol that addresses the weaknesses and acts as a sort of upgrade to WEP. WPA offers security enhancements such as dynamic encryption key generation (keys are issued on a per-user and per-session basis), an encryption key integrity-checking feature, user authentication through the industry-standard Extensible Authentication Protocol (EAP), and other advanced features that WEP lacks.

Wi-Fi Protected Access 2 (WPA2) An update to the WPA protocol that uses the Advanced Encryption Standard algorithm, making it much harder to crack.

WiMax *See* 802.16.

Windows Domain A group of computers controlled by a computer running Windows Server, which is configured as a domain controller.

Windows Firewall The firewall that has been included in Windows operating systems since Windows XP; originally named Internet Connection Firewall (ICF), but was renamed in XP Service Pack 2.

WINIPCFG A graphical program used on Windows 95, Windows 98, and Windows Me machines to display the current TCP/IP configuration of the machine; similar to more modern Windows's IPCONFIG and UNIX/Linux's IFCONFIG.

WINS (Windows Internet Name Service) A name resolution service that resolves NetBIOS names to IP addresses.

WINS Proxy Agent A WINS relay agent that forwards WINS broadcasts to a WINS server on the other side of a router to keep older systems from broadcasting in place of registering with the server.

Wired Equivalent Privacy (WEP) A wireless security protocol that uses a 64-bit encryption algorithm to scramble data packets.

Wireless Access Point (WAP) Connects wireless network nodes to wireless or wired networks. Many WAPs are combination devices that act as high-speed hubs, switches, bridges, and routers, all rolled into one.

Wireless Bridge Device used to connect two wireless network segments together, or to join wireless and wired networks together in the same way that wired bridge devices do.

Wireless Network *See* Wi-Fi.

Wiremap Term that techs use to refer to the proper connectivity of wires in a network.

Wireshark A popular packet sniffer.

Wiring Diagram A document, also known as a *wiring schematic*, that usually consists of multiple pages and that shows the following: how the wires in a network connect to switches and other nodes, what types of cables are used, and how patch panels are configured. It usually includes details about each cable run.

Wiring Schematic *See* Wiring Diagram.

Work Area In a basic structured cabling network, often simply an office or cubicle that potentially contains a PC attached to the network.

Workgroup A convenient method of organizing computers under Network/My Network Places in Windows operating systems.

Workstation A general-purpose computer that is small enough and inexpensive enough to reside at a person's work area for his or her exclusive use.

Worm A very special form of virus. Unlike other viruses, a worm does not infect other files on the computer. Instead, it replicates by making copies of itself on other systems on a network by taking advantage of security weaknesses in networking protocols.

WWW (World Wide Web) The (graphical) Internet that can be accessed using Gopher, FTP, HTTP, Telnet, USENET, WAIS, and some other tools.

X.25 The first generation of packet-switching technology, enables remote devices to communicate with each other across high-speed digital links without the expense of individual leased lines.

Yost Cable Cable used to interface with a Cisco device.

Zombie A single computer under the control of an operator that is used in a botnet attack. *See also* Botnet.

INDEX

D

D channels (Delta channels), 380
DAC (discretionary access control), 257
daily backups, 501
data backup. *See* backing up data
data encryption
    overview of, 438
    using WEP, 438–439
    using WPA, 439
    using WPA2, 439
Data Encryption Standard (DES), 282–283
data in Ethernet frames, 62
Data Link Layer, 11–13, 19
Data Over Cable Service Interface Specification (DOCSIS), 385
data throughput, 496–499
DCF (Distributed Coordination Function), 434
DDoS (Distributed Denial of Service) attacks, 463
dead spots, 432
decryption, 282, 284–285
dedicated connections, 389–390
dedicated lines, 376–377
dedicated servers, 315–316
default gateways, 144
default user names and passwords, 197–198
Delta channels (D channels), 380
demarc, 107–108
demilitarized zones (DMZs), 476–477
Denial of Service (DoS) attacks, 463
DES (Data Encryption Standard), 282–283
designated routers (DRs), 192
destination LAN IPs, 173–174
Destination NAT (Network Address Translation), 179
destination ports, 180
device IDs, 14
devices
    advanced. *See* advanced networking devices
    biometric, 466
    IDs of, 14
    overview of, 514–515
    security for, 519
    smart, 466
DHCP (Dynamic Host Configuration Protocol)
    IP addresses and, 161–164
    in IPv6, 350–351
    TCP/IP applications and, 212

diagnosing physical network problems
    cables, testing, 127–128
    lights, checking, 126–127
    NICs, checking, 127
    overview of, 126
    in telecommunication rooms, 128–129
    toners, 129
diagrams
    logical network, 487–488
    physical network, 486–487
    wiring, 485–486
dial-up connections, 377, 387
differential backups, 501–503
Diffie-Hellman key exchange, 283
DIG (domain information grouper), 266–267, 408–409
Digital Service Unit (DSU), 369–372
digital signal 1 (DS1), 370–371
digital signal level 0 (DSO), 369
digital signatures, 287
Digital Subscriber Line (DSL). *See* DSL (Digital Subscriber Line)
digital telephony, 368
dipole antennae, 442
direct-sequence spread-spectrum (DSSS), 433
directional antennae, 443
disassembly, 25–26
discretionary access control (DAC), 257
dispersion, 121
distance under 90 meters, 111
Distributed Coordination Function (DCF), 434
Distributed Denial of Service (DDoS) attacks, 463
DMZs (demilitarized zones), 476–477
DNAT (Dynamic Network Address Translation), 180
DNS (Domain Name System)
    Active Directory-integrated zones and, 264
    CIFS and, 263–264
    in IPv6, 351–352
    key terms, 274–275
    lab projects, 277
    load balancing in, 326–327
    name resolution with, 253–258
    name servers for, 251–253
    name spaces in, 248–251
    overview of, 245–247
    quizzes on, 275–277
    root servers, 247, 252
    servers, 258–262
    servers generally, 247

    summary of, 273–274
    TCP/IP utilities diagnosing, 269–272
    trees, 249–251
    troubleshooting, 264–267
    Windows and, 262–264
    WINS and, 267–269
    workings of, 247–248
DOCSIS (Data Over Cable Service Interface Specification), 385
documentation
    in change management, 490
    in configuration management. *See* configuration management documentation
    overview of, 30–33
    in troubleshooting, 416
domain information grouper (DIG), 266–267, 408–409
Domain Name System (DNS). *See* DNS (Domain Name System)
DoS (Denial of Service) attacks, 463
dotted decimal notation, 140–141, 155–157
drivers, 124
drops, 110
DRs (designated routers), 192
DS1 (digital signal 1), 370–371
DSL Access Multiplexer (DSLAM), 382
DSL (Digital Subscriber Line), 381–384
    ADSL, 381
    features of, 382
    installing, 382–384
    SDSL, 381
    VDSL, 382
DSL POTS filters, 382–383
DSLAM (DSL Access Multiplexer), 382
DSO (digital signal level 0), 369
DSSS (direct-sequence spread-spectrum), 433
DSU (Digital Service Unit), 369–372
Dynamic Host Configuration Protocol (DHCP). *See* DHCP (Dynamic Host Configuration Protocol)
dynamic IP addresses, 157, 161–164
Dynamic Network Address Translation (DNAT), 180
dynamic port numbers, 215
dynamic port usage, 470
dynamic routing
    BGP in, 189–190
    distance vectors in, 186–188
    EIGRP in, 194
    Internet and, 194
    IS-IS in, 194

quizzes on, 132–134
runs, mapping, 110
runs, testing, 117–122
solid vs. stranded core, 100–101
summary of, 130
in telecommunication rooms, 101–102, 111–112
topology of, 106–108
in work areas, 106
STS (Synchronous Transport Signal)
overhead, 372
payload, 372
for remote connectivity, 373
studying for certification exams, 5–7
subnet masks
in IP addresses, 145–149
in IPv6, 342
in routing tables, 173–175
in troubleshooting WINS, 270
subnets, 21
subnetting, 150–157
calculating subnets, 153–155
CIDR and, 150, 157
creating, 152–153
hosts, calculating, 151–152
manual dotted decimal to binary conversion in, 155–157
overview of, 150–151
summary of, 165
supplicants, 437–438
switched Ethernet networks, 71–75
switches
in Ethernet networks, 90
overview of, 72–75, 515
in VLANs, 322–324
switching loops, 419
Symmetric DSL (SDSL), 381
symmetric-key algorithm standards, 282–283
symptoms, identifying, 413
Synchronous Digital Hierarchy (SDH), 372
Synchronous Optical Network (SONET), 87, 372
Synchronous Transport Signal (STS), 373
system crashes, 459
System logs, 495

T

T-carriers, 376
T1 lines, 369–371
T3 lines, 371–372
TA (terminal adapter), 380
TACAS+ (Terminal Access Controller Access Control System Plus), 296
talking on networks, 26–28

TCP/IP applications
common, 222
communications, good vs. bad, 222
connection status of, 219–222
DNS and, 269–272
e-mail clients, 234–235
e-mail generally, 231
e-mail servers, 233–234
FTP, 235–238
HTTP, 224
HTTPS, 227–228
ICMP for, 213–214
IGMP for, 213–214
IMAP4, 232–233
Internet, 238
key terms, 240
lab projects, 243
overview of, 210–211
POP3, 232–233
port numbers in, 214–222
quizzes on, 241
RCP in, 231
registered ports in, 215–219
rlogin, 231
RSH in, 231
SMTP, 232–233
SSH and, 231
SSL, 227–228
summary of, 239–240
Telnet, 228–231
in Transport Layer, 211
UDP for, 212
World Wide Web, 223–228
TCP/IP applications, secure, 302–303
HTTPS, 303–304
NTP, 305
overview of, 303
SCP, 304
SFTP, 304–305
SNMP, 305
summary of, 308
TCP/IP networks, 358
TCP/IP networks, securing
AAA for, 294–295
applications in. See TCP/IP applications, secure
asymmetric-key algorithm standards in, 283–285
authentication in, 279, 291–299
authentication with encryption for, 302–303
authorization in, 291–292
digital signatures in, 287
EAP for, 297–299
encryption in, 279–285
hashes in, 286–287
IPSec for, 302–303
Kerberos, 296–297

key terms, 308–309
lab projects, 311
nonrepudiation in, 286
overview of, 278–279
PKI in, 287–291
PPP for, 292–294
quizzes on, 309–311
RADIUS, 295–296
SSL/TLS for, 302
standards for, 292
summary of, 306–308
symmetric-key algorithm standards in, 282–283
TACAS+, 296
TCP/IP (Transmission Control Protocol/Internet Protocol)
applications. See TCP/IP applications
CIDR, 150
class IDs, 149–150
introducing, 22–23
IP addresses, overview of, 139–143
IP addresses, subnetting, 150–157
IP addresses, supporting LANs and WANs, 143–149
IP addresses, using, 157–164
and IP, generally, 137–139
key terms, 166
lab projects, 168–169
overview of, 136
quizzes on, 166–168
securing applications. See TCP/IP applications, secure
securing networks. See TCP/IP networks, securing
subnetting, 150–157
summary of, 165
TCP (Transmission Control Protocol)
introducing, 22–23
ports, 510–511
TCP/IP applications using, 212–213
TCPView, 218
TDRs (time domain reflectometers), 118, 403–404
telecommunication rooms
defined, 99
diagnosis and repair of, 128–129
location of, 111–112
in structured cabling, 101–102
Telecommunications Industry Association (TIA), 47
telephone lines, 376–381
telephony
ATM in, 373–374
copper carriers in, 369–372
digital, 368